VOICE AND ARTICULATION

FIFTH EDITION

VOICE AND ARTICULATION

KENNETH C. CRANNELL, SR.

Emerson College

Professor Emeritus and Crannell Consulting

WADSWORTH
CENGAGE Learning™

Australia • Brazil • Japan • Korea • Mexico • Singapore • Spain • United Kingdom • United States

WADSWORTH
CENGAGE Learning™

Voice and Articulation, Fifth Edition
Kenneth C. Crannell, Sr., Professor Emeritus
and Crannell Consulting

Senior Publisher: Lyn Uhl

Publisher: Michael Rosenberg

Assistant Editor: Jillian D'Urso

Editorial Assistant: Erin Pass

Media Editor: Jessica Badiner

Marketing Director: Jason Sakos

Marketing Coordinator: Gurpreet Saran

Marketing Communications Manager:
Tami Strang

Content Project Management: PreMediaGlobal

Art Director: Linda Helcher

Print Buyer: Justin Palmeiro

Rights Acquisitions Specialist: Mandy Groszko
(Image and Text)

Cover Designer: Lisa Kuhn

Compositor: PreMediaGlobal

For product information and technology assistance, contact us at
Cengage Learning Customer & Sales Support, 1-800-354-9706

For permission to use material from this text or product,
submit all requests online at **www.cengage.com/permissions**
Further permissions questions can be e-mailed to
permissionrequest@cengage.com

Library of Congress Control Number: 2010932836

ISBN-13: 978-0-534-51499-0

ISBN-10: 0-534-51499-5

Wadsworth
20 Channel Center Street
Boston, MA 02210
USA

Cengage Learning is a leading provider of customized learning solutions with office locations around the globe, including Singapore, the United Kingdom, Australia, Mexico, Brazil, and Japan. Locate your local office at **www.cengage.com/global**

Cengage Learning products are represented in Canada by Nelson Education, Ltd.

To learn more about Wadsworth, visit **www.cengage.com/wadsworth**

Purchase any of our products at your local college store or at our preferred online store **www.cengagebrain.com**

Printed at CLDPC, USA, 09-18

Speech is a mirror of the soul:
As a man* speaks, so is he.
—PUBLILIUS SYRUS, Maxim MLXXIII

*also a woman!
—KCC, MCMXCIX

Dedication to

"Pop-Pop" and "Ma"   "Ed" and "Louise"
"Jack" and Bill   Ed III and Judy

and "Doris Iora"

Patricia

Chuck and Martha   Tracy and Paul
                          Allison and Elizabeth

CONTENTS

Speech is a mirror of the soul:
As a man* speaks, so is he.
—PUBLILIUS SYRUS, Maxim MLXXIII

*also a woman!
—KCC, MCMXCIX

Dedication to

"Pop-Pop" and "Ma"   "Ed" and "Louise"
"Jack" and Bill   Ed III and Judy

and "Doris Iora"

Patricia

Chuck and Martha   Tracy and Paul
                             Allison and Elizabeth

CONTENTS

APPENDIXES

APPENDIXES

PREFACE

ABOUT THE FIFTH EDITION

In the fifth edition of *Voice and Articulation,* I have deleted and added many new drills and exercises, including Audio Practicum Online (previously available by CD), that are available on the Premium Website. If student access was not included with this book as a bundle, it can be purchased at CengageBrain.com. I had a great deal of professional input in putting these exercises together.

I have always encouraged those who have worked with my text to give me input about what works and what might be improved in future edition. I have listened very carefully and have added:

- more diversity in the selections from world literature
- a total revision of Chapter 11, with a detailed discussion of various speaking occasions possible in professional and personal development
- new drills for Asian and Spanish students speaking English
- drills for additional blends
- extensive use of the Internet and YouTube for visuals and support information
- a section on the importance of listening and laryngitis
- updated Glossary and key terms
- new drills for vowels, consonants, and diphthongs
- a "sounder" difference between letters and sounds
- a more detailed discussion of homonyms, and homophones
- many more selections for oral performance
- and more bad jokes!

If the reader has additional comments or questions, please feel free to contact the author (www.speak@crannell.com).

>>>
THE STUDENT

This text is designed for beginning and advanced students in voice and speech classes. It is intended for, but not limited to, students who want to have a career in which strong oral skills are important. Because of its content and the techniques suggested within it, this text will also be very helpful to people who just want to improve their oral skills and to those studying English as a second language. The material is presented in a clear and concise manner but is sufficiently detailed to be used by advanced and beginning students alike.

Most voice and speech teachers acknowledge that changes take place very slowly. A teacher is successful if he or she is able to motivate students to the point where, with concerted effort, they are able to control their speech/voice during specific drills or exercises. However, it will take many months (and perhaps even years!) before positive changes have become a permanent part of a speaker's verbal patterns.

>>>
The Basics

This book makes no attempt to force students to rid themselves of regional speech or sound production. It is a recognized fact that some communication experts want to retain these cultural aspects of speech. I want to see them preserved as well, but not necessarily for use by those with careers in the communication arts and sciences. The emphasis in this text is on developing flexibility of voice and speech. Although an individual will never totally lose regional speech characteristics, a good communicator should be able to minimize them if they are a career disadvantage.

If the material is to be meaningful and is to remain with the reader, it must be understood. Key terms appear at the end of each chapter. They are boldfaced and explained the first time they are presented. In addition, appropriate anatomical and physiological discussions are included as needed for a student's basic understanding. A detailed glossary appears at the end of the book.

I want to emphasize that as students and their teacher progress through this text, they will need mechanical aids if they are to make significant progress. It is imperative, for example, that each student has access to audio recording equipment. Access to video recording equipment is also particularly useful, especially for speech occasions that will or might occur.

>>>
Approach and Application

This text differs from others in a number of important ways. First, students are encouraged to develop career speech through the exercise of a technique called negative practice, in which they become not only aware of the trained manner of speech and voice but also capable of reproducing on demand either old habits or just plain incorrect speech and voice.

Second, a basic principle governing this text is that both teacher and student can learn by experiencing vocal and articulatory extremes. When we achieve these extremes or exaggerations, we are more likely to make the discovery that the voice and speech we are currently using are inadequate or even inappropriate; we are unlikely to discover what is inappropriate or exaggerated until we have experienced it. Often students are in no position to determine what is overdone and feel self-conscious about any departure from habit. It sometimes takes feedback from objective or semiobjective observers (the teacher or peers), coupled with the student's willingness to experiment, before the right feeling is achieved. Being able to hear and reproduce vocal and articulatory extremes is an aid to developing flexibility in speech.

Third, the text encourages application of improved voice and speech skills to various communication occasions, as well as in personal development. Personal vocal changes are often easier and more effectively made when attention is given to communication situations and experiences that involve an audience. Standards of speech for the trained speaker are applied to oral performances and include oral readings of various kinds, from literature to oral reports. Because of this book's focus, selections appropriate for various types of speech occasions are also included

The text also discusses the acquisition and the elimination of common vocal habits, such as glottal shock and vocal fry. One chapter deals with the standard American dialects. Another details stage or British/London speech and selected foreign dialects that might be important to students' career goals. Asian dialects with accompanying exercises are presented in Appendix A.

Choices of the selections in this text have involved a conscious attempt to include literature that is not only interesting and vital but also allows students to achieve vocal techniques and flexibility with ease. A variety of selections from all over the world has been included, each of which has its own virtues. For those students who want to develop their performance abilities and apply their learned vocal skills, longer selections are included; many of them would be excellent selections to use in preparation for an oral final.

This text also differs from others with its focus on the role played by kinesics in the communication process. There is a very strong interaction between voice/speech and the use of the body in creating a whole communication experience. Speakers must appeal to both the ears (voice/speech) and the eyes (kinesics) of their audiences.

Many of the philosophical tenets of this text have their foundation in the teachings of Charles Wesley Emerson, the founder of Emerson College. Other concepts, drills, and exercises in this text are "Old Faithfuls." They are used because they work! A note about the use of news and sportscasts: A few have been included not because of their content, which often becomes outdated before they are even broadcast, but for their style of delivery.

>>>

ACKNOWLEDGMENTS

I want to emphasize my appreciation of a number of individuals without whose help and direction this text would still be in my lowest drawer.

To:

my students, undergraduates and graduates, and clients present and past, who have contributed their vocal strengths (and weaknesses) and encouragement to this project;

my colleagues at Emerson College, past and present—Professor Emerita Frances LaShoto, my dear friend, who taught and continues to teach me; Arthur Roidoulis; Barbara Ann Ferreira; Mary Sullivan; Nancy Newson Roos; Dr. Vito Silvestri; and Kay LaShoto Scinta—all of whom encouraged and gave me invaluable input;

Dr. Michele Drabant Perkins, President of New England College;

Denise Mallen, computer "specialist";

Dr. Allen and Judy Koenig, for their friendships and professional help through the years;

Salil K, Midha, M.D, and M. Akbarian, M.D, of Melrose–Wakefield Hospital, who gave invaluable information and assistance regarding relaxation and respiration techniques;

The reviewers of this edition, who provided valuable feedback: Steven Harders, Chowan University; Cindy Milligan, Kennesaw State University, and John M. Seogstoe-Northeast Community College;

Rainer Hoffmann, M.D.; Medizinische Klinikum 1, Klinikum RWTH, Aachen, Germany, for his counsel and anatomical expertise;

Inga Karetnikova of Boston University, Jürgen Hoffmann (special Freund), Ph.D. ABB Power Generation, Ltd., Consuela Roberta Valesquez and Diego Salazar of Emerson College, for their help with Russian, German, and Spanish pronunciations, respectively;

Tsun Ming Chmielinski (dear friend), Yoshikazu Ochi, and Ahn Hae Kyung, for their special help with the Chinese, Japanese, and Korean dialects, respectively;

Alfred Corona, for his personal support and artistic input;

Rett Rich, Professor Emeritus of Monmouth University, a close friend and colleague of great merit;

Fred Campagna, Meteorologist Extraordinaire at WLNE-TV ABC, for news, sports, and weather copy;

Jerome Lewis and the Newscenter Team, i 95.5 fm, Trinidad and Tabago;

Bob and Vangi Cathcart and Dan and Carole Gillette, for their substantial encouragement through the years;

Wilma (Becka) and Joseph Messina, for their technical knowledge and treasured friendship;

Dr. Lea Queener, Professor Emerita of Memphis State University, a long and trusted friend who played a most significant part in this project.

Our children, Ken, Jr. (Chuck), and Tracy, a constant source of encouragement, insight, inspiration and just plain fun; and finally, most important, Patricia, my wife, special friend, and confidant, who not only drew all of the illustrations for this text but also is my sounding board to whom I owe more than I can ever give back.

VOICE I

CHAPTER 1

MOTIVATION AND EXPECTATION

The purpose of **speech** is to communicate verbally, effectively. Everyone would agree that **voice** and **articulation** constitute an important part of that effectiveness. Not everyone would agree, however, on the importance of voice and articulation in the total communication process. This textbook maintains that voice and articulation play significant roles in communication. *Voice* is defined as the shades of tones that are produced by the vibration of the vocal folds within the larynx. These are then modified and amplified in the throat, mouth, and nose. *Articulation* is the procedure that allows the outgoing breath to be widened, narrowed, or closed off and categorized into various recognizable speech sounds.

Because of its importance, we will use the term *career speech* (or "preferred speech") to indicate the quality of speech that is the goal of this course. **Career speech** is the type of speech that is expected in a career in which oral communication plays a significant role. It is not necessarily the speech of the educated because one can be highly educated and yet make poor choices in terms of speech. It is speech that reflects the most appropriate vocal characteristics and exerts some control over regional speech patterns.

Remember that to others you are the way you sound. You want your voice and speech to say great things about you, don't you? Your voice and speech should reflect you at your best; and when they are effective, people will not only listen but remember.

A career in which **verbal** communication plays an integral part demands a different standard of speech and language than does a career that is not people-oriented. Some of the careers that should encourage preferred speech are teaching, theater, the media (radio, television, and so forth), business (sales, executive training), law, and the clergy.

>>>
Habit and Nature

Students often ask, "Why do we speak as we do?" The answer is somewhat complex. Speech (and often voice) is a learned process that becomes habitual if the speaker's intelligence and physical structure are relatively normal. **Habitual** refers to a pattern of behavior acquired by repetition, whereas **natural** can be defined as not artificial. In all probability, your current speech and voice are a result of habit. It will be difficult for you at first to distinguish habit from nature (and you will be frequently reminded to distinguish between the two terms).

Much habitual speech is determined and molded by factors that are both environmental and physiological. The local regionalisms that most of us have developed result from an idiosyncratic manner of speaking that we heard as infants. We learned to speak by observing those around us. If we heard poor speech most of the time, the chances are good that our speech is poor. If we were fortunate to be surrounded by those with good speech, our speech will reflect that as well. And so, if we were from Massachusetts and repeatedly during our childhood heard something like "*Lindar* had a great time in *Asiar*," it would sound quite **affected** when Aunt Matilda and Uncle Ned from Chicago said, "Linda had a great time in Asia."

Experts say that the best time for learning a foreign language is in the early, formative years of life. At that time you are a sand dune just waiting for a footprint. What you hear and mimic while learning to talk seems natural. Now, however, any and all attempts by you (and especially by your teacher) to modify or change your speech or voice will feel unnatural or affected. This class may be a kind of war between your habitual and trained speech habits.

So look at it this way: You are going to be asked to learn a new language called "career speech." It is yours to use when it is to your advantage.

In addition to environment, heredity plays an important part in determining the **pitch** and **quality** of a voice. *Pitch* is the ability to discriminate between the highs and lows of tones or sounds. Your voice *quality* is determined by those characteristics that individualize it or make it distinctive.

At birth, you were given **resonance cavities** (throat, mouth, and nose) and **muscles** that resemble those of your parents. This is an inherited phenomenon transmitted by genes, so the die has been cast. If your anatomical and physiological structure is similar to that of one of your parents, you are likely to sound like that parent. Thus, there is the great similarity between Liza Minnelli and her mother, Judy Garland. Ms. Minnelli has a Garlandesque quality of voice that she learned through manipulating and modifying the fundamental tone within her resonance cavities. In addition, her phrasing, pronunciation, and **inflection** in both singing and speaking are reminiscent of her mother and were in all probability made habitual through imitation, or **mimesis.** (*Inflection* is a vocal technique that brings attention to thoughts and ideas through variations of pitch, tempo, and stress without speech interruption.)

Although at present your voice reflects the momentary *habitual you,* it may not reflect the you whom you want heard and seen by yourself and others. The sound you produce now is created by muscles and **cartilages** manipulated by habit. As you progress in this class, you will experiment with new vocal and speech techniques. Try them all before you choose those that work, and eliminate those that do not. However, before you reject a suggestion, make certain that you do not do so merely because you are self-conscious. Unless you have perfect speech at the moment, which is unlikely, you are going to be self-conscious about making changes in your voice and speech until such modifications become habitual. Being self-conscious is a good sign because it shows that you are trying something new. You will be trying new speech and voice techniques in various exercises. Any self-consciousness should be regarded as a healthy feeling and should be encouraged in the early stages of change. If you do not feel a little self-conscious, there probably is little real change.

You will be spending an academic term working on voice and speech exercises. Exercise produces physical changes that are caused by the strengthening of muscles. You are going to make your voice and speech anatomy stronger through exercise.

Just for fun and to establish a goal or model for yourself, make a list of the positive aspects of voice in speakers you admire. What do you like about them? Surely one thing is the vocal individuality expressed by their voice and speech. But a distinctive voice is not necessarily a positive factor. We remember some distinctive voices and speech because they are produced with a great deal of tension or have such a whining inflection that they are irritating. The fact that we can identify an individual by his or her speech does not mean that that person uses preferred, or trained, speech. After all, Donald Duck's and Elmer Fudd's voices and speech are unique, but most people do not want to sound like them. On the other hand, to hear the voice of James Earl Jones is an aesthetic experience. The voice of Darth Vader needed to have confidence, power, and distinction. Therefore, Jones was selected to play the role rather than Dustin Hoffman!

Habits can be all-consuming, as you know. The strength of a habit depends on its nature and how long it has existed. Uncle Jake's habit of eating three packages of macadamia nuts per day began when he returned from his trip to the islands three years ago. His New England speech habits developed many decades before that. It will probably be easier for Uncle Jake to kick the macadamia nut habit than to alter his speech.

Your motivation ought to be influenced by the standard demanded by your chosen career. Many of the theories, discussions, and exercises in this text were designed for students who are planning careers in which human communication is vital and who want their speech and voice to reflect them accurately. No one wants to be accidentally misunderstood. Nor does one want to give out incorrect verbal or **nonverbal** cues. If you are angry, you may want to mask it (especially if the anger is directed at your teacher). This course is an opportunity for you to not be misunderstood while you refine your abilities to express your emotions.

Yes, your voice and speech ought to reflect you, but they ought to reflect what you *want* to reflect. You must be the one in control. Then, and only then, are you truly being reflected by the way you sound. How many times have you heard a voice on the radio or telephone and been shocked, appalled, or pleasantly surprised when you met or saw the person? To avoid disappointing their audiences, some radio personalities prefer not to have face-to-face contact with them. If a radio performer has a pleasant male voice and is personable, we are apt to associate an Alec Baldwin body with the voice, but in reality it may belong to someone who looks like Don Knotts.

Psychological considerations are essential in communication situations. In the 1880s two scientists, psychologist William James and physiologist Carl Lange, developed similar points of view regarding the origin of feelings; both felt feelings were physical in nature. They questioned the chronological order in the development of feelings. The scientists hypothesized that the physiological sensations preceded the actual feeling; put another way, the feeling follows the behavior. This was a reversal from the more popular view that the feeling caused the physiological changes. In a sense the James-Lange theory works from the outside to the inside. For example, we are sad because we cry, or we are afraid because we tremble.

Now let's apply this theory to the development of voice and speech and the communication situation. It suggests that during your "appearance" before an audience, the sweaty hands and increased heart rate are causing the fear rather than the fear of the audience causing the physical characteristics. If we can create voice and speech that indicate excellence and give the outward appearance of confidence and assuredness, then the appropriate changes are more likely to occur within the individual. Applying this theory might aid in reducing the apprehension caused by your appearance before that audience.

Although academically it might make more sense to develop inside to outside, some creative artists do advocate working from outside to inside. Actress Meryl Streep has often said that in the creative process she must first hear and develop the way her character speaks. The point is that if you sound and appear at ease, you will eventually be at ease. The Roman poet Virgil said that if you think you can do it, you *can* do it. So approach your drills and exercises with verve and nerve. It is amazing what this attitude can accomplish. Look what it did for Virgil!

This is perhaps one of the most important courses that you can select voluntarily (or nonvoluntarily!) for your own personal skills. When you have understood, practiced, and habituated the material, you will be more confident about your communication skills. You do not have to be fearful of lifelong speaking experiences. That is a choice that you make.

>>> COMMUNICATION APPREHENSION

All students who study voice/speech are quick to note that it is very difficult to alter one's vocal habits—and that to accomplish this in the presence of other "humanoid" beings is almost impossible. We are all much more successful and comfortable practicing our drills and exercises in our rooms or pulling into a rest area on the highway where no one will see us "ranting and raving." This is quite usual at the beginning. However, the time soon arrives where the classroom situation must be considered the "clinic" where the changes are observed and modified. At first it will be difficult for you to "perform" your exercises from your seat within the class. Then, to be expected to stand and face the audience and look into their faces is almost too traumatic to imagine.

Realize that everyone has this apprehension about speaking to an audience. There are not many speakers who cannot relate to the shaking knees, overall perspiration, racing pulse, adrenaline rush, shallow breathing, and eventual rigor mortis. Know that you are in very good company. Our Neanderthal ancestors felt the same way when they met a "beasty" in the forest. This is called the "fight or flight" response. It is very "natural"—a word, incidentally, that will be seldom used in this text. Success can be achieved only through hard work.

Speaking or even vocalizing in public can be a most horrifying experience. Each year in national and international surveys, speaking in public continues to be cited as the most feared experience. There is a great deal of current interest in researching ways of lowering this communication apprehension.

Every effective oral communicator has stage fright—that feeling of "butterflies in the stomach" often described by actors. The "horror" begins with anticipation and is soon magnified into full-scale terror. Too often, after the experience has passed, the speaker is embarrassed and, sometimes, humiliated. I have acquaintances who have changed their life's ambition because of this feeling of annihilation.

Be assured that everyone in your class in voice and speech has the jitters. If you do not, you will probably have a very unsuccessful communication experience. Your case of nerves indicates that you want to be successful. You care! When you are feeling nervous, your glands are secreting adrenaline into your blood just as they would if you were an Olympic athlete about to compete or a robber about to hold up the downtown branch of a bank! This stimulated, emotional state must be made to work for you. Otherwise, your thinking will become sloppy and your muscles will tighten excessively. The nervousness that you experience is an asset, not a liability. Your body is telling you that it is going to rise to the occasion, so to speak.

Remember, every good speaker has anxieties. You are not alone! There are only differences in degree. For example, even the great Sir Laurence Olivier speaks about stage fright in *On Acting:*

> [Stage fright] is an animal, a monster which hides in its foul corner without
> revealing itself, but you know that it is there and that it may come forward at

any moment. . . . [It] is always waiting outside the door, any door, waiting to get you. You either battle or walk away. . . . Suddenly there he is: the bogey-man comes along and tries to rob you of your living. He can come at any time, in any form. The dark shadow of fear. . . . Just when you think you've conquered it, there it is sitting at the end of the bed grinning at you.[1]

There are two extremes with many variations in between: the speaker who is so nervous that the butterflies have turned to mallard ducks, and the speaker who is so cool and confident that his or her performance will probably be boring because the apparent lack of concern about the communication act will likely lead to a lack of electricity during the communica-tion. I think we have all observed speakers who are "ducklike" or "zombielike."

Inexperienced speakers are often overwhelmed by their anxiety and focus energy in the wrong direction. They no longer concentrate on getting the message across. Uncle Ned's internal conversation goes something like this:

> I don't know what to do with my arms and legs. They're beginning to feel as heavy as concrete. Ah, I know . . . I'll put my hands in my pockets and look cool. Oh, boy, I can hear myself playing with the change in my pocket. Maybe if I put one hand on my hip . . . or better still, I'll cross my arms. . . . That'll look casual. . . . Oh, oh, my left knee is starting to shake. That guy in the front row noticed it, I know he did. . . . I'll shift my weight. . . . Now the shakes are in both legs. And starting to move up! . . . What am I doing here? Where am I? I forgot what I was saying. They're glaring at me; they're leav-ing their seats. They're coming after me. He-e-e-e-elp!

These thoughts are similar to those reported by many novice speakers. What went so cata-strophically wrong in Ned's case? He forgot his purpose and allowed his mind to wander; he began thinking about himself and his own reactions rather than keeping his concentra-tion where it ought to be—on getting that message across to the jury, congregation, poten-tial buyers, students, or whomever. He became self-conscious. These same fears are evident in the students who are taking this class. Controlling the fear is a difficult lesson to learn. If you have ever driven an automobile when the roads were slippery, you know that you are supposed to go with the skid and not apply the brakes. How many drivers can actually do that? Few can. Because of the tension experienced under these conditions, it is a difficult task even for the seasoned driver.

If you have prepared your vocal exercises or speeches or oral readings properly (and this is the key to being a successful communicator), no one in the audience knows the ma-terial better than you. You are the expert. You are the one who has been vocalizing the exercises in this text. Show your classmates and teacher that you have prepared. If you are making a speech, concentrate on getting that information across to the audience, whether the information is a sales presentation, a reading, a summary, or a report; whatever the "vehicle," your concentration must stay on the content.

Everyone is self-conscious and sensitive to some degree. These self-protective instincts are aroused when you are presenting yourself, under stress, to a class or audience. You are vulnerable! Think of yourself as having two antennae. One must never stray from yourself and the message you are presenting; the other must be aimed toward the audience so that it can pick up cues (**audience feedback**) about how effective your presentation is. Under the terror of the speaking situation, you must not succumb to the temptation of turn-ing both antennae toward yourself.

Don't try to inhibit the natural physical tension due to the anxiety caused by the situ-ation. Use it! Shift your weight. If you want to "connect" with your audience and you feel

---

[1] From Laurence Olivier, *On Acting* (New York: Simon & Schuster, 1986), 126.

so inclined, take a step *toward* (not away from) your audience. Use a gesture if it comes from within. Make your tense muscles useful. Remember that you cannot (nor should you want to) overcome the nervousness; you can only learn to control it.

Jerry Seinfeld is said to have commented on the Internet about the power of nervousness that we all share when presenting ourselves to more than one listener: "If it's true that the fear of public speaking is even greater than the fear of death, then—if you think about it—the average guy at a funeral would rather be in the casket than delivering the eulogy." (For exercises, refer to Dr. Herbert Benson's "Relaxation Response" in Chapter 4.)

>>>
LISTENING

Most people realize that listening is not the same as hearing. **Hearing** is a physiological phenomenon. **Listening**, loosely defined, is the use you make of hearing. It is a way to monitor your own speaking skills through imitating and modifying what you hear. It is a very important part of the communication process. It is also a way to acquire knowledge. This text focuses on all three areas, with an emphasis on the first two.

As you listen to other speakers, what voices carry more power? Which ones are more pleasant? What might you try to imitate? What might you try to avoid? Is the speaker's speech articulate and grammar proper? Listen to your instructor: What makes his or her voice and speech more acceptable than yours, for instance?

>>>
PREPARE . . . PREPARE . . . PREPARE

One of the best ways to control nervousness is thorough preparation. Know what it is you want to say and why. At first, your requirements will be to vocalize to your classmates, all of whom are in the same situation as you. If you do your drillwork at home, it will be much easier to present it to the teacher and your peers. Again, prepare! It is impossible to experience the horrors of hyperventilation when you are concentrating on your voice or speech or the message you are delivering and getting it across to your audience; anxiety attacks occur when you are unsure of what you are going to say. Your confidence in speaking increases when you begin to realize that your audience is listening because you not only have something important to say, you are saying it in the best vocal and speech mode available to you. You might want to take a quick look at Chapter 11, "Application to the Speech Occasion," to learn some healthy tricks that can help you.

>>>
STAGES OF DEVELOPMENT

All students studying voice and speech must pass through various stages or periods. Obviously, before you can do anything about modifying and correcting yourself, your vocal response must be analyzed. This is where your teacher's expertise is helpful. The evaluation may be written or oral. Some teachers prefer to make at least two copies of a written evaluation—one for the teacher and the other for the student. That way the student's progress can be monitored easily. It also helps in assigning individual drills to a student.

Finally, the list of problems that a student must overcome can be included in the evaluation. It is expected that you and your teacher will continue to analyze your progress as your awareness of your speech and voice increases. The evaluation given at the beginning of the term might well become your yardstick for measuring your improvement. There are evaluation forms in Appendix C.

Self-Appraisal Stages

After you become aware of your various problems, you must begin the first and second stages of improvement. These stages will take considerable time and can cause much frustration. *You must train your ear.* In the first stage it is helpful to listen to the voice and speech of others; it will be easier for you to hear errors and changes in others' speech than in your own. This listening process is critical. In the second stage, you must listen to and then apply voice and speech modifications to your voice. When you focus on listening to yourself, you must not be threatened by potential changes. The most important point is that you be motivated to make the changes necessary so that your speech and vocal skills can be the best possible. You have to be "ripe for change."

It is also important that you trust the expert ear of your teacher. At first, your teacher is in the best position to hear what you actually say. You will discover early on that what you think you say may be quite different from what you actually say. A cassette recorder comes in handy here, for at times your teacher will have to prove that you said a word in a particular way. It will take a good while for your mouth to catch up with your ear's perception. The important word is *trust*. It is important that you listen to your teacher. If any positive effect is to be achieved, a bonding must take place between you and your teacher.

Appraisal of Others

The third stage involves listening to the speech and vocal habits of people around you—your roommates, friends, family, classmates, and, yes, your teachers! The fact that twenty or thirty students are scrutinizing your speech teacher will keep his or her mind on the work at hand. After all, your teacher will set the standard for the class and should be your role model.

Also, a bit of tested advice—be patient with relatives and close friends. As your listening skills improve and you learn more principles of career speech, do not try to correct others' speaking habits. You will find that their responses are similar to yours right now: "What's wrong with my speech?" It might very well be that they like their speech as it is and do not want career speech. Many family members and friends have gone to war over a new voice student's desire to help by commenting, criticizing, correcting, and, worst of all, imitating their voice and speech. Remember that you are listening to their speech only to train your ear—not to teach them. If you want to continue to survive, leave them alone!

Listen to television, radio, theater, and movie personalities. Why do some of their voices "work"? What turns you off to others? Record your own voice on a cassette, play it back, and being as objective as you can, describe the person you hear. Now that takes both objectivity and courage! What do you look like according to your voice? Get a true image of yourself. Try to develop auditory accuracy.

Unfortunately, some students are unable to develop the necessary objectivity. Some students continue to be enamored of their own excellence (perhaps because they have been asked to read announcements over the loudspeaker in high school) when in reality their voice and speech are not very good; conversely, other students with positive characteristics feel insecure and self-conscious. Try to be objective, and listen to and trust your teacher's feedback.

Practice Situation

The fourth stage is to play around with the corrections and modifications suggested by your teacher. This can be a great deal of fun if you don't take yourself too seriously. (That is a helpful adage throughout this course: "Take the work seriously, but not yourself.") Try your new vocal skills in the privacy of your boudoir. Use a mirror. See how your mouth looks when you practice the new production or pronunciation. Risk it! It is different; yes, it does feel strange. But how did you feel in your first tuxedo or high heels (worn separately, it is hoped!)? You felt awkward and self-conscious, but you knew from Mom and Dad (as well as from Uncle Ned and Aunt Maude) that you looked great.

A word of warning—as you are experimenting with changes in your speech and voice, make certain that you do not develop an affected delivery. For example, to New Englanders it sounds rather affected to say "Carrrr" instead of the habitual "Caaaaaaaa." New Englanders are prone to making all sorts of grimaces while making certain that they pronounce the /r/ **phoneme** in certain words. (A single phonetic symbol appears between two slashes, / /.) The affectation is not in the sound but results from the speaker's inability to separate the sound he says habitually from the new sound. The same danger exists when you modify vocal quality, rhythm, inflection, or pitch. Use the mirror so you can make sure that you are not making exaggerated facial expressions. Time will take care of your self-consciousness.

Risk It!

This is the final stage before a speech modification becomes habitual. You must try out the new you on your friends, family, and acquaintances. Try to incorporate each new modification as you are working on it. Concentrate on one thing at a time. This is also the time for trial and error. Yes, you will make mistakes, and you may feel very self-conscious. But remember, laugh at yourself before anyone else can laugh at you. Yes, this takes courage, Mervin! Stick with the training that is being done in class. Begin to put it all together in rehearsal rather than during an actual speech occasion.

>>>
VOCAL AND VERBAL RECIDIVISM

As we previously noted, you are embarking on an extremely difficult and often frustrating path. You are attempting to modify **oral** behaviors that you have nurtured for many years. You will discover that these previous habits or behaviors are like giant hooks pulling you off the ground while you are trying to keep yourself firmly rooted in your attempt to establish these new habits. This is quite usual and to be expected. Those students who have been highly motivated and who have done the work on a regular basis will find the transition easier. After all, you are pitting many years of established vocal habits against fourteen or fifteen weeks of drills recently learned in a voice and articulation class. It is the special person who can control the old habits and apply the new behaviors after only a relatively short time. You cannot be expected to have habituated the new oral behaviors into your conversational speech. However, you should be able to control the new habits in prepared (and well-rehearsed) performance occasions.

The "normal" process of regression to previous modes of vocal behaviors (a process that we all experience, incidentally) could be called **oral recidivism.** (It is interesting to note that the original definition of *recidivism,* according to the *Oxford English Dictionary,* is "a relapse into sin, error, or crime." It is hoped that knowing about this will not motivate you in the wrong direction!) Although some highly motivated students continue to develop vocally, others forget everything before they have dramatically slammed the classroom door behind them for the last time.

This backsliding or oral recidivism is very evident, for example, when college students go home for the long Thanksgiving weekend. Their return to the classroom on Monday often challenges the instructor's decision to remain in the noblest of professions. The only difference between that Black Monday and the first day of class is that it does not take quite as long to bring a student back from the "black pit."

For the same reason, it is often more difficult for a commuter student to improve poor speech habits than it is for the dormitory student. Hearing the speech of family and friends at home does not always reinforce the precepts being learned in voice and articulation class. We tend to make more headway when quarantined, sequestered, or isolated from those who are our oral tempters. So if your roommate is from your hometown, your oral development is apt to take a little longer.

>>> VISUALIZATION

Visualization is a contemporary concept that is used in many areas to teach persons to feel good about themselves. It involves the summoning of a mental image or picture exactly as you want it to be. Psychologists and psychiatrists often have used the technique. They instruct a patient, for example, to visualize how he or she might feel if a particular fear were not present. In sports, football players visualize and recreate the feeling of throwing and completing a great pass. A figure skater, while sitting down, might visualize the approach and execution of a successful triple axel without leaving the chair. With her or his eyes closed, the skater sees the perfect entry into a lutz jump. The skater experiences the proper degree of muscular tension. Are the arms close to the body? Are the feet in position? Are you centered? At an audition an actor focuses on a situation in which there are no obstacles; the actor sees himself or herself giving a great reading and landing the role.

In this text, you are encouraged to use the concept of visualization at every stage of your development. Use it to deal with stage fright, for example. At home, on the day you are to get up in front of your peers, sit in a chair in a very relaxed position in a quiet room. Remove your shoes, unbutton your collar, and relieve yourself of any other obstruction made by your clothes. Let your arms rest at their sides. With your eyes closed, breathe slowly. In ten inhalations go from superficial to deep breathing. Remember what your mind and muscles were doing when you were in charge of a given situation, when you felt confident about yourself. Visualize being courageous and fearless. See yourself pleasantly excited about getting up in front of the class. Imagine yourself wanting to relate to your fellow students by looking into their eyes. It works. It is not a Mary Poppins delusion. As you are approaching the various elements of voice and speech production, take the time to visualize success and confidence. Visualize what is happening to you physically, mentally, and emotionally. Apply the technique in all of your oral work. Try to reproduce those responses that you achieved during the practice sessions.

>>> NEGATIVE PRACTICE

Negative practice is the process of consciously exaggerating and practicing an error and contrasting it with the desired behavior (also in exaggeration). This technique is somewhat controversial; some communication experts contend that it emphasizes the error and, thus, should be avoided. However, negative practice, when done properly and consciously, can be very helpful. It should be emphasized that the individual practicing negatively must always be aware of the problem and the process. For example, if one of your faults is vocal tension, fluctuating between relaxed and tense sounds underscores both the feeling and the sound of tension. When used properly, negative practice is a very effective tool. In this text, negative practice always occurs between examples of career speech.

>>>
APPROPRIATENESS

Speech that is clear and readily understood is not necessarily appropriate. Speech should not be developed in a vacuum; it must have a purpose, and you must be convinced that the purpose is justified. No one wants you to sound like a clone or a speech malcontent. You often hear speakers who are partially trained; their pronunciation is so careful and precise that they sound like cartoon characters. Even speech teachers err. How many times have you heard, "Danny, speak up! Pronounce every sound in the word"? Let's face it: Not every sound in a word is of equal importance. As a matter of fact, not every word in a sentence is of equal importance.

The term *appropriate* is applicable to any aspect of voice and speech you want to develop. Your pitch, quality, and **volume** ought to be appropriate. The sound of the voice ought to reflect an appropriateness of sex, age, and physical structure. If a speaker is a male, he wants to sound like one. He wants to sound mature unless he is a child; there is something rather humorous about a 35-year-old man with a powerful physique whose voice sounds like a teenager's.

Sometimes the appropriateness of speech is called the "working tone," defined as the quality that is appropriate for a particular speech occasion. Good taste dictates what is appropriate. When a person communicates with another, regardless of the occasion (a public speech, a telephone call, a conversation, or a theatrical performance), the occasion will determine the choice of vocal and verbal content. This is also called the **speech environment.** You must always be big enough to be seen and loud enough to be heard. You may ask, "How do you know if you are loud or big enough?" You must begin to tune in to your audience at this point. Read and interpret their facial expressions and their actions. Reading your audience is discussed in detail in Chapter 11.

The basis for all voice and articulation work should be a strong desire to develop **vocal flexibility.** A beautiful, resonating voice is worth little without flexibility, and there are voices that have excellent qualities in isolation but lack any excitement or interest.

In most cases, repetition establishes a habit. Thus, to change your speech and voice you must drill, drill, drill; practice, practice, practice; and quite possibly fail, fail, fail. You will make fewer and fewer errors, and one day your speech will be notably improved. Just when this happens depends on the quality of your practice.

As with dieting, the work may not always be exciting. Do you know anything duller than trying to lose weight? You do physical exercises a couple of times a day; you take in fewer calories because you know that by eating less and exercising, the pounds will come off. Your poor voice and speech habits "come off" in the same way. You must do those vocal sit-ups and deep knee-bends if you expect any change to take place. And, as in physical exercise, it takes a long time to see the effects. But then, all of a sudden, you begin dropping pounds. Likewise, in time your new speech habits will become established.

To make progress, you must practice the skills that are the means to the end. By the time actors are on the stage, it is too late for them to be concerned with vocal technique. They must at this point keep their minds on their characters. While you are selling a computer package to a company is not the time to concern yourself with proper articulation; stay with the thought or you will not make that sale.

If you are an anchor doing the evening news, you cannot take the time to think about how to deliver a story; you must stay with that story. Often, if you have not written the piece yourself, you must read it on sight and not be the least concerned about the quality of your voice or the presence of a regionalism.

However, all of the good thoughts and intentions in the world will not protect the actor from a bad performance, the priest or minister from a poor homily, or the salesperson from a lost sale if their basic oral skills are poor. They must put the time into perfecting those skills beforehand. It has been said that some preachers need not spend much time preparing to read the Scriptures because when they ascend the pulpit, the Spirit enters and leads them to read well. But it has also been said, "God helps those who help themselves"—by drilling, preparing, and rehearsing aloud.

You should practice frequently, but only for short periods of time. And you must practice every day. Pick a few times of the day when you are alone and can concentrate. Establish those times as your regular voice and speech times. At first, practice no more than fifteen minutes at a time, but do it conscientiously twice or three times a day—after your first cup of coffee in the morning and just before you go to sleep, for instance. Then, add a third time during midday. Eventually, you should increase your practice periods first to twenty minutes and then to half an hour. With proper concentration, an amazing amount of work can be done in thirty minutes.

The most effective way to teach voice and articulation is through the use of the **International Phonetic Alphabet (IPA),** which is an alphabet of sounds. The American-English sounds are a part of the sounds represented by the IPA; different sounds that occur in other recognized languages make up the rest. The concept of thinking in sounds rather than letters will likely be quite challenging until you get used to it. However, it is well worth the time spent because the IPA provides a clear, consistent way to represent sounds. English can be very confusing—letters can represent multiple sounds or even be silent. Just ask a person who is learning English! In the word *through,* for instance, there are seven letters but only three actual sounds; in the word *plumber* the letter *b* is silent; and in the word *palm* the preferred pronunciation omits the letter *l.*

Unless individuals learning English have a facility for hearing and producing speech sounds, they will probably only approximate those English sounds that do not appear in their native language. Thus, one way we can tell that people are not native English-speakers is that their **vowels** and **diphthongs** resemble those used in the production of their own language.

A few English **consonants** do not exist in some other languages, such as the "th" sound. Speakers of German or French who are learning English will substitute /t-d/ or /s-z /, respectively, depending upon their age. This is also true of speakers of Asian languages—in many Far Eastern cultures, it is not decorous to show the tongue; therefore, there are no "th" sounds.

How a normative speaker is able to learn English, a language peppered with exceptions in pronunciation and grammar, is beyond comprehension. The sentences that follow are part of a longer work, "Eve's Legend," by Lord Holland. Here, we've underlined only the letter *e* to point out the many different vowel sounds it can represent:

The terms perplexed Stephen, yet he jeered them. He resented the senseless credence, "Seers never err." Then he repented, knelt, wheedled, wept.

Another graphic example of the problems encountered when English is learned through spelling can be seen and heard in the following illustrations:

Dearest creature in Creation,

Studying English Pronunciation,

I will teach you in my verse:

Sounds like corpse, corps, horse and worse.

I will keep you, Susy, busy,

Make your head with heat grow dizzy,

Tear in eye your dress you'll tear,

So shall I!! Oh, hear my prayer,

Pray, console your loving poet,

Make my coat look new, dear, sew it!

Just compare heart, beard and heard,

Dies, diet lord and word,

Sword and sward, retain and Britain,

(Mind the letter, how it's written)

Made has not the sound of bade,

Say—said, pay—paid, laid, but plaid. . . .

River, rival, tomb, bomb, comb;

Doll and roll and some and home.

Stranger does not rhyme with anger,

Neither does devour with clangour.

Soul but foul and gaunt, but aunt

Font, front, wont; want, grand, and grant,

Shoes, goes, does. Now first say finger,

And then; singer, ginger, linger,

Real, zeal, mauve, gauze, and gauge;

Marriage, foliage, mirage, age,

Query does not rhyme with very,

Nor does fury sound like bury.

Dost, lost, post, and doth, cloth, loth.

Job, job, blossom, bosom, oath

Though the difference seems little,

We say actual but victual. . . .

Viscous, viscount; load and broad;

Toward, to forward, to reward,

And your pronunciation's O.K.

When you say correctly croquet;

Rounded, wounded; grieve and sleeve;

Friend and fiend; alive and live;

Liberty, library; heave and heaven;

Rachel, ache, moustache; eleven,

We say hallowed but allowed,

People, leopard; towed but vowed

Mark the difference moreover,

Between mover, plover, Dover; . . .

Finally: Which rhymes with "enough"

Though, through, plough, cough, hough, or tough?

Hiccough has the sound of "cup". . .

My advice is—give it up![2]

Since the last edition of this book there has been extensive technical and mechanical support given by the Internet and YouTube. At the end of each chapter you will find a web address that will lead you to web links and key search terms that will provide additional reference Material including current information and videos. Warning: Be discriminating about the material you consult. There is a great deal of misinformation on the Internet. Check out additional material with your Instructor.

You are embarking on a very challenging task: altering your voice and speech—two very personal habits. You are going to find it a difficult, humorous, confusing, but most of all, frustrating task. Don't give up! The time will come when these changes will become automatic. This is perhaps the most important course you can take for your personal development. Thousands have made it through successfully without lasting scars. The process is made easier if you maintain your sense of humor. Learn to laugh at yourself—nay, HOWL!

EXERCISES FOR THE RECORD

Purchase at least two blank cassette tapes and record selections 1 and 2 on both. You should keep one and give the other to your teacher for his or her files. (When you become a celebrity, the teacher can make copies of it and make you pay plenty!) By doing this, you will have a sample of your voice and speech before training. With the use of the tape, your teacher can monitor your progress during the home practice sessions throughout the term.

It is suggested that you make your first voice and speech presentation during the first week of class. *Speak to the members of your class.* This performance should be recorded (on audio- or videotape) by your teacher and will give you a fairly accurate representation of your current voice and speech mannerisms under stress. Tear out your blank Voice and Speech Evaluation and Rating Scale I forms and give them to your teacher for his or her comments. (See Appendix C for all of the forms in this section.) In addition, completely fill out the Student Information Sheet and give it to your teacher. This is very helpful information. The Voice and Speech Rating Scale II should be used for your final evaluation.

In the first part of the presentation you are to introduce yourself to the class and be prepared to speak for one-and-a-half minutes on one of the following questions:

What is your favorite food, and why?
What is your favorite song, and why?
What was one of your most embarrassing moments?
When you order pizza, what toppings do you select, and why?
Operas should be given in English.
Who is your favorite actor, and why?
What is your favorite movie, and why?

---

[2]From *Vrij Nederland*, 22 December 1945, 695.

For the remaining part of the evaluation, read the following selections. (Incidentally, the tape should be kept. It will become a great source of pleasure when it is compared with the most recent tape of the same material.)

1. A mouse went into a lion's cave by mistake, and before he knew what he was doing, he ran over the nose of the sleeping lion. The lion reached out his paw and caught the mouse and was about to eat him when the mouse said, "Forgive me, King of Beasts, I did not know where I was. I should never have been so proud as to come into this cave if I had known it was yours." The lion smiled at the poor frightened little mouse and let him go. Not long after this, the lion fell into a rope net left for him by some hunters, and his roars filled the forest. The mouse recognized the voice and ran to see if he could help him. He set to work nibbling the ropes, and soon the lion was free.

THE MOUSE AND THE LION
Aesop

2. It was the best of times, it was the worst of times, it was the age of wisdom, it was the age of foolishness, it was the epoch of belief, it was the epoch of incredulity, it was the season of Light, it was the season of Darkness, it was the spring of hope, it was the winter of despair, we had everything before us, we had nothing before us, we were all going direct to Heaven, we were all going direct the other way.

From A TALE OF TWO CITIES
Charles Dickens

Write the definitions for the following terms in the space below.

KEY TERMS	DEFINITIONS
Affected Speech/ Voice	
Articulation	
Audience feedback	
Career Speech	
Cartilage	
Consonant	
Diphthong	
Habitual	
Hearing	
Inflection	
International Phonetic Alphabet (IPA)	
Listening	
Mimesis	
Muscle	
Natural	
Negative Practice	

CHAPTER 2

>>>>>>>>>>>>>>>>>>>>>>>>>>>>>>>

BREATHING

If you have ever had singing lessons, you have heard your teacher say, "You must learn to breathe from here," as she pointed toward your abdominal region. No one argues with a singing teacher.

The same principle applies to speaking. Many students view this statement with more than a little suspicion. Why must we breathe that way? Surely we are not supposed to breathe that way all of the time? Won't we get tired? Isn't it unnatural? These common questions will be answered in this chapter. Keep in mind that the proper development and use of breath are basic to good voice and speech—breath is the foundation of good voice and speech.

For humans, there are two functions of breathing/**respiration.** Many voice and articulation teachers do not like to admit that the major function of breath involves **vegetative breathing;** that is, breathing keeps the organism alive so that it can fulfill the second function of breathing: speech. Whether we breathe for survival or for speech, the action of the muscles ought to be the same because breathing is a natural process. (Yes, the word *natural* is most appropriate in talking about diaphragmatic breathing!) Unfortunately, the process does not seem natural to many students studying speech and voice.

In vegetative breathing, the **inhalation** is active, whereas the **exhalation** is passive. In speech, both inhalation and exhalation are strong and controlled and, hence, are active processes.

In vegetative breathing, exhalation and inhalation usually take about the same time for all breaths. However, in breathing for speech, inhalation is usually of relatively short duration, whereas the duration of exhalation depends on the thought being expressed. In addition, breathing for speech is usually much deeper than respiration to sustain life.

>>>
TYPES OF BREATHING

There are three major types of breathing: (1) diaphragmatic (abdominal), (2) clavicular, and (3) upper thoracic.

1. **Diaphragmatic breathing** (abdominal breathing) is recommended for career speech by most trained voice and speech specialists. In this type of breathing, a downward movement of the diaphragm is accompanied by an expansion of the lower ribs. This technique provides greater control over exhalation.
2. In **clavicular breathing,** the speaker raises the shoulders and collarbones (clavicles) while inhaling. This can be a very exhausting habit. Because it adds tension to the laryngeal area, the resulting voice is often harsh and high-pitched.
3. In **upper thoracic breathing,** the sternum (breastbone) is elevated during inhalation and often pulls in the lower rib cage.

Swimming coaches often encourage clavicular or thoracic breathing in conjunction with diaphragmatic breathing to increase buoyancy. But in speech, obviously, this combination of respiratory processes would present problems for both speaker and listener. (Think of all of the naps we might be able to take in between thoughts and phrases.)

Because it is the escaping breath (the exhalation) that produces the sound for speech (as it goes between the slightly tense **vocal folds**), it is only reasonable to encourage the best (and the most natural) use of breath—diaphragmatic or abdominal breath. (See Chapter 3 for a detailed view of vocal folds.)

>>>
THE ANATOMY OF RESPIRATION

The **rib cage** is the bony structure of the **thorax,** or chest. It is composed of the spinal column (backbone or **vertebral column**), the **sternum** (breastbone), and twelve pairs of ribs, all of which are attached to the spinal column. The top six pairs of ribs are joined to the sternum in front by cartilage. The next four pairs of ribs are attached to the rib above it by cartilage. The two lower pairs, called the floating ribs, do not connect to anything in the front but are attached to the vertebral column in the back. They can move relatively freely. The sternum can be lifted with the rest of the thorax. The lower ribs can be moved outward and upward, thus allowing the thoracic cavity to enlarge.

In between the ribs are sets of muscles called the superior and inferior **intercostal muscles.** When they contract, they pull the entire rib cage upward and outward, an action that enables lung capacity to increase.

The **diaphragm** (Figure 2.1) is a double, dome-shaped muscle that forms the entire floor of the chest and the ceiling of the abdomen. Like any muscle, the diaphragm can contract or relax. And like any healthy muscle, if it is exercised, it will grow stronger.

The diaphragm is a large muscle that is attached to the vertebral column in the back, to the sternum in the front, and to the lower ribs along the sides. Obviously, you cannot place your hand directly on your diaphragm without its becoming a very messy (and painful) procedure. When you place your hand on your abdomen, you are actually feeling the sheath of muscle that goes from the sternum to the pelvic area just beneath the layers of skin. This sheath is called the **rectus abdominus.**

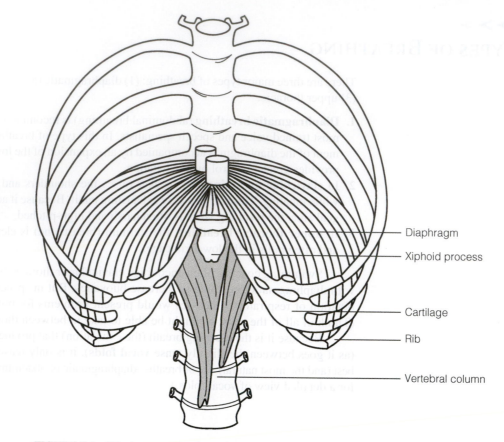

Diaphragm

Xiphoid process

Cartilage

Rib

Vertebral column

FIGURE 2.1   Diaphragm and points of attachment

The purpose of inhalation is to create as much space as possible in the thoracic cavity so that the lungs can sufficiently fill with air. Therefore, proper inhalation creates the appropriate space. The action of the rib cage is often compared to the action of a bellows. As the handles of the bellows are forced apart, the space is increased and a partial vacuum is created. Because the atmospheric pressure outside then becomes greater than the pressure inside, air rushes into the bellows to equalize the pressure. Similarly, as the rib cage elevates during inhalation, more room is created, a partial vacuum forms, and air rushes in to fill the space.

During this process the lungs are passive, like two partially deflated balloons. The central tendon of the diaphragm contracts, causing the diaphragm to descend and press down on the **viscera** below it. This process can be minimized if the ribs are allowed to move sideways. If you push down on an inflated balloon, it will expand at right angles to the direction of the pressure. This is similar to the effect on the viscera when they are pushed by the contracting diaphragm. During exhalation the abdominal muscles are contracted and the viscera return to their original position.

During inhalation, as the diaphragm is flattening and creating more space in the lower area of the thorax, the intercostal muscles cause the rib cage to move up and out. This in turn creates more space in the thoracic cavity. As the size of the chest cavity increases (both horizontally and vertically), the atmospheric pressure becomes greater outside the body

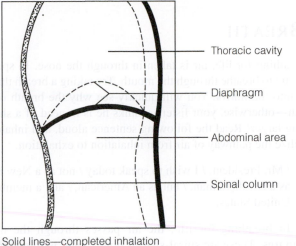

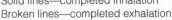
Solid lines—completed inhalation
Broken lines—completed exhalation

FIGURE 2.2   Side view of diaphragmatic action during breathing

than inside, and air rushes in to equalize the pressure. The natural advantage to this chest expansion is that the lungs can expand to their capacity. In exhalation the diaphragm and muscles between the ribs relax, allowing the diaphragm and rib cage to return to their original positions (Figure 2.2).

>>>

MAKING USE OF A NATURAL PROCESS

The movements just described are a result of a natural process. For example, look at a baby lying on its back. When the baby takes a breath, the abdominal region rises to an amazing degree and the rib area expands. The baby is "all stomach." Upon exhalation, the abdominal region returns to its passive state. Through the tool of visualization, close your eyes and see yourself lying on a cot duplicating the feeling that the baby has. You probably pull in your stomach and elevate your shoulders. Keep working at it until you can duplicate the natural abdominal process exemplified by the baby.

As you continue deep breathing, you may become a little dizzy. This occurs because your bloodstream is not accustomed to so much oxygen at once. This is a frequent complaint of students, but don't be alarmed. You are hyperventilating momentarily. If this occurs, sit down (before you fall down). Don't let this discourage you from doing your breathing exercises, however. You will build up a tolerance for the increased amount of oxygen in your lungs in no time at all. If you keep in mind that you breathe diaphragmatically when you breathe for life, the task will not seem so alien.

Posture is important in both breathing and vocal production. Good posture is nothing more than holding the parts of the body in their natural alignment. Standing tall makes it easier for the spine to support the body; it is the natural order. If you are stooped while breathing, you are inhibiting diaphragmatic activity. Freedom from tension and full control of the respiratory process are basic to effective breathing. For a more detailed discussion of the use of the body, see Chapter 10.

>>>

THE PATHWAY OF BREATH

In breathing for life, air is taken in through the nose. In speech, it is more practical and aesthetic to breathe through the mouth. Try taking a breath through the nose for speech and look into the mirror. You will quickly see why the breath ought to be taken through the mouth—otherwise, your listener thinks he is in need of a shower as he sees your nostrils getting larger! Read the following sentence aloud, and inhale orally at every slash. Try to visualize the pathway of air from inhalation to exhalation.

> / Mr. President, / I wish to speak today / not as a New Hampshire man, / nor as a Northern man, / but as an American, / and a member of the Senate of the United States.

In breathing for life, the air passes through the nostrils and enters the three **turbinates.** These are spiral-shaped bones lined with membrane out of which tiny hairs grow. The purpose of the turbinates is to warm the incoming air (accomplished by the spiral-shaped bones), moisten the air (accomplished by the membrane), and filter the air (accomplished by the hairs), thus making inhalation through the nose a healthier process. Whether the breath is taken in through the nose into the **nasal cavity** (vegetative breathing) or through the mouth into the **oral** (or buccal) **cavity** (breathing for speech), the next location for the breath is in the **pharynx** (throat). At this point, the air passes through the **larynx** (the voice box) and down the **trachea** (more commonly called the *windpipe*).

The trachea is a four- or five-inch-long tube that is held open by horseshoe-shaped cartilaginous rings approximately three-quarters to one inch in diameter. The open end of the horseshoe is in the back of the trachea. Across the open end of the cartilaginous rings is a band of muscle, behind which is located the esophagus, or food tube. The open end of the cartilaginous rings allows the food tube some room to expand, which is necessary in swallowing. The trachea is also capable of getting longer or shorter. Just below these rings the trachea divides, or bifurcates, into the left and right bronchi.

The right **bronchus** is shorter and slightly broader than the left because the right lung has one more lobe than the left and, thus, needs more room to expand. Because of this anatomical fact, foreign matter is more apt to be found in the right bronchus. Like the trachea, each bronchus is composed of horseshoe-shaped cartilaginous rings.

The ends of the bronchi branch out into many **bronchioles.** Located at the ends of the bronchioles are tiny air sacs called **alveoli** through which oxygen enters the bloodstream. Together these tissues and airways form the spongelike **lungs** (Figure 2.3).

There are, of course, two lungs in the thoracic cavity. The right lung has three lobes (curved projections); the left lung has only two to allow room for the heart. The lungs are passive; that is, they are incapable of moving on their own. When additional space is created within the thoracic cavity, the alveoli are filled with air. At this point oxygen is passed into the bloodstream and carbon dioxide is exchanged into the alveoli for exhalation.

The walls of the thorax and the lungs usually touch. The top of each lung is situated just above the collarbone, and the bottom of each touches the diaphragm. The lungs are lined with a serous, or watery, membrane called the *pleura.* When this coating is attacked by a virus, a very painful condition called *pleurisy* develops.

Breathing for life is involuntary and is dictated by the individual's brain stem. Inhalation is active, whereas exhalation is passive. The amount of air in each of a person's vegetative inhalations is about the same. In speech, inhalations and controlled exhalations are active, voluntary, and dependent upon the desired message of the speaker. We voluntarily take in the amount of air necessary to speak a complete thought. Thus, the depth of inhalation for shouting "Olé!" at a bullfight is significantly different from the amount of air necessary to impress friends with a lengthy tongue twister. This process is closely allied to the

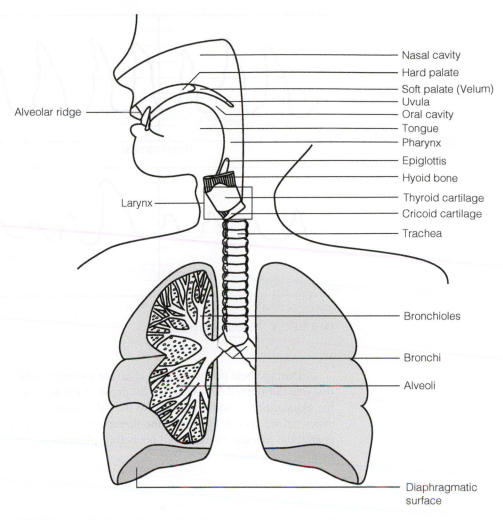

FIGURE 2.3   Basic anatomy for breathing, voice production, and articulation

psychology of speech, which is a major subject in itself. Inhalation is basically involuntary. However, the professional communicator sometimes takes a deeper breath voluntarily to achieve a desired effect. It is important that the depth of a breath be sufficient to support the intent, thought, or emotion to be conveyed.

>>> VISUALIZING RESPIRATION

It might be helpful to represent the process of respiration graphically. In Figure 2.4, the vertical scale indicates the depth (or volume) of the inhalation, and the horizontal scale indicates time. Thus, the graph reveals how an inhalation is used or controlled. The top chart illustrates the diaphragmatic breathing of an individual during vegetative breathing, and the bottom chart shows the thoracic breathing of an individual during vegetative breathing.[1] Note that the person breathing diaphragmatically gets more air into the lungs.

---

[1]Kenneth C. Crannell, "Breathing Patterns of the Individual with a Voice Problem as Compared to the Trained and Untrained Speaker," Master's thesis, Emerson College, 1957: 23.

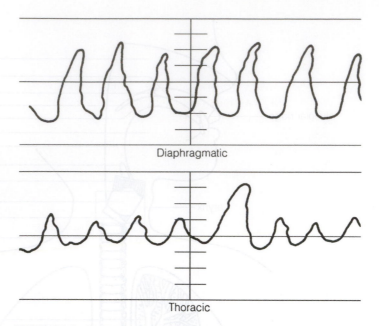

Diaphragmatic

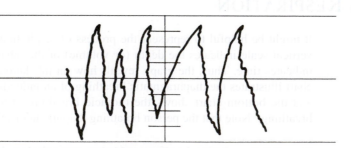

Thoracic

FIGURE 2.4   Vegetative breathing

During vocal production, the chart for a vocally trained person should look like the first one in Figure 2.5. Notice that the depth of the inhalation is about the same as that of the exhalation. In addition, because the exhalation is so well controlled, no breath escapes before speech begins. In the thoracic breathing of the untrained speaker (bottom chart), the amount of expended air before **phonation** varies, which greatly affects the quality of the voice.

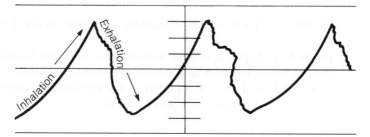

Diaphragmatic breathing during phonation
(speech begins on exhalation)

Thoracic breathing during phonation

FIGURE 2.5   Breathing during phonation

>>>

DIAPHRAGMATIC BREATHING FOR SPEECH

There are many misconceptions about diaphragmatic breathing. Sometimes one hears a director tell a cast member to "breathe from the stomach." This is not very helpful unless the director explains the process and underscores the training that is necessary for achieving change. We mentioned earlier that breathing for life is naturally diaphragmatic. For some inexplicable reason many untrained speakers (and, unfortunately, even some trained ones) shift from diaphragmatic to thoracic breathing when speaking.

To practice diaphragmatic/abdominal breathing, place your hand on your abdomen and inhale. If your hand moves out on the inhalation and back in on the exhalation, your breathing is diaphragmatic. Now stand up, place your hand on the same spot, and take a deep inhalation. Do your shoulders elevate? Does your hand go in when you inhale and return to the neutral position on the exhalation? If so, you are breathing thoracically. This kind of breathing can have a very negative effect on the speaking voice. The tone of the voice is not sustained, and there are problems with projection. But most important, there is a great deal of tension in the neck and shoulders that tends to "spill over" into the larynx, creating excessive vocal tension.

Keep in mind that diaphragmatic breathing is natural breathing. However, this does not mean that a speaker automatically uses it. As with speech, one must habituate oneself to diaphragmatic breathing. Because diaphragmatic breathing has a positive effect on amplification, relaxation, and pitch, it is vital to develop good respiration.

In time, the thoracic breather not only develops poor vocal habits but also tires easily. The abdominal breath is the most natural because the muscles involved in breathing can perform their function without restriction or added tension. To demonstrate this natural effect of diaphragmatic/abdominal breathing, do a series of aerobic exercises—push-ups or sit-ups—or run in place until you are breathing heavily. At that point, focus on how you are breathing. It is diaphragmatic, for this is the natural way!

You should do the diaphragmatic exercises every day if you want to improve your voice production. Set aside the same time each day. When you first awake and just before you retire are often practical times. Because some of the exercises do not involve vocal production, they can also be done while you walk to class or work.

The key to making diaphragmatic/abdominal breathing habitual is to understand why and how the process works. Then you must be highly motivated to do the repetitions necessary for the breathing to become second nature. The length of time required for habituation varies from person to person. In addition, it is important that you do not feel self-conscious. Again, do these exercises in privacy. But the sooner you can do all of the exercises in front of others (classmates, friends, or family), the better. Remember that all of your classmates in speech are similarly feeling inadequate, hesitant, and often foolish.

These are common reactions. You may feel as if everyone you meet is viewing you critically and wondering what your problem is. Just be careful about where you do the exercises, and, for your own sanity, develop your sense of humor and laugh at yourself. It truly makes the process go more speedily and smoothly, and with far less emotional trauma.

EXERCISES FOR DIAPHRAGMATIC BREATHING AND CONTROL

1. Stand up. Place the palm of your hand on your abdomen, stick out your tongue, and pant like a dog. (Remember that your classmates feel just as ridiculous as you do!) Feel the diaphragmatic action. When you inhale, the abdominal wall moves out; when you exhale, it returns to the relaxed position. This exercise gives you a good sense of the action of the diaphragm.

2. At home, lie down on your back on your plush Oriental carpet (regular carpets work almost as well) and place a book on your abdomen. When you inhale slowly through the mouth, make certain that the book is elevated slowly and evenly. When you exhale slowly through the mouth, the book should return smoothly to its former position. Do not allow the book to move jerkily. It should return to the neutral position at the same pace as it rose during inhalation.

3. Sit in a straight-back chair without arms. Hold the back legs of the chair so that your shoulders cannot be elevated. Breathing through the mouth, take a breath slowly to a silent count of five, hold your breath to a silent count of five, and exhale to a silent count of five. Choose your own rhythm of counting, but keep it consistent. Tension should be on the abdominal region, not on the throat or neck.

4. With your instructor establishing the beat, stand up and repeat the five count as in exercise 3. Your teacher might then count to six, seven, eight, and so on. Make certain that you keep the tension in the abdominal region. Also, be sure that you are inhaling, holding your breath, or exhaling all of the time that your teacher is counting. It is the tension followed by the relaxation that strengthens the diaphragm. Abdominal tension should also be maintained during the "hold" portion of the exercise. Your hand should move outward and inward slowly and evenly during respiration. Your instructor might want to alter the rhythm of the counting by increasing the time between each digit in the count. The instructor might set the pace for the class before vocalization begins.

5. This exercise is quite simple. Sit up on the floor with your legs bent. Lie back down slowly, keeping tension in the abdominal region. This reverse sit-up exercise helps to strengthen the rectus abdominus muscle.

Note: Make certain that you do not overdo any of these exercises. Obviously, you are exercising muscles and you do not want to injure or strain them.

It is of little use to develop diaphragmatic breathing unless one result is diaphragmatic control. It is the control of the outgoing breath that gives the voice volume, strength, and resonance. Proper diaphragmatic habits are essential to a full, resonant voice. To demonstrate the effect that controlling the breath has on the quality of a voice, record the following exercises on a cassette and then listen carefully and critically to the results.

6. Take a deep diaphragmatic breath and read the following without controlling the exhalation. Let the air escape as if you were a balloon that was just punctured. The sound that you produce is characterized by breathiness and is said to be "breathy." Recapture the feeling of your first meeting with your "significant other." Have fun with it and make it as sentimental as you can. Remember, in just one breath say:

I wish I could remember the first day,
First hour, first moment of your meeting me . . .

If your nervous and digestive systems can take more, feel free to look up the rest of Christina Rossetti's poem "The First Day."

7. Now read the selection in exercise 6 while controlling the output of the diaphragmatic breath. Bring tension to the abdominal area, and just think of filling with sound the room in which you are speaking. If you are controlling the breath properly, there should be a significant difference in the quality of your voice compared with the breathiness of the recording of the uncontrolled exhalation. Remember that both of the inhalations are diaphragmatic, but only the second exercise involves a controlled exhalation. Thus, controlled exhalation during phonation is almost as important as the original diaphragmatic breath.

((((· EXERCISES FOR BREATH CONTROL

When practicing these exercises, make certain that your vocalization begins immediately. Keep your loudness and pitch consistent in exercises 1 through 7. These exercises can be done alone or in a group.

Important: During the speech exhalation, your abdominal region must relax gradually. You control its movement back into place. It must return to its relaxed position. Do not try to keep your abdomen out during the entire process, for this creates additional tension. The abdomen must return because it is the escaping breath that causes the sound.

1. Stand and place the palm of your hand on your abdomen. With your instructor leading the exercise, take a deep diaphragmatic inhalation, and with a well-projected voice say, "One by one they went away." Exhale the remainder of the air through the mouth. Take another deep diaphragmatic inhalation and say, "One by one and two by two they went away." Repeat the exercise, increasing to "ten by ten they went away." If you begin to feel a little dizzy, sit down. You will gradually increase your lung capacity.

2. Stand and place the palm of your hand on your abdomen. With your instructor leading the exercise, take a deep diaphragmatic inhalation. Pick a comfortable pitch, and while exhaling, produce the vowel sound "ah" quietly. Increase the volume so that at the end of the exhalation the volume is at its loudest.

3. Complete exercise 2 again, but begin the "ah" at your greatest volume and decrease the projection until you are still sustaining the vowel but at your lowest volume. Make certain that you are bringing muscular tension to the abdominal region and not to the neck and shoulder muscles.

4. Complete exercise 2 again, but begin the "ah" quietly, build to your greatest volume, and return to the volume at which you began. Keep the tension in the abdominal region.

5. Complete exercise 2 again, but begin the vowel sound "ah" on the exhalation at your greatest volume, go to your minimal volume, and return to the loudest you can produce.

6. Take a deep diaphragmatic inhalation. At a rhythm of one count per second (set by your teacher) and with a good support of breath and volume, begin counting and aim for sixty. When you begin to feel a strain, drop out. Keep a record of your progress.

7. Substitute the alphabet for the numbers in exercise 6.

8. Take a deep diaphragmatic inhalation through the mouth, and read the following passages with as few breaths as possible. For your purposes, it is unimportant at present to consider the meaning. Read the selection with good articulation and intensity, if you like. Your teacher should set the rhythm. Keep a daily journal on your progress. How far into the selection can you get before you need to take a new breath? The lines of many exercises are numbered to make it easier to deal with segments of material. Be sure to keep the abdominal region tense as you speak. Do not force any part of the process. Go as quickly as you like, but make certain that you produce all of the sounds. The slash / indicates an inhalation.

   a. 1 When you're lying awake with a dismal headache, and repose is taboo'd by anxiety, /
       2 I conceive you may use any language you choose to indulge in, without impropriety; /
       3 For your brain is on fire—the bedclothes conspire of usual slumber to plunder you: /
       4 First your counterpane goes, and uncovers your toes, and your sheet slips demurely from under you; /

5   Then the blanketing tickles—you feel like mixed pickles—so terribly sharp is the pricking, /

6   And you're hot, and you're cross, and you tumble and toss till there's nothing 'twixt you and the ticking. /

7   Then the bedclothes all creep to the ground in a heap, and you pick 'em all up in a tangle; /

8   Next your pillow resigns and politely declines to remain at its usual angle! /

9   Well, you get some repose in the form of a doze, with hot eyeballs and head ever aching, /

10   But your slumbering teems with such horrible dreams that you'd very much better be waking. /

One breath

11   You're a regular wreck, with a crick in your neck, and no wonder you snore, for your head's on the floor, and you've needles and pins from your soles to your shins, and your flesh is a-creep, for your left leg's asleep, and you've cramp in your toes, and a fly on your nose, and some fluff in your lung, and a feverish tongue, and a thirst that's intense, and a general sense that you haven't been sleeping in clover; /

12   But the darkness has passed, and it's daylight at last, and the night has been long— ditto ditto my song—and thank goodness they're both of them over! /

THE NIGHTMARE SONG from *Iolanthe*
W. S. Gilbert

b.   1   Rats!/

2   They fought the dogs and killed the cats

3   And bit the babies in the cradles,

4   And ate the cheeses out of the vats,

5   And licked the soup from the cooks' own ladles,

One breath

6   Split open the kegs of salted sprats,

7   Made nests inside men's Sunday hats,

8   And even spoiled the women's chats

9   By drowning their speaking

10   With shrieking and squeaking

11   In fifty different sharps and flats.

From THE PIED PIPER OF HAMELIN
Robert Browning

9.   Take only the diaphragmatic breaths that are indicated by slashes in each reading. Keep a journal on your progress. How long did it take you to accomplish this? It can be done! In addition, these exercises are also excellent for articulation.

a. /21   Dividing and gliding and sliding,

22   And falling and brawling and sprawling,

23   And driving and riving and striving,

One breath

24   And sprinkling and twinkling and wrinkling,

25   And sounding and bounding and rounding,

26   And bubbling and troubling and doubling,

27   And grumbling and rumbling and tumbling,

28   And clattering and battering and shattering;/

/29   Retreating and beating and meeting and sheeting,

30   Delaying and straying and playing and spraying,

31   Advancing and prancing and glancing and dancing,

One breath

32   Recoiling, turmoiling and toiling and boiling,

33   And gleaming and streaming and steaming and beaming,

34   And rushing and flushing and brushing and gushing,

One breath

35 And flapping and rapping and clapping and slapping,
36 And curling and whirling and purling and twirling,
37 And thumping and plumping and bumping and jumping,
38 And dashing and flashing and splashing and clashing;

From THE CATARACT OF LODORE
Robert Southey

Try exercises (b) and (c) at the quickened pace that is usually used in breath control exercises. Then, repeat the exercise at a much slower pace. You should be able to complete it on one breath if you are able to do it at the faster pace. If you can't, the problem is psychological rather than physical.

b. /1 I am the very model of a modern Major-General,
2 I've information vegetable, animal, and mineral.
3 I know the kings of England, and I quote the fights historical,
4 From Marathon to Waterloo, in order categorical;
5 I'm very well acquainted too with matters mathematical.
6 I understand equations, both the simple and quadratical,
7 About binomial theorem I'm teeming with a lot o' news—
8 With many cheerful facts about the square of the hypotenuse.

/9 I'm very good at integral and differential calculus,
10 I know the scientific names of beings animalculus;
11 In short, in matters vegetable, animal, and mineral,
12 I am the very model of a modern Major-General.

From THE PIRATES OF PENZANCE
W. S. Gilbert

c. /1 There is beauty in the bellow of the blast,
2 There is grandeur in the growling of the gale,
3 There is eloquent out-pouring
4 When the lion is a-roaring,
5 And the tiger is a-lashing of his tail!
6 Yes, I'd like to see a tiger,
7 From the Congo or the Niger,
8 And especially when lashing of his tail!

From THE MIKADO
W. S. Gilbert

10. Take a diaphragmatic breath through the mouth and read the following selections, making certain that you do not allow any breath to escape before you begin speaking. While being mindful of each selection's meaning, keep the tone of your voice strong and resonant. These exercises use controlled exhalation more normally. As before, each inserted slash indicates a new diaphragmatic breath.

a. He didn't know which door (or well) or opening in the house to jump at, / to get through / because one was an opening that wasn't a door / and the other was a wall that wasn't an opening, / it was a sanitary cupboard of the same color.

From STUART LITTLE
E. B. White

b. 1 Call me Ishmael. / Some years ago—never mind how long precisely—
2 having little or no money in my purse, / and nothing particular to interest me
3 on shore, / I thought I would sail about a little and see the watery part of
4 the world. / It is a way I have of driving off the spleen, and regulating the

5 circulation. / Whenever I find myself growing grim about the mouth; when-
6 ever it is a damp, drizzling November in my soul; / [*Big breath and support*
7 *it!*] whenever I find myself involuntarily pausing before coffin warehouses,
8 and bringing up the rear of every funeral I meet; . . . / then, account it high
9 time to get to sea as soon as I can.

From MOBY DICK
Herman Melville

c. 1 It is impossible to say how first the idea entered my brain; but once conceived
2 it haunted me day and night. / Object there was none. Passion there was none.
3 I loved the old man. / He had never wronged me. He had never given me insult.
4 For his gold I had no desire. / I think it was his eye! yes, it was this! One of
5 his eyes resembled that of a vulture—a pale blue eye with a film over it. /
6 Whenever it fell upon me, my blood ran cold; and so by degrees—very gradually—
7 / I made up my mind to take the life of the old man, and thus rid myself
8 of the eye for ever. /
9 Now this is the point. You fancy me mad. Madmen know nothing. But you
10 should have seen me. You should have seen how wisely I proceeded—with
11 what caution—with what foresight—with what dissimulation I went to
12 work! / I was never kinder to the old man than during the whole week before I
13 killed him. / And every night, about midnight, I turned the latch of his door and
14 opened it— oh so gently! / And then, when I had made an opening sufficient for
15 my head, / I put in a dark lantern, all closed, closed, so that no light shone out,
16 and then I thrust in my head. / Oh, you would have laughed to see how cunningly
17 I thrust it in! / I moved it slowly—very, very slowly, so that I might not
18 disturb the old man's sleep. / It took me an hour to place my whole head within
19 the opening so far that I could see him as he lay upon his bed. / Ha!—would a
20 madman have been as wise as this?

From THE TELL-TALE HEART
Edgar Allan Poe

BREATHINESS

Obviously, much of the vocal characteristic of **breathiness** is eliminated by controlling diaphragmatic breaths and increasing the tension at the vocal folds and not in the muscles of the neck. *Breathiness* is a vocal quality in which excessive breath passes between the vocal folds during phonation because the folds are not close enough together. There are exercises for controlling breathiness that should be done in conjunction with those for controlling exhalation.

To build up tension on initial vowels and diphthongs for the breathy speaker, consult the section on glottal shock in Chapter 5. Practice the exercises there. In addition, here is another exercise for strengthening the muscles in your abdomen: Stand a couple of feet from a flat surface (a wall or a door), put your hands on the surface, and then lean forward. You may have to adjust the distance from the surface in order to feel muscular tension in the abdominal region. Then, complete a series of vertical push-ups using the wall or door.

A great deal of time has been spent in this chapter explaining how to control diaphragmatic action with increased phonation. However, there are instances in which it might be advantageous to be able to produce a breathy voice. Some of you may be taking voice and articulation as a beginning course for various majors in communication—speech communications, radio, television, or theater. Remember that one of the purposes of this text is to help you develop flexibility of voice and speech. Yes, eliminate the breathiness that is in your personal voice and speech, but realize that the flexible voice is the best voice. The individual who can do many things with his or her voice has more opportunities. As you are well aware, making a commercial or doing a voice-over can be very lucrative.

At any rate, you should be able to make the necessary physiological adjustments to the vocal apparatus so that you can adopt the voice appropriate to the kind of character you wish to present. As an example, if you are an actor in the role of Antigone, you will not want her to sound like the stereotypical "weathergirl" stating that "Rain is expected in the Athens/Piraeus area." No! Antigone is an assertive, definite, now kind of woman who knows where she is going and what she wants. Antigone's vocal traits ought to reflect these qualities. A breathy quality is often an outward manifestation of a very different sort of character. If you are playing Elvira in Noel Coward's *Blithe Spirit,* you might want to reflect her elegant earthiness at least partially through the use of a breathy voice. The point is that you want to make your vocal quality appropriate to the character.

The breathy quality is not limited to females. Most untrained (and, alas, too many trained) male speakers do not control their exhalation, which results in breathiness. The male voice may not sound as breathy as the female because of the differences in pitch and **resonance,** but breathiness can still be there. Sometimes you are unaware of breathiness until it has been reduced. (*Resonance* is the process that amplifies and modifies the intensity of tone. This takes place in the cavities of the mouth, nose, and throat.)

The following exercises have been designed to help you achieve breathiness. Understand why you are doing them, and feel what you are doing. This is a form of negative practice that may well be profitable for you sometime in your career.

EXERCISES FOR BREATHINESS

Take a diaphragmatic breath through the mouth before you read the following sentences and selections. Let the abdominal region collapse so that the breath rushes out. Then read the exercises with your career speech so that you will not forget what you want to be developing consciously. Record both voices on a cassette so that you also develop your listening acuity. And, as always, concentrate on what is happening to you physically during the process of phonation.

1. It is time to do those dreary exercises.

2. Life is, oh . . . so very long.

3. After I finished jogging I collapsed into this chair.

4. In Miami the weather is very sunny with 76 degrees.

5. There is sweet music here that softer falls
   Than petals from blown roses on the grass,
   Or night dews on still waters between walls
   Of shadowy granite, in a gleaming pass—,
   Music that gentlier on the spirit lies,
   Than tired eyelids upon tired eyes;
   Music that brings sweet sleep down from the blissful skies.

From THE LOTOS-EATERS
Alfred, Lord Tennyson

6. *FS:* Piping down the valleys wild
        Piping songs of pleasant glee
        On a cloud I saw a child
        And he laughing said to me.

SS: Pipe a song about a Lamb;
FS: So I piped with merry chear,
SS: Piper pipe that song again—
FS: So I piped, he wept to hear.

SS: Drop thy pipe thy happy pipe
        Sing thy songs of happy chear,
FS: So I sung the same again
        While he wept with joy to hear

SS: Piper sit thee down and write
        In a book that all may read—

FS: So he vanish'd from my sight.
        And I pluck'd a hollow reed.
        And I made a rural pen, And
        I stain'd the water clear,
        And I wrote my happy songs
        Every child may joy to hear.

From SONGS OF INNOCENCE
William Blake

FS (first speaker) more mature voice than SS (second speaker), who is the child.

Obviously, the FS voice would be your career voice and the SS voice would be the breathy voice of a child. Work for the simplicity inherent in the text of the poem.

7. Little Lamb, who made thee?
    Dost thou know who made thee?
    Gave thee life, and bid thee feed,
    By the stream and o'er the mead;
    Gave thee clothing of delight,
    Softest clothing, woolly bright;
    Gave thee such a tender voice,
    Making all the vales rejoice?
    Little Lamb, who made thee?
    Dost thou know who made thee?

    Little Lamb, I'll tell thee,
    Little Lamb, I'll tell thee;
    He is call-ed by thy name,
    For He calls Himself a Lamb.
    He is meek, and he is mild;
    He became a little child.
    I a child, and thou a lamb,
    We are call-ed by His name.
    Little Lamb, God bless thee!
    Little Lamb, God bless thee !

LITTLE LAMB
William Blake

In this poem a breathy voice could be used very effectively in creating the child's innocence.

W To locate URLs and search terms for weblinks relevant to this chapter, please go to the companion website at www.cengage.com/rtf/crannell/voiceandarticulation5e and select the proper chapter.

Write the definitions for the following terms in the space below.

KEY TERMS	DEFINITIONS
Alveoli	
Breathiness	
Bronchioles	
Bronchus	
Clavicular Breathing	
Diaphragm	
Diaphragmatic Breathing	
Exhalation	
Inhalation	
Intercostal Muscles	
Larynx	
Lungs	
Nasal Cavity	
Oral Cavity	
Pharynx	
Phonation	
Rectus Abdominus	
Resonance	
Respiration	
Rib Cage	
Sternum	
Thorax	
Trachea	
Turbinates	
Upper Thoracic Breathing	
Vegetative Breathing	
Vertebral Column	
Viscera	
Vocal Folds	

CHAPTER 3

THE VOICE

$\mathbf{P}$rior to a discussion of the mechanics of the voice, it is necessary to underscore the importance of keeping the voice box healthy. The larynx is a very delicate structure that can be permanently damaged through misuse of the voice. Therefore, as you progress through the following voice chapters, keep in mind that attaining the relaxed voice is not only a very healthy habit but also a criterion for good communication skills.

Before any sound can be produced, there must be something capable of being vibrated; that is, there must be a **vibrating agent.** In addition, a force must be applied to this vibrating agent. If the resulting sound is to be heard easily, there must also be some kind of cavity that can amplify this tone. In a clarinet, for example, the sound is produced by the action of the escaping breath on the vibrating agent, the reed. In a trumpet, the escaping breath acts on the trumpeter's lips to cause the vibration and thus the sound. In both instruments, its physical shape magnifies and colors the sounds. Breath rushing between the lips alone would not give Ravel's "Bolero" the same emotional power supplied by an amplifying trumpet.

In a piano, the vibrating agents are, of course, the strings of various tensions and lengths. The force is the amount of power applied to the keys. The pedals also influence the sound. The resonating, amplifying, or modifying cavity of the piano is the area surrounding the strings, and its size varies with the kind of piano: upright, baby grand, or grand.

The sound of musical instruments depends on the quality of the manufactured parts and the subsequent care given them. The same is true of the human voice. You are born with certain anatomical components. These, in conjunction with the care you give them, will determine the sound of your voice.

In the human voice, the vibrating agents are the folds of muscles called the **thyroarytenoids.** Not too many years ago these vibrating agents were known as the "vocal cords." The word *cords* implied that they were like strings or elastic bands, but the vocal folds are actually ligamentous tissue composed of folds of muscle. There are two vocal folds whose inner edges can be vibrated by the escaping air of exhalation. The vocal folds are housed in the **larynx,** commonly called the "voice box."

>>> STRUCTURE OF THE LARYNX

Although many voice teachers do not like to admit it, the larynx's primary function is not the production of resonant speech. Rather, it acts as a valve at the opening of the trachea. To demonstrate, if you try to lift yourself off a chair with your hands pushing on the seat, you will feel not only a strong closure at the larynx but also an increase in pressure there. During an effort such as lifting, the vocal folds contract tightly, and oxygenated air is retained beneath the closure to give the individual more physical strength. It is interesting to note that a person with a **laryngectomy** ("-ectomy" means removal by surgery) is physically weaker because such a person no longer has a valve to capture air.

The larynx is composed of five major cartilages as well as muscles other than the vocal folds (Figure 3.1). The five cartilages of the larynx are the cricoid, the two arytenoids, the thyroid, and the epiglottis. The **hyoid bone** is a small horseshoe-shaped bone (Figure 3.2), approximately one to one-and-a-half inches long, located horizontally in the **pharynx** near the base of the tongue. The open end of the horseshoe faces the back. The hyoid bone is considered the only truly floating bone in the body; it is not connected directly to the rest of the **skeleton,** but held in place by many muscles. Because of its floating quality, the hyoid is very movable. Its importance to voice production is evident when you realize that the larynx is suspended from this bone. When specific groups of muscles connected to the hyoid contract and relax, the hyoid can move upward or downward—a movement that makes certain sounds easier to produce. Even though the hyoid bone is an invaluable structure, it is not considered a part of the larynx.

The **cricoid** cartilage is the top ring of the trachea and forms a complete cartilaginous circle. You might remember from an earlier discussion that the other rings of the trachea are three-quarters-closed rings with the opening toward the back. The cricoid is often described as having the shape of a signet ring, with the narrow portion in the front and the wider portion in the back (Figure 3.3). This cartilage is the base of the larynx and gives the larynx some stability.

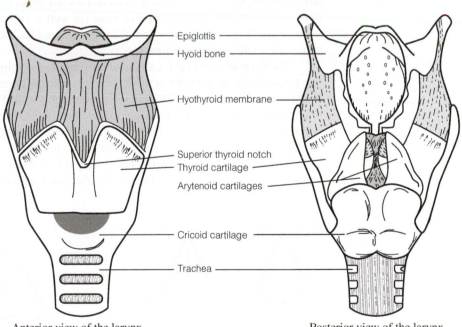

Epiglottis
Hyoid bone
Hyothyroid membrane
Superior thyroid notch
Thyroid cartilage
Arytenoid cartilages
Cricoid cartilage
Trachea

Anterior view of the larynx   Posterior view of the larynx

FIGURE 3.1   The five major cartilages of the larynx

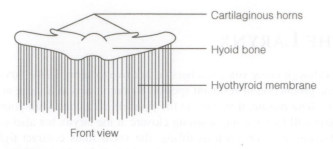

Cartilaginous horns

Hyoid bone

Hyothyroid membrane

Front view

FIGURE 3.2 Front view of the hyoid bone

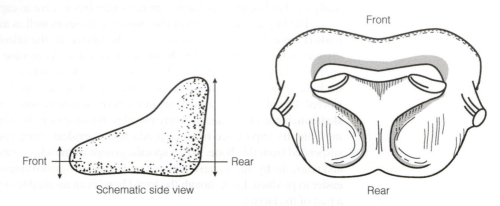

Front

Front — Rear

Schematic side view

Rear

FIGURE 3.3 Side view and sketch of front and rear views of cricoid cartilage

The two **arytenoids** are paired, pyramid-shaped cartilages whose bases rest on the back (posterior) portion of the cricoid cartilage. They look like a pyramid because they have three sides and a top, or apex (compare Figures 3.4 and 3.5).

The side corners of each arytenoid (A and B in Figure 3.5) are called the *muscular processes* (projections). To these are attached several important muscles that keep the larynx functioning. Because of the action of these (as well as other) muscles, the arytenoids can rotate, move from side to side, and slide forward and backward. The front corner of each arytenoid is called the **vocal process.**

The **thyroid cartilage** is a shield-shaped cartilage (composed of two **fused cartilages**) that forms the front and sides of the larynx. It is also the largest cartilage of the larynx. The frontal process on the thyroid cartilage is commonly called the **Adam's apple**, which is important because the vocal folds are located behind it. The front (anterior) portion of the vocal folds are attached to it; the Adam's apple helps to protect the vocal folds.

The true vocal folds are fused in the front (just below the thyroid notch; Figure 3.1) and separate into two folds, with each posterior end attached to the vocal process of the arytenoids (Figure 3.6). When the arytenoids slide forward or backward, the length and

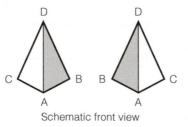

Schematic front view

FIGURE 3.4 Schematic pyramids

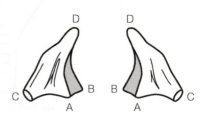

FIGURE 3.5 Arytenoid cartilages

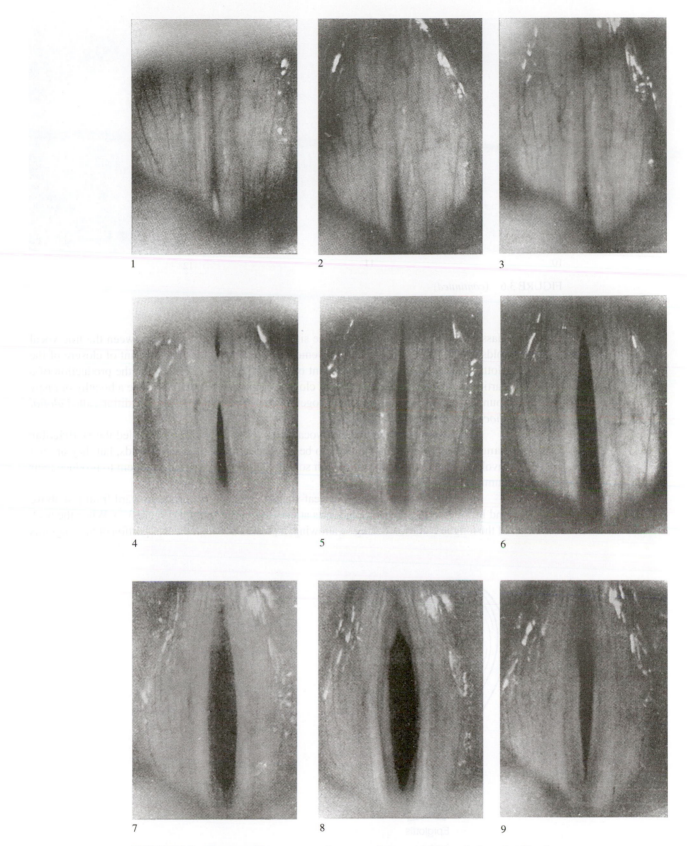

FIGURE 3.6   Photographic sequence of one complete vocal fold cycle (van den Berg)

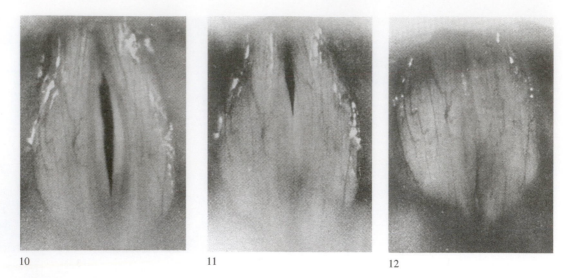

10   11   12

FIGURE 3.6   (*continued*)

mass of the vocal folds change. The size of the **glottis** (the space between the true vocal folds) is thus controlled by the movement of the arytenoids. The amount of closure of the glottis is dependent upon the amount of exhaled breath necessary for the production of a particular sound. If the folds are not close enough together, there will be a breathy or raspy sound. If they are too tightly drawn together, the voice will contain a condition called *glottal shock* (discussed in Chapter 5).

Growing just above the true vocal folds are false vocal folds called the **ventricular bands.** Their function is believed to be protection of the true vocal folds, but they are not involved in the production of speech sound. Ventriloquists often use them to produce their dummies' voices.

The **epiglottis** is a spoon- or leaf-shaped cartilage that grows upward from just above and inside the thyroid notch and rests at the base of the **tongue** (Figure 3.7). When the back of the tongue contracts during swallowing, it presses down on the leaf portion of the epiglottis

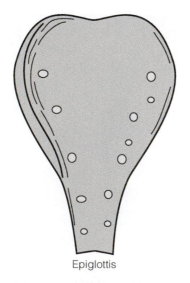

Epiglottis

FIGURE 3.7   Epiglottis

("epi-" means above, over, or covering), making it lean over the glottis to protect it from foreign matter. The epiglottis is not of great importance in the production of sound.

>>>
SOUND PRODUCTION

The exhaled breath causes vibration or a "buzzing sound" when the vocal folds are brought slightly together with just the right amount of tension. The sound that is then produced at the larynx is called the **fundamental tone;** it constitutes the general pitch of the voice, but this sound has little volume or resonance. For voice to have what we call **quality,** the sound must be amplified in the cavities of the mouth, throat, or nose with what is called **resonance,** or the "re-sounding" of the fundamental tone.

Resonance

Resonance can occur in the thorax and other structures, but it cannot be controlled as it can in the mouth, throat, and nose (see Figure 2.3). A number of factors contribute to how a cavity resonates a basic sound: the size of the cavity, the size of the opening into the cavity, and the condition of the lining of the cavity. There are three kinds of resonance: oral, nasal, and pharyngeal. **Oral resonance** is perhaps the most versatile because the size, shape, and opening of the oral cavity are more easily changed. For example, say the vowel sound "ah" and move slowly to the "ee" in "see." Feel what the tongue is doing during the transition. The tongue position, the size of the opening (determined by the lips and lower jaw), and the size of the oral cavity all change. The fundamental tone remains the same, but through a slight adjustment in the articulatory mechanism a different vowel sound is created.

The least mobile of the resonating cavities is the nasal cavity. Only the opening of this cavity can be controlled. The only three sounds in the English language that are legitimately re-sounded in the nose are /m/, /n/, and the sound of the letters *ng* in "long." Sometimes the nasal opening allows either too much or too little **nasal resonance,** and the quality of the voice changes accordingly.

Pharyngeal resonance is perhaps the most important to voice quality. Simple modification of the size and opening into the throat and of tongue placement can change vocal quality. To get an idea of pharyngeal resonance, constrict the muscles of the throat by making the throat area smaller. Sustain the vowel sound "ee." Listen to the quality of your voice, which becomes very tense, high-pitched, and thin. Now make the throat cavity as large as you can by yawning and producing a very relaxed throat. Slowly modify the sound by producing and sustaining the vowel sound "oo." The influence on the sound of the voice is unmistakable. You can feel the difference in the amount of tension in the throat and mouth cavities because of the changes in the size and shape of the pharyngeal cavity.

Forced and Sympathetic Vibration

Forced vibration results when one vibrating object is placed directly upon another, causing the second object to vibrate. A forced vibration occurs, for example, when a vibrating tuning fork is placed directly on another tuning fork, causing the second to vibrate as well. Helen Keller learned the concept of vibration by feeling it in the wood of a piano or in a floor upon which she stood. She also felt with her hand the vibration created within the larynx. Because forced vibration cannot be easily controlled, it is not important in developing voice for the average person.

Sympathetic vibration occurs when one frequency is in harmony with another. For example, when one tuning fork at a particular pitch is struck, it can cause another to vibrate at the same frequency without any direct contact. The cause of the vibration of the second tuning fork is indirect. Sympathetic vibration takes place in the three major cavities related to the production of speech sounds: the nose, throat, and mouth. By changing the size of the opening and the shape of the cavity, different choices of resonance can be made.

Factors of Sound

In addition to the fundamental tone produced at the vocal folds, four characteristics, or factors of sound, need to be considered: (1) pitch, (2) rate, (3) loudness, and (4) quality.

Pitch is determined by the number of vibrations per unit of time. In voice, this is determined by the thickness of the vocal folds (the pitch is lowered as the thickness increases), the length of the vocal folds (the pitch is lowered as the length decreases), the density of the vocal folds (the pitch is lowered as density increases), and the amount of tension in the vocal folds (the pitch is raised as the tension increases). The more vibrations per unit of time (also called "frequency") there are, the higher the pitch; the fewer vibrations, the lower the pitch (Figure 3.8). For example, the strings of a piano that produce the higher notes are shorter and thinner than those that produce the lower notes.

The second factor is the **rate,** or duration, of sound. *Rate* is a measure of both the length and number of pauses and the duration of syllables. A sound must be capable of being prolonged for a certain length of time for it to be heard and understood. If the duration of the sound is increased, the **tempo** slows. For example, if the vowel sound in the word *man* is prolonged, the tempo of the word is slowed down. When the duration is decreased, the tempo speeds up. One of the common characteristics of poor voice and speech habits, unintelligibility, results from not giving speech sounds (particularly vowels and diphthongs) enough time in production. Rate is also related to the number of words spoken during a certain period of time. Controlling the time factor is also used in making inflections (which will be discussed in Chapter 9).

The third characteristic of voice and speech is **loudness,** which involves the expansiveness of the vibration. The greater the expansion or amplification of the vibration, the louder the tone. The amount of power applied to the vibrating agent determines how far the vibrating body moves in its vibration and, consequently, how loud the sound produced will be. In the production of voice and speech, loudness is determined by the amount of breath during exhalation, the relative condition of the vocal folds, and the amplification by the resonance cavities. Figure 3.9 depicts loudness.

High
pitch

Medium
pitch

Low
pitch

FIGURE 3.8   Pitch

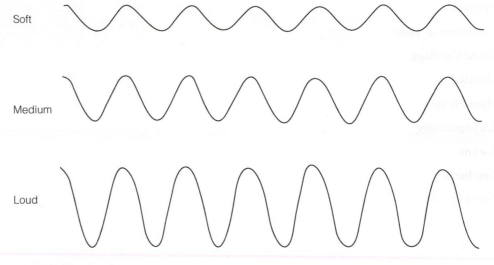

FIGURE 3.9   Loudness

Perhaps the most difficult factor to describe is *vocal quality,* which is determined by the amplitude and complexity of the vibration. The vocal folds, for example, vibrate as a whole, producing the aforementioned fundamental tone. The vocal folds also vibrate in "parts" called **partials,** *overtones, segmentals,* or *harmonics.* These parts are tuned to, or are in harmony with, different chambers in the resonance cavities. These chambers will select those partials with which they are sympathetic. It is the partials or segmentals that give each voice its unique vibration and make each voice recognizable. As a matter of fact, vowels are produced when the oral cavity size changes, and for each vowel certain partials are amplified rather than others. Two students may produce the same fundamental tone, but the differences between their voices will be determined by their partials and the resonators.

The anatomical structure of the larynx has been presented here in a most simplistic manner intentionally. You must be aware of the basic laryngeal structure if vocal exercises are to be at all meaningful.

To locate URLs and search terms for weblinks relevant to this chapter, please go to the companion website at www.cengage.com/rtf/crannell/voiceandarticulation5e and select the proper chapter.

Write the definitions for the following terms in the space below.

KEY TERMS

Adam's Apple

Arytenoids

Cricoid

DEFINITIONS

Epiglottis

Fundamental Tone

Fused Cartilage

Glottis

Hyoid Bone

Laryngectomy

Larynx

Loudness

Nasal Resonance

Oral Resonance

Partials

Pharyngeal Resonance

Pharynx

Pitch

Quality

Rate

Resonance

Skeleton

Sympathetic Vibration

Tempo

Thyroarytenoid Muscles

Thyroid Cartilage

Tongue

Ventricular Bands

Vibrating Agent

Vocal Process

CHAPTER 4

VOCAL RELAXATION

Human vocal communication can be categorized into three types: (1) conversational, (2) preferred or career, and (3) singing. Each communicator can use, in varying degrees, all of these voices. On a continuum, they would be represented in the following way:

conversational ⟵ preferred /career ⟶ singing

The type of public communication, the audience, and the material discussed all determine the speaker's proper voice. A public speech entitled "An End to MTV" would use a **career voice** toward the conversational end of the continuum instead of the singing end. On the other hand, a performance of Dylan Thomas's "Fern Hill," with all of its heightened use of sound, might be better served if the performer used career speech that leaned toward the singing end of the continuum. To find the career voice, the speaker would need to "pull away" from the **singing voice.**

Because **conversational speech** develops as one individual learns to communicate with another, the conversational voice usually develops accordingly and without the need for concentrated study. Conversational speech is a series of habits and a means of communication that is learned through observation, and it entails a great deal of trial and error.

For instance, say a child wants a drink of milk. He asks his mother for "moomoo." She laughs, thinks that the expression is cute, and gives him a glass of milk. As long as he gets his milk when he says "moo-moo," why does he need to say the word *milk?* Years pass. This particular **diction** (or choice of words) causes more than one raised eyebrow when the now teenager asks his football coach for "a glass of moo-moo" after the big game. Of course, such an expression might be acceptable from a person who has a speech or linguistic anomaly.

Unlike conversational speech, the singing voice and career speech require study because neither is a "natural" phenomenon, and your training must become habituated. Because speech differs from song in the same way that walking differs from dance, some people contend that no amount of practice will produce a pleasant singing voice. This may be a hard fact for a few people you know! Nevertheless, almost any singing voice can be improved through ear training and by properly producing vowels or diphthongs, for it is the vowel that gives language its projection and beauty of tone. Of course, the potential quality of the voice is also very important. The same is true with career speech, which, as we have noted, is not a natural phenomenon and must be habituated.

The differences among the three voices should be *quantitative* rather than *qualitative*. That is, you should not have a performance "sound" that is used exclusively for the performance occasion, and the changes in your voice and speech should vary in amount rather than in quality. The amount of articulation, voice quality, and dynamics in conversation might be less than in career speech, for example. How many times have you heard a person read a poem with a "poetry voice" that has no semblance to the conversational voice? The two voices should contain recognizable qualities; they should not sound like two different people.

An example using the singing voice and conversation/career speech might be helpful here. Our visual and auditory images of Jim Nabors's voice and speech are vividly identified with his portrayal of the character Gomer Pyle. Nabors often uses those characteristics when he is interviewed as Jim Nabors. However, when he sings he overarticulates and postures his mouth in an artificial manner that produces a quality of voice that appears affected. In reality he has a very well-trained singing voice that differs "qualitatively" from his speaking voice. And therefore, his conversational/career voice differs markedly from his singing voice.

Projection is a characteristic of both the career voice and the singing voice. At the foundation of projection is the proper use of breath. It is very important to learn to control exhalation. In addition to very definite differences in volume, controlled exhalation frequently changes the quality of the voice. A steadiness of tone results from supporting the breath. The voice without diaphragmatic control often wavers and sometimes cracks; this is true of both the singing and speaking voices. There is nothing more humiliating during speech than suffering from vocal tremors. They are insidious because you feel and hear them before your listeners do. Then your concentration on content is lost because you are expending all of your energies in covering up what is happening to you.

At any rate, career speech (which embodies voice) ought to possess a pleasant quality, appropriate projection, and vocal dynamics that suggest a thinking individual. Keep in mind, however, that the quality of any tone depends upon the use and structure of the resonance cavities (discussed in Chapter 3). It is important to note that resonance determines quality, breath control determines projection, and mind determines vocal dynamics. If you wish to improve your projection, work on your breath control. If you are unhappy with the quality of your voice because it is nasal (too much air through the nose) or denasal (not sufficient air through the nose), develop good resonance. The vocal dynamics that convey your meaning to your listeners depend upon intelligence as well as vocal quality and projection.

>>> OPEN THROAT

What are some of the more positive aspects of a pleasant speaking voice? First, the voice must be loud enough to be heard easily; thus, appropriate projection is necessary. A variation in the rate of speech is also important. Usually, an effective speaker slows down when delivering important points and passes over less important material relatively quickly. Frequently, a lower pitch is also characteristic of good speaking habits because it is more easily heard and, therefore, understood. Certainly, precise articulation is important to good voice and speech. You have already learned the importance of good diaphragmatic breathing habits. The last and perhaps most important factor is the degree of relaxation in a speaker's voice.

Generally, speakers should use what is called an **open throat**. When the throat is open (relaxed), the sound of the voice is not only more pleasant but can be sustained with the least effort. This does not mean that an open throat ought to be used all of the time; the intention of the thought will dictate the degree of openness. A performer needs to control the degree of relaxation according to the content. If you want to show a relaxed, caring, thoughtful person who is very much at ease in a given situation, the open throat—also called "the working tone"—is the sound to cultivate. The working tone should be appropriate for the event, the size of the room, the material, and the audience. Using a microphone makes choosing the appropriate working tone even more complex.

If as an actor or another type of performer you wish to reveal overt tension, you need to select the degree of tightness. The material dictates the appropriate vocal response.

However, for your habitual sound, the open throat (pharyngeal resonance) is strongly recommended. This is the best voice because when you want to appear relaxed in a tense situation (being interviewed for a job, for example), you want your voice and speech to behave accordingly. It is most unlikely that you will be able to achieve an open throat under pressure if it is not developed and made a habit. You will be too busy with other details, like words! Similarly, ministers or priests cannot use the open throat only in their gospel readings and sermons.

Part of the vocal tension in most trained and untrained speakers is decreased when they devote proper attention to getting all of their "systems" in a state of relaxation. A very effective exercise is the "Relaxation Response" designed by Dr. Herbert Benson,[1] a physician of international reputation and a leader in the field of stress reduction and management. The exercise was originally designed to reduce hypertension and cholesterol levels—vocal relaxation is a by-product. To achieve the Relaxation Response, Dr. Benson suggests the following daily routine:

1. Try to organize your schedule so that you will have twenty uninterrupted minutes.
2. Choose a quiet room. Sit erect in a comfortable chair with your feet on the floor.
3. Focus your awareness on a personal word or phrase.
4. Close your eyes.
5. Adopt a passive attitude toward your thoughts. This appears to be the most important element in eliciting the Relaxation Response. Thoughts, imagery, and feelings may drift into your awareness. Let them pass and return to your word or phrase, and you will discover that your diaphragmatic breathing becomes deeper.

Once you have completed the Relaxation Response exercise, you are in the best condition to perform your voice and speech exercises. The relaxed quality in an open throat can be achieved only when the pharynx is relaxed. Muscular tension must be taken away from the laryngeal area and moved to the abdominal region.

Your first act must be to compare the extremes. Tighten the voice. (Tense your neck with the lower jaw down.) Feel how this constriction physically affects your throat. Now relax the throat. Yawn out the sound and feel what your pharyngeal muscles do. This is called an **overly open throat.** Granted, this is not the most energetic-sounding quality; it is the sound you make when you talk while yawning at a dull lecture. In a relaxed position, take a quick breath through the mouth and quietly vocalize the exhalation. The sound produced is overly open. Yes, there is some tension in the yawning process, but it is natural and not excessive. Now say the following sentence with the same quality of overly open throat: "I am speaking with an overly open throat." No, this is not the new professional vocal quality that this text has been espousing. Nor should you let your family members hear it, or else you'll be handling your own tuition bills. Become aware of how an overly open throat is produced. Feel what the mouth, throat, and tongue are doing.

---

[1]Dr. Herbert Benson is chief of the Behavioral Medicine Section at the Beth Israel-Deaconess Medical Center in Boston. The materials presented here are adapted from notes and handouts taken and given to me at Dr. Benson's Hypertension Program. See Dr. Benson's books *The Relaxation Response* (New York: Avon Books, 1976) and *Beyond the Relaxation Response* (New York: Berkeley, 1985), and *Mind Your Heart,* Free Press, 2004.

Using negative practice, reverse this extreme again and speak the same material with a very contracted, tense throat. Do you feel the difference? Place your open hand around the front of your neck. While you repeat the exercise, focus on the difference in feeling between the two extremes of tension. Say the exercises with your habitual quality. Toward which end of the continuum do your voice and pharyngeal muscles lean—tight or overly relaxed? Remember that the overly open throat is merely an exercise, as is the overly tense throat. After you feel more comfortable with the sound of an overly open throat and can achieve it at will, you can learn how to pull away from that extreme to gain an open throat. For the moment, stick with the overly open throat so that you get used to the feeling of reduced muscular tension and the sound of exaggerated vocal relaxation.

Most untrained speakers (and too many trained speakers!) speak with too much vocal tension. Very little is achieved in acquiring the positive vocal habits cited unless excessive vocal tension is decreased. Therefore, it makes little sense to focus on articulatory problems or good inflection without minimizing the amount of tension first. A speaker may acquire excellent pitch, rate, and projection and still be abrasive if the voice is tense. In general, it is much easier to pull away from an overly open (overly relaxed) quality and gain good open throat than it is to add good voice and speech characteristics to a voice that is basically tense.

EXERCISES FOR OVERLY OPEN THROAT

There are three ways to achieve an overly open throat: (1) taking a quick breath through the mouth, (2) yawning, and (3) throwing up. Wouldn't you agree that of the three possibilities, a quick breath through the mouth seems the most desirable?

Exercises 1 through 5 can be used as warm-up exercises for each class.

1. Sitting in a chair with your feet firmly on the floor, tense the muscles of your forehead and elevate it; feel what is happening. Then relax the forehead. Feel what the muscles are doing. Then tighten the muscles of your cheeks and elevate them; feel them tense. Then relax the muscles of the cheeks; feel them relax. Follow the same procedure with:

   a. dropping the lower jaw

   b. elevating the shoulders

   c. tensing the muscles of the larynx

2. Begin each relaxation session by stimulating the area at the base of the **medulla oblongata** (the area where the base of the skull meets the vertebral column). With the middle three fingers of each hand, gently massage the area on each side of the spinal column. You will probably feel little balls of muscle. Gently massage the area until the "crunchies" are minimized.

3. Rotate the left shoulder six times; rotate the right shoulder six times; rotate both shoulders together six times. During this procedure, it is normal to experience the dreaded "crunchies."

4. Allow your head to fall forward slowly and gently as if you had no neck. Then slowly rotate your head to the right; do not force it all the way back. Reverse the rotation and continue all the way to the left; then return to the original position. Continue this movement five times around. Then reverse the direction five times around. Be careful that you do this gently, with no jarring or jerky movements; you do not want to end up in a neck brace. *Warning: People with neck or spinal problems should not do this exercise!*

5. Shake out both hands. With your shoulders back and down, pretend that you are trying to shake off a sticky piece of a "Milky Way" wrapper from the ends of your fingers. Then shake out your arms in the same manner. (Obviously, it was a bi-i-i-g candy bar!)

6. Now you are ready to yawn. After several yawns, introduce vibration of the vocal folds (this is a vocalized yawn). Then say, "I am yawning." Feel what is happening in the musculature of the pharynx.

7. Place your hands on your abdomen. After taking a quick diaphragmatic breath through the mouth, imitate popular television cartoon characters by saying "Yogi Baby," "Yabbadabba doo," and "Hey, Boo Boo." Make sure that you imitate the "cartoon style" of vocal presentation. You are not supposed to sound too intelligent (so you're safe)—that is part of the fun in this exercise. Gain the "speak on the yawn" quality. At first, complete this exercise in a group; that way everyone will feel ridiculous together.

8. Take a quick diaphragmatic breath through the mouth, pull your tongue back, and imitate the stereotypical punch-drunk fighter saying, "Gee, Ma, it was a great fight!" (Hear that bell ring in the background.)

9. Give your best ghost (or Homer Simpson) imitation as you recite the following passage from *Hamlet*. Use your face and let go with the overly open throat quality:

1 I am thy father's spirit;
2 Doom'd for a certain term to walk the night,
3 And for the day confin'd to fast in fires,
4 Till the foul crimes done in my days of nature
5 Are burnt and purg'd away. But that I am forbid
6 To tell the secrets of my prison-house,
7 I could a tale unfold whose lightest word
8 Would harrow up thy soul, freeze thy young blood,
9 Make thy two eyes, like stars, start from their spheres,
10 Thy knotted and combined locks to part
11 And each particular hair to stand on end,
12 Like quills upon the fretful porpentine:
13 But this eternal blazon must not be
14 To ears of flesh and blood.—List, list, O, list!
15 If thou didst ever thy dear father love— . . .
16 Revenge his foul and most unnatural murder.

Caution! Your quality of voice should not be strained or tense when doing this exercise. If it is, you are not vocalizing properly. Check with your instructor immediately. The overly open throat should be an easy sound to produce. If you have any doubt about the quality, don't do the exercise until you know you are producing it without strain. Otherwise, you might both damage your voice and make bad vocal characteristics habitual. Use your cassette recorder to hear the various qualities.

Speaking with an overly open throat becomes easier after using it in group exercises in class. Your instructor will help you attain it and make certain that you can reproduce it before you practice in private. The more frequently you exercise an overly open throat, the more quickly you will become accustomed to it.

The Desired Open Throat

After you can successfully produce an overly open throat, it is time to learn how to pull away from that quality to achieve the desired open throat, or "pharyngeal resonance." Nasal resonance is also a characteristic of an open throat. These are acquired, in part, by applying the rules of good diaphragmatic breathing while increasing the projection. Of course, this emphasizes the control of the exhalation. Record yourself as you compare and contrast vocal qualities. This may be a frustrating period for you; at times, you will not know which is which or what is what. This is quite usual. In time, as your awareness of **kinesthesis** and hearing acuity improve, you will be able to differentiate the vocal qualities.

You can develop the various types of relaxation by doing the following exercise several times a day: Take a diaphragmatic breath. With increased awareness of vowel and consonant production, say, "I am speaking with an overly open throat" as you attempt to do so. Then pull away from that quality and say, "I am speaking with an open throat." Then pull away more and say, "I am speaking with a tight throat." Feel the change in vocal and laryngeal tension as you increasingly pull away from an overly open throat.

In all probability, the pharyngeal resonance in an open throat is not characteristic of your habitual voice. The open throat must be made a habit if you want either the best sound that you can make or a profession in oral communications. This new vocal response is not the "you" with whom you are familiar. It is most usual to feel self-conscious, unnatural, and just plain silly, but it will be well worth it to you to take the time necessary to habituate yourself to the new sound that reveals the best elements of your voice. Those elements make up your "natural" voice that should become habitual.

However, you cannot save the open throat for those important moments when you want to sound your best. The faster you incorporate the open throat into your own speech patterns, the better. It must be emphasized repeatedly that you must tune into the kinesthetic as well as the **acoustic** elements. With an open throat, it is particularly important that you feel what the musculature is doing. It stands to reason that muscles that are constantly tense (as in a **tight throat**) must affect the quality of the voice.

EXERCISES FOR NASAL RESONANCE

Now that you have an open throat, at least theoretically, apply the principles that you have learned to the following exercises for developing good nasal resonance.

1. Produce a good humming sound. Do not clench the teeth. Bring the lips slightly and gently together to prepare for the hum. As you hum, get the sound in both the oral and nasal cavities. Feel the vibrating breath trying to get out between the two lips. Make sure that you feel strong vibration in the nasal cavity.

2. Hum the sounds /m/ and /n/ and the sound of the letters *ng,* changing from one to the next and then back again. This humming tone amplifies the nasal resonance. This exercise demonstrates that your mouth will open and close without altering the basic fundamental tone.

3. Sing the name of the Alaskan city Nome on one note. Prolong each of the sounds individually before going on to the next: /n:o:m:/. (The colon after a sound indicates that the sound is to be prolonged.) A less scientific way of representing it is NNNNN-NOOOOOOMMMMMM. Make sure that you glide from one sound to the next without interfering with the vocal quality.

4. Repeat exercise 3, but reverse the letters in the word *Nome* to get "moan."

5. Pick a note that is comfortable for you and sing the following words as they are written. Sustain the sung vowel sound. Then *speak* the word, retaining the appropriate nasal resonance. Make the difference in the *quantity* rather than the *quality.*

WORD	SINGING	SPEAKING
may	mmmmmmmmmmay-ay-ay-ay	may-may-may may
me	mmmmmmmmme-e-e-e-e	me-me-me me
my	mmmmmmmmmy-y-y-y-y	my-my-my my
ma	mmmmmmmmma-a-a-a-a	ma-ma-ma ma
mow	mmmmmmmmmo-o-o-o-o-o	mow-mow-mow mow
moo	mmmmmmmmmoo-oo-oo-oo	moo-moo-moo moo
neigh	nnnnnnnneigh-eigh-eigh	neigh-neigh-neigh neigh
knee	knknknknknee-ee-ee-ee	knee-knee-knee knee
nigh	nnnnnnnnnigh-igh-igh	nigh-nigh-nigh nigh
nab	nnnnnnnnah-ah-ah-ah-ab	nah-nah-nah nab
no	nnnnnnnno-o-o-o-o-o-o	no-no-no no
new	nnnnnnnnnew-ew-ew-ew	new-new-new new

6. Now add a consonant sound that is made in a similar way to the nasal sound. Follow what is written:

WORD	SINGING	SPEAKING
bay	mmmmmmmm-bay-ay-ay-ay	bay
bee	mmmmmmmm-bee-ee-ee-ee-ee-ee	bee
buy	mmmmmmmm-buy-uy-uy-uy-uy	buy
bah	mmmmmmmm-bah-ah-ah-ah-ah	bah
beau	mmmmmmmm-beau-eau-eau-eau	beau
boo	mmmmmmmm-boo-oo-oo-oo-oo	boo
day	nnnnnnnn-day-ay-ay-ay-ay-ay	day
dee	nnnnnnnn-dee-ee-ee-ee-ee-ee	dee
dye	nnnnnnnn-dye-eye-eye-eye-eye-eye	dye
dah	nnnnnnnn-da-a-a-a-a-a-a-a	dah
do	nnnnnnnn-do-o-o-o-o-o-o-o-o	do
gah	ng-ng-ng-ga-a-a-a-a-a	gah
geese	ng-ng-ng-gee-ee-ee-ee-ees	geese
guy	ng-ng-ng-guy-uy-uy-uy-uy	guy
go	ng-ng-ng-go-o-o-o-o-O-O-O	go
goon	ng-ng-ng-goo-oo-oo-oo-oon	goon

7. Read the following according to the way the words are printed:

beeeeeeeeeeeaaaaaammmmmmmmmm beam

paaaaaiiiiiiiiiiinnnnnnnnnnnn pain

gaaaaaaaaaaaaaaaaaangngngngngng gang

nnnnnnnnnnnnnnnnnnnnaaaaaaaaag nag

mmmmmmmmmmmmmmmmmmmaaaaaaaap map

nnnnnnnnnnnnnnnnnnnnaaaaaaaab nab

8. Say the following sound combinations with adequate projection, good open throat, one diaphragmatic breath, and solid nasal resonance on /m/. Try to keep the same feeling throughout the exercise, especially with the vocal attack on the isolated vowel sound in the final position. Also, make certain that there is vocal ease between the last two "ah" vowel sounds:

[m "ah"], [z "ah"], [sk "ah"], ["ah"]

The introduction of the consonants in this exercise brings attention to articulators in addition to the nasal and oral cavities: the lips "m," the tongue approximating the alveolar ridge "z," and the velum (or soft palate) "sk." This is also an excellent exercise for developing glottal or vocal shock (see pp. 72–73.).

9. Read each of the following selections using pharyngeal resonance. Do not worry about articulation or inflection; simply concentrate on attaining an open throat. Vary the tonal qualities intentionally. For example, read an entire selection, alternating the use of an overly open throat, open throat, and tight throat line by line. Then, reverse the procedure. Another pattern is to omit the tight throat and work exclusively with an overly open throat and open throat. In these important exercises, you should be learning to control voluntarily the quality of voice you produce. Finally, read the selections with an open throat exclusively and feel the comfort and ease in addition to hearing the difference in quality.

a. 1 Tomorrow, and tomorrow, and tomorrow,

2 Creeps in this petty pace from day to day,

3 To the last syllable of recorded time;

4 And all our yesterdays have lighted fools

5 The way to dusty death. Out, out, brief candle!

6 Life's but a walking shadow, a poor player

7 That struts and frets his hour upon the stage

8 And then is heard no more; it is a tale

9 Told by an idiot, full of sound and fury,

10 Signifying nothing.

From MACBETH
William Shakespeare

b. 1 Abou Ben Adhem (may his tribe increase!)

2 Awoke one night from a deep dream of peace,

3 And saw, within the moonlight in his room,

4 Making it rich, and like a lily in bloom,

5 An angel writing in a book of gold:—

6 Exceeding peace had made Ben Adhem bold,

7 And to the presence in the room he said,

8 "What writest thou?"— The vision raised its head,

9 And with a look made of all sweet accord,

10 Answered, "The names of those who love the Lord."

11 "And is mine one?" said Abou. "Nay, not so,"

12 Replied the angel. Abou spoke more low,

13 But cheerily still; and said, "I pray thee then,

14 Write me as one that loves his fellow-men."

15 The angel wrote, and vanished. The next night

16 It came again, with a great awakening light,

17 And showed the names whom love of God had blessed,

18 And lo! Ben Adhem's name led all the rest!

ABOU BEN ADHEM
Leigh Hunt

c. The following is a realistic view of love that is not typical of most sonnets:

1 My mistress' eyes are nothing like the sun;

2 Coral is far more red than her lips red;

3 If snow be white, why then her breasts are dun;

4 If hairs be wires, black wires grow on her head.

5 I have seen roses damask'd, red and white,

6 But no such roses see I in her cheeks;

7 And in some perfumes is there more delight

8 Than in the breath that from my mistress reeks.

9 I love to hear her speak, yet well I know

10 That music hath a far more pleasing sound;

11 I grant I never saw a goddess go;

12 My mistress, when she walks, treads on the ground.

13 And yet, by Heaven, I think my love as rare

14 As any she belied with false compare.

SONNET 130
William Shakespeare

10. Read aloud the following description of what an audition is like, voiced by a twenty-nine-year-old actress. Remember to keep your throat open.

Iris: You don't know what it's like though—God, to walk through those agency doors. . . . There's always some gal sitting on the other side, at a desk, you know, with a stack of pictures practically up to the ceiling in front of her. And they're always sort of bored, you know. Even the polite ones, the nice ones, I mean, they've seen five million and two like you and by the time you come through that door they are bored. And when you get past them, into the waiting room, there they are—the five million and two sitting there, waiting, and they look scared and mean and as competitive as you do. And so you all sit there, and you don't know anything: how you look, how you feel, anything. And least of all do you know how they want you to read. And when you get inside, you know less. There are just those faces. Christ, you almost wish that someone would make a pass or something; you could deal with that, you know—that's from life. But that almost never happens, at least not to me. All I ever see are those blank director-producer-writer faces just staring, waiting for you to show them something that will excite them. . . . And you just stand there knowing that you can't, no matter what, do it the way you did it at home in front of the mirror, the brilliant imaginative way you did it the night before. And all you can think is: What the hell am I doing standing here in front of these strangers, reading these silly words and jumping around for that fairy like some kind of nut . . . ? Sidney, I wish I had it in me to—be tougher. Like—like Gloria, I guess.

From THE SIGN IN SIDNEY BRUSTEIN'S WINDOW
Lorraine Hansberry

>>> PROJECTION

Projection is the carrying power of the voice. Appropriate projection is an important vocal component. Because projection is related to proper breathing habits, it might seem as if this subject more properly belongs in Chapter 2. However, projection is discussed here so that during your practice sessions you can incorporate it into an open throat. Be careful when you practice projection exercises! To practice full projection before relaxing the throat might prove harmful. You don't want to harm your voice by excessively increasing muscular tension in the pharyngeal area as you attempt to project. This tension may result in huskiness (sometimes permanent), hoarseness, or vocal strain. Remember how your throat felt (and sounded) after the yelling you did during your school's last big game. In addition to abusing physically the vocal mechanism, pharyngeal tension can also interfere with the aesthetics involved in communication. The emotions evoked by a soothing lyric poem cannot be conveyed with a brash and abrasive voice.

Again, use proper levels of projection. A speaker's vocal amplification ought to be appropriate to the message, the audience, and the site. A different kind of projection would be used for oration than for the reading of an Emily Dickinson poem. The audience must also be considered in adjusting projection, for it must always be able to hear (and see) the speaker easily. Nothing is more frustrating to an audience than not being able to hear a speaker; just imagine watching television with the volume off. Conversely, you must not overproject, overpowering your listeners. Experience and awareness will help you determine the appropriate projection for a communication event. Obviously, an important consideration is the amount of space involved, which may vary from a small conference room to a pulpit that has no microphone in a large church. Whenever possible, try speaking at the site in advance.

Many vocal factors work together to produce appropriate projection. The first thing the speaker must develop is adequate breath control, which is the foundation for all good voice and speech. You've heard this before, right? Proper breath control relates to many characteristics of the voice. To dramatize the influence of breath control on projection and vocal quality, select a wooden door in a classroom, house, or dorm that is in a relatively secluded area. Open it halfway. Plant your feet solidly on either side of the door and, with your hands on the doorknobs, place your abdominal area in firm contact with the edge of the door; keep your shoulders back and down. Take a deep but quick diaphragmatic breath, and while you are consciously controlling the exhalation, pretend that you are in a rather large theater. Having already taped the following excerpt of poetry to the door with masking tape (so that you don't damage the paint or stain on the door), read it at full volume:

> Roll on, thou deep and dark blue Ocean—roll!
> Ten thousand fleets sweep over thee in vain;
> Man marks the earth with ruin—his control
> Stops with the shore;—upon the watery plain
> The wrecks are all thy deed, nor doth remain

> A shadow of man's ravage, save his own,
> When for a moment like a drop of rain,
> He sinks into thy depths with bubbling groan,
> Without a grave, unknelled, uncoffined, and unknown.

From CHILDE HAROLD'S PILGRIMAGE
Lord Byron

Fill that room with sound! You will hear a tremendous difference in both the loudness and quality of the voice if you are using an open throat. If the tension goes from the abdomen to the throat, you are reciting the poem incorrectly.

Another important factor in good projection is how open the mouth is during phonation. All of your exercises should be completed with a conscious effort to articulate well. Don't overarticulate at this point, but do make certain that you are taking enough time to produce the sounds.

While doing the following projection exercises, keep your pitch level at your optimum range—neither too low nor too high. Also, make certain that you do not vary the pitch too much during the exercises. Read them with a good open throat. You will project more easily and comfortably when there is minimal tension in the pharyngeal area.

EXERCISES FOR PROJECTION

Say the following words and sentences with controlled exhalation at full projection. Make certain that you are using an open throat, however. If your voice hurts, chances are you are not using a relaxed tone.

1. You're on a golf course and want to warn players on the green ahead of you (or in the forest) that a ball is heading for them. Project the word *Fore!* so that it will be easily heard.

2. You have almost finished sawing down a giant tree and want to warn the villagers below. Take a good diaphragmatic breath, and project: "Tiiiimmmmmmbbeeerrr!"

3. Take a diaphragmatic breath, and project the following sentences on a controlled exhalation:

    Hey, look out for that car!

    I can't hear what you are saying. Speak up!

    Why do you always have to bring your mother with you?

After you have become familiar with the following exercises, recite them using the door technique previously described. Then reproduce the same vocal strength and ease of tone without the use of the door. While practicing, pretend that you are in a large hall and must reach the audience in the last row.

4. "A merry Christmas, uncle! God save you!" cried a cheerful voice. It was the voice of Scrooge's nephew, who came upon him so quickly that this was the first intimation he had of his approach.

    "Bah!" said Scrooge. "Humbug!"

    He had so heated himself with rapid walking in the fog and frost, this nephew of Scrooge's, that he was all in a glow; his face was ruddy and handsome; his eyes sparkled.

    "Christmas a humbug, uncle!" said Scrooge's nephew. "You don't mean that, I am sure?"

"I do," said Scrooge, "Merry Christmas! What right have you to be merry? You're poor enough."

"Come, then," returned the nephew gaily. "What right have you to be dismal? What reason have you to be morose? You're rich enough."

Scrooge, having no better answer ready on the spur of the moment, said "Bah!" again; and followed it up with "Humbug."

From A CHRISTMAS CAROL
Charles Dickens

5. In the following speeches from *Julius Caesar,* each man is using persuasion to quell a mob after the assassination of Caesar. Use your classmates to constitute the mob. This is a fine exercise for both males and females.

Brutus: Romans, countrymen, and lovers! hear me for my cause; and be silent, that you may hear: believe me for mine honour; and have respect to mine honour, that you may believe: censure me in your wisdom; and awake your senses, that you may the better judge. If there be any in this assembly, any dear friend of Caesar's, to him I say that Brutus' love for Caesar was no less than his. . . .

Antony: Friends, Romans, countrymen, lend me your ears;
I come to bury Caesar, not to praise him.
The evil that men do lives after them;
The good is oft interred with their bones;
So let it be with Caesar. The noble Brutus
Hath told you Caesar was ambitious:
If it were so, it was a grievous fault;
And grievously hath Caesar answered it.
Here, under leave of Brutus and the rest,—
For Brutus is an honourable man;
So are they all, all honourable men,—
Come I to speak in Caesar's funeral.
He was my friend, faithful and just to me:
But Brutus says he was ambitious;
And Brutus is an honourable man.
He hath brought many captives home to Rome,
Whose ransoms did the general coffers fill:
Did this in Caesar seem ambitious?

From JULIUS CAESAR
William Shakespeare

6. In the following selection from *Life with Father,* Father is a very proper Victorian whose views would hardly win a place in the hearts of women in the 2010s. He is strong, opinionated, and very definite about his "philosophies." He has just realized that his son, Clarence, has a romantic interest in a young woman. This exercise, like many others, is also good for vocal dynamics.

Father: Clarence, has your need for a suit of clothes anything to do with that young lady?

Clarence: Yes, Father.

Father: Why, Clarence! This comes as quite a shock to me.

Clarence: What does, Father?

Father:	You're being so grown up. Still, I might have known that if you're going to college this fall—yes, you're at an age when you'll be meeting girls—Clarence, there are things about women that I think you ought to know. . . . Yes—it's better for you to hear this from me than to have to learn it for yourself. . . . Clarence, women aren't the angels that you think they are. Well, now—first, let me explain this to you. You see, Clarence, we men have to run this world and it's not an easy job. It takes work, and it takes thinking. A man has to be sure of his facts and figures. He has to reason things out. Now you take a woman—a woman thinks—no, I'm wrong right there—she doesn't think at all. She just gets stirred up. And she gets stirred up about the damndest things. . . . Now, I love my wife just as much as any man, but that doesn't mean I should stand for a lot of folderol. . . . My God, I won't stand for it.
Clarence:	Stand for what, Father?
Father:	That is one thing I shall not submit myself to. Clarence, if a man thinks a certain thing is the wrong thing to do he shouldn't do it. If he thinks it's right, he should do it. But that has nothing to do with whether he loves his wife or not.
Clarence:	Who says it has, Father?
Father:	They do.
Clarence:	Who, sir?
Father:	Women. They get stirred up—and they try to get you stirred up, too—but don't you let them, Clarence. As long as you can keep reason and logic in the argument, no matter what it's about, a man can hold his own, of course. But if they can switch you—pretty soon the argument's about whether you love them or not. I swear I don't know how they do it. Don't you let 'em, Clarence, don't you let 'em.
Clarence:	I see what you mean, so far, Father. If you don't watch yourself, love can make you do a lot of things you don't want to do.
Father:	Exactly. . . . Now, Clarence—you know all about women. . . .
Clarence:	But, Father—
Father:	Yes, Clarence.
Clarence:	I thought you were going to tell me about—?
Father:	About what?
Clarence:	About—women.
Father:	Clarence, there are some things gentlemen don't discuss! I've told you all you need to know. The thing for you to remember is—be firm!

From LIFE WITH FATHER
Howard Lindsay and *Russel Crouse*

7. Antigone is confronting her sister Ismene:

Understand! The first word I ever heard out of any of you was that word "understand." Why didn't I "understand" that I must not play with water—cold, black, beautiful flowing water—because I'd spill it on the palace tiles. Or with earth, because earth dirties a little girl's frock. Why didn't I "understand" that nice children don't eat out of every dish at once; or give everything in their pockets to beggars; or run in the wind so fast that they fall down; or ask for a drink when they're perspiring; or want to go swimming when it's either too early or too late, merely because they happen to feel like swimming. Understand! I don't want to understand. There'll be time enough to understand when I'm old. . . . If I ever *am* old. But not now.

From ANTIGONE
Jean Anouilh

8. In the following selection, meek and mild-mannered Walter Mitty is daydreaming as he is driving his domineering wife to her appointment at the beauty parlor:

"We're going through!" The Commander's voice was like thin ice breaking. He wore his full dress uniform with the heavily braided white cap pulled down rakishly over one cold grey eye.

"We can't make it, Sir. It's spoiling for a hurricane, if you ask me."

"I'm not asking you, Lt. Berg. Throw on the power lights! Rev her up to 8500! We're going through!" The pounding of the cylinders increased: ta-pocket-ta-pocket-pock-ta-eta. The Commander stared at the ice forming on the pilot window. He walked over and twisted a row of complicated dials. "Switch on No. 8 auxiliary! Full strength in No. 3 turret!" The crew, bending to their various tasks in the huge, hurtling eight-engined navy hydroplane, looked at each other and grinned.

"The old man'll get us through," they said to one another. "The old man ain't afraid of hell!"

"Not so fast! You're driving too fast!" said Mrs. Mitty. "What are you driving so fast for?"

"H'mmm?" said Walter Mitty. He looked at his wife in the seat beside him with shocked astonishment. She seemed grossly unfamiliar, like a strange woman who had yelled at him in a crowd.

"You were up to 55. You know, I don't like to go more than 40. You were up to 55." Walter Mitty drove on toward Waterbury in silence, the roaring of the SN202 through the worst storm in 20 years of flying fading in the remote, intimate airways of his mind.

From THE SECRET LIFE OF WALTER MITTY
James Thurber

9. It was a bright cold day in April, and the clocks were striking thirteen. Winston Smith, his chin nuzzled into his breast in an effort to escape the vile wind, slipped quickly through the glass doors of Victory Mansions, though not quickly enough to prevent a swirl of gritty dust from entering along with him. The hallway smelt of boiled cabbage and old rag mats. At one end of it a coloured poster, too large for indoor display, had been tacked to the wall. It depicted simply an enormous face, more than a metre wide: the face of a man of about forty-five, with a heavy black moustache and ruggedly hand-some features. Winston made for the stairs. It was no use trying the lift. Even at the best of times it was seldom working, and at present the electric current was cut off during daylight hours. It was part of the economy drive in preparation for Hate Week. The flat was seven flights up, and Winston, who was thirty-nine and had a varicose ulcer above his right ankle, went slowly, resting several times on the way. On each landing, opposite the lift-shaft, the poster with the enormous face gazed from the wall. It was one of those pictures which are so contrived that the eyes follow you about when you move. BIG BROTHER IS WATCHING YOU, the caption beneath it ran. Inside the flat a fruity voice was reading out a list of figures which had something to do with the production of pig-iron. The voice came from an oblong metal plaque like a dulled mirror which formed part of the surface of the right-hand wall. Winston turned a switch and the voice sank somewhat, though the words were still distinguishable. The instrument (the telescreen, it was called) could be dimmed, but there was no way of shutting it off completely. He

moved over to the window: a smallish, frail figure, the meagreness of his body merely emphasized by the blue overalls which were the uniform of the party. His hair was very fair, his face naturally sanguine, his skin roughened by coarse soap and blunt razor blades and the cold of the winter that had just ended.

From 1984
George Orwell

>>> PITCH

Habitual Pitch

All of us incorporate several pitches into our speech. When under stress, people usually elevate the pitch. The pitch levels you use most frequently constitute your **habitual pitch,** which is sometimes called *modal pitch.* One usually begins phonation at one's habitual pitch. This pitch is the result of imitation and other factors.

Optimum Pitch

All of us have a pitch that is naturally best for us because it is the most efficient. "Best" here means that the pitch is the most anatomically comfortable for any given individual. This pitch is identified as the **optimum pitch,** which is not only the pitch at which the speaker is most physically comfortable but also the pitch at which muscles in the vocal mechanism function at their best. The most vibrant and resonant tones are produced at the optimum pitch. If there is a marked difference between your modal and optimum pitches, you will be psychologically more comfortable at your modal pitch because it is the pitch that you use most frequently. However, you have learned (we hope) not to mistake the habitual for what is appropriate or natural.

In addition to gaining comfort, a speaker can gain optimum projection using the optimum pitch. Remember that each resonance cavity selects certain partials with which it is in harmony (p. 41). When a speaker produces a very tense sound at the habitual rather than at the optimum pitch, the cavities will amplify those segmentals or partials with which there is sympathy, thus increasing the probability of producing an unpleasant sound. On the other hand, when the optimum pitch is used, the best partials are selected for amplification. Clearly, then, it is important that each speaker discover his or her optimum pitch.

Determining Habitual Pitch

Remember that your habitual pitch is the pitch that you use most of the time when you are not giving energized meaning to your speech. In other words, your habitual pitch is generally used in speech that has little inflection.

Record the following poem, Shakespeare's "Sonnet 18," and highlight those words that are underlined.

1 Shall I compare thee to a summer's day?

2 Thou art more lovely and more temperate:

3 Rough winds do shake the darling buds of May,

4 And summer's lease hath all too short a date:

5 Sometime too hot the eye of heaven shines,

6 And <u>often</u> is his <u>gold</u> <u>complexion</u> <u>dimmed</u>;

7 And <u>every</u> <u>fair</u> from <u>fair</u> <u>sometime</u> <u>declines</u>,

8 By <u>chance</u> or <u>nature's</u> <u>changing</u> <u>course</u> <u>untrimmed</u>;

9 But <u>thy</u> <u>eternal</u> summer shall <u>not</u> <u>fade</u>,

10 Nor <u>lose</u> <u>possession</u> of that <u>fair</u> thou <u>owest</u>;

11 Nor shall <u>Death</u> <u>brag</u> thou <u>wander'st</u> in his <u>shade</u>,

12 When in <u>eternal</u> <u>lines</u> to <u>time</u> thou <u>grow'st</u>;

13 So <u>long</u> as <u>men</u> can <u>breathe</u>, or <u>eyes</u> can <u>see</u>,

14 <u>So</u> <u>long</u> <u>lives</u> <u>this</u>, and <u>this</u> gives <u>life</u> to <u>thee</u>.

As you listen to your recording, become sensitive to the pitch that you use when you are not emphasizing meaning. This particular sonnet was selected because a "color" word—an important or highly descriptive word—often appears at the beginning and end of a line, leaving the middle for you to establish your habitual pitch. Focus your listening acuity on line 1 and lines 5 through 9. See if you can determine your habitual pitch on a piano, guitar, or pitch pipe. If none of these instruments is available to you, ask someone to help you determine the actual note. Keep in mind that this may or may not be your optimum pitch.

Determining Optimum Pitch

There are several ways to determine your optimum pitch. One of the easiest ways is to sing down the scale with the aid of a piano. With a good open throat, produce the vowel sound "ah"; if you use a tight throat, you will not get your true optimum pitch. At any rate, move down the scale to the lowest comfortable note you can sing with ease and duration. Then, go up three or four notes. That should be your optimum pitch. Experiment a little with the surrounding notes before you finally decide. You should be able to tell immediately when you have hit your optimum pitch, for there will be a stronger, more resonant, and more physically comfortable sound. Because the optimum pitch is easily heard by a listener, it is often helpful to work with a partner. A pitch pipe or another musical instrument may also help you determine your optimum pitch. The sketch of the piano keyboard in Figure 4.1 should help you identify the correct notes.

Make a notation of your optimum pitch. In addition, record the note from the piano or pitch pipe onto your cassette tape. Say "This is my optimum pitch," and play that note. You should not be interested in inflection at the moment. Get to the point at which you can reproduce your optimum pitch without the aid of the cassette tape.

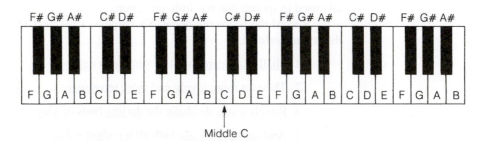

FIGURE 4.1   Section of piano keyboard indicating speaking/singing range

Of course, it is to your benefit if your modal or habitual pitch is the same as or close to your optimum pitch. Many boys intentionally lower their pitch during and immediately after that period of mystery known as puberty because they do not want to sound like (ugh!) girls. How many times have we males consciously turned on that macho sound to showcase our sexuality? Unfortunately, with such sociological and often self-imposed pressures, males often force their pitch well below the optimum level. Although we may be establishing our masculinity, our voices often sound gravelly and unpleasant.

Sometimes a female voice is too high for similar reasons. Girls are taught to be lady-like, and part of the stereotype includes a soft, high-pitched voice.

If there is a discrepancy of a full note or more between your modal and optimum pitches, it is important to make your optimum pitch a habit as quickly as possible. This is accomplished only through practice and conscious effort. Like all modifications, it will seem affected at first, and you may feel very ill at ease and self-conscious until the altered pitch becomes habitual. Keep in mind that it is important to develop the range of your pitch. Often males use only the bottom notes of their range while the women, who want to remain feminine, develop the upper ones.

EXERCISES FOR OPTIMUM PITCH

Quietly read the following exercises aloud using your optimum pitch. Include variations of pitch as dictated by the meaning. Concentrate on the sound and feeling while using the optimum pitch. If your **muscle memory** *is good, you should be able to reproduce the sound and feeling of the optimum pitch voluntarily.*

1. He doesn't seem to know what he wants, does he?

2. And now, friends, fellow citizens of Gettysburg and Pennsylvania, and you from remoter States, let me again, as we part, invoke your benediction on these honored graves. You feel, though the occasion is mournful, that it is good to be here.

   From the GETTYSBURG ADDRESS
   Abraham Lincoln

3. The following speech is a fictive confrontation between Queen Mary of Scotland and Queen Elizabeth of England. Mary has been imprisoned by her cousin Elizabeth. Mary's son James eventually became King of Scotland.

   Mary: And still I win.
   A demon has no children, and you have none,
   Will have none, can have none, perhaps. This crooked track
   You've drawn me on, cover it, let it not be believed
   That a woman was a fiend. Yes, cover it deep,
   And heap my infamy over it, lest men peer
   And catch sight of you as you were and are. In myself
   I know you to be an eater of dust. Leave me here
   And set me lower this year by year, as you promise
   Till the last is an oubliette, and my name inscribed
   On the four winds. Still, STILL I win! I have been
   A woman, and I have loved as a woman loves,
   Lost as a woman loses. I have borne a son,
   And he will rule Scotland—and England. You have no heir!
   A devil has no children.

   From MARY, QUEEN OF SCOTS
   Maxwell Anderson

4. The doctor led them down a corridor and *stopped* before a door. A nurse unlocked it. He held the door open.

Karen walked into a cell-like room. The room held a chair, a stand, and a bed. She looked around for a moment and then she stiffened. A man was sitting on the floor in a corner. He was barefooted and uncombed. He sat with his back against the wall and his arms around his knees and stared blankly at the opposite wall.

From EXODUS
Leon Uris

By now you have been able to produce a good open throat with your optimum pitch. It is now your responsibility to make it a speech habit. Keep in mind, furthermore, that you can modify that optimum pitch for variety. There are situations in which it would be appropriate to use a higher or lower pitch than the optimum.

How long it will take to habituate your optimum pitch depends exclusively on you. Yes, you may feel self-conscious at first, but frequent use of the optimum pitch will make it increasingly easy to produce and use. The easy feeling in your pharynx ought to encourage you. Your quality of voice is not only more pleasant; it feels better, too!

To locate URLs and search terms for weblinks relevant to this chapter, please go to the companion website at www.cengage.com/rtf/crannell/voiceandarticulation5e and select the proper chapter.

Write the definitions for the following terms in the space below.

KEY TERMS	DEFINITIONS
Acoustic	
Career Voice	
Conversational Speech	
Diction	
Habitual Pitch	
Kinesthesis	
Medulla Oblongata	
Open Throat	
Optimum Pitch	
Overly Open Throat	
Projection	
Singing Voice	
Tight Throat	

CHAPTER 5

COMMON VOICE PROBLEMS

This chapter deals with common vocal problems among untrained (and sometimes trained) speakers. The first group of errors is due to poor control of the velum; the second group is due to excessive tension in the laryngeal area. Exercises are provided to help minimize and correct the problems described. In addition, there are exercises to help you develop the desirable vocal characteristics needed to replace the vocal problems.

VELAR PROBLEMS

A variety of problems can result when the **velum**, or *soft palate* does not make appropriate contact with the pharyngeal wall. Next, we'll consider some of these velar problems.

Assimilation

Assimilation in speech is the influence of one sound upon another. Think of articulating the word *bow.* Feel the lips coming together for the closure on the sound /b/. What is the position of the tongue? Because it is not involved in the production of /b/, it is in all probability resting at the bottom of the mouth. Now form the word *brown,* but do not pronounce it. The tongue position has changed; instead of being in a relaxed position at the bottom of the mouth, the tongue has anticipated the production of the /r/ coming after the /b/. Now you should be aware that the tip of the tongue is slightly curled toward the roof of the mouth. The tongue is forming the /r/ in "brown" before the /b/ is exploded. Now form the word *blow* without vocalizing it. The tongue tip changes from being slightly curled to touching the ridge behind the upper teeth, anticipating the production of the sound /l/. These are just two examples of how assimilation works.

These actions happen because the second sound in each word can be produced without the lips. The plosive /b/ is a **bilabial** (made with the two lips) sound. In the first example ("bow"), there are two possible pronunciations: a bow on a dress or a bow of a boat. In either case, the tongue is free to begin the **articulatory adjustment** for the second sound, and there is a difference depending upon which pronunciation you make. There is a slight modification between the /o/ (as in "go") and the diphthong /aʊ/ (as in "house"). Can you feel the difference? The same principle applies to the other two examples, "brown" and "blow." The adjustments for the /r/ and /l/ are easier to feel because the tongue must be elevated for each sound.

Another example of assimilation occurs in the sentence "I don't have to go." The last sound in the word *have* is not pronounced /v/ but rather /f/. If the sentence were "I have won," the last sound in "have" would be /v/. In the first example, the /v/ becomes /f/ because in dynamic or conversational speech, the /v/ is often pronounced /f/ depending upon the sound that follows and the amount of stress on the word containing the /v/. If the sound following the /v/ is not vocalized (such as /t/ as in "to"), it is usually pronounced with the unvocalized /f/. The mechanism of the voice adapts to the easier production, whether it is correct or incorrect. Conversely, in the sentence "I have won," the sound /v/ is used because the next sound (/w/) is vocalized. This assimilation process occurs automatically because in general it is easier for the speaker to produce two voiceless sounds together or two voiced sounds together than it is to stop and start the vocal machinery each time. It should be made clear, however, that there are numerous exceptions to this generalization.

Nasality

Nasality (sometimes called *hypernasality* or *positive nasality*) is a vocal quality that occurs when too much sound resonation takes place in the nose. An extreme form is **cleft palate speech,** in which the palatal structure allows air to escape through the nose. Because the palate is used to block off the nasal cavity, individuals with a damaged palate often exhibit excessive nasality. People with a normal palate can also have nasal speech, but their degree of nasality is usually less than what occurs in cleft palate speech.

Check your own degree of nasality. Place a feather or several small pieces of paper or tissue on a piece of cardboard, and hold the cardboard above the upper lip and below the nose. Say the following sounds aloud several times: /t/, /d/, /s/, and /z/. The feather or pieces of paper should not move because the breath ought to escape through the mouth. Now say the sounds /m/ and /n/. The objects ought to move because each of these resonating sounds escapes through the nose. The good voice contains an appropriate amount of resonance in the nasal cavity. Figure 5.1 shows a side view of the oral, nasal, and pharyngeal cavities.

Place the tip of your tongue just behind the upper teeth on the hard ridge called the **alveolar ridge.** This ridge, which is composed of bone, is the bumpy area around the teeth. As the tongue tip leaves the ridge and moves back, it touches the **hard palate,** the bony portion of the roof of the mouth. Place the tip of the tongue farther back on the hard palate until you touch the *velum,* or "**soft palate**." Because the velum is composed of membrane and muscle, it can move. It is a valve made of muscle that controls the flow of breath. The hard palate and alveolar ridge are immovable and are extensions of the upper jaw (**maxilla**). At the end of the velum there is a hanging bulb called the **uvula.** This structure is not necessary in speaking English, but it is used in the production of kinds of /r/ phonemes that occur in German and French.

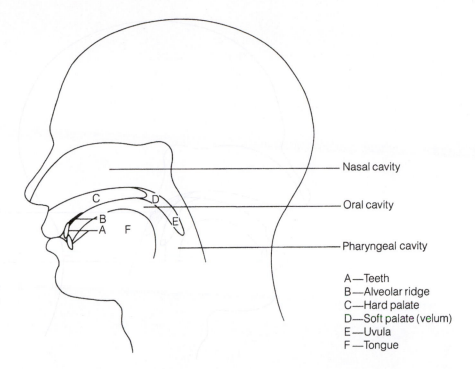

FIGURE 5.1   Oral, nasal, and pharyngeal cavities during breathing for life

In producing all the speech sounds except the nasals, the velum contracts and moves up and back while the muscles of the pharynx (throat) contract and move the pharyngeal wall down and forward, thereby closing off the nasal cavity. On the nasal sounds, the soft palate is actively lowered, allowing the vibrating breath to escape through the nasal cavity and out the nose (Figure 5.2).

Denasality

Denasality (sometimes called *negative nasality*) occurs when there is insufficient nasal resonance. When you are denasal, you are often told that you have a cold. (In this usage, the prefix *de-* means "away from"; thus, the literal meaning of *denasality* is "away from nasality.") There are many possible causes of denasality. When you have a cold, the mucous linings of the mouth and nose swell, preventing nasal resonance on the nasal sounds. Because of this swelling, the vibrations on these sounds are rerouted and escape through the mouth. This is why you can easily recognize the "cold in the head" quality that is characteristic of denasality.

There are a number of possible organic causes of denasality. Sometimes players of contact sports, such as boxing or wrestling, develop denasality if their **septum** (dividing wall of the nose) becomes deviated or turned. Basically, the nose is out of line. The nasal speech sounds cannot escape through the nose, and the resulting quality is denasal. Others become denasal because of other factors (colds, sinus infections, or allergies) that cause the nasal membranes to swell. Other possible causes are congestion, **nasal spurs** (growths), allergies, enlarged tonsils, or enlarged turbinates.

Many of these problems must be corrected surgically to make certain that whatever was blocking the passage is removed. However, some people are denasal because of vocal laziness and, in these cases, it is a functional problem. It is for these individuals that this section and the following exercises are intended.

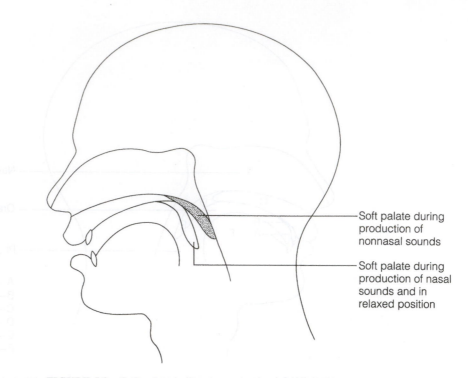

Soft palate during production of nonnasal sounds

Soft palate during production of nasal sounds and in relaxed position

FIGURE 5.2   Soft palate action

Regardless of the cause of denasality, the nasal sounds are the ones that are affected. Because the air is not escaping through the nose on these sounds, the nasals approximate different sounds:

/m/ becomes /b/
/n/ becomes /d/
"ng" becomes /g/

Read aloud the following poem as it is written. Then, while holding your nose, substitute the sounds that appear above the letters, thereby minimizing nasal resonance. You will produce denasality! Of course, if you wait until you have a bad cold, you will not need to hold your nose.

    b d   d b d
It was many and many a year ago,

d   g b
In a kingdom by the sea,

       b   d   b   b   d
That a maiden there lived whom you may know

      d b   d
By the name of Annabel[1] Lee:—

    d   b   d   d
And this maiden she lived with no other thought

---

[1]Notice that there is only one /n/ sound even though the word *Annabel* contains two *n* letters.

          d   d   b
Than to love and be loved by me.

                d
I was a child and she was a child,

         d   g   b
In this kingdom by the sea,

                   b   d
But we loved with a love that was more than love—

      d b d
I and my Annabel Lee—

                 g   d
With a love that the winged seraphs of heaven

              d b
Coveted her and me.

        b   d
From ANNABEL LEE

        d
Edgar Allan Poe

))) EXERCISES FOR ELIMINATING DENASALITY

1. Become aware of the action of the velum and uvula by alternating quickly between the letters *ng* as in "song" (/ŋ/) and the vowel sound "ah" (/ɑ/) ten times. Feel, hear, and visualize the muscular action.

2. The nasal resonance exercises in Chapter 4 are excellent for denasality because they exercise the velum and allow the opening into the nasal cavity to open and close (see pp. 47–51).

3. Place small pieces of tissue or paper on a piece of cardboard (as in testing for nasality), and place the cardboard just under the nostrils. Hum a quiet, sustained tone. Try to keep the pieces of paper on the cardboard rather than forcing them off with a spurt of air.

4. Read aloud the following passage, and prolong the underlined nasal sounds. Make certain that the transition to and from the nasal consonant is produced with as much nasal resonance as possible:

> And now, friends, fellow citizens of Gettysburg and Pennsylvania, and you from remoter States, let me again, as we part, invoke your benediction on these honored graves. You feel, though the occasion is mournful, that it is good to be here. . . . You now feel it a new bond of union, that they shall lie side by side, till a clarion, louder than that which marshalled them to the combat, shall awake their slumbers. God bless the Union;—it is dearer to us for the blood of brave men which has been shed in its defense. The spots on which they stood and fell; these pleasant heights; the fertile plain beneath them; the thriving village whose streets so lately rang with the strange din of war; the fields beyond the

ridge, where the <u>n</u>oble Rey<u>n</u>olds held the adva<u>nc</u>i<u>ng</u> foe at bay; a<u>n</u>d, while he gave up his ow<u>n</u> life, assured by his forethought a<u>n</u>d self-sacrifice the triu<u>mph</u> of the two succeedi<u>ng</u> days; the little strea<u>ms</u> which wi<u>n</u>d through the hills, o<u>n</u> whose ba<u>n</u>ks i<u>n</u> after ti<u>m</u>es the wo<u>n</u>deri<u>ng</u> plough<u>man</u> will tur<u>n</u> up, with the rude weapo<u>n</u>s of savage warfare, the fearful <u>m</u>issiles of <u>m</u>oder<u>n</u> artillery; Se<u>m</u>inary Ridge, the Peach Orchard, Ce<u>m</u>etery, Culp, a<u>n</u>d Wolf Hill, Rou<u>n</u>d Top, Little Rou<u>n</u>d Top, hu<u>m</u>ble <u>n</u>a<u>m</u>es, he<u>n</u>ceforward dear a<u>n</u>d fa<u>m</u>ous,—<u>n</u>o lapse of ti<u>m</u>e, <u>n</u>o dista<u>n</u>ce of space, shall cause you to be forgotte<u>n</u>. But they, I a<u>m</u> sure, will joi<u>n</u> us i<u>n</u> sayi<u>ng</u>, as we bid farewell to the dust of these <u>m</u>artyr-heroes, that wheresoever throughout the civilized world the accou<u>n</u>ts of this great warfare are read, a<u>n</u>d ow<u>n</u> to the latest period of recorded ti<u>m</u>e, i<u>n</u> the glorious a<u>nn</u>als of our co<u>mm</u>o<u>n</u> cou<u>n</u>try there will be <u>n</u>o brighter page tha<u>n</u> that which relates the battles of Gettysburg.

Edward Everett

>>>
ASSIMILATION NASALITY

We have discussed assimilation and nasality in detail; when they occur together, they create a rather common vocal quality that, when excessive, is quite unpleasant. **Assimilation nasality** often occurs when a vowel sound comes before or after nasal sounds. Say the words *apple* and *man*. Do the vowels in both words sound the same to you? If you were to look them up in a pronouncing dictionary, you would discover that both words contain the vowel /æ/ (as in "c<u>a</u>t"). However, to most people the vowels in the two words sound different. The reason is that the vowel in "man" is surrounded by two nasal sounds.

We identified the velum as the controller of the release of air and sound waves into the nasal cavity, and we noted that the velum contracts on all English sounds other than the three nasals. Because there are no nasal sounds in "apple," the velum remains contracted. However, in "man" the velum must first be actively lowered, allowing the sound vibrations to escape through the nose on /m/. For the next sound, /æ/ (as in "c<u>a</u>t"), the velum must contract upward, closing off the entrance into the nasal cavity; on the third sound, /n/, the velum must be lowered again. Because this movement is very rapid, a bit of nasal vibration normally escapes into the vowel. If the speaker is careless with this closure, the vowel absorbs too much nasal resonance and becomes too nasal. That is why the vowels in "apple" and "man" sound slightly different. It is the assimilation, or the influence of the nasal sound on the vowel, that produces the nasality, which must also be present in the good speaking voice. A good voice exhibits the proper degree of nasality.

Assimilation nasality is common. When it is *excessive,* the sound is most unpleasant. At this point, it is considered a problem of quality. Excessive assimilation nasality is not limited to any particular regional dialect, although it is quite typical of speech in the eastern United States. Because we are essentially lazy beings, the velum is often too relaxed during normal assimilation nasality. Therefore, too much vibrating air escapes through the nose, causing the vowel to contain excessive nasality. Although this condition may occur with any vowel or diphthong, the phoneme /æ/ (as in "c<u>a</u>t") is a particular favorite. Thus, the exercises that follow focus on that vowel combination with the nasal sounds. Excessive assimilation nasality is corrected by dropping the lower jaw (**mandible**) considerably and flattening the tongue for the low-front tongue placement of the vowel /æ/. You must make certain, however, that you are producing the same vowel. The common error is to substitute the /ɑ/ (as in "f<u>a</u>ther") for the /æ/ (as in "c<u>a</u>t"). To be clear, do not hesitate to overdo the production of the correct sound. As a matter of fact, such exaggeration is to be encouraged. When the exaggerated movement is easy, it is a simple task to pull away and produce the sound appropriately. Remember to work with negative practice.

EXERCISES FOR ELIMINATING EXCESSIVE ASSIMILATION NASALITY

1. In pronouncing the following words, drop the lower jaw and flatten the tongue (if necessary, with a tongue depressor or spoon) on the vowel /æ/. Make certain that the underlined vowel is produced in the front of the mouth. Use negative practice by reading the three columns across for each word. "Career" indicates career speech. Although you will notice that all of the words contain the vowel /æ/, excessive assimilation nasality can occur on any vowel. The first ten words begin with the vowel /æ/ so you can more easily feel and hear the error. The next ten words begin with the consonant /h/, which is produced with breath escaping through the mouth. The remaining words are more difficult to produce without excessive assimilation nasality.

	CAREER	ERROR	CAREER
<u>a</u>nd	[ænd]	[æ̃nd]²	[ænd]
<u>A</u>ndes	[ˈændiz]	[ˈæ̃ndiz]	[ˈændiz]
<u>A</u>ndrew	[ˈændru]	[ˈæ̃ndru]	[ˈændru]
<u>a</u>nnex	[ˈænɛks]	[ˈæ̃nɛks]	[ˈænɛks]
<u>a</u>nimal	[ˈænəml̩]³	[ˈæ̃nəml̩]	[ˈænəml̩]
<u>A</u>ndrea	[ˈændrɪə]	[ˈæ̃ndrɪə]	[ˈændrɪə]
<u>a</u>mnesty	[ˈæmnəstɪ]	[ˈæ̃mnəstɪ]	[ˈæmnəstɪ]
<u>a</u>ngry	[ˈæŋgrɪ]	[ˈæ̃ŋgrɪ]	[ˈæŋgrɪ]
<u>a</u>mble	[ˈæmbl̩]	[ˈæ̃mbl̩]	[ˈæmbl̩]
<u>a</u>ntler	[ˈæntlɚ]	[ˈæ̃ntlɚ]	[ˈæntlɚ]
h<u>a</u>ndle	[ˈhændl̩]	[ˈhæ̃ndl̩]	[ˈhændl̩]
h<u>a</u>m	[hæm]	[hæ̃m]	[hæm]
h<u>a</u>mburger	[ˈhæmbɜˑgɚ]	[ˈhæ̃mbɜˑgɚ]	[ˈhæmbɜˑgɚ]
h<u>a</u>nger	[ˈhæŋɚ]	[ˈhæ̃ŋɚ]	[ˈhæŋɚ]
H<u>a</u>mpshire	[ˈhæmpʃɪr]	[ˈhæ̃mpʃɪr]	[ˈhæmpʃɪr]
h<u>a</u>ndball	[ˈhændbɔl]	[ˈhæ̃ndbɔl]	[ˈhændbɔl]
H<u>a</u>ncock	[ˈhænkɑk]	[ˈhæ̃nkɑk]	[ˈhænkɑk]
h<u>a</u>ndicap	[ˈhændɪkæp]	[ˈhæ̃ndɪkæp]	[ˈhændɪkæp]
h<u>a</u>ngman	[ˈhæŋmæn]	[ˈhæ̃ŋmæn]	[ˈhæŋmæn]
h<u>a</u>ndsome	[ˈhænsəm]	[ˈhæ̃nsəm]	[ˈhænsəm]
D<u>a</u>nny	[ˈdænɪ]	[ˈdæ̃nɪ]	[ˈdænɪ]
Fl<u>a</u>nnery	[ˈflænərɪ]	[ˈflæ̃nərɪ]	[ˈflænərɪ]

---

²The symbol ˜ indicates nasality.
³See p. # for an explanation of the syllabic [l̩] mark.

	CAREER	ERROR	CAREER
Spanish	[ˈspænɪʃ]	[ˈspæ̃nɪʃ]	[ˈspænɪʃ]
tango	[ˈtæŋgo]	[ˈtæ̃ŋgo]	[ˈtæŋgo]
mammal	[ˈmæml̩]	[ˈmæ̃ml̩]	[ˈmæml̩]
family	[ˈfæməlɪ]	[ˈfæ̃məlɪ]	[ˈfæməlɪ]
scandal	[ˈskændl̩]	[ˈskæ̃ndl̩]	[ˈskændl̩]
Pamela	[ˈpæmələ]	[ˈpæ̃mələ]	[ˈpæmələ]
understand	[ˈʌndɚstænd]	[ˈʌndɚstæ̃nd]	[ˈʌndɚstænd]
jam	[ʤæm]	[ʤæ̃m]	[ʤæm]
lame	[lem]	[lẽm]	[lem]
can't	[kænt]	[kæ̃nt]	[kænt]
Vangi	[ˈvænʤɪ]	[ˈvæ̃nʤɪ]	[ˈvænʤɪ]
nag	[næg]	[næ̃g]	[næg]
Stanley	[ˈstænlɪ]	[ˈstæ̃nlɪ]	[ˈstænlɪ]
panda	[ˈpændə]	[ˈpæ̃ndə]	[ˈpændə]
handmaiden	[ˈhændmedn̩]	[ˈhæ̃ndmẽdn̩]	[ˈhændmedn̩]
gamble	[ˈgæmbl̩]	[ˈgæ̃mbl̩]	[ˈgæmbl̩]
manger	[ˈmenʤɚ]	[ˈmẽnʤɚ]	[ˈmenʤɚ]
banister	[ˈbænɪstɚ]	[ˈbæ̃nɪstɚ]	[ˈbænɪstɚ]

Because negative practice and visualization are quite valuable, go back and see (and hear) yourself produce exaggerated assimilation nasality, and then immediately visualize (and hear) yourself saying the word again with appropriate assimilation nasality. This should give you a contrast between a careless and a preferred production of the vowel sound.

2. In the following sentences, make certain that you drop the lower jaw and flatten the tongue on the underlined vowel sounds.

   a. Nancy, hand the man the dandy candy.

   b. His name is Stanley and he comes from Manchester, New Hampshire.

   c. Don't raise the banner with your left hand, Randall.

   d. Samantha Anderson is living on Hancock Street.

   e. Andrea rants and raves about the answer.

   f. Vangi never crammed for her examination.

   g. Sandra and Frank smelled the rancid cheese.

   h. The Colonel had a dandy Handy Andy in his pocket.

   i. Mandy, handle the candle carefully.

   j. Frannie, do you like candied yams with your ham?

   k. Robert, have you ever used canned pineapple on your hamburger and linguiça sandwiches?

   l. Consult "hammer and nails" in your handyman manual.

   m. The Hanniford family came from Amsterdam, New Hampshire.

Now read the sentences using negative practice. Say the sentences properly, then with excessive assimilation nasality, and then properly again. Feel and hear the contrasting production of sounds.

3. In the following poems, pay close attention to the underlined vowels. Remember to drop your jaw and keep your tongue position flat. After you have read the poems with appropriate assimilation nasality, read them again using negative practice (that is, say them properly, then with excessive assimilation nasality, and then properly again).

  a. I met a traveller from an antique land
      Who said: "Two vast and trunkless legs of stone
      Stand on the desert. Near them, on the sand
      Half sunk, a shattered visage lies, whose frown
      And wrinkled lip and sneer of cold command
      Tell that its sculptor well those passions read
      Which yet survive, stamped on these lifeless things.
      The hand that mocked them and the heart that fed.
      And on the pedestal these words appear:
      'My name is Ozymandias, king of kings:
      Look on my works, ye Mighty, and despair!'
      Nothing beside remains. Round the decay
      Of that colossal wreck, boundless and bare,
      The lone and level sands stretch far away."

      OZYMANDIAS
      Percy Bysshe Shelley

  b. Once upon a midnight dreary, while I pondered, weak and weary,
      Over many a quaint and curious volume of forgotten lore—
      While I nodded, nearly napping, suddenly there came a tapping,
      As of some one gently rapping, rapping at my chamber door—
      "'Tis some visitor," I muttered, "tapping at my chamber door—
      Only this and nothing more."

      From "The Raven"
      Edgar Allan Poe

  c. Thy summer's play,
      My thoughtless hand
      Has brushed away
      Am I not
      A fly like thee?
      Or art not thou
      A man like me?
      For I dance
      And drink and sing.

      LITTLE FLY
      William Blake

  d. *Crystal:* Now get this straight, Mrs. Haines. I like what I've got and I'm going to keep it. You handed me your husband on a silver platter. But I'm not returning the compliment. I can't be stampeded by gossip.

      From THE WOMEN
      Clare Boothe

   e. There was a young man from Japan
   Whose limericks never would scan;
   When they said it was so,
   He replied, "Yes, I know,
   But I always try to get as many words in the last line as ever I possibly can."

   Anonymous

>>>
EXCESSIVE VOCAL TENSION

Glottal Shock or Glottal Stop

Glottal shock, or **stop,** is a voice problem often caused by poor breathing habits and excessive tension. It occurs when the subglottal breath (breath below the opening between the vocal folds) does not escape evenly because of tension at the vocal folds. The tension is most easily heard during the production of initial vowels and diphthongs. Breathiness could be considered the opposite of glottal shock. In breathiness, because there is a lack of tension at the vocal folds, the air escapes with no perceptible tension. To get the feel of glottal shock, bring the vocal folds together as in the beginning of a cough. Habitual glottal shock may cause severe vocal problems. When there is glottal shock, there is usually a tight throat, and the sound produced is harsh and strident. However, used carefully and purposefully, glottal shock can add color to your speech.

Elimination of Glottal Shock or Glottal Stop

To eliminate glottal shock, you must get rid of the tension in the vocal area that is causing the problem. This can be easily accomplished by incorporating the /h/ consonant, which is produced by breath escaping through the glottis. Because it is a completely aspirated or breathy sound, there is little tension in its production.

    Read aloud the following list of words using negative practice. Increase the tension on the first vowel of the word that appears in the first column. Cause a slight explosion or click of breath on the initial vowel. Feel what is happening; this is glottal shock! Does it feel at all natural or habitual? Do you identify glottal shock as part of your speech? You probably have glottal shock to some degree. Next, place an aspirated /h/ before the initial vowel sound: "Apple" becomes "/h/apple." Feel the release of the breath and the reduction in tension at the vocal area. Then say the word in the third column, attempting to duplicate the feeling of the second column but without the /h/.

ever	/h/ever	ever	eel	/h/eel	eel
all	/h/all	all	ace	/h/ace	ace
elk	/h/elk	elk	east	/h/east	east
epic	/h/epic	epic	ate	/h/ate	ate
injury	/h/injury	injury	even	/h/even	even
irritate	/h/irritate	irritate	active	/h/active	active
urgent	/h/urgent	urgent	us	/h/us	us
orange	/h/orange	orange	inch	/h/inch	inch
also	/h/also	also	easy	/h/easy	easy
into	/h/into	into	only	/h/only	only

EXERCISES FOR ELIMINATING GLOTTAL SHOCK OR GLOTTAL STOP

1. Place an /h/ phoneme in front of each of the following words; then, repeat each without the /h/, attempting to maintain the same relaxation of the attack: outgrowth, Irvine, envelope, email, equal, Elsie, interest, oxygen, Ella, alternate, all night, anything, urban, optimist, image, and interval.

2. Sometimes a speaker uses glottal shock before a consonant (usually /t/ or /d/) in the middle of a multisyllabic word. Read the following list of words, and make certain that you do not glottalize before a consonant: bottle, rattle, mitten, mountain, Hutton, important, subtle, button, little, metal, written, battle, mutton, and rattle.

Read the following sentences and lines of poetry using negative practice. The first time you read them, concentrate on the feeling of tension in the larynx. You might even consciously build up the pressure in the larynx before uttering the first word to underscore the production of glottal shock. During the second reading, place the /h/ on the initial vowels, then remove it on the third reading but maintain a similar feeling.

3. Even Edna couldn't tell him everything.
/h/Even /h/Edna couldn't tell him /h/everything.
Even Edna couldn't tell him everything.

4. The aim of the course was to interest everyone.
The /h/aim /h/of the course was to /h/interest /h/everyone.
The aim of the course was to interest everyone.

5. How awful it is to eat everything.
How /h/awful /h/it /h/is to /h/eat /h/everything.
How awful it is to eat everything.

6. Oil is oozing under our oven.
/h/Oil /h/is /h/oozing /h/under /h/our /h/oven.
Oil is oozing under our oven.

7. Andrea admires Arthur more than anyone else.
/h/Andrea /h/admires /h/Arthur more than /h/anyone /h/else.
Andrea admires Arthur more than anyone else.

8. He always acts that way.
He /h/always /h/acts that way.
He always acts that way.

9. I never admit when I am wrong.
/h/I never /h/admit when /h/I /h/am wrong.
I never admit when I am wrong.

10. Everyone arrived at the party early and upset Agnes.
/h/Everyone /h/arrived /h/at the party /h/early /h/and /h/upset /h/Agnes.
Everyone arrived at the party early and upset Agnes.

11. Keep your eye on "Edgy Al" all the time.
Keep your /h/eye /h/on "/h/Edgy /h/Al" /h/all the time.
Keep your eye on "Edgy Al" all the time.

12. I was born an American; I live an American; I shall die an American; and I intend to perform the duties incumbent upon me in that character to the end of my career.

/h/I was born /h/an /h/American; /h/I live /h/an /h/American; /h/I shall die /h/an /h/ American; /h/and /h/I /h/intend to perform the duties /h/incumbent /h/upon me /h/in that character to the /h/end /h/of my career.

I was born an American; I live an American; I shall die an American; and I intend to perform the duties incumbent upon me in that character to the end of my career.

Daniel Webster

13. In the afternoon they came unto a land
In which it seemed always afternoon.

/h/In the /h/afternoon they came /h/unto /h/a land
/h/In which /h/it seemed /h/always /h/afternoon.

In the afternoon they came unto a land
In which it seemed always afternoon.

From THE LOTOS-EATERS
Alfred, Lord Tennyson

14. O Jehovah, our Lord,
How excellent is thy name in all the earth.

/h/O Jehovah, /h/our Lord,
How /h/excellent /h/is thy name /h/in /h/all the /h/earth.

O Jehovah, our Lord,
How excellent is thy name in all the earth.

From PSALM 8:1
(*ARV*)

15. Out of the mouth of babes and sucklings
hast thou established strength.

/h/Out /h/of the mouth /h/of babes /h/and sucklings
hast thou /h/established strength.

Out of the mouth of babes and sucklings
hast thou established strength.

From PSALM 8:2
(*ARV*)

Producing Glottal Shock

Glottal shock used sparingly and intentionally can support your oral communication. In a performance career, you might need to create a character who speaks with glottal shock. For example, a Scottish dialect requires glottal shock. But, it is important to know when you are using glottal shock. Furthermore, you must handle your production of glottal shock with great care, for it is, after all, caused by vocal tension that you are encouraged to eliminate. Extended use of glottal shock can be damaging to your vocal folds!

EXERCISES FOR GLOTTAL SHOCK

In the following exercises, produce a glottal shock or attack on the underlined vowels and diphthongs. Remember that the larynx functions primarily as a valve; allow the pressure to build up a bit, and then force the vocal folds apart in a short spurt or click of air. However, be careful that you do not project a great deal.

1. I told you to get out of my sight!

2. Under the bamboo bamboo bamboo
   Under the bamboo tree

   From FRAGMENT OF AN AGON
   T. S. Eliot

3. It was an awful automobile accident.

4. Even Eddie knew everything Agnes argued was wrong.

5. Always I tell you this they learned—
   Always at night when they returned.

   "House Fear" from THE HILL WIFE
   Robert Frost

6. It stuck in a barb wire snare.
   Ich, ich, ich, ich,
   I could hardly speak.

   From DADDY
   Sylvia Plath

7. OOOOOOO, but he was a tight-fisted hand at the grindstone, Scrooge!

   From A CHRISTMAS CAROL
   Charles Dickens

Vocal Fry

Vocal fry is generally caused by improper breathing. The speaker runs out of breath before the speech is finished and often creates excessive tension at the vocal folds. Fry is characterized by a lowering of pitch (sometimes up to a full octave) at the end of a thought, and the quality of the voice is often described as breathy, scratchy, and unsustained. The name came from the sound of hot frying grease. Excessive vocal fry can cause vocal damage. Because vocal fry results from a breathing problem, continue to develop your breath control.

EXERCISES FOR ELIMINATING VOCAL FRY

Read aloud the following exercises, sustaining your voice to the next inhalation mark (slash). Breathe at each inhalation mark, even though its placement may not agree with your interpretation of the selection. As you work at your own pace, you may find that you need to take more inhalations than are indicated; that is perfectly acceptable. Build up your capacity. Remember, it is very important to support your breath throughout the thought. Control your exhalation.

1. A squeezing, wrenching, grasping, scraping, clutching, covetous old sinner. / Hard and sharp as flint, / from whom no steel had ever struck out generous fire; / secret and self-contained and solitary as an oyster. / The cold within him froze his old features, / nipped

his pointed nose, shrivelled his cheek, stiffened his gait, made his eyes red, his thick lips blue; / and spoke out shrewdly in his grating voice.

From A CHRISTMAS CAROL
Charles Dickens

2. A strong and determined middle-aged mother is very unhappy when her son plans to marry. In this passage, she is telling him of her displeasure:

So it's come at last! / At last it's come! / The day I knew would come at last has come at last! / My sonnyboy doesn't need me anymore. Well, what are you waiting for? / Get rid of me! / (*And she indicates the garbage can.*) Put me out with the garbage! / Just throw me out with the used grapefruits and the empty cans from the Bumble-Bee salmon. / Never mind putting a lid on. / Leave it open so a hundred thousand pussycats can walk all over a Mother. / And by the way, sweetheart darling, I got some good news for you. / I got the report from the hospital. / It's absolutely definite. / I got a condition. / Never mind what kind of condition, / a condition. / And the one thing doctors can't cure is a condition. / I don't want you to worry though. Fancy funerals are for rich people. / I don't want you to spend a cent. Just wait 'til Mother's Day, wrap me in a flag, and dump me in the river! / (*Then rising from garbage can.*) Well. I feel better now. / Everything is as it should be. / A mother is lying on top of a Sanitation truck bound for the City Dump, / and a son is running around in saloons with a Mexicali Rose who came over for the fruit picking season / and stayed to ruin an American woman's life!

From BYE BYE BIRDIE
Michael Stewart

3. The Lord is my shepherd / I shall not want. / He makes me lie down in green pastures; / he leads me beside still waters. / He restores my soul; / he leads me in paths of righteousness / for his name's sake. Even though I walk through the valley of the shadow of death, / I fear no evil; / for thou art with me. / Thy rod and thy staff they comfort me. / Thou preparest a table before me / in the presence of my enemies; / thou anointest my head with oil. / My cup overflows. / Surely goodness and mercy / shall follow me all the days of my life, / and I shall dwell in the house of the Lord forever.

PSALM 23
(*Revised Standard Version*)

4. 1 No doubt I now grew very pale. / But I talked more fluently / and with a heightened
   2 voice. Yet the sound increased / —and what could I do? / It was a low, dull, quick
   3 sound— / much like the sound a watch makes when enveloped in cotton. I gasped
   4 for breath and yet the officers heard it not. / I talked more quickly, / more
   5 vehemently, / but the noise steadily increased. / I arose and argued about trifles, / in a
   6 high key and with violent gesticulations, / but the noise steadily increased. / Why
   7 would they not be gone? / I paced the floor to and fro with heavy strides, / as if
   8 excited to fury by the observation of the men— / but the noise steadily increased. / O
   9 God! / What could I do? / I foamed— / I raved— / I swore! / I swung the chair upon
   10 which I had been sitting, / and grated it upon the boards, / but the noise arose
   11 overall and continually increased. / It grew louder— / louder / louder—! / And still the
   12 men chatted pleasantly, / and smiled. Was it possible they heard not? / Almighty
   13 God! / —no, no. / They heard! / They suspected! / They were making mockery of
   14 my horror! / But anything was better than this agony! / Anything was more tolerable
   15 than this derision! / I could bear those hypocritical smiles no longer! / I felt that
   16 I must scream or die! / And now— / again! / Hark! / Louder! / Louder! / Louder!
   17 / Louder! / "Villains!" I shrieked, / "dissemble no more! / I admit the deed! / Tear up
   18 the planks! / Here, / here! / It is the beating of his hideous heart!"

From THE TELL-TALE HEART
Edgar Allan Poe

5. Read aloud the following exercises, and mark the breath slash to reflect your meaning.

a. A rather bizarre young woman of nineteen attempts to explain her philosophy of life. Make certain that you sustain the resonance through good breath control.

1 *Jill*: I guess it was right after my marriage. I used to hang around Sunset Strip
2 and smoke pot and say things like, "Down with the fuzz" and "Don't trust any-
3 one over thirty." The whole bit. I just did it because everybody was doing it. Then
4 I stopped because everybody was doing it. I felt I was losing my individuality—
5 whatever that is. The main thing, of course, was to protest against my mother, but
6 it didn't work. I mean I walked in one day with my hair long and stringy, wearing
7 far-out clothes and beads and sandals. . . . she LOVED it. Next day, she had
8 stringy hair and far-out clothes and beads and sandals. Well, I mean how can you
9 protest against someone who's doing the same thing you are? Right? So, I went
10 the other way and joined the Young Republicans for Ronald Reagan. Another
11 mistake. There's no such thing as a young Republican.

From BUTTERFLIES ARE FREE
Leonard Gershe

b. Just married, Patsy, a woman of twenty-seven, is determined to change her husband.

1 *Patsy:* Honey, I don't want to hurt you. I want to change you. I want to save you.
2 I want to make you see that there is some value in life, that there is some beauty,
3 some tenderness, some things worth reacting to. Some things worth feeling—
4 (*Snaps fingers in front of his eyes.*) Come back here! I swear, Alfred, nobody is
5 going to kill you. But you've got to take some chances sometime! What do you
6 want out of life? Just survival? It's not enough! It's not, not, not enough! I'm not
7 going to have a surviving marriage, I'm going to have a flourishing marriage! I'm
8 a woman! Or, by Jesus, it's about time I became one. I want a family! Oh, Christ,
9 Alfred, this is my wedding day—(*Pause. Regains composure.*) I want—I want
10 to be married to a big, strong, protective, vital, virile, self-assured man. Who I
11 can protect and take care of. Alfred, honey, you're the first man I've ever gone to
12 bed with where I didn't feel he was a lot more likely to get pregnant than I was.
13 (*Desperate.*) You owe me something! I've invested everything I believe in you.
14 You've got to let me mold you. Please let me mold you. (*Regains control.*) You've
15 got me begging. You've got me whining, begging and crying. I've never behaved
16 like this in my life. Will you look at this? (*Holds out finger.*) That's a tear. I never
17 cried in my life. I never cried because I was too tough—but I felt everything.
18 Every slight, every pressure, every vague competition—but I fought. And I won!
19 There hasn't been a battle since I was five that I haven't won. And the people I
20 fought were happy that I won! Happy! After a while. Alfred, do you have any idea
21 how many people in this town worship me? Maybe that's the attraction—you
22 don't worship me. (*Shakes head.*) Maybe I'd lose all respect for you if you did all
23 the things I want you to do. (*Thinks on it.*) Alfred, you've got to change! (*Regains
24 calm.*) Listen. (*Pause.*) I'm not saying I'm better or stronger than you are. It's just
25 that we—you and I have different temperaments. (*Explodes.*) And my tempera-
26 ment is better and stronger than yours! (*Frantic.*) You're a wall! You don't fight!
27 You hardly ever listen! Dear God, will somebody please explain to me why I
28 think you're so beautiful.

From LITTLE MURDERS
Jules Feiffer

c. The following speech is given by Sammy, who attends a military school. His world is filled with strangers, which has forced him to develop his interpersonal skills. He is dating young Reenie for the first time and wants to be liked.

1 *Sammy:* I always worry that maybe people aren't going to like me, when I go to
2 a party. Isn't that crazy? Do you ever get a kind of a sick feeling in the pit of your
3 stomach when you dread things? Gee, I wouldn't want to miss a party for anything.
4 But every time I go to one, I have to reason with myself to keep from feeling
5 that the whole world's against me. See, I've spent almost my whole life
6 in military academies. My mother doesn't have a place for me, where she lives.
7 She . . . she just doesn't know what else to do with me. But you musn't
8 misunderstand about my mother. She's really a very lovely person. I guess every boy
9 thinks his mother is very beautiful, but my mother really is. She tells me in every
10 letter she writes how sorry she is that we can't be together more, but she has to
11 think of her work. One time we were together, though. She met me in San
12 Francisco once, and we were together for two whole days. She let me take her to
13 dinner and to a show and to dance. Just like we were sweethearts. It was the most
14 wonderful time I ever had. And then I had to go back to the old military academy.
15 Every time I walk into the barracks, I get kind of a depressed feeling. It's got hard
16 stone walls. Pictures of generals hanging all over . . . oh, they're very fine gentlemen,
17 but they all look so kind of hard-boiled and stern . . . you know what I mean.

From THE DARK AT THE TOP OF THE STAIRS
William Inge

Producing Vocal Fry

Many comedians use vocal fry for their characters. Many of the cartoon voices created by the great Mel Blanc (the voice of Bugs Bunny and many other characters) gained much of their impact through the use of vocal fry. Characters like Gloria Upson, the narrator of the unforgettable ping pong match in *Auntie Mame*, or even Agnes Gooch from the same play, incorporate much vocal fry in their vocal responses. Vocal fry sounds like the voice of the wonderful Margaret Hamilton, who played the wicked witch in *The Wizard of Oz*. Remember "I'm m-e-e-l-t-t-t-ti-i-i-n-n-ng-g-g-g!"

Imitate the stereotypical witch's voice in this excerpt from Shakespeare's *Macbeth*:

1 Witch: When shall we three meet again,
              In thunder, lightning, or in rain?

2 Witch: When the hurlyburly's done,
              When the battle's lost and won.

3 Witch: That will be ere the set of sun.

1 Witch: Where the place?

2 Witch: Upon the heath.

3 Witch: There to meet with Macbeth. . . .

All: Fair is foul, and foul is fair:
              Hover through the fog and filthy air.

In "Mr. Flood's Party," Edwin Arlington Robinson presents a very long opening primary cadence (sentence):

Old Eben Flood, / climbing alone one night
Over the hill between the town below
And the forsaken upland hermitage
That held as much as he should ever know
On earth again of home, / paused warily.

The poet helps the performer communicate Mr. Flood's spent and tired physical state by forcing the effective inhalation before "paused warily." A performer might support the tone with some vocal fry near the end ("On earth again of home").

Record the following description of the first four days of the creation of the world from the Torah (Genesis 1). As you listen to the recording, tune in to the number of times you used vocal fry to enhance and amplify the meaning. Then, reread those sections without vocal fry. Which readings were more effective?

1 When God began to create the heaven and the earth—the earth being unformed
2 and void, with darkness over the surface of the deep and a wind from God sweeping
3 over the water—God said, "Let there be light"; and there was light. God saw
4 that the light was good, and God separated the light from the darkness. God called
5 the light Day, and the darkness He called Night. And there was evening and there
6 was morning, a first day.
7   God said, "Let there be an expanse in the midst of the water, that it may separate
8 water from water." God made the expanse, and it separated the water which
9 was below the expanse from the water which was above the expanse. And it was
10 so. God called the expanse Sky. And there was evening and there was morning, a
11 second day.
12   God said, "Let the water below the sky be gathered into one area, that the dry
13 land may appear." And it was so. God called the dry land Earth, and the gathering
14 of waters He called Seas. And God saw that this was good. And God said,
15 "Let the earth sprout vegetation: seed-bearing plants, fruit trees of every kind on
16 earth that bear fruit with the seed in it." And it was so. The earth brought forth
17 vegetation: seed-bearing plants of every kind, and trees of every kind bearing
18 fruit with the seed in it. And God saw that this was good. And there was evening
19 and there was morning, a third day.
20   God said, "Let there be lights in the expanse of the sky to separate day from
21 night; they shall serve as signs for the set times—the days and the years; and they
22 shall serve as lights in the expanse of the sky to shine upon the earth." And it was
23 so. God made the two great lights, the greater light to dominate the day and the
24 lesser light to dominate the night, and the stars. And God set them in the expanse
25 of the sky to shine upon the earth, to dominate the day and the night, and to sepa-
26 rate light from darkness. And God saw that this was good. And there was evening
27 and there was morning, a fourth day.

Hoarseness

Hoarseness is a kind of breathiness caused by strain. A common source of hoarseness is laryngitis. There is, however, another kind of hoarseness that is chronic and that is some-times caused by vocal abuse. Remember what cheerleaders sounded like after the big game? Their voices probably had that strained sound of hoarseness. If they spoke little afterward, their voices healed until the next Saturday, when the misuse and abuse began again. In some cases, the abuse that causes hoarseness can injure the voice permanently.

Hoarseness results because the vocal folds cannot close the glottis effectively and the vocal muscles are strained. Characteristics of the hoarse voice are an unsteady pitch that favors the lower registers, a weak voice, and a voice that frequently cracks. If vocal rest does not clear up hoarseness within a week, see a laryngologist or consult a voice therapist. The cause of the hoarseness or huskiness may be physical.

With the advent of rock and roll and of singers who brag that they have never had a singing lesson and can be easily heard over the guitars and drums, there has been a marked increase in the incidence of hoarseness. This hoarseness can be either momentary or long-lasting. Sometimes this kind of vocal abuse creates *nodules* on or near the vocal folds. **Nodules** are types of polyps that are benign rather than malignant. They are caused by ex-cessive strain or friction. Often called **singer's nodes,** such nodules continue to grow as long as the abuse continues. Nodules can be removed surgically if necessary, but they grow back if the speech habits that create tension continue. Therefore, it is of great importance that a speech pathologist be consulted so that bad vocal habits can be eliminated. Other causes of hoarseness are allergies, air pollution caused by cigarette smoke, automobile and industrial fumes, and other irritants.

Individuals with hoarseness can benefit from exercises in relaxation and proper breathing habits.

Harshness

Harshness is often present when the vocal quality sounds very strained and inflexible and is accompanied by breathy noises. Projection is loud; pitches are low. It is a very difficult sound to listen to because of the gross tension that is present in the laryngeal area. You can feel this tension by placing an opened hand on the larynx. If this quality remains for any length of time, it is important that you visit a laryngologist. If the cause of the harshness is functional rather than physical, you might have to relearn and apply some of the positive vocal relaxation techniques discussed in this text.

Stridency

A **strident** voice is harsh, unpleasant, tinny, and generally high-pitched. People with strident voices are often labeled neurotic, whether they are male or female. Another group of individuals who often have strident voices are the hearing-impaired. Many speakers with a hearing loss cannot hear their stridency.

To help correct hoarse and strident voices, consult the following exercises: Exercises for Breath Control (pp. 25–30), Overly Open Throat Exercises (pp. 46–47), Nasal Resonance Exercises (pp. 48–52), and Optimum Pitch Exercises (pp. 59–60).

Laryngitis

Laryngitis is a different matter. Laryngitis is the inflammation of the larynx (voice box). It is generally short-lived. It might be caused by a cold or shouting at a neighbor to turn down the volume of his television set.

Usually, the problem will clear up itself through whispering, vocal rest, and drinking plenty of liquids. If the laryngitis persists, it might be a more serious medical condition.

The "-itis" part of the word indicates inflammation of the vocal folds that are swollen for some reason and cannot approximate each other. Therefore, the sound of your voice is rather hoarse, but only temporarily. Other causes of laryngitis are allergies and singing or speaking loudly for an extensive period of time.

If the hoarse quality lasts for more than two weeks, there may be reason for you to see your doctor, who can easily check your vocal folds to make certain there are no nodules present.

To locate URLs and search terms for weblinks relevant to this chapter, please go to the companion website at www.cengage.com/rtf/crannell/voiceandarticulation5e and select the proper chapter.

Write the definitions for the following terms in the space below.

KEY TERMS   DEFINITIONS

Alveolar Ridge

Articulatory Adjustment

Assimilation

Assimilation Nasality

Bilabial

Cleft Palate Speech

Denasality

Glottal Shock or Stop

Hard Palate

Harshness

Hoarseness

Laryngitis

Mandible

Maxilla

Nasality

Nasal Spurs

Nodules

Septum

Singer's Nodes

Soft Palate

Strident

Uvula

Velum

Vocal Fry

SPEECH II

CHAPTER 6

THE PRODUCTION OF VOWELS

In Chapter 1 (1-11), we looked at ways that letters can be misleading (they can represent multiple sounds). That is the reason the IPA (International Phonetic Alphabet), which deals exclusively with sounds, was published in 1888 by the International Phonetic Association. Although several phonetic alphabets existed at the time, the Broad Romic was selected to form the basis for the IPA (see the front inside cover). A group of international scholars developed an alphabet that assigned a written symbol to each of the produced sounds within a given language. Today, the association has expanded to include the symbols and sounds of the main languages of the world. The symbol representing the assigned sound is the same regardless of the language or spelling.

Each symbol stands for an entire family of sounds. For example, all /l/ sounds are not made entirely the same; one may produce that sound with the tongue tip either up or down. However, each one would have a similar acoustic characteristic. Our traditional alphabet can be used to create words and, therefore, meaning, but pronouncing words can be very confusing. The IPA is a common system of notation that simplifies our study of the sound of language. This study is called **phonetics,** the science of speech sounds.

Before we isolate English speech sounds and learn their symbols in the phonetic alphabet, we must clarify a few terms. Speech sounds are composed of *phonemes*. A **phoneme** is the smallest unit of recognizable speech sound; it is a sound family. Not everyone produces a phoneme in exactly the same way. In addition, as indicated in our discussion on assimilation (Chapter 5), the location of sounds in a word and the transition from one sound to another are also relevant. In the words *theme, seat, bean,* and *peach,* the only similarity is that all of the words contain the same vowel phoneme; every consonant phoneme in the words is different.

There are a number of ways to produce a phoneme, depending on the sounds that surround it and the capability of the speaker. The /d/ in "deal" is not produced in exactly the same way as the /d/ in "drown." You can easily feel the difference between the productions of these sounds by going back and forth between the two words. These varieties of the phoneme /d/ are called *allophones*. An **allophone** is a recognizable variation of a phoneme. An allophone can be acceptable or unacceptable, depending on the standard for the particular dialect or profession in question. For example, an unacceptable allophone would be the substitution of "th" for /s/ and /z /. Not many would accept the pronunciation of the following sentence: "I think that thoup ith one of my favorite luncheth." On the other hand, there are many other acceptable ways to say the consonants /s/ and /z/.

SENSE STIMULI

Four senses are of particular importance in developing good articulation: the auditory, visual, tactile, and kinesthetic senses. Everyone has a favorite sense through which much information can be obtained. All can be developed, however.

Because of the impact of the printing press, many people believe that the strongest sense is the **visual sense.** For many others, the **auditory sense** is the most important because it prevailed before printed material existed. Both the visual and auditory senses are important in the production of speech, but hearing the differences among sounds is particularly valuable. After all, you distinguish the difference between /o/ (as in "go") and /u / (as in "true") through **auditory discrimination** rather than through visual clues.

Visualization is used not only in the production of sounds, but also—and more importantly—in the communication process as a whole. Much of the information received by a listener is visual, including sound production (such as the difference between /f/ as in "fun" and /θ/ as in "thing"), gestures, and attitude.

The **tactile sense** concerns touch and the sensation of physical contact. The differences among suede, burlap, and cashmere are most dramatically perceived through the tactile sense. When you buy fruit or vegetables, it is recommended (but not by the store owner!) that you touch and gently squeeze as well as smell each item. In sound production, it is often very helpful to feel what your tongue is doing when you articulate an /l/ or a /t/. The tactile sense is especially useful in producing consonant sounds.

The **kinesthetic sense** involves the feeling or tension of the muscles and the awareness of the resulting movement. (The word is from the Greek *kine,* meaning "movement" or "motion," and *thesis,* meaning "concept.") For example, you can tell whether or not your lips are rounded in the production of /u/ (as in "true").

The four senses work together, of course. Although you sometimes favor one or two of the senses, all four are very helpful in learning and distinguishing among sounds. They are also very helpful in the general communication process.

ARTICULATION

Articulation in the context of this book is defined as the production of vowels, diphthongs, and consonants. Clearly, there is a strong relationship between this definition and the more usual definitions, such as the ability to speak clearly and skillfully. The term *articulation* was chosen over its synonym *enunciation* because another of its meanings is "to join"; articulators are frequently "joined" one with another to produce a sound. At the end of the nineteenth century and the early part of the twentieth century, articulation was primarily considered to be the study of consonants, whereas enunciation was the study of vowels and diphthongs. Today, the term *articulation* is used to include vowels, diphthongs, and consonants. **Pronunciation** is the combining of vowels, diphthongs, and consonants to form words.

The *articulators* (organs that work alone or in conjunction with another organ and are responsible for producing speech sounds) are either active (those that are capable of moving) or passive (those that are immovable):

ACTIVE	PASSIVE
Tongue (largest and most active articulator)	Maxilla (upper jaw)
	Alveolar ridge
Velum	Teeth (passive . . . in most cases!)
Muscles of the cheeks	Hard palate
Muscles of the pharynx	
Lips	
Mandible (lower jaw)	

Usually, one of these articulators comes in contact with another in producing a speech sound, especially in the production of consonants.

All sounds, whether they are vowels, diphthongs, or consonants, are composed of either (1) breath (with no vibration of the vocal folds) or (2) vibration of the vocal folds. Breath must be present to produce all sounds, whether voiced or voiceless. One of the classifications of English sounds is based on whether the vocal folds vibrate. If just breath is used with no vibration of the vocal folds, the sound is referred to as **voiceless,** surd, atonic (without tone), nonphonating, or nonvibrating. If the sound is produced with breath plus vibration, it is referred to as **voiced,** sonant, tonic, phonating, or vibrating. All vowels and diphthongs are voiced.

VOWELS

A **vowel** is a speech sound formed from a free and unobstructed flow of vibrating breath. A **diphthong** is a speech sound composed of two vowels coming together within the same syllable. Vowels and diphthongs are important in English because they not only provide the basis of the syllable but also give the language carrying power and beauty. Although the fricative /f/, for example, is a helpful sound, particularly if you want to say the words *friend* or *after,* few people would disagree that prolonging the /f/ sound is not very pleasant. On the other hand, prolonging the vowel in "calm" gives increased loudness and certainly a difference in auditory pleasure. Part of this response, however, is related to the word's suggestive meaning, or its **connotation.** For example, separate the meaning (that is, the **denotation**) from the pronunciation in the word *confusion.* Again, the vowels give the sound of the word carrying power and a degree of pleasure, partly because of the combinations of consonants and vowels. The words *cellar door* are reputed to constitute one of the most pleasant sound combinations in English when their meaning is separated from the sound.

The major organ in vowel production is the tongue (Figure 6.1). The tongue is divided into three areas: the front, the center, and the back (Figure 6.2). The most frontal portion of the tongue is called the *tip;* it can be pointed. The blade of the tongue is that portion just behind the tip. Vowels are produced by altering both the position of and the amount of

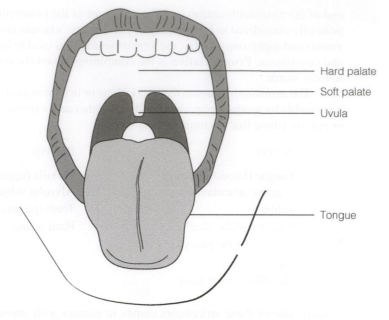

FIGURE 6.1   The mouth cavity

tension in the tongue. Other active articulators are (1) the cheek and lip muscles, (2) the lower jaw (mandible), and (3) the tensed velum (because all vibrating air is resonated through the mouth in producing vowels and diphthongs). Compared with the precision required to articulate consonants, more latitude is allowable for vowels.

All vowels are voiced **continuants;** that is, they are produced without a complete closure of the breath passage. Some vowels are produced with similar articulatory

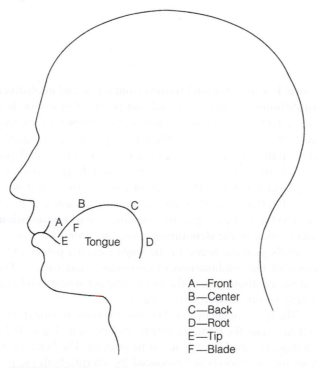

A—Front
B—Center
C—Back
D—Root
E—Tip
F—Blade

FIGURE 6.2   Parts of the tongue

adjustments. By shifting the position of the tongue, in some cases very slightly, and by increasing or decreasing the amount of tension in the tongue, different vowels are enunciated. Prolong the vowels in the words *beet* and *bit,* and feel the differences in tongue placement and amount of tension.

Producing vowel sounds requires less articulatory movement than that required for most consonant sounds. Several vowel charts have been designed to illustrate these adjustments. In the accompanying chart, "High," "Middle," and "Low" refer to the position of the peak of the tongue's arch. If the arch is high and almost touching the palate, two cavities are created within the mouth. The less arch in the tongue there is, the larger the oral cavity. "Front," "Central," and "Back" indicate where in the mouth (buccal cavity) the resonance is produced. Clearly, considerably more vowels than the famous "a, e, i, o, u, and sometimes y" have been included here.

SITE OF RESONANCE IN MOUTH

		Front	Central	Back
ARCH OF THE TONGUE	High	/i/—s<u>ee</u>: *tongue tense* /ɪ/—b<u>i</u>t: *tongue relaxed*		/u/—tr<u>ue</u>: *tongue slightly tense* /ʊ/—p<u>u</u>t: *tongue relaxed*
	Middle	/e/—m<u>a</u>ke: *tongue tense* /ɛ/—m<u>e</u>t: *tongue relaxed*	/ɝ/—h<u>er</u>: *tongue tense* /ɜ/—b<u>ir</u>d: *tongue slightly tense* (New England / British) /ɚ/—aft<u>er</u>: *tongue slightly tense* /ʌ/—c<u>u</u>t: *tongue relaxed* /ə/—<u>a</u>bout: *tongue relaxed*	/o/—g<u>o</u>: *tongue tense*
	Low	/æ/—c<u>a</u>t: *tongue relaxed* /a/—h<u>a</u>lf: *tongue relaxed* (New England/British)		/ɔ/—l<u>aw</u>: *tongue slightly tense* /ɒ/—w<u>a</u>lnut: *tongue slightly tense* (New England) /ɑ/—f<u>a</u>ther: *tongue relaxed*

Each of the vowel sounds is **transcribed** into a phonetic symbol and accompanied by a key word containing that vowel. Words can often be pronounced in more than one way; therefore, using the key words as indicators of standard pronunciation provides general agreement on sounds. There will not be problems with many sounds, but remember that for some there are a number of correct pronunciations and that speakers from different parts of the country might use different pronunciations. As its authority on pronunciation, this text uses the standard reference book, *A Pronouncing Dictionary of American English,* by John S. Kenyon and Thomas A. Knott (Springfield, Mass.: Merriam, 1953). Errors in the production of vowels and diphthongs (substitutions, additions, and distortions) are primarily due to regionalisms (this subject will be discussed in Chapter 12). Other errors will be detailed here.

In the exercises that appear in the next section, a variety of vowel sounds can be used for the underlined vowels. However, you will learn to differentiate vowel sounds more quickly by pronouncing the vowel under discussion as indicated rather than voicing your **habitual** vowel sound. Remember that people in your area might use a variant pronunciation that is also acceptable.

It is also suggested that for purposes of differentiation you keep the tip of your tongue against the lower front teeth for all of the vowels except /ɜ/ (as in "h<u>er</u>") and /ɚ/ (as in "aft<u>er</u>"). This will help you focus on the changes in the curve of the tongue.

In practice, always visualize the production of the sound; then, exaggerate the production and feeling of the sound. Get a visual and kinetic sense of what the articulators are doing. To help develop the appropriate sound, first exaggerate and then pull away only slightly from the exaggerated articulation.

>>> FRONT VOWELS

/i/

Production

In the production of /i/ (as in "s<u>ee</u>"), the muscles of the tongue tense. The tongue is slightly arched, and the front of the tongue is raised. The mouth is almost closed, and the lips are slightly tensed and spread. *The vowel /i/ occurs only in **stressed** syllables.*

(((EXERCISES

The first time you read aloud exercises 1 through 3, exaggerate the production of all of the sounds in the words, giving special attention to the vowels. Feel what is happening to both the lips and the tongue. Be careful; to develop the appropriate pronunciation in later readings, do not pull away too much from the overarticulation when practicing these exercises.

1. k<u>ee</u>n   rel<u>ea</u>se
   f<u>ee</u>d   l<u>ei</u>sure
   s<u>ea</u>l   pl<u>ea</u>sing
   m<u>ea</u>l   rec<u>ei</u>ve
   m<u>ea</u>n   str<u>ea</u>mers
   cr<u>ee</u>d   fr<u>e</u>quent
   r<u>ea</u>d   t<u>ea</u>cher
   s<u>ee</u>n   <u>ea</u>gles
   n<u>ee</u>d   m<u>ea</u>ning

2. f<u>ee</u>d the <u>ea</u>gles   n<u>ee</u>d l<u>ei</u>sure time
   pl<u>ea</u>sing s<u>ea</u>ls   fr<u>ee</u> the b<u>ee</u>s
   n<u>ee</u>d p<u>eo</u>ple   gr<u>ee</u>n l<u>ea</u>ves
   r<u>ea</u>ding t<u>ea</u>cher   <u>Ea</u>stern pol<u>i</u>ce

3. a. Oscar chased thr<u>ee</u> <u>ea</u>gles under the tr<u>ee</u>.

   b. The police agr<u>ee</u>d to pl<u>ea</u>se the p<u>eo</u>ple.

   c. In the <u>Ea</u>st, the gr<u>ee</u>n l<u>ea</u>ves are falling.

  d. Mugsy's d<u>ee</u>ds were appr<u>e</u>ciated by the t<u>ea</u>m.

  e. Malic <u>ea</u>sed his way into the s<u>e</u>cret melon patch.

  f. The g<u>ee</u>se were f<u>ee</u>ding on the b<u>ea</u>ns in Midnite's garden.

  g. We had s<u>ee</u>n the th<u>ie</u>f stuff the wh<u>ea</u>t into the b<u>ee</u>hive.

  h. Christ<u>i</u>ne's scr<u>ea</u>ms were heard from the village gr<u>ee</u>n.

  i. Vin made his usual sc<u>e</u>ne about undercooked linguiça.

4. Aye thought yew awl night depr<u>e</u>ciate this . . .
Eye have a spelling checker,
It came with my <u>PC</u>;
It plainly marks four my revue
Mistakes I cannot s<u>ea</u>.

I've run this poem threw it,
I'm sure your pl<u>ea</u>sed to no,
Its letter perfect in it's weigh,
My checker told m<u>e</u> sew.

The following selections are by W. S. Gilbert. It may seem that his works appear frequently in this text (and they do!), but they happen to be among the best for developing good breath control and appropriate articulation.

5. With base dec<u>ei</u>t
You worked upon our f<u>ee</u>lings!
Revenge is sw<u>ee</u>t,
And flavours all our d<u>ea</u>lings!
With courage rare
And resolution manly,
For death prepare,
Unhappy General Stanley.

From THE PIRATES OF PENZANCE
W. S. Gilbert

6. Over the ripening p<u>ea</u>ch
Buzzes the b<u>ee</u>.
Splash on the billowy b<u>ea</u>ch
Tumbles the s<u>ea</u>.
But the p<u>ea</u>ch
And the b<u>ea</u>ch
They are <u>ea</u>ch
Nothing to m<u>e</u>!

From RUDDIGORE
W. S. Gilbert

/ɪ/

Production

In the production of /ɪ/ (as in "b<u>i</u>t") the muscles of the tongue are relaxed, which lowers the hump in the tongue slightly from the /i/ position. The teeth are slightly farther apart, and the sound is usually shorter in duration. The lips are spread.

EXERCISES

The first time you read aloud the following exercises, exaggerate all of the sounds in each word, giving special attention to the vowels. Feel how this vowel differs from /i/.

1. Read aloud the following words, alternating between the /ɪ/ and /i/ columns. The purpose of the word list is not only to present the new vowel sound but also to compare it with the one that you have just learned. This technique will be used throughout this chapter. Make certain that you don't pull away too much from the overarticulation when trying to develop appropriate pronunciation.

/ɪ/	/i/	/ɪ/	/i/
itch	each	hitting	heating
slit	sleet	filling	feeling
dim	deem	mitten	meetin'
list	least	whisper	whee spur
will	we'll	chipper	cheaper
mitt	meet	bitter	beater
rid	read	dipper	deeper
sin	scene	kipper	keeper
kid	keyed	liver	leave her
mill	meal	pitcher	peacher[1]
been	bean	riches	reaches
sit	seat	shipping	sheeping
Tim	team	living	leaving

2. Follow the same procedure with these phrases.

Christmas thistle	the kid's list
Mister Rip Van Winkle	the river's mist
the whispering twins	a thin fist
since Steve wished it	middle of the film

3. A number of languages do not contain the vowel /ɪ/ (as in "bit"), and the vowel /i/ is often substituted for /ɪ/. The following limerick is a good exercise to contrast and compare /i/ and /ɪ/.

There was a faith healer of Deal,
Who said, "Although pain isn't real,
If I sit on a pin
And it punctures my skin,
I dislike what I fancy I feel."

Read aloud the selections in exercises 4 and 5.

4. **a.** Patricia was knitting little mittens for him.

   b. "Miss Brill" is not a simple story.[2]

   c. We got a tin of mixed biscuits for Christmas.

   d. Rip Van Winkle is my favorite literary[2] character.

---

[1]Would you believe a farmer who raises peaches? No? Oh well.
[2]The vowel in the last syllable of these words (represented by the letter *y*) is pronounced /ɪ/ (as in "bit").
 In **dynamic speech**, many /i/ vowels become /ɪ/, particularly in the final position.

    e. Silly Millie went fishing with Willie.[3]

    f. Thin vinegar is often used in salads.

    g. Steve wished that Katy[2] would tickle Mister Greenjeans.

    h. Phil picks thick chickens for his soup.

    i. Gristle on liver is particularly[2] offensive.

    j. The twins swam in flimsy[2] bathing suits.

5. You have to marvel at the unique lunacy of a language in which your house can burn up as it burns down, in which you fill in a form by filling it out and in which, an alarm goes off by going on.

/e/

Production

In the production of /e/ (as in "make"), the tongue is lowered slightly from the /ɪ/ position. There is a curve in the tongue that is raised slightly toward the palate. The muscles of the tongue are tense. The mouth is opened wider than for /ɪ/, and the lips are spread. When used in stressed syllables in particular, the vowel /e/ often becomes the diphthong /eɪ/ rather than the pure vowel. The use of this diphthong is encouraged in career speech *even though* the pure vowel symbol is often used in transcription.

EXERCISES

In the following exercises, feel the increased tension in the tongue compared with the /ɪ/ position. The tongue is also slightly lowered. Exaggerate the pronunciation of the words. To produce the sounds appropriately, make certain you do not pull away too much from the practiced overarticulation.

1. Alternate reading aloud the words in the /e/ and /ɪ/ columns, and feel the adjustment. In addition, prolong the vowel. The polysyllabic nonsense words in the /ɪ/ column continue to contrast the two vowels. Don't try to make sense out of these words, simply pronounce them; the pronunciation of the phonetic symbols will prove helpful.

/e/	/ɪ/	/e/	/ɪ/
bait	bit	satiate	['sɪʃijɪt]
steak	stick	later	litter
rain	Rin[4]	ungrateful	[əngrɪtf̩l]
mate	mitt	famous	[fɪməs]
gave	give	taping	tipping
take	tick	ancient	[ɪnʃənt]
hate	hit	Hemingway	hemming[wɪ]
break	brick	casing	kissing
stale	still	vacation	[vɪkɪʃən]
fail	fill	tornado	[tɔrnɪdo]
sale	sill	ailment	ill mint

---

[3]It was my choice to emphasize the rhyme in this sentence, and that brought more muscular tension to the articulators. Therefore, the vowel is /i / in the final syllables in the proper names.

[4]The given name of Mr. Tin Tin.

taint	tint	display	[dɪsplɪ]
skate	skit	relation	[rɪlɪʃən]

Read aloud the selections in exercises 2 through 6.

2. table and tray   Mabel's famous sales
   waiters and waitresses   wake up and shake hands
   crayfish and brains   a Hemingway vacation
   the neighbor's aim   a crazy relation

3. a. Mabel and Abe went on a vacation to Angel, Texas.

b. They gave a great deal of help to their neighbors during the rainstorm.

c. Robert's birthday cake was ordered in May.

d. With the aid of a cane Sabre can walk.

e. The weathervane indicated a rainy day.

f. Tracy raked the cranberries with a gray rake.

g. Apple taste very smooth with Tasty Choice coffee.

h. Maiden Denise made a strange mistake on the paper.

i. Hazel would always remain faithful to the family name.

4. There was a young lady of Spain
   Who was dreadfully sick in a train,
   Not once, but again
   And again and again,
   And again and again and again.

5. The long June twilight faded into night. Dublin lay enveloped in darkness but for the dim
   light of the moon that shone through fleecy clouds, casting a pale light. . . .

   From THE SNIPER
   Liam O'Flaherty

/ɛ/

Production

In the production of /ɛ/ (as in "met"), the muscles of the tongue are relaxed and the tip of
the tongue is positioned behind the lower teeth—lower in the mouth than for /e/. The lips
are slightly spread, while the lower jaw drops slightly from the /e/ position.

Problems

One of the most common problems with this sound is the substitution of /ɪ/ for /ɛ/. Although
this error is especially prevalent in the South and the Southwest, it is very common in all
parts of the country.

   You probably have not heard all of the following transcribed words pronounced this
way. On the other hand, you have certainly heard some of them—and frequently (and *you*
might even use such pronunciations!). In the following word list, use negative practice and
feel the error.

	CAREER	ERROR	CAREER
get[5]	[gɛt]	[gɪt]	[gɛt]
met	[mɛt]	[mɪt]	[mɛt]

---

[5]Many speakers use the substandard "git" for "get."

	CAREER	ERROR	CAREER
forget	[forˈgɛt]	[fəˈgɪt][6]	[forˈgɛt]
better	[ˈbɛtɚ]	[ˈbɪtə]	[ˈbɛtɚ]
relish	[ˈrɛlɪʃ]	[ˈrɪlɪʃ]	[ˈrɛlɪʃ]
fetch	[fɛtʃ]	[fɪtʃ]	[fɛtʃ]
let	[lɛt]	[lɪt]	[lɛt]
next	[nɛkst]	[nɪkst]	[nɛkst]
very	[ˈvɛrɪ]	[ˈvɪrɪ]	[ˈvɛrɪ]
chest	[tʃɛst]	[tʃɪst]	[tʃɛst]

Forget about it [forˈgɛt əˈbaʊt ɪt] [fəˈgɪt əˈbaʊt ɪt] [forˈgɛt əˈbaʊt ɪt]

Get it, please! [gɛt ɪt pliz] [gɪt ɪt pliz] [gɛt ɪt pliz]

Call next time. [kɔl nɛkst taɪm] [kɔl nɪkst taɪm] [kɔl nɛkst taɪm]

Let me do it. [lɛt mi du ɪt] [lɪt mi du ɪt] [lɛt mi du ɪt]

Fetch the ball. [lɛtʃ ðə bɔl] [fɪtʃ ðə bɔl] [fɛtʃ ðə bɔl]

 EXERCISES

The first time you read aloud the following exercises, exaggerate the production of all of the sounds, giving special attention to the vowels. Feel how the vowel /ɛ/ differs from /e/.

1. Alternate reading aloud the words in the /ɛ/ and /e/ columns. The words enclosed in brackets are nonsense words transcribed into phonetics; sound them out. Make certain you do not pull away too much from the overarticulation when trying to develop the appropriate pronunciation.

/ɛ/	/e/	/ɛ/	/e/
Ed's	aids	testing	tasting
pen	pain	spectra	spake [trə]
met	mate	America	[əmɛrəkə]
fez	phase	wetter	waiter
sex	sakes	henpecked	[hɛnpɛkt]
best	baste	intention	[ɪntɛnʃən]
yell	Yale	utensils	[jutɛnsəlz]
led	laid	emphasis	aim [fəsɪs]
sped	spade	breakfast	break [fəst]
fed	fade	wretched	Ray [tʃəd]
kept	caped	repentance	[rɪpɛntəns]
men	mane	penthouse	paint house
bed	bade[7]	repent	repaint

---

[6]I know, "I would never say that!"

[7]A common error occurs in the pronunciation of this word. The only acceptable pronunciation of "bade" is [bæd], as if it were spelled "bad."

Read aloud the selections in exercises 2 through 7.

2. Ned's relish   the sheriff's intention
Fred's epic   rest your leg
pegs and tents   September checking
eggs for breakfast   pleasant memories

3. a. It is a pleasure to remember that debt.

b. The keg was held by Trevor and Fred.

c. *High Noon* is a Western epic that will be remembered forever.

d. Helen was selling the shells for a penny.

e. After eating the yellow melons, David and Adam felt helpless.

f. Rett and Ellen's cosmic energy was felt for several days after we met them.

g. Steve pretended that he did not feel the intense pain.

h. Infamous Uncle Ned had a large welt on his leg when he arrived.

i. Heather always said that the well-bred horse was the best.

4. Now what is this, and what is that, and why does father leave his rest
At such a time of night as this, so very incompletely dressed?
Dear father is, and always was, the most methodical of men!
It's his invariable rule to go to bed at half-past ten.
What strange occurrence can it be that calls dear father from his rest
At such a time of night as this, so very incompletely dressed?

From THE PIRATES OF PENZANCE
W. S. Gilbert

5. We build monuments in memory of our heroes. Washington, Jefferson, and Lincoln live on in our nation's capital. We erect monuments to honor our martyrs.

From THE "MONUMENT" AT WOUNDED KNEE
Cecile Larson

6. The cellar smelled of dust and old moisture. The beams were fuzzed with cobwebs. There was only one light, a dim one in the corner. A little rivulet was running darkly down the wall and already had formed a footsquare pool on the floor.

From THE STORM
McKnight Malmar

7. Freddie the Frog would wed.
He needed a frog in his bed.
Every froggie said "No!"
Every froggie said "Go!"
So Fred wed a tadpole instead.

FREDDIE THE FROG
Edward Lear

/æ/

Production

In the production of /æ/ (as in "cat"), the muscles of the tongue are relaxed. The front and back of the tongue are low, and the tip is behind the lower front teeth. The mouth is opened wider than for /ɛ/. The lips are in a neutral position.

Problems

The most common error in the production of this vowel is too much tension in the tongue, resulting in the substitution of /ɛə/ for the correct vowel /æ/. This error is common in the speech of New Yorkers and Midwesterners, particularly Chicagoans. For exercises, see pages 311–312 in Chapter 12.

EXERCISES

The first time you read aloud the following exercises, exaggerate the production of all of the sounds in the words, giving special attention to the vowels.

1. Read aloud the following words, alternating between the /æ/ and /ɛ/ columns. The words enclosed in brackets are nonsense words transcribed into phonetics. Sound them out, keeping the same stress as in the related /æ/ word. Make certain you don't pull away too much from the overarticulation when trying to develop appropriate pronunciation.

/æ/	/ɛ/	/æ/	/ɛ/
Pat	pet	balance	bell [ləns]
can	Ken	galaxy	[gɛləksɪ]
had	head	latter	letter
bag	beg	chattering	[tʃɛtɚɪŋ]
sand	send	graduate (v)	[grɛdʒuet] (v)
Danny	Denny	gallon	[gɛlən]
land	lend	pastoral	pest [ərəl]
and	end	expansive	expensive
sad	said	bombastic	bomb [bɛs] tick
band	bend	sandman	send men
add it	edit	diagram	[daɪəgrɛm]
than	then	gnatting[8]	netting
Annie	any	batting	betting

2. The following is a list of words that contrasts /æ/ with /e/ and /ɛ/, vowels that are frequently incorrectly used in conjunction with /ŋ/ (as in "rang"). In career speech, the /æ/ is used. (However, /ɛ/ is used in words like *length* [lɛŋθ], *penguin* ['pɛŋgwɪn], and *strength* [strɛŋθ].) The lower jaw is lower than in the production of the vowels /e/ or /æ/.

	CAREER	/e/ ERROR	/ɛ/ ERROR	CAREER
bank	[bæŋk]	[beŋk]	[bɛŋk]	[bæŋk]
thank	[θæŋk]	[θeŋk]	[θɛŋk]	[θæŋk]
hang	[hæŋ]	[heŋ]	[hɛŋ]	[hæŋ]
Frank	[fræŋk]	[freŋk]	[frɛŋk]	[fræŋk]
rang	[ræŋ]	[reŋ]	[rɛŋ]	[ræŋ]
spanking	['spæŋkɪŋ]	['speŋkɪŋ]	['spɛŋkɪŋ]	['spæŋkɪŋ]
flank	[flæŋk]	[fleŋk]	[flɛŋk]	[flæŋk]

---

[8]The act of going on safari to shoot tiny, annoying insects.

sank	[sæŋk]	[seŋk]	[sɛŋk]	[sæŋk]
blank	[blæŋk]	[bleŋk]	[blɛŋk]	[blæŋk]
Hank	[hæŋk]	[heŋk]	[hɛŋk]	[hæŋk]

Read aloud the selections in exercises 3 through 5.

3. *C̲a̲ndid C̲a̲mera*   Spanish gr̲a̲nd pi̲a̲no
   f̲a̲st c̲a̲ts   beg̲a̲n cl̲a̲pping h̲a̲nds
   Harold's b̲a̲nner   cr̲a̲ss ̲a̲ttitude
   bl̲a̲ck c̲a̲scading hair   fl̲a̲t l̲a̲nd

4. **a.** C̲a̲role gave D̲a̲n a b̲a̲ck scratcher.

   b. Vangi b̲a̲ttered the r̲a̲dical purse sn̲a̲tcher.

   c. D̲a̲n ̲a̲sked ̲A̲ndrea if she saw the t̲a̲n c̲a̲t att̲a̲ck the dog.

   d. *C̲a̲ndid C̲a̲mera* is a very popular progr̲a̲m.

   e. Darnell, the m̲a̲sked b̲a̲ndit, gr̲a̲bbed h̲a̲lf the c̲a̲lf and r̲a̲n.

   f. Cr̲a̲mming for ex̲a̲minations is a b̲a̲d h̲a̲bit.

   g. My ̲A̲unt P̲a̲t's ̲a̲ttic is filled with ̲a̲ntiques.

   h. There is a gr̲a̲nd pi̲a̲no for sale in M̲a̲nchester.

   i. C̲a̲ndied ̲a̲pples are traditional ̲a̲t Th̲a̲nksgiving.

   j. C̲a̲rrie h̲a̲s been called a tough t̲a̲skmaster by her students.

5. Produce the vowel without the additional tension in the following exercises:

   a. She beg̲a̲n to drink the coffee. While she was drinking, holding the cup in both hands, she beg̲a̲n to make the sound again. She made the sound into the cup and the coffee spl̲a̲shed out onto her h̲a̲nds ̲a̲nd her dress.

   From THAT EVENING SUN
   William Faulkner

   b. There was an old M̲a̲n of Madrás,
   Who rode on a cream-coloured ̲a̲ss;
   But the length of its ears, so promoted his fears,
   Th̲a̲t it killed that Old M̲a̲n of Madrás.

   From A BOOK OF NONSENSE
   Edward Lear

>>>
REVIEW OF FRONT VOWELS

/i/	/ɪ/	/e/	/ɛ/	/æ/
m̲e̲an	M̲i̲n	m̲ai̲n	m̲e̲n	m̲a̲n
k̲ee̲n	k̲i̲n	c̲a̲ne	K̲e̲n	c̲a̲n
b̲e̲an	b̲ee̲n	b̲a̲ne	B̲e̲n	b̲a̲n
m̲e̲al	m̲i̲ll	m̲a̲le	M̲e̲l	M̲a̲l
r̲e̲ap	r̲i̲p	r̲a̲pe	R̲e̲p.	wr̲a̲p

leased	list	laced	lest	last
peel	pill	pale	Pell	pal
seal	sill	sale	sell	Sal
read	rid	raid	red	rad
feast	fist	faced	fest	fast
beat	bit	bait	bet	bat
mead	mid	made	Med	mad
seat	sit	sate	set	sat
seeks	six	sakes	sex	sacks
deal	dill	Dale	dell	Dal
seen	sin	sane	Sen.	San
keel	kill	kale	Kell	Cal
Pete	pit	pate	pet	Pat

/a/

Production

The muscles of the tongue are relaxed, and the front and the back of the tongue are low in the mouth. The tongue lies midway between the positions used to produce /æ/ and /ɑ/ (as in "father"). The lips are in a neutral position. The vowel /a/ (as in "half") is primarily a New England sound, used when the letters *a* and *au* come before /s/, /n/, /θ/, and /f/. (Most speakers would pronounce the key word *half* with /æ/.) This sound is also prevalent in some parts of the Midwest, as well as in upstate New York, in words like *hot, Tom, cot,* and *Bob.* It is often used in the South in words like *night* [nat], *fright* [frat], *fire* [far], and *tire* [tar]. The phoneme /a/ is heard as the first sound in the diphthong /aɪ/, as in "I," "cry," and "might."

It can be a useful sound for the performer to use in reading some poems by Robert Frost, Eugene O'Neill's *Desire Under the Elms,* and other New England literature. It is a good sound to use for any communication occasion when there is the need for New England speech. This sound can be unpleasant to the ear, especially when produced with too much tension, and it is not recommended for career speech because it is regional and potentially abrasive.

EXERCISES

The first time you read aloud exercises 1 through 5, exaggerate the production of all of the sounds in the words, giving special attention to the vowels. Feel how this vowel differs from /æ/.

1. Alternate reading aloud the words in the /a/ and /æ/ columns. Sound them out. Make certain you don't pull away too much from the exaggerated articulation when trying to develop the appropriate pronunciation. Remember that most of these words are also pronounced with /æ/.

/a/	/æ/	/a/	/æ/
bath	bath	disaster	disaster
salve [sav][9]	salve [sæv]	bombastic	bombastic
fast	fast	laughter	laughter

---

[9]Notice that the letter *l* is silent.

aunt	aunt /ant	pasture	pasture
can't	can't	grasping	grasping
class	class	answer	answer
glass	glass	plasterer	plasterer
path	path	afterward	afterward
aft	aft	advantage	advantage
ask	ask	blaspheme	blaspheme

2. pass out   glass of water
master electrician   ask everyone
class reunion   hot dog
Tom's task   comfortable cot

3. a. There is an advantage to granting him his wish.

  b. Colonel command the child to stay off the grass.

  c. My Aunt Doris thinks that the draft would be ghastly.

  d. The cast gave Jack a set of brass candlesticks.

  e. The photograph of Frances and Hank amazed the class.

  f. They gasped when they heard I had returned from France.

  g. On behalf of Uncle Ned, I thank you for the staff's canister you were asked to bring.

  h. Wilma pranced down the path like a real dancer.

  i. Nana took a chance and glanced at Vangi.

  j. Joseph advanced into his alabaster bathroom.

4. The flowers that bloom in the spring,
Tra la,
Breathe promise of merry sunshine—
As we merrily dance and we sing,
Tra la.

From THE MIKADO (as pronounced by a New Englander)
W. S. Gilbert

>>>
CENTRAL VOWELS

/ɝ/

Production

The vowel /ɝ/ (as in "her") is used only in *stressed* syllables. It may occur in a **monosyllabic** word like "fur" or in a **polysyllabic** word like "usurping." The muscles of the tongue are tense, the sides of the tongue are positioned against the upper rear **molars** (teeth with a flattened surface), and the tongue tip is free and slightly tense. The lips are slightly rounded. The position of the tongue is similar to that for the semivowel /r/.

((((· EXERCISES

The first time you read aloud exercises 1 through 9, exaggerate the production of all of the sounds in the words. Feel how the vowel /ɜ/ is produced compared with other vowels. Make certain you don't pull away too much from the overarticulation when trying to develop the appropriate pronunciation.

1. earth   verdict
    nerve   furnace
    stir   deserving
    heard   churlish
    term   disturb
    work   confirm
    curl   mercy
    surge   irksome
    err   cursing
    swerve   rehearse

2. surge of energy[10]   perfect manner[10]
    heard the bell   church service
    working hard   burst of light
    wordy essay   flirting behavior[10]

3. a. Richard[10] Burton purchased some ermine furs.

    b. Shirley was sure she would smirk at the sermon.

    c. The verb occurs in the first verse of the poem.

    d. Many girls are learning to assert themselves.

    e. The Colonel works miracles with persons who search for truth.

    f. Herb the herbman prepares the meals for all the servants.

    g. The nurse was irked by the less than perfect patient.

    h. Research the records for Myrtle's birthday.

    i. The cowboy's stirrup was made of sterling.

    j. The blackbird was sitting on the perch.

4. O'er the season vernal,
    Time may cast a shade;
    Sunshine, if eternal,
    Makes the roses fade!

    From TRIAL BY JURY
    W. S. Gilbert

5. There was an Old Lady of Chertsey,
    Who made a remarkable curtsey;
    She twirled round and round, till she sank underground,
    Which distressed all the people of Chertsey.

    From A BOOK OF NONSENSE
    Edward Lear

―――――――――――
[10]These words contain an unstressed "er" and, therefore, a *different* vowel sound!

6. For anything so overdone is from the p<u>ur</u>pose of playing, whose end, both at the f<u>ir</u>st and now, was and is to hold as 'tw<u>ere</u> the mirror up to Nature.

From HAMLET
William Shakespeare

7. W<u>or</u>kers <u>ear</u>n it,
Spendthrifts b<u>ur</u>n it, . . .

From MONEY
Richard Armour

8. The flowers appear on the <u>ear</u>th; the time
of the singing of b<u>ir</u>ds is come, and the voice
of the t<u>ur</u>tle is h<u>ear</u>d in our land.

SONG OF SOLOMON 2:12
(*KJV*)

9. There was an old party of Lyme
Who married three wives at one time.
When asked: "Why the th<u>ir</u>d?"
He replied: "One's abs<u>ur</u>d,
And bigamy, s<u>ir</u>, is a crime."

Anonymous

/ɚ/

Production

The vowel /ɚ/ (as in "after") sounds the same as /ɝ/ except in the degree of stress; /ɚ/ occurs only in "unstressed" or minimally stressed syllables. (Remember that an unstressed syllable is a misnomer, for every syllable must have some degree of stress.) The production of /ɚ/ is almost identical to that of /ɝ/ except that the muscles of the tongue are more relaxed and the sound is shorter in duration. The sides of the tongue are pressed against the upper molars, and the tongue tip is free and slightly tense.

EXERCISES

The first time you read aloud the following exercises, exaggerate the production of all of the sounds in the words, giving special attention to the vowels.

1. a. Your instructor will pronounce the following words with particular attention to the unstressed syllable containing the "er" sound. Then, repeat them after your instructor:

lab<u>or</u>	ex<u>er</u>cise
conc<u>er</u>t	earli<u>er</u>
flav<u>or</u>	int<u>er</u>net
post<u>ure</u>	listen<u>er</u>
cent<u>er</u>	p<u>er</u>fection
diff<u>er</u>	int<u>er</u>national
speak<u>er</u>	conv<u>er</u>sation
numb<u>er</u>	int<u>er</u>fere
tens<u>er</u>	sev<u>er</u>al
flow<u>er</u>s	gen<u>er</u>al

b. The words in column I use the unstressed /ɚ/. (In isolated words, /ɚ/ occurs only in words of more than one syllable. A monosyllabic word may contain /ɚ/ in dynamic speech if the syllable is unstressed. Refer to exercises 2 and 10.) How would the words in column I sound if the syllables containing /ɚ/ were stressed? This is called shifted stress, or **wrenched stress.** Such a pronunciation is transcribed into phonetics in column II. Compare and contrast the pronunciation of the words in both columns.

	I	II
sister	['sɪstɚ]	[sɪs'tɝ]
brother	['brʌðɚ]	[brʌð'ɝ]
average[11]	['ævɚədʒ]	[æv'ɝ-ədʒ]
boundary[11]	['baʊndɚɪ]	[baʊn'dɝɪ]
comfortable[12]	['kʌmfɚtəbl̩]	[kəm'fɝtəbl̩]
southern	['sʌðɚn]	[səð'ɝn]
razor	['rezɚ]	[re'zɝ]
suffer	['sʌfɚ]	[sə'fɝ]
perhaps	[pɚ'hæps]	['pɝhæps]
governor	['gʌvɚnɚ]	[gəv'ɝ'nɝ]

Read aloud the selections in exercises 2 and 3.

2. master carpenter   sister's decision
    everlasting spirit   Robert's former roomer
    actor's role   ordering mackerel
    Arthur's fencing sword   Cardos' picture

3. a. Louise lost her feathers in her dance number.

   b. The state government has a great deal of power.

   c. Mother cooked my favorite dinner—liver.

   d. Arthur ordered butter for his lobster.

   e. The banker put the picture of the thief on the posterboard.

   f. Perhaps the chair was comfortable, but it looked uncomfortable to me.

   g. Wait for her in the doctor's office.

   h. His father was studying to be an actor.

   i. I wonder what the average grade was in her class?

   j. Robert called Lydia a super baker.

4. The following English words contain the stressed /ɝ/ and the unstressed /ɚ/, depending upon the degree of stress:

STRESSED /ɝ/	UNSTRESSED /ɚ/
I earn [aɪ] [ɝn]	iron ['aɪɚn]
large err [lɑrdʒ] [ɝ]	larger ['lɑrdʒɚ]

---

[11]If pronounced with three syllables.
[12]If pronounced with four syllables.

nay burr [ne] [bɝ]   neighbor ['nebɚ]

lay burr [le] [bɝ]   labor ['lebɚ]

cub bird [kʌb] [bɝd]   cupboard ['kʌbɚd]

5. Read aloud the following bisyllabic words containing both the stressed /ɝ/ and the un-stressed /ɚ/. Then, reverse the vowel sounds in the word.

server ['sɝvɚ] [sɚ'vɝ]   merger ['mɝdʒɚ][mɚ'dʒɝ]

murder ['mɝdɚ][mɚ'dɝ]   worker ['wɝkɚ][wɚ'kɝ]

stirrer ['stɝɚ] [stɚ'ɝ]   learner ['lɝnɚ]] [lɚ'nɝ]

murmur ['mɝmɚ][mɚ'mɝ]   burner ['bɝnɚ][bɚ'nɝ]

Herbert ['hɝbɚt] [hɚ'bɝt]   discerner [dɪ'zɝnɚ] [dɪzɚn'ɝ]

Read aloud the selections in exercises 6 through 13. The appropriate vowel symbols are written above the words.

6. Her nurse brought her a stirrer for her coffee.

7. Herbert loved raspberry sherbet.

8. Valerie's workers perverted the aims of the organization.

9. The governor of New York talked about a merger with New Jersey.

10. The courtroom was filled with murmurs when the murder er learned of the jur ors'

    verdict.

11. I love him—I love him—with fervour unceasing

    I worship and madly adore;

    My blind adoration is always increasing,

    My loss I shall ever deplore.

    Oh, see what a blessing, what love and caressing

    I've lost, and remember it, pray,

    When you I'm addressing, are busy assessing

    The damages Edwin must pay!

    From TRIAL BY JURY

    W. S. Gilbert

12. Cold in the e<u>ar</u>th—and fifteen wild Decemb<u>er</u>s

From those brown hills have melted into spring:

Faithful, indeed, is the spirit that remembers

Aft<u>er</u> such years of change and suff<u>er</u>ing!

From REMEMBRANCE
Emily Brontë

13. But the dance itself had been enjoyable. The best people w<u>er</u>e there, and Ivan

Ilych has danced with Princess Trufonova, as sist<u>er</u> of the distinguished found<u>er</u>

of the Society "Bear My B<u>ur</u>den."

From ANNA KARENINA
Count Leo Tolstoy

/ɜ/   Production

The vowel /ɜ/ (as in "b<u>ir</u>d") is used by some New England and Southern speakers. Like /ɝ/, the vowel /ɜ/ is used only in stressed syllables. A speaker who uses /ɝ/ would not use /ɜ/ in conversational speech. For career speech, the /ɝ/ is recommended. The vowel /ɜ/ is preferred in British speech, notably stage speech.

    To produce the sound for /ɜ/, the arch of the tongue is high, but the tip is slightly tense and resting behind the lower front teeth. For practice, refer to the exercises for the stressed /ɝ/. Using those word lists, compare and contrast the stressed /ɝ/ with /ɜ/.

/ʌ/   Production

The vowel /ʌ/ (as in "c<u>u</u>t") is also used only in *stressed* syllables; it occurs both in monosyllabic words ("b<u>u</u>t") and words of more than one syllable ("b<u>u</u>tter," "m<u>o</u>ther," and "fl<u>u</u>ttering"). The muscles of the tongue are relaxed, and the central portion of the tongue is slightly raised. The tongue tip remains behind the lower teeth, and the lips are in a neutral position.

((((EXERCISES

The first time you read aloud the following exercises, exaggerate the production of all the sounds in the words, giving special attention to the vowels. Make certain that you do not pull away too much from overarticulation when trying to develop the appropriate pronunciation.

1. j<u>u</u>st   m<u>o</u>ther
   l<u>o</u>ve   d<u>o</u>uble
   r<u>u</u>sh   m<u>o</u>ney
   c<u>o</u>me   f<u>u</u>nding
   h<u>u</u>sk   m<u>u</u>ttering
   s<u>u</u>ch   p<u>u</u>nish

s<u>o</u>me	<u>u</u>nderlying
<u>u</u>s	<u>u</u>tterly
fl<u>oo</u>d	h<u>u</u>ndred
y<u>ou</u>ng	j<u>u</u>dgment

2. M<u>u</u>tt and Jeff   justice[13] prevails
m<u>u</u>ddy river fl<u>oo</u>d   J<u>u</u>dgment[13] Day
d<u>ou</u>ble bl<u>u</u>nder   b<u>u</u>bble g<u>u</u>m
m<u>u</u>gging faces   a[13] Betty H<u>u</u>tton b<u>u</u>tton

3. a. The[13] y<u>ou</u>ng p<u>u</u>ppy named M<u>u</u>gsy d<u>u</u>g in the[13] dirt.

b. A[13] sk<u>u</u>nk stood on a[13] st<u>u</u>mp. The[13] st<u>u</u>mp th<u>u</u>nk the[13] sk<u>u</u>nk st<u>u</u>nk.

c. "Sh<u>u</u>cks," m<u>u</u>ttered S<u>o</u>nny, "I can j<u>u</u>mp and t<u>ou</u>ch the[13] ceiling."

d. Ed's tr<u>u</u>ck was[13] j<u>u</u>st c<u>o</u>vered with rep<u>u</u>lsive words.

e. Louise asked the[13] j<u>u</u>dge to make the[13] p<u>u</u>nishment fit the[13] crime.

f. Have you st<u>u</u>died m<u>u</u>ch about[13] the[13] h<u>u</u>mmingbird?

g. M<u>o</u>ther and L<u>u</u>dwig r<u>u</u>shed to the[13] d<u>u</u>mbwaiter for the[13] f<u>u</u>dge.

h. The[13] hamburg was[13] on an <u>u</u>gly-looking b<u>u</u>n covered with m<u>u</u>stard. H<u>u</u>mb<u>u</u>g!

i. B<u>u</u>ster gr<u>u</u>mbled that there was[13] s<u>o</u>me m<u>o</u>ney in h<u>o</u>ney.

j. There is a special s<u>o</u>me<u>o</u>ne s<u>o</u>mewhere for H<u>u</u>mphrey.

4. Olympus is now in a terrible m<u>u</u>ddle,
The deputy deities all are at fault;
They spl<u>u</u>tter and splash like a pig in a p<u>u</u>ddle,
And dickens a <u>o</u>ne of 'em's earning his salt,
For Thespis as Jove is a terrible bl<u>u</u>nder,
Too nervous and timid—too easy and weak—
Whenever he's called on to lighten or th<u>u</u>nder,
The thought of it keeps him awake for a week!

From THESPIS
W. S. Gilbert

5. J<u>u</u>dge not, that ye be not j<u>u</u>dged.
For with what j<u>u</u>dgment ye j<u>u</u>dge,
ye shall be j<u>u</u>dged: and with what measure
ye mete, it shall be measured to you again.
And why beholdest thou the mote
that is in thy br<u>o</u>ther's eye, b<u>u</u>t considerest
not the beam that is in thine own eye?

MATTHEW 7:1–3
(*KJV*)

6. All hail great J<u>u</u>dge!
To your bright rays
We never gr<u>u</u>dge
Ecstatic praise.

From TRIAL BY JURY
W. S. Gilbert

---

[13]These syllables are not stressed and, therefore, do not contain the stressed /ʌ/ (as in "c<u>u</u>t").

7. *Judge:*   For now I am a Judge!

    All: And a good Judge too.

    Judge: Yes, now I am a Judge!

    All: And a good Judge too!

    Judge: Though all my law is fudge,
            Yet, I'll never, never budge,
            But I'll live and die a Judge!

    All: And a good Judge too!

From TRIAL BY JURY
W. S. Gilbert

8. Double, double, toil and trouble;
Fire burn and cauldron bubble.

From MACBETH
William Shakespeare

9. It's a song of a merryman, moping mum,
Whose soul was sad, and whose glance was glum,
Who sipped no sup, and who craved no crumb,
As he sighed for the love of a ladye.

From THE YEOMEN OF THE GUARD
W. S. Gilbert

/ə/   Production

The vowel /ə/ (as in "about") has its own name—the **schwa.** The schwa, the most common vowel in English, is a neutral-sounding vowel that occurs only in unstressed syllables. The relationship between /ʌ/ and /ə/ is the same as that between /ɜ/ and /ɚ/. They differ in the degree of stress: the vowel /ʌ/ occurs only in stressed syllables, whereas the schwa is used in unstressed syllables.

Any unstressed vowel sound can turn into the schwa. Say the word *America* aloud as transcribed: [ə'mɛrɪkə]. Now increase the speed. You probably said [ə'mɛrəkə]. To the New Englander, it is quite acceptable to say [sɪstə] for [sɪstɚ], turning the unstressed /ɚ/ into the schwa. When you are not quite sure what vowel is being said, it is most likely the schwa. In New England and Southern speech, when the /ɜ/ is used, the unstressed /ɚ/ is replaced by the schwa ([mɜdə] for [mɜ˞dɚ]).

As in producing /ʌ/, the central portion of the tongue is raised slightly and the muscles of the tongue are relaxed. The tongue tip rests behind the lower teeth, and the lips are in a neutral position. The /ə/ sound is usually shorter in duration than the /ʌ/ sound (as in "cut").

 **EXERCISES**

The first time you read aloud the following exercises, exaggerate the production of all of the sounds in the words, giving special attention to the vowels. Listen to how this vowel differs from /ʌ/. Remember that the major difference between /ʌ/ and /ə/ is the degree of stress.

1. a'lert   po'tato
   a'lone   'miracle
   a'fraid   'moment

pₐ'rade   'presidₑnt
'poₑtry   underline{u}'pon
underline{o}'ccur   'fam<u>ou</u>s

2. The pronunciations of each of the words in the following list are transcribed properly in column I. In column II, the words are transcribed with shifted or wrenched stress. Read both columns, making certain that you accurately vocalize what is transcribed. Focus on the differences in stress. Make certain that you do not pull away too much from the over-articulation when trying to develop the appropriate pronunciation.

	I	II
around	[ə'raʊnd]	['ʌraʊnd]
poetry	['poətrɪ]	[po'ʌtrɪ]
suppose	[sə'poz]	['sʌpoz]
connect	[kə'nɛkt]	['kʌnɛkt]
banana	[bə'nænə]	['bʌnæ'nʌ]
aloud	[ə'laʊd]	['ʌlaʊd]
method	['mɛθəd]	[mɛ'θʌd]
apply	[ə'plaɪ]	['ʌplaɪ]
society	[sə'saɪətɪ]	['sʌsaɪ'ʌtɪ]
possibly	['pasəblɪ]	[pa'sʌblɪ]

Read aloud the following sentences. Pay close attention to the placement of the stress. The symbol [˘] indicates minimal stress. Note that a monosyllabic word can contain the schwa in connected speech when the syllable is unstressed.

3. a. Allₑn's famᵢly was frŏm Californiă.

   b. The ideₐ ŏf going to Australiₐ excitₑd Minervₐ.

   c. Have you ever been to ă travₑling circ<u>u</u>s?

   d. Here is ă book by thĕ fam<u>ou</u>s author Williₐm Sₐroyₐn.

   e. It is ₐbout time that performₐnce wăs stressed in literₐture classₑs.

   f. Abdul could better underline{u}nderstand thĕ dilemmₐ facing thĕ group.

   g. Presidₑnt Kennₑdy had strong views ₐbout Cubₐ.

   h. Generₐlly speaking, thĕ sophₒmore year at collₑge is quite differₑnt frŏm high school.

   i. Thĕ momₑnt he saw Veronicₐ he knew whăt to do. (Now read this sentence with an increased stress on "what." You would now use /ʌ/ or /ɑ/, and the meaning would be slightly different.)

   j. Robert wăs ă master in growing thĕ best butternut squash.

Many of the schwas used in the previous sentences can be replaced by different vowels in the unstressed syllables. For example, in the word dilemma, the first vowel could be pronounced as /ɪ/ (as in "bi<u>t</u>") as well as with a schwa.
Read aloud the following selections.

4. Sing ă song ŏf sixpₑnce,
   Ă pockₑt full ŏf rye,
   Four ănd twenty blackbirds
   Baked in ă pie.

When thĕ pie wăs opĕned,
Thĕ birds began to sing;
Wasn't that ă dainty dish
To set before thĕ king?

Frŏm MOTHER GOOSE

5. God be thanked, thĕ meanĕst ŏf his creatures
   Boasts two soul-sides, one to face thĕ world with,
   One to show ă womăn when he loves her!

   Frŏm ONE WORD MORE
   Rŏbert Browning

6. My garden will never make me famŏus,
   I'm ă horticultural ignoramŭs.

   Frŏm HE DIGS, HE DUG, HE HAS DUG
   Ogden Nash

Read aloud the selections in exercises 7 through 14, which contain /ʌ/ and /ə/.

    ʌ ə   ə ʌ ə   ə ʌ   ə ʌ   ʌ   ə
7. husband   abutment   above   another   umbrella

   ʌ ə   ʌ ə   ʌ ə   ʌ ə   ʌ ə
hubbub   cultivate   onion   company   buffalo

    ə ʌ ə ə   ə ʌ ə   ə   ə
8. The cultivation of onions is a difficult task.

    ə   ʌ ə   ə   ʌ
9. Animal husbandry is an interesting study.

     ə   ə ʌ ə   ʌ
10. The buildings abutted each other.

     ə   ʌ   ə ə   ə
11. Ezra had fun playing with Irma and Thomas.

     ə ʌ   ə   ʌ   ə
12. The vulture is a bird that is rarely up to charitable deeds.

     ə   ə   ʌ
13. He was used to both, to dreams and mistakes. How often, in that other world, had

                 ə   ʌ ə   ʌ   ʌ   ə   ə
he not dreamed that he was wildly shoveling up money from the street. . . .

    ə   ə   ə   ə
From BONTSHA THE SILENT
I. L. Peretz

    ə   ə   ʌ   ə ʌ   ʌ
14. The camel's hump is an ugly lump

                            ə
Which well you may see at the Zoo;

   ə ʌ   ə ʌ
But uglier yet is the Hump you get

     ə
From having little to do.

    ə   ə   ʌ
From HOW THE CAMEL GOT HIS HUMP

     ʌ
Rudyard Kipling

The following reading emphasizes /ɜ˞/ and /ə˞/ and /ʌ/ and /ə/.

15.   *Plaintiff:*   I l**o**ve him—I l**o**ve him—with f**er**v**our** **u**nceasing

I w**or**ship and madly **a**dore;

My blind adorat**io**n is always increasing,

My loss I shall ev**er** deplore.

Oh, see wh**a**t **a** blessing, wh**a**t l**o**ve **a**nd c**a**ressing

I've lost, and rememb**er** it, pray,

When you I'm **a**ddressing, are busy **a**ssessing

Th**e** dam**a**ges Edwin m**u**st pay!

Defendant: I smoke like **a** f**ur**n**a**ce—I'm always in liqu**or**

A r**u**ffi**a**n—**a** bully—**a** sot;

I'm sure I should thrash h**er**, p**er**haps I should kick h**er**,

I am s**u**ch a very bad lot!

I'm not prep**o**ssessing, as you may be guessing,

She couldn't endure me **a** day;

Recall my professing, when you are **a**ssessing

Th**e** dam**a**ges Edwin m**u**st pay!

Fr**o**m TRIAL BY JURY
W. S. Gilb**er**t

>>> BACK VOWELS

/u/

Production

In the production of /u/ (as in "true"), the muscles of the tongue are slightly tense; the back of the tongue is high toward the palate, and the tip rests behind the lower front teeth. The lips are rounded and slightly protruded.

(((EXERCISES

The first time you read aloud exercises 1 through 8, exaggerate the production of all the sounds in the words, giving special attention to the vowels. Make certain that you do not pull away too much from the overarticulation when you're trying to develop the appropriate pronunciation.

1. | zoo | balloon |
    |-----|---------|
    | through | peruse |
    | fruit | voodoo |
    | June | blueberry |
    | roof | fruition |
    | school | spoonerism |
    | lose | kangaroo |
    | glue | wounded |
    | choose | recruit |
    | bruise | festoon |

2. | spoon in June | croon a tune[14] |
    |---------------|------------------|
    | one who did | truth of the matter |
    | fools rush in | spools of thread |
    | pick fruit | cruel man |

3. **a.** The troops in the platoon were crouching in a festoon of blooms. (Oh, boy!)

    b. Every noontime, the boys loosen the balloons.

    c. Daniel Boone had nothing to do with the hole in the canoe.

    d. The recruits got tattooed in July.

    e. The prudent woman told the truth about the cruel crew.

    f. I assume[14] that his orders will be resumed[14] in June.

    g. Choose the right glue for the roof.

    h. The frost bruised the fruit trees, especially the blueberries.

    i. The kangaroo was wounded by the foolish troops.

    j. The train's caboose worked itself loose and went through the wall.

    k. The noon balloon from Rangoon arrives soon.

---

[14]Career speech would feature the diphthong /ju/ (see pp. 124–126 for details).

4. There was a young lady in blue,
Who said, "Is it you?[15] Is it you?"[15]
When they said, "Yes it is,"
She replied only, "Whizz!"
That ungracious young lady in blue.

From MORE NONSENSE PICTURES, ETC.
Edward Lear

5. They intend to send a wire
To the moon—to the moon;
And they'll set the Thames on fire
Very soon—very soon.

Anonymous

6. In Rangoon the heat of noon is just what the natives shun.

From MAD DOGS AND ENGLISHMEN
Noel Coward

7. She left the web, she left the loom,
She made three paces through the room,
She saw the water lily bloom,
They saw the helmet and the plume— . . .

From LADY OF SHALLOT
Alfred, Lord Tennyson

8. Oh, Georgia booze is mighty fine booze,
The best yuh ever poured yuh.

From THE MOUNTAIN WHIPPOORWILL
Stephen Vincent Benét

/ʊ/

Production

In the production of /ʊ/ (as in "put"), the muscles of the tongue are relaxed. The back of the tongue is high toward the palate, and the tip rests behind the lower front teeth. The lips are less rounded than for /u/. The sound created by /ʊ/ is of shorter duration than that of /u/ (as in "true").

EXERCISES

The first few times you read aloud exercises 1 through 5, exaggerate the production of all of the sounds in the words, giving special attention to the vowels. Feel how this vowel differs from /u/.

1. Alternate reading aloud the words in the /ʊ/ and /u/ columns. The words enclosed in brackets are nonsense words transcribed into phonetics; sound them out. Make certain you do not pull away too much from the overarticulation when trying to develop the appropriate pronunciation.

/ʊ/	/u/	/ʊ/	/u/
pull	pool	cushion	['kuʃən]
stood	stewed	sugar	['ʃugɚ]
could	cooed	mistook	[mɪs'tuk]

---
[15]Use the diphthong /ju/.

f<u>u</u>ll	f<u>oo</u>l	Br<u>oo</u>klyn	['br<u>u</u>klɪn]
s<u>oo</u>t	s<u>ui</u>t[16]	b<u>u</u>lletin	['b<u>u</u>lətən]
sh<u>ou</u>ld	sh<u>oe</u>d	p<u>u</u>lpit	['p<u>u</u>lpɪt]
c<u>oo</u>k	k<u>oo</u>k	c<u>oo</u>kies	['k<u>u</u>kiz]
w<u>oo</u>d	w<u>oo</u>ed	b<u>u</u>shel	['b<u>u</u>ʃl]
h<u>oo</u>d	wh<u>o</u>'d	neighborh<u>oo</u>d	['nebɚˌh<u>u</u>d]
h<u>oo</u>f[17]	h<u>oo</u>f	b<u>o</u>som	['b<u>u</u>zəm][18]

2. t<u>oo</u>k the broom   p<u>u</u>sh and shove
    sh<u>ou</u>ld know   c<u>oo</u>kie jar
    c<u>oo</u>ked dinner   l<u>oo</u>ks c<u>ou</u>ld kill
    s<u>u</u>gar and spice   got the h<u>oo</u>k

3. **a.** The c<u>oo</u>k t<u>oo</u>k the s<u>u</u>gar and p<u>u</u>t it in the p<u>u</u>dding.

    b. Reverend W<u>oo</u>ds read the b<u>u</u>lletin from the p<u>u</u>lpit.

    c. Ferdinand the B<u>u</u>ll p<u>u</u>shed the flowers into[19] the b<u>u</u>shes.

    d. The neighborh<u>oo</u>d children were happy with their w<u>oo</u>len p<u>u</u>llovers.

    e. Dot p<u>u</u>lled the h<u>oo</u>d over the horse's head and checked his h<u>oo</u>f.

    f. Charlie st<u>oo</u>d in his w<u>oo</u>lies as long as he c<u>ou</u>ld.

    g. Mrs. F<u>u</u>lton said she w<u>ou</u>ld always suffer from g<u>oo</u>d l<u>oo</u>ks.

    h. The w<u>oo</u>den keg was f<u>u</u>ll of beer.

    i. He sh<u>oo</u>k the h<u>oo</u>k from the p<u>u</u>shcart.

    j. The w<u>o</u>lf stole the p<u>u</u>llet and fors<u>oo</u>k the farm.

4. In May, when the sea-winds pierced our solitudes,
I found the fresh Rhodora in the w<u>oo</u>ds,
Spreading its leafless blooms in a damp n<u>oo</u>k,
To please the desert and the sluggish br<u>oo</u>k.

From THE RHODORA
Ralph Waldo Emerson

/o/

Production

In the production of /o/ (as in "g<u>o</u>") the muscles of the tongue are tense. The back of the tongue is raised midway to the palate, and the tip rests behind the lower front teeth. The lips are rounded. When used in stressed syllables, /o/ often becomes the diphthong /oʊ/. This is particularly true when the single vowel appears in the final position, as in the word *go*, or when it is used in stressed syllables. In career or trained speech, the use of this diphthong is encouraged. It is produced when the lips are relaxed after the production of /o/.

Problem

The major problem in producing the /o/ vowel is evident in the speech of, among others, natives from the New York City and Philadelphia areas. These speakers often substitute the

---

[16]Professional speech would feature the diphthong /ɪu/ (see pp. 125–126 for details).

[17]This [hʊf] is the predominant pronunciation in the North, East, and South (and in Canada).

[18]This [buzəm] is a secondary pronunciation and is reminiscent of the days of yore. Actors, remember that!

[19]Because this word is minimally stressed and the sound precedes another consonant, career speech uses the schwa rather than /ʊ/ or /u/. However, before a different vowel sound, the /ʊ/ is preferred in trained speech (such as "to Atlanta" [tʊ ætlæntə]).

diphthong /ɛʊ/ for /o/ or /oʊ/. To correct the error, relax and round your lips and do not allow them to move before or after you produce the sound. Of course, the production of the /o/ will be exaggerated at first. Refer to page 314 for exercises for this substitution.

EXERCISES

The first time you read aloud exercises 1 through 7, exaggerate the production of all of the sounds in the words, giving special attention to the vowels. Feel how this vowel differs from /u/.

1. Alternate reading aloud the words in the /o/ and /ʊ/ columns. The words enclosed in brackets are nonsense words transcribed into phonetics; sound them out. Make certain that you do not pull away too much from the overarticulation when trying to develop the appropriate pronunciation.

/o/	/ʊ/	/o/	/ʊ/
bowl	bull	obey	[ʊ'beɪ]
foal	full	soldier	['sʊldʒɚ]
pole	pull	frozen	[frʊzn̩]
showed	should	Ohio	[ʊ'haɪjʊ]
stowed	stood	Oklahoma	[ʊklə'hʊmə]
Coke	cook	piano	[pɪ'ænʊ]
goad	good	woeful	['wʊfʊl]
code	could	open	[ʊpn̩]

2. bowl of cereal   if Joe folds the paper
   black angry crows   showing the bureau
   Coals to Newcastle   following the fold
   "Over the Rainbow"   holding the phone

3. **a.** Joe was the only one at the bowling alley.

   b. Go and bring me both folders from the desk.

   c. The short stories by Poe are often odious and sorrowful.

   d. Snow White sang "Heigh Ho" along with Dopey.

   e. The opening of *Oklahoma* was loaded with celebrities.

   f. Joan broke the woeful silence with a friendly "Hello."

   g. Coal costs almost double what it did only ten years ago.

   h. In poker the joker does not count.

   i. Otto was catching toads and putting them into bowls of flowers.

   j. The phony old man was rowing toward the other rowboat.

4. I grow old . . . I grow old . . .
   I shall wear the bottom of my trousers rolled.

   From THE LOVE SONG OF J. ALFRED PRUFROCK
   T. S. Eliot

5. In vain to us you plead—
   Don't go!
   Your prayers we do not heed—
   Don't go!

It's true we sigh,
But d<u>o</u>n't supp<u>o</u>se
A tearful eye
Forgiveness sh<u>ow</u>s.
Oh, n<u>o</u>!

From IOLANTHE
W. S. Gilbert

6. Sweet and l<u>ow</u>, sweet and l<u>ow</u>,
Wind of the western sea,
L<u>ow</u>, l<u>ow</u>, breathe and bl<u>ow</u>,
Wind of the western sea!
<u>O</u>ver the r<u>o</u>lling waters g<u>o</u>,
Come from the dying moon, and bl<u>ow</u>,
Bl<u>ow</u> him again to me.

From THE PRINCESS
Alfred, Lord Tennyson

7. <u>O</u>ld King C<u>o</u>le
Was a merry <u>o</u>ld s<u>ou</u>l,
And a merry <u>o</u>ld s<u>ou</u>l was he;
He called for his pipe,
And he called for his b<u>ow</u>l,
And he called for his fiddlers three.

From MOTHER GOOSE

/ɔ/ Production

In the production of /ɔ/ (as in "l<u>aw</u>"), the muscles of the tongue are slightly tense. The back of the tongue is lower than for /o/, and the tip rests behind and touches the lower front teeth. The lips are less rounded than in /o/ but still pursed forward.

EXERCISES

The first few times you read aloud exercises 1 through 8, exaggerate the production of all of the sounds in the words, giving special attention to the vowels. Feel how this vowel differs from /o/.

1. Alternate reading aloud the words in the /ɔ/ and /o/ columns. The words enclosed in brackets are nonsense words transcribed into phonetics; sound them out. Make certain you do not pull away too much from the exaggerated articulation when trying to develop appropriate pronunciation. It is important to note that the following words can be pronounced using different vowels, but for the purpose of learning this sound, use /ɔ/.

/ɔ/	/o/	/ɔ/	/o/
cl<u>au</u>se	cl<u>o</u>se	l<u>au</u>nder	['lond<u>ə</u>˞]
P<u>au</u>l	p<u>o</u>le	L<u>a</u>wrence	l<u>ow</u> rents
g<u>au</u>ze	g<u>o</u>es	colesl<u>aw</u>	['kolsl<u>o</u>]
gn<u>aw</u>	kn<u>ow</u>	st<u>a</u>lling	['st<u>o</u>lɪŋ]
b<u>a</u>ll	b<u>ow</u>l	<u>aw</u>ning	<u>ow</u>ning
fl<u>aw</u>	fl<u>ow</u>	withdr<u>aw</u>	[wɪð'dr<u>o</u>]
l<u>aw</u>n	l<u>oa</u>n	<u>A</u>ustralian	[<u>o</u>'streljən]

chalk	choke	authentic	[oˈθɛntɪk]
scald	scold	caucus	coke us
walk	woke	caution	co shun
shawl	shoal	because	[bɪˈkɔz]
fawn	phone	automobile	[ˈotəmobil]
bossed	boast	auspicious	[osˈpɪʃəs]
Saul	soul	authority	[əˈθɔrətɪ]
saw	sew	Boston	[ˈbɔstn̩]

2. authentic Boston baked beans   drawing board
Austrian Alps   forgotten dreams
apple blossoms   just because
withdraw the sword   a hot sauce

3. a. There are many auspicious authors in Boston.

   b. The Australian and the Austrian met because of chance.

   c. Yvonne's Southern drawl called attention to her speech.

   d. DeShaw thought that the longer song was better.

   e. The automobile I bought had many flaws.

   f. The newscaster authenticated the awful details.

   g. Some people caution against putting salt on the fish.

   h. Audrey insisted upon an audit.

   i. The fawn was walking in the wrong direction.

   j. Saul forgot he fought for the lost cause.

4. In beauty may I walk.
All day long may I walk.
Through the returning seasons may I walk.
On a trail marked with pollen may I walk.
With grasshoppers about my feet may I walk.
With dew about my feet may I walk.
With beauty may I walk.
With beauty before me, may I walk.
With beauty behind me, may I walk.
With beauty above me, may I walk.
With beauty below me, may I walk.
With beauty all around me, may I walk.
In old age wandering on a trail of beauty, lively, may I walk.
In old age wandering on a trail, living again, may I walk.
It is finished in beauty.
It is finished in beauty.

From THE NIGHT CHANT
Navajo Ceremonial Chant, translated by Washington Matthews

5. It isn't the cough
That carries you off;
It's the coffin
They carry you off in.

Anonymous

6. There is only one way to achieve happiness on this terrestrial b<u>a</u>ll,
And that is to have either a clear conscience, <u>or</u> none at <u>a</u>ll.

From INTER-<u>O</u>FFICE MEMORANDUM
<u>O</u>gden Nash

7. I know not whether L<u>aws</u> be right,
Or whether L<u>aws</u> be wrong;
<u>A</u>ll that we know who lie in gaol
Is that the w<u>a</u>ll is str<u>o</u>ng;
And that each day is like a year,
A year whose days are l<u>o</u>ng.

From THE BALLAD OF READING GAOL
<u>O</u>scar Wilde

8. He shall treat us with <u>awe</u>,
If there isn't a fl<u>aw</u>,
Singing so merrily—Trial-la-l<u>aw</u>!
Trial-la-l<u>aw</u>—Trial-la-l<u>aw</u>!
Singing so merrily—Trial-la-l<u>aw</u>!

From TRIAL BY JURY
W. S. Gilbert

/ɒ/ Production

This is often a most difficult and problematic sound. "W<u>a</u>lnut" has been chosen to represent the vowel /ɒ/. Other words like "w<u>a</u>nder," "h<u>o</u>t," "w<u>a</u>nt," and "w<u>a</u>llet" could also be used. However, there is no key word that would clarify the sound for everyone. The sound /ɒ/ is primarily Eastern and Southern, but it is used in both British speech and stage speech, which is why it is considered acceptable for the trained speaker. It is an Eastern substitution for /ɔ/ (as in "l<u>aw</u>") or /ɑ/ (as in "f<u>a</u>ther"). Continue to use the sound if it is part of your speech. It is not important to use it, however, unless your goal is professional acting or performance.

The muscles of the tongue are slightly tense; the back of the tongue is low, and the tip of the tongue rests behind the lower front teeth. The mandible is lowered from the /ɔ/ position. The lips are slightly rounded but not as much as in /ɔ/.

EXERCISES

The first few times you read aloud exercises 1 through 6, exaggerate the production of all of the sounds in the words, giving special attention to the vowels. Feel how this vowel differs from /ɔ/.

1. Alternate reading aloud the words in the /ɒ/ and /ɔ/ columns; sound them out. Make certain you do not pull away too much from the exaggerated articulation when trying to develop the appropriate pronunciation. Incidentally, both pronunciations of the words in the columns are acceptable for the trained speaker.

	/ɒ/	/ɔ/		/ɒ/	/ɔ/
l<u>o</u>st	[lɒst]	[lɔst]	al<u>o</u>ng	[ə'lɒŋ]	[ə'lɔŋ]
c<u>ou</u>gh	[kɒf]	[kɔf]	fr<u>o</u>sty	['frɒstɪ]	[frɔstɪ]
t<u>o</u>ssed	[tɒst]	[tɔst]	m<u>o</u>ral	['mɒrəl]	['mɔrəl]
b<u>o</u>ss	[bɒs]	[bɔs]	<u>o</u>range	['ɒrəndʒ]	['ɔrəndʒ]
s<u>o</u>ft	[sɒft]	[sɔft]	<u>O</u>regon	['ɒrəgɑn]	['ɔrəgɑn]
sc<u>o</u>ff	[skɒf]	[skɔf]	<u>o</u>ffice	['ɒfəs]	['ɔfəs]

broth	[brɒθ]	[brɔθ]	salty	['sɒltɪ]	['sɔltɪ]
cloth	[klɒθ]	[klɔθ]	Florence	['flɒrəns]	['flɔrəns]
crossed	[krɒst]	[krɔst]			

2. Robin Hood's band   not a plot
a hacking cough   worn a smock
a plot in the grotto   the rusting lock
Bob's soft cloth   the officer's watch

3. a. Eviston's office windows were frosted.

   b. Don't shut the hall closet.

   c. He coughed when he lost his medicine.

   d. Dorothy fostered a love for horse watching.

   e. He tossed the ball in the fog.

   f. The cloth was filled with moth holes.

   g. Does the cake have chocolate frosting?

4. Hickory, dickory, dock,
The mouse ran up the clock,
The clock struck one,
The mouse ran down,
Hickory, dickory, dock.

From MOTHER GOOSE

5. "Who killed Cock Robin?"
"I," said the sparrow,
"With my bow and arrow,
I killed Cock Robin."

From MOTHER GOOSE

/ɑ/

Production

In the production of /ɑ/ (as in "father"), the muscles of the tongue are relaxed, the back of the tongue is low, and the tip rests behind the lower front teeth. The mandible is dropped from the /ɒ/ position, and the mouth is wide open. This sound often precedes the semivowel /r/. See the section on New England regionalisms in Chapter 12 for a detailed discussion of this sound combination. You may have noticed that in producing the back vowels from high to low, the lips become increasingly unrounded as the mouth opens more.

EXERCISES

The first few times you read aloud the following exercises, exaggerate the production of the sounds in the words, giving special attention to the vowels.

1. park   [pɑrk]   balmy[20]   ['bɑmɪ]
   Psalms[20]   [sɑmz]   alarmed   [ə'lɑrmd]

---

[20]In these words, the letter *l* is silent. For a more detailed list of words, see pages 199–200.

honor	['ɑnɚ]	accomplish	[ə'kɑmplɪʃ]
John	[dʒɑn]	doctor	['dɑktɚ]
carve	[kɑrv]	darkened	['dɑrkn̩d]
bomb	[bɑm]	common	['kɑmən]
prompt	[prɑmpt]	possibility	[pɑsə'bɪləti]
box	[bɑks]	economics	[ɛkən'ɑmɪks]
shock	[ʃɑk]	population	[pɑpju'leʃən]
harm	[hɑrm]	Harvard	['hɑrvɚd]
Sarge	[sɑrdʒ]	partner	['pɑrtnɚ]
palm[20]	[pɑm]	guardian	['gɑrdɪjən]
cart	[kɑrt]	farmer	['fɑrmɚ]
charm	[tʃɑrm]	harvest	['hɑrvəst]
calm[20]	[kɑm]	articulation	[ɑrtɪkju'leʃən]
alms[20]	[ɑmz]	Arkansas	['ɑrkənsɔ]

2. There is often confusion between /ɑ/ (as in "father") and /ɔ/ (as in "law"). The following words compare the two sounds:

	/ɑ/		/ɔ/
hock	[hɑk]	hawk	[hɔk]
farm	[fɑrm]	form	[fɔrm]
car	[kɑr]	core	[kɔr]
collar	['kɑlɚ]	caller	[kɔlɚ]
moll	[mɑl]	maul	[mɔl]
popper	['pɑpɚ]	pauper	['pɔpɚ]
body	['bɑdɪ]	bawdy	['bɔdɪ]

3.
Tommy's dart board a pretty charm bracelet
the calm ocean the Arkansas farmer's cart
a smart palm reader very salty popcorn
Robert's clam broth the doctor's partnership

4. **a.** Arthur was originally from Arkansas.

   b. The ardent students charged out of the stacks in the archives.

   c. Jacob Marley was Scrooge's smart partner.

   d. They argued that they would not harm the cargo.

   e. Farmers are known as the guardians of the harvest.

   f. The Artful Dodger is a character from Charles Dickens.

   g. Bobbie was elected the sergeant at arms.

   h. It is a hard task to read the Psalms with good articulation.

   i. King Arthur's knights wore carved armor.

   j. Park your proverbial car in Harvard Yard!

5. As a beauty I am not a great star,
   There are others more handsome, by far,
   But my face—I don't mind it
   For I am behind it,
   It's the people in front get the jar!

   Anonymous

6. All that I know
Of a certain st<u>a</u>r
Is, it can throw
(Like the angled sp<u>a</u>r)
Now a d<u>a</u>rt of red,
Now a d<u>a</u>rt of blue;
Till my friends have said
They would fain see, too,
My st<u>a</u>r that d<u>a</u>rties the red and the blue!

From MY ST<u>A</u>R
Robert Browning

7. The following word lists compare /ɒ/ (as in "h<u>o</u>t"), /ɑ/ (as in "f<u>a</u>ther"), and /a/ (as in "h<u>a</u>lf").

	/ɒ/	/ɑ/	/a/
R<u>o</u>bert	[ˈrɒbɚt]	[ˈrɑbɚt]	[ˈrabɚt]
T<u>o</u>m	[tɒm]	[tɑm]	[tam]
gr<u>o</u>tto	[ˈgrɒto]	[ˈgrɑto]	[ˈgrato]
pr<u>o</u>bably	[ˈprɒbəblɪ]	[ˈprɑbəblɪ]	[ˈprabəblɪ]
m<u>o</u>tto	[ˈmɒto]	[ˈmɑto]	[ˈmato]
l<u>o</u>cked	[lɒkt]	[lɑkt]	[lakt]
g<u>o</u>t	[gɒt]	[gɑt]	[gat]
c<u>o</u>t	[kɒt]	[kɑt]	[kat]
d<u>o</u>ctor	[ˈdɒktɚ]	[ˈdɑktɚ]	[ˈdaktɚ]

>>> DIPHTHONGS

A diphthong (notice the pronunciation: [ˈdɪfθɑŋ]) is the combination of two vowels within the same syllable. One of the vowels has more emphasis because its duration is longer. Although any two vowels can constitute a diphthong, some are acceptable in career speech and some are not. This section will introduce and discuss both kinds.

Many speakers commonly diphthongize the vowels /e/ and /o/, especially in stressed syllables, to /eɪ/ and /oʊ/, respectively. It is difficult to control the action of the tongue in making the first vowel. Besides, for the trained speaker, this process is encouraged. The diphthongs in "go and stay" ([goʊ ænd steɪ]) are caused by the rhythm of the language and are difficult to isolate from the individual vowel.

The phonemic diphthongs that will be discussed in detail are /aɪ/, /aʊ/, /ɔɪ/, /ju/, and /ɪu/.

/aɪ/

Production

The diphthong /aɪ/ (as in "<u>i</u>ce") is sometimes transcribed as /ɑɪ/, which is a most acceptable allophone of the /aɪ/ diphthong. It might be a good idea for New Englanders to use /ɑɪ/ to discourage them from using /a/ in their speech.

In the production of /aɪ/, the first vowel requires a low tongue and a lowered jaw. The muscles of the tongue are relaxed, and the tip rests behind the lower front teeth. From that position the tongue moves to a high-front position. If the allophone is used, the first vowel is produced with a low-back tongue position /ɑ/ before moving into the /ɪ/.

Problems

Three errors are common in the production of /aɪ/. The first is to omit the /ɪ/ component completely, a trait that is quite common in some Southern and Eastern speech. In the following word list, use negative practice.

	/aɪ/	/a/	/aɪ/
fine	[faɪn]	[fan]	[faɪn]
blind	[blaɪnd]	[bland]	[blaɪnd]
final	['faɪnl̩]	['fanl̩]	['faɪnl̩]
tribe	[traɪb]	[trab]	[traɪb]
sight	[saɪt]	[sat]	[saɪt]
spite	[spaɪt]	[spat]	[spaɪt]
I'm	[aɪm]	[am]	[aɪm]
right	[raɪt]	[rat]	[raɪt]
line	[laɪn]	[lan]	[laɪn]
crime	[kraɪm]	[kram]	[kraɪm]

The second error is to use excessive tension on the /a/, which gives the sound an abrasive and very unpleasant quality. To correct this problem, use /ɑ/ (as in "father") for the first vowel. Keep the tongue flat in the mouth, and produce the sound with an open throat. After you feel the difference between the productions of the sounds /ɑɪ/ and /aɪ/, you may want to go back to using /a/ in /aɪ/ but retain a relaxed quality. If you choose /ɑɪ/, make certain that you do not exaggerate the production of the /ɑ/.

The third error is the New York pronunciation of the diphthong. Refer to Chapter 12 (pp. 312–313) for an additional discussion of this problem and corrective exercises.

EXERCISES

Record the selections in exercises 1 through 7, focusing on the production of /aɪ/.

1.
eye	[aɪ]	spinal	['spaɪnl̩]
pile	[paɪl]	playwright	['pleraɪt]
mice	[maɪs]	island	['aɪlənd]
spies	[spaɪz]	daylight	['delaɪt]
wide	[waɪd]	stylish	['staɪlɪʃ]
right	[raɪt]	finite	['faɪnaɪt]
twice	[twaɪs]	diary	['daɪərɪ]
guide	[gaɪd]	certify	['sɝtəfaɪ]
high	[haɪ]	license	['laɪsəns]
rise	[raɪz]	biography	[baɪ'ɑgrəfɪ]

2.
rise and shine	the final examination
Lord Byron's bicycle	Dan's high rise
the climber's guide	a mighty fine ending

3. **a.** The bicycle arrived just in time.

b. Diane L. didn't realize the biography was by Myers.

c. Tyrone told us to turn right twice.

d. Iris got a diamond ring from Byron.

e. At the height of the lightning storm they arrived.

f. Midnite liked to chase hiding Tigers.

g. The license certified that they could photograph the lions.

h. The ivory jewelry was mine.

i. The sky was clear and bright blue.

j. I'll not ask the guide to drive the Jeep.

4. The world stands out on either side
No wider than the heart is wide.

From RENASCENCE
Edna St. Vincent Millay

5. "Who saw him die?"
"I," said the Fly,
"With my little eye,
I saw him die."

From WHO KILLED COCK ROBIN?
Mother Goose

6. Madame Arcati *(a medium):* When I was quite tiny. My mother was a medium before me, you know, and so I had every opportunity of starting on the ground floor as you might say. I had my first trance when I was four years old and my first protoplasmic manifestation when I was five and a half—what an exciting day that was, I shall never forget it—of course the manifestation itself was quite small and of very short duration, but, for a child of my tender years, it was most gratifying.

From BLITHE SPIRIT
Noel Coward

7. Had I been afraid? I couldn't say. I had witnessed a strange sight. What strange sight? I couldn't say. The sky was blue and the sea was white. I felt I ought to tell someone about it since I was back from so far away! But I had no grip on what I had been through.

From WIND, SAND, AND STARS
Antoine de Saint Exupéry

8. early morning
best time to fish
think clearly, organize, run

early evening
good time to fish
relax, unwind, have fun

night time
great time to fish
read, watch, listen, or sleep

early and late extend many choices
choose as you wish when you want
time not important to keep

TIME
Robert H. Cathcart

/aʊ/

Production

In the production of /aʊ/ (as in "house"), the first vowel requires a low tongue position and a lowered jaw. (For the preferred allophone, /ɑʊ/, the first vowel requires a low-back tongue position.) The muscles of the tongue are relaxed. The tongue tip starts at rest behind the lower front teeth; the tongue then moves to a high-back position, but the muscles stay relaxed. The lips are rounded.

Problems

The most common error in the production of /aʊ/ is the substitution of /æ/ for the vowel /a/. What results is the wrong sound, and it is also very unpleasant. The error is found in a number of dialects, which is why it appears here rather than in the section on regionalisms.

The best way to correct this error is to substitute /ɑ/ (as in "f<u>a</u>ther") for the /æ/ (as in "c<u>a</u>t"). Although the diphthong is made with the low-front /a/ (as in "<u>a</u>sk"), it is often produced with the accepted allophone /aʊ/ using the low-back /ɑ/ (as in " f<u>a</u>ther").

If you have difficulty with this diphthong, produce /æ→u/ and /ɑ→u/ before making the correct sound /aʊ/. When you pronounce this diphthong properly, /u/ becomes /ʊ/ because the first vowel outweighs the second in importance, and there is less stress in the production of /ʊ/ than in the production of /u/. To get a sense of this error, record the following transcribed sounds:

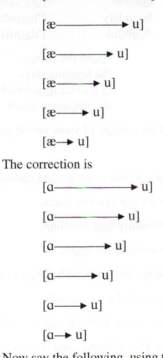

[æ————► u]

[æ———► u]

[æ——► u]

[æ—► u]

[æ—► u]

[æ► u]

The correction is

[ɑ————► u]

[ɑ———► u]

[ɑ——► u]

[ɑ—► u]

[ɑ—► u]

[ɑ► u]

Now say the following, using the correct phoneme /aʊ/ with negative practice.

	CAREER	ERROR	CAREER
b<u>ou</u>nd	[ba<u>ʊ</u>nd]	[bæʊnd]	[ba<u>ʊ</u>nd]
h<u>ow</u>l	[ha<u>ʊ</u>l]	[hæʊl]	[ha<u>ʊ</u>l]
n<u>ow</u>	[na<u>ʊ</u>]	[næʊ]	[na<u>ʊ</u>]
s<u>ou</u>r	[sa<u>ʊ</u>r]	[sæʊr]	[sa<u>ʊ</u>r]
v<u>ow</u>	[va<u>ʊ</u>]	[væʊ]	[va<u>ʊ</u>]
c<u>ou</u>nt	[ka<u>ʊ</u>nt]	[kæʊnt]	[ka<u>ʊ</u>nt]
m<u>ou</u>th	[ma<u>ʊ</u>θ]	[mæʊθ]	[ma<u>ʊ</u>θ]

wow	[waʊ]	[wæʊ]	[waʊ]
hour	[aʊr]	[æʊr]	[aʊr]

Remember, do not pull away too much from the exaggeration when trying to develop appropriate pronunciation.

EXERCISES

The first few times you work with these exercises, exaggerate the pronunciation of the words and phrases. Feel how the diphthong is produced. Make certain you don't pull away too much from the overarticulation when trying to develop the appropriate pronunciation.

1.

shout	[ʃaʊt]	housekeeper	['haʊskipɚ]
foul	[faʊl]	ourselves	[aʊr'sɛlvz]
bough	[baʊ]	devout	[dɪ'vaʊt]
owl	[aʊl]	tower	['taʊɚ]
south	[saʊθ]	counterfeit	['kaʊntɚfɪt]
flour	[flaʊr]	Browning	['braʊnɪŋ]
drown	[draʊn]	mountains	['maʊntənz]
crowd	[kraʊd]	outside	[aʊt'saɪd]
bounce	[baʊns]	boundary	['baʊndərɪ]
mouth	[maʊθ]	doubtful	['daʊtfʊl]

2.

bouncing the flowered ball	round the corner
The Sound and the Fury	the howling dogs
outside the boundary	cows that found shelter
owl heard mouse	the sun down south

3. a. How do you account for the amount of snow on the ground?

   b. Shout at the crowd!

   c. Howard thought it was about time to go around the house.

   d. Browning and Housman are our favorite poets.

   e. The brown cows are particularly foul smelling.

   f. Now the flowers are blooming in the south.

   g. The housekeeper came down the stairs with a frown on her face.

   h. When she scowled and pouted, I went outside.

   i. The mountainous terrain made it doubtful that we could go south.

   j. The chowder was filled with cauliflower and flounder.

4. Hark, the hour of ten is sounding:
Hearts with anxious fears are bounding,
Hall of Justice crowds surrounding,
Breathing hope and fear—
. . . .
Oh, joy unbounded,
With wealth surrounded,
The knell is sounded
Of grief and woe.

From TRIAL BY JURY
W. S. Gilbert

5. A gourmet dining in St. Lou
   F<u>ou</u>nd quite a large m<u>ou</u>se in his stew.
   Said the waiter: "Don't sh<u>ou</u>t
   And wave it ab<u>ou</u>t,
   Or the rest will be wanting one too."
   Anonymous

6. The <u>ow</u>l looked d<u>ow</u>n with his great r<u>ou</u>nd eyes
   At the lowering cl<u>ou</u>ds and the darkening skies,
   "A good night for sc<u>ou</u>ting," says he,
   "With never a s<u>ou</u>nd I'll go pr<u>ow</u>ling ar<u>ou</u>nd.
   A m<u>ou</u>se or two may be f<u>ou</u>nd on the gr<u>ou</u>nd
   Or a fat little bird in a tree."
   So d<u>ow</u>n he flew from the old church t<u>ow</u>er,
   The m<u>ou</u>se and the birdie cr<u>ou</u>ch and c<u>ow</u>er,
   Back he flies in half an h<u>ou</u>r,
   "A very good supper," says he.

   THE HUNGRY <u>OW</u>L
   Anonymous

/ɔɪ/

Production

In the production of /ɔɪ/ (as in "b<u>oy</u>"), the first vowel requires the tongue to be in a low-back position with a lowered jaw. The muscles of the tongue are tense, and the tip rests touching the lower front teeth; the lips are rounded and pursed forward. The tongue moves to a high-front position, the muscles of the tongue are relaxed, and the lips are retracted.

EXERCISES

Exaggerate the production of the diphthong in addition to each sound in the selections in the following exercises. Feel how the blending of the vowels is produced. Do not pull away too much from the exaggeration while developing the appropriate pronunciation.

1.
f<u>oi</u>l	[fɔɪl]	sirl<u>oi</u>n	['sɚˌlɔɪn]
j<u>oi</u>n	[dʒɔɪn]	r<u>oy</u>alty	['rɔɪəlti]
b<u>oi</u>l	[bɔɪl]	app<u>oi</u>ntment	[ə'pɔɪntmənt]
v<u>oi</u>ce	[vɔɪs]	rej<u>oi</u>ce	[rɪ'dʒɔɪs]
t<u>oy</u>	[tɔɪ]	embr<u>oi</u>l	[ɛm'brɔɪl]
j<u>oi</u>st	[dʒɔɪst]	b<u>oi</u>sterous	['bɔɪstərəs]
ch<u>oi</u>ce	[tʃɔɪs]	destr<u>oy</u>	[dɪ'strɔɪ]
s<u>oi</u>l	[sɔɪl]	p<u>oi</u>gnant	['pɔɪnjənt]
<u>oi</u>l	[ɔɪl]	<u>oy</u>ster	['ɔɪstɚ]
n<u>oi</u>se	[nɔɪz]	thyr<u>oi</u>d	['θaɪrɔɪd]

2. b<u>oi</u>led peanut <u>oi</u>l   br<u>oi</u>led <u>oy</u>sters
   rej<u>oi</u>cing for the ch<u>oi</u>ce   ann<u>oy</u>ing the b<u>oy</u>
   "J<u>oy</u> to the World"   p<u>oi</u>nting to the j<u>oi</u>nt
   the n<u>oi</u>sy empl<u>oy</u>ees   making real app<u>oi</u>ntments

3. **a.** Did you enj<u>oy</u> the ch<u>oi</u>ce of <u>oy</u>sters on the menu?

   b. R<u>oy</u>, av<u>oi</u>d the sirl<u>oi</u>n steak in the <u>oi</u>ly restaurant.

   c. The <u>oi</u>l s<u>oi</u>led Mrs. Fl<u>oy</u>d's rug.

   d. J<u>oy</u> had an adr<u>oi</u>t way of av<u>oi</u>ding empl<u>oy</u>ment.

   e. The n<u>oi</u>se of the b<u>oy</u>s made her av<u>oi</u>d the den.

   f. The people rej<u>oi</u>ced when the r<u>oy</u>al family entered.

   g. Don't destr<u>oy</u> the old <u>oi</u>ntment.

   h. Although the s<u>oi</u>l was m<u>oi</u>st, it was too deep.

   i. The b<u>oi</u>sterous and n<u>oi</u>sy crowd made him rec<u>oi</u>l in terror.

   j. Don't disapp<u>oi</u>nt your l<u>oy</u>al fans.

4. There was a fellow from R<u>oi</u>ling
   Whose temper was quick to come b<u>oi</u>ling;
   He'd leap and he'd hum as he banged on his drum,
   That b<u>oi</u>ling old fellow from R<u>oi</u>ling.

   Edward Lear

5. Music to hear, why hear'st thou music sadly?
   Sweets with sweets war not, j<u>oy</u> delights in j<u>oy</u>.
   Why lov'st thou that which thou receiv'st not gladly?
   Or else receiv'st with pleasure thine ann<u>oy</u>?

   From SONNET 8
   William Shakespeare

6. If somebody there chanced to be
   Who loved me in a manner true,
   My heart would p<u>oi</u>nt him out to me,
   And I would p<u>oi</u>nt him out to you.
   But here it says of those who p<u>oi</u>nt,
   Their manners must be out of j<u>oi</u>nt
   You "may" not p<u>oi</u>nt—
   You "must" not p<u>oi</u>nt—
   It's manners out of j<u>oi</u>nt, to p<u>oi</u>nt!

   From RUDDIGORE
   W. S. Gilbert

/ju/

Production

In the production of this diphthong (/ju/ as in "<u>u</u>se"), the tongue begins in a high-front position and ends in a high-back position. The muscles of the tongue are tense, and the diphthong ends with the lips rounding. The /ju/ diphthong is often found in the initial position in words of more than one syllable.

EXERCISES

In order to differentiate between /ju/ and the next diphthong, /ɪu/, it is important to exaggerate the articulation. Do not pull away from this exaggeration too much when you develop the appropriate pronunciation.

1. h<u>ue</u>   [hj<u>u</u>]   <u>u</u>nison   ['j<u>u</u>nəsən]
    f<u>ew</u>   [fj<u>u</u>]   <u>u</u>niversity   [j<u>u</u>nə'vɝˌsɪtɪ]

Ute	[jut]	eulogy	['juləʤɪ]
youth	[juθ]	value	['vælju]
huge	[hjuʤ]	unit	['junɪt]
mute	[mjut]	uniform	['junəfɔrm]
Hugh	[hju]	usurp	[ju'sɝp]
fuel	[fjul]	future	['fjutʃɚ]
you'll	[jul]	community	[kə'mjunətɪ]

2. Hugh's dirty uniforms
unduly prosecuted
usually beautiful rainbows
nuclear energy

future community spirit
Utah's Zion National Park
you'll enjoy ducks
unit of fuel

3. **a.** Few institutions are without constitutions.

   b. Tune in Tuesday's news.

   c. The lute player's enthusiasm was infectious.

   d. Unitarians' eulogies are usually short.

   e. Hugh renewed his interest in nuclear fusion.

   f. The nuisance was caused by the weak test tubes.

   g. The tutor's duties were established by the university officials.

   h. Eulalia's teaching imbued the students with confidence.

   i. Humility is a human characteristic.

   j. He was duly amused by the duplication of the huge manuscript.

4. No woman would ever be quite accurate about her age. It looks so calculating.

From THE IMPORTANCE OF BEING EARNEST
Oscar Wilde

5. Ignorance of the law excuses no man; not that all men know the law, but because 'tis an excuse every man will plead, and no man can tell how to refute him.

From TABLE TALK
John Selden

/ɪu/

Production

This is an alternative diphthong to /ju/, and in many situations in trained speech it is preferred to /ju/. It is produced like /ju/ except that the muscles of the tongue are more relaxed. Remember that in the production of a diphthong one sound outweighs the other. The /j/ in /ju/ is stronger than the /ɪ/ in /ɪu/, which makes the latter sound more subtle. In many words, such as "tune," "institution," and "constitution," the singular vowel /u/ or the diphthongs /ju/ and /ɪu/ may be used. However, /u/ is the third choice. In career speech, the diphthong /ju/ is used at the beginning of a word, as in "unison" and "unit"; the diphthong /ɪu/ is preferred when the sound occurs within a word. In that case, if /ju/ is used pronunciation may become labored and seem showy. The diphthong /ɪu/ contains very little of the gliding movement produced by the semivowel /j/.

EXERCISES

1. Produce the three acceptable pronunciations transcribed for the following words. Remember that for career speech, you should develop a preference for /ɪu/.

	/u/	/ju/	/ɪu/
new	[nu]	[nju]	[nɪu]
Tuesday	['tuzdeɪ]	['tjuzdeɪ]	['tɪuzdeɪ]
dew	[du]	[dju]	[dɪu]
nude	[nud]	[njud]	[nɪud]
tune	[tun]	[tjun]	[tɪun]
astute	[æ'stut]	[æ'stjut]	[æ'stɪut]
neuter	['nutɚ]	['njutɚ]	['nɪutɚ]
neurosis	[nu'rosɪs]	[nju'rosɪs]	[nɪu'rosɪs]

2. Compare the /ɪu/ diphthong with /ju/ in the following sentences.

   a. Few institutions are without constitutions.

   b. Tune in Tuesday's news.

   c. The lute player's enthusiasm was infectious.

   d. Unitarians'[21] eulogies[21] are usually[21] short.

   e. Hugh renewed his interest in nuclear fusion.

3. Distinguish between /u/ and /ɪu/ in the following word pairs.

stoop–stupid	[stup]–['stɪupɪd]
noon–new	[nun]–[nɪu]
two–tune	[tu]–[tɪun]
do–dew	[du]–[dɪu]
moo–mew	[mu]–[mɪu]
pooh–pew	[pu]–[pɪu]
who–hew	[hu]–[hɪu]
tooter–tutor	['tutɚ]–['tɪutɚ]
Tudor	['tudɚ]–['tɪudɚ]

/eɪ/ and /oʊ/

You will remember that the pure vowels /e/ and /o/ are rarely used. Instead, they are turned into the diphthongs /eɪ/ and /oʊ/, especially in stressed syllables. Compare the pronunciation of /e/ with the diphthong /eɪ/ and that of /o/ with the diphthong /oʊ/ in the following words.

	/e/	/eɪ/		/o/	/oʊ/
tray	[tre]	[treɪ]	so-and-so	['soænso]	['soʊænsoʊ]
maybe	['mebɪ]	['meɪbɪ]	moan	[mon]	[moʊn]
daylight	['delaɪt]	['deɪlaɪt]	float	[flot]	[floʊt]
way	[we]	[weɪ]	suppose	[sə'poz]	[sə'poʊz]
mayonnaise	[meə'nez]	[meɪə'neɪz]	cosy	['kozɪ]	['koʊzɪ]

(For additional exercises, see the material on the pure vowels /e/ and /o/ on pp. 91–92 and 112–113.)

---

[21]The only acceptable pronunciations of these words use the diphthong /ju/ because the sound is stressed and appears initially.

EXERCISES FOR VOWELS AND DIPHTHONGS

The following selections use numerous vowels and diphthongs. As you read aloud the selections, make certain you take sufficient time to produce the vowels and diphthongs.

1.   1   I was quiet. Sitting there, I saw that my father looked like an older, thinner image of
     2   Uncle. His face was more stern, also more intelligent-looking. He wore glasses with
     3   round gold rims, a dark Western suit with a Chinese vest underneath. He was not
     4   very tall, although he had the air of a large man, the way he slowly turned his head
     5   halfway back toward a servant, then slowly waved the servant forward with his hand.
     6   But instead of telling the servant something, he turned to me.
     7   "Daughter, you decide. Should we have Chinese snacks or English biscuits with
     8   our tea?" My mind felt like two horses running off in opposite directions. Which
     9   one? Which answer was correct?
     10   "Something simple," I finally whispered.
     11   And he smiled. "Of course, that's what you always prefer." He waved his hand
     12 once again to the servant, told him to bring English biscuits, Chinese pears, and
     13 Belgian chocolates.

From THE KITCHEN GOD'S WIFE
Amy Tan

2.   1   Scrooge lived in chambers which had once belonged to his deceased partner. . . .
     2   Now, it is a fact that there was nothing at all particular about the knocker on the door,
     3   except that it was very large. It is also a fact, that Scrooge had seen it, night and
     4   morning, during his whole residence in that place; also that Scrooge had as little of
     5   what is called fancy about him as any man in the city of London. . . . Then let any
     6   man explain to me, if he can, how it happened that Scrooge, having his key in the
     7   lock of the door, saw in the knocker, without its undergoing any intermediate
     8   process of change—not a knocker, but Marley's face.
     9   Marley's face. . . . It . . . had a dismal light about it and its livid color, made it
     10 horrible. As Scrooge looked fixedly at this phenomenon, it was a knocker again. To say
     11 that he was not startled, or that his blood was not conscious of a terrible sensation
     12 would be untrue.

From A CHRISTMAS CAROL
Charles Dickens

3.   1   The rain set early in tonight,
     2   The sullen wind was soon awake,
     3   It tore the elm-tops down for spite,
     4   And did its worst to vex the lake:
     5   I listened with heart fit to break.
     6   When glided in Porphyria; straight
     7   She shut the cold out and the storm,
     8   And kneeled and made the cheerless grate
     9   Blaze up, and all the cottage warm;
     10 Which done, she rose, and from her form
     11 Withdrew the dripping cloak and shawl,
     12 And laid her soiled gloves by, untied
     13 Her hat and let the damp hair fall,
     14 And last, she sat down by my side
     15 And called me. When no voice replied,
     16 She put my arm about her waist,

17   And made her smooth white shoulder bare
18   And all her yellow hair displaced,
19   And, stooping, made my cheek lie there,
20   And spread, o'er all, her yellow hair,
21   Murmuring how she loved me—she
22   Too weak, for all her heart's endeavor,
23   To set its struggling passion free
24   From pride, and vainer ties dissever,
25   And give herself to me forever.
26   But passion sometimes would prevail,
27   Nor could tonight's gay feast restrain
28   A sudden thought of one so pale
29   For love of her, and all in vain:
30   So, she was come through wind and rain.
31   Be sure I looked up at her eyes
32   Happy and proud; at last I knew
33   Porphyria worshipped me; surprise
34   Made my heart swell, and still it grew
35   While I debated what to do.
36   That moment she was mine, mine, fair,
37   Perfectly pure and good: I found
38   A thing to do, and all her hair
39   In one long yellow string I wound
40   Three times her little throat around,
41   And strangled her. No pain felt she;
42   I am quite sure she felt no pain.
43   As a shut bud that holds a bee,
44   I warily oped her lids: again
45   Laughed the blue eyes without a stain.
46   And I untightened next the tress
47   About her neck; her cheek once more
48   Blushed bright beneath my burning kiss:
49   I propped her head up as before,
50   Only, this time my shoulder bore
51   Her head, which droops upon it still:
52   The smiling rosy little head,
53   So glad it has its utmost will,
54   That all it scorned at once is fled,
55   And I, its love, am gained instead!
56   Porphyria's love: she guessed not how
57   Her darling one wish would be heard.
58   And thus we sit together now,
59   And all night long we have not stirred,
60   And yet God has not said a word!

PORPHYRIA'S LOVER
Robert Browning

4.

1

1   They went to sea in a sieve, they did;
2   In a sieve they went to sea;
3   In spite of all their friends could say,
4   On a winter's morn, on a stormy day,
5   In a sieve they went to sea.
6   And when the sieve turned round and round,

7   And every one cried, "You'll all be drowned!"
8   They called aloud, "Our sieve ain't big,
9   But we don't care a button; we don't care a fig:
10 In a sieve we'll go to sea!"
11 Far and few, far and few,
12 Are the lands where the Jumblies live:
13 Their heads are green, and their hands are blue;
14 And they went to sea in a sieve.

2

15 They sailed away in a sieve, they did,
16 In a sieve they sailed so fast,
17 With only a beautiful pea-green veil,
18 Tied with a ribbon, by way of a sail,
19 To a small tobacco-pipe mast.
20 And every one said who saw them go,
21 "Oh! won't they be soon upset, you know?
22 For the sky is dark, and the voyage is long;
23 And, happen what may, it's extremely wrong
24 In a sieve to sail so fast."
25 Far and few, far and few,
26 Are the lands where the Jumblies live:
27 Their heads are green, and their hands are blue;
28 And they went to sea in a sieve.

From THE JUMBLIES
Edward Lear

VOWELS AND DIPHTHONGS[22]

IPA	Symbol	Classification	Tongue Action	Articulatory Adjustment
/i/	see	front vowel	tense	high-front
/ɪ/	bit	front vowel	relaxed	high-front
/e/	make	front vowel	tense	middle-front
/ɛ/	met	front vowel	relaxed	middle-front
/æ/	cat	front vowel	relaxed	low-front
/a/	half	front vowel	relaxed	low-front
/ɝ/	her	central vowel	tense	middle-central
/ɜ/	bird	central vowel	slightly tense	middle-central
/ɚ/	after	central vowel	slightly tense	middle-central
/ʌ/	cut	central vowel	relaxed	middle-central
/ə/	about	central vowel	relaxed	middle-central
/u/	true	back vowel	slightly tense	high-back
/ʊ/	put	back vowel	relaxed	high-back
/o/	go	back vowel	tense	middle-back
/ɔ/	law	back vowel	slightly tense	low-back
/ɒ/	walnut	back vowel	slightly tense	low-back
/ɑ/	father	back vowel	relaxed	low-back
/aɪ/	ice	diphthong	relaxed	low-high front
/aʊ/	house	diphthong	relaxed	low-front, high-back
/ɔɪ/	boy	diphthong	relaxed	low-back, high-front
/ju/	huge	diphthong	tense	lingua-velar[23], high-back

[22]Vocal fold action is *voiced* for all entries.
[23]See page 131 for an explanation of *lingua-velar.*

/ɪu/	new	diphthong	relaxed	high-front, high-back
/eɪ/	may	diphthong	tense	middle-front
			relaxed	high-front
/oʊ/	go	diphthong	tense	middle-back
			relaxed	high-back

To locate URLs and search terms for weblinks relevant to this chapter, please go to the companion website at www.cengage.com/rtf/crannell/voiceandarticulation5e and select the proper chapter.

Write the definitions for the following terms in the space below.

KEY TERMS   DEFINITIONS

Allophone

Articulation

Auditory Discrimination

Auditory Sense

Connotation

Continuant

Denotation

Diphthong

Dynamic Speech

Habitual

Kinesthetic Sense

Molar

Monosyllabic

Phoneme

Phonetics

Polysyllabic

Pronunciation

Schwa

Stress

Tactile Sense

Transcribe

Visual Sense

Voiced Sound

Voiceless Sound

Vowel

Wrenched Stress

CHAPTER 7

THE PRODUCTION OF CONSONANTS

CONSONANT CLASSIFICATIONS

Two consonant sounds, one voiced and one unvoiced, having the same articulatory adjustment are called **cognate pairs.** These consonant sounds are made in the same way, but in the first one the vocal folds vibrate and in the other there is just breath (/v/ and /f/, for example). Two classifications of consonant sounds contain cognate pairs: plosives and fricatives.

Plosives

An American-English sound is either a **continuant** (capable of being prolonged) or a **plosive** (short for *explosive*). If it is a plosive, there is breath under pressure, which peaks in the articulatory mold and is released in a small puff of sound when the articulators are relaxed. There are eight plosives composed of four cognate pairs. All of the remaining sounds in English are continuants.

ARTICULATORY ADJUSTMENT	UNVOICED	VOICED
Bilabial (two lips)	/p/ as in "put"	/b/ as in "bad"
Lingua-alveolar (tip of tongue on alveolar ridge)	/t/ as in "take"	/d/ as in "day"
Lingua-velar (back of the tongue and velum)	/k/ as in "cake"	/g/ as in "gun"
Lingua-alveolar and **lingua-palatal** (tongue against front and sides of palate)	/tʃ/ as in "chain"	/dʒ/ as in "joint"

Remember that each pair of sounds (/p-b/, /t-d/, /k-g/, and /tʃ-dʒ/) have the same articulatory adjustment and differ only in the presence or absence of vibration of the vocal folds.

Although /tʃ/ and /dʒ/ are classified as plosives, they are also known as **affricates,** a combination of a plosive followed by a *fricative.*

The following word list presents each plosive in the three possible positions in a word:

	INITIAL	MEDIAL	FINAL
/p/	pout, punch, pick	apply, apart, apple	slap, step, clip
/b/	but, bunch, back	about, rubble, mobbing	slab, sub, crab
/t/	toy, talk, tub	matter, hurting, plotter	sweet, night, mint
/d/	dine, deal, den	toddler, middle, rudder	add, tied, fled
/k/	keep, kill, kind	picket, pocket, ankle	hawk, book, zinc
/g/	get, gone, game	ago, beggar, anger	bag, pig, drag
/tʃ/	chip, check, chop	butcher, catcher, matches	birch, witch, etch
/dʒ/	jump, Jim, juggle	agile, angel, budget	age, garbage, rampage

Fricatives

A **fricative** is a speech sound in which breath passes through a narrow opening in the articulatory mold (between the upper teeth and the lower lip), creating frictional noises. Most fricatives occur as cognate pairs.

ARTICULATORY ADJUSTMENT	UNVOICED	VOICED
Labio-dental (lower lip and upper teeth)	/f/ as in "fun"	/v/ as in "vine"
Lingua-dental (tongue between upper and lower teeth)	/θ/ as in "thing"	/ð/ as in "them"
Glottal (takes on articulatory characteristics of the sound that follows)	/h/ as in "hop"	
Bilabial	/ʍ/ as in "while"	
Lingua-alveolar	/s/ as in "save"	/z/ as in "zoo"
Lingua-palatal	/ʃ/ as in "shape"	/ʒ/ as in "treasure"

The last four fricatives in this list (/s/, /z/, /ʃ/, and /ʒ/) are also called *sibilants.* A **sibilant** is a sound in which breath passes through a narrow opening, creating a hissing noise. A speaker with a whistling /s/ is sometimes described incorrectly as having a sibilant /s/. Because a sibilant is a type of sound, and not a production error, it is redundant to say that someone has a "sibilant /s/." All /s/ phonemes are sibilants.

The following list presents the fricatives in the three possible positions in a word:

	INITIAL	MEDIAL	FINAL
/f/	fine, fit, phone	after, afraid, offer	hoof, half, beef
/v/	vouch, very, vain	average, avenue, cover	stove, cave, above
/θ/	theme, thought, three	author, birthday, anything	sheath, birth, breath
/ð/	there, that, thou	bathing, bother, other	clothe, writhe, breathe
/h/	hoe, hay, home	ahoy, behind, beehive	(does not occur)

	INITIAL	MEDIAL	FINAL
/ʍ/	<u>wh</u>ere, <u>wh</u>en, <u>wh</u>ite	mean<u>wh</u>ile, any<u>wh</u>ere, every<u>wh</u>ere	(does not occur)
/s/	<u>s</u>ay, <u>s</u>ail, <u>s</u>ign	a<u>s</u>leep, ba<u>s</u>ket, fa<u>s</u>ter	cla<u>ss</u>, fa<u>ce</u>, che<u>ss</u>
/z/	<u>z</u>ebra, <u>z</u>ipper, <u>z</u>ero	ha<u>z</u>el, ra<u>z</u>or, ama<u>z</u>ed	a<u>s</u>, pha<u>se</u>, brui<u>se</u>
/ʃ/	<u>sh</u>ip, <u>sh</u>ell, <u>sh</u>ore	la<u>sh</u>ing, a<u>sh</u>es, bru<u>sh</u>es	blu<u>sh</u>, cra<u>sh</u>, di<u>sh</u>
/ʒ/	(does not occur)	a<u>z</u>ure, lei<u>s</u>ure, mea<u>s</u>ure	gara<u>ge</u>, mira<u>ge</u>, espiona<u>ge</u>

Lateral

There is one *lateral* speech sound—/l/ as in "leg." "Lateral" refers to the passage of breath over the sides of the tongue. The sound is produced with the tip of the tongue against the alveolar ridge, with the sides of the tongue free from contact. It can appear in any position within a word:

ARTICULATORY ADJUSTMENT		PHONEME
Lingua-alveolar		/l/ as in "<u>l</u>ike"

	INITIAL	MEDIAL	FINAL
/l/	<u>l</u>ie, <u>l</u>ick, <u>l</u>amp	a<u>l</u>ong, a<u>ll</u>ow, a<u>l</u>ibi	fi<u>ll</u>, whi<u>le</u>, ho<u>le</u>

Semivowels

A **semivowel**, or **glide**, is a speech sound in which there is a gliding movement of the tongue, the lips, or both. Because of the gliding movement, the semivowels maintain characteristics of vowels (see Chapter 6). There are three semivowels: /r/, /w/, and /j/. There are no cognate pairs among the semivowels because all of them are voiced.

ARTICULATORY ADJUSTMENT	PHONEME
Lingua-palatal (gliding movement of lips and tongue)	/r/ as in "<u>r</u>ed"
Bilabial (gliding movement of lips)	/w/ as in "<u>w</u>ay"
Lingua-palatal (gliding movement of tongue)	/j/ as in "<u>y</u>et"

	INITIAL	MEDIAL	FINAL
/r/	<u>r</u>un, <u>r</u>ig, <u>r</u>obbed	a<u>r</u>range, a<u>r</u>ound, ca<u>rr</u>iage	ta<u>r</u>, bo<u>re</u>, fea<u>r</u>
/w/	<u>w</u>edge, <u>w</u>illow, <u>w</u>eb	a<u>w</u>ay, for<u>w</u>ard, co<u>w</u>ard	(does not occur)
/j/	<u>y</u>onder, <u>y</u>ell, <u>y</u>oung	bill<u>i</u>ard, be<u>y</u>ond, law<u>y</u>er	(does not occur)

Nasals

A **nasal** sound is a speech sound in which the vibrating breath escapes through the nose because the velum is relaxed. All nasal sounds are sonant (voiced), so there are no cognate pairs. The three nasal sounds are /m/, /n/, and /ŋ/. The last nasal is the sound that corresponds to the pronunciation of the two letters *ng*. This sound poses difficulties for speakers for whom English is a second language.

ARTICULATORY ADJUSTMENT	PHONEME
Bilabial with relaxed velum	/m/ as in "<u>m</u>itt"
Lingua-alveolar with relaxed velum	/n/ as in "<u>n</u>o"
Lingua-velar with relaxed velum (back of tongue against velum)	/ŋ/ as in "ri<u>ng</u>"

	INITIAL	MEDIAL	FINAL
/m/	may, marsh, mug	amid, camel, camera	same, crumb, clam
/n/	nice, knife, numb	annoy, annual, candle	tan, sane, been
/ŋ/	(does not occur)	singer, hanger, length	rang, fling, lung

In subsequent sections each sound will be presented and discussed in terms of its articulatory production, frequent problems in its production, and exercises for improvement.

>>> PLOSIVES

/p/ and /b/

Production

The phonemes /p/ (as in "pie") and /b/ (as in "big") are a cognate pair that are made with the lips coming together and the teeth slightly apart. Pressure is built up behind the lips; when they are pushed apart so that the air or sound waves escape, sound is produced. The sound produced varies with the amount of air expended and the amount of pressure built up behind the lips. Another variable is the location of the sound within the words. For example, there is more pressure in the initial /p/ (as in "Pat") than in the final /p/ ("up"), and there is more pressure in the initial /b/ ("ball") than in the medial /b/ ("robbed").

Problems

The phonemes /p/ and /b/ are usually not problematic unless there is some difficulty with the bite. If there is a fairly severe overbite, for example, the upper teeth may touch the lower lip when /p/ and /b/ are produced. (This **dental** problem would affect the production of other sounds as well.) Make certain that your lips touch when you say these phonemes. Use a mirror in addition to your tactile and kinesthetic senses.

(((EXERCISES

1. Read aloud the following word lists, exaggerating your production of /p/ and /b/. Build up the pressure so that you can feel and see in a mirror the production of the sounds. Make certain that you do not pull away too much from the overarticulation when trying to develop the appropriate sound. Chances are you are an underarticulator!

INITIAL	MEDIAL	FINAL
pot	clapping	top
pay	apart	cup
paid	report	tape
paste	stepping	strap
pray	rupture	hope
bought	above	dab
base	rebound	disturb
back	stable	crab
beggar	rebel	slab
blame	habit	stub

Read aloud the selections in exercises 2 through 9.

2. passing the <u>b</u>utter   <u>P</u>unch and <u>B</u>uddy
  a<u>pp</u>ealing ha<u>b</u>it   a<u>pp</u>le and cran<u>b</u>erry juice
  u<u>p</u> on the cur<u>b</u>   the ma<u>p</u>le caro<u>b</u> <u>b</u>ean

3. a. Ro<u>b</u>ert <u>p</u>ut the <u>p</u>ackage of coupons in his safe.

 b. <u>P</u>at put a da<u>b</u> of <u>p</u>aste on the <u>b</u>roken cu<u>p</u>.

 c. <u>P</u>ost the "Do Not Distur<u>b</u>" sign on the <u>b</u>ack of the door.

 d. Chi<u>p</u> <u>p</u>laced the <u>b</u>lame on <u>P</u>eggy.

 e. It is <u>p</u>roper to clap hands when you're ha<u>pp</u>y about a <u>p</u>erformance.

4. <u>P</u>atricia walked through the empty house, finding herself alone in all of its comfort. She was the owner now, <u>b</u>ut loss surrounded her, footsteps echoed in her mind, eyes filled with <u>p</u>atterns that were now a few ashes scattered over a mountain. <u>B</u>en was gone, <u>b</u>ut the house didn't seem to know this. O<u>b</u>jects waited for his touch.

From IN <u>B</u>LACK AND WHITE
Ann Jones

5. Five weeks have gone <u>b</u>y, and still no news of Naema. Nothing at all. Some <u>p</u>eople think she's imprisoned in the <u>B</u>edeau <u>b</u>arracks. The <u>B</u>edeau <u>b</u>arracks . . . the <u>p</u>risoners held there are considered to <u>b</u>e hostages; dreadful things are said a<u>b</u>out what ha<u>pp</u>ens to them.

 How to <u>b</u>e sure? It's im<u>p</u>ossible to get any definite news; no one has ever returned home from that <u>p</u>lace. Wait, that's all—for some news to trickle through, for Naema, <u>b</u>y some miracle, to <u>b</u>e <u>b</u>rought to trial. Wait—that's all that's left to us.

From NAEMA—WHEREA<u>B</u>OUTS UNKNOWN
Mohammed Di<u>b</u>

6. The <u>b</u>aby <u>b</u>oy grew older and <u>b</u>ecame very smart. He had to <u>b</u>e, to <u>b</u>e able to remember his own name. Like all other children he was always trying to avoid work. He discovered that <u>b</u>y the time his mother had finished calling his name for chores, he could <u>b</u>e far, far away.

From TAHOTAHONTANEKENTSERATKERONTAKWENHAKIE
Salli <u>B</u>enedict

7. <u>B</u>ack from the <u>b</u>ath, she got out some ice from the icebox, crushed it finely, wrapped it in a double layer of gauze and s<u>p</u>ent ten minutes with it <u>b</u>efore the mirror, massaging her face all over.

From LATE CHRYSANTHEMUM
Hayashi Fumiko

8. <u>B</u>ack in the days when everyone was old and stu<u>p</u>id or young and foolish, and me and Sugar were the only ones just right, this lady moved on our <u>b</u>lock with na<u>pp</u>y hair and <u>p</u>roper s<u>p</u>eech and no make-u<u>p</u>.

From THE LESSON
Toni Cade <u>B</u>am<u>b</u>ara

9. Then taking out his field dressing, he ri<u>pp</u>ed o<u>p</u>en the <u>p</u>acket with his knife. He <u>b</u>roke the neck of the iodine <u>b</u>ottle and let the <u>b</u>itter fluid dri<u>p</u> into the wound. A <u>p</u>aroxysm of pain swept through him. He <u>p</u>laced the cotton wadding over the wound and wra<u>pp</u>ed the dressing over it.

From THE SNI<u>P</u>ER
Liam O'Flaherty

/t/
and
/d/

Production

The phonemes /t/ (as in "<u>t</u>o") and /d/ (as in "<u>d</u>o") are a cognate pair that are made with the tip of the tongue against the alveolar ridge behind the upper teeth. Pressure is built up between the tongue tip and the alveolar ridge, and the sound is produced when the tongue tip is dropped. The sound produced varies with the amount of air expended and the amount of pressure behind the ridge. There is more pressure when the sound is produced in the initial position ("<u>t</u>ale") than in the final position ("eigh<u>t</u>").

Problems

The most common problem in the production of /t/ and /d/ is contact of the blade of the tongue with the back of the upper teeth rather than with the gum ridge. Thus, even though these sounds are lingua-alveolar, they are often made lingua-dentally. The problem sound that is produced is said to be **dentalized** and is transcribed as /t̪/ and /d̪/, respectively. Instead of saying "<u>t</u>oo<u>t</u>" [tut] or "<u>d</u>u<u>d</u>e" [dud] with just the tongue tip, the person who dentalizes says /t̪ut̪/ or /d̪ud̪/ by placing the blade of the tongue on the back of the upper teeth. This is how many New Yorkers sound. Use a mirror to see the position of the tongue that results in dentalization.

A major problem for the Southern speaker (especially young girls) is the substitution of the glottal stop ['] for the /t/ and /d/ in the medial position in the contractions of "did not" and "could not." However, this error is not limited only to the South! If this is one of your errors, see "Explosion and Implosion" in Chapter 8.

 EXERCISES

1. Read aloud the following word lists, exaggerating your production of /t/ and /d/. Build up the pressure so that you can feel and see in a mirror the production of the sounds. Make certain that you do not pull away too much from overarticulation when trying to develop the appropriate sound.

INITIAL	MEDIAL	FINAL
<u>t</u>ongue	swea<u>t</u>er	poli<u>t</u>e
<u>t</u>oll	le<u>tt</u>uce	frui<u>t</u>
<u>t</u>ea	si<u>tt</u>er	clapp<u>ed</u>
<u>t</u>owel	la<u>t</u>ely	dir<u>t</u>
<u>t</u>elevision	pain<u>t</u>ing	boa<u>t</u>
<u>d</u>iaper	a<u>dd</u>ing	si<u>d</u>e
<u>d</u>are	bu<u>dd</u>y	learn<u>ed</u>
<u>D</u>anny	un<u>d</u>er	fin<u>d</u>
<u>d</u>onor	fee<u>d</u>er	sign<u>ed</u>
<u>d</u>ivine	we<u>dd</u>ing	avi<u>d</u>

BLENDS: /tr/, /dr/, /tw/, AND /dw/

/tr/	/dr/	/tw/	/dw/
<u>tr</u>ip	<u>dr</u>ip	<u>tw</u>ice	<u>dw</u>indle
<u>tr</u>y	<u>dr</u>y	<u>tw</u>irl	<u>dw</u>arf
<u>tr</u>ain	<u>dr</u>ain	<u>tw</u>in	<u>dw</u>ell

true	drew	twenty	Dwight
trade	hydrant	twit	Dwayne
Patrick	adrift	twine	sandwich
attribute	drape	between	
trait	cathedral	twig	
actress	drool	twist	
electric	hundred	twitch	

Read aloud the selections in exercises 2 through 10. Many of them are also good for breath control.

2. tricks or treats   twirling batons
red drapes   dripping towels
mind-altering drug   dwelling place
dwindling fortune   Andrea's sister's toys

3. a. The Trojan horse attracted many true stories.

b. Have you ever tried racing twin trains?

c. Dwight drew over twenty sketches.

d. Try and drink the twirling water before it goes down the drain.

e. Donna warned the children not to drag the blankets.

4. Refer to "Modern Major-General" (from *The Pirates of Penzance*) in the breath control section (p. 29). This exercise is also good for the articulation of the /l/ phoneme as well. Make certain that you do not substitute the /d/ phoneme for the /t/ in such words as "Waterloo," "categorical," and "matters mathematical."

5. He didn't say he wouldn't, and he didn't say he couldn't or shouldn't, but he didn't.

6. And I had to go and tell him that I'd adore to dance with him. I cannot understand why I wasn't struck dead.

From THE WALTZ
Dorothy Parker

7. Oh, somewhere in this favored land the sun is shining bright;
The Band is playing somewhere, and somewhere hearts are light.

From CASEY AT THE BAT
Ernest Lawrence Thayer

8. Deep into that darkness peering, long I stood there, wondering, fearing,
Doubting, dreaming dreams no mortal ever dared to dream before;
But the silence was unbroken, and the stillness gave no token,
And the only word there spoken was the whispered word "Lenore!"
This I whispered, and an echo murmured back the word "Lenore!"
Merely this and nothing more.

From THE RAVEN
Edgar Allan Poe

9. A silly young fellow named Hyde
In a funeral procession was spied;
When asked, "Who is dead?"
He giggled and said,
"I don't know; I just came for the ride."

Anonymous

10. I dreamed that I died: that I felt the cold close to me;
and all that was left of my life was contained in your presence:
your mouth was the daylight and dark of my world,
your skin, the republic I shaped for myself with my kisses.

From XC
Pablo Neruda

/k/ and /g/

Production

The phonemes /k/ (as in "kit") and /g/ (as in "get") are a cognate pair that are made with the back of the tongue firmly against the velum. Pressure should be built up between the tongue and velum; when the tongue is relaxed and the air escapes, the sounds are produced.

Problems

The two most frequent difficulties in producing /k/ and /g/ are (1) the failure to make firm contact between the tongue and the velum and (2) the omission of the /k/ in certain words ("breafast" for "breakfast") and in conversational speech ("Don't 'ass' questions!"), making the speech sound stereotypically uneducated.

EXERCISES

1. *Weakness in Contact.* Read aloud the following word lists, exaggerating your production of /k/ and /g/. Build up the pressure so that you can feel and see in a mirror the production of the sounds. This is more difficult than in /p/ and /b/ because the position required for the production of those sounds is easier to see. Make certain that you do not pull away from the articulation too much when trying to develop the appropriate sound.

Initial	Medial	Final
count	lucky	back
care	bunker	book
crunch	become	fork
chemistry	looking	bake
quite	turkey	stork
goose	begin	bag
guess	forget	rig
guard	regulate	vague
goat	trigger	iceberg
gift	beggar	intrigue

BLENDS: /kr/, /gr/, /kw/, /kl/, and /gl/

/kr/	/gr/	/kw/	/kl/	/gl/
crow	grow	quick	cloud	glad
cruel	gruel	quaint	click	glide
crew	grew	Quayle	clear	glutton
crab	grab	acquaint	clone	gloat
crate	great	quiet	clam	glance

craft	grin	quite	clasp	glass
Socrates	outgrowth	quaver	clarity	aglow
fulcrum	grits	quarter	acclaim	gland
Chris	grief	quench	classify	glottal
crutch	angry	quill	cliché	glory

2. climbing crabapple trees   kiss the goat
great oaks   cloudy skies
Grover's Corners   Thanksgiving turkey
getting the books   tiger's claws

3. *Omission of /k/.* Read aloud and record the following list of words and phrases, making certain that all of the sounds in the words are produced. For the present purposes, you should explode all of the underlined /k/ sounds so that you feel the production of the sound. Use negative practice, and make sure that you omit the /k/ phoneme in the second pronunciation. In career speech, you would use implosion, which is discussed in Chapter 8.

asked him	desktop	risks everything
Masked Marvel	disk drive	white tusks
car flasks	heavy tasks	asks him

Read aloud the selections in exercises 4 through 12.

4. **a.** Count the lucky numbers on the book.

    b. Give the basket of baked goods to Karen.

    c. The goat got a stomachache eating the iceberg lettuce.

    d. The guard tried to regulate the flow of traffic.

    e. The hunter was quite angry when the gun's trigger wouldn't work.

5. Mrs. Ericson . . . subsided after a glance at the girl's set profile. Marain drove the car slowly through the shady streets. It was one of the first hot days in June, and when they reached the boulevard they found it crowded with cars headed for the beaches.

From THE TEST
Angelica Gibbs

6. Children begin by loving their parents; after a time they judge them; rarely, if ever, do they forgive them.

7. I can't help detesting my relations, I suppose it comes from the fact that we can't stand other people having the same faults as ourselves.

8. Where my grandfather came from, most of the people lived by working in the flax sheds. For five generations they had been breathing in the dust which rose from the crushed flax stalks, letting themselves be killed off by slow degrees, a race of long-suffering, cheerful people who ate goat cheese, potatoes, and now and then a rabbit; . . .

From THE BALEK SCALES
Heinrich Boll

9. A fancy young dandy from Niger
Went out for a ride on a tiger.
They returned from the ride
With the dandy inside
And a smile on the face of the tiger.

Edward Lear

10. There was a young lady of <u>C</u>rete
Who was e<u>x</u>ceedingly neat.
When she got out of bed
She stood on her head
To ma<u>ke</u> sure of not soiling her feet.

Edward Lear

11. <u>K</u>iss me in the <u>c</u>as<u>k</u>et
Before they <u>c</u>lose the lid.
To say <u>g</u>oodbye to a wonderful <u>g</u>uy
Who doesn't know he's dead.
Don't be forlorn
My thoughts are gone
There's nothing in my head.
The end has <u>c</u>ome
And stru<u>ck</u> me dumb
Never to <u>c</u>are a<u>g</u>ain.
Please thin<u>k</u> of me
Twi<u>xt</u> land and sea
Just blowing in the wind.

From <u>K</u>ISS ME IN THE <u>C</u>AS<u>K</u>ET
Robert H. Cath<u>c</u>art

12. The following poem should be read when you feel a little cocky about your importance
on this earth.
1   "Ah, are you di<u>gg</u>ing on my <u>g</u>rave
2   My beloved one?—planting rue?"
3   —"No: yesterday he went to wed
4   One of the brightest wealth has bred,
5   'It cannot hurt her now,' he said,
6   'That I should not be true.'"
7   "Then who is di<u>gg</u>ing on my <u>g</u>rave?
8   My nearest, dearest <u>k</u>in?"
9   —"Ah, no: They sit and thin<u>k</u>, 'What use!
10 What <u>g</u>ood will planting flowers produce?
11 No tendance of her mound can loose
12 Her spirit from Death's gin.'"

13 "But someone di<u>g</u>s upon my <u>g</u>rave—
14 My enemy?—prodding sly?"
15 —"Nay: When she heard you had passed the <u>G</u>ate
16 That shuts on all flesh soon or late,
17 She thought you no more worth her hate,
18 And <u>c</u>ares not where you lie."

19 "Then, who is di<u>gg</u>ing on my <u>g</u>rave?
20 Say—since I have not <u>g</u>uessed!"
21 —"O, it is I, my mistress dear,
22 Your little dog who still lives near,
23 And much I hope my movements here
24 Have not disturbed your rest?"

25 "Ah, yes! You dig upon my <u>g</u>rave. . . .
26 Why flashed it not on me

27 That one true heart was left behind!
28 What feeling do we ever find
29 To equal among human kind
30 A dog's fidelity!"

31 "Mistress, I dug upon your grave
32 To bury a bone, in case
33 I should be hungry near this spot
34 When passing on my daily trot.
35 I am sorry, but I quite forgot
36 It was your resting-place."

AH, ARE YOU DIGGING ON MY GRAVE?
Thomas Hardy

/tʃ/ and /dʒ/

Production

The phonemes /tʃ/ (as in "church") and /dʒ/ (as in "judge") are a cognate pair that are made with the tip and blade of the tongue pressed firmly against the alveolar ridge. The sides of the tongue touch the inner edges of the upper back teeth along the palate. Pressure is built up behind the tongue, and the sound is produced when the air escapes and the tip and blade of the tongue drop down, causing a small groove. The sides of the tongue remain along the inner edges of the palate and upper teeth to prevent air from escaping over the sides of the tongue.

Problems

The biggest problem in the production of /tʃ/ and /dʒ/ is the escape of air over the sides of the tongue rather than over the tip. This problem is called **lateralization.** Make believe that you are going to phonate the consonant /l/. Place the tip of your tongue on the alveolar ridge, and blow air over the sides of the tongue. This is lateralization.

 EXERCISES

1. To correct lateralization, a good exercise is to increase the feeling of lingua-alveolar closure. As in the other exercises for initial plosives, exaggerate the buildup of pressure as you read aloud the following word lists. Round the lips as you exaggerate the production of the sound. Using a mirror, pay attention to the visual aspects of the production of the sounds.[1]

INITIAL	MEDIAL	FINAL
cheerful	butcher	pitch
Chuck	benches	batch
chin	beaches	witch
chopping	matches	beach
chain	furniture	match

---

[1]These affricates are particularly difficult for nonnative speakers learning English. Because many languages do not contain /tʃ/ and /dʒ/, nonnative speakers sometimes substitute the fricatives /ʃ/ and /ʒ/. These are discussed in detail on page 353. A German or French speaker is apt to say "sheet" for "cheat" and "ship" for "chip." Other nonnatives like Greeks or Japanese are likely to substitute /ts/ or /dz/ for /tʃ/ and /dʒ/, respectively. Further difficulty stems from the inconsistency in the English spelling of the sound /dʒ/: "soldier," "rage," "general," "jump," and "grandeur."

jail	besieger	average
jump	stranger	Madge
joke	regent	lunge
jelly	major	merge
gem	plunging	marriage

Read aloud the selections in exercises 2 through 8.

2. church and chapel   jumping on the judge
butcher and baker   the strange badger
Jennifer and Marjorie   furniture store chain
the changing guard   a major decision

3. a. Charlie was the name of the cheerful butcher you met.

b. Marjorie said that the furniture was cheap for cherrywood.

c. Tsun Ming jumped on the park bench and told a joke.

d. Midge brought a cheap batch of matches to the beach.

e. Pitch the jam and jelly sandwiches!

f. A cheap, changeable, childlike chimpanzee champion was playing checkers with Chuck.

g. The angels wrote down the strategy for the old major.

4. The reverend Mr. Chippler, who had organized the revival which would wind up this afternoon, was a leaping little man, fuller of friendliness, optimism, go, zip, imagination, ingenuity, cheeriness, and oratory than the nobler and slower animals. In joy over his camp meeting, he was jammed with exuberant wrath at sinners, this bountiful June morning. His text was from Job: . . .

From THE GOD-SEEKER
Sinclair Lewis

5. *Gwendolyn*: Jack? No, there is very little music in the name Jack, if any at all, indeed. It does not thrill. It produces absolutely no vibrations. I have known several Jacks, and they all, without exception, were more than usually plain. Besides, Jack is a notorious domesticity for John! And I pity any woman who is married to a man called John. She would probably never be allowed to know the entrancing pleasure of a single moment's solitude. The only really safe name is Ernest.

From THE IMPORTANCE OF BEING EARNEST
Oscar Wilde

6. Cheddar and jack cheese can be cheap.

7. Speech teachers are often accused of teaching gibberish.

8. Jenny kissed me when we met,
Jumping from the chair she sat in;
Time, you thief, who loves to get
Sweets into your list, put that in:
Say I'm weary, say I'm sad,
Say that health and wealth have missed me,
Say I'm growing old, but add
Jenny kissed me.

JENNY KISSED ME
Leigh Hunt

>>> FRICATIVES

/f/
and
/v/

Production

The phonemes /f/ (as in "<u>f</u>ed") and /v/ (as in "<u>v</u>et") are a cognate pair made by bringing the inner edges of the lower lip against the upper teeth. The sounds are produced when the breath or voice escapes through a narrow opening between the upper teeth and lower lip.

Problems

The most common error in the production of /f/ and /v/ is too much or too little contact between the upper teeth and the lower lip. If there is too much contact and a pressing down of the teeth on the lip, the sound resembles plosive sounds. If there is too little contact or the teeth touch too low on the lip, the sounds become "slushy."

 EXERCISES

In reading the following word lists and exercises, exaggerate the articulation before you attempt to pull away. Using a mirror, watch the formation of the sounds; maintain good articulation when you pull away from exaggerated sound production.

1.

INITIAL	MEDIAL	FINAL
<u>f</u>ame	in<u>f</u>amous	belie<u>f</u>
<u>f</u>erment	in<u>f</u>luence	Cli<u>ff</u>
<u>ph</u>oto	tele<u>ph</u>one	lau<u>gh</u>
<u>f</u>ood	co<u>ff</u>ee	cou<u>gh</u>
<u>f</u>unny	chau<u>ff</u>eur	enou<u>gh</u>
<u>v</u>anity	e<u>v</u>il	e<u>ve</u>
<u>V</u>enus	de<u>v</u>il	groo<u>ve</u>
<u>v</u>ictory	Da<u>v</u>id	shel<u>ve</u>
<u>v</u>alley	pre<u>v</u>ent	sto<u>ve</u>
<u>v</u>ain	a<u>v</u>oid	lo<u>ve</u>

BLENDS: /fr/, /fl/

/fr/	/fl/
<u>fr</u>ee	<u>fl</u>ee
<u>fr</u>eeze	<u>fl</u>eas
<u>fr</u>ies	<u>fl</u>ies
<u>fr</u>ost	<u>fl</u>ossed
<u>fr</u>ill	<u>fl</u>attery
<u>fr</u>olic	<u>fl</u>ood
<u>fr</u>ugal	<u>fl</u>apjack
a<u>fr</u>aid	<u>fl</u>aw
re<u>fr</u>action	<u>fl</u>oat
<u>fr</u>ump	<u>fl</u>autist

2. <u>f</u>ace the <u>v</u>erdict   a <u>v</u>ery <u>f</u>unny e<u>v</u>ent
<u>f</u>ollow the <u>f</u>old   a <u>v</u>ictorious ad<u>v</u>enture

Vincent van Gogh's canvas   forever drinking coffee
foretelling the future   falling in love

3. **a.** David gave Vera the famous photo.

   b. The chauffeur telephoned the food store for coffee.

   c. Avoid eating any fish that isn't fresh.

   d. The French love eating frog's legs.

   e. If I laugh enough I can't avoid coughing.

4. The holy passion of Friendship is of so sweet and steady and loyal and enduring a nature that it will last through a whole lifetime, if not asked to lend money.

   From PUDD'NHEAD WILSON
   Mark Twain

5. I am a first-generation Korean American. On my first trip to Korea at age twenty-six, I found that I had two fathers. One was the Dad I'd always known, but the second was a Korean father I'd never seen before—one surprising and familiar at the same time, like my homeland.

   From MY TWO DADS
   Marie G. Lee

6. Faint heart never won fair lady!
   Nothing venture, nothing win—
   Blood is thick, but water's thin—
   In for a penny, in for a pound—
   It's Love that makes the world go round!

   From IOLANTHE
   W. S. Gilbert

/θ/ and /ð/

Production

The phonemes /θ/ (as in "thin") and /ð/ (as in "them") are a cognate pair that are produced with the tip of the tongue lightly placed between the teeth. The breath or voice that escapes through the space between the tongue and the teeth causes the frictional noise.

Problems

The major problems in producing these phonemes are (1) the substitution of /t/ or /d/ for /θ/ and /ð/, respectively, and (2) their omission. For example, the stereotypical street kid says, "Ya bedda go wid me!" substituting the /d/ plosive for the /ð/ fricative. In words like "widths," "sixths," "baths," and "clothes," you don't have to be a thug to omit /θ/ and /ð/—care is necessary to articulate all of the sounds. Career speech requires this kind of precision. Carefully articulating some of these words will probably make you feel somewhat self-conscious. It's almost like learning a foreign language. But your speech is supposed to be that of a trained communicator!

These fricative sounds can be problematic for individuals learning English as a second language. In many languages, including German, French, Italian, Chinese, and Spanish, there are no /θ/ and /ð/ sounds. When native speakers of these languages learn English, they usually substitute /t-d/ or /s-z/. Speakers of Black English often substitute /f/ for /θ/ when it occurs in the final position.

EXERCISES FOR /θ/ AND /ð/

1. Read aloud the following word lists with exaggerated articulation. Take the time to feel and see the production of all of the sounds, particularly /θ/ and /ð/.

INITIAL	MEDIAL	FINAL
theme	bathroom	breath
thought	pathetic	wrath
think	Catholic	mouth
thanks	pathway	cloth
thin	youthful	bath
them	father	tithe
those	leather	breathe
though	either	soothe
there	weather	lithe
that	feather	with

 BLEND: /θr/

/θr/

thrash
thread
three
threw
thrift
thrive
throb
throne
throttle
thrust

2. Read aloud the following pairs of words, exaggerating the articulation. Take the time to feel and see the production of the fricative sounds, both without and with the sibilant. Repeat the words with the appropriate articulation, making certain that you do not pull away too much from the overarticulation.

myth, myths	wreath, wreaths
breathe, breathes	wreathe, wreathes
teethe, teethes	writhe, writhes
clothe, clothes	depth, depths
lathe, lathes	earth, earths
length, lengths	north, norths

Read aloud the selections in exercises 3 through 7.

3. this and that   thick foggy weather
   birds of a feather   with Miss Smith
   through the thicket   withering leather
   those soothing hands   either stay there or go

4. **a.** That is the theme of the book.

   b. He never thought to say thanks to the youth.

   c. Father gave them that feather.

   d. The weather was either snow or sleet.

   e. Theodore thought that the pathway led to the river.

5. The minister gave out his text and droned along monotonously through an argument that was so prosy that many a head by and by began to nod—and yet it was an argument that dealt in limitless fire and brimstone and thinned the predestined elect down to a company so small as to be hardly worth the saving.

   From THE ADVENTURES OF TOM SAWYER
   Mark Twain

6. When I hear people say they have not found the world and life so agreeable or interesting as to be in love with it, or that they look with equanimity to its end, I am apt to think they have never been properly alive nor seen with clear vision the world they think so meanly of, or anything in it—not a blade of grass.

   From FAR AWAY AND LONG AGO
   W. H. Hudson

7. I sing the body electric;
   The armies of those I love engirth me, and I engirth them;
   They will not let me off till I go with them, respond to them,
   And discorrupt them, and charge them full with the charge of the Soul.

   From I SING THE BODY ELECTRIC
   Walt Whitman

8. May those who love us, love us.
   And those that don't love us,
   May God turn their hearts;
   And if He doesn't turn their hearts,
   May He turn their ankles,
   So we'll know them by their limping!

   OLD GAELIC BLESSING

/h/ Production

Because the glottal sound /h/ (as in "house") has no articulatory adjustment, it takes on the adjustment of the vowel or diphthong that follows it. The frictional sound is produced at the glottis with slight tension but with no vibration of the vocal folds.

Problems

Difficulties with /h/ are rare for the native English speaker; most problems are found among people learning English as a second language. Sometimes the letter *h* is silent, as in words like *honor* or *hour.* Some words like *humor* or *human* can be said with or without the phoneme /h/.

 **EXERCISES**

1. Read aloud the following word lists with exaggerated articulation. Take the time to feel and see the assimilation that takes place during the production of /h/. Do not pull away

too much when you read the exercises with appropriate articulation. Be guided visually more than by your kinesthetic sense.

INITIAL	MEDIAL	FINAL
home	somehow	(does not occur)
who	inhuman	
honey	behave	
hill	beehive	
half	bohemian	
hear	unheard	
head	prehistorical	
hair	exhale	
hospital	unholy	
hall	cohort	

2. The following is a partial list of words that may be pronounced with or without the /h/ phoneme, according to *Webster's New Collegiate Dictionary*. However, for the trained speaker, the /h/ should be pronounced.

humanity	humane	humidify
huge	humor	humiliate
humid	humorist	humble
humidor	Hugh	homage
human	humorous	humongous

Read aloud the selections in exercises 3 through 6.

3. hide and seek   Harry's humiliating experience
   a great head of hair   a humorous movie
   inhale and exhale   holding Herbert's hand

4. **a.** Let's hail that hale and hearty he-man.

   b. Somehow it is inhuman to hurt animals.

   c. Half the hair on his head was short.

   d. Hank took the honey from the beehive.

   e. High on the hill there lived a huge dog.

5. 1   Little Harry stole a dollar
   2   From his mother's dearest friend;
   3   He was caught but never punished,
   4   And they hoped it there would end.
   5   Harry smiled and slyly whispered
   6   "Oh, the law is made to bend."
   7   Having learned this useful lesson,
   8   He went on to bigger game,
   9   Ripping off his aunts and uncles,
   10 Signing checks with teacher's name;
   11 All agreed, "Let's have no scandal."
   12 And protected him from shame.

   13 Harry started up a business,
   14 Made a bundle, how it grew!
   15 Clergy had him in for supper,

16   Though the bankers really knew,
17   <u>H</u>arry cut most every corner,
18   "But <u>h</u>e's useful," sad, but true.

19   Then <u>h</u>e slipped, got caught red-<u>h</u>anded;
20   Creditors let out a gasp,
21   "Why, we stand to lose a bundle,
22   Better close <u>h</u>im down, and fast.
23   Wait! That might be bad for business;
24   License <u>h</u>im, forget the past."

25   <u>H</u>arry told <u>h</u>is latest girlfriend,
26   "Lil, I've found the system's flaw. . . .
27   Now, I'm gonna run for Congress,
28   Where the action's rough and raw,
29   Where with lies, and bribes, and blackmail,
30   <u>H</u>eck, I'll get to make the law!"

31   <u>H</u>arry always says <u>h</u>e's sorry,
32   But <u>h</u>e never says what for,
33   So, I <u>h</u>ope somewhere in <u>h</u>eaven
34   There's an angel keeping score,
35   For <u>h</u>is mother says <u>h</u>er <u>H</u>arry
36   Never even thought of sin,
37   If Saint Peter isn't careful,
38   Lord, she's gonna sneak <u>h</u>im in!

HARRY'S GAME
Eugene F. Lyttle

6. <u>H</u>ere comes a candle to light you to bed,
Here comes a chopper to chop off your <u>h</u>ead.

/ʍ/
or
/hw/

Production

The phoneme /ʍ/ (as in "<u>wh</u>en") is sometimes transcribed /hw/. However, the sound should not be separated into /h/ and /w/ because the latter component is voiced, whereas /h/ is unvoiced. Notice that the symbol looks something like the nasal /m/, with which it is often confused. In this text, /ʍ/ is classified as an unvoiced fricative having the **aspirate** (or breathy) characteristics of the /h/ phoneme. Like /h/, the phoneme /ʍ/ is influenced by the vowel or diphthong that it precedes. The sound is produced as the breath escapes between the slightly tensed vocal folds, which causes the frictional sound. In addition, upon production, the lips are rounded and the cheeks are blown out slightly. This adjustment of the cheeks feels most alien to Americans, but it is one of those characteristics that you are strongly encouraged to make a habit. Perhaps we need a "Save the /ʍ/ Phoneme" crusade.

Problems

Many Americans do not use this sound in their speech because they do not know that it exists. Instead, they use only the phoneme /w/. Others, because of sloppy articulation, poor auditory discrimination, or both, use the semivowel /w/ instead of /ʍ/. Believe it or not, there is a difference in the pronunciation (as well as in the meaning) between "weather" and "whether." The phoneme /ʍ/ is truly an endangered sound.

(((**EXERCISES**

In practicing the following exercises, it is natural to feel self-conscious while you learn how to produce an English sound you never realized existed! Use a mirror and make certain that when the sound is produced, your cheeks blow out a bit. Hold a piece of yarn (or some confetti, but only if you have maid service) ten to twelve inches from your mouth. Make the yarn move as you pronounce the /ʍ/ words. If you are producing the sound properly, you can see the action of your cheeks clearly. If you are beginning to look like Dizzy Gillespie, the trumpeter, you are overinflating your cheeks. However, that is a fine way to feel the sensation necessary for the production of this sound.

1. INITIAL   MEDIAL   FINAL

<u>wh</u>ip   some<u>wh</u>at   (does not occur in English)
<u>wh</u>ittle   no<u>wh</u>ere
<u>wh</u>isker   every<u>wh</u>ere
<u>wh</u>imper   bull<u>wh</u>ip
<u>wh</u>irl   else<u>wh</u>ere
<u>wh</u>istle   buck<u>wh</u>eat
<u>wh</u>eeze   free<u>wh</u>eeling
<u>wh</u>isper   a<u>wh</u>ile
<u>wh</u>ale   a<u>wh</u>irling
<u>wh</u>ere   bob<u>wh</u>ite

2. In the following word pairs, "Gillespie-ize" the second word, which contains the /ʍ/ phoneme. As in all introductory exercises, overdo the articulation. This sound, incidentally, occurs only in front of a vowel or diphthong. Make certain that when you pull away from the overarticulation, you maintain the same accuracy of articulation.

witch, <u>wh</u>ich   wither, <u>wh</u>ither
wear, <u>wh</u>ere   wen, <u>wh</u>en
wit, <u>wh</u>it   wine, <u>wh</u>ine
way, <u>wh</u>ey   Wight, <u>wh</u>ite
wail, <u>wh</u>ale   wile, <u>wh</u>ile
we'll, <u>wh</u>eel   wig, <u>Wh</u>ig
world, <u>wh</u>irled   woe, <u>wh</u>oa
wax, <u>wh</u>acks   Y, <u>wh</u>y
word, <u>wh</u>irred   wet, <u>wh</u>et
weather, <u>wh</u>ether   were, <u>wh</u>ir

3. Read aloud the following selections.

a. <u>Wh</u>ich witch is <u>wh</u>ich?

b. <u>Wh</u>en do wens go away?

c. Curds and <u>wh</u>ey

d. in a short <u>wh</u>ile

e. <u>Wh</u>at do <u>wh</u>ale wails sound like?

f. <u>Wh</u>y not join the Y instead of <u>wh</u>ining?

g. There are <u>wh</u>ite cliffs on the Isle of Wight.

h. Many <u>Wh</u>igs wore wigs.

i. The world is in a <u>wh</u>irl.

In the remaining exercises, compare /ʍ/ with /w/. The double underline is under the phoneme /ʍ/; the single underline is under the phoneme /w/. Yes, the pronunciation of /ʍ/ feels incorrect; look up the pronunciation of the words in the dictionary. And remember to blow out your cheeks.

4. What whim led Whitey White to whittle, whistle, whisper, and whimper near the wharf where a whale might wheel and whirl?

5. Oh, what a tangled web we weave,
   When first we practice to deceive!

   From MARMION
   Sir Walter Scott

6. We look forward to a world founded upon four essential human freedoms. The first is freedom of speech and expression— everywhere in the world. The second is freedom of every person to worship God in his own way— everywhere in the world. The third is freedom from want—anywhere in the world.

   From THE FOUR FREEDOMS
   Franklin D. Roosevelt

7. To go home and wear shorts forever
   in the enormous paddocks, in that warm climate,
   adding a sweater when winter soaks the grass.

   From THE DREAM OF WEARING SHORTS FOREVER
   Les A. Murray

8. I'll walk where my own nature would be leading—It vexes me to choose another guide—Where the grey flocks in ferny glens are feeding, Where the wild wind blows on the mountain-side.

   From OFTEN REBUKED
   Emily Brontë

9. This is the way the world ends
   Not with a bang but a whimper.

   From THE HOLLOW MEN
   T. S. Eliot

10. Whither, o splendid ship, thy white sails crowing,
    Leaning across the bosom of the urgent West,
    Whither away, fair rover, and What thy quest?

    From A PASSER-BY
    Robert Bridges

11. Home is the place where, when you have to go there,
    They have to take you in.

    From THE DEATH OF THE HIRED MAN
    Robert Frost

12. See the mermaid on the whale,
    "Whoa!" she cries, "Don't whisk your tail!"
    "Whoa!" she cries, "It makes me slip.
    Must I whack it with my whip?"
    Said the whale with a mournful whine,
    "Your tail whisks as well as mine;

Tails were made to <u>wh</u>isk and flop,
<u>Wh</u>acking will not make them stop."

Anonymous

>>>
FRICATIVE SIBILANTS

/s/
and
/z/

Production

The phonemes /s/ (as in "<u>s</u>ew") and /z/ (as in "<u>z</u>oo") are a cognate pair that are made with the blade of the tongue contacting the alveolar ridge. In addition, the sides of the tongue touch the inner edges of the upper teeth. A small groove is created down the middle of the tongue over which the escaping breath or voice is forced, causing the frictional sound. Some speakers produce the sounds with the tongue tip raised, others with the tongue tip remaining behind the lower teeth. The preferred production depends on the surrounding sounds.

Problems

There are perhaps more difficulties in the production of these cognates than in the production of any other sounds. Although the sounds are not classified as dental, the teeth are essential for proper production. Thus, a child learns to "speak" long before the permanent front teeth come in. As a result, some children develop a frontal lisp—the substitution of /θ/ and /ð/ for /s/ and /z/.

If for the /s/ or /z/ a child produces the /l/ formation and blows the air out over the sides of the tongue, he or she is exhibiting lateralization.

In producing /s/ or /z/, some people bring the top and bottom teeth together and make the groove down the center of the tongue too narrow, causing the sound to be too sharp. In males, the resulting sound is considered effeminate.

Another common error is the whistling /s/. If this is a problem, shorten the length of the sound during production. The whistle often results from the groove down the blade of the tongue being too narrow.

All too often a speaker touches the lower lip to the upper teeth in producing /s/ or /z/. This is another form of dentalizing. The lip should not be used in the formation of sibilants.

(((EXERCISES

Read aloud the following exercises, using overarticulation. Use a mirror to see how you produce the sounds. When you pull away from the overarticulation, make certain to produce your sounds precisely. To develop flexibility in producing /s/ and /z/, you might also read the exercises (1) with a frontal lisp, (2) with a lateral lisp, (3) with the top and bottom teeth together, and (4) using the lower lip. In creating characterizations, these faulty productions of /s/ and /z/ might prove helpful.

1. INITIAL	MEDIAL	FINAL
<u>s</u>eem	an<u>s</u>wer	noti<u>ce</u>
<u>S</u>unday	u<u>s</u>eful	hou<u>se</u>
<u>s</u>uddenly	ex<u>c</u>ited	gra<u>ss</u>
<u>s</u>oon	ex<u>c</u>ellent	ni<u>ce</u>
<u>c</u>ircle	ho<u>s</u>pital	jui<u>ce</u>

zipper	hazing	phase
zoo	lazy	chaise
xylophone	razor	craze
zink	sneezing	pays
zany	Caesar	prize

BLENDS: /sp/, /spl/, /sm/, /sn/, /st/, /stj/, /str/, /sl/, /sw/, /sk/, /skl/, /skr/, /skj/, /skw/, /spr/, AND /spj/

2.

/sp/	/spl/	/sm/	/sn/	/st/	/stj/	/str/[2]	/sl/
spider	splash	Smith	snip	step	stupid	strict	slash
spend	split	smell	snore	style	stew	street	slow
spell	splendid	small	snare	stare	Stewart	straight	slight
spite	splint	smooth	snap	store		strip	slime
spill	splurge	smart	sneeze	stamp		strength	slumber

/sw/	/sk/	/skl/	/skr/	/skj/	/skw/	/spr/	/spj/
swell	scare	sclerosis	scream	skewer	squid	spring	spew
sweet	skirt	sclera	scrunch	askew	square	sprain	spurious
swarm	scan	scleroid	scramble	skewbald	squash	sprig	sputum
swim	scarf		describe		squeeze	spray	
Sweden	skate		script		squirt	spread	

3.

seek and serve	aspirin please
selling roses	false advertising
fixed earnings	Saturdays and Thursdays
boys assisting	staring at stars

4. **a.** Sally sold the same materials every Saturday and Sunday.

   b. Snoopy spends most of his money in the spring.

   c. Chris has such super girls and grandsons.

   d. Nickolas speaks slowly and with special care.

   e. Sometimes there are pets in the zoo that can be raised in a house.

5. The little Reed, bending to the force of the wind, soon stood upright again when the storm had passed over.

   Aesop

6. Susan Simpson strolled sedately,
   Stifling sobs, suppressing sighs,
   Seeing Stephen Slocum, stately,
   She stopped, showing some surprise.

   "Say," said Stephen, "Sweetest sighter,
   Say, shall Stephen spouseless stay?"
   Susan, seeming somewhat shyer,
   Showed submissiveness straightaway.

   Summer's season slowly stretches,
   Susan Simpson Slocum she—

---

[2]Make certain that this blend /str/ is not pronounced /ʃtr/. Americans sometimes use this mispronounciation, making the speech sound uneducated. Germans are also apt to pronounce /str/ as /ʃtr/ as in the German word *Strasse*.

So she sighed some simple sketches—
Soul sought soul successfully.

Six Septembers Susan swelters;
Six sharp seasons snow supplies;
Susan's satin sofa shelters
Six small Slocums side by side.

Anonymous

7. I'm the last one. Still strapped in the chair in the corner. McMurphy stops when he gets to me and hooks his thumbs in his pockets again and leans back to laugh, like he sees something funnier about me than about anybody else.

From ONE FLEW OVER THE CUCKOO'S NEST
Ken Kesey

8. Left to herself Salomy Jane stared a long while at the coffee pot, and then called the two squaws who assisted her in her household duties to clear away the things while she went up to her own room to make her bed.

From SALOMY JANE'S KISS
Bret Harte

9. My mother danced all night and Roberta's was sick. That's why we were taken to St. Bonny's. People want to put their arms around you when you tell them you were in a shelter, but it really wasn't bad. No big long room with one hundred beds like Bellevue. There were four to a room, and when Roberta and me came, there was a shortage of state kids, so we were the only ones assigned to 406 and could go from bed to bed if we wanted to. And we wanted to, too. We changed beds every night and for the whole four months we were there we never picked one out as our own permanent bed.

From RECITATIF
Toni Morrison

/ʃ/ and /ʒ/

Production

The phonemes /ʃ/ (as in "ship") and /ʒ/ (as in "measure") are a cognate pair that are made by placing the tongue farther back in the mouth than for the production of /s/ and /z/ and by bringing the sides of the tongue in direct contact with the upper back teeth. The blade of the tongue almost touches the area of the palate just behind the alveolar ridge. When the breath or voice is forced through a groove down the center of the tongue and out through a narrow aperture between the upper and lower teeth, a frictional sound results. The lips should be slightly rounded and pursed forward.

Problems

Review the discussions of problems in articulating the fricative sibilants /s/ and /z/ and the plosive affricates /tʃ/ and /dʒ/. Many of the same errors made in producing those sounds are applicable here, including lateralization, whistling, and lower lip action.

(((EXERCISES

1. Read aloud the following word lists, exaggerating your production of /ʃ/ and /ʒ/. Make certain that you do not pull away too much from the overarticulation when trying to develop the appropriate sound.

INITIAL	MEDIAL	FINAL
ship	assure	wash
sheet	fissure	crash
Chicago	patient	mash
shack	cashier	leash
shirt	precious	dish
(No English	lesion	corsage
words begin	casual	mirage
with /ʒ/.)	confusion	camouflage
	occasion	barrage
	treasure	garage

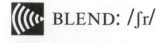 BLEND: /ʃr/

/ʃr/

shrink
shred
shrew
shriek
shrike
shrill
shrine
shrimp
shrivel
shrub

German speakers of English might have a little difficulty with the "sch" letters in English because they are pronounced with the /sk/ blend (see /sk/ blend on p. 152). In German, "sch" is pronounced /ʃ/ as in "ship." A few words spelled with the letters "schm" and "schn" have made their way into English from the German and Hebrew languages. The following words are found in English dictionaries and pronounced using the /ʃ/ as in "ship." These words are used in informal conversation.

schnauzer [ʃnauzəˈ]	schmaltz [ʃmaltz]	schnapps [ʃnaps]
schmo [ʃmo]	schnorkel [ʃnork]	
schmeer [ʃmɪr]	schlock [ʃlak]	

Germans will find the production of this consonant sound very difficult. Make certain to sufficiently drill sound discrimination. Exaggerate the articulation in the following exercises. However, do not pull away too much from the overarticulation when trying to develop the appropriate sound. Prolong the underlined letters.

2. washing dishes   confusion reigns
   harsh and windy oceans   seeking treasures
   wishing for more leisure time   casual shop

3. a. Trish ironed the freshly washed shirt.

   b. Frank Walsh took a short leisurely shower.

   c. The ocean liner *Shanghai* had a ship-to-shore radio on the shelf.

   d. Barbara finished the usual television treasure hunt.

   e. A lot of Asian sugar is sent to Iora in Chicago.

4. This har<u>sh</u> and untimely interrup<u>ti</u>on of summer is brought to you by Middlesex Bank. If your house could use a little ventila<u>ti</u>on and winterizing, summer is the time to do it.

5. <u>Sh</u>op for furni<u>sh</u>ings at <u>Ch</u>icago's newest <u>sh</u>opping mall.

6. Gustave A<u>sch</u>enbach—or von A<u>sch</u>enbach, as he had been known officially since his fifteenth birthday—had set out alone from his house in Prince Regent Street, Munich, for an extended walk.

From DEATH IN VENICE
Thomas Mann

7. Bob and Vangi put <u>Z</u>a<u>z</u>a's leash in the garage.

8. At Blair's lei<u>s</u>ure he ordered a corsa<u>ge</u> for Beverly.

>>>
LATERAL
/l/

Production

In the production of the voiced lateral /l/, the tip of the tongue touches the alveolar ridge and the sound escapes over the sides of the tongue. The /l/ phoneme is deceptive because its production cannot be easily seen.

There are two allophones of the phoneme /l/, a fact that complicates the situation even further. These are called the *light,* or *clear,* /l/ and the *dark* /l/. The dark /l/ is formed with the tongue farther back and lower than for the production of the light /l/. The light /l/ is used when the sound appears initially and is followed by a front vowel or diphthong. The dark /l/ is used in the medial and final positions or preceding a back vowel, as in the words *lower* and *lost.*

Problems

Sometimes /w/ is substituted for /l/ ("<u>w</u>ion" for "<u>l</u>ion"), although this pronunciation is rather rare among college-age students. Of course, another problem is the mixture of clear and dark allophones; this occurs more frequently among speakers learning English as a second language than among native speakers.

A fairly common error is to produce /l/ with the tip of the tongue behind the lower front teeth instead of touching the alveolar ridge. This unacceptable allophone of /l/ is called the **lambda**.

Care must be taken to produce the /l/ in the final position properly. Make certain that the tip of the tongue touches the alveolar ridge when pronouncing the words in the third column in exercise 1.

 EXERCISES

1. Read aloud the following word lists, exaggerating your articulation while prolonging the /l/. Make certain that you do not pull away too much from the overarticulation when trying to develop the appropriate sound.

INITIAL	MEDIAL	FINAL
<u>l</u>augh	a<u>l</u>one	broi<u>l</u>
<u>l</u>ong	a<u>l</u>as	mi<u>ll</u>

light	follow	kneel
late	hailed	motel
lawn	squalor	deal
lower	squealer	keel
lucky	believe	hall
learn	balloon	style
lunch	below	cruel
liver	bellow	pill

Read the lists again, but this time use the lambda by keeping the tongue tip down behind the lower front teeth during the production of the sound. Feel what the tongue is doing, and listen to the sound that the error produces. It has no place in career speech, even though some national communicators have this speech defect. Captain Hook's comment about Peter Pan also applies to the lambda: "That is the canker that g-naws!"

The easiest way of eliminating the lambda is to produce the proper /l/ phoneme in the initial position. This is because production is more easily seen when the phoneme is in the initial rather than the final position. Make certain that the back of the tongue is free from the velum and that you are using the front of the tongue to produce the sound. (The "Lambda People" can be very clever in lifting the tongue to touch the alveolar ridge, but they still produce the sound with the back of the tongue and velum.) After you have mastered the production of /l/ in the initial position, say the following words and connect them as indicated without changing the position of the tongue to any great degree. As you say the /l/ in the final position of the first word ("full"), think of the /l/ in the initial position (in "love").

full (of) → love	love → full
cool → lock	lock → cool
ball → lost	lost → ball
male → lady	lady → male
oil → lock	lock → oil
veal → lamb	lamb → veal
bale → late	late → bale
bowl → low	low → bowl

 # BLENDS: /pl/, /bl/, /fl/, /gl/, /kl/, AND /sl/

/pl/	/bl/	/fl/
plate	blink	flip
plume	blood	flock
plant	blew	fly
plenty	blister	flat
fireplace	blush	aflame
airplane	bland	flower

/gl/	/kl/	/sl/	/rl/ (in final position)
globe	clock	slipper	Karl
glide	clothes	slap	spiral
glance	clever	sleep	hurl
glacier	clear	sled	pearl
glimpse	clipper	slide	snarl
glory	clerk	slippery	carl

Read aloud the following selections, and prolong the underlined letters.

2. lovely Lucy Lake   believe in learning
   leaving all alone   pull the balloons
   place broiler in oven   lucky in love

3. a. Lea and Lew are lovely people.

   b. The balloon flew below the lightning clouds.

   c. Lunch is served with great style at the Hotel Cecil Clayton.

   d. Elizabeth walked[3] all alone on the yellow line.

   e. When will someone reveal the hidden secrets of life?

4. José María Rivera always read important letters with a red pencil in his hand. They were letters written in *castellano*[4]—he sometimes called it *cristiano*, his eyes rolling, his voice serious—by people who knew or should have known the language as well or better than he did, which is what made the letters important. He read first for spelling errors, rapidly, crossing out, adding, changing, circling, then he went back for a second reading to seize anything that had escaped his initial sweep. In repeated readings, finally, he concentrated on what the letters said.

From LEARN! LEARN!
Hugo Martinez-Serros

5. New York! At first your beauty confused me, and your great longlegged golden girls.
   I was so timid at first under your blue metallic eyes, your frosty smile
   So timid. And the disquiet in the depth of your skyscraper streets
   Lifting up owl eyes in the sun's eclipse.

From NEW YORK
Léopold Sédar Senghor

6. Braving the bitter cold, I traveled more than seven hundred miles back to the old home I had left over twenty years before.
   It was late winter. As we drew near my former home the day became overcast and a cold wind blew into the cabin of our boat, while all one could see through the chinks in our bamboo awning were a few desolate villages, void of any sign of life, scattered far and near under the somber yellow sky. I could not help feeling depressed.

From MY OLD HOME
Lu Xün

7. Inem was one of the girls I knew. She was eight years old—two years older than me. She was no different from the others. And if there was a difference, it was that she was one of the prettier little girls in our neighborhood. People liked to look at her. She was polite, unspoiled, deft, and hard-working—qualities which quickly spread her fame even into other neighborhoods as a girl who would make a good daughter-in-law.

From INEM
Pramoedya Ananta Toer

8. The low, undulating Danish landscape was silent and serene, mysteriously wide-awake in the hour before sunrise. There was not a cloud in the pale sky, not a shadow along the dim, pearly fields, hills and woods. The mist was lifting from the valleys and hollows, the air was cool, the grass and the foliage dripping wet with morning-dew. Unwatched

---

[3]Nonnative speakers often incorrectly produce the silent *l* in "walked."
[4]The double *ll* letters in Spanish are pronounced /j/ (as in "yellow").

by the eyes of man, and undisturbed by his activity, the country breathed a timeless life, to which language was inadequate.

From SORROW-ACRE
Isak Dinesen (Karen Blixen)

9. He had traversed plow-furrowed fields when silence, imminent with violence, weighted him down like a pack. He had traversed shell-pelted fields when fear tangled his legs like a barricade. He had seen his enemy and his comrades sprawled grotesque and cold in the neutrality of death, as impersonal as the cows among them, angling stiff legs to the sky.

From THE HUNTERS
Harris Downey

10. [Phoenix Jackson] . . . was very old and small and she walked slowly in the dark pine shadows, moving a little from side to side in her steps, with the balanced heaviness and lightness of a pendulum in a grandfather clock. She carried a thin, small cane made from an umbrella, and with this she kept tapping the frozen earth in front of her.

From A WORN PATH
Eudora Welty

Semivowels

/r/

Production

The phoneme /r/ (as in "run") is a voiced semivowel produced with tension in the center of the tongue; the tongue tip is elevated toward the hard palate, and the lips are slightly rounded.

Problems

One of the reasons that /r/ is a problem for many speakers is that proper production of the sound requires a gliding movement of the tongue and lips. The tongue tip is elevated toward the alveolar ridge and glides downward when the sound is completed. The lips are slightly pursed at the beginning of production and are relaxed when the sound is completed. It is impossible to put the articulators in a set position and produce the sound, as in /p/ or /v/. Another cause of difficulty is that the sound cannot be seen in production; the action of the tongue can only be described and felt.

Some speakers curl the tongue tip too much toward the hard palate, producing a very heavy-sounding /r/. This is quite characteristic of some Midwesterners. If you have this heavy-sounding /r/, bring the tongue tip forward but not down.

Other speakers produce the /r/ phoneme with the tongue tip down behind the lower front teeth. The difficulty in this case is in getting the speaker to feel the action of the tongue because the only portion of the sound's production that can be observed is the slight rounding of the lips. Often the sound becomes labialized through the excessive use of the lips. This is particularly evident in some Eastern speech. This articulation certainly has its advantages in creating a character type—a character that does not reflect trained speech.

New Englanders (and others) tend to make additional efforts relating to the /r/ phoneme, such as adding or omitting the /r/. These characteristics will be discussed in a subsequent chapter.

 EXERCISES

Read aloud the following exercises without the accustomed exaggerated articulation. Because the production of the sound is visually obstructed and an exaggeration of the sound might promote the heavy Midwestern /r/, you should articulate the phoneme appropriately. However, your habitual production of the sound may be inappropriate. If so, get used to increasing the articulatory movements.

1. A helpful way of teaching the /r/ phoneme is to introduce the vowel sound "er" before /r/ in the initial position. It is very important not only to prolong the vowel sound but also to feel the tension in the lips before moving on to the production of the consonant /r/. The consonant is produced through the release of the lips. Do not take a pause or a break between the end of the vowel and the beginning of the consonant. Say the following:

run	"eeerrrrrr" → [rʌn]
rough	"eeerrrrrr" → [rʌf]
red	"eeerrrrrr" → [rɛd]
roll	"eeerrrrrr" → [rol]
race	"eeerrrrrr" → [res]
rave	"eeerrrrrr" → [rev]

BLENDS: /fr/, /pr/, /tr/, /dr/, /kr/, /br/, /gr/, /θr/, /str/, AND /spr/

frame	/f/	"eeerrrrrr" → [rem] [frem]
pray	/p/	"eeerrrrrr" → [re] [pre]
train	/t/	"eeerrrrrr" → [ren] [tren]
dream	/d/	"eeerrrrrr" → [rim] [drim]
cream	/k/	"eeerrrrrr" → [rim] [krim]
brown	/b/	"eeerrrrrr" → [raʊn] [braʊn]
gross	/gr/	"eeerrrrrr" → [ros][gros]
thrill	/θ/	"eeerrrrrr" → [rɪl] [θrɪl]
strong	/st/	"eeerrrrrr" → [rɔŋ] [strɔŋ]
spring	/spr/	"eeerrrrrr" → [rɪŋ][sprɪŋ]

2. The first time you read the following word lists, add the "er" vowel sound before each word in the first column. Feel, visualize, and listen to the production of each sound.

INITIAL	MEDIAL	FINAL
ripe	arrive	care
rent	carpet	hear
really	carriage	wear
rant	horrible	jar
rim	around	fire
right	garbage	par
rave	very	scare
rotten	bearing	there
rough	barren	tour
rhyme	oral	four

3. Because the phoneme /r/ does not appear in Asian languages, it presents real difficulties for nonnative Asians learning the English language. This phoneme is very common in

English (just look at the number of times Vanna White has to turn it around); therefore, it is important to learn its production. Because this phoneme is such a rascal, the following word lists include the consonant blends involving the phoneme /r/. As with the previous word lists, the first time you read aloud the exercise you should exaggerate the /r/ to get the feeling of the blend, although you are actually producing the vowel /ɝ/ (as in "her"). (For a more detailed discussion of the vowel /ɝ/, see pp. 98–100.)

/pr/	/br/	/tr/	/dr/	/kr/
proud	brown	trip	drip	cream
print	brought	trump	drum	cringe
prom	bright	trick	droop	crime
problem	brim	trim	dram	crone
pram	brash	troop	drawn	crown
promote	bring	truck	dreary	crag
prim	Bret	trollop	draft	crunch
pronto	brag	tray	dream	crowd
preppy	bray	trunk	dragon	crepe
prattle	brother	tram	dry	craft

/gr/	/fr/	/θr/	/str/	/spr/
grim	frown	thrive	strong	spray
ground	frame	thrill	struggle	spry
great	frump	throne	streak	sprout
grant	Frances	threat	stroll	sprain
grudge	frill	thrust	street	spring
green	front	throttle	strip	sprawl
grand	friend	through	stripe	spread
greet	French	throb	stream	spruce
graft	freeze	thrown	strict	sprinkle
grown	fragile	thrash	strap	bedspring

Read aloud the following selections.

4. right and wrong   strapping the spring
a graft to the fragile branch   against the grain
a thorough sprinkle of rain   the rotting railing and step

5. a. Are the brakes the problem with the brown truck?

b. Around the ground are located the frozen patches.

c. Through the round circle[5] you can see the right cross.

d. Bret's bicycle has a great big bright stripe.

e. Frances and Margaret strapped themselves in and hit the throttle.

6. All religion, all life, all art, all expression come down to this: to the effort[5] of the human soul to break through its barrier of loneliness, of intolerable loneliness, and make some contact with another seeking soul.

From CHAPTERS FOR THE ORTHODOX
Donald Marqui

7. John Gray jerked[5] his head towards Rose. Minni's bare heels struck her[5] horse's belly. With a turn[5] of the wrist she swung her horse off from the mob, turned,[5] leaned forward,

---

[5]In this word, and in many others in this exercise, the *r* letters are often a vowel (either /ɚ/ or /ɝ/) instead of a consonant.

rising in her stirrups,[5] and came up with Rose. But the glitter[5] and tumult of Rose's eyes, Minni looked away from them.

From THE COOBOO
Katharine Susannah Prichard

8. He rolled over[5] the roof to a chimney stack in the rear, and slowly drew himself up behind it, until his eyes were level with the top of the parapet.

From THE SNIPER
Liam O'Flaherty

9. Dancing is wonderful[5] training for girls;[5] it's the first[5] way you learn[5] to guess what a man is going to do before he does it.

From KITTY FOYLE
Christopher[5] Morley

10. Mother's[5] stress may be caused in part by

a
Teenage Attitude
like
I don't have to listen to you!
You can't tell me what to do!
I'll smoke, and drink, and pierce my ears
and dress real cool just like my peers,
with chains, and gloves, and colored[5] hair,
that causes folks to stop and stare
and mutter[5] ugly things at me
but I don't care! I'm young; I'm free!

I know my grades are not the best,
but I won't study for a test.
Why should I waste my time that way?
I'd rather just "hang out" all day.

So, Ma, get off my case—ask Dad—
he'll tell you I'm not really bad.
Just going through a stage, you see.
I'm young; I'm cool, and oh, so free.
(But Ma, please Ma, take care of me.)

From TEENAGE ATTITUDE
Father Eugene F. Lyttle

/w/

Production

The bilabial, voiced /w/ (as in "well") is made with a gliding movement of the lips that is similar to the pursed position of the lips used in producing the vowel /u/ (as in "true"). The tongue is elevated toward the back. In English, /w/ is found only before a vowel sound.

Problems

The phoneme /w/ is not a difficult sound either to produce or to teach. The major difficulty with the sound occurs when it is substituted for the voiceless /ʍ/. Reread aloud the exercises for discriminating between /w/ and /ʍ/ on pages 148–151.

In addition, nonnative English speakers sometimes substitute /v/ for /ʍ/ ("vade" for "wade").

EXERCISES

Read aloud the following exercises with exaggerated articulation before pulling away to the appropriate articulation.

1.

INITIAL	MEDIAL	FINAL
witty	upward	(does not occur)
walk	awake	
worm	award	
wife	unwind	
wash	anyone	
wonder	liquid	
weigh	highway	
woman	inquest	
with	require	
wall	unworthy	

2. without winding the watch   require a liquid
   with a watchful eye   Wild Will from Wyoming
   "Wishing Will Make It So"   wall-to-wall carpeting

3. **a.** Warren's witty wife was very willing to tell a joke.

   b. Would the woman require a pass to get into the White House?

   c. Juanita wishes that her wallet were made of walnut wood.

   d. The award was for winning the high jump.

   e. Winifred wondered what the requirements would be.

4. Those who have wealth must be watchful and wary.

   From I'D BE A BUTTERFLY
   Thomas Bayly

5. The witch said she was from Walla Walla, Washington.

6. They were going to throw her away when she was a baby. The doctors said she was too tiny, too frail, that she wouldn't live. They performed the baptism right there in the sink between their pots of boiling water and their rows of shining instruments, chose who would be her godparents, used water straight from the tap. Her father, however, wouldn't hear one word of it.

   From MY MOTHER'S STORIES
   Tony Ardizzone

7. Was ever woman in this humour wooed?
   Was ever woman in this humour won?

   From RICHARD III
   William Shakespeare

8. Long time ago
   in the beginning
   there were no white people in this world
   there was nothing European.
   And this world might have gone on like that
   except for one thing:

<u>w</u>itchery.
This <u>w</u>orld <u>w</u>as already complete
even <u>w</u>ithout white people.
There <u>w</u>as everything
including <u>w</u>itchery.

From [LONG TIME AGO]
Leslie Marmon Silko

9. If love <u>w</u>ere what the rose is,
And I <u>w</u>ere like the leaf,
Our lives <u>w</u>ould grow together
In sad or singing <u>w</u>eather.

A MATCH
Algernon Swinburne

10. He <u>w</u>ent through the <u>W</u>et <u>W</u>ild <u>W</u>oods, <u>w</u>aving his <u>w</u>ild tail, and <u>w</u>alking by his <u>w</u>ild
lone. But he never told anybody.

From THE CAT THAT <u>W</u>ALKED BY HIMSELF
Rudyard Kipling

/j/

Production

The voiced semivowel /j/ (as in "yard") glides from the /i/ position (as in "s<u>ee</u>") toward the
vowel that follows it. The front portion of the tongue is elevated and tense. In English, /j/,
like /w/, is found only before a vowel sound.

Problems

Most of the problems associated with the production of this sound are found among nonnative speakers of English.

EXERCISES

*Read aloud the following exercises, and overarticulate. For your own speech standard,
make certain that you do not pull away too much.*

1.

INITIAL	MEDIAL	FINAL
<u>y</u>ard	on<u>i</u>on	(does not occur)
<u>y</u>et	compan<u>i</u>on	
<u>y</u>ellow	jun<u>i</u>or	
<u>y</u>awn	mill<u>i</u>on	
<u>E</u>urope	can<u>y</u>on	
<u>Y</u>ankee	un<u>i</u>on	
<u>y</u>oung	bun<u>i</u>on	
<u>y</u>esterday	stall<u>i</u>on	
<u>y</u>ear	be<u>y</u>ond	
<u>y</u>es	gen<u>i</u>us	

2. *The <u>Y</u>oung and the Restless*   *Yankee Clipper*
<u>y</u>esterday's <u>y</u>outh   <u>y</u>our colorful cra<u>y</u>ons
the Grand Can<u>y</u>on   <u>Y</u>osemite National Park
be<u>y</u>ond the limit   <u>y</u>onder in the <u>y</u>ard

3. **a.** The mayor of York was very young.

   b. Daniel's companion was a senior.

   c. William yawned at yesterday's boring lecture.

   d. He yearns for yams and a Yankee dinner.

   e. Yoke Yellow is a strange color for a yacht.

   f. Yesterday, William Gilbert Junior was yearning for a bigger backyard.

4. In winter I get up at night
   And dress by yellow candle-light.

   From BED IN SUMMER
   Robert Louis Stevenson

5. Children of yesterday,
   Heirs of tomorrow.

   From SONG OF HOPE
   Mary Lathbury

6. Oh, yer's yer good old whiskey,
   Drink it down.

   From TWO MEN OF SANDY BAR
   Bret Harte

7. Bards of Passion and of Mirth,
   Ye have left your souls on earth!
   Have ye souls in heaven too?

   From ODE: BARDS OF PASSION AND OF MIRTH
   John Keats

>>> NASALS

/m/

Production

The voiced nasal sound /m/ (as in "my") is made by closing the lips and relaxing the velum, which pulls it down and allows the sound to resonate through the nose. In the production of /m/, the teeth are slightly apart.

Problems

The main difficulty in producing the /m/ phoneme occurs when there is an obstruction interfering with the nasal emission of breath; in such cases a physician should be consulted. The exercises for eliminating denasality might also prove helpful. (See pp. 65–66.)

 EXERCISES

Read aloud the following exercises with exaggerated articulation. Feel what is occurring as the nasal sound is produced. Remember—do not pull away too much in order to achieve appropriate articulation.

1.

INITIAL	MEDIAL	FINAL
mate	demean	form
middle	demolish	climb
mine	someday	home
Monday	cement	column
make	terminal	game
march	umbrella	groom
month	semester	autumn
mob	comfortable	phlegm
myth	teamwork	foam
murder	humanity	grime

2. removing many spots climbing the mountains

the comfortable sofa Monday, March 10

summertime fun humane transformation

camel coat framing portraits

3. a. Jim and Matthew swam a mile or more.

  b. Becka's "Mighty Meal" was mashed potatoes and roasted lamb.

  c. Mary's mouth has been painful for a month.

  d. Mark's sense of humor must be remembered.

  e. Many animals are meant to roam.

  f. maggie and milly and molly and may
    went down to the beach (to play one day)

From MAGGIE AND MILLY AND MOLLY AND MAY
e. e. cummings

4. Call me Ishmael. Some years ago—never mind how long precisely—having little or no money in my purse, and nothing particular to interest me on shore, I thought I would sail about a little and see the watery part of the world.

From MOBY DICK
Herman Melville

5. A gentleman friend and I were dining at the Ritz last evening and he said that if I took a pencil and paper and put down all of my thoughts it would make a book. This almost made me smile as what it would really make would be a whole row of encyclopedias. I mean I seem to be thinking practically all the time.

From GENTLEMEN PREFER BLONDES
Anita Loos

6. Dear Ma, January, 1980

I was depressed over Christmas, and when New Year's rolled around, do you know what one of my resolves was? Not to come by and see you as much anymore. I had to ask myself why I get so down when I'm with you, my mother, who has focused so much of her life on me, who has endured so much; one who I am proud of and respect so deeply for simply surviving.

From LETTER TO MA
Merle Woo

7. As Gregor Samsa awoke one morning from uneasy dreams he found himself transformed in his bed into a gigantic insect. He was lying on his hard, as if it were armor-plated, back and when he lifted his head a little he could see his dome-like brown belly divided into stiff arched segments on top of which the quilt could hardly keep in position and was about to slide off completely. His numerous legs, which were pitifully thin compared to the rest of his bulk, waved helplessly before his eyes.

From THE METAMORPHOSIS
Franz Kafka

8. The young man's impression of his prospective pupil, who had first come into the room, as if to see for himself, as soon as Pemberton was admitted, was not quite the soft solicitation the visitor had taken for granted. . . . Pemberton was modest—he was even timid; and the chance that his small scholar might prove cleverer than himself had quite figured, to his nervousness, among the dangers of an untried experiment.

From THE PUPIL
Henry James

/n/   Production

The voiced nasal sound /n/ (as in "no") is made with a closure created by the tongue tip touching the alveolar ridge; the relaxed velum allows the breath to escape through the nose.

Problems

In some words the letter *n* is improperly pronounced as the phoneme /m/. This assimilation takes place because the sound that follows is a bilabial, and imprecise articulation is easier for the vocal mechanism. Examples of such words include the following:

unpleasant	unblessed	unpatriotic
unbutton	unborn	unbolt
unpardonable	unburden	unpolished
unbind	unbaptized	unbridled
unbending	unbleached	unbrushed

Sometimes the lingua-velar nasal /ŋ/ should be substituted for /n/, but sometimes it is substituted erroneously. In all of these instances, the /n/ phoneme is followed by either /k/ or /g/, which, except for the nasality, has the same articulatory adjustment as /ŋ/. Again, because of assimilation, it is easier to pronounce these words using /ŋ/, whether it is correct or not. Check with your dictionary to determine whether /ŋ/ should be used. Using negative practice, exaggerate the incorrect pronunciation and then exaggerate the proper pronunciation in the following list of words:

congressional[6]	include
congruent[7]	incapacity
congratulate	incantation
incomplete	incline
enclose	inclement
inclusive	incoherent
incognito	income

(For additional words, refer to p. 200.)

Often the /n/ phoneme turns into a dentalized /m/ when followed by a labio-dental /f/ or /v/. Feel how easy it is to say "imfant" for "*infant*." The symbol /m̪/ indicates an /m/ with dentalization. Therefore, the word *infant* would be transcribed as ['ɪm̪fənt].

---

[6]Notice that *congress* maintains the /ŋ/ phoneme.
[7]*Congruent* may be pronounced with /n/ or /ŋ/.

Using negative practice, say each of the following words, first exaggerating the error and then exaggerating the articulation:

confer	infernal	invade
confess	infant	inveigle
confetti	infantile	invert
confident	infect	invest
confine	infest	invisible
confirm	infinite	invite

(For additional words, refer to p. 201.)

Sometimes /n/ is erroneously omitted, particularly when /n/ is followed by /m/. This is one of the sound combinations that you ought to develop if you desire trained speech. Using negative practice, omit the /n/ phoneme in each of the following words. Feel what is wrong as you intentionally exaggerate the error. Then, repeat the list producing the /n/ phoneme with exaggeration. When you pull away, make certain that you don't underarticulate the production of the word.

government	adjournment
environment	assignment
lean more	adornment
earn more	consignment
can make	corn meal
Ann Miller	Ben Macy

EXERCISES

1. Overarticulate the correct pronunciation of the words in the following lists. Then, pull away from the overarticulation, but not too much!

INITIAL	MEDIAL	FINAL
knowledge	grinning	spoon
knit	announce	open
nimble	annual	heaven
neck	demand	crown
nice	Danny	began
nothing	fence	token
nail	funny	scene
nasal	standing	main
natural	bench	swoon
never	blond	burn

Read aloud the selections in exercises 2 through 9.

2. dinner on the menu   demand an answer
   standing on the corner   nothing is new
   Never on Sunday   beginnings and endings
   sincere analysis   Flannery O'Connor

3. **a.** Norman's painful knees stop him from kneeling.

   b. Nelson didn't mean to knock down the bean garden.

   c. The burning bundle was found near the fender of the car.

d. Pneumonia is a dangerous and nasty disease.

e. Natalie's niece Anne knew better than to run down the lane.

4. Once upon a sunny morning a man who sat in a breakfast nook looked up from his scrambled eggs to see a white unicorn with a gold horn quietly cropping the roses in the garden.

From THE UNICORN IN THE GARDEN
James Thurber

5. No man is an island, entire of itself; every man is a piece of the continent, a part of the main.

From DEVOTIONS UPON EMERGENT OCCASIONS
John Donne

6. The Gentleman Caller in this play is attempting to instill some confidence in his friend Tom's sister Laura, a young lame woman who was "intrigued" by Jim in high school.

1 Jim (*sits on the arm-chair right, faces Laura*): I'm glad to see that you have a sense
2 of humor. You know—you're . . . different from anybody else I know! Do you mind
3 me telling you that? I mean it. . . . You make me feel sort of—I don't know how to
4 put it! . . . Has anybody ever told you that you were pretty? (*rises, crosses to Laura*)
5 Well, you are! In a very different way from anyone else. And all the nicer because of
6 the difference, too. I wish that you were my sister. I'd teach you to have some
7 confidence in yourself. . . . Being different is nothing to be ashamed of. Because
8 other people are not such wonderful people. They're one hundred times one thousand.
9 You're one times one! They walk all over the earth. You just stay here. They're
10 common as—weeds, but—you, well you're—Blue Roses!

From THE GLASS MENAGERIE
Tennessee Williams

7. How do you do?
No, I am not Chinese.
No, not Spanish.
No, I am American Indi-uh, Native American.
No, not from India.
No, not Apache.
No, not Navajo.
No, not Sioux.
No, we are not extinct.
Yes, Indin.

From SURE YOU CAN ASK ME A PERSONAL QUESTION
Diane Burns

8. I want live things in their pride to remain.
I will not kill one grasshopper vain.

From THE SANTA FE TRAIL
Vachel Lindsay

9. My apple trees will never get across
And eat the cones under his pines, I tell him.

From MENDING WALL
Robert Frost

/ŋ/

Production

This is a voiced nasal with strong contact between the back of the tongue and the velum. The velum is relaxed, allowing the sound to resonate through the nose.

Problems

The nasal /ŋ/ (as in "ri<u>ng</u>") is a single sound, like /m/ or /n/. The most common confusion in its production stems from its expression as two letters, *n* and *g*. However, there is no sound of the phoneme /n/ in the phoneme, nor of the phoneme /g/. Three common errors are made in the production of /ŋ/. Many untrained speakers (and, alas, even some trained ones) make the first error: substituting /n/ for /ŋ/. Such speech thieves say "goin'" for "going" and "comin'" for "coming." Unfortunately, the error is so prevalent that writers indicate the substituted sound with the apostrophe. But you are not leaving off the "g"—you are using a full-fledged sound-for-sound substitution!

The second error is to pronounce the /ŋ/ (as in "ri<u>ng</u>") and then add the plosive /g/, as in "He is a singer's singer" ([hi ɪz ə sɪŋɡɚz sɪŋɡɚ]). This error is often called the "ng" click. It is caused partly by a misconception of the sound and partly from the bad habit of producing a sound as the tongue drops down from the velum. The letters *ing* are misleading (especially to someone who is still learning English) because they imply two sounds where only one exists. This error is *never* accepted in career speech; in fact, it sometimes arouses ethnic prejudice, even though no one ethnic or religious group makes this error more than other groups. Generally, anyone who has learned English as a second language makes this error, which can be passed along to subsequent generations. As has been mentioned time and time again, habit is immeasurably strong!

The third error involves the substitution of /in/ for /ŋ/ in the "ing" combination. This is true particularly when the sound combination occurs in the final position.

EXERCISES

1. *Substitution of /n/ for /ŋ/.* In the following exercise, use negative practice when you pronounce each word in the middle column. Exaggerate the pronunciations, and make certain that you do not pull back too much to gain the appropriate articulation.

	CAREER	ERROR	CAREER
going	[goɪŋ]	[goɪn] [goən]	[goɪŋ]
doing	[duɪŋ]	[duɪn] [duən]	[duɪŋ]
walking	[wɔkɪŋ]	[wɔkɪn] [wɔkən]	[wɔkɪŋ]
following	[fɑloɪŋ]	[fɑloɪn] [fɑloən]	[fɑloɪŋ]
jumping	[dʒʌmpɪŋ]	[dʒʌmpɪn] [dʒʌmpən]	[dʒʌmpəŋ]

2. *Addition of /g/ or /k/.* To understand the kinesics involved, make a strong closure in producing /ŋ/ and then add the /g/ or /k/ after you have held the nasal for a few seconds. Repeat this several times. Feel the addition of the /g/ and /k/ each time. (These pronunciations are transcribed as /ŋːg/ and /ŋːk/. The modifying mark placed after a sound prolongs it.)

/ŋː → g/	/ŋː → k/
/ŋː → g/	/ŋː → k/
/ŋː → g/	/ŋː → k/
/ŋː → g/	/ŋː → k/
/ŋː → g/	/ŋː → k/

anger	[ˈæŋɡɚ][8]	anchor	[ˈæŋkɚ]
angle	[ˈæŋɡl̩][8]	ankle	[ˈæŋkl̩]
tingle	[ˈtɪŋɡl̩][8]	tinkle	[ˈtɪŋkl̩]
spangle	[ˈspæŋɡl̩][8]	strength[9]	[strɛŋkθ][8] [strɛŋθ]
wangle	[ˈwæŋɡl̩]	length[9]	[lɛŋkθ] [lɛŋθ]
mingle	[ˈmɪŋɡl̩]	mink	[mɪŋk]
linger	[ˈlɪŋɡɚ]	pharynx[9]	[ˈærɪŋks]
English	[ˈɪŋɡlɪʃ]	sank	[sæŋk]

3. The correct pronunciation of /ŋ/ is made more complicated by the fact that there are a few words in which a /g/ "should" follow /ŋ/ (including those in column 1 in exercise 2). After you overarticulate and use negative practice in pronouncing the following comparative adjectives, repeat the exercise with appropriate articulation. Remember not to pull away too much.

	CAREER	ERROR	CAREER
strong	[strɔŋ]	[strɔŋɡ]	[strɔŋ]
stronger	[strɔŋɡɚ]	[strɔŋɚ]	[strɔŋɡɚ]
strongest	[strɔŋɡɪst]	[strɔŋɪst]	[strɔŋɡɪst]
long	[lɔŋ]	[lɔŋɡ]	[lɔŋ]
longer	[lɔŋɡɚ]	[lɔŋɚ]	[lɔŋɡɚ]
longest	[lɔŋɡɪst]	[lɔŋɪst]	[lɔŋɡɪst]
young	[jʌŋ]	[jʌŋɡ]	[jʌŋ]
younger	[jʌŋɡɚ]	[jʌŋɚ]	[jʌŋɡɚ]
youngest	[jʌŋɡɪst]	[jʌŋɪst]	[jʌŋɡɪst]

4. Generally, when a suffix is added to a root word, the /g/ is not added. In the word *ringer*, the suffix is added to the root word *ring*, which is a recognizable English word. Therefore, /g/ is not added to the /ŋ/. The same rule applies to a gerund, a noun using the "ing" form of the verb (for example, cooking). Use negative practice and overarticulation in the pronunciation of the following words; then repeat with appropriate articulation.

	CAREER	ERROR	CAREER
longing	[lɔŋɪŋ]	[lɔŋɡɪŋ]	[lɔŋɪŋ]
singer	[sɪŋɚ]	[sɪŋɡɚ]	[sɪŋɚ]
coat hanger	[kot hæŋɚ]	[kot hæŋɡɚ]	[kot hæŋɚ]
swinger	[swɪŋɚ]	[swɪŋɡɚ]	[swɪŋɚ]
bringer	[brɪŋɚ]	[brɪŋɡɚ]	[brɪŋɚ]
laughing	[læfɪŋ]	[læfɪŋɡ]	[læfɪŋ]
coaxing	[koksɪŋ]	[koksɪŋɡ]	[koksɪŋ]
singing	[sɪŋɪŋ]	[sɪŋɡɪŋ]	[sɪŋɪŋ]
belonging	[bɪlɔŋɪŋ]	[bɪlɔŋɡɪŋ]	[bɪlɔŋɪŋ]

---

[8]When "ng" comes together in the same syllable, usually only the /n/ is used alone. There are exceptions as in "strength" [strɛŋkθ]. In words of two syllables (like anger and tingle), the /g/ is added to begin the second syllable.
[9]The first pronunciation of these words contains the /k/ phoneme. However, the words may be legitimately pronounced with or without the /k/.

ringing	[rɪŋɪŋ]	[rɪŋgɪŋ]	[rɪŋɪŋ]
clinging	[klɪŋɪŋ]	[klɪŋgɪŋ]	[klɪŋɪŋ]

5. If the letters *ng* occur in a nonsense syllable, the /g/ is added to the /ŋ/; examples are the words *linger* and *finger*. To most of us "to ling" and "to fing" would not be acceptable infinitives. They are a part of the entire word. Use negative practice and overarticulation in the following word lists. Then, repeat the exercise with appropriate articulation.

	CAREER	ERROR	CAREER
linger	[lɪŋgɚ]	[lɪŋɚ]	[lɪŋgɚ]
finger	[fɪŋgɚ]	[fɪŋɚ]	[fɪŋgɚ]
mangle	[mæŋgl̩]	[mæŋl̩]	[mæŋgl̩]
jungle	[dʒʌŋgl̩]	[dʒʌŋl̩]	[dʒʌŋgl̩]
Congress	[kɑŋgrəs]	[kɑŋrəs]	[kɑŋgrəs]
tangle	[tæŋgl̩]	[tæŋl̩]	[tæŋgl̩]
penguin	[pɛŋgwɪn]¹⁰	[pɛŋwɪn]	[pɛŋgwɪn]
language	[læŋgwɪdʒ]	[læŋwɪdʒ]	[læŋgwɪdʒ]
wrangle	[ræŋgl̩]	[ræŋl̩]	[ræŋgl̩]
bingo	[bɪŋgo]	[bɪŋo]	[bɪŋgo]
distinguish	[dɪstɪŋgwɪʃ]	[dɪstɪŋwɪʃ]	[dɪstɪŋgwɪʃ]
shingle	[ʃɪŋgl̩]	[ʃɪŋl̩]	[ʃɪŋgl̩]
Singapore	[sɪŋgəpor]¹¹	[sɪŋəpor]	[sɪŋgəpor]

6. Use overarticulation as you read aloud the following list of words that contain /ŋ/, /g/, and /k/ combinations; these words are transcribed into career speech. Then, repeat the exercise using appropriate articulation. Feel what is happening as you produce these various sounds.

monkey	[ˈmʌŋkɪ]	larynx	[ˈlærɪŋks]
singing	[ˈsɪŋɪŋ]	elongate	[iˈlɔŋget]
tongue	[tʌŋ]	sinker	[ˈsɪŋkɚ]
Brinker	[ˈbrɪŋkɚ]	wrangle	[ˈræŋgl̩]
Frankfort	[ˈfræŋkfɚt]	stringy	[ˈstrɪŋɪ]
meringue	[məˈræŋ]	gangway	[ˈgæŋwe]
gangrene	[ˈgæŋgrin]	clinging	[ˈklɪŋɪŋ]
clinker	[ˈklɪŋkɚ]	Ming	[mɪŋ]

7. Use negative practice and overarticulation as you read aloud the following phrases. Then, repeat the exercise with appropriate articulation. Feel what is happening as you produce these various sounds.

	CAREER	ERROR	CAREER
going out	[goɪŋ aʊt]	[goɪŋg aʊt]	[goɪŋ aʊt]
wrong answer	[rɔŋ ænsɚ]	[rɔŋg ænsɚ]	[rɔŋ ænsɚ]
ringing a bell	[rɪŋɪŋ ə bɛl]	[rɪŋgɪŋ ə bɛl]	[rɪŋɪŋ ə bɛl]
Long Island	[lɔŋ aɪlənd]	[lɔŋg aɪlənd]	[lɔŋ aɪlənd]
hang on	[hæŋ ɑn]	[hæŋg ɑn]	[hæŋ ɑn]
coming in	[kʌmɪŋ ɪn]	[kʌmɪŋg ɪn]	[kʌmɪŋ ɪn]
singing a song	[sɪŋɪŋ ə sɔŋ]	[sɪŋgɪŋ ə sɔŋg]	[sɪŋɪŋ ə sɔŋ]
running along	[rʌnɪŋ əlɔŋ]	[rʌnɪŋg əlɔŋg]	[rʌnɪŋ əlɔŋ]
baking a pie	[bekɪŋ ə paɪ]	[bekɪŋg ə paɪ]	[bekɪŋ ə paɪ]
walking up	[wɔkɪŋ ʌp]	[wɔkɪŋg ʌp]	[wɔkɪŋ ʌp]

---

¹⁰This is a secondary pronunciation.
¹¹Yes, this is the preferred pronunciation.

trying it	[traɪɪŋ ɪt]	[traɪɪŋg ɪt]	[traɪɪn ɪt]
swing on	[swɪŋ ɑn]	[swɪŋg ɑn]	[swɪn ɑn]
looking up	[lʊkɪŋ ʌp]	[lʊkɪŋg ʌp]	[lʊkɪn ʌp]
riding around	[raɪdɪŋ əraʊnd]	[raɪdɪŋg əraʊnd]	[raɪdɪn əraʊnd]

8. *Substitution of* /in/ *for* /ɪŋ/. Use overarticulation and negative practice in producing the following sound combinations (the second production is incorrect for the "ing" combination): /ɪŋ/, /in/, /ɪŋ/. Repeat this several times.

9. Use negative practice and overarticulation in reading aloud the following words. The middle pronunciation is the substitution of /in/ for /ɪŋ/. Then, repeat the exercise with appropriate articulation.

	CAREER	ERROR	CAREER
going	[goɪŋ]	[goin]	[goɪŋ]
doing	[duɪŋ]	[duin]	[duɪŋ]
singing	[sɪŋɪŋ]	[sɪŋin]	[sɪŋɪŋ]
following	[fɑloɪŋ]	[fɑloin]	[fɑloɪŋ]
sitting	[sɪtɪŋ]	[sɪtin]	[sɪtɪŋ]
walking	[wɔkɪŋ]	[wɔkin]	[wɔkɪŋ]
flinging	[flɪŋɪŋ]	[flɪŋin]	[flɪŋɪŋ]

retreating and beating and meeting and sheeting

CAREER: [rɪtritɪŋ ænd bitɪŋ ænd mitɪŋ ænd ʃitɪŋ]

ERROR: [rɪtritin ænd bitin ænd mitin ænd ʃitin]

CAREER: [rɪtritɪŋ ænd bitɪŋ ænd mitɪŋ ænd ʃitɪŋ]

Read aloud the selections in exercise 10.

10. **a.** Uncle Frank's language mingled with the soft breeze.

   b. The young bird's wings were long and strong.

   c. During the evening the bells ring a lot.

   d. Even though Inga was laughing she kept singing the sad song.

   e. Bring the springer pups for their morning run.

Read aloud the stanzas from the following poems, concentrating on the words ending in "ing." Make certain that the back of your tongue comes in contact with the velum. If the front of your tongue touches the alveolar ridge, prolong the "ing" (/ɪŋ/) endings and stick out your tongue tip; this will give you an exaggerated feeling of the correct placement of the tongue for the /ŋ/.

11. 1   I'm sure I'm no ascetic; I'm as pleasant as can be;
   2   You'll always find me ready with a crushing repartee,
   3   I've an irritating chuckle, I've a celebrated sneer,
   4   I've an entertaining snigger, I've a fascinating leer.
   5   To everybody's prejudice I know a thing or two;
   6   I can tell a woman's age in half a minute—and I do.
   7   But although I try to make myself as pleasant as I can,
   8   Yet everybody says I am a disagreeable man!
   9   And I can't think why!

   From PRINCESS IDA
   W. S. Gilbert

12.

1 There was a rustling that seemed like a bustling
2 Of merry crowds justling at pitching and hustling;
3 Small feet were pattering, wooden shoes clattering,
4 Little hands clapping and little tongues chattering,
5 And, like fowls in a farm-yard when barley is scattering,
6 Out came the children running.

From THE PIED PIPER OF HAMELIN
Robert Browning

13. Recite aloud the stanzas from "The Cataract of Lodore" (p. 24); they are excellent to test your /ŋ/ nasal.

>>>

SYLLABIC CONSONANTS

Sometimes the consonants /l/, /m/, and /n/ form syllables without the aid of a full vowel. These consonants are called *syllabic* and are identified by a mark underneath the sound: /l̩/, /m̩/, and /n̩/. In the word *button* there is a slight vowel component between /t/ and /n/. If the syllable were prolonged, it would contain the schwa, or /ə/ (as in <u>a</u>bout). Listen to the tape and develop auditory discrimination in the following words in which the full vowel and the syllabic consonant are compared. (If you want more details, see the discussion of implosion on pp. 191–195.)

	FULL VOWEL	SYLLABIC CONSONANT
bottle	[ˈbɑtəl]	[ˈbɑtl̩]
bottom	[ˈbɑtəm]	[ˈbɑtm̩]
button	[ˈbʌtən]	[ˈbʌtn̩]
single	[ˈsɪŋgəl]	[ˈsɪŋgl̩]
cycle	[ˈsaɪkəl]	[ˈsaɪkl̩]
prison	[ˈprɪzən]	[ˈprɪzn̩]
mitten	[ˈmɪtən]	[ˈmɪtn̩]
Latin	[ˈlætən]	[ˈlætn̩]

The use of the syllabic consonant is quite appropriate in career speech, and in some circles it is preferred, especially in words in which the syllabic sound follows /t/, such as in *cotton* ([ˈkɑtn̩]) and *little* [ˈlɪtl̩].

EXERCISES FOR GENERAL ARTICULATION

In practicing these exercises, remember the technique of overarticulating and then pulling away for appropriate articulation. Too many speakers revert to their habitual production, which as a rule is underarticulated.

Begin slowly and build up speed. When you "go into a skid," it is usually caused by an unopened mouth, too fast a pace, or inadequate preparation! In the following selections by W. S. Gilbert, maintain a pace and stay with the rhythm. Then, increase your pace.

The next six exercises are for focusing your listening acuity. For purposes of auditory discrimination it is important for you to distinguish among the syllables containing the major and minor stresses, which will heighten your sense of rhythm while listening.

1. In the following selection there are three primary, or heavy, stresses in each line. Maintain the heavy stress and your pace will increase. However, remember that this exercise is for articulation, so keep your concentration on sound production.

   1 I'm the sláve of the góds, néck and heéls,
   2 And I'm boúnd to obéy, though I ráte at 'em;
   3 And I not ónly órder their méals,
   4 But I coók 'em, sérve 'em, and wáit at 'em.
   5 Then I máke all their néctar—I dó—
   6 (Which a térrible líquor to ráck us is)
   7 And whenéver I míx them a bréw,
   8 Why áll the thanksgívings are Bácchus's!

   From THESPIS
   W. S. Gilbert

2. In this selection, the rhythm alternates between four stresses in the odd-numbered lines and three in the even-numbered ones.

   1 In Westmínster Háll I dánced a dánce,
   2 Like a sémi-despóndent fúry;
   3 For I thóught I should néver hít on a chánce
   4 Of addréssing a Brítish Júry—
   5 But I sóon got tíred of thírd-class jóurneys,
   6 And dínners of bréad and wáter;
   7 So I féll in lóve with a rích attórney's
   8 Élderly, úgly daúghter.

   (Mark the accents in the next stanza yourself.)

   9   The rich attorney, he jumped with joy,
   10 And replied to my fond profession:
   11 "You shall reap the reward of your pluck, my boy,
   12 At the Bailey and Middlesex Sessions.
   13 You'll soon get used to her looks," said he,
   14 "And a very nice girl you'll find her!
   15 She may very well pass for forty-three
   16 In the dusk, with a light behind her!"

   From TRIAL BY JURY
   W. S. Gilbert

3. The rhythm in the next selection is slightly different from those in the preceding selections. Each line has four primary (unmarked) stresses. Keep up the pace and rhythm, but remember that the purpose of these exercises is to improve your articulation. Mark the stressed syllables in the lines.

   1   When I was a lad I served a term
   2   As office boy at an Attorney's firm.
   3   I cleaned the windows and I swept up the floor,
   4   And I polished up the handle of the big front door.
   5   I polished up the handle so carefullee,
   6   That now I am the Ruler of the Queen's Navee!

   7   As office boy I made such a mark
   8   That they gave me the post of a junior clerk. (pronounced like [klark])
   9   I served the writs with a smile so bland,
   10 And I copied all the letters in a big round hand—
   11 I copied all the letters in a hand so free,

12 That now I am the Ruler of the Queen's Navee!
13 In serving writs I made such a name
14 That an articled <u>clerk</u> I soon became; (pronounced like [klark])
15 I wore clean collars and a brand-new suit
16 For the pass examination at the Institute,
17 And that pass examination did so well for me,
18 That now I am the Ruler of the Queen's Navee! . . .

19 I grew so rich that I was sent
20 By a pocket borough into Parliament.
21 I always voted at my party's call,
22 And I never thought of thinking for myself at all.
23 I thought so little, they rewarded me
24 By making me the Ruler of the Queen's Navee!

From H. M. S. PINAFORE
W. S. Gilbert

4. In the following selection, the rhythm is composed of four primary stresses in lines 1 through 3 followed by three major stresses in line 4.
   1 It's a song of merryman, moping mum,
   2 Whose soul was sad, and whose glance was glum,
   3 Who sipped no sup, and who craved no crumb,
   4 As he sighed for the love of a ladye.

From THE YEOMEN OF THE GUARD
W. S. Gilbert

5. Notice that in the following selection there is only one major stress in lines 1 through 4.
   1 That celebrated,
   2 Cultivated,
   3 Underrated,
   4 Nobleman
   5 The Duke of Plaza Toro!

From THE GONDOLIERS
W. S. Gilbert

6. Unlike the preceding selections, the rhythm in the following selection is less structured.

You must lie upon the daisies and discourse in novel phrases of your
complicated state of mind,
The meaning doesn't matter if it's only idle chatter of a transcendental kind.
And everyone will say,
As you walk your mystic way,
"If this young man expresses himself in terms too deep for me,
Why, what a very singularly deep young man this deep young man must be!"

From PATIENCE
W. S. Gilbert

7. The following poem is a fine example of *consonance,* which is the use of the same or similar consonant sounds with differing vowels. For those of you who think that a poet works by inspiration exclusive of perspiration, this poem ought to be of some interest. (It is a *little* labored, though, isn't it!)
   1 Leaves
   2 Murmuring by myriads in the shimmering trees.
   3 Lives
   4 Wakening with wonder in the Pyrenees.
   5 Birds

 6   Cheerily chirping in the early day.
 7   Bards
 8   Singing of summer, scything thro' the bay.
 9   Bees
10   Shaking the heavy dews from bloom and frond.
11   Boys
12   Bursting the surface of the ebony pond.
13   Flashes
14   Of swimmers carving thro' the sparkling cold.
15   Fleshes
16   Gleaming with wetness to the morning gold.
17   A mead
18   Bordered about with warbling water brooks,
19   A maid
20   Laughing the love-laugh with me; proud of looks.
21   The heat
22   Throbbing between the upland and the peak.
23   Her heart
24   Quivering with passion to my pressed cheek.
25   Braiding
26   Of floating flames across the mountain brow.
27   Brooding
28   Of stillness; and sighing of the bough.
29   Stirs
30   Of leaflets in the gloom; soft petal-showers;
31   Stars
32   Expanding with the starr'd nocturnal flowers.

From MY DIARY, JULY 1914
Wilfred Owen

In the next selection, play with the repetitions.

8. From birth to age eighteen, a girl needs good parents. From eighteen to thirty-five, she needs good looks. From thirty-five to fifty-five, she needs a good personality. From fiftyfive on, she needs good cash.

Sophie Tucker

9. 1   The Sockslurp is friendly and playful;
  2   It loves heat and tumbles for thrills;
  3   It lives in a cozy, clothes dryer,
  4   Avoiding most weather that chills.
  5   It slurps just one sock or the other,
  6   But never would slurp a whole pair.
  7   It knows other creatures are hungry,
  8   And usually tries to be fair.
  9   When forced to live out of the dryer,
 10   Where socks are protected by shoes,
 11   It hardly gets by in the winter,
 12   Just slurping the socks people lose.
 13   So nature decided to help it,
 14   And found it a food that it loves,
 15   It spends the cold months slurping mittens,
 16   And ear muffs, and tiny wool gloves.
 17   Small people who lose one new tennie,

18   Should know that the Sockslurp's aware,
19   That if it finds one small sock straying,
20   A tennie is usually there.
21   So Sockslurps slurp small socks for some suppers,
22   Then always alert for a treat,
23   Will probably try a new tennie,
24   And tickle the owner's bare feet.

THE SOCKSLURP
Father Eugene F. Lyttle

TONGUE TWISTERS

The following tongue twisters are for the brave and pure of heart. They will test your ability at **diadochokinesis** *(producing difficult sound combinations rapidly)! Don't be afraid to open your mouth and articulate the consonant sounds. Pronounce the words slowly at first, and then increase the speed. If you make an error and your mouth goes on the* articulatory skids*, go back to the problem word and spend some time feeling the production of the sound. Perhaps a visualization of where the sound is produced in the mouth or throat will help. Then, go back and put the word or phrase into the presented context.*

1. Pronounce the following word combinations slowly at first. When you feel that you have them "firmly in your mouth," say them quickly five times each:

    a. rubber buggy

    b. buggy bumpers

    c. rubber buggy bumpers (Feel: front /b/ back /g/ front /mp/)

    d. red rubber buggy bumpers

    e. rubber baby buggy bumpers

    f. red rubber baby buggy bumpers

    g. toy boat

    h. Wayne went to Wales to watch walruses.

    i. unique New York

    j. luge sluiceway

    k. What noise annoys an oyster? A noisy noise annoys an oyster.

    l. Northeast Optic Network, Inc.

    m. philosophically, psychologically, and philologically sound

    n. What a terrible tongue twister.

    Only for the courageous:

2. Will you William?

    a. I saw the six thick thumbs

    b. ophthalmological ophthalmologist

    c. Guy Gargoyle, Girl Gargoyle

  d. abominable abdominal

  e. Sushi Chef

  f. damp canned clams

  g. <u>P</u>eter <u>P</u>an <u>p</u>urposely <u>p</u>laced <u>P</u>olly's <u>p</u>arrots <u>p</u>roximate to the <u>p</u>recipitous <u>p</u>recipices. (Thanks to Mark Stewart)

3. /bl/ *blend*:

  a. A big <u>bl</u>ack bug bit a big <u>bl</u>ack bear, made a big <u>bl</u>ack bear <u>bl</u>eed <u>bl</u>ood.

  b. Big <u>bl</u>ue jeans in a brown <u>bl</u>own <u>bl</u>adder.

4. The following exercise is designed to get your mouth around the sounds while producing them at a fast pace. Make certain that you do not turn /t/ into /d/. Be guided by the underline.

  a. <u>Bet</u>ty <u>Bot</u>ter bough<u>t</u> a bi<u>t</u> of bu<u>tt</u>er. "Bu<u>t</u>," she said, "This bu<u>tt</u>er's bi<u>tt</u>er. If I pu<u>t</u> i<u>t</u> in my ba<u>tt</u>er, i<u>t</u> will make my ba<u>tt</u>er bi<u>tt</u>er." So <u>Bet</u>ty <u>Bot</u>ter bough<u>t</u> a bi<u>t</u> of be<u>tt</u>er bu<u>tt</u>er, and i<u>t</u> made her ba<u>tt</u>er be<u>tt</u>er.

  b. How many <u>c</u>oo<u>k</u>ies could a good <u>c</u>ook <u>c</u>ook
   If a good <u>c</u>ook <u>c</u>ould <u>c</u>ook <u>c</u>ookies?
   A good <u>c</u>ook <u>c</u>ould <u>c</u>ook as much <u>c</u>ookies
   As a good <u>c</u>ook who <u>c</u>ould <u>c</u>ook <u>c</u>ookies.

5. *Common* /f/ *blends*:
  <u>F</u>anny <u>F</u>inch <u>fr</u>ied <u>f</u>ive <u>fl</u>oundering fish <u>f</u>or <u>F</u>rancis <u>F</u>owler's <u>f</u>ather.

6. /f/, /l/, /fl/ *blend:*
  I never <u>f</u>el<u>t</u> <u>f</u>el<u>t</u> <u>f</u>eel <u>fl</u>at like that <u>f</u>el<u>t</u> <u>f</u>el<u>t</u>.

7. /k/, /p/, *and* /t/ *in all positions*:
  A <u>p</u>rope<u>r</u>, <u>p</u>urple <u>p</u>orta-<u>p</u>o<u>t</u>ty in the park.

  <u>T</u>homas <u>T</u>a<u>tt</u>er<u>t</u>oo<u>t</u> <u>t</u>ook <u>t</u>au<u>t</u> <u>t</u>wine <u>t</u>o <u>t</u>ie <u>t</u>en <u>t</u>wigs <u>t</u>o <u>t</u>wo <u>t</u>all <u>t</u>rees.

8. /s/, /sl/, /sm/, /sn/, /sk/, /st/, /sw/, *and* /skr/ *blends:*

  a. A <u>sn</u>ifter of <u>sn</u>uff is enough <u>sn</u>uff for a <u>sn</u>iff for the <u>sn</u>uff <u>sn</u>iffer.

  b. <u>S</u>inful <u>S</u>ydney <u>s</u>ipped his <u>s</u>oda, <u>s</u>eized his <u>sn</u>oot, and <u>sn</u>eezed.

  c. <u>S</u>i<u>x</u>teen <u>st</u>ainle<u>ss</u>-<u>st</u>eel twin-<u>scr</u>ew cruisers.

  d. Two twin-<u>scr</u>ew <u>st</u>eel cruisers <u>st</u>eamed up the Thames.

  e. <u>Sl</u>ippery <u>sl</u>eds <u>sl</u>ide <u>sm</u>oothly down the <u>sl</u>uiceway.

  f. <u>S</u>ixty-two <u>s</u>ick chick<u>s</u> <u>s</u>at on <u>s</u>ix <u>sl</u>im <u>sl</u>ick <u>sl</u>ender <u>s</u>aplings.

  g. A <u>sk</u>unk <u>st</u>ood on a <u>st</u>ump. The <u>st</u>ump thunk the <u>sk</u>unk <u>st</u>unk, but the <u>sk</u>unk thunk the <u>st</u>ump <u>st</u>unk.
   The following is a comparison of /m/ and /w/.

  <u>Wh</u>y do you cry, <u>W</u>illy? <u>Wh</u>y do you cry? <u>Wh</u>y, <u>W</u>illy? <u>Wh</u>y, <u>W</u>illy? <u>Wh</u>y, <u>W</u>illy? <u>Wh</u>y?

9. *Fricatives*:

  a. The <u>six</u><u>th</u> <u>sh</u>eik's <u>six</u><u>th</u> <u>sh</u>eep'<u>s</u> <u>s</u>ick.

  b. <u>S</u>e<u>v</u>enty <u>s</u>e<u>v</u>en bene<u>v</u>olent <u>el</u>ephants.

  c. Henry the <u>S</u>ixth'<u>s</u> three advi<u>s</u>ers.

d. I slit the sheet. The sheet I slit. Upon the slitted sheet I sit.

e. The sun shines on shop signs.

f. Does this shop stock short socks with spots?

g. I wish to wish the wish you wish to wish, but if you wish the wish the witch wishes, I won't wish the wish you wish to wish.

10. The following lines are particularly good for the New England and New York City accents.

To sit in solemn silence in a dull, dark, dock,
In a pestilential prison, with a life-long lock.
Awaiting the sensation of a short, sharp shock.
From a cheap and chippy chopper, on a big black block.

From THE MIKADO
W. S. Gilbert

11. Cognates /θ-ð/:

a. 1 Theophilus Thistledown, the successful thistle sifter, in sifting a sieve full of unsifted
2 thistles, thrust three thousand thistles through the thick of his thumb. Now
3 if Theophilus, the successful thistle sifter, in sifting a sieve full of unsifted
4 thistles, thrust three thousand thistles through the thick of his thumb, see that
5 thou, in sifting a sieve full of unsifted thistles, thrust not three thousand thistles
6 through the thick of thy thumb. Success to the successful thistle sifter, Theophilus
7 Thistledown.

b. Beneath the length and breadth of the booth Seth found cloths, sheaths, moths, wreathes, paths, and lathes.

c. Elizabeth's birthday is on the third Thursday of this month.

d. Something in a thirty-acre thermal thicket of thorns and thistles thumped and thundered threatening the three-D thoughts of Matthew the thug — although, theatrically, it was only the thirteen-thousand thistles and thorns through the un derneath of his thigh that the thirty year old thug thought of that morning.

12. /r/ *and* /gr/ *blend*:

a. Around the rough and rugged rock the ragged rascal ran.

b. If you meet a rapid, rabid rabbit, wrap it.

c. Three gray geese in the green grass grazing; gray were the geese, and green was the grazing.

The following tongue twisters are a mixed bag of sounds. Feel the placement of the articulators. Begin slowly, and increase your speed while articulating the sounds with gusto!

13. a. She stood on the steps inexplicably mimicking his hiccuping and amicably welcoming him in.

b. Are you copperbottoming 'em, my man? No, I'm aluminizing 'em, ma'am.

c. The seething sea ceaseth—it sufficeth sufficiently that the seething sea ceaseth.

d. She stood on the steps of Burgess's Fish Sauce Shop in the Strand, welcoming him in.

e. I saw Susie sitting in a shoe shine shop. Where she sits she shines, and where she shines she sits.

14. A tutor who tooted the flute
    Tried to tutor two tooters to toot.
    Said the two to the tutor,
    "Is it harder to toot or
    To tutor two tooters to toot?"

15. Denise sees the fleece,
    Denise sees the fleas.
    At least Denise could sneeze and feed and freeze the fleas.

16. I bought a batch of baking powder and baked a batch of biscuits. I brought a big basket of biscuits back to the bakery and baked a basket of big biscuits. Then I took the big basket and the basket of big biscuits and mixed the big baskets with the basket of biscuits that was next to the big basket and put a bunch of biscuits from the baskets into a box. Then I took the box of mixed biscuits and a biscuit mixer and the biscuit basket and brought the basket of biscuits and the box of mixed biscuits and the biscuit mixer back to the bakery and opened up a can of tuna.

17. To help you be successful with the following classic mouthful, it would be a good idea to look up the meanings and pronunciations of those words that are new to you. Then, pray a lot! This makes a fine oral examination for articulation. It is also a good challenge for your classroom professional—the professor!

    1 In promulgating your esoteric cogitations, or articulating your superficial
    2 sentimentalities, and amicable, philosophical, or psychological observations, beware of
    3 platitudinous ponderosity. Let your conversational communications possess a
    4 clarified conciseness, a compacted comprehensibleness, coalescent consistency, and
    5 a concatenated cogency. Eschew all conglomerations of flatulent garrulity, jejune
    6 babblement, and asinine affectations. Let your extemporaneous descantings
    7 and unpremeditated expatiations have intelligibility and voracious vivacity, without
    8 thrasonical bombast. Sedulously avoid all polysyllabic profundity, pompous
    9 prolixity, ventriloquial verbosity, and vain vapidity. In other words, say what you
    10 mean and mean what you say, and don't use big words.

>>>

THREE-POINT ANALYSES OF ENGLISH SOUNDS

The following chart identifies the consonants, vowels, and diphthongs that appear in the English language. A three-point analysis appears with each sound:

1. *Flow of breath* (Is the sound a plosive or a continuant? If it is a continuant, what kind? Fricative? Nasal? Semivowel?)

2. *Action of vocal folds* (Is the sound surd [voiceless] or sonant [voiced]?)

3. *Articulatory adjustment* (With what articulators is the sound produced?)

THREE-POINT ANALYSES OF ENGLISH SOUNDS

Phonetic Symbol	Cognate	Flow of Breath	Action of Vocal Folds	Articulatory Adjustment
Consonants				
/p/	/b/	plosive	voiceless	bilabial
/b/	/p/	plosive	voiced	bilabial
/t/	/d/	plosive	voiceless	lingua-alveolar
/d/	/t/	plosive	voiced	lingua-alveolar

/k/	/g/	plosive	voiceless	lingua-velar
/g/	/k/	plosive	voiced	lingua-velar
/tʃ/	/dʒ/	plosive	voiceless	lingua-alveolar/palatal
/dʒ/	/tʃ/	plosive	voiced	lingua-alveolar/palatal
/f/	/v/	continuant fricative	voiceless	labio-dental
/v/	/f/	continuant fricative	voiced	labio-dental
/θ/	/ð/	continuant fricative	voiceless	lingua-dental
/ð/	/θ/	continuant	voiced	lingua-dental
/h/		continuant fricative	voiceless	glottal
/ʍ/		continuant fricative	voiceless	bilabial
/s/	/z/	continuant fricative sibilant	voiceless	lingua-alveolar
/z/	/s/	continuant fricative sibilant	voiced	lingua-alveolar
/ʃ/	/ʒ/	continuant fricative sibilant	voiceless	lingua-palatal
/ʒ/	/ʃ/	continuant fricative sibilant	voiced	lingua-palatal
/l/		continuant lateral	voiced	lingua-alveolar
/r/		continuant semivowel	voiced	lingua-palatal bilabial (slight)
/w/		continuant semivowel	voiced	bilabial
/j/		continuant semivowel	voiced	lingua-palatal
/m/		continuant nasal	voiced	bilabial
/n/		continuant nasal	voiced	lingua-alveolar
/ŋ/		continuant nasal	voiced	lingua-velar

Vowels

/i/		vowel	voiced	high-front tense
/ɪ/		vowel	voiced	high-front relaxed
/e/		vowel	voiced	mid-front tense
/ɛ/		vowel	voiced	mid-front relaxed
/æ/		vowel	voiced	low-front relaxed
/a/		vowel	voiced	low-front relaxed
/ɝ/		vowel	voiced	mid-central tense
/ɜ/		vowel	voiced	mid-central slightly tense
/ɚ/		vowel	voiced	mid-central slightly tense

Phonetic Symbol	Cognate	Flow of Breath	Action of Vocal Folds	Articulatory Adjustment
Vowels				
/ʌ/		vowel	voiced	mid-central relaxed
/ə/		vowel	voiced	mid-central relaxed
/u/		vowel	voiced	high-back slightly tense
/ʊ/		vowel	voiced	high-back relaxed
/o/		vowel	voiced	mid-back tense
/ɔ/		vowel	voiced	low-back slightly tense
/ɒ/		vowel	voiced	low-back slightly tense
/ɑ/		vowel	voiced	low-back relaxed
Diphthongs				
/aɪ/		diphthong	voiced	low-front to high-front
/aʊ/		diphthong	voiced	low-front to high-back
/ɔɪ/		diphthong	voiced	low-back to high-front
/ju/		diphthong	voiced	lingua-velar to high-back
/ɪu/		diphthong	voiced	high-front to high-back
/eɪ/		diphthong	voiced	mid-front to high-front
/oʊ/		diphthong	voiced	mid-back to high-back

W W
To locate URLs and search terms for weblinks relevant to this chapter, please go to the companion website at www.cengage.com/rtf/crannell/voiceandarticulation5e and select the proper chapter.

Write the definitions for the following terms in the space below.

KEY TERMS   DEFINITIONS

Affricate

Aspirate

Bilabial

Cognate Pairs

Continuant

Dental

Dentalized

Diadochokinesis

Fricative

Glide

Glottal

Labio-dental

Lambda

Lateralization

Lingua-alveolar

Lingua-dental

Lingua-palatal

Lingua-velar

Nasal

Plosive

Semivowel

Sibilant

PRONUNCIATION

("Granite": People have always taken me for granite.)

In dynamic or conversational speech, three processes are necessary. First, sound must be produced at the larynx (discussed in Chapters 2, 3, and 4). Second, the sound must be resonated into various speech sounds (Chapters 6 and 7). Third, the speech sounds must be combined into syllables that are transformed into words (Chapter 8), which eventually are used to form vital or fluid speech (Chapters 11, 12, and 13).

The combination of vowels and consonants creates *pronunciation*. It has been said that a word is a picture to the ear, with the vowel as the painting and the consonant as the frame; one is of little use without the other. This chapter deals with **pronunciation**—combining consonants and vowels into words that are uttered correctly and that work together to create dynamic speech.

("Next cheer": What school are you planning to attend next cheer?)

English is based on a phonemic writing system. That means that there is a definite relationship between its spoken and written forms. Most of the written letters in English have some relationship to their sound productions.

This is not true in many Asian languages that are derived from ancient Chinese. In these cases, the written symbols convey an idea rather than relate to sounds. Most scholars agree that in earlier times English writing was more phonetic than it is today.

Regarding this relationship between letters and sounds in English, everyone speaking the language (including American-born-speaker) must cope with the problems presented by the use of silent letters. This problem of a letter with no phonemic value is a fairly common occurrence in English. The following lists indicate a letter that is silent in English:

t	p	g	k
mois*t*en	*p*neumonia	diaphra*g*m	*k*night
has*t*en	*p*neumonic	*g*nat	*k*nock
lis*t*en	recei*p*t	*g*nome	*k*now
fas*t*en	*p*sychology	rei*g*n	*k*nee
sof*t*en	*p*tomaine	fei*g*n	*k*nead

l	b	h	w
ca<u>l</u>f	dum<u>b</u>	<u>h</u>eir	<u>w</u>rite
ha<u>l</u>f	crum<u>b</u>	<u>h</u>onest	<u>w</u>rong
ta<u>l</u>k	thum<u>b</u>	<u>h</u>eirloom	<u>w</u>rath
cha<u>l</u>k	clim<u>b</u>	herb	<u>w</u>restle
pa<u>l</u>m	de<u>b</u>t	herbage	<u>w</u>ry

e	gh
din<u>e</u>	thou<u>gh</u>t
som<u>e</u>	thorou<u>gh</u>
sinc<u>e</u>	throu<u>gh</u>
complet<u>e</u>	sou<u>gh</u>t
gon<u>e</u>	wrou<u>gh</u>t

>>> STRESS

Although a discussion of **stress**—the emphasis we give to certain spoken syllables— could have been included earlier in the text, it appears here because stress is a relatively sophisticated concept, and hearing it in speech requires a developed ear. Intelligence has little relevance in the ability to use stress correctly, and its incorrect use has been the downfall of many voice and speech students. Without some training, stress can cause great frustration.

There are two main types of stress in the English language. *Primary stress* is indicated by the placement of an acute accent [´] over the vowel in the syllable receiving the strongest emphasis; *minimal,* or weak, *stress* is indicated by the placement of a breve [˘] over the vowel in the syllable receiving less stress. Sometimes a weak or minimally stressed syllable is said to be "unstressed." This is a misnomer, for any spoken syllable must receive some stress. However, many teachers still use the term *unstressed,* and everyone comes to understand what is meant.

Every spoken word contains some kind of stress. If a word of one syllable is uttered aloud by itself, it receives primary stress because it cannot be heard in relation to another syllable. Thus, in the sentence

Í ám á bíg trée

the primary stress marks indicate either that there is a significant pause after each word or that the speaker is an oak that talks like a robot. If the adjective were *little* instead of *big,* a decision would have to be made regarding the degree of stress.

In English, there are several other systems for indicating stress. There is the four-stress system, in which [´] signifies primary stress (the syllables receiving the greatest degree of stress), the circumflex [ˆ] signifies secondary stress (or the next greatest degree of stress), the grave accent [`] signifies tertiary stress (the third greatest degree of stress), and [˘] signifies minimal or weak stress. In a three-stress system, [´] represents primary, [`] represents secondary, and [˘] represents minimal stress.

The syllable that contains the primary stress (and there is usually only one primary stress in a word or phrase) is also the loudest syllable. Read aloud the following sentences as marked. The parenthetical matter indicates the situations, which will determine the proper stress.

(You brought me the pencils, paper, and ink, but . . .)
Whêre àre thĕ boóks?

(I did not ask you, What are the books; I want to know . . .)
Whére àre thĕ boôks?

(I give up . . .)
Whêre áre thĕ boòks?

And so stress is related not only to the loudness of the surrounding syllables but also to the underlying meaning. Using the four-stress system, read aloud the following phrases as transcribed.

1. *Thĕ Côrn Ìs Gréen*

2. Ĭ mèt ă grêat gírl.

3. Thĕ tîme ĭs nów.

4. *Gône wìth thĕ Wínd*

5. Whàt ĭs thĕ mêanĭng ŏf thát phrâse?

6. Dò yôu bĕlîeve ĭn thĕ stárs?

7. Hòoráh fŏr thĕ lîttlĕ màn!

8. Gô ănd càtch ă fâllĭng stár.

9. Thàt wăs nót vêrў smârt.

10. Î knòw. Lèt's âll gò skíĭng!

What changes of meaning are there in the following four pairs of sentences?

1. The president lives in the Whíte Hôuse.
    Did you like the whíte hòuse?

2. She is a líghthòuse kêepĕr.
    She is a lîght hóusekeèpĕr.

3. These are hôthòuse flówĕrs.
    This is a hôt hóuse.

4. He is a bóokkêepĕr.
    Marian, the librarian, called herself a bôok kéepĕr.

Throughout this text we have noted that the criteria for your standard of speech are determined by the demands made by your career. The appropriateness is further determined by your personality, the audience, and the speech occasion. As you move along in this chapter, you will be dealing with some sophisticated speech principles. Do not minimize their importance. Many of the principles presented here make the difference between being a trained and an untrained speaker.

("Neck Store": I am in love with the woman who lives neck store.)

RESTRESSING

In English, a number of words can be pronounced in two possible ways depending on the degree of stress given to them. These words are sometimes called strong or weak, depending on the meaning of the sentence. A speaker would use the *strong form* when the word is given by itself or if it receives emphasis in the sentence. The *weak form* is often used in connected, or dynamic, speech in which the stress on the word is minimal.

Novelists will often use an apostrophe with these weak syllables: "cup o' java," and "love 'n such."

Certain words usually contain minimal stress in conversational speech because they are less important than other words in the same phrase or sentence. These words very often contain the unstressed schwa, /ə/. If, to clarify meaning, these words are given additional stress, the original vowel should be retained. In Chapter 6, it was stated that any unstressed vowel can become a schwa. However, if this **restressing** occurs, which often happens in career speech, the speaker should use the original vowel. Read aloud the following sampling of words that are examples of both weak and strong forms. The words containing the unstressed form cannot be pronounced by themselves (or in isolation).

	UNSTRESSED (WEAK)	RESTRESSED (INCORRECT VOWEL)	RESTRESSED WITH ORIGINAL VOWEL (CAREER SPEECH—STRONG FORM)
because	[bɪkəz]	[bɪkʌz]	[bɪkɔz]
was	[wəz]	[wʌz]	[wɑz], [wɒz]
of	[əv]	[ʌv]	[ɑv], [ɒv]
for	[fɚ]	[fɝ]	[fɔr]
from	[frəm]	[frʌm]	[frɑm], [frɒm]
can	[kən],[kn̩]	[kʌn]	[kæn]
must	[məst]		[mʌst]
some	[səm]		[sʌm]
have	[həv], [həf]	[hʌv], [hʌf]	[hæv], [hæf]
to	[tə], [tu]	[tʌ]	[tu]
his	[ɪz]		[hɪz]

It is quite acceptable for the trained communicator to use the unstressed form when the words are truly unstressed. However, it is important to use the career form when the unstressed words are restressed for emphasis. The possibly familiar chats between Father and Son and Teacher and Student that follow are examples of both forms used correctly. The words that contain strong stress are in italics.

1.   *Son:*   *I* went because [bɪkəz] *I wanted* to go.

    Father: *Why?*

    Son: *Because* [bɪkɔz]. (Never [bɪkʌz]!)

2.   *Son:*   I was [wəz] *going* to tell you.

    Father: *Likely story.*

    Son: Well, I *was* [wɑz] (or [wɒz], not [wʌz])!

3.   *Father:*   I can [kən] *beat* you at *poker.* It's a *piece* of [əv] *cake.*

    Son: *No* you *can't!*

    Father: *Yes I can* [kæn]! *Yóu're a* [ə] *píece óf* ([ɑv] or [ɒv]; not [ʌv]!) *cáke!*

4. *Teacher:*   You *must* [mʌst] attend my class!

    Student: *Why* must [məst aɪ] I go *every day?*

    Teacher: From [frəm] where *I* stand it is your *only* chance to [tə] *pass.*

    Student: *How* am I supposed to [tʊ] *get to* [tʊ] and [ænd] *from* [frəm] the class without a *car?*

    Teacher: *Use* your *legs! What* kind of a [əv ə] question is that?

Here is the familiar story of Fuzzy Wuzzy. The first transcription highlights the re-stressed form; the second transcription is the career speech form.

	RESTRESSED (INCORRECT VOWEL)	CAREER (CORRECT VOWEL)
Fuzzy Wuzzy was a bear.	[fʌzɪ wʌzɪ wʌz ə ber]	[fʌzɪ wʌzɪ wɑz ə ber]
Fuzzy Wuzzy had no hair.	[fʌzɪ wʌzɪ hæd no her]	[same]
Fuzzy Wuzzy wasn't	[fʌzɪ wʌzɪ wʌzn̩t]	[fʌzɪ wʌzɪ wɑzn̩t]
Fuzzy, was he?	[fʌzɪ wʌz hɪ]	[fʌzɪ wɑz hɪ]

Even though this transcription uses career speech, it is not as much fun and loses a good deal of the merriment, doesn't it?

("Forced": In South America there are many problems in a rain forced.)

>>> ASSIMILATION

We have already discussed assimilation as a basic principle in the production of speech sounds; in this chapter, we will deal more extensively with both the positive and negative influences of assimilation. As defined earlier in Chapter 5, **assimilation** is the influence of one sound upon another. In producing sounds, words, and dynamic speech, the mouth ordinarily assumes the simplest and easiest articulation. The results may be acceptable or unacceptable pronunciation.

In a sentence, the incorrect use of one voiced sound for an unvoiced one can have very interesting results. Look at the following two sentences and their phonetic transcriptions. Two changes are made in dynamic speech in the second sentence: the use of /f/ instead of /v/ and the use of the schwa /ə/ for the tense /u/ (as in "true").

I have two (books).
[aɪ hæv tu bʊks]

I have to (go home now).
[aɪ hæf tə go hom naʊ]

Any individual who pronounces both sentences the same way is not likely to be considered a native speaker. Say "I have two of them" using /f/ in "have" and "of." Now say "I have to go home now" using /v/ in "have" and /u/ in "to." Don't you sound like a KGB agent? A simple little change of sound will give you the beginnings of a very subtle accent.

When people learn English, they learn that the letter *f* is pronounced /f/ and the letter *v* is pronounced /v/, but not always! In the first example sentence, the major stress is on "two." In the second sentence the major stress is elsewhere. And so assimilation takes place.

In the words in the following exercise, the last sound becomes /s/ or /z/, or /t/ or /d/, depending upon the preceding sound. If an unvoiced sound (or surd) precedes the last sound, /s/ or /t/ is used because they, too, are unvoiced. Conversely, if the next-to-last sound is voiced (or sonant), the /z/ or /d/ is used. In general, it is easier for the articulatory mechanism to say two consecutive voiced or unvoiced sounds than to switch on and off between them. This principle does not apply in all cases, however. Exaggerate the production of the following words before pulling away in order to develop the appropriate articulation.

(((• EXERCISES

In the following lists, pay close attention to the unvoiced and voiced endings.

2. These mistakes

UNVOICED–UNVOICED ENDINGS

flakes [fleks]	omits [omɪts]	lips [lɪps]
tops [taps]	shakes [ʃeks]	shirts [ʃɝts]
Grasped [græspt]	thinks [θɪŋks]	floats [flots]

VOICED–VOICED ENDINGS

raved [revd]	paths [pæðz]	deeds [didz]
clothes [kloðz]	thrills [θrɪlz]	tongues [tʌŋz]
snows [snoz]	thieves [θivz]	cabs [kæbz]

Omission of /t/ and /d/

An untrained speaker often omits the /t/ and /d/ phonemes.

 **EXERCISES**

1. In the following word list, exaggerate the production of each word so that you feel the articulation of /t/ and /d/. Use negative practice. Do not pull away too much from the overarticulation when trying to develop the appropriate pronunciation.

	CAREER	ERROR	CAREER
interval	[ˈɪntɚvl̩]	[ˈɪnɚvl̩]	[ˈɪntɚvl̩]
interface	[ɪntɚˈfes]	[ɪnɚˈfes]	[ɪntɚˈfes]
interlace	[ɪntɚˈles]	[ɪnɚˈles]	[ɪntɚˈles]
enter	[ˈɛntɚ]	[ˈɛnɚ]	[ˈɛntɚ]
cantaloupe	[ˈkæntəlop]	[ˈkænəlop]	[ˈkæntəlop]
intermix	[ɪntɚˈmɪks]	[ɪnɚˈmɪks]	[ɪntɚˈmɪks]
interlunar	[ɪntɚˈlɪunɚ]	[ɪnɚˈlɪunɚ]	[ɪntɚˈlɪunɚ]
renter	[ˈrɛntɚ]	[ˈrɛnɚ]	[ˈrɛntɚ]
interlude	[ˈɪntɚlɪud]	[ˈɪnɚlɪud]	[ˈɪntɚlɪud]
antics	[ˈæntɪks]	[ˈænɪks][1]	[ˈæntɪks]
enterprise	[ˈɛntɚpraɪz]	[ˈɛnɚpraɪz]	[ˈɛntɚpraɪz]
frantic	[ˈfræntɪk]	[ˈfrænɪk]	[ˈfræntɪk]
intermingle	[ɪntɚˈmɪŋgl̩]	[ɪnɚˈmɪŋgl̩]	[ɪntɚˈmɪŋgl̩]
interjection	[ɪntɚˈdʒɛkʃən]	[ɪnɚˈdʒɛkʃən]	[ɪntɚˈdʒɛkʃən]
intersperse	[ɪntɚˈspɝs]	[ɪnɚˈspɝs]	[ɪntɚˈspɝs]
entertain	[ɛntɚˈten]	[ɛnɚˈten]	[ɛntɚˈten]
holding	[ˈholdɪŋ]	[ˈholɪŋ]	[ˈholdɪŋ]
underling	[ˈʌndɚlɪŋ]	[ˈʌnɚlɪŋ]	[ˈʌndɚlɪŋ]
underneath	[ˈʌndɚniθ]	[ˈʌnɚniθ]	[ˈʌndɚniθ]
wonder	[ˈwʌndɚ]	[ˈwʌnɚ]	[ˈwʌndɚ]
blond	[blɔnd]	[blɔn]	[blɔnd]
hand	[hænd]	[hæn]	[hænd]
spend	[spɛnd]	[spɛn]	[spɛnd]
Internet	[ɪntɚnɛt]	[ɪnɚnɛt]	[ɪntɚnɛt]
Interpole	[ɪntɚpol]	[ɪnɚpol]	[ɪntɚpol]

---

[1]Have you made the discovery that "annex" is not "antics"?

2. These mistakes are more prevalent in phrases and sentences than in isolated words. Some of you may believe that you made no mistakes in the preceding list. See if you can hear any changes as you say the following phrases and sentences:

Hold my hand!	[hold maɪ hænd]	[hol maɪ hæn]	[hold maɪ hænd]
a blond wig	[ə blɔnd wɪg]	[ə blɔn wɪg]	[ə blɔnd wɪg]
entertain me	[ɛntɚˈten mi]	[ɛnɚˈten mi]	[ɛntɚˈten mi]
spend some time	[spɛnd sʌm taɪm]	[spɛn sʌm taɪm]	[spɛnd sʌm taɪm]
underneath the dirt	[ʌndɚˈniθ ðə dɝ˞t]	[ʌnɚˈniθ ðə dɝ˞t]	[ʌndɚˈniθ ðə dɝ˞t]

("Pitcher": Do you have Mom's pitcher in your wallet?)

Substitution of /d/ for /t/

In many words, a /t/ phoneme is changed to a /d/ phoneme because of assimilation. To produce the unvoiced phoneme /t/, the vocal mechanism must shut off the vibration. When /t/ is placed between two voiced sounds, the vocal mechanism tends to substitute the phonating /d/ for the unvoiced /t/, as in "little" ([ˈlɪdl̩] for [ˈlɪtl̩]). Remember that we are basically lazy animals; career speech requires attention to this error.

 **EXERCISES**

The following list is exemplary rather than exhaustive. Make your own list; doing so will aid in your listening and articulatory reinforcement. Use negative practice. Note that this error is very common in the pronunciation of numbers. Read aloud the words as they are transcribed in order to hear and feel the differences.

	CAREER	ERROR	CAREER
metal	[ˈmɛtl̩]	[ˈmɛdl̩]	[ˈmɛtl̩]
sixty[2]	[ˈsɪkstɪ]	[ˈsɪksdɪ]	[ˈsɪkstɪ]
otter	[ˈɑtɚ]	[ˈɑdɚ]	[ˈɑtɚ]
fraternity	[frəˈtɝ˞nətɪ]	[frəˈtɝ˞nədɪ]	[frəˈtɝ˞nətɪ]
accreditation	[əkrɛdəteʃən]	[əkrɛdədeʃən]	[əkrɛdəteʃən]
entirety	[ɛnˈtaɪrtɪ]	[ɛnˈtaɪrdɪ]	[ɛnˈtaɪrtɪ]
creditor	[ˈkrɛdətɚ]	[ˈkrɛdədɚ]	[ˈkrɛdətɚ]
dirty	[ˈdɝ˞tɪ]	[ˈdɝ˞dɪ]	[ˈdɝ˞tɪ]
ninety	[ˈnaɪntɪ]	[ˈnaɪndɪ]	[ˈnaɪntɪ]
eighty	[ˈetɪ]	[ˈedɪ]	[ˈetɪ]
seventy	[ˈsɛvəntɪ]	[ˈsɛvəndɪ]	[ˈsɛvəntɪ]
fritter	[ˈfrɪtɚ]	[ˈfrɪdɚ]	[ˈfrɪtɚ]
Betty	[ˈbɛtɪ]	[ˈbɛdɪ]	[ˈbɛtɪ]
actor	[ˈæktɚ]	[ˈækdɚ]	[ˈæktɚ]
thirsty	[ˈθɝ˞stɪ]	[ˈθɝ˞sdɪ]	[ˈθɝ˞stɪ]
meteor	[ˈmitɪɚ]	[ˈmidɪɚ]	[ˈmitɪɚ]

Omission of /d/

When the /nd/ combination occurs in a word, the /d/ phoneme is often omitted. Even trained speakers commit this "sin." In the following list of words, take the time to produce the /d/.

---

[2]Can you feel that the /t/ is easier to produce in this word than in the others? This is because the /t/ continues the voiceless adjustment begun with the /k/ phoneme. However, there must be vibration of the vocal folds in the production of the last sound in that word, the vowel /ɪ/.

 **EXERCISES**

	CAREER	ERROR	CAREER
grandfather	['grændfɑðɚ]	['grænfɑðɚ][3]	['grændfɑðɚ]
handful	['hændfʊl]	['hænfʊl][3]	['hændfʊl]
sandwich	['sændwɪtʃ]	['sænwɪtʃ][3]	['sændwɪtʃ]
handout	['hændaʊt]	['hænaʊt]	['hændaʊt]
handicap	['hændɪkæp]	['hænɪkæp]	['hændɪkæp]
handgrip	['hændgrɪp]	['hæŋgrɪp][3]	['hændgrɪp]
sandbag	['sændbæg]	['sænbæg][3]	['sændbæg]

("Less": The math professor wouldn't less study for the examination.)

> > >

EXPLOSION AND IMPLOSION

A plosive sound may be imploded (unaspirated) or exploded (aspirated). In **explosion,** breath is built up behind the articulators and then released in a puff of air. The amount of air released (explosion) depends on the placement of the plosive in the word. Place a piece of paper in front of your mouth and say the word *pan;* now say the word *span.* Does the movement of the paper show less aspiration in "span" than in "pan"?

In **implosion,** the articulators come together and (as in explosion) pressure is built up, but the articulators do not release the puff of air into that sound. Instead, the air is absorbed into the next sound. This is a sophisticated process, and it is an important one for the communication specialist. A few examples should help to clarify the distinction between implosion and explosion. In this text, the mark indicating explosion is ['], and it is placed to the right of the plosive: /pʻ/, /bʻ/, and /kʻ/. Implosion is designated by ['] as in /pʼ/, /bʼ/, and /kʼ/.

Read aloud the following sentence as indicated by the transcriptions. Focus your attention on the underlined portions:

I don't know.	[aɪ do<u>n</u>o]	(omission of /t/)
	[aɪ do<u>nt'n</u>o]	(exploded /t/)
	[aɪ do<u>nt'n</u>o]	(imploded /t/)

Which pronunciation is preferred in career speech? If you use the first one, you talk like Bullwinkle the Moose. The third pronunciation is preferred. Whenever all plosives are exploded in speech, the impression created is one of pedantic prissiness. How many times have you heard a director of a play say, "Pronounce all of the consonants distinctly and clearly"? In following this suggestion, often all of the plosive sounds are exploded.

In the following discussion, the guidelines that are suggested should not be considered unbreakable rules; there are too many exceptions.

Plosives are usually exploded when they are either the initial sound in a word or the last sound when no thought continues immediately.

Implosion can be thought of as generally occurring medially. In the following sentence, *E* represents explosion and *I* represents implosion. Pay close attention to the position of the plosive sounds:

```
E  E     E I      I E I I E  E
```
Bob . . . I told you that I didn't do it.

Explosion also occurs when a plosive is located in a stressed syllable.

---

[3]In *A Pronouncing Dictionary,* authors John S. Kenyon and Thomas A. Knott allow these as secondary pronunciations. (Merriam-Webster Inc: Springfield, MA., U.S.A., 1953.)

What is the importance of explosion?

The /p/ phonemes in "importance" and "explosion" are exploded because they occur in the initial position in a stressed syllable.

Meaning can be lost or muddled when sounds that ought to be imploded are entirely omitted. Which is the preferred pronunciation of the following phrase:

"the next sound" [ðə nɛk saʊnd] (the sound that is made by your stiff neck, no doubt!)

or

[ðə nɛkst saʊnd]

The tendency to omit imploded sounds (as in the first transcription) is a "pain in the neck" for many trained speakers.

EXERCISES

Explode all of the plosives in pronouncing the following words. Feel what the articulators are doing.

cup	[kʰʌpʰ]
coast	[kʰostʰ]
gift	[gʰɪftʰ]
took	[tʰʊkʰ]
Kent	[kʰɛntʰ]
toast	[tʰostʰ]
brunch	[bʰrʌntʃʰ]
bridge	[bʰrɪdʒʰ]
peep	[pʰipʰ]
cheap	[tʃʰipʰ]

In an imploded plosive, the articulators come together and pressure builds up behind the articulators, but the breath is released into the next sound.

EXERCISES

1. In the following words, a pronunciation using explosion is followed by a pronunciation using implosion; the implosion occurs immediately before a syllabic consonant. Make both of the pronunciations for each word, and *feel* what the breath is doing upon its release.

	EXPLOSION	IMPLOSION
Latin	[ˈlætʰən]	[ˈlæt’n̩]
mitten	[ˈmɪtʰən]	[ˈmɪt’n̩]
middle	[ˈmɪdʰəl]	[ˈmɪd’l̩]
Hutton	[ˈhʌtʰən]	[ˈhʌt’n̩]
muddle	[ˈmʌdʰəl]	[mʌd’l̩]

2. As you pronounce the following phrases, exaggerate the explosion and implosion so that you feel what is happening in sound production.

	EXPLOSION	IMPLOSION
don't know	[dont‛no]	[dont' no]
won't go	[wont‛ go]	[wont' go]
quick temper	[kwɪk‛ tɛmpɚ]	[kwɪk' tɛmpɚ]
book store	[bʊk‛ stɔr]	[bʊk' stɔr]
Cape clam	[kep‛ klæm]	[kep' klæm]
Spot Pond	[spɑt‛ pɑnd]	[spɑt' pɑnd]
right hand	[raɪt‛ hænd]	[raɪt' hænd]
put it	[pʊt‛ ɪt]	[pʊt' ɪt]
talk fast	[tɔk‛ fæst]	[tɔk' fæst]
sank quickly	[sæŋk‛ kwɪk'lɪ]	[sæŋk' kwɪk'lɪ]

When one plosive is followed by another the first is imploded and the second is exploded.

(((EXERCISES

Say the following words twice. The first time explode all of the plosives. The second time use implosion followed by explosion; this latter pronunciation should be used in career speech. Hold the implosion for a long beat.

	EXPLOSION ONLY	IMPLOSION AND EXPLOSION
loo<u>ked</u>	[lʊk‛t‛]	[lʊk't‛]
as<u>ked</u>	[æsk‛t‛]	[æsk't‛]
hus<u>ked</u>	[hʌsk‛t‛]	[hʌsk't‛]
bas<u>ked</u>	[bæsk‛t‛]	[bæsk't‛]
rob<u>bed</u>	[rɑb‛d‛]	[rɑb'd‛]
ga<u>ped</u>	[gep‛t‛]	[gep't‛]
gras<u>ped</u>	[græsp‛t‛]	[græsp't‛]

When a word ends with a plosive sound and the next word begins with a plosive (whether the same or a different one), the first plosive is imploded and the second is exploded.

The duration of the implosion creates the two separate sounds.

(((EXERCISES

1. In the following words, first explode the final plosive in the first word; then, implode the final plosive in the first word and hold the implosive long enough to feel and hear the production.

	EXPLOSION ONLY	PROLONGED IMPLOSION AND EXPLOSION
<u>black</u> <u>cat</u>	[b‛læk‛ k‛æt‛]	[blæk' k‛æt‛]
ri<u>pe</u> <u>b</u>erries	[raɪp‛ b‛ɛriz][4]	[raɪp' b‛ɛriz]
re<u>d</u> <u>p</u>ajamas	[rɛd‛ p‛ədʒ‛æməz]	[rɛd' p‛ədʒ‛æməz]
rhubar<u>b</u> <u>p</u>ie	[rub‛ɑrb‛ p‛aɪ]	[rub‛ɑrb' p‛aɪ]
a<u>ct</u> <u>t</u>wo	[æk‛t‛ t‛u]	[æk‛t' t‛u]

---

[4]The plosives do not have to be the same ones, even though they were in "black cat."

	EXPLOSION ONLY	PROLONGED IMPLOSION AND EXPLOSION
<u>coo</u>ked <u>d</u>inner	[kʰʊkˀtˀdˀɪnɚ]	[kʰʊkˀtˀ dˀɪnɚ]
as<u>ked</u> me	[æskˀtˀ mi]	[æskˀtˀ mi]
<u>J</u>immy cra<u>cked</u> <u>c</u>orn	[ʤˀɪmɪ kˀrækˀtˀ kˀɔrn]	[ʤˀɪmɪ kˀrækˀtˀ kˀɔrn]

2. In the following lists, say the phrases three times as indicated and feel the explosion and implosion in the plosives. The first time use straight explosion; the second time exaggerate the length of the implosion; the third time give the implosion the proper amount of time. Note that the modifying mark [ː] after a plosive signifies that it is prolonged. (Although the *sound* of a plosive cannot be prolonged, its buildup of pressure can be prolonged.)

	EXPLOSION ONLY	PROLONGED IMPLOSION AND EXPLOSION	PROPER IMPLOSION AND EXPLOSION
bla<u>ck</u> <u>c</u>at	[blæk ˀkˀætˀ]	[blækˀːkˀætˀ][5]	[blækˀ kˀætˀ]
<u>ri</u>pe <u>b</u>erries	[raɪpˀ bˀɛriz]	[raɪpˀː bˀɛriz]	[raɪpˀ bˀɛriz]
re<u>d</u> <u>p</u>ajamas	[rɛdˀ pˀəʤˀæməz]	[rɛdˀː pˀəʤˀæməz]	[rɛdˀ pˀəʤˀæməz]
rhu<u>bar</u>b <u>p</u>ie	[rubˀarbˀ pˀaɪ]	[rubˀarbˀː pˀaɪ]	[rubˀarbˀ pˀaɪ]
a<u>ct</u> <u>t</u>wo	[ækˀtˀ tˀu]	[ækˀtˀː tˀu]	[ækˀtˀtˀu]
<u>coo</u>ked <u>d</u>inner	[kˀʊkˀtˀ dˀɪnɚ]	[kˀʊkˀtˀː dˀɪnɚ]	[kˀʊkˀtˀ dˀɪnɚ]
as<u>ked</u> me	[æskˀtˀ mi]	[æskˀtˀː mi][6]	[æskˀtˀmi]
<u>J</u>immy cra<u>cked</u> <u>c</u>orn	[ʤˀɪmɪ kˀrækˀtˀ kˀɔrn]	[ʤˀɪmɪ kˀrækˀtˀː kˀɔrn]	[ʤˀɪmɪ kˀrækˀtˀ kˀɔrn]

One very common error is the omission of medial plosives. Sometimes these incorrect pronunciations create unintended but legitimate words, such as "paining" for "painting."

EXERCISES

Using negative practice, pronounce the following words and phrases.

	CAREER	ERROR	CAREER
rental	[ˈrɛntl̩]	[ˈrɛnl̩]	[ˈrɛntl̩]
problem	[ˈprɑbləm]	[ˈprɑləm]	[ˈprɑbləm]
mental	[ˈmɛntl̩]	[ˈmɛnl̩]	[ˈmɛntl̩]
painting	[ˈpentɪŋ]	[ˈpenɪŋ]	[ˈpentɪŋ]
gentle	[ˈʤɛntl̩]	[ˈʤɛnl̩]	[ˈʤɛntl̩]
Bedford	[ˈbɛdfɚd]	[ˈbɛfəd]	[ˈbɛdfɚd]
probably	[ˈprɑbəblɪ]	[ˈprɑblɪ]	[ˈprɑbəblɪ]
dental	[ˈdɛntl̩]	[ˈdɛnl̩]	[ˈdɛnl̩]
chanting	[ˈʧæntɪŋ]	[ˈʧænɪŋ][7]	[ˈʧæntɪŋ]
splinter	[ˈsplɪntɚ]	[ˈsplɪnɚ]	[ˈsplɪntɚ]
breakfast	[ˈbrɛkfəst]	[ˈbrɛfəst]	[ˈbrɛkfəst]
Medford	[ˈmɛdfɚd]	[ˈmɛfəd]	[ˈmɛdfɚd]

---

[5]Say the following as written: [bˀlækˀætˀ] and [bˀlækˀ kˀætˀ]. You should feel the difference between the single exploded /k/ in the first pronunciation and the two /k/ phonemes (one imploded and one exploded) in the second.
[6]There is no explosion.
[7]Carol, right?

That's a problem.	[ðæts ə 'prɑbləm]	[ðæts ə 'prɑləm]	[ðæts ə 'prɑbləm]
a mental trick	[ə 'mɛntl̩ trɪk]	[ə 'mɛnl̩ trɪk]	[ə 'mɛntl̩ trɪk]
painting a house	['pentɪŋ ə haʊs]	['penɪŋ ə haʊs]	['pentɪŋ ə haʊs]
Gently does it.	['ʤɛntlɪ dʌz ɪt]	['ʤɛnlɪ dʌz ɪt]	['ʤɛntlɪ dʌz ɪt]
probably true	['prɑbəblɪ tru]	['prɑblɪ tru]	['prɑbəblɪ tru]
a dental plan	[ə 'dɛntl̩ plæn]	[ə 'dɛnl̩ plæn]	[ə 'dɛntl̩ plæn]

("Bar": Joe, may I bar your car tomorrow night?)

/nd/ and /md/ Clusters

In connected speech, the combinations /nd/ and /md/ are often produced carelessly. Sometimes the plosives should be imploded and aren't, and sometimes they should be exploded but aren't.

EXERCISES

1. In the following selections, make certain that the plosive is imploded before you proceed to the next word. The flow of the nasal continuant before the plosive must be interrupted. Many of the clusters can also be pronounced with exploded plosives.

the end of the story	*without plosive*	[ðɪ ɛn əv ðə 'stɔrɪ]
	with plosive	[ðɪ ɛnd' əv ðə 'stɔrɪ]
My hand aches.	*without plosive*	[maɪ hæn eks]
	with plosive	[maɪ hænd' eks]
Find the way!	*without plosive*	[faɪn ðə weɪ]
	with plosive	[faɪnd' ðə weɪ]
Don't hound me!	*without plosive*	[don haʊn mi]
	with plosive	[dont' haʊnd' mi]
Andrea blamed Dan.	*without plosive*	['ɑndrɪjə blem dæn]
	with plosive	['ɑndrɪjə blemd' d'æn]
Helen claimed the box.	*without plosive*	['hɛln̩ klem ðə bɑks]
	with plosive	['hɛln̩ klemd' ðə bɑks]
Jake commanded his troops.	*without plosive*	['ʤek kə'mænəd hɪz trups]
	with plosive	['ʤek kə'mænd'əd' hɪz trups]

2. The following sentences contain identical plosives. Implode the first one, and explode the second.

   a. In order to keep' pʰeace Ted' Dʰexter took' Kʰaren and Bob to dinner.

   b. Please meet' Tʰom with a cab' bʰanner.

   c. You'd better walk' cʰarefully and not kick' cʰorn stalks.

   d. Bad' dʰog! Don't' tʰake' cʰandy.

   e. Frank' kʰeeps cheap' pʰarts of cars in the back' cʰamper.

   f. Polly is a bag' gʰirl at the big' gʰrocery store.

   g. Bob' bʰrought Jack', Kʰen, and Tom to the wrestling match.

   h. That was a big' gʰolf cart that Fred' Dʰonnelly bought.

i. Mar̲k̲' c̲'aught̲' t̲'wo long bluefish.

j. I found' D̲'ee Dee to be a tight̲' t̲'ongued' d̲'aughter.

("Inner view": Professor Rich said he would give me an inner view for a job.)

/ts/ and /dz/ Clusters

The /ts/ and /dz/ combinations are frequently mispronounced. The /t/ and /d/ are often omitted, or the combination is sloppily produced.

EXERCISES

Overarticulate each of the following words. Do not pull away too much when you practice. To make closure in the production of /t/ and /d/, feel the tongue in contact with the alveolar ridge. The tongue tip then drops, and the escaping air is forced through the narrow groove down the front of the tongue in the production of /s/ and /z/.

/ts/		/dz/	
goa̲ts̲	[gots]	goa̲ds̲	[godz]
bi̲tes̲	[baɪts]	bi̲des̲	[baɪdz]
to̲tes̲	[tots]	toa̲ds̲	[todz]
coa̲ts̲	[kots]	co̲des̲	[kodz]
righ̲ts̲	[raɪts]	ri̲des̲	[raɪdz]
ca̲ts̲	[kæts]	ca̲ds̲	[kædz]
insigh̲ts̲	[ˈɪnsaɪts]	insi̲des̲	[ˈɪnsaɪdz]
no̲tes̲	[nots]	no̲des̲	[nodz]
cu̲ts̲	[kʌts]	cu̲ds̲	[kʌdz]
ma̲tes̲	[mets]	mai̲ds̲	[medz]
sligh̲ts̲	[slaɪts]	sli̲des̲	[slaɪdz]
bu̲tts̲	[bʌts]	bu̲ds̲	[bʌdz]

/sts/ Clusters

Although this is a difficult combination that takes practice to make habitual, in career speech /sts/ is one of the most important combinations in the language. Its correct pronunciation reflects a speaker of precision and care. Anyone interested in a communications career should master this combination. The most common error is to omit the imploded /t/ plosive and, instead, make one long /s/ phoneme.

EXERCISES

1. The following words appear in singular and plural verb forms. Exaggerate the articulation of each. As you pronounce each, feel what the articulators are doing. If you have difficulty inserting the plosive in the plural form, separate the cluster /sts/ into /s/ and /ts/. Prolong the first /s/ in "hosts," for example, but stop the flow of breath by producing an imploded /t/ before proceeding with the production of the second /s/. Go back to the preceding /ts/ word list, and feel what is happening in the production of the cluster. Remember that the modifying mark [ː] prolongs the production of the phoneme.

SINGULAR		PLURAL	
host	[host]	hosts	[hosːts]
blast	[blæst]	blasts	[blæsːts]
priest	[prist]	priests	[prisːts]
boast	[bost]	boasts	[bosːts]
coast	[kost]	coasts	[kosːts]
mast	[mæst]	masts	[mæsːts]
frost	[frɔst]	frosts	[frɔsːts]
taste	[test]	tastes	[tesːts]
cast	[kæst]	casts	[kæsːts]
thrust	[θrʌst]	thrusts	[θrʌsːts]
wrist	[rɪst]	wrists	[rɪsːts]
insist	[ɪnsɪst]	insists	[ɪnsɪsːts]
last	[læst]	lasts	[læsːts]
fist	[fɪst]	fists	[fɪsːts]
post	[post]	posts	[posːts]
assist	[əˈsɪst]	assists	[əˈsɪsːts]

2. In the following tongue twisters, work first to exaggerate the proper production of the sounds. When you have that under control, quicken the pace. When you have succeeded in producing the difficult sound combinations with rapidity and clarity, you are exemplifying diadochokinesis (as you also are when you pronounce this word successfully!). Additional tongue twisters appear on pages 177 through 180.

> Amidst the mists and coldest frosts,
> With barest wrists and stoutest boasts,
> He thrusts his fists against the posts,
> And still insists he sees the ghosts.

> A Swiss wrist wrestler's watch lasts longer when it rests on the wrestler's
> wrists rather than on his fists.

("Mere": I'll bet that Whitney Houston looks into her mere every morning.)

/θs/ and /ðz/ Clusters

 EXERCISES

Read aloud the following words and phrases using negative practice. The untrained speaker tends to omit the fricative before /s/ and /z/ phonemes. Exaggerate the production of the sound, and feel the placement of the articulators. When you try to develop the proper pronunciation, make certain that you do not pull away too much from the over-articulation.

1.

	CAREER	ERROR	CAREER
mouths (n)	[maʊθs]	[maʊz]	[maʊθs]
mouths (v)	[maʊðz]	[maʊz]	[maʊðz]
fourths	[fɔrθs]	[fɔrs] (force)	[fɔrθs]
fifths	[fɪfθs]	[fɪfs]	[fɪfθs]
lengths	[lɛŋkθs]	[lɛŋks]	[lɛŋkθs]
sixths	[sɪksθs]	[sɪks] (six)	[sɪksθs]
depths	[dɛpθs]	[dɛps]	[dɛpθs]
breaths	[brɛθs]	[brɛs]	[brɛθs]

	CAREER	ERROR	CAREER
brea<u>the</u>s	[briðz]	[briz] (breeze) [bridz] (breeds)[8]	[briðz]
wri<u>the</u>s	[raɪðz]	[raɪz] (rise) [raɪdz] (rides)	[raɪðz]
ti<u>the</u>s	[taɪðz]	[taɪz] (ties) [taɪdz] (tides)	[taɪðz]
clo<u>the</u>s	[kloðz]	[klodz][9]	[kloðz]
tee<u>the</u>s	[tiðz]	[tiz] (tease)	[tiðz]

2.

	CAREER	ERROR	CAREER
leng<u>th</u>s of cord	[lɛŋkθs əv kɔrd]	[lɛŋks əv kɔrd]	[lɛŋkθs əv kɔrd]
brea<u>the</u>s some air	[briðz səm er]	[briz səm er] [bridz səm er]	[briðz səm er]
washes clo<u>the</u>s	['wɑʃəz kloðz]	['wɑʃəz klodz]	['wɑʃəz kloðz]
wri<u>the</u>s with pain	[raɪðz wɪð pen]	[raɪz wɪð pen] [raɪdz wɪð pen]	[raɪðz wɪð pen]
brea<u>the</u>s diaphragmatically	[briðz daɪəfræg'mætɪklɪ]	[briz daɪəfrə'mædɪglɪ]	[briðz daɪəfræg'mætɪklɪ]

When you think you are ready, recite one of Carl Sandburg's definitions of poetry with speed and continuity:

Poetry is the synthesis of hyacinths and biscuits.

("Mill": My father threw me right in the mill of the pond.)

Repeated Consonants

The following phrases illustrate the use of identically repeated continuant consonant sounds, the first appearing in the final position of a word and the second appearing in the initial position of the next word. It is important to notice that the underlined consonant sounds are repeated. The first time these phrases are pronounced, take a slight pause between the words with underlined sounds to demonstrate the presence of two consonant sounds. The second time prolong the underlined sound of the first word in the pair so that a break does not occur between the two sounds. Prolong the sound long enough to indicate that the pronunciation is of two separate sounds. This would be preferred for career speech.

/f/	a li<u>fe</u> <u>f</u>orce	chie<u>f</u> <u>f</u>inancial officer	to laug<u>h</u> <u>f</u>ully
/v/	li<u>ve</u> <u>v</u>itally	to lo<u>ve</u> <u>v</u>ibrantly	mo<u>ve</u> <u>v</u>oluntarily
/θ/	bo<u>th</u> <u>th</u>ieves	brea<u>th</u> <u>th</u>at reeks	uncou<u>th</u> <u>th</u>ought
/ð/	loa<u>the</u> <u>th</u>at	soo<u>the</u> <u>th</u>em	brea<u>the</u> <u>th</u>ere
/s/	si<u>x</u> <u>s</u>enses	fa<u>ce</u> <u>C</u>ynthia	ni<u>ce</u> <u>s</u>cenery
/z/	doe<u>s</u> <u>z</u>ero	buz<u>z</u> <u>Z</u>anzibar	i<u>s</u> <u>z</u>ipping
/ʃ/	pu<u>sh</u> <u>sh</u>eep	ra<u>sh</u> <u>sh</u>all itch	lea<u>sh</u> <u>sh</u>op
/ʒ/	No English words with /ʒ/ in the initial position		
/h/	No English words with /h/ in the final position		
/l/	Li<u>l</u> <u>l</u>oves	Phi<u>l</u> <u>l</u>ongs	ba<u>ll</u> <u>l</u>ost
/r/	sto<u>re</u> <u>r</u>eady	fou<u>r</u> <u>r</u>ipe bananas	hea<u>r</u> <u>r</u>hyme
/w/	No English words with /w/ in the final position		
/j/	No English words with /j/ in the final position		

---

[8]There clearly is a distinct difference between "breathing" and "breeding."
[9]There are two acceptable pronunciations of the noun *clothes:* [kloz] and [kloðz]. The former is used by most and is considered the cultivated colloquial pronunciation. The second is preferred in career speech.

/m/	home mate	climb mountains	autumn memories
/n/	Maine native	green knit	token neighbor
/ŋ/	No English words with /ŋ/ in the initial positon		

("Mince": Leave the office in exactly fifteen mince!)

Omission of /l/

 EXERCISES

1. In the following words, the /l/ phoneme is correctly omitted, even though some trained speakers say it. Consult your dictionary.

	CAREER	ERROR	CAREER
salmon	['sæmən]	['sælmən]	['sæmən]
half	[hæf]	[hælf]	[hæf]
walk	[wɔk]	[wɔlk]	[wɔk]
calf	[kæf]	[kælf]	[kæf]
Salk	[sɔk]	[sɔlk]	[sɔk]
palm	[pɑm]	[pɑlm]	[pɑm]
behalf	[bɪ'hæf]	[bɪ'hælf]	[bɪ'hæf]
psalms	[sɑmz]	[sɑlmz]	[sɑmz]
folklore	['foklɔr]	['folklɔr]	['foklɔr][10]
balk	[bɔk]	[bɔlk]	[bɔk]
almond	['amənd]	['almənd]	['amənd]
calm	[kam]	[kalm]	[kam]
chalk	[tʃɔk]	[tʃɔlk]	[tʃɔk]
folks	[foks]	[folks]	[foks]
embalm	[ɛm'bam]	[ɛm'balm]	[ɛm'bam]

2. On the other hand, sometimes the /l/ phoneme is omitted when it should be articulated. Practice pronouncing the following words.

	CAREER	ERROR	CAREER
milk	[mɪlk]	[mɪuk]	[mɪlk]
welcome	['wɛlkəm]	['wɛukəm]	['wɛlkəm]
railroad	['relrod]	[reurod]	['relrod]
million	['mɪljən]	['mɪujən] ['mɪjən]	['mɪljən]
William	['wɪljəm]	['wɪujəm] ['wɪjəm]	['wɪljəm]
trillion	['trɪljən]	['trɪujən] ['trɪjən]	['trɪljən]
help	[hɛlp]	[hɛup]	[hɛlp]
build	[bɪld]	[bɪud]	[bɪld]
bulb	[bʌlb]	[baʊb]	[bʌlb]

On his popular television program, Milton Berle used to say:

"I'll kill you a million times!" [aʊ kɪu ju ə mɪujən taɪmz]

A popular politician of the past was once called:

---

[10]Only one /l/ phoneme is pronounced in "folklore."

Wendell L. Willkie [ˈwɛndɪu ɛu ˈwɪukɪ]

Now say it correctly:

[ˈwɛndl̩ ɛl ˈwɪl̩kɪ]

("Intensive": For all intensive purposes we just shouldn't meet like this.)

Substitution of /ŋ/ for /n/

The problem of substituting /ŋ/ for /n/ arises when /n/ precedes the plosives /k/ and /g/. Because /ŋ/ has an articulatory adjustment similar to that of /k/ and /g/, it is easier to anticipate the plosives by changing the /n/ to /ŋ/.

EXERCISES

Although many of the word lists in this chapter may seem like overkill, they serve a most useful purpose. Remember that modification of speech behaviors occurs only after a great deal of practice, and only at that point can these behaviors become habit. The extended lists give variety as well as practice.

Read aloud the following words, and use negative practice. Exaggerate the production of the words, and feel what the articulators are doing. Do not pull away too much from the overarticulation.

	CAREER	ERROR	CAREER
in̠come	[ˈɪn̠kəm]	[ˈɪŋkəm]	[ˈɪn̠kəm]
in̠congruous	[ɪn̠ˈkɑŋgruəs]	[ɪŋˈkɑŋgruəs]	[ɪn̠ˈkɑŋgruəs]
in̠cantation	[ɪn̠kænˈteʃən]	[ɪŋkænˈteʃən]	[ɪn̠kænˈteʃən]
in̠capable	[ɪn̠ˈkepəbl̩]	[ɪŋˈkepəbl̩]	[ɪn̠ˈkepəbl̩]
in̠ case	[ɪn̠ ˈkes]	[ɪŋ ˈkes]	[ɪn̠ ˈkes]
in̠coming	[ˈɪn̠kʌmɪŋ]	[ˈɪŋkʌmɪŋ]	[ˈɪn̠kʌmɪŋ]
in̠close	[ɪn̠ˈkloz]	[ɪŋˈkloz]	[ɪn̠ˈkloz]
in̠complete	[ɪn̠kəmˈplit]	[ɪŋkəmˈplit]	[ɪn̠kəmˈplit]
in̠crease (n.)	[ˈɪn̠kris]	[ˈɪŋkris]	[ˈɪn̠kris]
in̠correct	[ɪn̠kəˈrɛkt]	[ɪŋkəˈrɛkt]	[ɪn̠kəˈrɛkt]
in̠credible	[ɪn̠ˈkrɛdəbl̩]	[ɪŋˈkrɛdəbl̩]	[ɪn̠ˈkrɛdəbl̩]
in̠nkeeper	[ˈɪn̠kipɚ]	[ˈɪŋkipɚ]	[ˈɪn̠kipɚ]
in̠grain	[ˈɪn̠gren]	[ˈɪŋgren]	[ˈɪn̠gren]
in̠grate	[ˈɪn̠gret]	[ˈɪŋgret]	[ˈɪn̠gret]
in̠going	[ˈɪn̠goɪŋ]	[ˈɪŋgoɪŋ]	[ˈɪn̠goɪŋ]
in̠gredient	[ɪn̠ˈgridiənt]	[ɪŋˈgridiənt]	[ɪn̠ˈgridiənt]

Substitution of /m̪/ for /nf/ and /nv/

You will remember that the symbol /m̪/ indicates that the phoneme is produced with **dentalization;** that is, it is produced with the upper teeth touching the lower lip rather than by its usual **bilabial** production. When either /nf/ or /nv/ follows /m/, the /m/ is often dentalized because of assimilation. For instance, it is easier to articulate /m̪f/ than /nf/ in the word *confine,* and whatever is easier is usually the route taken by the untrained speaker.

EXERCISES

In the following words, make certain that you take the time to produce the /n/ before moving to the fricative /f/ or /v/ or to the plosive /p/ or /b/. Exaggerate the pronunciation using negative practice. During exhalation, make certain that you do not pull away too much from the overarticulation.

	CAREER	ERROR	CAREER
Sta<u>n</u>ford	[ˈstæ<u>n</u>fɚd]	[ˈstæm̩fɚd]	[ˈstæ<u>n</u>fɚd]
cra<u>n</u>berry	[ˈkræ<u>n</u>bɛrɪ]	[ˈkræm̩bɛrɪ]	[ˈkræ<u>n</u>bɛrɪ]
co<u>n</u>fine	[kən̩ˈfaɪn]	[kəm̩faɪn]	[kən̩ˈfaɪn]
co<u>n</u>fection	[kən̩ˈfɛkʃən]	[kəm̩ˈfɛkʃən]	[kən̩ˈfɛkʃən]
co<u>n</u>federate	[kən̩ˈfɛdɚət]	[kəm̩ˈfɛdɚət]	[kən̩ˈfɛdɚət]
co<u>n</u>fess	[kən̩ˈfɛs]	[kəm̩fɛs]	[kən̩ˈfɛs]
co<u>n</u>fer	[kən̩ˈfɝ]	[kəm̩ˈfɝ]	[kən̩ˈfɝ]
co<u>n</u>firm	[kən̩ˈfɝm]	[kəm̩ˈfɝm]	[kən̩ˈfɝm]
co<u>n</u>fuse	[kən̩ˈfɪuz]	[kəm̩ˈfɪuz]	[kən̩ˈfɪuz]
co<u>n</u>vert	[kən̩ˈvɝt]	[kəm̩ˈvɝt]	[kən̩ˈvɝt]
co<u>n</u>verge	[kən̩vɝʤ]	[kəm̩vɝʤ]	[kən̩vɝʤ]
co<u>n</u>vey	[kən̩ˈveɪ]	[kəm̩ˈveɪ]	[kən̩ˈveɪ]
co<u>n</u>vince	[kən̩ˈvɪns]	[kəm̩ˈvɪns]	[kən̩ˈvɪns]
i<u>n</u>firm	[ɪn̩ˈfɝm]	[ɪm̩ˈfɝm]	[ɪn̩ˈfɝm]
i<u>n</u>fection	[ɪn̩ˈfɛkʃən]	[ɪm̩ˈfɛkʃən]	[ɪn̩ˈfɛkʃən]
i<u>n</u>ference	[ˈɪnfɚəns]	[ˈɪm̩fɚəns]	[ˈɪnfɚəns]
i<u>n</u>fidel	[ˈɪnfədl̩]	[ˈɪm̩fədl̩]	[ˈɪnfədl̩]
i<u>n</u>finitive	[ɪn̩ˈfɪnətɪv]	[ɪm̩ˈfɪnətɪv]	[ɪn̩ˈfɪnətɪv]
i<u>n</u>flate	[ɪn̩ˈflet]	[ɪm̩ˈflet]	[ɪn̩ˈflet]
i<u>n</u>fringe	[ɪn̩ˈfrɪnʤ]	[ɪm̩ˈfrɪnʤ]	[ɪn̩ˈfrɪnʤ]
i<u>n</u>fluence	[ˈɪnfluəns]	[ˈɪm̩fluəns]	[ˈɪnfluəns]
i<u>n</u>formal	[ɪn̩ˈfɔrməl]	[ɪm̩ˈfɔrməl]	[ɪn̩ˈfɔrməl]
u<u>n</u>fit	[ʌn̩ˈfɪt]	[ʌm̩fɪt]	[ʌn̩ˈfɪt]
u<u>n</u>fold	[ˈʌn̩fold]	[ˈʌm̩fold]	[ˈʌn̩fold]
u<u>n</u>flinch	[ˈʌn̩flɪntʃ]	[ˈʌm̩flɪntʃ]	[ˈʌn̩flɪntʃ]
u<u>n</u>feeling	[ʌn̩ˈfilɪŋ]	[ʌm̩ˈfilɪŋ]	[ʌn̩ˈfilɪŋ]
ha<u>n</u>dbag	[ˈhæ<u>n</u>dbæg]	[ˈhæm̩bæg]	[ˈhæ<u>n</u>dbæg]
sa<u>n</u>dbag	[ˈsæ<u>n</u>dbæg]	[ˈsæm̩bæg]	[ˈsæ<u>n</u>dbæg]

Dentalization of /p/ and /b/

 EXERCISES

1. In pronouncing the words in the following list, use negative practice. When making the correction, do not allow the upper teeth to touch the lower lip on the bilabial plosive before articulating the fricatives /f/ and /v/, as in the words *stop fast* [stɑp'fæst]. Give the plosive sounds their full bilabial adjustment. Hold the imploded plosive longer than usual so that you can feel the bilabial adjustment. Remember that [ː] after a sound usually indicates prolongation. For this exercise the modifying mark indicates that the plosive is being imploded.

	CAREER	ERROR	CAREER
step first	[stɛpʼː fɝˑst]	[stɛp ː fɝˑst]	[stɛpʼː fɝˑst]
top value	[tɑpʼː vælju]	[tɑp ː vælju]	[tɑpʼː vælju]
obvious	[ɑbʼːvɪəs]	[ab̥ ːvɪəs]	[ɑbʼːvɪəs]
stop Frank	[stɑpʼː fræŋk]	[stɑp ː fræŋk]	[stɑpʼː fræŋk]
mob violence	[mɑbʼː vaɪələns]	[mɑb̥ ː vaɪələns]	[mɑbʼː vaɪələns]
rob Verne	[rɑbʼː vɝˑn]	[rɑb̥ ː vɝˑn]	[rɑbʼː vɝˑn]
Fab vendors	[fæbʼː vɛndɚz]	[fæb̥ ː vɛndɚz]	[fæbʼː vɛndɚz]
group fatigue	[grupʼː fətig]	[grup ː fətig]	[grupʼː fətig]
Stepford Wives	[stɛpʼːfɚd waɪvz]	[stɛp ːfɚd waɪvz]	[stɛpʼːfɚd waɪvz]

2. In the following phrases, the underlined sounds highlight continuant cognate pairs. A slight pause must be taken between the cognates to voice or unvoice the consonant sound.

/f/ and /v/	love Fred	massive phone	safe vaults	leaf vanished
/θ/ and /ð/	loathe thin lips	soothe Thelma	breathe through	smooth things
/s/ and /z/	six zoos	rose smells	eyes sing	place zinc
/ʃ/ and /ʒ/	massage Shelley	beige shoes	camouflage shawls	wash Zsa Zsa

>>>
SYLLABLE OMISSION AND ADDITION

There are a number of words whose pronunciations have been altered through the omission of a syllable. Obviously, enough speakers have made the change in pronunciation that the changes are reflected in the dictionary. The following list of words is divided into "career" and "conversational." "Conversational" is defined as "informal." Thus, actors might present themselves with career speech but use conversational speech when in character. Trained speakers would obviously use the career pronunciations. You are encouraged to maintain flexibility in communication in your career.

	CAREER	CONVERSATIONAL
literature	[ˈlɪtɚrətʃur]	[ˈlɪtrətʃur][11]
interesting	[ˈɪntərɛstɪŋ]	[ˈɪntrɪstɪŋ]
sophomore	[ˈsɑfəmɔr] or [ˈsɑfmɔr]	[ˈsɑfmɔr]
traveling	[ˈtrævəlɪŋ] or [ˈtrævlɪŋ]	[ˈtrævlɪŋ]
scenery	[ˈsinərɪ]	[ˈsinrɪ]
camera	[ˈkæmərə]	[ˈkæmrə]
veteran	[ˈvɛtərən]	[ˈvɛtrən]
family	[ˈfæməlɪ]	[ˈfæmlɪ]
boundary	[ˈbaʊndərɪ]	[ˈbaʊndrɪ][12]
difference	[ˈdɪfərəns]	[ˈdɪfrəns]
salary	[ˈsælərɪ]	[ˈsælrɪ]
temperamental	[tɛmpɚrəˈmɛntl̩]	[tɛmprəˈmɛntl̩][13]
liberal	[ˈlɪbərəl]	[ˈlɪbrəl]
memory	[ˈmɛmərɪ]	[ˈmɛmrɪ]
misery	[ˈmɪzərɪ]	[ˈmɪzrɪ]

---

[11]Often mispronounced as "lidercher" [ˈlɪdɚtʃɚ].

[12]According to *The American Heritage Dictionary,* the first and second pronunciations are [ˈbaʊndrɪ] and [ˈbaʊndərɪ], respectively.

[13]According to *The American Heritage Dictionary,* the first and second pronunciations are [tɛmprəˈmɛntl̩] and [tɛmpərəˈmɛntl̩], respectively.

The following words are pronounced with their full sound values according to *The American Heritage Dictionary:*

federal	['fɛdərl̩] *not* ['fɛdr̩l]
victory	['vɪktərɪ] *not* ['vɪktr̩ɪ]
regular	['rɛgjulɚ] *not* ['rɛgəlɚ]
considerable	[kən'sɪdərəbl̩] *not* [kən'sɪdrəbl̩]
bakery	['bekərɪ] *not* ['bekr̩ɪ]
liable	['laɪəbl̩] *not* ['laɪbl̩]
privilege	['prɪvəlɪdʒ] *not* ['prɪvlɪdʒ]
grocery	['grosərɪ] *not* ['grosr̩ɪ]
poem	['poəm] *not* [pom]
mathematics	[mæθə'mætɪks] *not* [mæθ'mætɪks]
history	['hɪstərɪ] *not* ['hɪstr̩ɪ]
celery	['sɛlərɪ] *not* ['sɛlr̩ɪ]
delivery	[dɪ'lɪvərɪ] *not* [dɪ'lɪvr̩ɪ]
miniature	['mɪnɪətʃur] *not* ['mɪnətʃur]
criminal	['krɪmɪnl̩] *not* ['krɪmnl̩]
General Delivery	['dʒɛnərl̩ dɪlɪ'vərɪ] *not* ['dʒɛnr̩l̩ dɪl'ɪvr̩ɪ]

Often the secondary pronunciation becomes the preferred one because the pronunciation that contains the omitted syllable is easier to say (and we know how lazy some speakers can be!). This has occurred with "laboratory," whose preferred pronunciation is now [læbrə'tɔrɪ], rather than ['læbərə'tɔrɪ], which this text prefers.

("Win": When the win blows the temperature drops 20 degrees.)

>>>
ANAPTYXIS

Sometimes speakers produce an additional vowel, often the schwa, between two consonants. This linguistic error is called **anaptyxis**.

(((EXERCISES

Use negative practice on the following list of frequently mispronounced words, and add new words to the list.

	CAREER	ERROR	CAREER
triathlon	[traɪ'æθlɔn]	[traɪ'æθələn]	[traɪ'æθlɔn]
pentathlon	[pɛn'tæθlɔn]	[pɛn'tæθələn]	[pɛn'tæθlɔn]
disastrous	[dɪz'æstrəs]	[dɪz'æstərəs]	[dɪz'æstrəs]
umbrella	[ʌm'brɛlə]	[ʌm'bərɛlə]	[ʌm'brɛlə]
chimney	['tʃɪmnɪ]	['tʃɪmənɪ]	['tʃɪmnɪ]
mischievous	['mɪstʃɪvəs]	[mɪs'tʃivɪəs]	['mɪstʃɪvəs]
ambidextrous	[æmbɪ'dɛkstrəs]	[æmbɪ'dɛkstərəs]	[æmbɪ'dɛkstrəs]
toward	[tɔrd]	['towɚd]	[tɔrd]
lightning	['laɪtnɪŋ]	['laɪtənɪŋ]	['laɪtnɪŋ]
remembrance	[rɪ'mɛmbrəns]	[rɪ'mɛmbərəns]	[rɪ'mɛmbrəns]
sparkling	['spɑrklɪŋ]	['spɑrkəlɪŋ]	['spɑrklɪŋ]

	CAREER	ERROR	CAREER
athletic	[æθˈlɛtɪk]	[æθəˈlɛtɪk]	[æθˈlɛtɪk]
laundry	[ˈlɔndrɪ]	[ˈlɔndərɪ]	[ˈlɔndrɪ]
troubling	[ˈtrʌblɪŋ]	[ˈtrʌbəlɪŋ]	[ˈtrʌblɪŋ]
heartrending	[ˈhɑrtˌrɛndɪŋ]	[ˈhɑrtˌrɛndərɪŋ]	[ˈhɑrtˌrɛndɪŋ]
evening	[ˈivnɪŋ]	[ˈivənɪŋ]	[ˈivnɪŋ]
bubbling	[ˈbʌblɪŋ]	[ˈbʌbəlɪŋ]	[ˈbʌblɪŋ]
grievous	[ˈgrivəs]	[ˈgriviəs]	[ˈgrivəs]
business	[ˈbɪznəs]	[ˈbɪzənəs][14]	[ˈbɪznəs]
chuckling	[ˈtʃʌklɪŋ]	[ˈtʃʌkəlɪŋ]	[ˈtʃʌklɪŋ]
please	[pliz]	[pəliz]	[pliz]

("Lays": Lays and genlmen of the jury, have you reached your verdict?)

>>>

THE SNEEZING ERROR

One of the most common errors made by untrained (and too many trained) speakers is as-similation when the pronoun "you" (or its variations) follows a plosive, particularly /t/ and /d/. The resulting sound often imitates the sneeze [əˈtʃu]. This error is exemplified in the following:

Speaker 1:   [dʒitjɛt]

Speaker 2:   [nodʒu]

Speaker 1:   [no skwit]

The translation of this is:

Speaker 1:   [dɪd ju it jɛt]
           Did you eat yet?

Speaker 2:   [no dɪd ju]
           No, did you?

Speaker 1:   [no lɛts go it]
           No. Let's go eat.

Or the following:

Speaker 1:   [dʒu wɔŋˈgo]
           Do you want to go?

Speaker 2:   [kmɪr fɚ ˈmɪnɪt] [dʒu no wʌd ˈmin]
           Come here for a minute. Do you know what I mean?

This error must be corrected for it is the basest of sound combinations. Such errors might even be considered barbaric and bestial utterances—and they are not used by trained speak-ers! In correcting this speech deviation, first give attention to the imploded plosive. Then, you move into the /j/ or into the diphthong /ju/.

---

[14]In some areas of the country, [ˈbidnəs] is also heard.

(((**EXERCISES**

1. In the following exercises, hold the indicated imploded plosive in practice for a full second before moving into the /ju/ diphthong. This will help you focus on the proper articulatory adjustment. Then, give appropriate timing to the plosives as they appear in the right-hand column.

	PRACTICE	CORRECT
Did you?	[dɪd'ːju]	[dɪd'ju]
Won't you?	[wont'ː ju]	[wont'ju]
He didn't cast you.	[hɪ dɪdn̩t kæst'ː ju]	[hɪ dɪdn̩t kæst' ju]
Couldn't you do it?	[kʊdn̩t'ː ju du ɪt]	[kʊdn̩t' ju du ɪt]
It's the cat you mean.	[ɪts ðə kæt'ː ju min]	[ɪts ðə kæt' ju min]
Let the baby pat you.	[lɛt ðə bebɪ pæt'ː ju]	[lɛt ðə bebɪ pæt' ju]
the pad you bought	[ðə pæd'ː ju bɔt]	[ðə pæd' ju bɔt]

2. Use negative practice in the following exercise. Exaggerate the articulation of the error as well as the correct pronunciation. Make certain that you do not pull away too much from the overarticulation when you speak correctly.

	CAREER	ERROR	CAREER
Don't you	[don't' ju]	[dontʃu] (Gesundheit!)	[don't' ju]
makes you	[meks ju]	[mekʃu] (You're a cobbler?)	[meks ju]
Won't you?	[wont' ju]	[wontʃu]	[wont' ju]
Did you?	[dɪd' ju]	[dɪdʒu]	[dɪd' ju]
Can't you?	[kænt' ju]	[kæntʃu]	[kænt' ju]
trust you	[trʌst' ju]	[trʌstʃu]	[trʌst' ju]
but you	[bʌt' ju]	[bʌtʃu]	[bʌt' ju]
Would you?	[wud ju]	[wudʒu]	[wud ju]
Bite your nails.	[baɪt jɔr nelz]	[baɪtʃɚ nelz]	[baɪt jɔr nelz]
Lift your leg.	[lɪft jɔr lɛg]	[lɪftʃɚleg]	[lɪft jɔr lɛg]
Hold your temper.	[hold jɔr 'tɛmpɚ]	[holdʒɚ 'tɛmpɚ]	[hold jɔr 'tɛmpɚ]
Could you?	[kʊd ju]	[kʊdʒu]	[kʊd ju]
What's your name?	[ʍʌts jɔr nem]	[ʍʌtʃɚ nem]	[ʍʌts jɔr nem]
Change your mind.	[tʃendʒ jɔr maɪnd]	[tʃendʒɚ maɪnd]	[tʃendʒ jɔr maɪnd]
May I go with you?	[meɪ aɪ go wɪð ju]	[meɪ aɪ go wɪtʃu]	[meɪ aɪ go wɪð ju]

3. Say the following sentences being careful to substitute /t/ or /d/ for the underlined Sneezing Error:

   a. Perhaps she wouldn't want you to go with her.

   b. You said I convinced you to stay with me.

   c. Did you see the way Juergen smiled at you?

   d. Would you try hard not to be so darn bossy?

   e. That is what you said to Martha.

4. As you read aloud this paragraph, make certain that you are pronouncing the underlined sounds properly. Keep in mind that the speaker is, obviously, not one of Rob's best buddies!

   Did you do it, Rob? Or did you not? I told you on Tuesday that you really ought to audition for that commercial. And don't say, "Mind your own business!" Won't you do it as a special favor for a friend? If you will, could you or rather would you give me a call? And what's your part in the commercial? If you make a mistake hold your temper. And don't let this upset you. It happened last year because you couldn't put the fight with Alex behind you. That's the reason Dr. Ashermann didn't cast you in the last play. Can I trust you to have a positive attitude? And remember, if you change your mind, be sure and give me a buzz. (Sure!)

("Winner": My mother-in-law always gets cold in the winner.)

>>> HOMONYMS, HOMOPHONES, AND HOMOGRAPHS

The Spelling Chequer
(oar, poet tree without miss takes)

Eye have a spelling checker,
It came with my pea see;
It plainly marks four my revue
Miss steaks I cannot sea.

Each thyme when I have struck the quays
Eye weight four it two say
If watt eye rote is wrong or rite …
It shows me strait a weigh.

As soon as a mist ache is maid
It nose bee fore too late
And eye can put the error rite.
Eve really fined it grate.

I've run this poem threw it,
I'm sure your pleased to no,
Its letter perfect in it's weight.
My checker tolled me sew.

Anonymous

A **homonym** is one of two or more words that have the same sounds and often the same spelling but have differences in meaning. They can be a problem in both spelling and pronunciation for those speaking English and those learning it. The words can be very confusing, and there are many of them in our language. There are so many more!

sewer Sue her	tear	wind
number Numb her	close	bass
object	invalid	sow
does	row	desert
wound	dove	polish

A **homophone** is a type of homonym in which the sounds are the same but the words are spelled differently. There are so many more than those using the letters a and b.

Refer to additional homophonous words on p. 270.

acts	axe	ade	aid	aide
aero	arrow	ale	ail	

air	e'er	ere	heir	aisle	isle	I'll
allowed	aloud			Ann	an	
ant	aunt			ascent	assent	
aught	ought			aural	oral	
away	aweigh			awed	odd	
awful	awful	offal		aye	eye	I
bear	bare	bair		baron	barren	
bald	bawled	balled		based	baste	
band	banned			bait	bate	
bar	barre			beach	beech	
bard	barred			beau	bow	
blew	blue			bred	bread	
bier	beer			but	butt	
by	bye	buy		bused	bussed	bust

A **homograph** is one of two or more words that are spelled in the same way but differ in meaning, pronunciation, or derivation. Many of the pronunciations differ according to their part of speech. A syllable might be stressed when it appears in a noun but unstressed when used in a verb.

Trained speakers must know these differences. Even though secondary pronunciations appear in dictionaries, reflect the best possible standard. Join the campaign to keep your language as pure as possible.

In conclusion, all homographs are homonyms but not all homonyms are homographs. A homograph is a subdivision of a homonym. Got it?

(((**EXERCISES**

1. Read aloud the following list of homographs, paying close attention to the shifts in stress. The stress marks for primary ['] and secondary [ˌ] appear before the syllable.

	NOUN	VERB	ADJECTIVE
progress	['prɑˌgrɛs]	[ˌprəˈgrɛs]	
ally	['æ laɪ]	[əˈlaɪ]	
content	['kɑnˌtɛnt]	[ˌkənˈtɛnt]	
estimate	['ɛs tə ˌmɪt]	['ɛs tə ˌmet]	
combat	['kɑmˌbæt]	[ˌkəmˈbæt]	
permit	['pɝˌmɪt]	[ˌpɝˈmɪt]	
discharge	['dɪsˌtʃɑrdʒ]	[ˌdɪsˈtʃɑrdʒ]	
object	['ɑbˌdʒɪkt]	[ˌəbˈdʒɛkt]	
pervert	['pɝˌvɝt]	[ˌpɝˈvɝt]	
conduct	['kɑnˌdəkt]	[ˌkənˈdʌkt]	
convict	['kɑnˌvɪkt]	[ˌkənˈvɪkt]	
recall	['riˌkɔl][15]	[ˌrɪˈkɔl]	
research	[ˌrɪˈsɝtʃ]	[ˌrɪˈsɝtʃ]	
	['riˌsɝtʃ][15]		
conflict	['kɑnˌflɪkt]	[ˌkənˈflɪkt]	
convert	['kɑnˌvɝt]	[ˌkənˈvɝt]	
insult	['ɪnˌsəlt]	[ˌɪnˈsʌlt]	
overflow	['ovɚˌfloʊ]	[ˌovɚˈfloʊ]	

---

[15]These are the primary pronunciations in Kenyon and Knott, *A Pronouncing Dictionary*. Variations of these pronunciations appear in other dictionaries.

	NOUN	VERB	ADJECTIVE
digest	['daɪ ˌʤɛst]	[də 'ʤɛst]	
present	['prɛ ˌzn̩t]	[ˌprɪ 'zɛnt]	
contrast	['kɑn ˌtræst]	[ˌkən 'træst]	
torment	['tɔr ˌmɛnt]	[ˌtɔr 'mɛnt]	
lament	[ˌlə 'mɛnt]	[ˌlə 'mɛnt][16]	
survey	['sɝ ˌveɪ]	[ˌsɚ 'veɪ]	
rebel	['rɛ ˌbl̩]	[ˌrɪ 'bɛl]	
extract	['ɛk ˌstrækt]	[ˌɛk 'strækt]	
appropriate		[ə 'propri ˌet]	[ə 'propriɪt]
articulate		[ɑr 'tɪk jə ˌlet]	[ɑr 'tɪk jə lɪt]
perfect		[ˌpɚ 'fɛkt]	['pɝ fɪkt]
frequent		[ˌfri 'kwɛnt]	['fri ˌkwənt]
consummate		['kɑn sə ˌmet]	[ˌkən 'sʌm ɪt]
intimate	['ɪn tə met]	['ɪn tə ˌmet]	['ɪn tə mɪt]

2. Pronounce the following sentences using the preceding pronunciations. (This exercise will also force you to refresh your knowledge of the parts of speech.)

They wouldn't *permit* me to buy a *permit*.
All *rebels* are supposed to *rebel!*
He's a *pervert* with very *perverted* ideas.
Vanilla *extract* was *extracted* from the beans.
The *surveyors' survey surveyed* the back forty!
Waldo not only *insulted* me, but he gave Frieda the worst *insults* of her life.
Robert *intimated* that they were *intimate* friends.
The sink *overflow* was so bad that the water *overflowed* and the ceiling fell down.
Chris and Helen made *frequent* stops at all of the stores they had *frequented* over the years looking for pistachio nuts from Crete.
The battery was *discharging* and just wouldn't start.
The hose's *discharge* was a green misty gas.
The *convict* was *convicted* of heinous crimes.
He could *lead* if he could get the *lead* out.
Since there is no time like the *present*, he thought it was time to *present* the *present*.
The dump was very full and had to *refuse* any more *refuse*.
The Sheik decided to *desert* his *dessert* in the *desert*.
The stag *does* strange things when the *does* are present.

3. Copy this page and transcribe the following homographs into phonetics, including the primary and secondary stresses.

	NOUN		VERB		ADJECTIVE	
abuse	[	]	abuse	[	]	
bow	[	]	bow	[	]	
confine	[	]	confine	[	]	
addict	[	]	addict	[	]	
buffet	[	]	buffet	[	]	
conserve	[	]	conserve	[	]	
			approximate	[	]	approximate [ ]
combine	[	]	combine	[	]	
consort	[	]	consort	[	]	

[16]Notice that the noun and verb are pronounced the same.

attribute	[	]	attribute	[	]			
contest	[	]	contest	[	]			
August	[	]				august	[	]
base	[	]	base	[	]	base	[	]
bass	[	]				bass	[	]
compact	[	]	compact	[	]	compact	[	]
delegate	[	]	delegate	[	]			
import	[	]	import	[	]	import	[	]
suspect	[	]	suspect	[	]	suspect	[	]

("Inner net": Please show me how to get on the Inner net.)

>>>
METATHESIS AND HAPLOLOGY

Two common errors in pronunciation are *metathesis* and *haplology*. **Metathesis** is the reversal of sounds within the same word. Recently, politicians have been talking about the possibility of a ['nu kju lɚ] (instead of a ['njuklɪɚ]) war. This slip of the tongue, which is often highlighted on radio and television "blooper" shows, is similar to a **spoonerism**, in which sounds in different words are transposed (as in "getting your mords wixed," "hutterly artless," "shake a tower [unless you're Goliath or Samson]," and "slopped her dripper")*.

The second error, **haplology**, is the omission of a repeated sound or syllable ([hæp 'alədʒɪ] for [hæp 'lalədʒɪ].

 EXERCISES FOR METATHESIS

As you read aloud the following word lists, use negative practice. Exaggerate the correct and incorrect pronunciations. When developing the correct pronunciation, use a mirror, and do not pull away too much from the overdone articulation. Let the visual image determine to what degree you add to or minimize articulation.

	CAREER	ERROR	CAREER
sibilant	['sɪbələnt]	['sɪləbənt]	['sɪbələnt]
deficit	['dɛfəsɪt]	['dɛsəfɪt]	['dɛfəsɪt]
strategy	['strætədʒɪ]	['strædʒətɪ]	['strætədʒɪ]
synonymous	[sɪn'anəməs]	[sɪn'amənəs]	[sɪn'anəməs]
sepulcher	['sɛpulkɚ]	['sɛpləkɚ]	['sɛpulkɚ]
officer	['afɪsɚ]	['asɪfɚ]	['afɪsɚ]
cavalry	['kævəlrɪ]	['kælvərɪ]	['kævəlrɪ]
calvary	['kælvərɪ]	['kævəlrɪ]	['kælvərɪ]
fraternize	[frætɚnaɪz]	[frætrənaɪz]	[frætɚnaɪz]
relevant	['rɛləvənt]	['rɛvələnt]	['rɛləvənt]
hospital	['haspɪtl̩]	['hapsɪtl̩]	['haspɪtl̩]
I asked her	[aɪ æskt hɚ]	[aɪ ækst hɚ][17]	[aɪ æskt hɚ]

---

[17][ænd naʊ aɪm ɪn prɪzn̩]

	CAREER	ERROR	CAREER
s<u>p</u>aghetti	[spə 'gɛtɪ]	[pəs 'gɛtɪ]	[spə 'gɛtɪ]
trage<u>dy</u>	['træ<u>ʤ</u>ədɪ]	['trædədʒɪ]	['træ<u>ʤ</u>ədɪ]
asteri<u>sk</u>	['æstərɪ<u>sk</u>]	['æstərɪ<u>ks</u>]	['æstərɪ<u>sk</u>]
		['æ<u>kt</u>əˈɪ<u>ks</u>]	
int<u>r</u>oduction	[ɪn<u>tr</u>ə'dʌkʃən]	[ɪn<u>tɚ</u>'dʌkʃən]	[ɪn<u>tr</u>ə'dʌkʃən]
jewe<u>lr</u>y	['ʤuə<u>lr</u>ɪ]	['ʤulərɪ]	['ʤuə<u>lr</u>ɪ]
jeo<u>par</u>dy	['ʤɛpɚdɪ]	['ʤɛprədɪ]	['ʤɛpɚdɪ]
<u>per</u>spire	[pɚ'spaɪr]	[prə'spaɪr]	[pɚ'spaɪr]
a<u>pr</u>on	['eprən]	['epɚn]	['eprən]
<u>per</u>spiration	[pɚspɪ'reʃən]	[prɛspɪ'reʃən]	[pɚspɪ'reʃən]
hund<u>red</u>	['hʌnd<u>r</u>əd]	['hʌndɚd]	['hʌnd<u>r</u>əd]
p<u>r</u>ofessor	[prə'fɛsɚ]	[pɚ'fɛsɚ]	[prə'fɛsɚ]
child<u>ren</u>	['tʃɪld<u>r</u>ən]	['tʃɪldɚn]	['tʃɪld<u>r</u>ən]
p<u>r</u>escribe	[prə'skraɪb]	[pɚ'skraɪb]	[prə'skraɪb]
<u>per</u>form	[pɚ'fɔrm]	[prə'fɔrm]	[pɚ'fɔrm]
<u>per</u>haps	[pɚ'hæps]	[prə'hæps]	[pɚ'hæps]
Chris Eve<u>rt</u>	[krɪs 'ɛvɚt]	[krɪs 'ɛvrət]	[krɪs 'ɛvɚt]
conve<u>r</u>sation	[,kɑnvɚ'seʃən]	[,kɑnsɚ'veʃən]	[,kɑnvɚ'seʃən]
conse<u>r</u>vational	[,kɑnsɚ'veʃənl̩]	[,kɑnvɚ'seʃənl̩]	[,kɑnsɚ'veʃənl̩]
po<u>r</u>tray	[po<u>r</u>'tre]	[pro'tre]	[po<u>r</u>'tre]

(((EXERCISES FOR HAPLOLOGY

Follow the same procedure with these lists.

	CAREER	ERROR	CAREER
A<u>t</u>lan<u>t</u>a	[æt̬'læn<u>t</u>ə]	[æ'læn<u>t</u>ə]	[æt̬'læn<u>t</u>ə]
		[æt̬'læn<u>ə</u>]	
quan<u>t</u>ity	['kwɑn<u>t</u>ətɪ]	['kwɑnətɪ]	['kwɑn<u>t</u>ətɪ]
p<u>r</u>erogative	[prə'rɑgətɪv]	[pɚ'ɑgətɪv]	[prə'rɑgətɪv]
an<u>t</u>ecedent	[ænt̬ɪ'sidn̩t]	[ænə'sidn̩t]	[ænt̬ɪ'sidn̩t]
den<u>t</u>istry	['dɛn<u>t</u>əstrɪ]	['dɛnəstrɪ]	['dɛn<u>t</u>əstrɪ]
in<u>t</u>eract	[ɪntɚ'ækt]	[ɪnə'ækt]	[ɪntɚ'ækt]
in<u>t</u>erject	[ɪntɚ'ʤɛkt]	[ɪnə'ʤɛkt]	[ɪntɚ'ʤɛkt]
en<u>t</u>ertain	[ɛntɚ'ten]	[ɛnɚ'ten]	[ɛntɚ'ten]
twen<u>t</u>y	['twɛn<u>t</u>ɪ]	['twɛnɪ]	['twɛn<u>t</u>ɪ]
in<u>t</u>eresting	[ɪntɚ'rɪstɪŋ][18]	[ɪnɚrɪstɪŋ]	[ɪntɚrɪstɪŋ]
in<u>t</u>erdepa<u>rt</u>mental	[ɪntɚdɪpart'mɛnl̩]	[ɪnɚdɪpart'mɛnl̩][19]	[ɪntɚdɪpart'mɛnl̩]
		[ɪnɚdɪpar'mɛnl̩][20]	
an<u>t</u>idote	['æntədot]	['ænədot]	['æntədot]
proba<u>b</u>ly	['prɑbəblɪ]	['prɑlɪ]	['prɑbəblɪ]
		['prɑblɪ]	
gove<u>r</u>nor	['gʌvɚnɚ]	['gʌvnɚ]	['gʌvɚnɚ]
Feb<u>r</u>uary	['fɛbruɛrɪ]	['fɛbjuɛrɪ]	['fɛbruɛrɪ]
lib<u>r</u>ary	['laɪbrɛrɪ]	['laɪbɛrɪ]	['laɪbrɛrɪ]
sec<u>r</u>e<u>t</u>ary	['sɛkrətɛrɪ]	['sɛkətɛrɪ]	['sɛkrətɛrɪ]

---

[18] The pronunciation [ɪntə'rɛstɪŋ] is generally considered pedantic speech.

[19] Notice that only one /t/ phoneme remains.

[20] Notice that *no* /t/ phonemes remain!

particularly	[pɑr'tɪkjələrlɪ]	[pɑr'tɪkjəlɪ]	[pɑr'tɪkjələrlɪ]
ophthalmology	[ɑfθəl'mɑlədʒɪ]	[ɑfθə'mɑlədʒɪ]	[ɑfθəl'mɑlədʒɪ]
arctic	['ɑrktɪk]	['ɑrtɪk]	['ɑrktɪk]
substitute	['sʌbstətɪut]	['sʌbsətɪut]	['sʌbstətɪut]
tentative	['tɛntətɪv]	['tɛnətɪv]	['tɛntətɪv]
candidate	['kændədet]	['kænədet]	['kændədet]
fifths	[fɪfθs]	[fɪθs]²¹	[fɪfθs]
		[fɪfs]	

There is another form of anaptyxis in which sounds or syllables in words are repeated, but incorrectly. For example, the words *familiarity* [fəmɪlɪ'ærətɪ] and *auxiliary* [ɔg'zɪljərɪ] are often mispronounced with an additional /r/, as in [fəmɪljə'rærətɪ] and [ɔg'zɪljərɛrɪ].

There are also common errors in the pronunciation of words that use the verb and noun forms. For example, how many speakers correctly pronounce and spell the verb *pronounce* [prə'naʊns] but mispronounce and misspell the noun as [prə,naʊnsɪ'eʃən] rather than [prə,nʌnsɪ'eʃən] (pronunciation)? Fewer speakers have pronunciation difficulty with "explain" and "explanation," although their spelling is often sacrificed.

>>> FOREIGN WORDS

("Pal": I am tired of paling the canoe.)

The following is a list of foreign words and phrases that are commonly used both in conversation and in the communication professions. The American-English pronunciations appear in career speech phonetics. Look up their meanings. The following abbreviations indicate the original language: French, Fr.; Hebrew, H.; Italian, It.; Japanese, Jp.; Latin, L.; Spanish, Sp.; and German, Ger.

a cappella (It.) ['ɑkə'pɛlə]
adagio (It.) [ə'dɑdʒɪo]
ad hoc (L.) ['æd 'hɑk]
adieu (Fr.) [ə'dju]
aficionado (Sp.) [əfɪsɪə'nɑdo]
aide-de-camp (Fr.) ['edda'kɑ̃]
andante (It.) [æn'dæntɪ] [ɑn'dɑnte]
a priori (L.) ['e praɪ'oraɪ]
apropos (Fr.) [æprə'po]
arpeggio (It.) [ɑr'pɛdʒɪo] [ɑr'pɛdʒo]
attaché (Fr.) [ætə'ʃe] [ə'tæʃe]
au gratin (Fr.) [o'grɑtn̩] [o'grɑ'tæ̃]
avant-garde (Fr.) ['ɑvənt 'gɑrd]

bel canto (It.) [bel 'kɑnto]
belles-lettres (Fr.) [bɛl 'lɛtrə]
blasé (Fr.) [blɑ'ze]
bona fide (L.) ['bonə faɪdɪ]
bon appetit (Fr.) ['bon ɑpətit]
bon mot (Fr.) [bō'mo]
bon vivant (Fr.) [bōvi'vɑ̃]

---

²¹Usually, the first of the doubled sounds is omitted. In this instance, the second /f/ is omitted.

bon voyage (Fr.) [bõvwaˈjaːʒ]
bravado (Sp.) [brəˈvɑdo]
bourgeois (Fr.) [bʊrˈʒwa]

cachet (Fr.) [kæˈʃɛ] [ˈkæʃe] [kaˈʃɛ]
Candide (Fr.) [kanˈdid]
carpe diem (L.) [ˈkarpɪ ˈdəɪɛm]
cause célèbre (Fr.) [ˈkɔz sɛlˈɛb]
c'est la vie (Fr.) [seɪ lə ˈviː]
chef (Fr.) [ʃɛf]
chic (Fr.) [ʃik]
coiffure (Fr.) [kwaˈfjʊr]
concierge (Fr.) [kɑnsɪˈɛrʒ]
connoisseur (Fr.) [kɑnəˈsɝ]
coup de grace (Fr.) [kudeˈgrɑːs]
coup d'état (Fr.) [ˈkudeˈta]
crescendo (It.) [krɛˈʃɛndo]
crouton (Fr.) [kruˈtɑn] [kruˈtõ]
cuisine (Fr.) [kwɪˈzin]
cul-de-sac (Fr.) [ˈkʌldəˈsæk]

debonair (Fr.) [dɛbəˈnɛr]
de facto (L.) [dɪˈfækto]
denouement (Fr.) [deˈnumɑ̄]
détente (Fr.) [deˈtant]
deus ex machina (L.) [ˈdiəs ɛks ˈmækɪnə]

effete (Fr.) [ɛˈfit]
élan (Fr.) [eˈlɑ̃]
esprit de corps (Fr.) [ɛˈspridəˈkor]
ex post facto (L.) [ˈɛks post ˈfækto]

façade (Fr.) [fəˈsɑd]
fait accompli (Fr.) [fɛtakɑmˈpli]
faux pas (Fr.) [ˈfo ˈpɑ]
forte (It.) [fort]; music: [fɔrˈte]

gauche (Fr.) [goʃ]
gourmet (Fr.) [gurˈmɛ]

in medias res (L.) [ɪn ˈmidɪæs ˈriz]
in toto (L.) [ɪn ˈtoto]
in vacuo (L.) [ɪnˈvækjʊo]

Jacques (Fr.) [ʒɑk]
Jahweh (H.) [ˈjɑwɛ]
jai alai (Sp.) [ˈhaɪ laɪ]
jujitsu (Jp.) [ʤuˈʤɪtsu]
junta (Sp.) [ˈʤʌntə] [ˈhʊntə]

laissez-faire (Fr.) [lɛseˈfɛr]
lieu (Fr.) [lu]
liqueur (Fr.) [lɪˈkɝ]

machete (Sp.) [mɑˈʧete] [məˈʃɛtɪ]
machismo (Sp.) [mɑˈkizmo]
malaise (Fr.) [mæˈlez]

maraschino (It.) [mærəˈskino]
marijuana (Sp.) [mɑrɪˈhwɑnə]
mélange (Fr.) [meˈlɑ̃ʒ]
melee (Fr.) [meˈle] [ˈmele]
milieu (Fr.) [miˈljø]

niche (Fr.) [nɪtʃ]
non sequitur (L.) [nɑn ˈsɛkwɪtɚ]
nouveau riche (Fr.) [nuvoˈriʃ]

pièce de résistance (Fr.) [pjɛs də rezisˈtɑ̃ːs]
pique (Fr.) [pik]

queue (Fr.) [kju]
quo warranto (L.) [ˈkwo wɔˈrænto]

raison d'être (Fr.) [ˈrezɔn ˈdɛt]
repartee (Fr.) [rɛpɚˈti] [rɛpɑrˈte]

savoir faire (Fr.) [ˈsævwɑrˈfɛr]

tête-à-tête (Fr.) [ˈtetəˈtet]
tour de force (Fr.) [tʊr də fors]

wunderkind (Ger.) [ˈvʊndərkɪnt]

>>>

FREQUENTLY MISPRONOUNCED WORDS (1)

Copy the following page(s) so you can hand in the assignments and quizzes.

The following words are frequently mispronounced. Write the preferred pronunciation in phonetics within the brackets next to each word. Mark the major stress within the word.

abdomen	[	]	acumen	[	]
alma mater	[	]	amenable	[	]
amicable	[	]	amphetamine	[	]
anachronism	[	]	androgynous	[	]
anonymity	[	]	antithesis	[	]
bestial	[	]	chasm	[	]
clandestine	[	]	conversant	[	]
culinary	[	]	demoniac	[	]
err	[	]	flaccid	[	]
gala	[	]	gratis	[	]
grimace	[	]	heinous	[	]
impious	[	]	incognito	[	]
indefatigable	[	]	indict	[	]
inexplicable	[	]	inveigle	[	]
irrefutable	[	]	irreparable	[	]
politic	[	]	pronunciation	[	]
quixotic	[	]	respite	[	]
schism	[	]	scion	[	]
secretive	[	]	statistician	[	]
statistics	[	]	succinct	[	]
vagary	[	]			

>>> FREQUENTLY MISPRONOUNCED WORDS (2)

Transcribe the following words, and then record them using the phonetic transcription.

aberrant	[	]	caches	[	]
cannabis	[	]	censure	[	]
chasm	[	]	comely	[	]
dais	[	]	deluxe	[	]
facetious	[	]	fungi	[	]
genuine	[	]	heinous	[	]
hirsute	[	]	indict	[	]
misogynist	[	]	niche	[	]
penchant	[	]	posthumous	[	]
propitiate	[	]	pugilist	[	]
renege	[	]	sadist	[	]
sagacious	[	]	surrogate	[	]
titular	[	]	ubiquitous	[	]
vermicelli	[	]	voluminous	[	]

>>> TOUGH WORDS TO PRONOUNCE

Look up the meanings and record the pronunciations of each of the following difficult words:

abstemiousness	[	]	academician	[	]
algebraical	[	]	ammoniacal	[	]
anathematize	[	]	anesthetize	[	]
antipathetic	[	]	antiphlogistic	[	]
conciliatory	[	]	consanguinity	[	]
contiguity	[	]	corroborative	[	]
diocesan	[	]	elucidatory	[	]
genealogical	[	]	hieroglyphic	[	]
immeasurably	[	]	incendiary	[	]
inefficacious	[	]	malleability	[	]
masticatory	[	]	peremptorily	[	]
pertinacity	[	]	plenipotentiary	[	]
pusillanimity	[	]	sedentariness	[	]
synthesis	[	]	undulatory	[	]

((((EXERCISES FOR TRANSCRIPTION

The following section contains worksheets and /or quiz sheets for phonetic transcription. Copy the pages so you can hand in the exercises. It is not important that you be able to transcribe what you hear quickly. If you are able to transcribe what you hear with some degree of accuracy, you have good listening skills. You were told earlier that you will be unable to modify your own speech unless you are able to distinguish the differences between spelling and hearing. If you spell the word there as "there" but hear it as [ˈðejə] or spell the word Hannah as "Hannah" but hear it as [ˈhænɚ], you are less than accurate and little advance can be made on your New England dialect.

I. PHONETICS TO ENGLISH

Written 1

Monosyllabic Words (highlighting vowels *and* diphthongs*)*

Name: _____

Fill in the blank spaces with the appropriate letters that spell the phonetically written word.

1. [mæn]   _____
2. [min]   _____
3. [mɛn]   _____
4. [mun]   _____
5. [maɪn]   _____
6. [strænd]   _____
7. [straɪk]   _____
8. [stren]   _____
9. [ston]   _____
10. [stʊd]   _____
11. [strɔŋ]   _____
12. [strɪkt] _____
13. [blæŋk]   _____
14. [blɑnd]   _____
15. [blaɪnd] _____
16. [praʊd]   _____
17. [flem]   _____
18. [plʌm]   _____
19. [plum]   _____
20. [hid]   _____
21. [hɝd]   _____
22. [hʊd]   _____
23. [haɪd]   _____
24. [kraɪd]   _____
25. [kraʊd]   _____

I. PHONETICS TO ENGLISH

Written 2

Bisyllabic Words

Name: _____

Fill in the blank spaces with the appropriate letters that spell the phonetically written word.

1. [ˈhæpɪ]   _____

2. [ˈmɛlo]   _____

3. [ˈfɛzn̩t]   _____

4. [ˈkaʊntɚ]   _____

5. [ɪˈmɝʤ]   _____

6. [ˈfɪdl̩]   _____

7. [ˈhɛlmɪt]   _____

8. [ˈsɑrʤənt]   _____

9. [sɚˈmaɪz]   _____

10. [ˈtɑmˌbɔɪ]   _____

11. [ˈʌndɚ]   _____

12. [ˈtrɪbjun]   _____

13. [ˈdɑŋkɪ]   _____

14. [ˈhɑrtˌek]   _____

15. [ɪnˈtwaɪn]   _____

16. [ʃæmˈplen]   _____

17. [ˈkɑstjum]   _____

18. [ˈfɪgjɚ]   _____

19. [ˈɪnˈtɝn]   _____

20. [ˈkɑnvɪkt]   _____

21. [ˈʧɪkɪn]   _____

22. [ˈdaɪət]   _____

23. [ˈfɝˈvənt]   _____

24. [ˈlaɪtˈwet]   _____

25. [ˈprɑdəkt]   _____

I. PHONETICS TO ENGLISH

Written 3

Polysyllabic Words

Name: _____

Fill in the blank spaces with the appropriate letters that spell the phonetically written word.

1. [ˈflætərɪ]   _____

2. [ˈaɪdḷˌaɪz]   _____

3. [ɪˈmidɪɪt]   _____

4. [ˈmʌðərɪnlɔ]   _____

5. [ˈmɑrʤɪnḷ]   _____

6. [ˈʃɛrətn̩]   _____

7. [ˈtɛmpəˌrɛrɪ]   _____

8. [dɪˈplomə]   _____

9. [ɪkˈsplorɪŋ]   _____

10. [ˈækjərɪt]   _____

11. [ˈbɪʧˌkomɚ]   _____

12. [ˈkæntḷˌop]   _____

13. [ˌkɔrəˈneʃən]   _____

14. [ˈfaɪrˈprufɪŋ]   _____

15. [ˈθɝməˌstæt]   _____

16. [ˈjunəsn̩]   _____

17. [ˌovɚˈhɔl]   _____

18. [ˌnɛvɚðəˈlɛs]   _____

19. [ˈfɪləˌpin]   _____

20. [rɪˈsaɪtḷ]   _____

21. [ˌsæljʊˈteʃən]   _____

22. [ˈʧɛkɚˌbord]   _____

23. [dɪˈskʌʃən]   _____

24. [ˌkæbəˈre]   _____

25. [ɪˌlɛkˈtrɪsətɪ]   _____

(((I. PHONETICS TO ENGLISH

Written 4

Proper Names

Name: _____

Fill in the blank spaces with the appropriate letters that spell the phonetically written word.

1. [ˈgrɛgərɪ pɛk]   _____

2. [ˈrabɚt frɔst]   _____

3. [glɛn klos]   _____

4. [ˈdʌbl̩ju etʃ ɔdn̩]   _____

5. [ˈɛml̩ɪ ˈdɪkn̩sən]   _____

6. [ˈgwɛndl̩ɪn brʊks]   _____

7. [ˈaɪvənho]   _____

8. [ˈoklənd ez]   _____

9. [nju ˈʤɝˑzi]   _____

10. [bɛn ʤansn̩]   _____

11. [ˈarnl̩d ˈpamɚ]   _____

12. [ˈvɪn dɪˈbonə]   _____

13. [ˈrɪtʃɚd ˈdaɪsart]   _____

14. [ˈmægnə ˈkartə]   _____

15. [ˈhibru]   _____

16. [pɔˈtʌkɪt rod ˈaɪlənd] _____

17. [ˈɝˑnɪst ˈhɛmɪŋwe]   _____

18. [ˈɛdgɚ ˈælən po]   _____

19. [fræŋk sɪˈnatrə]   _____

20. [ˈrɛdɪŋ pi eɪ]   _____

21. [ˈlæpˌlændɚ]   _____

22. [ˈdɛnɪs ˈlɪrɪ]   _____

23. [ˈhɛnrɪ ˈwɪŋklɚ]   _____

24. [ˈmarɪo kænˈton]   _____

25. [arˈlin ˈsorkɪn]   _____

I. PHONETICS TO ENGLISH

Written 5

Phrases

Name: _____

Fill in the blank spaces with the appropriate letters that spell the phonetically written words.

1. ['ɪntʊ ðə wʊdz]   _____

2. [krɑs ɪg͵zæmə'neʃən]   _____

3. ['sloɪŋ daʊn ðə kɑr]   _____

4. [ɪn ə 'mɪnɪt]   _____

5. [ə'gɛnst 'særəz æd'vaɪs]   _____

6. ['risənt 'ɛvədəns]   _____

7. ['kwɛstʃənz æskt]   _____

8. ['taɪtḷ əv ðə kors]   _____

9. ['saɪnɪŋ fræŋks bʊk]   _____

10. [ə 'dɪzmḷ 'feljɚ]   _____

11. [ɪn spaɪt əv ɪt ɔl]   _____

12. [wɪð'aʊt ɪn'ʌf 'wɔrnɪŋ]   _____

13. ['wɪlɪŋnəs tʊ draɪv fæst]   _____

14. [bɪ'twin boθ 'pɪktʃɚz]   _____

15. [θɪk 'rɛnɪ klaʊdz]   _____

16. [rɪ'pit ʃɔrt 'frezɪz]   _____

17. ['iðɚ 'steɪŋ ɔr 'goʊɪŋ]   _____

18. [strɔŋ lɛŋθs əv rop]   _____

19. [kən'fɝ·ɪŋ dɪ'griz]   _____

20. ['traɪɪŋ ɪn ven]   _____

21. ['prɑfɪtəbḷ 'bɪznɪsɪz]   _____

22. ['mʌtɚ·ɪŋ rɪ'trit]   _____

23. ['kændḷ flem]   _____

24. ['stɪmjʊlet 'θɪŋkɪŋ]   _____

25. ['ʃɔkɪŋ ru'tin]   _____

(((I. PHONETICS TO ENGLISH

Reading and Speaking Exercise

In the following exercise, the phrases are transcribed into phonetics. The columns indicate how the phrases are to be pronounced. Make certain that you pay attention to the stressed and unstressed vowel sounds.

		STRESSED	UNSTRESSED
1.	in the mood	[ɪn ðʌ mud]	[ɪn ðə mud]
2.	between the rocks	[bə'twin ðʌ rɑks]	[bə'twin ðə rɑks]
3.	a time to speak	[ʌ taɪm tu spik]	[ə taɪm tə spik]
4.	the whole thing	[ðʌ hol θɪŋ]	[ðə hol θɪŋ]
5.	because of you	[bɪ'kɔz ʌv ju]	[bɪ'kəz əv ju]
6.	cash and carry	[kæʃ ænd 'kærɪ]	[kæʃ ənd 'kærɪ]
7.	chase the dog	[ʧes ðʌ dɔg]	[ʧes ðə dɔg]
8.	a piece of cake	[ʌ pis ʌv kek]	[ə pis əv kek]
9.	calling the cops	['kɔlɪŋ ðʌ kɑps]	['kɔlɪŋ ðə kɑps]
10.	fixes the bumper	['fɪksɪz ðʌ bʌmpɚ]	['fɪksɪz ðə bʌmpɚ]
11.	a bottle of soda	[ʌ batl̩ ʌv 'sodə]	[ə batl̩ əv 'sodə]
12.	from time to time	[frʌm taɪm tu taɪm]	[frəm taɪm tə taɪm]
13.	timing her lessons	['taɪɪŋ hɝ 'lesɪz]	['taɪɪŋ hɚ 'lesɪz]
14.	cooks the dinner	[kʊks ðʌ dɪnɚ]	[kʊks ðə dɪnɚ]
15.	but Pat can	[bʌt pæt kæn]	[bət pæt kn̩]

(((I. PHONETICS TO ENGLISH

Written 6

Sentences

Name: _____

Fill in the blank lines with the appropriate sentences indicated by their phonetic transcription.

1. ['wɪlmə ænd 'ʤosəf lɪv haɪ ən ðə hɪl]

_____

2. [ʍʌt ɪz ðə 'minɪŋ əv truθ]

_____

3. [maɪ 'brʌðɚ ɪz 'wɝkɪŋ fɚ maɪ dæd]

_____

4. ['bɒstən ɪz ðə 'kæpɪtl̩ əv mæsə'ʧusɪts]

_____

5. [flɔɪd hæd bɪn 'gɪvn̩ ə ʧæns tə go tə ðə gem]

_____

6. ['sæli 'kʌvɚd hɚ kɑr wɪð ə 'kænvəs]

_____

7. [hɪz 'tiʧɚ rɪ'fiuzd tʊ 'ænsɚ ðə 'kwɛsʧənz]

_____

8. ['kɛnɪθ kɔzd hɪz 'pærənts ə lɑt əv kən'sɝnz]

_____

9. ['flɔrəns wəz ɪ'lɛktɪd tə ðə kə'mɪti ɑn sɪ'kjurəti]

_____

10. [no rul ɪz so 'ʤɛnɚl̩ ʍɪʧ æd'mɪts nɒt sʌm ɪk'sɛpʃən]

_____

II. ENGLISH TO PHONETICS

Since this is not a phonetic text, the exercises are geared toward listening skills important for the development of voice and speech. With that in mind, the following exercise reverses the focus. You have demonstrated that you are able to "translate" from phonetics to English. Now let's see how successful your listening skills are as you transcribe from English to phonetics.

Monosyllabic Words

Written 1

Name: _____

Record the following list of words. Listen to each word and repeat what you have heard three times before you transcribe it. There may be a few acceptable pronunciations for a word. Refer to Kenyon and Knott's A Pronouncing Dictionary *for the possibilities. Fill in the blank spaces with the appropriate phonetic transcriptions that spell the words.*

1. same   _____

2. chip   _____

3. fleet   _____

4. push   _____

5. dive   _____

6. farm   _____

7. jump   _____

8. hurt   _____

9. left   _____

10. cramp   _____

11. search   _____

12. shame   _____

13. joist   _____

14. trout   _____

15. mush   _____

16. church   _____

17. knap   _____

18. pole   _____

19. link   _____

20. call   _____

21. butt   _____

22. smile   _____

23. Nice (France) _____

24. nice   _____

25. shake   _____

II. ENGLISH TO PHONETICS

Monosyllabic Nonsense

Written 2

Name: _____

The ability to transcribe nonsense syllables is very valuable in developing listening acuity and sound differentiation. Listen to the following list of nonsense syllables delivered by your instructor or on tape. The syllables will be pronounced three times. The first time, listen. The second time, transcribe what you heard. The third time, read what you have written.

1. [   ]

2. [   ]

3. [   ]

4. [   ]

5. [   ]

6. [   ]

7. [   ]

8. [   ]

9. [   ]

10. [   ]

11. [   ]

12. [   ]

13. [   ]

14. [   ]

15. [   ]

16. [   ]

17. [   ]

18. [   ]

19. [   ]

20. [   ]

II. ENGLISH TO PHONETICS

Two-Syllabic Words

Written 3

Name: _____

Record the following list of words. Listen to each word and repeat what you have heard three times before you transcribe it. There may be a few acceptable pronunciations for a word. Refer to Kenyon and Knott's A Pronouncing Dictionary *for the possibilities. Fill in the blank spaces with the appropriate phonetic transcriptions that spell the words. Mark the primary syllables.*

1. shepherd _____

2. rerun _____

3. snowdrift _____

4. demise _____

5. flagstone _____

6. heartburn _____

7. impart _____

8. bishop _____

9. asthma _____

10. athlete _____

11. button _____

12. custard _____

13. differ _____

14. martyr _____

15. brother _____

16. passion _____

17. something _____

18. flutter _____

19. yearning _____

20. wretched _____

21. vista _____

22. tardy _____

23. schism _____

24. rascal _____

25. smoker _____

II. ENGLISH TO PHONETICS

Two-Syllabic Nonsense

Written 4

Name: _____

The ability to transcribe nonsense syllables is very valuable in developing listening acuity and sound differentiation. Listen to the following list of nonsense syllables delivered by your instructor or on tape. They will be pronounced three times. Transcribe what you hear into phonetics.

1. [   ]

2. [   ]

3. [   ]

4. [   ]

5. [   ]

6. [   ]

7. [   ]

8. [   ]

9. [   ]

10. [   ]

11. [   ]

12. [   ]

13. [   ]

14. [   ]

15. [   ]

16. [   ]

17. [   ]

18. [   ]

19. [   ]

20. [   ]

II. ENGLISH TO PHONETICS

Polysyllabic Words

Written 5

Name: _____

Record the following list of words. Listen to each word and repeat what you have heard three times before you transcribe it. There may be a few acceptable pronunciations for a word. Refer to Kenyon and Knott's A Pronouncing Dictionary *for the possibilities. Fill in the blank spaces with the appropriate phonetic transcriptions that spell the words. Mark the primary syllables.*

1. ransacking   _____
2. sensitize   _____
3. parachute   _____
4. ninepenny   _____
5. paternal   _____
6. identify   _____
7. larynx   _____
8. murderer   _____
9. hyphenated   _____
10. microwave   _____
11. conclusion   _____
12. bricklayer   _____
13. Barbara   _____
14. adversary   _____
15. downhearted   _____
16. flamingo   _____
17. gentlewoman   _____
18. housebreaking _____
19. catharsis   _____
20. hunky-dory   _____
21. mountainside   _____
22. plantation   _____
23. ragamuffin   _____
24. harp player   _____
25. sheepherder   _____

II. ENGLISH TO PHONETICS

Phrases

Written 6

Name: _____

Record the following phrases. Listen to each word and repeat what you have heard three times before you transcribe it. There may be a few acceptable pronunciations for a word. Refer to Kenyon and Knott's A Pronouncing Dictionary *for the possibilities. Fill in the blank spaces with the appropriate phonetic transcriptions that spell the words. Mark the primary syllables.*

1. in school _____

2. singing songs _____

3. mother's house _____

4. frankfurter roll _____

5. something beautiful _____

6. cleaning ovens _____

7. wash dishes _____

8. figure out problems _____

9. inside story _____

10. study mathematics _____

11. Martha's office _____

12. huckleberry pie _____

13. great-uncle Joe _____

14. epic poem _____

15. destroying hornet's nests _____

16. examining crisp leaves _____

17. buttermilk candies _____

18. emphasizes points _____

19. internal strife _____

20. mainsheet computation _____

21. privacy concerns _____

22. star-crossed lovers _____

23. brand new car _____

24. women's movement _____

25. luncheon special _____

Write the definitions for the following terms in the space below.

KEY TERMS   DEFINITIONS

Anaptyxis

Assimilation

Bilabial

Dentalization

Explosion

Haplology

Homograph

Homonym

Homophone

Implosion

Metathesis

Pronunciation

Restressing

Spoonerism

Stress

CHAPTER 9

VOCAL DYNAMICS

The basic tools of voice and speech have been discussed in previous chapters. However, open throat, good diaphragmatic control, and good pronunciation are relatively useless in and of themselves; they must be applied to the communication of some message to an audience (even if the audience is yourself). Otherwise, no meaningful message is imparted.

However, having good tools does not ensure successful communication. The tools of a Shakespearean actor, for example, certainly include the play's content. But if the audience is bored by the delivery, this content has little value. How many of us have had a professor (or two!) who clearly knew the subject matter but was unable to communicate this knowledge to an audience?

Obviously, truly effective communication must include a melding of materials with delivery. Although there are many components of good delivery, among the most important are the choices available to the speaker for underscoring and amplifying meaning. How can certain words and ideas be colored to clarify the meaning and attitude of the speaker? These techniques, which are learned behaviors rather than innate ones, can ensure that the speaker will not be monotonous (that is, will not use the same pitch and intensity).

Speakers must consider vocal dynamics to be a priority. If allowed to take only three vocal or speech concepts to a "desert island," they ought to be open throat, diaphragmatic breathing, and vocal dynamics. A listener will overlook a great many speaking faults, but boredom is the number one sin.

There are a number of reasons why a speaker may be monotonous; the most important one is a lack of variety in thought and emotion. Therefore, it is fundamental for a speaker to understand thoroughly the content of his or her communication. Washington Irving mused that "at sea, everything that breaks the monotony of the surrounding expanse attracts attention."[1] The study of **prosody** tells us that the meter in a poem may not be as

---

[1]Washington Irving, *The Sketch Book* (New York: United States Book Company, 1819), 13.

significant to meaning as the foot that breaks the pattern. Our eyes and ears are more alert when a pattern is broken. For a detailed discussion of variety in poetry, refer to *Oral Interpretation* by Timothy Gura and Charlotte Lee.[2]

In the early 1880s, Charles Wesley Emerson identified four forms of speech emphasis that are useful in contemporary speech and help give a speaker vocal dynamics: stress, slide, pace or tempo, and pause. Emerson felt that stress or force was the most primitive form of emphasis, changes of pitch and inflection followed. Then came modifications of pitch. The most artistic form of emphasis is the "ellipse" or pause, all forms should work together.[3]

In Chapter 3, we discussed the difficulty in separating the factors of voice (quality, pitch, rate, and volume). These factors work together to form a "whole" voice. Similarly, the forms of speech emphasis should not be separated in the communication process. Indeed, they, too, are parts of the whole and work together to energize the entire speech performance. To learn to communicate effectively, however, the forms of speech emphasis must first be isolated, identified, and discussed. When these elements are then combined and used to express the intended meaning, appropriate inflection is achieved. **Inflection** is defined as the variations of vocal techniques that support, enhance, reflect, and amplify meaning.

STRESS

A natural progression takes place when you begin studying stress, or force, and proceed through slide, tempo, and pause. **Stress** (force or *punching*) is one of the most basic and primitive forms of speech emphasis. In this kind of emphasis, the speaker selects the most important words and images and stresses them, usually through increased volume but sometimes through decreased volume. The danger with using only one of these forms of emphasis exclusively throughout a message (presentation, performance, reading, or sermon) is that the communication becomes colorless. As with any other art form, attention is drawn to the meaning through the use of variations.

Ordinarily, the words that receive attention are those that give a thought clarity and dynamism: nouns, both proper and common, action verbs, adverbs ("quietly," "frankly," "quickly"), conjunctive adverbs (*also, furthermore, however, consequently*), interjections ("Huh!" "Ugh!" "Shhh!"), adjectives, and digital or pointing words (*this, that, there*). Interrogative pronouns ("whose," "which," "what"), demonstrative pronouns ("this," "that," "those"), and indefinite pronouns ("everyone," "someone," "everybody") are most frequently stressed. The parts of speech that are usually unstressed are personal pronouns (including personal, relative pronouns like *that, which, and who*); possessive and reflexive pronouns; linking and auxiliary verbs ("must," "have," "been," "is" "being," "can," "would," "used to"); definite and indefinite articles; most conjunctions (*and, but, in order to, until, if, because, though, that*); and single and multiword prepositions ("for," "in" "out," "over," "instead of," "because of," "near to," "in spite of," "in accordance with").

Of course, there are exceptions. Television stations, for example, often prescribe their own style of delivery. At one radio station the on-air talent often identifies the station's call letters by saying, "This *is* WWWW." As a frequent listener I find myself saying, "Well, who says it isn't?" The emphasis on "is" suggests that someone has charged that the station call letters are not WWWW. As another example, suppose you ask your roommate to put the wastebasket on the desk so that you will not forget to empty it but your roomie places it under the desk; you might

---

[2]Timothy Gura and Charlotte Lee, *Oral Interpretation*, 12/E (Needham, MA: 2010).

[3]Charles Wesley Emerson, *The Evolution of Expression* (Boston: Emerson College Press, 1881), 26.

respond, "No, I said to put it *on* the desk." In this case stressing a preposition is important to the meaning. Ordinarily, of course, the preposition *on* would not receive a great deal of stress.

 EXERCISES FOR STRESS

1. In this poem, color or expressive words are underscored according to one person's interpretation. You may have a few additions or deletions of your own according to your understanding. Read the poem aloud and record yourself, stressing the underscored words. As you listen to the playback, make certain that you accomplished your intention.

    1 Come <u>live</u> with <u>me</u> and <u>be</u> my <u>love</u>,
    2 And <u>we</u> will <u>all</u> the <u>pleasures</u> <u>prove</u>,
    3 That <u>hills</u> and <u>valleys</u>, <u>dales</u>, and <u>fields</u>,
    4 And <u>all</u> the <u>craggy</u> <u>mountains</u> <u>yields</u>.

    5 <u>There</u> we will <u>sit</u> upon the <u>rocks</u>,
    6 And <u>see</u> the <u>shepherds</u> <u>feed</u> their <u>flocks</u>,
    7 By <u>shallow</u> <u>rivers</u> to whose <u>falls</u>
    8 <u>Melodious</u> <u>birds</u> sing <u>madrigals</u>.

    9 And I will <u>make</u> thee <u>beds</u> of <u>roses</u>
    10 With a <u>thousand</u> <u>fragrant</u> <u>posies</u>,
    11 A <u>cap</u> of <u>flowers</u>, and a <u>kirtle</u>
    12 <u>Embroidered</u> <u>all</u> with <u>leaves</u> of <u>myrtle</u>;

    13 A <u>Gown</u> made of the <u>finest</u> <u>wool</u>
    14 Which from our <u>pretty</u> <u>lambs</u> we <u>pull</u>;
    15 <u>Fur</u> <u>lined</u> <u>slippers</u> for the <u>cold</u>,
    16 With <u>buckles</u> of the <u>purest</u> <u>gold</u>;

    17 A <u>belt</u> of <u>straw</u> and <u>ivy</u> <u>buds</u>,
    18 With <u>coral</u> <u>clasps</u> and <u>amber</u> <u>studs</u>:
    19 And if these <u>pleasures</u> may thee <u>move</u>,
    20 <u>Come</u> <u>live</u> with <u>me</u> and be my <u>love</u>.

    21 The <u>shepherd</u> <u>swains</u> shall <u>dance</u> and <u>sing</u>
    22 For thy <u>delight</u> <u>each</u> <u>May</u> <u>morning</u>:
    23 If <u>these</u> delights thy <u>mind</u> may <u>move</u>,
    24 Then <u>live</u> with <u>me</u> and <u>be</u> my <u>love</u>.

        THE PASSIONATE SHEPHERD
        Christopher Marlowe

In exercises 2 and 3, underline the important words according to your interpretation. Then, record your reading according to what you have underlined.

2. 1 If all the world and love were young,
    2 And truth in every shepherd's tongue,
    3 These pretty pleasures might me move,
    4 To live with thee, and be thy love.

    5 Time drives the flocks from field to fold,
    6 When rivers rage, and rocks grow cold,
    7 And Philomel becometh dumb,
    8 The rest complains of cares to come.

    9 The flowers do fade, and wanton fields,

10 The wayward winter reckoning yields,
11 A honey tongue, a heart of gall,
12 Is fancy's spring, but sorrow's fall.

13 Thy gowns, thy shoes, thy beds of roses,
14 Thy cap, thy kirtle, and thy posies,
15 Soon break, soon wither, soon forgotten:
16 In folly ripe, in reason rotten.

17 Thy belt of straw and ivy buds,
18 Thy coral clasps and amber studs,
19 All these in me no means can move,
20 To come to thee, and be thy love.

21 But could youth last, and love still breed,
22 Had joys no date, nor age no need,
23 Then these delights my mind might move,
24 To live with thee and be thy love.

THE NYMPH'S REPLY TO THE SHEPHERD
Sir Walter Raleigh

3. 1 The stone rests comfortably in the grass,
2 Planted in the hill like it was always there . . .
3 I stand silent, eyes closed,
4 I grab onto any warmth I can find.

5 My bones rattle,
6 My teeth chatter,
7 And from my throat hums a dry solemn song,
8 A musical march to the ceremony of death.

9 Only the few scattered trees and the many stones,
10 Only the scraggly grass, and the shovel matted dirt,
11 And only the cool breeze and the gray tinted clouds
12 Bear witness to my stern frame gone to pieces.

13 My tears water the sandpaper like grass,
14 My knees buckle,
15 Falling to an inevitable state of reverence,
16 Staring head on into the abyss like epitaph.

17 "Never was there a man more proud to be an American,
18 Lt. Colonel Donald Kieran—a patriot to the very end."
19 The end . . .
20 The end—it has passed.

21 Never did I imagine the vehicle of death to be so swift.
22 Like an arrow darting through the heart,
23 Piercing the soul that was once whole,
24 And then subsiding just as quick.

25 The pain, the hurt—it's all gone,
26 Isn't it?
27 Then why do I still cry?
28 I should be finished shedding my tears should I not?

29 The answer is directly in front of me,
30 Scribed in stone "to the very end."

31 The burial is over and the time for grieving is well passed
32 But I wasn't ready.

33 It all happened so fast,
34 The tears came so suddenly,
35 My throat choked on this sudden absence so badly,
36 That I never got a chance to really say "Good-bye."

DON'T FORGET TO SAY GOOD-BYE
Thomas Myers-Kieran

4. In the following selections, use as much force and stress as you can in your first reading without distorting the meaning as determined by the color words.

a. This is the bricklayer; hear the thud
Of his heavy load dumped down on stone.
His lustrous bricks are brighter than blood. . . .

From SANCTUARY
Elinor Wylie

b. 1 *Oswald (to his mother, Mrs. Alving):* I had one attack while I was away. It didn't
2 last long, but it filled me with . . . terror. If it had only been an ordinary illness—
3 even a fatal one—I wouldn't have minded so much. I'm not afraid of death. But to
4 become a child again—a helpless child—to have to be fed! I can't stand the
5 thought of lingering on like that! And if you die, Mother, I would be left alone. The
6 doctor said I might live for years. He called it softening of the brain. What a way
7 to put it! It makes me think of cherry-colored velvet curtains—soft and delicate to
8 the stroke!

From GHOSTS
Henrik Ibsen

c. 1 During the night the seas piled up and became really fierce. Often it was quite
2 uncanny to stand on the creaking, swaying steering bridge and see nothing in the
3 world but a lighted patch of sail and the lamp at the masthead, which swung like
4 an unruly moon among the stars when one glimpsed their light between racing
5 storm clouds. Now and then a venomous snake seemed to be hissing right at one's
6 back and a foaming wave crest would come rushing along at the height of one's
7 head, invisible in its blackness apart from the white foam on top that seemed
8 to be sailing along through the air, whispering to itself. The pursuing creature
9 reached us and lifted us in the air with its huge watery muscles, only to let us go
10 again and drop us so deep that the next white phantom following behind hovered
11 over us at a still greater height. We were worn out, dead tired, after two hour's
12 intensive night watch at the two rudder-oars, even though we were generally using
13 only one of them, allowing the other to work in a fixed position.

From KON-TIKI
Thor Heyerdahl

d. 1 *Mary:* I am Mary of Scotland—and I came to you for mercy. This you have denied
2 me. You tore me from my people. You cast me into a prison. However, let us
3 forget all the cruelties I have suffered. You will never use the power you have to kill
4 me. I give up all claims to your throne. You've done your worst. You have destroyed
5 me. My sins were human. Can as much be said of yours? You did not inherit
6 virtue from your mother. We know only too well what brought the head
7 of Anne Boleyn to the block! If there were justice, you would be kneeling here

8   before me because I am your lawful queen. The English have been cheated by a
9   juggler! A bastard—yes, a bastard, soils the British throne!

From MARY STUART
Friedrich von Schiller

e. 1   Although it was so brilliantly fine—the blue sky powdered with gold and great
    2   spots of light like white wine splashed over the Jardin Publiques—Miss Brill was
    3   glad that she had decided on her fur. The air was motionless, but when you opened
    4   your mouth there was just a faint chill, like a chill from a glass of iced water before
    5   you sip, and now and again a leaf came drifting—from nowhere—from the
    6   sky. Miss Brill put up her hand and touched her fur. Dear little thing! It was nice
    7   to feel it again.

From MISS BRILL
Katherine Mansfield

>>> SLIDE

A **slide** is a form of speech emphasis in which pitch always changes; often vocal quality and volume change as well. The use of this vocal technique is dictated by the speaker's intended meaning.

The interval between two adjoining pitches is called a **step.** The term *slide is* particularly vivid because of its implicit visual imagery. A slide provides vocal movement and energy. This movement is evident when the intended meaning is conveyed. For example, say the following "pitch graphic" as it appears on the page:

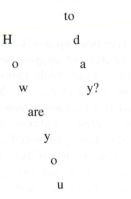

When spoken as written, this sentence carries little meaning; even though changes in pitch are designated, there is no thought behind these changes in pitch. It is a sentence that could be said by an android or a robot.

When appropriate and thoughtful inflection is used, there is usually not only a change in pitch but also a change in the quality and projection of the voice. Exaggerate and record the following pitch graphic:

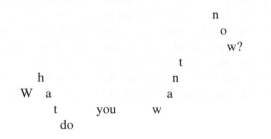

If you have produced the sentence as written, there will be a change of pitch on the words *what, want,* and *now.* Can you detect a difference in the quality and projection of your voice in addition to the more obvious change in pitch? These changes in pitch as dictated by the meaning are slides. This sliding effect between words (and frequently within a word) is a more sophisticated form of emphasis than is either stress or tempo.

The use of the slide can be illustrated easily if you imagine yourself reading a child's story to a kindergarten class. The slides become exaggerated. (Most kindergarten students do not like this technique because they feel that the reader is talking down to them. Nevertheless, this exaggeration will clarify the slide.)

The following question-and-answer technique will provide you practice with the slide. Record yourself as you read aloud the following sentence:

The sky is blue.

Now ask yourself, "What color is the sky?" Then give the answer.

```
                              bl

                           u

           sky          u
  The                    u
           is          ue.
```

On the last word, you probably used a slide. Listen to it again.

Record this sentence: *"Quietly* put your *paper* on the *table."* In preparation for the recording, speak the following questions and their answers:

How?	quietly
Put the what?	paper
Where?	on the table

The sentence you just recorded might be graphed with the actual words or "slide graffiti." However, it is important to keep in mind that each person would have his or her own pitch graphics, depending on the desired meaning and personal preferences. Using the graphics is encouraged to ensure that the exercises do not become mechanical.

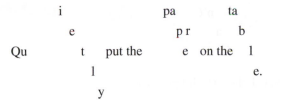

Read aloud the following sentences using the pitch graphic as your source of meaning:

1. What is going on?

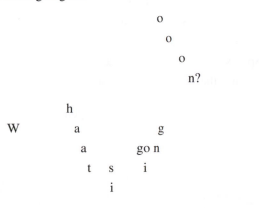

2. And don't slam the door when you leave!

d nt   l
                   e
         d   o   do r   l e   b
    n   sl m the   o   yo   e
A   a   when   a
                                  ve!

3. Can't you do anything right?

                              t?
                         gh
                       i
                     i
                   r
                ng
              i
            i
          th
        y
      n
    a
  o
d
u
o
y
n't
a
C

4. Speak the speech I pray you.

                r
               p
         p I a
      s e ch   a
   e   e   a
Sp   k   a
  a   the   a
                      y
                   you.

5. There are strange things done in the midnight sun.

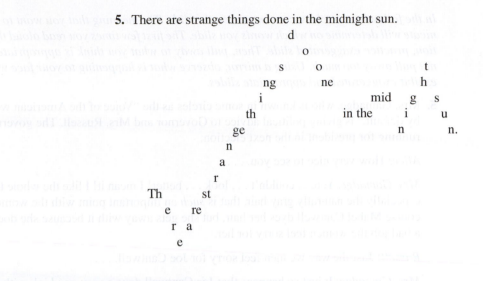

EXERCISES FOR THE SLIDE

> *In the following exercises, ask a question that has to be answered by the underscored words. Record your answer, and listen carefully to what you have said. If there was a change of pitch (and perhaps of quality and projection), you probably "slid"! If not, repeat your answer and exaggerate the slide. Then, graph what you have recorded. You should be able to see the variety in expression. Record the exercises another possible way, maintaining the integrity of the meaning. Can you see expressive differences in your graphs?*

1. Go, Sir, gallop, and don't forget that the world was made in six days. You can ask me for anything you like, except time.

Napoleon Bonaparte

2. Three years she grew in sun and shower,
Then Nature said, "A lovelier flower
On earth was never sown.
This Child I to myself will take;
She shall be mine, and I will make
A Lady of my own."

From LUCY
William Wordsworth

3. Near this spot are deposited the remains of one who possesses Beauty without Vanity, Strength without Insolence, Courage without Ferocity, and all the Virtues of Man, without his Vices. This Praise, which would be unmeaning Flattery if inscribed over human ashes, is but a just tribute to the Memory of Boatswain, a Dog.

INSCRIPTION ON THE MONUMENT OF A NEWFOUNDLAND DOG
Lord Byron

4. Therefore to this dog will I,
Tenderly not scornfully,
Render praise and favor:
With my hand upon his head,
Is my benediction said
Therefore and for ever.

From TO FLUSH, MY DOG
Elizabeth Barrett Browning

In the following exercises, concentrate on the slide. The meaning that you want to communicate will determine on which words you slide. The first few times you read aloud the selection, practice exaggerated slide. Then, pull away to what you think is appropriate, but do not pull away too much. Using a mirror, observe what is happening to your face while you exhibit exaggerated and appropriate slides.

5. Mrs. Gamadge, who is known in some circles as the "Voice of the American woman, by default," is giving political advice to Governor and Mrs. Russell. The governor is running for president in the next election:

Alice: How very nice to see you. . . .

Mrs. Gamadge: You. . . couldn't . . . look . . . better! I mean it! I like the whole thing . . . especially the naturally gray hair, that is *such* an important point with the women. Of course Mabel Cantwell dyes her hair, but she gets away with it because she does such a bad job the women feel sorry for her.

Russell: Just the way we men feel sorry for Joe Cantwell. . . .

Mrs. Gamadge: It just so happens that Joe Cantwell does a very good job with his hair. Almost as good a job as Ronnie Reagan does with his and Ronnie's is just scrumptious. Oh, I know you have a million things to do! Anyway, I just want you to know that I'm for you, Governor, and I'm sure that you and Mrs. Russell are a winning team. When you're the First Lady, just remember this: don't talk too much . . . like Mrs. Ford. The women don't like that. On the other hand, don't talk too little, like Mrs. Kennedy. The women don't like that either. When you get right down to the nitty gritty, Pat Nixon was just about perfect considering all the agony she had to go through. My husband had such a crush on Pat.

Adapted from THE BEST MAN
Gore Vidal

6. *Elvira (a beautiful ghost talking to her former husband):* I sat there, on the other side, just longing for you day after day. I did really—all through your affair with that brassy-looking woman in the South of France I went on loving you and thinking truly of you—then you married Ruth and even then I forgave you and tried to understand because all the time I believed deep inside that you really loved me best . . . that's why I put myself down for a return visit and had to fill in all those forms and wait about in draughty passages for hours—if only you'd died before you met Ruth everything might have been all right—she's absolutely ruined you—I hadn't been in the house a day before I realized that. Your books aren't a quarter as good as they used to be either.

From BLITHE SPIRIT
Noel Coward

7. The vitriolic Captain is ranting at Mr. Roberts, who has asked the Captain for a transfer and liberty for the crew.

1   *Captain:* I think you're a pretty smart boy. I may not talk very good, Mister, but
2   I know how to take care of smart boys. Let me tell you a little secret. I hate your
3   guts. . . . You think you're better than I am! You think you're better because you've
4   had everything handed to you! Let me tell you something, Mister—I've worked
5   since I was ten years old, and all my life I've known you superior bastards. I knew
6   you people when I was a kid in Boston and I worked in eating-places and you ordered
7   me around. . . . "Oh, bus-boy! My friend here seems to have thrown up on the
8   table. Clean it up, please." I started going to sea as a steward and I worked for you
9   then . . . "Steward, I don't like your looks. Please keep out of my way as much as

10   possible!" Well, I took that crap! I took that for years from pimple-faced bastards who
11   weren't good enough to wipe my nose! And now I don't have to take it any more!
12   There's a war on, and I'm the Captain, Mister, I'm the Captain, and you're welcome
13   to wipe my nose! The worst thing I can do to you is keep you on this ship! And that's
14   where you're going to stay! Now get out of here!

From MISTER ROBERTS
Thomas Heggen, Joshua Logan

8. A middle-aged woman is talking to a psychiatrist about her brother Elwood.

1   *Veta:* Doctor— do I have to keep repeating myself? My brother insists that his closest
2   friend is this big white rabbit. This rabbit is named Harvey. Harvey lives at our
3   house. Don't you understand? He and Elwood go every place together. Elwood buys
4   railroad tickets, theater tickets, for both of them. As I told Myrtle Mae—if your
5   uncle was so lonesome he had to bring something home—why couldn't he bring
6   home something human? He has me, doesn't he? He has Myrtle Mae, doesn't he? I'm
7   going to tell you something I've never told anybody in the world before. Every once
8   in a while I see that big white rabbit myself. Now isn't that terrible? I've never even
9   told that to Myrtle Mae.

From HARVEY
Mary Chase

9. Obviously, the following poem was written with a serious intention. Read it that way,
even though you may be trying to hold back a grin. This selection will supply you with
excellent examples of slide in spite of its sentimentality.

1   One more little spirit to heaven has flown,
2   To dwell in that mansion above.
3   Where dear little angels, together roam,
4   In God's everlasting love.

5   Her sweet silvery voice no more is heard
6   In the home where she once roamed;
7   Her place is vacant around the hearth,
8   Where her friends are mourning lone.

9   One morning in April, a short time ago,
10   Libbie was active and gay;
11   Her Savior called her, she had to go,
12   E're the close of that pleasant day.

13   While eating dinner, this dear little child
14   Was choked on a piece of beef.
15   Doctors came, tried their skill awhile,
16   But none could give relief.

17   She was ten years of age, I am told,
18   And in school stood very high.
19   Her little form now the earth enfolds,
20   In her embrace it must ever lie.
21   Her friends and schoolmates will not forget
22   Little Libbie that is no more;
23   She is waiting on the shining step,
24   To welcome home friends once more.

LITTLE LIBBIE
Julia Moore

10. In this selection, Lady Bracknell, a Victorian aristocrat, has just come upon Jack Worthing, who is proposing marriage (on his knees, of course!) to her daughter Gwendolen. Lady Bracknell speaks first to her daughter, then to Jack:

1   Pardon me, you are not engaged to anyone. When you do become engaged to some
2   one, I, or your father, should his health permit him, will inform you of the fact. An
3   engagement should come on a young girl as a surprise, pleasant or unpleasant, as
4   the case may be. It is hardly a matter that she should be allowed to arrange herself. . . .
5   And now I have a few questions to put to you, Mr. Worthing. While I am making
6   these inquiries, you, Gwendolen, will wait for me below in the carriage. . . .
7   Mr. Worthing, I confess I feel somewhat bewildered by what you have just told
8   me. To be born, or at any rate bred, in a hand-bag, whether it had handles or not,
9   seems to me to display a contempt for the ordinary decencies of family life that
10   remind one of the worst excesses of the French Revolution. And I presume you
11   know what that unfortunate movement led to? As for the particular locality in
12   which the handbag was found, a cloak-room at a railway station might serve to
13   conceal a social indiscretion—has probably, indeed, been used for that purpose
14   before now—but it could hardly be regarded as an assured basis for a recognized
15   position in good society. . . . You can hardly imagine that I and Lord Bracknell
16   would dream of allowing our only daughter—a girl brought up with the utmost
17   care—to marry into a cloak-room, and form an alliance with a parcel? Good morning,
18   Mr. Worthing!

From THE IMPORTANCE OF BEING EARNEST
Oscar Wilde

11. Eliza Doolittle's father goes to Henry Higgins's house to make a deal with him.

1   *Alfred Doolittle:* I ask you, what am I? I'm one of the undeserving poor, that's what
2   I am. Think of what that means to man. It means that he's up agen middle class
3   morality all the time. If there's anything going, and I put in for a bit of it, it's always
4   the same story: "You're undeserving: so you can't have it."
5   But my, needs is as great as the most deserving
6   widow's that ever got money out of six different charities in one week for the death
7   of the same husband. I don't need less than a deserving man: I need more. I don't
8   eat less hearty than him; and I drink a lot more. I want a bit of amusement, cause
9   I'm a thinking man. I want cheerfulness and a song and a band when I feel low.
10   Well, they charge me just the same for everything as they charge the deserving.
11   What is middle class morality? Just an excuse for never giving me anything. Therefore,
12   I ask you, as two gentlemen, not to play that game on me. I'm playing straight
13   with you. I ain't pretending to be deserving. I'm undeserving; and I mean to go on
14   being undeserving. I like it; and that's the truth. Will you take advantage of a man's
15   nature to do him out of the price of his own daughter what he's brought up and fed
16   and clothed by the sweat of his brow until she's growed big enough to be interesting
17   to you two gentlemen? Is five pounds unreasonable? I put it to you; and I leave
18   it to you.

From PYGMALION
George Bernard Shaw

12. Do not worry about giving the characters accents. However, do pay attention to the crisp and accurate articulation.

To my extreme annoyance, Poirot was not in, and the old Belgian who answered my knock informed me that he believed he had gone to London.

I was dumbfounded. What on earth could Poirot be doing in London! Was it a sudden decision on his part, or had he already made up his mind when he parted from me a few hours earlier?

I retraced my steps to Styles in some annoyance. With Poirot away, I was uncertain how to act. Had he foreseen this arrest? Had he not, in all probability, been the cause of it? Those questions I could not resolve. But in the meantime what was I to do? Should I announce the arrest openly at Styles, or not? Though I did not acknowledge it to myself, the thought of Mary Cavendish was weighing on me. Would it not be a terrible shock to her? For the moment, I set aside utterly any suspicions of her. She could not be implicated—otherwise I should have heard some hint of it.

Of course, there was no possibility of being able permanently to conceal Dr. Bauerstein's arrest from her. It would be announced in every newspaper on the morrow. Still, I shrank from blurting it out. If only Poirot had been accessible, I could have asked his advice. What possessed him to go posting off to London in this unaccountable way?

In spite of myself, my opinion of his sagacity was immeasurably heightened. I would never have dreamt of suspecting the doctor, had not Poirot put it into my head. Yes, decidedly, the little man was clever.

After some reflecting, I decided to take John into my confidence, and leave him to make the matter public or not, as he thought fit.

He gave vent to a prodigious whistle, as I imparted the news.

"Great Scott! You were right, then. I couldn't believe it at the time."

"No, it is astonishing until you get used to the idea, and see how it makes everything fit in. Now, what are we to do? Of course, it will be generally known tomorrow."

John reflected.

"Never mind," he said at last, "we won't say anything at present. There is no need. As you say, it will be known soon enough."

But to my intense surprise, on getting down early the next morning, and eagerly opening the newspapers, there was not a word about the arrest! There was a column of mere padding about "The Styles Poisoning Case," but nothing further. It was rather inexplicable, but I supposed that, for some reason or other, Japp wished to keep it out of the papers. It worried me just a little, for it suggested the possibility that there might be further arrests to come.

After breakfast, I decided to go down to the village, and see if Poirot had returned yet; but, before I could start, a well known face blocked one of the windows, and the well known voice said:

"Bon jour, mon ami!"

"Poirot," I exclaimed, with relief, and seizing him by both hands, I dragged him into the room. "I was never so glad to see anyone. Listen, I have said nothing to anybody but John. Is that right?"

"My friend," replied Poirot, "I do not know what you are talking about."

"Dr. Bauerstein's arrest, of course," I answered impatiently.

"Is Bauerstein arrested, then?"

"Did you not know it?"

"Not the least in the world." But, pausing a moment, he added: "Still, it does not surprise me. After all, we are only four miles from the coast."

From MYSTERIOUS AFFAIR AT STYLES
Agatha Christie

>>>

PACE OR TEMPO

From slide we proceed to a change in tempo or pace. **Pace** in speech is akin to emotion; the **tempo** of a voice is often an outward manifestation of what is happening emotionally inside the speaker. Therefore, it is extremely important to control your tempo so that it reflects what is desired. For example, a person's pace usually speeds up as pressure or emotional intensity increases. A slower pace is associated with serenity, which may or may not in fact exist within the speaker.

Frequently, the importance of a message is reflected in the pace used in delivering it. Usually, the important parts of a message are delivered slowly; less important parts are usually delivered more quickly. However, sometimes the opposite technique is used. For example, a comedian may deliver a punch line with rapid-fire speech and then slow up the pace while the audience responds to the joke. This is a delivery technique that Bob Hope often uses. Thus, a change in tempo can frequently underscore meaning or indicate a change in thought. In addition, an increase in tempo and volume in speech, as in music, often builds to a climax followed by a decrescendo.

Various effects can be achieved through changing the pace. Sometimes, as in the opening of Robert Frost's "The Death of the Hired Man," a certain mood can be emphasized by using a relatively slow pace. In this poem, the slow pace works with the tone color (use of sounds) to create an atmosphere of contemplation. After the musing mood has been established in the first two lines, the poet continues:

> She ran on tip-toe down the darkened passage
> To meet him in the doorway with the news
> And put him on his guard.

The mood changes from meditation to action, a fact amplified by the poet's use of plosive sounds and run-on lines. By using these devices and increasing the tempo, you can effectively suggest a character's movements in an oral performance.

 ## EXERCISES FOR TEMPO

1. The opening lines from Alfred, Lord Tennyson's "Ulysses" are contemplative in mood. Read them aloud using a slow pace to emphasize the discontent and dissatisfaction with life that Ulysses felt. Lines 6 through 11 build in emotional tension to the epigram "I am become a name"; this climactic moment can be realized for an audience by increasing the tempo, along with other forms of speech emphasis.

   In the third part of the poem, Ulysses is trying to convince his mariners to follow him back into the life of adventure. Varying pace can very successfully highlight meaning.

   1   It little profits that an idle king,
   2   By this still hearth, among these barren crags,
   3   Matched with an aged wife, I mete and dole
   4   Unequal laws unto a savage race,
   5   That hoard, and sleep, and feed, and know not me.
   6   I cannot rest from travel; I will drink
   7   Life to the lees. All times I have enjoyed
   8   Greatly, have suffered greatly, both with those
   9   That loved me, and alone; on shore, and when

10   Through scudding drifts the rainy Hyades—[4] ['haɪədiz]
11   Vext the dim sea: I am become a name.

....

44   There lies the port; the vessel puffs her sail:
45   There gloom the dark broad seas. My mariners,
46   Souls that have toiled, and wrought, and thought with me
47   That ever with a frolic welcome took
48   The thunder and the sunshine, and opposed
49   Free hearts, free foreheads—you and I are old;
50   Old age hath yet his honor and his toil.
51   Death closes all; but something ere the end,
52   Some work of noble note, may yet be done,
53   Not unbecoming men that strove with Gods.
54   The lights begin to twinkle from the rocks;
55   The long day wanes; the slow moon climbs; the deep
56   Moans round with many voices. Come, my friends,
57   'Tis not too late to seek a newer world.
58   Push off, and sitting well in order smite
59   The sounding furrows; for my purpose holds
60   To sail beyond the sunset, and the baths
61   Of all the western stars, until I die.
62   It may be that the gulfs will wash us down;
63   It may be we shall touch the Happy Isles,
64   And see the great Achilles, whom we knew.
65   Though much is taken, much abides; and though
66   We are not now that strength which in old days
67   Moved earth and heaven, that which we are, we are:
68   One equal temper of heroic hearts,
69   Made weak by time and fate, but strong in will
70   To strive, to seek, to find, and not to yield.

From ULYSSES
Alfred, Lord Tennyson

2. Record the following selection and create varieties of pace to convey the poet's meaning.

1   Into the street the Piper stept,
2   Smiling first a little smile,
3   As if he knew what magic slept
4   In his quiet pipe the while;
5   Then, like a musical adept,
6   To blow the pipe his lips he wrinkled,
7   And green and blue his sharp eyes twinkled
8   Like a candle-flame where salt is sprinkled
9   And ere three shrill notes the pipe uttered,
10   You heard as if an army muttered;
11   And the muttering grew to a grumbling;
12   And the grumbling grew to a mighty rumbling;
13   And out of the houses the rats came tumbling.
14   Great rats, small rats, lean rats, brawny rats.
15   Brown rats, black rats, gray rats, tawny rats.
16   Grave old plodders, gay young friskers,
17   Fathers, mothers, uncles, cousins,
18   Cocking tails and pricking whispers,

---

[4]"Hyades" is a cluster of stars believed by the ancients to indicate rainy weather when they rose with the sun.

19   Families by tens and dozens,
20   Brothers, sisters, husbands, wives—
21   Followed the Piper for their lives.
22   From step to step he piped advancing,
23   And step for step they followed dancing,
24   Until they came to the river Weser [veze],
25   Wherein all plunged and perished!

From THE PIED PIPER OF HAMELIN
Robert Browning

3. 1   She pierced her ears,
2   She pierced her nose,
3   Had roses tattooed where it shows,
4   (And other places? Gad! Who knows?)
5   She dyed her hair both green and blue,
6   And combed it high, a foot or two,
7   (Or styled it in a Mohawk crew.)
8   For shadowing her eyes she'd use
9   Chalk white and bold, fluorescent hues,
10   (Her orange lips made local news.)
11   She draped her anorectic frame
12   With clothes Goodwill refused to claim,
13   Like shawls, and beads, and heavy chain.
14   Long, silver nails took time and pain
15   To grow, and paint, and now it's plain
16   She'd do most anything for thrills—
17   It's Grandson *Bob!* Oh, Maude, my pills!

A MODERN CHILD: AS SEEN BY A MODERN GRANDPA!
Father Eugene F. Lyttle

4. 1   Good Heavens! what was that which sent the blood tingling to his heart and deprived
2   him of his voice and of power to move! There—there—at the window— close before
3   him—so close, that he could have almost touched him before he started back—with
4   his eyes peering into the room and meeting his—there stood Fagin! And beside
5   him, white with rage or fear, or both, were the scowling features of the very man
6   who had accosted him in the inn yard.
7   It was but an instant, a glance, a flash, before his eyes; and they were gone.
8   But they recognized him, and he them; and their look was firmly impressed upon his
9   memory. He stood transfixed for a moment; then, leaping from the window into the
10   garden, called loudly for help.

From OLIVER TWIST
Charles Dickens

5. A linguistics professor was lecturing to his class one day. "In English," he said, "A
double negative forms a positive. In some languages, though, such as Russian, a double
negative is still a negative. However, there is no language wherein a double positive
can form a negative."
    A voice from the back of the room piped up, "Yeah, right."

6. Jesse Kiplinger, a Hollywood producer, is talking to Muriel Tate, a married acquain-
tance whom he hasn't seen in many years.

1   Why did I call you yesterday? After seventeen years? Okay, let's start with, "Yes, I'm
2   a Famous Hollywood Producer. Yes, I never made a picture that lost money. Yes, I

3   got that magic touch, call it talent, whatever you want, I don't know." . . . The fact is,
4   ever since I was old enough to sneak into the Ridgewood Theatre in Tenafly, I've
5   been a movie nut. Not only have I seen every Humphrey Bogart movie he ever made
6   at least eight times, I now own a print of all those pictures. Why do you think I was
7   so crazy to buy his house? So crazy to buy this house? So I went to Hollywood and
8   was very lucky and extremely smart and presto, I became a producer. I love making
9   movies. Some are good, some are bad, most of them are fun. I hope I can continue
10 doing it for the next fifty years. That's one half of my life. The other half is that in
11 the last fourteen years I've been married three times—to three of the worst bitches
12 you'd ever want to meet.

From PLAZA SUITE
Neil Simon

7. Annie Sullivan, the teacher of Helen Keller, describes the asylums that her student
might have to enter in the future if she does not learn how to communicate.

1   I grew up in such an asylum. The state alms-house. Rats—why, my brother Jimmie
2   and I used to play with rats because we didn't have any toys. Maybe you'd like to
3   know what Helen will find there, not on visiting days? One ward was full of the—
4   old women, crippled, blind, most of them dying. But even if what they had was
5   catching there was nowhere else to move them, and that's where they put us. There
6   were younger ones across the hall, prostitutes mostly, with T.B., and epileptic fits,
7   and a couple of the kind who—keep after other girls, especially young ones, and
8   some insane. Some just had the D.T.'s. The youngest were in another ward to have
9   babies they didn't want, they started at thirteen, fourteen. They'd leave afterwards,
10 but the babies stayed and we played with them, too, though a lot of them had—sores
11 all over from diseases you're not supposed to talk about, but not many of them lived.
12 The first year we had eighty, seventy died. The room Jimmie and I played in was the
13 deadhouse, where they kept the bodies till they could dig—the graves. No, it made
14 me strong. But I don't think you need send Helen there. She's strong enough.

From THE MIRACLE WORKER
William Gibson

8. Lorraine Sheldon, star of stage, screen, radio (and television—had it existed at the
time for public consumption) visits her dear friend Sheridan Whiteside, another gem
in the world of the theatrical and notorious.

1   *Lorraine:* You look perfectly wonderful—I never saw you look better. My dear, do
2   I look a wreck? I just dashed through New York. Didn't do a thing about Christmas.
3   Hattie Carnegie and had my hair done, and got right on the train. And the Normandie
4   coming back was simply hectic. Fun, you know, but simply exhausting. Jock
5   Whitney, and Cary Grant, and Dorothy de Frasso—it was *too* exhausting. And of
6   course London before that was so magnificent, my dear—well, I simply never got
7   to bed at all. Darling, I've so much to tell you I don't know where to start. . . . Let
8   me see. Sybil Cartwright was thrown right out of Ciro's—it was the night before I
9   left. She was wearing one of those new cellophane dresses, and you could absolutely
10 see Trafalgar Square. And Sir Harry Montross—the painter, you know—is suing
11 his mother for disorderly conduct. It's just shocked *everyone*. And oh! before I forget:
12 Anthony Eden told me he's going to be on your New Year's broadcast, Sherry,
13 and Beatrice Lillie gave me a message for you. She says for you to take off twenty five
14 pounds right away and send them to her by parcel post. She needs them.

From THE MAN WHO CAME TO DINNER
Moss Hart, George S. Kaufman

9. What I so greatly feared, happened! Miss Whiteside, the dean of our college, withheld my diploma. When I came to her office, and asked her why she did not pass me, she said that she could not recommend me as a teacher because of my personal appearance.

She told me that my skin looked oily, my hair unkempt, and my fingernails sadly neglected. She told me that I was utterly unmindful of the little niceties of the well-groomed lady. She pointed out that my collar did not set evenly, my belt was awry, and there was a lack of freshness in my dress. And she ended with: "Soap and water are cheap. Anyone can be clean."

In those four years while I was under her supervision, I was always timid and diffident. I shrank and trembled when I had to come near her. When I had to say something to her, I mumbled and stuttered, and grew red and white in the face with fear.

Every time I had to come to the dean's office for a private conference, I prepared for the ordeal of her cold scrutiny, as a patient prepares for a surgical operation. I watched her gimlet eyes searching for a stray pin, for a spot on my dress, for my un-polished shoes, for my uncared-for fingernails, as one strapped on the operating table watches the surgeon approaching with his tray of sterilized knives.

She never looked into my eyes. She never perceived that I had a soul. She did not see how I longed for beauty and cleanliness. How I strained and struggled to lift myself from the dead toil and exhaustion that weighed me down. She could see nothing in people like me, except the dirt and the stains on the outside.

But this last time, when she threatened to withhold my diploma because of my appearance, this last time when she reminded me that "Soap and water are cheap. Anyone can be clean," this last time, something burst with me.

From SOAP AND WATER
Anzia Yezierska

PAUSE

A **pause** is the absence of speech before or after an utterance. It is a temporary stop in verbalization with a continuation of thought; it is not a break in the continuity of the thought. The pause is an integral part of meaning. It is in the speaker's speech and not the thought. A true pause is the "loud" silence that intensifies a communication, during which the thought is maintained until vocalization resumes. This bridge of thought is usually emphasized through facial expression (particularly the eyes) and tension in the body.

A pause may be likened to an electric arc (Figure 9.1). When an uncharged wire is slowly brought closer to a wire plugged into a live socket, an arc of electricity springs from the live wire to the other when the charge is great enough. A similar situation occurs with the use of the pause (Figure 9.2). If the thought before the pause is sufficiently energized, the thought will be maintained and intensified until it is verbally "discharged." The pause is "the servant of the thought."[5]

The pause is the most artistic form of speech emphasis. There are three types of pauses: (1) reflection, (2) anticipation, and (3) implication. The pause of reflection stimulates the listener to think back on something that has been said. This technique is often used by comics. Frequently, the expression on the face is an indication or tip-off that something significant has been said. The response of the audience comes after a couple of beats.

The pause of anticipation is used when the audience anticipates something that is about to be said. Again, a comic uses this form of pause very frequently. Sometimes the audience itself completes the thought.

---

[5]Charles Wesley Emerson, *The Evolution of Expression,* vol. 4 (Boston: Emerson College of Oratory, 1919), 8.

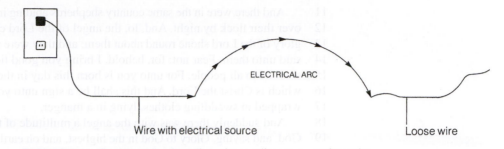

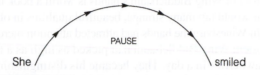

FIGURE 9.1   Current arcing from live wire to adjacent, powerless wire

FIGURE 9.2   Pause providing energized meaning between two words

The third type of pause (and perhaps the most meaningful) is the pause of implication, in which the pause implies something more than has been said. As an example, suppose Aunt Maude and Uncle Ned had been invited to a party on Friday night, but Aunt Maude did not attend. So the next morning Uncle Ned says, "Maudie, you missed [pause of implication] quite a party last night." This pause would probably be accompanied by some form of nonverbal communication, perhaps a nod of the head or widened eyes.

It is very important to underscore that all of the forms of speech emphasis (stress, slide, pace, and pause) work together to create an appropriate whole. Using all of the inflective forms gives the speaker variety, energy, and (above all) clarity. No one form of emphasis should be used to the exclusion of the others. Obviously, the material presented here can help you determine which forms of emphasis to use.

EXERCISES FOR PAUSE

Tape the following selections, and determine the location and duration of your own pauses. You will, of course, use additional forms of emphasis, but highlight the use of the pause.

1. 1   And it came to pass in those days, that there went out a decree from Caesar Augustus,
    2   that all the world should be taxed. . . . And all went to be taxed, every one into
    3   his own city. And Joseph also went up from Galilee, out of the city of Nazareth, into
    4   Judea, unto the city of David, which is called Bethlehem (because he was of the
    5   house and lineage of David) to be taxed with Mary his espoused wife, being great
    6   with child.
    7   And so it was, that, while they were there, the days were accomplished that she
    8   should be delivered. And she brought forth her firstborn son, and wrapped him in
    9   swaddling clothes, and laid him in a manger, because there was no room for them
    10 in the inn.

11   And there were in the same country shepherds abiding in the field, keeping watch
12   over their flock by night. And, lo, the angel of the Lord came upon them, and the
13   glory of the Lord shone round about them: and they were sore afraid. And the angel
14   said unto them, Fear not: for, behold, I bring you good tidings of great joy, which
15   shall be to all people. For unto you is born this day in the city of David a Saviour,
16   which is Christ the Lord. And this shall be a sign unto you; Ye shall find the babe
17   wrapped in swaddling clothes, lying in a manger.
18   And suddenly there was with the angel a multitude of the heavenly host praising
19   God, and saying, Glory to God in the highest, and on earth peace, good will toward
20   men.

LUKE 2:1–14

2.
1   The story of Wing Biddlebaum's hands is worth a book in itself. Sympathetically set
2   forth it would tap many strange, beautiful qualities in obscure men. It is a job for a
3   poet. In Winesburg the hands had attracted attention merely because of their activity.
4   With them Wing Biddlebaum had picked as high as a hundred and forty quarts
5   of strawberries in a day. They became his distinguishing feature, the source of his
6   fame. Also they made more grotesque an already grotesque and elusive individuality.
7   Winesburg was proud of the hands of Wing Biddlebaum in the same spirit in which
8   it was proud of banker White's new stone house and Wesley Moyer's bay stallion,
9   Tony Tip, that had won the two-fifteen trot at the fall races in Cleveland.

From THE BOOK OF THE GROTESQUE in *WINESBURG, OHIO*
Sherwood Anderson

3. *Mama:* Son—how come you talk so much 'bout money? . . . *(Quietly)* Oh—*(Very
quietly)* So now it's life. Money is life. Once upon a time freedom used to be
life—now it's money. I guess the world really do change. . . . No . . . something
has changed. *(She looks at him.)* You something new, boy. In my time we was worried about not being lynched and getting to the North if we could and how to stay
alive and still have a pinch of dignity too . . . Now here come you and Beneatha—
talking 'bout things we ain't even thought about hardly, me and your daddy. You
ain't satisfied or proud of nothing we done. I mean that you had a home; that we
kept you out of trouble till you was grown; that you don't have to ride to work on
the back of nobody's streetcar—You my children—but how different we done become. . . . Son—do you know your wife is expecting another baby? That's what
she wanted to talk to you about. This ain't for me to be telling—but you ought to
know. *(She waits)* I think Ruth is thinking 'bout getting rid of that child. . . .
When the world gets ugly enough—a woman will do anything for her family. *The
part that's already living.* . . . Well—(Tightly) Well—son, I'm waiting to hear you
say something . . . I'm waiting to hear how you be your father's son. Be the man
he was . . . Your wife say she going to destroy your child. And I'm waiting to hear
you talk like him and say we a people who give children life, not who destroys
them—*(She rises)* I'm waiting to see you stand up and look like your daddy and
say we done give up one baby to poverty and that we ain't going to give up nary another
one . . . I'm waiting. . . . If you are a son of mine, tell her! *(Walter looks at her and
can say nothing. She continues bitterly)* You . . . you are a disgrace to your father's
memory. Somebody get me my hat.

From A RAISIN IN THE SUN
Lorraine Hansberry

4. Christine, a mother, finally realizes that her young daughter Rhoda may be a murderer:

1   You used to go up to see her every afternoon. She was very old, and liked to show
2   you all her treasures. The one you admired most was a crystal ball, in which
3   opals floated. The old lady promised this treasure to you when she died. One afternoon
4   when the daughter was shopping at the supermarket and you were alone with
5   Mrs. Post, she somehow managed to fall down the spiral backstairs and break her
6   neck. You said she heard a kitten mewing outside and went to see about it and somehow
7   missed her footing and fell five flights to the courtyard below. Then you asked
8   the daughter for the crystal ball. She gave it to you, and it's still hanging at the head
9   of your bed. Rhoda, did you have anything to do, anything at all, no matter how little
10 it was, with Claude getting drowned?

From THE BAD SEED
Maxwell Anderson

5.   1   Cliff Klingenhagan had me in to dine
2   With him one day; and after soup and meat,
3   And all the other things there were to eat,
4   Cliff took two glasses and filled one with wine
5   And one with wormwood. Then, without a sign
6   For me to choose at all, he took the draught
7   Of bitterness himself, and lightly quaffed
8   It off, and said the other one was mine.
9   And when I asked him what the deuce he meant
10 By doing that, he only looked at me
11 And smiled, and said it was a way of his.
12 And though I know the fellow, I have spent
13 Long time a-wondering when I shall be
14 As happy as Cliff Klingenhagen is.

From CLIFF KLINGENHAGEN
Edwin Arlington Robinson

6. The dirt yards, carefully swept and sprinkled in Haven, became lawns in Ruby until, finally, front yards were given over completely to flowers for no good reason except there was time in which to do it. The habit, the interest in cultivating plants that could not be eaten, spread, and so did the ground surrendered to it. Exchanging, sharing a cutting here, a root there, a bulb or two became so frenetic a land grab, husbands complained of neglect and the disappointingly small harvest of radishes, or the too short rows of collards, beets. The women kept on with their vegetable gardens in back, but little by little its produce became like the flowers—driven by desire, not necessity. Iris, phlox, rose and peonies took up more and more time, quiet boasting and so much space new butterflies journeyed miles to brood in Ruby. Their chrysalises hung in secret under acacias, and from there they joined blues and sulphurs that had been feeding for decades in buckwheat and clove. The red bands drinking from sumac competed with the newly arrived creams and whites that loved jewel flowers and nasturtiums. Giant orange wings covered in black lace hovered in pansies and violets. Like the years of garden rivalry, the butterflies were gone that cool October evening, but the consequence remained—fat, overwrought yards; clumps and chains of eggs. Hiding. Until spring.

From PARADISE
Toni Morrison

EXERCISES FOR EMPHASIS

Tape the following selections using the separate forms of emphasis. This is a very difficult challenge. Apply stress (punching) the first time. Then, read them with changes of pace. Then, add inflection, and finally, pause. This procedure may well be very mechanical and in many cases humorous, but the purpose here is to isolate and highlight the separate forms. Then, read aloud the selections with a mixture of all four forms of emphasis. Remember that an overused technique diminishes its effectiveness. Determine your choices according to the meaning you desire to convey to your audience.

1. "Hallelujah" was the only observation
That escaped Lieutenant-Colonel Mary Jane,
When she tumbled off the platform in the station,
And was cut in little pieces by the train.
Mary Jane, the train is through yer:
Hallelujah, hallelujah!
We will gather up the fragments that remain.

HALLELUJAH
A. E. Housman

2. When Sir Joshua Reynolds died
All nature was degraded;
The King dropped a tear into the Queen's ear,
And all his pictures faded.

SIR JOSHUA REYNOLDS
William Blake

3. Try these limericks.

a. There was a young maid who said, "Why
Can't I look in my ear with my eye?
If I put my mind to it,
I'm sure I can do it.
You never can tell till you try."

b. A decrepit old gas man named Peter,
While hunting around for the meter,
Touched a leak with his light.
He arose out of sight,
And, as anyone can see by reading this, he also destroyed the meter.

c. I sat next to the Duchess at tea.
It was just as I feared it would be:
Her rumblings abdominal
Were simply abominable,
And everyone thought it was me.

d. There was an old man of Peru
Who dreamed he was eating his shoe.
He awoke in the night
In a terrible fright,
And found it was perfectly true.

e. There was a young lady of Lynn
Who was so uncommonly thin

That when she essayed
To drink lemonade
She slipped through the straw and fell in.

EXERCISES FOR VOCAL DYNAMICS

In the following exercises, try each of the four forms of speech emphasis. Read aloud the exercises and tape them. You are encouraged to exaggerate your use of the forms at first. However, when you pull away from the exaggeration, make certain that you retain appropriate vocal dynamics. Remember that after you have isolated each form of speech emphasis, you must put the four back together again; one form should not be used to the exclusion of the others.

1. Amanda Wingfield sells magazine subscriptions in order to meet the monthly bills. She is on the telephone in the living room.

   Amanda: Ida Scott? This is Amanda Wingfield. We missed you at the D.A.R. last Monday. Oh, first I want to know how's your sinus condition? You're just a Christian martyr. That's what you are. You're just a Christian martyr. Well, I was just going through my little red book, and I saw that your subscription to the "Companion" is about to expire just when that wonderful new serial by Bessie Mae Harper is starting. It's the first thing she's written since "Honeymoon for Three." Now, that was unusual, wasn't it? Why, Ida, this one is even lovelier. It's all about the horsey set on Long Island and a debutante is thrown from her horse while taking him over the jumps at the—regatta. Her spine—her spine is injured. That's what the horse did—he stepped on her. Now, there is only one surgeon in the entire world that keep her from being completely paralyzed, and that's the man she's engaged to be married to and he's tall and he's bond and he's handsome. That's unusual, too, huh? Oh, he's not perfect. Of course he has a weakness. He has the most terrible weakness in the entire world. He just drinks too much. What? Oh, no, Honey, don't let them burn. You go take a look in the oven and I'll hold on . . . Why, that woman! Do you know what she did? She hung up on me.

   From THE GLASS MANAGERIE
   Tennessee Williams

2. His *(Burt's)* eyes widened.
   My God, there aren't any weeds!
   Not a single one. Every foot and a half the corn plants rose from the earth. There was no witchgrass, jimson, pikeweed, whore's hair, or poke salad. Nothing.
   Burt stared up, eyes wide. The light in the west was fading. The raftered clouds had drawn together. Below them the golden light had faded to pink and ocher. It would be dark soon enough.
   It was time to go down to the clearing in the corn and see what was there—hadn't that been the plan all along? All the time he had thought he was cutting back to the highway, hadn't he been being led to this place?
   Dread in his belly, he went on down to the row and stood at the edge of the clearing. There was enough light left for him to see what was here. He couldn't scream. There didn't seem to be enough air left in his lungs. He tottered in on legs like slats of splintery wood. His eyes bulged from his sweaty face.
   "Vicky," he whispered, "Oh, Vicky, my god—" . . .

   From CHILDREN OF THE CORN
   Stephen King

3. The following comic essay, "Stamp Out Fadspeak!" by Richard Lederer, is an excellent selections for reading aloud. The work gives you plenty of opportunity to make use of the forms of emphasis. You would be "fadspeaking" directly to the members of your audience.

Some people lament that speaking and writing these days are simply a collection of faddish cliches patched together like the sections of prefabricated houses made of ticky-tacky. They see modern discourse as a mindless clacking of trendy expressions, many of them from movies and television sitcoms.

Why is English discourse in such a parlous state? Maybe it's because verbal knee-jerkery requires no thought. It's so much easier not to think, isn't it? It's so much easier to cookie-cut the rich dough of the English language. It's so much easier to microwave a frozen dinner than to create a meal from scratch. After all, when we were children, we loved to pull the string on the doll that said the same thing over and over, again and again.

That's what fadspeak is—the unrelenting mix of mimicry and gimmickry. Fadspeak comprises vogue phrases that suddenly appear on everybody's tongues—phrases that launch a thousand lips. Before you can say, "yada yada yada," these throwaway expressions become instant cliches, perfect for our throwaway society, like paper wedding dresses for throwaway marriages.

Fadspeak cliches lead mayfly lives, counting their duration in months instead of decades. They strut and fret their hour upon the stage of pop culture and then are heard no more.

Now, would I, your faithful, drop-dead-good-looking language columnist, your poster boy for user-friendly writing, ever serve you anything totally bogus like fadspeak? I don't think so. Not a problem. That just lowers the bar for what makes good writing.

I know that I wear many hats, but I'm not talking trash here. I'm not the 800-pound gorilla out to bust your chops. I feel your pain, and I'm your new best friend. At this point in time, I've got you on my radar screen, and I know you da man! Yessss!

Hey, people, this isn't rocket science or brain surgery. It's simply a no-brainer—a drop kick and a slam dunk. I, the mother of all language writers, will go to the mat 24-7 for fresh, original language because I get more bang for the buck when I avoid those new cliches. I want to level the playing field and give something back to the community.

So I'm making you an offer you can't refuse. I'm never going to slip into those hackneyed faddish expressions that afflict our precious American language. How about we run that one up the flagpole and give it a salute? Sound like a plan? I bring a lot to the table. I come to play, and the ball's in your court.

Sheeesh, Don't you just hate it when a writer or speaker gives you that same old same old? Doesn't it just send you on an emotional roller coaster? Doesn't it just blow you out of the water and make you want to scream, "Oh, puh-leeze! In your dreams! Excuuuuse me! It's my way or the highway! You're history! You're toast! That's so twentieth century! Put a sock in it!"?

As for me, I'm like, "Are you the writer from Hell? Lose the attitude, man. You are so-o-o-o busted. Maybe it's a guy thing, but get real! Read my lips! Get a life! And while you're at it, why don't you knock yourself out and get a vocabulary?"

Anyhoo, off the top of my head, the bottom line is that fadspeakers and fadwriters are so clueless. They just don't get up to speed, go the whole nine yards, and take it to another level. They're afraid to push the envelope and think out of the box. All they do is give you that same-old-same-old, been-there-done-that kind of writing.

Tell me about it. Fadspeakers and fadwriters just play the old tape again and again, and their ideas just fall through the cracks. They're not playing with a full deck. The light's on, but nobody's home. Elvis has left the building. Go figure.

Hel-lo-oh? Duuuh. Boooring. What's wrong with this picture? Are we on the same page? Are we having fun yet? Are you having some kind of a bad-hair day? Are you having a midlife crisis? A senior moment? Maybe it's time for a wake-up call? Or maybe a reality check? I don't think so. In your dreams. Not even close.

O-o-k-a-a-a-y. You wanna talk about it? You wanna get with the program? I feel your pain, but why don't you wake up and smell the coffee? How about we cut right to the chase? Deal with it. You got that right. Or maybe I'm just preaching to the choir. Whatever.

Now that I've got your attention, here's the heads-up on communication. Whenever I find one of these snippets of fadspeak strewn about a sentence, I'm in your face. I'm your worst nightmare. Strings of pop phrases just make me go ballistic, even to the point of going postal. After all, what goes around comes around.

Okay, okay. I understand that you're not a happy camper and maybe you just don't want to go there. But I do because I've got all my ducks in a row. I mean, at the end of the day, is this a great, language—or what? I mean, It's a language to die for.

Gimme a break. Cut me some slack. What am I, chopped liver? Hey, what do I know? And now that I've thrown my hissy fit about fadspeak, here's what's going down.

Thanks a bunch you for letting me share. Now that I've been able to tell it like it is, I'm outta here. Buh-bye. Talk to you soon—and have a nice day.

STAMP OUT FADSPEAK!
Richard Lederer

4. In *The Color Purple,* Celie is writing a letter to God:

Dear God,

Shug Avery is coming to town! She coming with her orkestra. She going to sing in the Lucky Star out on Coalman road. Mr. _____ going to hear her. He dress all up in front the glass, look at himself, then undress and dress all over again. He slick back his hair with pomade, then wash it out again. He been spittin on his shoes and hitting it with a quick rag.

He tell me, Wash this. Iron that. Look for this. Look for that. Find this. Find that. He groan over holes in his sock.

I move round darning and ironing, finding hanskers. Anything happening? I ast.

What you mean? He say, like he mad. Just trying to git some of the hick farmer off myself. Any other woman be glad.

I'm is glad, I say.

What you mean? He ast.

You looks nice, I say. Any woman be proud.

You think so? He say.

First time he ast me. I'm so surprise, by time I say Yeah, he out on the porch, trying to shave where the light better.

I walk round all day with the announcement burning a hole in my pocket. It pink. The trees tween the turn off to our road and the store is lit up with them. He got bout five dozen in his trunk.

Shug Avery standing upside a piano, elbow crook, hand on her hip. She wearing a hat like Indian Chiefs. Her mouth open showing all her teef and don't nothing seem to be troubling her mind. Come one, come all, it say. The Queen Honeybee is back in town.

Lord, I wants to go so bad. Not to dance. Not to drink. Not to play card. Not even to hear Shug Avery sing. I just be thankful to lay eyes on her.

From THE COLOR PURPLE
Alice Walker

5. 1   *Valvert (to Cyrano de Bergerac):* Ah-hem—your nose—your nose is rather large.
2   *Cyrano:* Rather. That is all? [*Valvert merely shrugs.*] Tis not enough. You might
3   have said a multitude of things by varying the tone. . . . As for example: *Aggressively:*
4   —"Sir, if I had such a nose I'd amputate it at once!" *Friendly:*—"How do you
5   drink with such a nose? You ought to have a medieval goblet made for it." *Descriptive:*
6   —"Tis a rock! . . . a peak . . . a cape! . . . a cape, forsooth! Tis a peninsula!"
7   *Curious:*—"How serves that oblong capsular? For scissor case? or pot to hold
8   your ink?" or *Graciously:*—"I see that you are fond of little birds—you give them
9   this to rest their little feet." Or *Insolently:*—"When you smoke your pipe . . . suppose
10 that the tobacco smoke spouts from your nose—do not the neighbors, as the fumes
11 rise higher, cry terror struck: 'The Chimney is afire!'" *Warning:*—"Careful, this
12 weight will drag you down." *Tender:*—"Pray, get a small umbrella made, lest its
13 bright color should fade in the sun." *Pedantic:*—"That beast Aristophanes named
14 Hippocamelele-phantoles must have possessed just such a lump of flesh and bone."
15 *Dramatic:*—"When it bleeds, the Red Sea!" *Admiring:*—"What a sign for a perfumer!"
16 *Naive:*—"This monument is interesting; what are the visiting hours?"
17 *Rustic:*—"That thing a nose? Na-na—that is a turnip or a dwarf pumpkin."
18 *Practical:*—"Put it in a lottery!" These, then are the things you might have said—had
19 you some learning or some wit. Of wit you never had an atom, and of letters you have
20 three only—they spell ass!

Adapted from CYRANO DE BERGERAC
Edmond Rostand

6. 1   The black man placed his tea on the tray. He rose, patted his lips with the napkin,
2   placed the napkin beside his cup and went to the piano. He sat on the piano stool and
3   immediately he rose and twirled it till the height was to his satisfaction. He sat down
4   again, played a chord and turned to them. This piano is badly in need of a tuning, he
5   said. Father's face reddened. Oh yes, Mother said, we are terrible about that. The
6   musician turned again to the keyboard. "Wall Street Rag," he said. Composed by the
7   great Scott Joplin. He began to play. Ill-tuned or not the Aeolian had never made
8   such sounds. Small clear chords hung in the air like flowers. The melodies were like
9   bouquets. There seemed to be no other possibilities for life than those delineated by
10 the music. When the piece was over Coalhouse Walker turned on the stool and found
11 in his audience the entire family, Mother, Father, the boy, Grandfather and Mother's
12 Younger Brother, who had come down from his room in shirt and suspenders to see
13 who was playing. Of all of them he was the only one who knew ragtime. He had
14 heard it in his nightlife period in New York. He had never expected to hear it in his
15 sister's home.
16   Coalhouse Walker Jr. turned back to the piano and said "The Maple Leaf." Composed
17 by the great Scott Joplin. The most famous rag of all rang through the air. The
18 pianist sat stiffly at the keyboard, his long dark hands with their pink nails seemingly
19 with no effort producing the clusters of syncopating chords and the thumping octaves.
20 This was a most robust composition, a vigorous music that roused the senses
21 and never stood still a moment. The boy perceived it as light touching various places
22 in space, accumulating in intricate patterns until the entire room was made to glow
23 with its own being. The music filled the stairwell to the third floor where the mute
24 and unforgiving Sarah sat with her hands folded and listened with the open door.
25   The piece was brought to a conclusion. Everyone applauded. Mother then introduced
26 Mr. Walker to Grandfather and to Younger Brother, who shook the black
27 man's hand and said I am pleased to meet you. Coalhouse Walker was solemn.
28 Everyone was standing. There was a silence. Father cleared his throat. Father was
29 not knowledgeable in music. His taste ran to Carry Jacob's Band. He thought Negro
30 music had to have smiling and cakewalking. Do you know any coon songs? he said.

31 He did not intend to be rude— coon songs was what they were called. But the pianist
32 responded with a tense shake of the head. Coon songs are made for minstrel shows,
33 he said. White men sing them in blackface. There was another silence. The black
34 man looked at the ceiling. Well, he said, it appears as if Miss Sarah will not be able
35 to receive me. He turned abruptly and walked through the hall to the kitchen. The
36 family followed him. He had left his coat on a chair. He put it on and ignoring them
37 all, he knelt and gazed at the baby asleep in its carriage. After several moments he
38 stood up, said good day and walked out the door.

From RAGTIME
E. L. Doctorow

7. In the following poem, make certain that you decide on a meaning for the made-up
words, which Lewis Carroll called "portmanteau words." For example, "slithy" melds
the words *slimy* and *lithe,* and "brunch" is a combination of *breakfast* and *lunch.*
Create a character/narrator and a fictive world or environment for this reading.

1 'Twas brillig, and the slithy toves
2 Did gyre and gimble in the wabe;
3 All mimsy were the borogoves,
4 And the mome raths outgrabe.

5 "Beware the Jabberwock, my son!
6 The jaws that bite, the claws that catch!
7 Beware the Jubjub bird, and shun
8 The frumious Bandersnatch!"

9 He took his vorpal sword in hand:
10 Long time the manxome foe he sought—
11 So rested he by the Tumtum tree,
12 And stood awhile in thought.

13 And, as in uffish thought he stood,
14 The Jabberwock, with eyes of flame,
15 Came whiffling through the tulgey wood,
16 And burbled as it came!

17 One, two! One, two! And through and through
18 The vorpal blade went snicker-snack!
19 He left it dead, and with its head
20 He went galumphing back.

21 "And hast thou slain the Jabberwock?
22 Come to my arms, my beamish boy!
23 O frabjous day! Callooh! Callay!"
24 He chortled in his joy.

25 'Twas brillig, and the slithy toves
26 Did gyre and gimble in the wabe;
27 All mimsy were the borogoves,
28 And the mome raths outgrabe.

JABBERWOCKY
Lewis Carroll

8. Joan is attempting to motivate France's Charles, the "wimpy" Dauphin, to loan her his
army to fight the British. She asks Charles if he is afraid:

1 *Charles:* Yes: I am afraid. It's no use preaching to me about it. It's all very well for
2 these big men with their armor that is too heavy for me, and their swords that I can

3 hardly lift, and their muscle and their shouting and their bad tempers. They like
4 fighting: most of them are making fools of themselves all the time they are not fighting;
5 but I am quiet and sensible; and I don't want to kill people: I only want to be left
6 alone to enjoy myself in my own way. I never asked to be king: it was pushed on me.
7 So if you are going to say "Son of St. Louis: gird on the sword of your ancestors, and
8 lead us to victory," you may spare your breath to cool your porridge; for I cannot do
9 it. I am not built that way; and there is an end of it.

10 *Joan: (earnestly)* Charlie: I come from the land, and have gotten my strength working
11 on the land; and I tell thee that the land is thine to rule righteously and keep God's
12 peace in, and not to pledge at the pawnshop as a drunken woman pledges her children's
13 clothes. And I come from God to tell thee to kneel in the cathedral and
14 solemnly give thy kingdom to Him for ever and ever, and become the greatest king
15 in the world as His steward and His bailiff, His soldier, and His servant. The very
16 clay of France will become holy: her soldiers will be the soldiers of God: the rebel
17 dukes will be rebels against God: the English will fall on their knees and beg thee let
18 them return to their lawful homes in peace. Wilt be a poor Judas, and betray me and
19 Him that sent me?

From SAINT JOAN (Scene 2)
George Bernard Shaw

9. See if you can suggest the three characters' speech and vocal attitudes in the following scene:

1 *Mrs. Candour, a rather viperous woman, enters:* My dear Lady Sneerwell, how have
2 you been this century?—Mr. Surface, what news do you hear?—though indeed it is
3 no matter, for I think one hears nothing else but scandal—
4 *Surface:*   Just so, indeed, Madam.
5 *Mrs. C:*   Ah, Maria, child—what, is the whole affair off between you and
6   Charles?—His extravagance, I presume— The town talks of nothing
7   else—
8 *Maria:*   I am very sorry, ma'am, the town has so little to do.
9 *Mrs. C:*   True—true, child but there's no stopping people's tongues. I own I was
10   hurt to hear it—as I indeed was to learn from the same quarter that your
11   guardian, Sir Peter, and Lady Teazle have not agreed lately so well as
12   could be wished.
13 *Maria:*   'Tis strangely impertinent for people to busy themselves so.
14 *Mrs. C:*   Very true child; but what's to be done? People will talk—there's no
15   preventing it. Why it was but yesterday, I was told that Miss Gadabout had
16   eloped with Sir Filagree Flirt. But, Lord! there's no minding what one
17   hears; though, to be sure, I had this from very good authority.
18 *Maria:*   Such reports are highly scandalous.
19 *Mrs. C:*   So they are, child—shameful, shameful! But the world is so censorious,
20   no character escapes. Lord, now who would have suspected your friend,
21   Miss Prim, of an indiscretion? Yet such is the ill nature of people that they
22   say her uncle stopped her last week just as she was stepping into the York
23   diligence with her dancing master.
24 *Maria:*   I'll answer for it. There are no grounds for the report.
25 *Mrs. C:*   Oh, no foundation in the world, I dare swear, no more probably than for
26   the story circulated last month, of Mrs. Festino's affair with Colonel
27   Cassino—though, to be sure, that matter was never rightly cleared up.

From THE SCHOOL FOR SCANDAL
Richard Brinsley Sheridan

10.

1 Musical melodies of my younger years
2 When I know not the sweetness
3 But only the tears.
4 Sad memories of Tchaikovsky and Chopin
5 A pen, a notebook, a metronome.
6 Tremulous fingers and unsteady hands
7 Stumbled on the keyboard, a foreign land.

8 "Sit up straight, no slouching
9 Smile on face, stop sweating
10 The recital's tomorrow
11 You keep forgetting."

12 Sweet melodies.
13 Sad memories.

14 Vivid pictures dance in my mind
15 Of those practice sessions,
16 Endless, agonizing lesions.
17 A cold, damp studio on the second floor
18 No view from the solo window
19 Only the piece of music before me
20 That tedious score.
21 The ebony Steinway, so grands,
22 A virtuoso I was told
23 With hammers of silk
24 And foot pedals in gold.

25 *Sotto voce*, Staccato,
26 Arpeggios played *Pianissimo*.
27 "Not that way, no!
28 Play again, repeat once more
29 As *I* played it before."

30 What do you want
31 From my amateur hands?
32 I practice everyday
33 As I promised at the start
34 To achieve the perfection
35 Of your incessant demands.

36 This dream
37 Is not mine
38 It belongs to you.
39 The experienced teacher
40 With her clever advice has failed.
41 Please, unmask the disguise.
42 I still see clearly your aching face—
43 Experience and loss defined your anguish
44 Determined dark eyes, regret, and sadness.
45 Gray and silver streaks formed a mane of hair
46 That flowed down your back
47 And framed your despair.
48 "Musical memories of my younger years
49 I remember only sweetness
50 There were never tears.

51 Sweet melodies of Chopin and Tchaikovsky
52 And fingers lithely flowing
53 Over black & white keys.
54 As the orchestra played behind me,
55 I soloed on a Steinway grand
56 Dazzling crowds with
57 The *Grande Polonaise.*

58 "And then one day
59 The streets filled with storm troopers
60 In brown and black.
61 They silenced the orchestras
62 Shut down the hallowed halls
63 Banned Jews from performing
64 And I never turned back.
65 In time, I escaped
66 This nightmare
67 From over there
68 To this dream—over here.

69 "This dream
70 Is not yours
71 It belongs to me.
72 The experienced teacher
73 With her clever advice
74 Has failed.
75 Please, forgive the disguise.
76 I Surrender my anger
77 And offer my sorrow,
78 Get some sleep, don't forget,
79 Your recital's tomorrow."

80 Sweet melody
81 Sad memory
82 Of Chopin and Tchaikovsky.

PIANO LESSONS
Judith Lynn Antelman

11. 1 It was a bright cold day in April, and the clocks were striking thirteen. Winston
2 Smith, his chin nuzzled into his breast in an effort to escape the vile wind, slipped
3 quickly through the glass doors of Victory Mansions, though not quickly enough to
4 prevent a swirl of gritty dust from entering along with him. The hallway smelt of
5 boiled cabbage and old rag mats. At one end of it a coloured poster, too large for
6 indoor display, had been tacked to the wall. It depicted simply an enormous face,
7 more than a metre wide: the face of a man of about forty-five, with a heavy black
8 moustache and ruggedly handsome features. Winston made for the stairs. It was
9 no use trying the lift. Even at the best of times it was seldom working, and at
10 present the electric current was cut off during daylight hours. It was part of the
11 economy drive in preparation for Hate Week. The flat was seven flights up, and
12 Winston, who was thirty-nine and had a varicose ulcer above his right ankle, went
13 slowly, resting several times on the way. On each landing, opposite the lift-shaft,
14 the poster with the enormous face gazed from the wall. It was one of those
15 pictures which are so contrived that the eyes follow you about when you move.
16 BIG BROTHER IS WATCHING YOU, the caption beneath it ran. Inside the flat a
17 fruity voice was reading out a list of figures which had something to do with the

18 production of pig-iron. The voice came from an oblong metal plaque like a dulled
19 mirror which formed part of the surface of the right-hand wall. Winston turned a
20 switch and the voice sank somewhat, though the words were still distinguishable.
21 The instrument (the telescreen, it was called) could be dimmed, but there was no
22 way of shutting it off completely. He moved over to the window: a smallish, frail
23 figure, the meagreness of his body merely emphasized by the blue overalls which
24 were the uniform of the party. His hair was very fair, his face naturally sanguine,
25 his skin roughened by coarse soap and blunt razor blades and the cold of the
26 winter that had just ended.

12. 1 Withal a meagre man was Aaron Stark,—
2 Cursed and unkempt, shrewd, shrivelled, and morose.
3 A miser was he, with a miser's nose,
4 And eyes like little dollars in the dark.
5 His thin, pinched mouth was nothing but a mark;
6 And when he spoke there came like sullen blows
7 Through scattered fangs a few snarled words and close,
8 As if a cur were chary[6] of its bark.

9 Glad for the murmur of his hard renown,
10 Year after year he shambled through the town,—
11 A loveless exile moving with a staff;
12 And oftentimes there crept into his ears
13 A sound of alien pity, touched with tears,—
14 And then (and only then) did Aaron laugh.

AARON STARK
Edwin Arlington Robinson

13. 1 I looked out over the beautiful expanse, bathed in soft yellow moonlight till it was
2 almost as light as day. In the soft light the distant hills became melted, and the
3 shadows in the valleys and gorges of velvety blackness. The mere beauty seemed to
4 cheer me; there was peace and comfort in every breath I drew. As I leaned from the
5 window my eye was caught by something moving a storey below me, and
6 somewhat to my left, where I imagined, from the order of the rooms, that the windows
7 of the Count's own room would look out. The window at which I stood was tall and
8 deep, stone-mullioned, and though weather worn, was still complete; but it was
9 evidently many a day since the case had been there. I drew back behind the stonework,
10 and looked carefully out.
11   What I saw was the Count's head coming out from the window. I did not see the
12 face, but I knew the man by the neck and the movement of his back and arms. In
13 any case I could not mistake the hands which I had had so many opportunities of
14 studying. I was at first interested and somewhat amused, for it is wonderful how
15 small a matter will interest and amuse a man when he is a prisoner. But my very
16 feelings changed to repulsion and terror when I saw the whole man slowly emerge
17 from the window and begin to crawl down the castle wall over that dreadful abyss,
18 *face down,* with his cloak spreading out around him like great wings. At first I
19 could not believe my eyes. I thought it was some trick of the moonlight, some weird
20 effect of shadow; but I kept looking, and it could be no delusion. I saw the fingers
21 and toes grasp the corners of the stones, worn clear of the mortar by the stress of
22 years, and by thus using every projection and inequality move downwards with
23 considerable speed, just as a lizard moves along a wall.
24   What manner of man is this, or what manner of creature is it in the semblance of

---

[6]Wary, cautious.

25 man? I feel the dread of this horrible place overpowering me; I am in fear—in awful
26 fear—and there is no escape for me. . . .

From DRACULA
Bram Stoker

14. The beginning of the short story or the novel is used to pique the reader to investigate the entire literary work. This is not as easily achieved when the beginning of a play is presented.

1 Lovely ladies, kind gentlemen:
2 Please to introduce myself.
3 Sakini by name.
4 Interpreter by profession.
5 Education by ancient dictionary.
6 Okinawan by whim of gods.
7 History of Okinawa reveal distinguished record of conquerors.
8 We have honor to be subjugated in fourteenth century by Chinese pirates.
9 In sixteenth century by English missionaries.
10 In eighteenth century by Japanese war lords.
11 And in twentieth century by American Marines.
12 Okinawa very fortunate.
13 Culture brought to us. . . . Not have to leave home for it.
14 Learn many things.
15 Most important that rest of world not like Okinawa.
16 World filled with delightful variation.
17 Illustration.
18 In Okinawa . . . no locks on doors.
19 Bad manners not to trust neighbors.
20 In America . . . lock and key big industry.
21 Conclusion?
22 Bad manners good business.
23 Okinawa . . . wash self in public bath with nude lady quite proper.
24 Picture of nude lady in private home . . . quite improper.
25 In America . . . statue of nude lady in park win prize.
26 But nude lady in flesh in park win penalty.
27 Conclusion?
28 Pornography question of geography.

From THE TEAHOUSE OF THE AUGUST MOON
John Patrick

15. 1 From the madding crowd they stand apart,
2 The maidens four and the Work of Art;

3 And none might tell from sight alone
4 In which had culture ripest grown—

5 The Gotham Millions fair to see,
6 The Philadelphia Pedigree,

7 The Boston Mind of azure hue,
8 Or the Soulful Soul from Kalamazoo;

9 For all loved Art in a seemly Way,
10 With an earnest soul and a capital A.

11 Long they worshipped; but no one broke
12 The sacred stillness, until up spoke

13 The Western one from the nameless place,
14 Who, blushing, said, "What a lovely vace!"

15 Over three faces a sad smile flew,
16 And they edged away from Kalamazoo.

17 But Gotham's haughty soul was stirred
18 To crush the stranger with one small word;

19 Deftly hiding reproof in praise,
20 She cries, "'Tis, indeed, a lovely vaze!"

21 But brief her unworthy triumph, when
22 The lofty one from the home of Penn,

23 With the consciousness of two grandpapas,
24 Exclaims, "It is quite a lovely vahs!"

25 And glances round with an anxious thrill,
26 A waiting the word of Beacon Hill.

27 But the Boston maid smiles courteouslee,
28 And gently murmurs, "Oh, pardon me!

29 "I did not catch your remark, because
30 I was so entranced with that charming vaws!"

THE V-A-S-E
James Jeffrey Roche

W To locate URLs and search terms for weblinks relevant to this chapter, please go to the companion website at www.cengage.com/rtf/crannell/voiceandarticulation5e and select the proper chapter.

Write the definitions for the following terms in the space below.

KEY TERMS	DEFINITIONS
Inflection	
Pace	
Pause	
Prosody	
Slide	
Step	
Stress	
Tempo	

CHAPTER 10

KINESICS

T hus far, this text has dealt with incorporating voice and speech into the communication process. There is another important component in communication, a nonverbal one called *kinesics,* a kind of action language. Some theoreticians maintain that the nonverbal portion of a spoken message is as much as 65 percent.[1]

The great American nineteenth-century dancer Isadora Duncan (Vanessa Redgrave in the movie) is supposed to have said: "If I could tell you what it meant, there would be no point in dancing it." And likewise, in presentation, "If you can vocalize your total meaning there would be no reason to use your body." Why, I could legitimately sit tied, glued, or even nailed to my stool and not have to move my body at all. We have come to realize that the words provide only the verbal portion of the text, and they are supported and amplified by subtext whose intentions and emotions may be more fully expressed physically.

You may be familiar with the phrase "kinesthetic sense image," which refers to the awareness of muscular movement. **Kinesics** is the study of bodily movement, which in this text means gestures, countenance (the use of the face), and body stance. We will not attempt to discuss other nonverbal cues, which are numerous. We have chosen these topics because of their practicality and relevance to career communication.

Public speaking, presentation, acting, reading aloud are all acts of joining words with meanings, meanings with emotions, and emotions with various states of the body. The expressive states of the body can be broken down into three major areas of concentration: (1) facial expressions, with particular emphasis on the effect of the eyes; (2) gesturing, with the reinforcement of expression through bodily movements; and (3) posture, which refers to the projected attitude of body stance.

As in the study of the factors involved in sound and voice, it is difficult to separate the various components of kinesics because they all work together to form the entire communication experience. However, to better understand the components we will deal with them individually.

---

[1]For a more detailed discussion of nonverbal and interpersonal communication, see Joseph Devito, *The Interpersonal Communication Book* (Boston: Allyn and Bacon, 2006), and Vito N. Silvestri, *Interpersonal Communication: Perspectives and Interfaces* (Boston: American Press, 1987).

⟫⟫⟫
Gesture

Gesture as the term is used here refers to the underscoring or amplification of words through the speaker's upper body movements, including movements of the arms and hands. It should be stressed at the outset that gestures, like other positive nonverbal components, should result naturally from the desire to get a message across. Although specific gestures should not be taught, a speaker should be encouraged to explore physical alternatives (to have physical freedom, if you will) that might clarify or amplify a spoken message. However, this should not be attempted until the speaker has total mastery of the verbal material.

Some individuals use **autistic mannerisms,** which are unconscious gesticulations that reveal nervousness and interfere with the communication process. These mannerisms should be pointed out to a speaker and eliminated. Begin by minimizing all gestures; before you can concentrate on what is right for you, you must rid yourself of those gestures that stand in the way of good communication. Because of the tension involved in speaking, people are usually not composed enough to control their gestures and their message. During delivery, however, total concentration must be on getting the message across. The accompanying amplification of that message, whether through vocal technique or body movement, should be encouraged.

Gestures that are prescribed are often mechanical and usually false because they are imposed from the outside. In time, however, freeing gestures can be developed and become habitual. As in developing voice and speech, one should be loath to say, "But that's not me!" You don't know who you are "gesticulatively" until you have investigated the possibilities. The major point is to eliminate those gesticulations that do not clarify your message and use those that are appropriate for it and supportive of it.

Although specific gestures should not be taught, you are encouraged to explore all possibilities through exercises. Here we are promoting physical freedom rather than pre-scribed gestures. If a speaker is open to the content of his or her message and has processed the message intellectually and emotionally, the physical response will likely be sincere and appropriate. Inhibiting a physical response through nervousness, a lack of control of the content, or some other fault does a great disservice to the communication experience as well as to the speaker.

There is a place for the mechanical gesture—not, however, in an actual performance—in exercises or rehearsals before the communication event. Students who are controlled by fear tend to restrict their physical movement. It is sometimes helpful to force yourself to make a particular gesture with your arm and hand. For example, in the sentence "I will not do it!" try stressing the *not* with a jab of a pointed index finger on your dominant hand. Make certain that the tension that is in the message gets into the muscles of that finger. The gesture must be viewed as an extension of you. If the wrist is weak, the listener will get a confused message. Repeat the sentence until your gesture feels comfortable. If necessary, try using your fist rather than a pointed finger; perhaps that gesture expresses your feelings more successfully. Ultimately, even though the gesture was imposed mechanically, it will have been made to work effectively for you. Besides, any mimetic gesture must be processed through the speaker's own perceptions.

An autistic gesture can reflect the speaker's nervousness about the oral performance. Each of us has autistic mannerisms that reveal our "self." The teacher who tosses and catches a piece of chalk during a lecture reveals something of himself. As students we get caught up not in taking notes but, instead, in hoping that the teacher will drop the chalk, which will shatter into a million pieces! What about the speaker who twists his wedding ring throughout a presentation? Does that mean that he is unhappily married?

Before you can correct these distracting types of mannerisms, you have to become aware of them. As an exercise, videotape an informative speech about yourself. Discuss your hobbies or what you hope to be doing professionally in ten years. Do not use notes or a lectern. During the playback, note those gestures that distract from your intended message. We all have certain idiosyncratic mannerisms. Among the most common are shifting the weight from one foot to the other, brushing hair out of the eyes, clearing the throat, and the dreaded interjections "ah . . . like y'know," "whatever," and "right."

Every speaker faces the problem of dealing with nonverbal symbols. Sometimes they are in the form of *paralanguage,* such as the vocalized pause, nervous giggling, an unusual inflection, or the use of silences. With some speakers the physical process of dealing with nonverbal symbols is more difficult than dealing with either the intellectual or emotional factors involved in speaking. One of the great dangers in teaching gestures is that speakers may become so concerned with their bodies that their physical responses become self-conscious and out of proportion, thus interfering with the message. As a result, when a speaker must think of gesturing on a particular word, the most important activity in getting a message across to an audience—concentration—is disrupted. But if a speaker is encouraged to "em-body" the message, then the mind, the emotions, and the body must work together.

The speaker's body should significantly amplify the thought. According to some experts, "gestures are used to illustrate, to emphasize, to point, to explain, or to interrupt; therefore, they cannot be isolated from the verbal components of speech. The understanding of most spoken messages is dependent upon the observation of both verbal and nonverbal codifications, and any isolation of oratorical or conversational gesture is out of the question."[2]

>>>
THE "WHEN YOU SAY IT DON'T DO IT" PRINCIPLE

One of the dangers in concentrating on gesturing is using too many, many of which are inappropriate to that speaking occasion. Don't use gestures to support an obvious verbal message. For example, how many times have you heard a politician or a cleric say, "There are three reasons for this. One (accompanied by one finger, of course), two (you guessed it!), and three (yup!)." We can all be grateful that there were not eleven reasons! What would the speaker have done then? A more extreme example would be singing the song "Tea for Two" while sipping from an imaginary cup on the word *tea* and holding up two fingers on the word *two*. We might call this the "do it as you say it" game.

These kinds of actions may be quite humorous, and their use is an effective technique when laughter is the desired response. Be very careful, however, to use this technique with discrimination and for the proper effect.

 EXERCISES FOR GESTURE

As you read aloud the following selections before a full-length mirror, play the "do it as you say it" game. Underscore the message with descriptive gestures. Keep in mind that these exercises are forms of negative practice, and make certain that you understand why each accompanying gesture is inappropriate! A comic effect is not the intent, although it likely will be the result. Then, read the exercises with appropriate gestures; and this time use the "when you say it don't do it" principle.

---

[2]Jurgen Ruesch and Weldon Kees, *Nonverbal Communication: Notes on the Visual Perception of Human Relations* (Berkeley: University of California Press, 1970), 37.

1. *Hjalmar:*   It's Father's old shot-gun. It doesn't shoot any more; something's gone wrong with the lock. But it's quite fun to have it, all the same, because we can take it to pieces and clean it every now and then, and grease it and put it together again. Of course, it's mostly Father who plays with that sort of thing.

   Hedvig: Now you can see the wild duck properly.

   Gregers: I was just looking at it. She seems to me to drag one wing a little.

   Hjalmar: Well, that's not very surprising; she's been wounded.

   Gregers: And she's a little lame in one foot, too.

   From THE WILD DUCK
   Henrik Ibsen

2. By the cigars they smoke, and the composers they love, ye shall know the texture of men's souls.

   From INDIAN SUMMER OF A FORSYTE
   John Galsworthy

3. The poet is like the prince of the clouds who haunts the tempest and laughs at the man with the bow; exiled on the ground amid the hue and cry, his giant's wings prevent him from walking.

   From FLEURS DU MAL
   Charles Baudelaire

4. Othello is talking about his wife, Desdemona, who is asleep:

   It is the cause, it is the cause, my soul,—
   Let me not name it to you, you chaste stars!—
   It is the cause.—Yet I'll not shed her blood;
   Nor scar that whiter skin of hers than snow,
   And smooth as monumental alabaster.
   Yet she must die, else she'll betray more men.
   Put out the light, and then put out the light.

   From OTHELLO
   William Shakespeare

5. Sometimes it is appropriate to say it and do it! Notice in the following selection how the use of gestures can be supportive and effective in clarifying the despicable nature of the speaker's (Volpone's) character. In this case, comedy is desirable.

   Ah, Mosca, you clever puppy, what a fool you are, how little you have learned of me! Do you really think you have to let the ducats fly in order to have everything? No, you fool! Let them rest quietly, side by side. Then, people will come of their own accord to offer you everything. Get this through your head: the magic of gold is so great that its smell alone can make men drunk. They only need to sniff it, and they come creeping here on their bellies; they only need to smell it, and they fall into your hands like moths in a flame. I do nothing but say I am rich—they bow their backs in reverence. Then I make a pretense at mortal illness. Ah, then the water drips off their tongues, and they begin to dance for my money. And how they love me: Friend Volpone! Best beloved friend! How they flatter me! How they serve me! How they rub against my shins and wag their tails! I'd like to trample the life out of these cobras, these vipers, but they dance to the tune of my pipe.

   From VOLPONE
   Ben Jonson

>>>
COUNTENANCE

Countenance actions are movements of the head and face, particularly the eyes, "the orbs of the soul." It is through the use of the eyes that the proper relationship between the speaker and the audience is established.

Making direct eye contact with the audience is perhaps the best advice, even though people talking to each other actually look at each other only about 35 percent of the time, according to some psychologists. But remember that a speech occasion is not conversation. It is your responsibility to make contact at some level with everyone in your audience. It is also one of the most difficult things for the beginning speaker to do. The tendency is to look almost anywhere except into the eyes of the listeners—you don't want them to discover that you are uncomfortable and nervous. But your momentary neurosis keeps you from seeing that you relate your tensions to an audience by *not* looking at them.

Older textbooks used to advise speakers not to look directly into the eyes of audience members: "Look over their heads!" Poppycock! One of the reasons for looking into the eyes of an audience member is to read the feedback. This is perhaps the most important technique to be learned. On the other hand, speakers should not be glued to the eyes of their listeners; that kind of intensity should be avoided. And there are appropriate times for a speaker's gaze to wander. Observe a conversation between two friends. Do they constantly stare at each other? No! However, their eyes probably do make frequent connections. What techniques do you use when you don't want to listen to someone? You do not make direct eye contact; perhaps you take a quick glance at your wristwatch or smile at someone else who is passing by. The point is that direct eye contact indicates an interest on the parts of both the speaker and the listener.

Historically, a great deal of attention has been given to the power in the look of an eye. In grade B movies, a look is often used to hypnotize and gain control over another. Popular adages tell us that "a person who does not look directly into your eyes when speaking should not be trusted" and suggest dire consequences in "if looks could kill." In the Latin American and Native American cultures, there is *ojo de dios,* or the "eye of god," which protects against evil. The opposite meaning appears in Robert Browning's dramatic monologue "The Laboratory," in which the female speaker gives the evil eye to her competition in romance:

> For only last night, as they whispered, I brought
> My own eyes to bear on her so, that I thought
> Could I keep them one half minute fixed, she would fall
> Shrivelled; she fell not; yet this does it all!

The absence of direct eye contact becomes an especially important technique when it is dictated by the material. In a reading, for example, if you are addressing an imagined character or listener, you should not look into the eyes of the actual audience. Thus, Elizabeth Barrett Browning's "How Do I Love Thee?" should not be read directly to the fellow in the third row; he might feel a little uncomfortable.

Facial expression, or countenance, should be reinforced by gesture to create a total message that amplifies the verbal content. Facial expression is often used to cue an audience for a desired response. For example, a speaker would not smile if an atmosphere of gloom were desired. Conversely, a somber expression is rarely the best cue to create a comedic environment. For our purposes the movements of the arms, hands, and head (with particular emphasis on facial expression) work together to perform "an additional function that is interpreted as a meta-communicative instruction accompanying verbal messages."[3]

---

[3]Ruesch and Kees, *Nonverbal Communication,* 64.

People with hearing problems must develop the ability to read nonverbal cues given by speakers. A person with a serious hearing loss must gain much information from the visual component of the messages. He or she relies more on **speechreading,** a term that has supplanted the term *lipreading.* Experts in the field of communication disorders recognize that there is more to speechreading than a total focus on the lips. Because the impaired person is unable to hear the sounds produced, "the cues provided by the general situation are very helpful. Facial expressions, gestures, and reactions are frequently more expressive than the words that are uttered."[4]

Speechreading techniques can be extremely helpful to people with normal hearing as well. Why shouldn't the hearing community benefit from techniques used by the hearing-impaired?

Everyone interested in speechreading soon becomes aware of the difficulties posed by **homophenous sounds**—sounds that look alike on the lips when they are pronounced. The following sets of English consonants are considered homophenous sounds.[5]

GROUP	CONSONANTS
I	/p/, /b/, /m/
II	/f/, /v/
III	/ʍ/, /w/, /r/
IV	/tʃ/, /dʒ/
	/ʃ/, /ʒ/
V	/t/, /d/, /l/, /n/, /s/, /z/, /θ/, /ð/
VI	/k/, /g/, /ŋ/, /h/

The acoustic components in these sounds are either unvoiced, voiced, or nasal. In Group I, all three consonants are bilabial; because the hearing-impaired or deaf person cannot perceive the acoustic components, the three sounds appear to be the same. Both of the consonant sounds in Group II are fricative labio-dental sounds (sounds articulated with the lower lip and upper teeth); the acoustic components vary in terms of the action of the vocal folds. In Group III, /ʍ/ and /w/ are both bilabials, but they differ in terms of the action of the vocal folds (/ʍ/ is voiceless, /w/ is voiced). In addition, there is more observable cheek movement with /ʍ/. Although the tongue plays an important part in the production of the semivowel /r/, the primary visual cue is the movement of the two lips. Group IV consists of two sets of cognate pairs, /tʃ/ and /dʒ/ and /ʃ/ and /ʒ/. In Group V, all of the sounds are considered lingua-alveolar (articulated with the tip of the tongue against the hard ridge behind the upper teeth), except for the last set of cognates, /θ/ and /ð/. The articulatory adjustment for these sounds is lingua-dental (articulated with the tip of the tongue touching the upper teeth). However, because of assimilation, Group V sounds can be mistaken for other sounds in dynamic speech. Group VI includes the cognate plosives /k/ and /g/, the nasal /ŋ/, and the fricative /h/.

It is very difficult for people with impaired hearing to differentiate sounds made in the back of the throat, because the visual cues for such sounds are indistinct. Remember that people with significant hearing losses must rely almost exclusively on speechreading for communication, but rarely can they see either differences in the flow of breath or the action of the vocal folds. It is easy to appreciate the problems faced by the hearing-impaired when they try to distinguish visually among these homophenous sounds in dynamic speech; the difficulties are compounded when the same vowel is used with these homophenous sounds.

---

[4]Miriam D. Pauls, "Speechreading," in *Hearing and Deafness,* rev. ed., ed. Hallowell Davis and S. Richard Silverman (New York: Holt, Rinehart & Winston, 1964), 356.

[5]This classification of homophenous sounds was suggested by John J. O'Neill and Herbert J. Oyer, *Visual Communication for the Hard of Hearing* (Englewood Cliffs, N.J.: Prentice Hall, 1961), 46.

Homophenous words are words that use homophenous consonants, which look alike on the lips, with the same vowel or diphthong. Examples are *fault* and *vault; tan, Dan,* and *Nan;* and *chin* and *shin.* **Homophonous words,** on the other hand, sound exactly alike; examples are *ate* and *eight; vale* and *veil;* and *vein, vane,* and *vain.* Kenneth Walter Berger has dramatized the problems with distinguishing among homophenous words in the sentence "I sat down and wrote a letter to my mother."[6] Homophonous words are in parentheses:

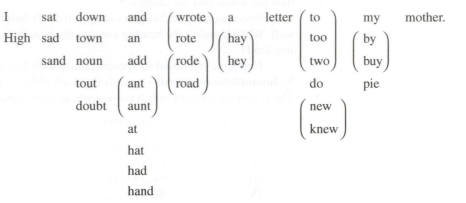

Silently mouth this sentence (and use only minimal facial expression) to people with normal hearing and ask them what you "said"; you'll likely gain much appreciation of the difficulties facing the hearing-impaired.

Exercises using speechreading principles can help people with normal hearing to develop freedom in using the body for gesturing. In using exercises composed of homophenous words, it becomes necessary to communicate with the body as well as with the voice and speech. Consequently, such exercises increase our awareness of our bodies.

EXERCISES FOR HOMOPHENOUS SOUNDS

1. The following is a list of homophenous words. Although the consonants are different, all of the words contain the same vowel, /æ/:

man	pan	ban
mat	Pat	bat
mad	pad	bad

   Before an audience, articulate each of the words in order, but do not vocalize. Do not use your countenance, especially the eyes. Because the words look alike on the lips, your listeners should experience a healthy confusion about which words you articulated. Repeat the exercise, but this time skip around the list. Your audience's confusion should increase.

2. The homophenous words in exercise 1 are used in the following sentences:

   He is the man who did it!
   Watch out! The pan is hot!
   Have you ever tried Ban deodorant?
   The bathroom mat is still wet.
   Be careful! Don't pat the dog. It might bite you!

---

[6]Kenneth Walter Berger, *Speechreading: Principles and Methods* (Baltimore: National Educational Press, 1972), 101.

I could have belted him with a baseball bat.
Don't be mad at me.
Come up to my pad when the class is over.
My brother was a very bad boy.

Select one of these sentences to present to classmates without vocalization. The first time you present the sentence, be careful that you do not use any kinesic clues in your delivery.

3. Repeat each of the sentences in exercise 2 with nonverbal amplifications, but do not exaggerate the use of gesture. Deliver the sentences in a conversational, natural manner. After you can do this effectively and accurately, maintain the same degree of kinesic behavior while you vocalize the sentences.

4. Take a short stanza from a poem, speech, short story, or monologue, and present it before an audience without vocalizing. Rely exclusively on the nonverbal components to convey the meaning or at least the emotion inherent in the segment. Do not exaggerate your gestures. Maintain a natural, conversational manner.

 ## EXERCISES FOR ADDITIONAL HOMOPHENOUS WORDS AND SENTENCES

The following combinations of sounds are additional homophenous words and sentences.

1. Initial position: palatal sounds /ʧ/, /ʤ/, /ʃ/, /ʒ/, /j/
   Final position: bilabial sounds /p/, /b/, /m/
   Medial vowel: /æ/

   chap: What is that <u>chap's</u> name?
   Jap(anese): The <u>Japanese</u> are very musical people.
   yap: All his dog does is <u>yap</u>, <u>yap</u>, <u>yap</u>.
   jab: He gave Tom a quick <u>jab</u> to the head and another jab to the stomach.
   jam: My mother makes the best strawberry <u>jam</u> in the world!
   sham: I found the whole contest a big <u>sham</u>.

2. Initial position: labio-dental sounds /f/, /v/
   Final position: lingua-alveolar sounds /t/, /d/, /n/
   Medial vowel: /æ/

   fat: Boy, am I getting <u>fat</u>!
   vat: Please place the <u>vat</u> in the far corner.
   fad: Long hair was just a passing <u>fad</u>.
   fan: It's so hot. Where is the <u>fan</u>?
   van: I think the moving <u>van</u> will be a big help.

3. Initial position: lingua-alveolar sounds /l/, /s/, /z/, /t/, /d/, /n/
   Final position: bilabial sounds /m/, /p/, /b/
   Medial vowel: /æ/
   (Homophonous words are in parentheses.)

   tam: Why do you like to wear a <u>tam</u>?
   tap: What is that <u>tap</u> <u>tap</u> <u>tapping</u> on my window pane?
   tab: It is your turn to pay the <u>tab</u>.
   (dam): Boulder <u>Dam</u> is incredibly huge!
   (damn): I really don't give a <u>damn</u>.

dab: Put a little <u>dab</u> of blue in the paint.

(nap): I'm very tired. I think that I'll take a little <u>nap</u>.

(knap): We can climb that <u>knap</u> without any trouble. But this <u>knapsack</u> is mighty heavy!

nab: Don't let the police <u>nab</u> you for speeding.

(lamb): I don't like <u>lamb</u> chops.

(lam): Hey, Mugsy, we better take it on the <u>lam</u>.

lap: Get off my <u>lap</u>. You're too heavy.

lab: Meet me in the <u>lab</u> in an hour.

Sam: Who doesn't love Uncle <u>Sam</u>?

sap: The blasted <u>sap</u> is all over my hands and clothes.

4. Initial position: lingua-velar sounds /k/, /g/; glottal /h/
   Final position: lingua-alveolar-palatal sound /tʃ/; lingua-palatal sound /ʃ/
   Medial vowel: /æ/

catch: You'd better <u>catch</u> the ball before it breaks the window!

hatch: Batten down the <u>hatch</u>!

cash: Why didn't you <u>cash</u> the check?

gash: He had a two-inch <u>gash</u> in his leg.

hash: My favorite meal is corned beef <u>hash</u>.

5. Initial position: lingua-velar sounds /k/, /g/; glottal /h/
   Final position: lingua-alveolar sounds /t/, /d/, /n/, /l/, /s/, /z/
   Medial vowel: /æ/

cat: I wouldn't have a <u>cat</u> in my house!

gat: OK, Bugsy, put the <u>gat</u> back in its holster.

hat: What a beautiful <u>hat</u> you're wearing, Michele!

cad: Mark, you're a rat and a <u>cad</u>!

has: Does Karen have the flu? Yes, she <u>has</u> it.

gad: Oh, Chuck and Tracy are just <u>gadabouts</u>!

Remember, the major purpose of homophenous word drills, with and without vocalization, is to encourage you to develop a flexible, meaningful physical response during the speech process.

EXERCISE FOR ADDITIONAL HOMOPH<u>O</u>NOUS WORDS

Put the following homophonous words in a sentence, and test each other's speechreading skills:

break, brake	cite, sight, site	coarse, course
descent, dissent	dual, duel	fair, fare
hear, here	passed, past	minor, miner
patients, patience	plain, plane	waist, waste
presents, presence	principal, principle	prey, pray
their, there, they're	gorilla, guerilla	feat, feet
gun, knew, new	rain, reign, rein	forth, fourth
raise, rays, raze	plum, plumb	gene, jean
hew, hue, Hugh	bridle, bridal	hole, whole
browse, brows	seas, sees, seize	idle, idol
links, lynx	mane, main, Maine	colonel, kernel
meat, meet, mete	prints, prince	friar, fryer

>>>

BODY STANCE

The final aspect of bodily movement in communication is the stance of the body. This is important because often the reason speakers fail to get their points across is too little attention to this factor. Stance is closely related to posture.

Make certain that in performance you stand with your weight evenly distributed on both feet. Avoid the tendency to bend one knee because it looks more casual. The danger is that under the tension of the situation, you will continually shift your weight from one leg to the other. That is the surest way of revealing your tension to the audience.

The attitude of a speaker is also transmitted through stance. A timid, ill-prepared image is conveyed by slouched shoulders, hanging arms, and lowered head and eyes. This is the judge-me-severely-because-I-am-unworthy-to-be-in-front-of-you-wasting-your-valuable-time syndrome. Spare all audiences from such poor wretches!

On the other hand, there is the speaker who stands erectly with chest out, looking down his nose and communicating such an arrogant "you're so incredibly lucky to have the opportunity of seeing and hearing me that even I can't believe I'm here" attitude that the audience wants to see the person self-destruct. Both of these stances represent negative extremes.

Stand tall (but not too tall!) with your shoulders back (but not too far back!), your feet shoulder-width apart and your weight on both legs, and your head in a comfortable position so that you can see the audience easily. And keep those knees unlocked. Take a few deep breaths before you approach your audience, and use that controlled breath support that you developed earlier.

Also, be neither a pacer nor a meandering nomad. If you take a step, it ought to be because you want to get closer to some member of the audience. Do not move just for the sake of moving, because that is exactly what it will look like. Any movement should come as a result of a desire to communicate either a message or a transition between messages. That is what prompts movement—the desire to communicate a message to that audience, at that time, and in that place. No other message, time, place, or audience matters! That is what gives the performance dynamism and vitality!

Many of the selections in this text have been chosen with body movement in mind. Therefore, choose some selections from other chapters, and apply the principles of kinesics to them as you read them aloud.

(((EXERCISES FOR FREEDOM OF MOVEMENT

All scenes from plays within this text may be read by one reader, one reader per character, or several speakers for each character. You are encouraged to use your imagination and free your body. Use kinesics as much as is necessary to communicate the message.

1. In the following dialogue, see how much of the scene you can create for your audience through the use of body movements. Make the audience see the pained lion. The setting is a jungle path during the first century A.D. Androcles and his domineering wife, Megaera, are confronted by a limping lion that gives a great groan of pain. She faints.

1	*Androcles:*	[*quaking, but keeping between the lion and Megaera*] Dont you come
2		near my wife, do you hear? [*The lion groans. Androcles can hardly*
3		*stand for trembling.*] Meggy: run. Run for your life. If I take my eye
4		off him, its all up. [*The lion holds up his wounded paw and flaps it*
5		*piteously before Androcles.*] Oh, he's lame, poor old chap! He's got a
6		thorn in his paw. A frightfully big thorn. [*Full of sympathy*] Oh, poor

7   old man! Did um get an awful thorn into um's tootsums wootsums?
8   Has it made um too sick to eat a nice little Christian man for um's
9   breakfast? Oh, a nice little Christian man will get um's thorn out for
10 um; and then um shall eat the nice Christian man and the nice Christian
11 man's nice big tender wifey pifey. [*The lion responds by moans of*
12 *self-pity.*] Yes, yes, yes, yes, yes. Now, now [*taking the paw in his*
13 *hand*] um is not to bite and not to scratch, not even if it hurts a very,
14 very little. Now make velvet paws. That right. [*He pulls gingerly at the*
15 *thorn. The lion, with an angry yell of pain, jerks back his paw so*
16 *abruptly that Androcles is thrown on his back.*] Steadee! Oh, did the
17 nasty cruel little Christian man hurt the sore paw? [*The lion moans*
18 *assentingly but apologetically.*] Well, one more little pull and it will be
19 all over. Just one little, little, leetle pull; and then um will live happily
20 ever after. [*He gives the thorn another pull. The lion roars and snaps*
21 *his jaws with a terrifying clash.*] Oh, mustnt frighten um's good kind
22 doctor, um's affectionate nursey. That didnt hurt at all: not a bit. Just
23 one more. Just to shew how the brave big lion can bear pain, not like
24 the little crybaby Christian man. Oopsh! [*The thorn comes out. The*
25 *lion yells with pain, and shakes his paw wildly.*] Thats it! [*Holding up*
26 *the thorn.*] Now its out. Now lick um's paw to take away the nasty
27 inflammation. See? [*He licks his own hand. The lion nods intelligently*
28 *and licks his paw industriously.*] Clever little liony-piony! Understands
29 um's dear old friend Andy Wandy. [*The lion licks his face.*] Yes,
30 kissums Andy Wandy. [*The lion, wagging his tail violently, rises on his*
31 *hind legs and embraces Androcles, who makes a wry face and cries.*]
32 Velvet paws! Velvet paws! [*The lion draws in his claws.*] Thats right.
33 [*He embraces the lion, who finally takes the end of his tail in one paw,*
34 *places that tight around Androcles' waist, resting it on his hip. Androcles*
35 *takes the other paw in his hand, stretches out his arm, and the*
36 *two waltz rapturously round and round and finally away through the*
37 *jungle.*]

38 *Megaera:*   [*who has revived during the waltz*] Oh, you coward, you havnt danced
39 with me for years; and now you go off dancing with a great brute beast
40 that you havnt known for ten minutes and that wants to eat your own
41 wife. Coward! Coward! Coward! [*She rushes off after them into the*
42 *jungle.*]

From ANDROCLES AND THE LION (Prologue)
George Bernard Shaw

2. In the following scene, Gwendolen and Cecily have discovered that they love the same
   man. Their kinesics reveal much more about their attitudes than does their speech in
   this incredibly civilized conversation about the virtues of the city and the country.

1   *Gwendolen:*   Are there many interesting walks in the vicinity, Miss Cardew?
2   *Cecily:*   Oh, yes! a great many. From the top of one of the hills quite close one
3   can see five counties.
4   *Gwendolen:*   Five counties! I don't think I should like that; I hate crowds.
5   *Cecily:*   [*sweetly*] I suppose that is why you live in town? [*Gwendolen bites*
6   *her lip, and beats her foot nervously with her parasol.*]
7   *Gwendolen:*   [*looking round*] Quite a well-kept garden this is, Miss Cardew.
8   *Cecily:*   So glad you like it, Miss Fairfax.
9   *Gwendolen:*   I had no idea there were any flowers in the country.
10   *Cecily:*   Oh, flowers are as common here, Miss Fairfax, as people are in
11   London.

12	*Gwendolen:*	Personally I cannot understand how anybody manages to exist in the
13		country, if anybody who is anybody does. The country always bores
14		me to death.
15	*Cecily:*	Ah! This is what the newspapers call agricultural depression, is it
16		not? I believe the aristocracy are suffering very much from it just at
17		present. It is almost an epidemic amongst them, I have been told.
18		May I offer you some tea, Miss Fairfax?
19	*Gwendolen:*	[*with elaborate politeness*] Thank you. [*aside*] Detestable girl! But
20		I require tea!
21	*Cecily:*	[*sweetly*] Sugar?
22	*Gwendolen:*	[*superciliously*] No, thank you. Sugar is not fashionable anymore.
23		[*Cecily looks angrily at her, takes up the tongs and puts four lumps*
24		*of sugar into the cup.*]
25	*Cecily:*	[*severely*] Cake or bread and butter?
26	*Gwendolen:*	[*in a bored manner*] Bread and butter, please. Cake is rarely seen at
27		the best houses nowadays.
28	*Cecily:*	[*cuts a very large slice of cake and puts it on the tray*] Hand that
29		to Miss Fairfax. [*Gwendolen drinks the tea and makes a grimace.*]

From THE IMPORTANCE OF BEING EARNEST
Oscar Wilde

3. Captain Robert De Baudricourt, a military squire, handsome and physically energetic but with no will of his own, is disguising that defect in his usual fashion by storming terribly at his steward, a trodden worm—the sort of man whom age cannot wither because he has never bloomed.

1	*Robert:*	No eggs! No eggs! Thousand thunders, man, what do you mean by no
2		eggs?
3	*Steward:*	Sir: it is not my fault. It is the act of God.
4	*Robert:*	Blasphemy. You tell me there are no eggs; and you blame your Maker
5		for it.
6	*Steward:*	Sir: what can I do? I cannot lay eggs.
7	*Robert:*	[*sarcastic*] Ha! You jest about it.
8	*Steward:*	No, sir, God knows. We all have to go without eggs just as you have,
9		sir. The hens will not lay.
10	*Robert:*	Indeed! [*rising*] Now listen to me, you.
11	*Steward:*	[*humbly*] Yes, Sir.
12	*Robert:*	What am I?
13	*Steward:*	What are you, sir?
14	*Robert:*	[*coming at him*] Yes: what am I? Am I Robert, squire of Baudricourt
15		and captain of this castle of Vaucouleurs; or am I a cowboy?
16	*Steward:*	Oh, sir, you know you are a greater man here than the king himself. . . .
17	*Robert:*	You have not only the honor of being my steward, but the privilege of
18		being the worst, most incompetent, drivelling snivelling jibbering
19		jabbering idiot of a steward in France.
20	*Steward:*	Yes, sir: to a great man like you I must seem like that.
21	*Robert:*	My fault, I suppose. Eh?
22	*Steward:*	Oh, sir: you always give my most innocent words such a turn!
23	*Robert:*	I will give your neck a turn if you dare tell me, when I ask you how many
24		eggs there are, that you cannot lay any.
25	*Steward:*	Oh sir, oh sir—
26	*Robert:*	No: not oh sir, oh sir, but no sir, no sir. My three Barbary hens and the
27		black are the best layers in Champagne. And you come and tell me that

28   there are no eggs! Who stole them? Tell me that, before I kick you out
29   through the castle gate for a liar and a seller of my goods to thieves.

From SAINT JOAN (Scene 1)
George Bernard Shaw

4. In the following dramatic monologue by Robert Browning, the speaker, an unidenti-
fied woman, is recounting her hatred for her lover's new romantic interest. She is talking to an old man who is in the process of mixing and selling her poison.

The speaker must create a total environment. She is, obviously, surrounded by all
kinds of poisons. What kinds of aromas are present? Can the speaker taste some of the
powders that, no doubt, permeate the air How is she dressed? Perhaps she has a cloak
with a hood to help disguise her departure from the laboratory? What kind of panto-
mime might be used in developing the scene? Where is the "soft phial"? . . . the "old
man"? Your analysis of the poem will give you clues to the kinetics that are occurring
in the scene.

1   Now that I, tying thy glass mask tightly,
2   May gaze thro' these faint smokes curling whitely,
3   As thou pliest thy trade in this devil's-smithy—
4   Which is the poison to poison her, prithee?

5   He is with her; and they know that I know
6   Where they are, what they do: they believe my tears flow
7   While they laugh, laugh at me, at me fled to the drear
8   Empty church, to pray God in, for them!—I am here.

9   Grind away, moisten and mash up thy paste,
10   Pound at thy powder,—I am not in haste!
11   Better sit thus, and observe thy strange things,
12   Than go where men wait me and dance at the King's.

13   That in the mortar—you call it a gum?
14   Ah, the brave tree whence such gold oozings come!
15   And yonder soft phial, the exquisite blue,
16   Sure to taste sweetly,—is that poison too?

17   Had I but all of them, thee and thy treasures,
18   What a wild crowd of invisible pleasures!
19   To carry pure death in an earring, a casket,
20   A signet, a fan-mount, a filligree-basket!

21   Soon, at the King's, a mere lozenge to give
22   And Pauline should have just thirty minutes to live!
23   But to light a pastille, and Elise, with her head
24   And her breast and her arms and her hands, should drop dead!

25   Quick—is it finished? The colour's too grim!
26   Why not soft like the phial's, enticing and dim?
27   Let it brighten her drink, let her turn it and stir,
28   And try it and taste, ere she fix and prefer!

29   What a drop! She's not little, no minion like me—
30   That's why she ensnared him: this never will free

31   The soul from those masculine eyes,—say, 'no!'
32   To that pulse's magnificent come-and-go,

33   For only last night, as they whispered, I brought
34   My own eyes to bear on her so, that I thought
35   Could I keep them one half minute fixed, she would fall,
36   Shrivelled; she fell not; yet this does not all!

37   Not that I bid you spare her the pain!
38   Let death be felt and the proof remain;
39   Brand, burn up, bite into its grace—
40   He is sure to remember her dying face!

41   Is it done? Take my mask off! Nay, be not morose
42   It kills her, and this prevents seeing it close:
43   The delicate droplet, my whole fortune's fee—
44   If it hurts her, beside, can it ever hurt me?

45   Now, take all my jewels, gorge gold to your fill,
46   You may kiss me, old man, on my mouth if you will!
47   But brush this dust off me, lest horror it brings
48   Ere I know it—next moment I dance at the King's!

THE LABORATORY
Robert Browning

To locate URLs and search terms for weblinks relevant to this chapter, please go to the companion website at www.cengage.com/rtf/crannell/voiceandarticulation5e and select the proper chapter.

Write the definitions for the following terms in the space below.

KEY TERMS	DEFINITIONS
Autistic Mannerisms	
Countenance	
Gesture	
Homophenous Sounds	
Homophenous Words	
Homophonous Words	
Kinesics	
Speechreading	

CHAPTER 11

APPLICATION TO THE SPEECH OCCASION

Thus far, this text has dealt mainly with the individual parts of speech—the individual sounds, the common vocal errors, and suggestions for creating dynamism. We turn now to the oral performance. The purpose of this chapter is to discuss the application of voice and speech to the speaking event. Excellent voice and speech that occur in a vacuum are worth little individually unless they are applied together in a communication act.

For our purposes, there are four styles of oral presentations:

1. *Memorized.* The entire presentation is memorized. The most common form of this presentation might be one speaker's performance of literature (poems, a play, or a novel or short story).[1]

2. *Read from text.* The presentation is read aloud. This style is often criticized because so frequently the presentation sounds "as if it were being read," a pejorative commentary. Believe it or not, a reading from text can be a very effective style of performance if the material is designed to be presented orally. We accept a reader of poetry or fiction. We also accept an extended quotation being read. If a commencement speech or a clerical homily is created in the oral tradition—with oral diction—it can be delivered most successfully to an audience.

3. *Extemporaneous.* This is perhaps the best form for a traditional presentation. It may or may not begin with a written form. From it, after much practice aloud, the speaker may make short notes to have with him or her at the delivery as a reminder. The presentation is never exactly the same twice. It will vary in degrees. The point is you have complete

---

[1]For many years, I gave one-man presentations of complete plays, poetry, and fiction lasting from one to one-and-a-half hours. The plays and novels were cut to the desired time and memorized. It was called the art of interpretation.

control over the material because you have practiced, practiced, practiced. A simple word on a card could remind you of your material.

4. *Impromptu*. Impromptu speaking is done "off the cuff." A more extensive description of this type of speaking appears later in this chapter.

>>> PERFORMANCE OCCASIONS

There are two major types of performance occasions: *direct* and *indirect,* which have also been called *open* and *closed* situations. In the **direct performance occasion,** there is direct contact between the speaker and the audience, in which the speaker expresses his or her own ideas and emotions. Any form of public speaking is a direct occasion because the speaker is relating to a specific audience in a specific place at a specific time. Other direct occasions include:

> the oral reading of some kinds of literature
> the cleric's homily
> the businessperson's presentation
> the lawyer's opening argument
> the politician's debate
> the professor's lecture
> the salesperson's presentation
> the anchor's newscast
> just plain conversation and discussion

In the second kind of performance occasion, the **indirect performance occasion,** the ideas and emotions expressed by the speaker are not necessarily his or her own. The audience addressed may be present or one only imagined by the speaker. An actor's performance of a scene from a play, for example, would be an indirect performance occasion. Within the context of the play, Macbeth and Lady Macbeth are alone when they are plotting the death of King Duncan. Although the performers must never forget that an actual audience is present and therefore they must not turn their backs to it, their characters are alone in the castle. Other indirect occasions might include:

> the actor's monologue
> a character's direct discourse in a novel, play, or short story
> a recorded commercial
> the dialogue in a cleric's scriptural reading
> the storyteller's narrative

A performance occasion can be both direct and indirect. For instance, a narrator in a conventional story acknowledges the presence of the audience and directs the narrative to them, but when the characters are speaking, the audience "disappears." In this instance, the ideas and emotions that the narrator has may or may not be the narrator's own.

>>> SPEECH OCCASION AS DRAMA

Every speech occasion should be viewed as a play. If you are giving a business presentation, you are narrator/character. Like a play, you have created a story that has a beginning, a middle, and an end. You are its main character, and you will introduce other characters, perhaps through a relevant story or humorous anecdote. These characters may speak in their own person, with their own dialogue, or through you as the "storyteller." That story is told to an audience or a listener.

This narrator/character should have at his or her disposal all of the techniques that a good actor uses in the performance of a play in addition to a well-trained voice and career speech.

>>> ANALYSIS OF THE AUDIENCE

Before any performance, you should if at all possible know who your audience is. This information is certain to affect the content of your performance. If you are speaking to the inmates at a house of correction, a speech on the values of capital punishment would probably be inappropriate. Knowing the demographics of the group—race, sex, occupation, education, economic status, social standing, and religion—may be invaluable in determining what material to communicate. This knowledge helps you to decide which figures of speech to use, what illustrations to have, which senses to appeal to, and how sophisticated to be.

>>> THE INTRODUCTION

An **introduction** begins when you present yourself or are presented to an audience; *this is very much a part of the performance.* How you are dressed and your attitude as you walk to the front of the room influence your audience. Do you walk briskly to the front of the room or do you meander? Are you happy to be there? Do you appear confident? Are you making faces that indicate you're nervous or ill-prepared? Are you anxious to communicate? Are you compensating for your nervousness by appearing cocky? Remember that as long as the audience can see or hear you, you are being monitored and communication is taking place. (In fact, you continue to communicate long after your oral presentation is over. Even as you leave the performance environment you are metaphorically still on stage. Audience members can tell if you are disappointed or pleased with your presentation, so be on guard.)

The second part of the introduction is the verbal component, although nonverbal communication continues. The verbal aspects of the introduction are designed to introduce you and your content to the audience. The length of the introduction will depend on the content being performed. If you are reading a scene from a play or a section from a novel, more time must be devoted to informing the audience of plot and characters or other information necessary to the scene. Generally speaking, however, the introduction ought to be brief.

It is usually inadvisable and counterproductive to read your introduction. The introduction ought to present you in relation to your audience. The major purpose of an introduction is to prepare the audience for your presentation. *You* and *your* content are that presentation. When you read your introduction, the sense of **spontaneity** between you and your audience is diminished. Obviously, your full attention cannot be where it ought to be. Even if your purpose is to read a report, you should still make certain that your introduction is conversational and is not read. This is your first opportunity to relate, so take advantage of it!

Directing the introduction to the audience also gives you an opportunity for reading audience feedback. Remember that the first impression is the most important one. Are they listening? How hard do you have to work to gain and maintain their attention? Seeing a smiling face can work miracles for a nervous speaker. Use that time to get to know your listeners. Look into their eyes and begin to read their feedback.

Because the introduction is an important part of the performance, it should be well prepared. If it is necessary to memorize your introduction, make it seem spontaneous and conversational just as the actor should make the audience feel that he or she is saying the lines of the character for the very first time. Above all, do not allow yourself to use a **canned speech!**

There are at least three purposes for a good introduction. First, an introduction should prepare the audience for the kind of material to be presented. Is it literature? What is the subject matter under consideration? Is it a presentation at the Toastmasters? What can the audience members expect to hear?

Second, the introduction should set the appropriate mood. If the presentation is light and humorous, you don't want to get the audience into a serious frame of mind; if, on the other hand, the content is strongly emotional, you should be careful about using humor. Sometimes, however, the surgeon giving a lecture on vascular diseases, for example, might want to introduce a little levity. Of course, any lightness depends on the makeup of the audience; thus, you would relate differently to your peers than to consumers of your product.

Both you the performer and your audience can benefit from the introduction. Accordingly, the third purpose of an introduction is to channel some of that nervous energy and settle yourself down. Sometimes, because of nervousness (and who of us is not!), the speaker will over-compensate for this condition. He or she might become "cocky" in both body language and attitude, to show the audience that everything is under control. On the other hand, sometimes the speaker approaches the stage or front of the class in a semicatatonic state, totally oblivious to his or her environment. The best approach is to be your most decorous self. Realize that you have spent those tiring hours preparing your delivery. You should know what you are capable of doing better than anyone. The success that you achieved in the "privacy of your boudoir" must be transmitted to the present environments. As you are practicing your speech or selection, imagine the room or hall in which you will be working.[2] If the presentation is properly prepared, you should have acquired a degree of confidence. Of course, if your work lacks adequate preparation, take a deep breath and do a lot of praying. Sometimes a student loses his or her audience before a word has been uttered. This usually occurs because the speaker's body language, whether conscious or unconscious, draws attention to this nervous condition.

>>>
EYE CONTACT

Although direct and indirect **eye contact** were mentioned in Chapter 10, it is so important to the direct performance occasion that we'll elaborate on them here. The eyes are the most important part of the face. Ralph Waldo Emerson said, "The alleged power to charm down . . . the ferocity in beasts, is a power behind the eye." Others have said that "the eyes are the mirrors of the soul" and have referred to the "evil eye."

One of the most common behaviors by nervous, inexperienced speakers is failing to make direct eye contact with the audience. The speaker neither wants the audience to see his or her nervousness nor desires to see that his or her inept delivery has been detected. The speaker believes that if direct eye contact were made, the audience would discover his or her worthlessness.

Force yourself to look into the eyes of your audience. They are not the enemy, believe it or not! Most of them are in that audience because they want to be. Some speech texts have

---

[2]Refer to visualization on [page 11].

recommended that you focus on the foreheads of your audience, but by doing this you miss the **audience feedback** (and you may also develop a forehead fetish). Foreheads give little feedback; their communicative powers are minimal. Instead, pick out a few friendly faces at first and gradually include more. You must also maintain eye contact long enough for communication to take place. Sometimes a speaker looks but does not see while the audience hears but does not listen. An audience will respond to the degree that the speaker demands. The responsibility begins with the speaker; if the speaker reaches out to the audience, they will respond.

>>>
Signature Story

A **signature story** is usually a narrative that is used in a presentation or performance that helps to identify the speaker. Sometimes the story is told as a whole, and other times it takes the form of short narratives that inform the audience who the speaker is. It might be presented as an anecdote or a reference. It is a way of making the presentation yours. Put your stamp on it. No one else on earth can use your story with any sort of legitimacy, ethos, or truth. It may or may not contain characters. It might be serious, humorous, or a combination of both.

In some companies, the policy is to write out the presentation and a salesperson is expected to memorize and deliver it to an audience in that fashion. This is *not* a signature story, and this form of presentation is fraught with dangers. As the deliverer, you cannot really own it. A much more successful way is to give your sales people information about the product (material that should be covered in the presentation), and it is up to the speaker to make the presentation his or her own by allowing his or her personality to be expressed. The success of a sale is often a result of a personable presentation. Each of us has a life filled with signature stories!

An offshoot of a signature story is the use of a metaphor—a figure of speech that compares one thing to another without the use of *like* or *as*. Shakespeare's line "All the world's a stage" is a metaphor. It is **not like** a stage. It **is** a stage.

I once worked with a client who was presenting at a UN function, and our goal was to personalize his speech. No, he had no hobbies. No, he had no unforgettable characters in his life. Nothing much had happened to him. During the process of putting the speech together the subject of time came up. He said that quick second judgments were necessary in his flying. "Nothing much ever happened" because every leisure hour was spent flying his airplane. The entire speech was rewritten with the metaphor of comparing his role as the president of his company to his piloting a large aircraft. His speech was most memorable.

Signature stories do a great deal to color your presentation.

>>>
Motivated Movement (or the "Frontal Assault" versus "Retrograde")

There are many theories concerning the presence and amount of movement while a speaker is involved in a performance occasion. Kinesics were discussed in detail in Chapter 10. It is worth repeating, however, that movement should be governed by propriety; all movements should be appropriate for the content, the occasion, and the speaker.

At this point it is important to state that movement ought also to be motivated by a speaker's goal. In some public-speaking texts, speakers are told that it is okay to pace back and forth in front of the audience. Avoid this approach because such movement conveys little positive meaning. Movement is encouraged as long as it is *motivated* by your desire to communicate some information to your listeners. In a speech occasion the audience is in front of you. Therefore, most of your movement should have a forward thrust.

Allow enough distance between you and your audience so that you can move toward them. Yes, some "retrograde" or retreating may occur, but only to set up your next advance toward your audience. This "frontal assault" truly gives your audience the feeling that you want to talk to them; it underscores your desire to communicate with them. A constant retrograde might indicate cowardice—and you'll probably be captured by the enemy! Remember, take those steps only when you are motivated to do so.

>>>
DOLCE ET UTILE

Your audience presumes that you know your content and that you have something important to say. Audiences take that for granted. However, as you put your program together, you want to have balance—a **dolce et utile**. In Italian, *dolce* means "sweet." I like to think of *dolce* as "entertaining." *Utile* means "useful," or "informational and educational." Both of these should be present in varying degrees in all presentations. The degree of "entertainment" will vary with the degree of "information," which is dependent upon the purpose of the presentation.

You should not have to be told that a significant portion of your *dolce* will be your voice, speech, and kinesics—those elements that are fostered and preached so strongly in the first two-thirds of this text. Your job as speakers is to make an accurate assessment of the message and audience and then structure your blend accordingly. The balance will be determined by the content and the event. How many of you had an English teacher who took all of the joy and *dolce* out of Shakespeare? (By the way, "*et*" means "and" in Italian.)

>>>
PASSION

The role played by passion is extremely important. Oral communication ends with a high degree of passion. Your audience must feel that you are passionate about that subject. If you are not, how can you presume that the audience will respond in kind? Everyone talks about and wants passion. But for the speaker, the passion is that tremendous *desire* to communicate your message to your audience. Nothing should get in the way of that strong desire to communicate. But the passion must be controlled. The technique must work along with the passion. The technique controls the passion. You see, passion without technique is barbarous and primitive and often embarrassing, and technique without passion is just plain boring.

>>>
ANGLES OF DIRECTION

How does a speaker in an indirect performance occasion stay in contact with the audience when not looking directly into their eyes? This is accomplished by using a technique called the **projected scene.** During a projected scene, the audience receives the information through characters in the scene. For example, when a cleric is reading the Scriptures, there are moments when one character might be talking to another character instead of to the audience. The cleric would not want to look at a member of the audience and make him Pilate (to whom Jesus is speaking). Instead, Jesus (as played by the cleric) would "see" Pilate in a scene "projected" over the heads of the audience. When Pilate answers Jesus, the speaker would focus at another spot in the projected scene. The speaker's different positions form *angles of direction.*

This technique is useful for both the speaker and the audience whenever a character is involved in direct discourse within drama, prose, or poetry. In such a situation, the speaker suggests one character is speaking to himself or herself or to another character who is positioned slightly above and beyond the heads of the audience. Therefore, the audience is right in the middle of the action in the imagined scene. The speaker supplies the major dynamics in the scene through controlling what the audience hears and observes. When the speaker, in suggesting each character, focuses on a different point, each character is distinguished for the audience. Each character is given a different angle of direction. The "interpersonal distance" between characters depends on the emotional makeup of the scene and the characters' relationship. The success of the performance is dependent upon the degree to which the audience is able to identify with the characters and experiences presented by the speaker. In an indirect speaking occasion that is dramatic in nature, speaking directly to an audience member might make him or her uncomfortable.

For example, read these first few lines from Elizabeth Barrett Browning's sonnet aloud to your roommates as you look deeply into their eyes:

How do I love thee? Let me count the ways.
I love thee to the depth and breadth and height.
My soul can reach . . .

At about this time, our roommates are laughing or punching you in the nose. Now place the receiver of the loving tribute at your height but over the heads of your roommates, who now are becoming observers rather than receivers. If you are giving a true reading, your roommates are seeing your responses to those lines that are being given to your imagined sweetheart and not to them. This is called *aesthetic distance.* In this case it is the appropriate distance that the speaker has from his audience and poem.

A related example is the story teller whose narrative might include the presence of other characters. We often see the narrator in a presentation turning his or her body to indicate each of the character who is speaking. Not only does this take time, it also brings negative attention to the narrator. It is much easier to employ angles of direction.

The simplest way of using the angles of direction is to position yourself as the speaker at the apex of a triangle (Figure 11.1). Under ordinary circumstances, the characters the speaker is addressing would not be located outside this triangle. The size of the triangle depends on the number of characters in the performance, the dimensions of the room, and the size and arrangement of the audience. In determining the size of the triangle, always keep in mind that the audience should be able to see at least a three-quarter profile of the speaker. Nothing is more frustrating to an audience than seeing half a speaker's face! Also, keep in mind that the character speaking determines the angle of direction, not the character being addressed.

Figure 11.1 illustrates the three most common types of rooms used for speaking occasions. The shape of the room and the position of the audience determine the shape of the triangle. Figure 11.1a represents the most common rectangular-shaped room, with the speaker working in the center of one of the longer sides of the rectangle. The base of this triangle is smaller than the one in Figure 11.1b, in which the audience is spread more widely. In Figure 11.1c, the audience is sitting in arcs, which requires the speaker to use a smaller base to maintain the suggested three-quarter profile. These angles of direction are

W—Speaker at apex of triangle; character angles form triangle
X—Location of characters in scene
Y—Back wall
Z—Audience

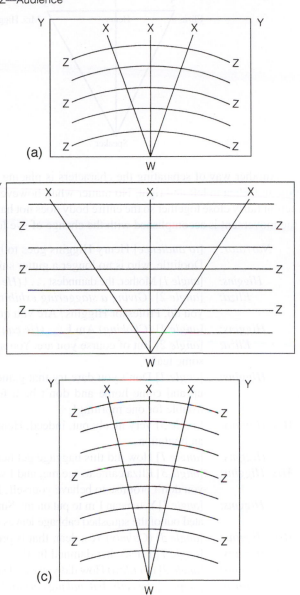

FIGURE 11.1   Most common performance arenas

simply suggestions; make your own if you wish. And if you have occasion to speak in an arena theater in which the audience truly surrounds you, good luck!

In some situations in which angles of direction are used, the speaker may also deal directly with the audience. In the following selection, the performer/narrator relates the narrative portions directly to the audience. A projected scene using (notated) angles of direction is used during the direct discourse portions. In this scene, the speaker might want to separate the characters by gender placing Henry Higgins at the center angle with the women (Eliza and Mrs. Higgins) on either side of him. The triangle would look like this:

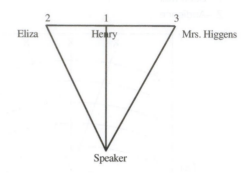

Another way of separating the characters is placing Mrs. Higgins in the center and Henry and Eliza to left and right. No matter what, however, be sure to make the angles of direction fairly close together so the entire body does not have to move back and forth. Most of the movement is accomplished with the change of eye location.

Narrator:	[*to audience*] Henry Higgins goes to his mother's house to find Eliza Doolittle, who is no longer a gutter snipe.
Higgins:	[*angle 1*] Mother, the damndest . . . ! (*He sees Eliza. Amazed, angry*) You!
Eliza:	[*angle 2*] (*Giving a staggering exhibition of ease of manner*) How do you do, Professor Higgins? Are you quite well?
Higgins:	[*angle 1*] (*Choking*) Am I . . . (*He can say no more*)
Eliza:	[*angle 2*] But of course you are. You are never ill. Would you care for some tea?
Higgins:	[*angle 1*] Don't you dare try that game on me! I taught it to you! Get up and come home and don't be a fool! You've caused me enough trouble for one morning!
Mrs. Higgins:	[*angle 3*] Very nicely put, indeed, Henry. No woman could resist such an invitation.
Higgins:	[*angle 1*] How did this baggage get here in the first place?
Mrs. Higgins:	[*angle 3*] Eliza came to see me, and I was delighted to have her. And if you don't promise to behave yourself, I shall have to ask you to leave.
Higgins:	[*angle 1*] You mean I'm to put on my Sunday manners for this thing I created out of the squashed cabbage leaves of Covent Garden?
Mrs. Higgins:	[*angle 3*] (*Calmly*) Yes, dear, that is precisely what I mean.
Higgins:	[*angle 1*] I'll see her damned first!
Mrs. Higgins:	[*angle 3*] (*To Eliza*) How did you ever learn manners with my son around?
Eliza:	[*angle 2*] (*Sweetly, but making certain her voice carries*) It was very difficult. I should never have known how ladies and gentlemen behave if it hadn't been for Colonel Pickering. He always showed me that he felt and thought about me as if I were something better than a common flower girl. You see, Mrs. Higgins, apart from the things one can pick up, the difference between a lady and a flower girl is not how she behaves, but how she is treated. I shall always be a flower girl to Professor Higgins because he always treats me as a flower girl and always will; but I know that I shall always be a lady to Colonel Pickering because he always treats me as a lady and always will.
Mrs. Higgins:	[*angle 3*] Henry, please don't grind your teeth.

From MY FAIR LADY
Alan Jay Lerner and Frederick Loewe

For those of you who perform mainly in the open situation or direct performance occasion (presenter, cleric, or public speaker), there are often times when you might switch to the indirect technique. For example, if you are telling a short narration, or a humorous joke or story that includes characterizations, there is no better technique than the use of angles of direction with the use of changes of voice and physical demeanor.

As an exercise, read the following portion from the opening paragraph of Robert Penn Warren's "The Patented Gate and the Mean Hamburger," and pay attention to the markings of the script. It should be emphasized that this is simply *one* way to employ the use of the open and closed situations. Try other possible readings using the same material:

```
————— open ————————— open ——
You have seen him a thousand times. You have seen him
——————— closed ————————— open ¬
standing on the street corner on Saturday afternoon, in the little
— open ——— closed ——— open ———
county-seat towns. He wears blue jean pants, or overalls washed
—— open —————— closed ———
to a pale pastel blue like the color of sky after a shower
— closed ——— open ——— closed ——
in spring, but because it is Saturday he has on a wool coat,
——— open ———
an old one, perhaps the coat left from the suit he got married
—— open ————— closed ———
in a long time back. His long wrist bones hang out from the
——————— closed —————
sleeves of his coat, the tendons showing along the bone
——— open ———
like the dry twist of grapevine still corded on the stove-length
——————— open ———
of hickory sapling you would find in his wood box beside
——————— open ———
his cookstove among the split chunks of gum and red oak.
——— closed ———
The big hands, with the knotted, cracked joints and the
——— closed ———
square, horn-thick nails, hang loose off the wrist bone
——— open ———
like clumsy, home-made tools hung on the wall of a shed
— open ¬
after work.
```

THE GOLDEN TRIANGLE

Charles Wesley Emerson referred to the Golden Triangle in dealing with speakers utilizing both the direct and indirect performance occasion. The triangle refers to the speaker, the audience, and the content. These three components working together "create something far greater than any two can without the third."[3]

We have all seen great actors or presenters who outdistance their material. I am certain that Sir Anthony Hopkins has accepted a movie role to pay some bills. He waltzes through the film, and it isn't even a musical! At other times, the material gobbles up the

[3]Charles Wesley Emerson, *The Evolution of Expression*, vol. 4, (Boston: The Barta Press, 1905), 10

actor. Sometimes, an audience would not respond adequately to the Fonz! We as performers can control the quality of our content and work to excel in our performance, but we cannot do much about the audience. All we can do is hope that our competent work will reach them and help them forget their trials and problems. Our responsibility is to put together content that will be effective when delivered to the audience.

>>>
ORAL DICTION AND WRITTEN DICTION

As mentioned in Chapter 4, *diction* means "choice of words." It is very important in presentations and public speaking to use oral diction as opposed to the choice of words that appear in written diction. *Oral diction* is composed of words that are somewhat easily understood because the audience members must get the message immediately. There is no chance to go back and look up the difficult diction. In *written diction,* we are able to take all the time we need to clarify the message that was presented.

If the performance is a presentation of literature, it would be wise for you to analyze the audience. You would not perform the same material for a high school audience that you might utilize at a meeting of the American Association of University Women.

>>>
MEMORIZATION VERSUS USING NOTES

The material in a speech determines the style of presentation. One of the considerations, of course, is whether the material is performed from memory or read from a script. Generally, if the material allows the speaker to address the audience directly (a direct performance occasion), detailed notes should not be used. Very brief notes are acceptable for a sales presentation that includes complicated details. However, when you're speaking directly to an audience, the less you have to rely on notes, the better. The continuity of thought that develops in the communication process between the speaker and audience is broken if the speaker keeps looking down at notes.

On special occasions, such as the presentation of an annual report, the text is meant to be read aloud. In those cases, the principles governing a direct performance occasion are applied. However, if you are reading a report or commencement speech, make certain that it is concealed within a black folder so that the audience can't count the pages with you or see how thick the text is. As audience members, how many times have you looked forward to seeing the speaker holding the final lonely page?

Other than in a theatrical event like a play or interpretation recital, memorization should be used with great discrimination. If you want to memorize introductions or transitions, make certain that they sound spontaneous and unstudied; canned speech is very uninteresting. That does not mean that some of the thoughts cannot be memorized; material recited from memory can still appear to be spontaneous. After all, actors in long-running shows must make each performance appear as if it were the first. But don't memorize large chunks. The danger is that if someone sneezes or coughs or otherwise breaks your concentration, your chances of continuing from memory are rather slight. Then what do you do— start the paragraph over? It might be necessary to go back to the beginning like a novice at a piano recital because that is how you rehearsed your speech. These dangers of memorization also apply to poems, monologues, and other material made more pleasing when presented from memory. It is an extra pressure you certainly do not need.

If you use notes in a direct performance occasion, they should be sparse, containing single words or phrases to remind you about organization or content. A quick look down ought to do the trick because you must be very familiar with your material. Nothing will help you if you do not have considerable mastery over your material.

In indirect performance occasions (in which the audience is not addressed directly), the speaker is speaking in character. For example, in an interpretative reading of a dramatic monologue, the speaker presents (with or without a copy of the text) the words and thoughts of one character to another character in a fictional world (rather than to the actual audience). If you choose to read from a text in such a case, make certain that you do not rely too heavily on it. Be very familiar with the material. Nothing takes the place of having mastery over the content. Hold the text high enough so you must merely lower your eyes to glance at the script. If you hold the text in your less dominant hand, your gestures may be stronger because you will be free to use your stronger side. Many readers hold the text too low and must peek at the audience. A great deal of the performance is missed when the speaker's face cannot be seen.

If you use a script, be sure to mark it so that when your eyes go to the text, you do not have to waste time searching for your place. You might put a large colored arrow at the place to begin reading. It is important for you to look down at the script at the same times during each rehearsal; that way reading the script becomes a part of the technique you use in your performance. If you look down only when your memory "dries up," you will not know exactly where you are and may panic unnecessarily. Such unsureness will be revealed in your performance. Remember always to keep eye contact with your audience members. They are the reason for your communication, and your main objective is to get that communication across to them.

A cleric's homily mixes direct and indirect performance occasions. The reading of the Scriptures, of course, is from text. The narrative elements of the text, which include the characters in the biblical scene, are spoken directly to the audience. When one character speaks to another character, the occasion becomes indirect. The cleric's sermon or remarks should be a direct performance occasion with as few glances at the notes as possible. Remember that nothing takes the place of preparation, rehearsal, and mastery over the content.

>>> LECTERNS

By its very existence, a **lectern** poses a barrier between the speaker and the audience. The term *lectern* comes from the Latin *lector,* meaning "reader." Its purpose is not to provide an object to clutch until your knuckles turn white, to hide behind, or to play "peekaboo" behind, but to hold a book—especially the Bible. Used properly, the lectern presents no problems in presentational decorum. Unfortunately, many untrained speakers feel more comfortable when they can lean on, wrap around, or hold on to the edges of the lectern in neurotic desperation.

Frequently, lecterns in churches are located in awkward places away from the audience, which simply contributes to the division between the speaker and the audience. A cleric's first job is to remove or at least avoid using those huge wooden structures. Sermons should be given to the congregation in full view and as close to them as possible. For the reading, hold the book in your nondominant hand and rehearse. The Spirit of the Lord doesn't enter in and make the lazy reader successful; God continues to help those who help themselves.

The same advice applies to the speaker who has to perform in a hotel meeting room. Usually, lecterns in such rooms are large boxes resting on a table. Because you can't be seen, the lectern becomes a distraction. Get rid of it and get closer to your audience. Bring notes if you really need them, but refer to them as infrequently as possible. Prepare yourself well, and always remember that you should rid yourself of anything that distances you—physically or psychologically—from your audience.

If it is necessary that you use a lectern, there are some aesthetic techniques that might prove helpful. If you are speaking at a memorial, the service is rather somber and formal. Standing behind the lectern will help to achieve that feeling of formality. This is most appropriate if a reading from Scriptures is being presented. Antony's oration before the crowd from *Julius Caesar* might begin behind the lectern, giving a feeling of distance. The lectern acts as a barrier between him and the unhappy crowd. As Antony begins to make his points to the audience, he might come out from behind this barrier as he becomes more relaxed. Moving away from the lectern promotes the feeling of security.

As a general rule, the speaker who uses a lectern throughout a presentation indicates a lack of security, especially if the lectern is used to support more than notes or a script. Conversely, a speaker who frees himself or herself from a lectern appears more secure and confident to the audience.

>>>

MICROSOFT POWERPOINT

PowerPoint was developed as a tool to underscore and amplify an oral presentation. It was meant as a support. It was not supposed to take on a life of its own. Too often, the untrained speaker allows the instrument to become the message instead of highlighting the message. Too many speakers use PowerPoint to hide behind. Much of the time, they are safely in the dark, with the listener's attention on the lighted screen. The speaker simply reads what the audience sees on the screen. Many of us loathe the use of PowerPoint as viewed in badly presented speeches. Bullets were meant to be in guns, not read in oral presentations! Too many speakers use the tool as a teleprompter.

Use PowerPoint with care. It is a great tool for giving the audience information that a speaker would have difficulty accomplishing, like cartoons, statistics, colored photographs, and other kinds of documents.

When you are speaking (and that should be most of the time), you are in the light. The overhead machine is off so there is no competitive hum! Turn it on when needed. Nothing is more powerful than the power of good speech presentation.

>>>

MICROPHONES

The microphone is one of the greatest inventions of the twentieth century, but it also imposes limitations on many speaking situations. Of course, microphones are necessary for the media, but in most halls, small theaters, churches, and hotels, they are unnecessary because the human voice can be trained rather easily to be heard clearly. A microphone anchored to the heinous lectern imposes a limitation because it inhibits a speaker's movements. Or, if you use a lapel mike, you must be sure not to turn your head from side to side, or your voice disappears. If you are lucky enough to have a cordless mike, your audience may wonder when you'll break into song.

Whether you have a mike or not, you must still reach your audience visually, aurally, and aesthetically, but a certain energy is created when the human voice is heard without mechanical amplification. And, unfortunately, microphone systems are frequently run by people who know nothing more than how to turn on the switch. As a result, distortion and a lack of intelligibility often occur when a speaker uses a microphone.

One of the most frustrating things about going to the theater today is that everything is miked! In a musical, we know who is going to do the big tap number because we hear the tapping long before the first step is danced. Every actor should get vocal training. How much nicer it is for the audience and easier for the actor when the speaker is unhampered by a microphone. Of course, the worst thing that can happen to you in using a microphone is that it does not work when you arrive there or it gives tremendous feed back that takes time to fix. Develop that voice.

Microphones are important to news anchors and others who make a career in the mass media. If you must use a microphone, certain microphone deportment, or behavior, is suggested: (1) If you use a lavalier microphone you should make certain that it is clipped fairly tightly on a collar or lapel so the sound will not be muffled or stifled. Otherwise it might disappear or fall off. When you are finished, make certain that you do not walk away without unclipping the microphone or you might come to a sudden stop. (2) If you are near a mike in use, remember that unwanted movements such as clapping or loud speech will be picked up by the sensitive instrument. Any sudden change in projection as you read copy will be amplified. Carefully modulate your voice. (3) If you are using a script, do not use staples or paper clips. Make sure that the script contains numbered pages. Type on one side of the page, double- or triple-spaced, which allows you to move the pages aside gently rather than turning them over.

>>>
IMPROMPTU SPEAKING

You cannot escape from taxes or your in-laws or speaking at one time or other. And most people are forced into a speaking situation during their lives in which they are called upon to speak immediately. How many of us have been called upon at a faculty meeting and asked to "make a few remarks." Or in a business meeting when the boss says. "Ken, give us some background on the project" or "Would you mind summarizing that for us?" Panic overwhelms you as you glare at your boss for not having told you that you were going to speak. When you go to a meeting ask yourself the following question: "Is that guy or gal likely to call on me today to address the group? If so, what might the boss want me to talk about?"

Don't panic! Accept the request with a smile. Look assured and definite. This is called impromptu speaking—speaking at the moment. If you are called upon "to say a few words," keep the following old axiom in mind: *Tell them what you are going to tell them, tell them, and then tell them what you told them.* This is a very wise statement.

Impromptu Topics

1. Operas should (should not) be translated into English.
2. Comment on your favorite movie.
3. What is your favorite food, and why?
4. What was one of your most embarrassing moments?
5. Discuss a person who has had tremendous influence on your life.
6. Discuss three entertainers who have helped to mold your appreciation of the arts.

7. What is your worst vocal or speech error, and what are you doing about it?
8. What is your favorite song, and why?
9. What professor or administrator has had the greatest influence on you?
10. How do you recover from jet lag?
11. "Good fences make (do not make) good neighbors."
12. We can be strangers in a familiar land.
13. What was your most embarrassing moment?
14. Relate a "special" moment.
15. Do you believe in the colorization process for black-and-white movies?
16. Should an automobile driver feel hesitant about closing his or her eyes during a sneeze?
17. What is your favorite Broadway musical and why?
18. Is listening to an iPod a dangerous pastime?
19. There will never be another Fred Astaire.
20. What happened to the good old barber?

Extemporaneous Topics

1. How do you see technology in the future?
2. Of what importance should SAT scores be in college entrance requirements?
3. Should drugs be legalized?
4. No one can rob us of our free will!
5. English should (should not) be the primary language of the United States.
6. A trial should (should not) take place in the state in which the crime was committed.
7. The two-party system is (not) politically limiting.
8. Urban living has its drawbacks.
9. Human nature is to be good (bad).
10. The line between tax shelter and fraud is very fine.
11. The economic problem is (not) going to improve.
12. There should (not) be capital punishment.
13. The destruction of the rain forest should (not) cease.
14. Speak to the following Shakespearean quotation: "What is past, is prologue."
15. The more we label something, the less clearly we see it.
16. All wild animal killing should be declared illegal by international law.
17. Too much of our tax dollar is (not) going into military spending.
18. You are nothing in the job market today unless you can market skill.
19. We are what we are because they were what they were.
20. Comment on the following definition by Robert Frost: "Home is the place where, when you have to go there, they have to take you in."

REHEARSAL

If you want to be a successful communicator, you must rehearse—and you must rehearse aloud and to an imaginary audience. If at all possible, rehearse at least once in the room in which you will be speaking. Also, acquire as much information as you can about your audience. When you rehearse in the room, visualize your audience in that setting.

It is also a good idea to tape your rehearsals and study the tape. Of course, a videotape of your rehearsal is preferable. It is important that you be objective when you review such a tape; look at what you actually did—not at what you intended to do. It is too late now.

Watch your body. Did it communicate what you wanted? What about your face? If you used visuals in your presentation, did they detract, or did you use them wisely? Did your audience concentrate on your visuals, or did they listen to what you were saying? Were you looking at your audience? Were you including everyone? By anticipating problems and rehearsing your presentation well, you will probably be able to handle any calamity that arises during the actual performance.

>>>

EMPATHY

Empathy is feeling what another person feels. In the communications process, you want your audience to have empathy with you and with what you are saying, and you want to have an empathic response to the audience. Essentially, empathy has three components: (1) the intellectual, (2) the emotional, and (3) the physical. First, you want your audience to understand what you are presenting, whether it is a speech of instruction, a lecture, a homily, or a poem. Second, you want your audience to feel—to have an emotional reaction to what they understand intellectually. Third, you want a physical response from that audience. Learn to read their feedback. Are they leaning forward because they are highly interested in your speech, or are they leaning forward because they can't hear you easily? Are they smiling, or do their glazed eyes signify boredom? Have you caused them to feel what you want them to feel?

The empathic response is easy to see in the young boy who leaves the movie theater pretending that he is riding off into the sunset as the hero of an old Western movie. The youngster's make-believe horseback ride indicates that all three components of empathy have taken place.

>>>

GUIDELINES FOR PRESENTATIONS

- Remember, you are communicating from the time you leave your seat until you arrive back.
- Regardless of what is happening inside of you, step up with confidence and show authority. "As people speak, so are they!" Audience perception of you must be strong!
- Get yourself in the mood of communicating before you speak.
- Do not look at your notes before you begin. Make contact with your audience first.
- Maintain direct eye contact! Do not merely look at your audience—you must see them! Do not look at their foreheads—or, over their heads! You will learn how long to stay with your audience members. If the audience is large and you cannot make contact with all of them, choose someone in various areas of the room.
- Stand with support by your feet, legs, and trunks. Your feet should be at least one foot apart. You want to look like a fortified building!
- If you gesture, make certain you communicate something other than nervousness. Be definite and strong. Fill your space!
- Make certain there is a strong conclusion to your presentation. Do not verbally "fade away." Let your audience know that you are finished by a strong conclusion followed by a definite "holding beat." Then move. Do not say "Thank you." Your audience should be thanking you! Do not show relief until you go to the lavatory. Too often, speakers end mentally and envision themselves back in their seats before all the words are spoken.

>>>

SPEECH ELEMENTS

- Use *oral* and not *written* diction.
- Use simplified but vivid sentences with active language.
- Use the active voice in your grammatical structure:

  Passive: It was told to me that I was an appreciated speaker at the last meeting.
  Active: John, I am happy to hear that I made a good impression the last time I spoke. At least no one left the room . . . to my knowledge. (This statement is more interesting and dynamic.)

- Use contractions. They are more casual and friendly.
- Be careful in covering mistakes. Everyone is nonfluent. If you sound as if you know what you are saying, often the audience will not even hear the error. Do not call additional attention to the error. However, if it is a bad mistake, do not be afraid to acknowledge it and make the correction. The severity of the error is the question here. There is nothing wrong with saying, "I had better correct that one!"

>>>

TASTE

Good taste is difficult to define. It is far easier to define bad taste. Charles Wesley Emerson said that "anything that interferes with the flow of the vitalized picture is in bad taste."[4] Taste is a very personal characteristic. What is tasteful for one person may not be to another. Bad taste can manifest itself in a performer, the material, an audience, or an occasion. Analyze the audience, the material, and most of all your participation in the occasion.

A speaker can be dressed in bad taste. For example, it is perfectly acceptable to wear a diamond pendant to a cocktail party, but the lights in a hotel ballroom where you are speaking may make the necklace sparkle so much that attention is drawn away from your message.

A priest might wear a liturgical garment that is particularly full and flowing, causing him to pull constantly at his sleeves to free his arms or hands, or he might frighten a congregation by getting too close to a lighted candle. Either action is very distracting and would interfere with the energized picture. To avoid this kind of costume dilemma, a priest should first wear the garment during rehearsal to get used to it.

In another example, material might be in bad taste because it is inappropriate for an audience. Thus, one would probably not discuss the virtues of MTV with an audience composed of elderly people.

>>>

ASSIGNMENTS

1. *Speech of Introduction.* In four minutes introduce yourself to your audience. At the end of the speech, your audience should have a good idea of what you're all about.
2. *Personal Narrative.* Tell a personal story (four minutes) about your professional of work experience in chronological order. You are expected to select a situation in which other people are involved. Characterization is an important component in this assignment.

---

[4]Charles W. Emerson, *Evolution of Expression*, vol. 3 (Millis, Mass: Emerson, 1920), 11.

3. *Narrative Humorous Anecdote.* Tell a story, or joke (three minutes) in which character-ization and use of the body are highlighted.

4. *Forms of Speech Emphasis Exercises.* Choose a selection to demonstrate the four forms of emphasis.

5. *Novel or Short Story.* Reading the opening paragraph of a novel or short story, (three minutes).

6. *Speech of Demonstration.* Demonstrate a concept, action, or principle (five to seven minutes) with a beginning, a middle, and an end. The members of your audience ought to be able to reproduce, fairly accurately, the demonstration.

7. *Multi media Presentation.* Use one or more special media devices (five to seven min-utes), such as an overhead projector, slides, music, posters, etc.

EXERCISES FOR THE SPEECH OCCASION

The following selections have been included so that you can apply the principles of good speech and voice that have been presented. Comments on performance are made when appropriate.

1. In The Hague, Netherlands, when the temperature is about 46 degrees and the humidity is just right, toads cross a road to get to their mating grounds. Many were killed by cars until a Herr Bleumink obtained permission to put up a gate during the mating time. It was also noted that at the height of the mating period, females carry the smaller male toads piggyback to the breeding grounds. Such newsworthy happenings should not go uncelebrated:

A passionate toad crossing Duinlaan Road
In the land of the Zuider Zee,
So preoccupied with the other side,
That he failed to hear or see
A car or a jeep that didn't beep,
But caught him by surprise.
Pffhht! he died on that road, an ugly toad,
With the lovelight still in his eyes.
Now, will he be missed at the annual tryst
In the ditch by the North Sea dune,
In March when the temperature's forty-six
And the toads start to moon and croon?
"Well," said his mate as she passed Bleumink's gate
With a toad piggyback, "You can see,
In the pale moonlight on a humid night,
All toads look alike to me."

ODE TO A TOAD WHO DIED ON THE ROAD
Father Eugene F. Lyttle

2. In the following sonnet, pay attention to the poet's use of sound, particularly alliteration (/g/, /r/, /l/, /f/, and /w/), assonance (/e/, /ɛ/, /æ/, and /o/), onomatopoeia, end-of-line rhymes, and internal rhymes.

The world is charged with the grandeur of God.
It will flame out, like shining from shook foil;
It gathers to a greatness like the ooze of oil
Crushed. Why do men then now not reck his rod?
Generations have trod, have trod, have trod;

And all is seared with trade; bleared, smeared with toil;
And wears man's smudge and shares man's smell: the soil
Is bare now, nor can foot feel, being shod.
And for all this, nature is never spent;
There lives the dearest freshest deep down things;
And though the last lights off the black West went
Oh, morning at the brown brink eastward springs—
Because the Holy Ghost over the bent
World broods with warm breast and with ah! bright wings.

GOD'S GRANDEUR
Gerard Manley Hopkins

3.   *Sir Peter:*   [*angle 1*] Lady Teazle, Lady Teazle, I'll not bear it!

Lady Teazle: [*angle 2*] Sir Peter, Sir Peter, you may bear it or not, as you please; but I ought to have my own way in everything, and what's more, I will too.— What! though I was educated in the country, I know very well that women of fashion in London are accountable to nobody after they are married.

Sir Peter: [*angle 1*] Very well, ma'am, very well,—so a husband is to have no influence, no authority?

Lady Teazle: [*angle 2*] Authority! No, to be sure—if you wanted authority over me, you should have adopted me, and not married me; I am sure you were old enough.

Sir Peter: [*angle 1*] Old enough!—aye, there it is!—Well, well, Lady Teazle, though my life may be made unhappy by your temper, I'll not be ruined by your extravagance.

Lady Teazle: [*angle 2*] My extravagance! I'm sure I'm not more extravagant than a woman of fashion ought to be.

Sir Peter: [*angle 1*] No, no madam, you shall throw away no more sums on such unmeaning luxury. 'Slife! to spend as much to furnish your dressing-room with flowers in winter as would suffice to turn the Pantheon into a greenhouse, and give a fete champetre at Christmas!

Lady Teazle: [*angle 2*] Lord, Sir Peter, am I to blame because flowers are dear in cold weather? You should find fault with the climate, and not with me. For my part, I am sure I wish it was spring all the year round, and that roses grew under one's feet!

Sir Peter: [*angle 1*] Oons! madam—if you had been born to this, I shouldn't wonder at your talking thus.—But you forget what your situation was when I married you.

Lady Teazle: [*angle 2*] No, no, I don't; 'twas a very disagreeable one, or I should never have married you.

From THE SCHOOL FOR SCANDAL
Richard Brinsley Sheridan

4. Lucy Westenra's Diary. [use indirect occasion]

12 September.—How good they all are to me. I quite love that dear Dr. Van Helsing. I wonder why he was so anxious about these flowers. He positively frightened me, he was so fierce. And yet he must have been right, for I feel comfort from them already. Somehow, I do not dread being alone tonight, and can go to sleep without fear. I shall not mind any flapping outside the window. Oh, the terrible struggle that I have had against sleep so often of late; the pain of the sleeplessness, or the pain of the fear of sleep, and with such unknown horror as it has for me! How blessed are some people, whose lives have no fears, no dreads; to whom sleep is a blessing that comes nightly, and brings nothing but sweet dreams. Well, here I am tonight, hoping for sleep, and lying like Ophelia in the play with "virgin crants and maiden strewmeats." I never liked the garlic before, but tonight it is delightful! There is peace in its smell; I feel sleep coming already. Goodnight everybody.

From DRACULA
Bram Stoker

5. In this dialogue poem, two former friends from the country meet in town.

—"O Amelia, my dear, this does everything crown!
Who could have supposed I should meet you in Town?
And whence such fair garments, such prosperi-ty"—
"O didn't you know I'd been ruined?" said she.

—"You left us in tatters, without shoes or socks,
Tired of digging potatoes, and spudding up docks;
And now you've gay bracelets and bright feathers three!"—
"Yes: that's how we dress when we're ruined," said she.

—"At home in the barton you said 'thee' and 'thou,'
And 'this oon,' and 'theas oon,' and 't'other'; but now
Your talking quite fits 'ee for high compa-ny!"
"Some polish is gained with one's ruin," said she.

—"Your hands were like paws then, your face blue and bleak
But now I'm bewitched by your delicate cheek,
And your little gloves fit as on any la-dy!"—
"We never do work when we're ruined," said she.

—"You used to call home-life a hag-ridden dream.
And you'd sigh, and you'd sock; but at present you seem
To know not of megrims or melancho-ly!"
"True. One's pretty lively when ruined," said she.

—"I wish I had feathers, a fine sweeping gown,
And a delicate face, and could strut about Town!"
"My dear—a raw country girl, such as you be,
Cannot quite expect that. You ain't ruined," said she.

THE RUINED MAID
Thomas Hardy

6. The following testimony in the Salem witch trials is taken from actual court records:

a. An examination of the accused Bridget Bishop by Judge Hawthorne:

Judge: Bridget Bishop, what do you say? You here stand charged with sundry acts of witchcraft made upon the bodies of Mercy Lewis and Ann Putnam and others.

Bishop: I am innocent. I know nothing of it. I have done no witchcraft.

Judge: Look upon this woman and see if this be the woman that you have seen hurting you. [*to Bishop*] What do you say now that you see they charge you? Do you confess?

Bishop: I never hurt them in my life. I never seen these persons before. I am as innocent as the child unborn.

Judge: What contract have you made with the devil?

Bishop: I have made no contract with the devil. I never saw him in my life.

Mercy Lewis: Oh Goody Bishop, did you not come to my house the last night and did you not tell me that you would torment me?

> *Judge:* Tell the truth in this matter. How come this person to be tormented and to charge you with doing it?
>
> *Bishop:* I am not come here to say that I am a witch and to take away my life.

b. William Stacy, age 36, thereupon said:

1 About 14 years gone I had the small pox and Bridget Bishop did visit me and profess
2 a great love for me in my affliction. After I got well, Bridget Bishop got me
3 to do some work for her for which she gave me threepence, which seemed to me
4 as if it had been good money, but I had not gone over three or four rods before I
5 looked into my pocket where I put the money but could not find it. After that in
6 the winter about midnight I felt something between my lips pressing hard against
7 my teeth and it was very cold insomuch that it did wake me, and I got up and set
8 upon my bed and at the same time I did see the said Bridget Bishop or her shape
9 at the foot of the bed and it was as light as if it had been day. And the said Bishop
10 or her shape clapped her coat close to the legs and hopped upon the bed and about
11 the room . . . and then went out.

12   I fully believe that the said Bishop was instrumental in the death of my daughter
13 Priscilla about two years ago. The child was a lively, thriving child and suddenly
14 screeched out and so continued in this unusual manner for about a fortnight
15 and so died in a lamentable manner.

c. Sal Shaltoch, age about 41 years, testified:

1 In the year 1680, Bridget Bishop did come to my house pretending to buy an old
2 hog which they asked for, while after she went away with it and at sundry other
3 times she came in a smooth manner and I have often thought she came to make
4 mischief.

5   About that time our eldest child, who promised as much as any other of the
6 children, was taken in a very drooping condition and as Bridget Bishop came oftener
7 to the house he grew worse and worse. As he would be standing at the door
8 he would fall out and bruise his face upon the step, as if he had been pushed out
9 by an invisible hand. After that she brought me a pair of fleeces to dye. After that,
10 sundry pieces of lace, some of which were so short I could not judge they were
11 of any use. . . .

12   Just after this, our child was taken with a terrible fit. His mouth and eyes turned
13 aside in such a manner as if he was taken upon in death. After this he grew worse
14 in his fits, and he would be almost always crying. For many months he would be
15 daily crying until his strength was spent, and then he would fall asleep and wake
16 and fall to crying and moaning. Ever since, he has been stupefied and void of reason,
17 his fits still following him, and I cannot judge otherwise but that he is bewitched
18 and that Bridget Bishop is the cause of it all.

7. Let civilian voices argue the merits or demerits of our processes of government; whether our strength is being sapped by deficit financing, indulged in too long, by federal paternalism grown too mighty by power groups grown too arrogant, by politics grown too corrupt, by crime grown too rampant, by morals grown too low, by taxes grown too high, by extremists grown too violent; whether our personal liberties are as thorough and complete as they should be. These great national problems are not for your professional participation or military solution. Your guidepost stands out like a ten-fold beacon in the night: *Duty, Honor, Country.*

You are the leaven which binds together the entire fabric of our national system of defense. From your ranks come the great captains who hold the nation's destiny in their hands the moment the war tocsin sounds. The Long Gray Line has never failed us. Were you to do so, a million ghosts in olive drab, in brown khaki, in blue and gray, would rise from their white crosses thundering those magic words: *Duty, Honor, Country.*

This does not mean that you are war mongers.

On the contrary, the soldier, above all other people, prays for peace, for he must suffer and bear the deepest wounds and scars of war.

But always in our ears ring the ominous words of Plato, that wisest of all philosophers: "Only the dead have seen the end of war."

The shadows are lengthening for me. The twilight is here. My days of old have vanished, tone and tint. They have gone glimmering through the dreams of things that were. Their memory is one of wondrous beauty, watered by tears, and coaxed and caressed by the smiles of yesterday. I listen vainly, but with thirsty ears, for the witching melody of faint bugles blowing reveille, of far drums beating the long roll. In my dreams I hear again the crash, of guns, the rattle of musketry, the strange, mournful mutter of the battlefield.

But in the evening of my memory, always I come back to West Point.

Always there echoes and re-echoes: *Duty, Honor, Country.*

Today marks my final roll call with you, but I want you to know that when I cross the river my last conscious thoughts will be of The Corps, and The Corps, and The Corps.

I bid you farewell.

From DUTY, HONOR, COUNTRY
General Douglas MacArthur

8. This selection would be considered a direct performance occasion by most, where you as the narrator would speak directly to the audience members, who become characters. However, you might choose to relate the story to an imagined listener(s), thereby making it an indirect performance occasion. The aesthetics are slightly different depending upon your choice.

1 I have often heard it scream. No, I am not nervous, I am not imaginative, and I
2 never believed in ghosts, unless that thing is one. Whatever it is, it hates me almost
3 as much as it hated Luke Pratt, and it screams at me.
4 If I were you, I would never tell ugly stories about ingenious ways of killing
5 people, for you never can tell but that some one at the table may be tired of his or her
6 nearest and dearest. I have always blamed myself for Mrs. Pratt's death, and I suppose
7 I was responsible for it in a way, though heaven knows I never wished her anything
8 but long life and happiness. If I had not told that story she might be alive yet.
9 That is why the thing screams at me, I fancy.
10 She was a good little woman, with a sweet temper, all things considered, and a
11 nice gentle voice; but I remember hearing her shriek once when she thought her little
12 boy was killed by a pistol that went off, though every one was sure that it was not
13 loaded. It was the same scream; exactly the same, with a sort of rising quaver at the
14 end; do you know what I mean? Unmistakable.
15 The truth is, I had not realised that the doctor and his wife were not on good terms.
16 They used to bicker a bit now and then when I was here, and I often noticed that little
17 Mrs. Pratt got very red and bit her lip hard to keep her temper, while Luke grew pale
18 and said the most offensive things. He was that sort when he was in the nursery, I
19 remember, and afterward at school. He was my cousin, you know; that is how I came
20 by this house; after he died, and his boy Charley was killed in South Africa, there
21 were no relations left. Yes, it's a pretty little property, just the sort of thing for an old
22 sailor like me who has taken to gardening.

From THE SCREAMING SKULL
F. Marion Crawford

9. In the following selection Evy, a mother in her forties, is teaching the facts of life to her seventeen-year-old daughter.

 1 *Evy:* You're seventeen years old, it's time you judged me. I just don't want you to get
 2 the idea that a hundred and eighty-three pounds of pure alcohol is something called
 3 Happy Fat. . . . Many a night I would have thrown myself out that window if I could
 4 have squeezed through. . . . I'm not what you'd call an emotionally stable person.
 5 You know how many times I was *really* in love since your father and I broke up? I
 6 met the only man who ever really meant anything to me about seven, maybe eight,
 7 times. Mr. Right I meet at least twice a week. . . . I sure know true love when I see
 8 it. It's wherever I happen to look. . . . I want you to know everything, Polly, before
 9 you make up your mind. I lived here with that guitar player for eight of the happiest
 10 months of my life. Well, why not? He was handsome, funny, ten years younger than
 11 me, what more could a woman want? . . . He sat in that chair all day working and
 12 writing and I fed him and clothed him and loved him for eight incredible months. . . .
 13 And then that dirty bastard—I'm sorry, I'm going to try not to do that any more. . . .
 14 No, the hell with it. That dirty bastard. He walked out on me in the middle of the
 15 night for an eighteen-year-old Indian hippie. "Princess-Screw-the-Other Woman.". . .
 16 Wait'll she gets old and starts looking like the face on the nickel. And he doesn't have
 17 a penny, not a cent. Well, her moccasins'll wear out, we'll see how long that affair
 18 lasts. . . . But I sat at that window for six weeks, waiting and hoping while I ran
 19 through two liquor stores in this neighborhood alone. . . . Finally, Toby came in one
 20 day and found me face-down in the bathtub. . . . I woke up in a sanitarium in Long
 21 Island, and the rest isn't very interesting unless you like stories about human torture.
 22 . . . But I went through it and I'm here. And I figure, pussycat, that I have only one
 23 more chance at this human being business . . . and if I blow it this time, they'll probably
 24 bury me in some distillery in Kentucky. . . . And if this is the kind of person
 25 you'd like to live with, God has cursed me with one of the all-time-great schmucks
 26 for a daughter.

From THE GINGERBREAD LADY
Neil Simon

10. A girl stood on the shingle that fringes Millbourne Bay, gazing at the red roofs of the little village across the water. She was a pretty girl, small and trim. Just now some secret sorrow seemed to be troubling her, for on her forehead were wrinkles and in her eyes a look of wistfulness. She had, in fact, all the distinguishing marks of one who is thinking of her sailor lover.

But she was not. She had no sailor lover. What was she thinking of was that at about this time they would be lighting up the shop-windows in London, and that of all the deadly, depressing spots she had ever visited this village of Millbourne was the deadliest.

The evening shadows deepened. The incoming tide glistened oilily as it rolled over the mud flats. She rose and shivered.

"Goo! What a hole!" she said, eyeing the unconscious village morosely. "*What* a hole!"

This was Sally Preston's first evening in Millbourne. She had arrived by the afternoon train from London—not of her own free will. Left to herself, she would not have come within sixty miles of the place. London supplied all that she demanded from life. She had been born in London; she had lived there ever since—she hoped to die there. She liked fogs, motor-buses, noise, policemen, paper-boys, shops, taxi-cabs, artificial light, stone pavements, houses in long, grey rows, mud, banana-skins, and moving-picture exhibitions. Especially moving-picture exhibitions. It was, indeed, her taste for these that had caused her banishment to Millbourne.

The great public is not yet unanimous on the subject of moving-picture exhibitions. Sally, as I have said, approved of them. Her father, on the other hand, did not. An austere ex-butler, who let lodgings in Ebury Street and preached on Sundays in Hyde Park, he looked askance at the "movies." It was his boast that he had never been inside a theatre in his life, and he classed cinema palaces with theatres as wiles of the devil. Sally, suddenly unmasked as an habitual frequenter of these abandoned places, sprang with one bound into prominence as the Bad Girl of the Family. Instant removal from the range of temptation being the only possible plan, it seemed to Mr. Preston that a trip to the country was indicated.

He selected Millbourne because he had been butler at the Hall there, and because his sister Jane, who had been a parlourmaid at the Rectory, was now married and living in the village.

Certainly he could not have chosen a more promising reformatory for Sally.

From SOMETHING TO WORRY ABOUT
P. G. Wodehouse

11. Eudora Welty's "Why I Live at the P.O." is the story of a woman who has had a spat with her family and leaves home. The dramatic monologue is the humorous and pathetic story of a Southern speaker who is frantic and must deliver her story . . . to anyone.

I was getting along fine with Mama, Papa-Daddy and Uncle Rondo until my sister Stella-Rondo just separated from her husband and came back home again. Mr. Whitaker! Of course I went with Mr. Whitaker first, when he first appeared here in China Grove, taking "Pose Yourself" photos, and Stella-Rondo broke us up. Told him I was one-sided. Bigger on one side than the other, which is a deliberate, calculated falsehood: I'm the same. Stella-Rondo is exactly twelve months to the day younger than I am and for that reason she's spoiled.

She's always had anything in the world she wanted and then she'd throw it away. Papa-Daddy gave her this gorgeous Add-a-Pearl necklace when she was eight years old and she threw it away playing baseball when she was nine, with only two pearls.

So as soon as she got married and moved away from home the first thing she did was separate! From Mr. Whitaker! This photographer with the popeyes she said she trusted. Came home from one of those towns up in Illinois and to our complete surprise brought this child of two.

Mama said she like to made her drop dead for a second. "Here you had this marvelous blonde child and never so much as wrote your mother a word about it," says Mama. "I'm thoroughly ashamed of you." But of course she wasn't.

Stella-Rondo just calmly takes off this *hat,* I wish you could see it. She says, "Why, Mama, Shirley-T.'s adopted, I can prove it."

"How?" says Mama, but all I says was, "H'm!" There I was over the hot stove, trying to stretch two chickens over five people and a completely unexpected child into the bargain, without one moment's notice.

"What do you mean 'H'm!'?" says Stella-Rondo, and Mama says, "I heard that, Sister."

I said that oh, I didn't mean a thing, only that whoever Shirley-T. was, she was the spit-image of Papa-Daddy if he'd cut off his beard, which of course he'd never do in the world. Papa-Daddy's Mama's papa and sulks.

> To locate URLs and search terms for weblinks relevant to this chapter, please go to the companion website at www.cengage.com/rtf/crannell/voiceandarticulation5e and select the proper chapter.

Write the definitions for the following terms in the space below.

KEY TERMS	DEFINITIONS
Audience Feedback	
Canned Speech	
Direct Performance Occasion	
Dolce et utile	
Empathy	
Eye Contact	
Extemporaneous Speech	
Impromptu Speech	
Indirect Performance Occasion	
Introduction	
Lectern	
Projected Scene	
Signature Story	
Spontaneity	

CHAPTER 12

THE FOUR MAJOR DIALECTS OF AMERICAN ENGLISH

A **dialect** is the general pronunciation practiced in a particular region by people who speak the same language. Within and outside the continental United States there are a number of dialects. The American English in Hawaii, for example, is highly influenced by Asian languages. As you study dialects, remember that some speakers will have stronger dialects than others.

Obviously, a text on voice and articulation must limit its discussion to the most common dialects. The four dialects of American English that will be presented here are New England, New York City, Southern, and General American, which is the prevailing dialect in the Midwest, West, and Northwest.

Dialects develop for many reasons. The most important, perhaps, is the influence of another language used by previous generations. A couple whose primary language is Italian are likely to speak English with an accent. Consequently, their children, although born in the United States, will be influenced by their parents' speech.

The early settlers in New England were primarily British. Accordingly, New England speech contains strong elements of British speech along with its own concoctions. British characteristics are also present in Southern speech, which includes additional Southern characteristics. Within a dialect there are standard and substandard pronunciations.

Whether you are a "regional culturist" (a person who wishes to retain the best standards of speech within a particular region) or someone who does not want regional elements in your speech, it is important to know the voice and speech characteristics of different geographic locations. For example, there are many kinds of radio stations: hard rock, classical, country, gospel, and so on. If you are interested in becoming an on-air personality, you will want to know the recommended style of speech for the type of station for which you want to work. Program requirements within a market will usually dictate appropriate speech or dialect.

You want your speech to be flexible, to be able to adapt to different styles and environments. Maintain your Down East or Southern speech if it is helpful and "natural" or required for the people with whom you interact—your listening or viewing audience, your students, the members of your congregation, or your clients.

On the national level, the speech used by the professional communicator is heard on television and radio, in motion pictures, on the stage, and elsewhere. However, many of these professionals have speech that does not reflect the standards of a trained speaker. In some cases, their speech is even defective and, therefore, far from appropriate. It is important to realize that the speech of professional speakers substantially affects the average listener. Radio and television personalities often inadvertently become role models and set our communication standards. Because we tend to imitate the speech of personalities we admire, it would be beneficial for everyone to mimic someone with a professional standard.

The material on dialects in this chapter is by no means exhaustive, nor does it deal with dialectical variations. Your teacher will determine the dialectical standards for your class. The purpose of the chapter is simply to introduce you to the most obvious characteristics of the four major dialects of American English. The discussions and drills are helpful if you want to control or eliminate a dialect or to adopt a dialect for professional purposes.

The following modifying marks will be used in this and the following chapter to furnish additional information regarding the production of the sounds:

1. The symbol [ː] appearing after the sound indicates that the sound is prolonged.
2. The symbol [ʔ] appearing before a sound indicates that the sound is glottalized. The breath is stopped with increased subglottal pressure and then the glottis is relaxed, allowing the breath to escape freely. The glottal stop is often used in place of the plosive /t/ (for example, [bɑʔ l] for [ˈbɑtl]) in the pronunciation of "bottle"). This sound occurs frequently in the cockney and Scottish dialects.
3. The symbol [˜] placed over a sound indicates that the sound is produced with nasality. This modifying mark frequently appears with the vowel /æ/ and indicates excessive assimilation nasality. It is also quite evident in French.
4. The symbol ['] set high before a syllable indicates a primary accent on that syllable; set low before a syllable, it indicates secondary stress on that syllable. Obviously, these marks are used with bisyllabic and polysyllabic words only (for example, [ɪˈvækjuˌet] for "evacuate" and [ˈsɪmpləˌfaɪ] for "simplify").
5. The symbol [.] placed beneath a vowel indicates greater tension than usual.
6. The symbol [ˌ] under a consonant signifies that the sound is dentalized (the blade of the tongue is against the alveolar ridge with the tip touching the upper teeth).
7. The symbol [ɾ] indicates a single trill of the tongue tip on the consonant /r/.
8. The symbol [ř] indicates a multiple trill of the tongue tip on the consonant /r/. (Imitate the stereotypical English duchess and roll that /r/!)
9. The symbol [ɻ] indicates an /r/ for which the tip of the tongue is curled too far back toward the palate (for example, some Midwesterners might say [ɻʌn] for [rʌn]).
10. The symbol [⊥] indicates that the tongue position is higher than usual.
11. A slash [/] through a letter indicates its omission in pronunciation ("with us" is pronounced "wi us").

In most of the exercises that follow, the dialectical substitution of the sound will appear above the appropriate letters. Each dialectical characteristic will be presented one at a time, and only sounds that have been discussed will be included in the examples.

>>> NEW ENGLAND

My Mar 'n Pop came from Reveea, not too fah from Lynn.

The speech of New Englanders is heavily influenced by their ancestors, the British. New Englanders not only use **sound addition** and **sound omission;** they often create an abrasive vocal quality quite unlike British English, leading to **sound distortion.** In addition, New England speech makes several **sound substitutions.**

Omission of /r/ and Substitution of /a/ for /ɑ/

One of the most distinguishing characteristics of New England speech is the omission of the semivowel /r/ and the substitution of the vowel /a/ (as in "<u>a</u>sk") for /ɑ/ (as in "f<u>a</u>ther").

Using negative practice as indicated by the column headings, read aloud the following word list. If your speech is a New England dialect, record the following exercises as presented and then reverse the procedure—rerecord the exercise using New England, career, and then New England pronunciations. This will sensitize you to the correct and incorrect sounds.

	CAREER	NEW ENGLAND	CAREER
park	[pɑrk]	[pak]	[pɑrk]
Harvard	[hɑrvɚd]	[havəd]	[hɑrvɚd]
sharp	[ʃɑrp]	[ʃap]	[ʃɑrp]
farm	[fɑrm]	[fam]	[fɑrm]
far	[fɑr]	[fa]	[fɑr]
army	[ɑrmɪ]	[amɪ]	[ɑrmɪ]
harm	[hɑrm]	[ham]	[hɑrm]
harp	[hɑrp]	[hap]	[hɑrp]
cart	[kɑrt]	[kat]	[kɑrt]
Arthur	[ɑrθɚ]	[aθə]	[ɑrθɚ]
partridge	[pɑrtrɪdʒ]	[patrɪdʒ]	[pɑrtrɪdʒ]
marvelous	[mɑrvələs]	[mavələs]	[mɑrvələs]
garter	[gɑrtɚ]	[gadə]	[gɑrtɚ]
harmonize	[hɑrmənaɪz]	[hamənaɪz]	[hɑrmənaɪz]
arson	[ɑrsən]	[asən]	[ɑrsən]
pardon	[pɑrdn̩]	[padn̩]	[pɑrdn̩]

In trying to correct this regionalism, very frequently the New Englander adds the consonant /r/ but retains the vowel /a/. This is not sufficient; the vowel must also be changed to /ɑ/.

Read aloud the following word lists.

	NEW ENGLAND	/a/ PLUS /r/	CAREER SPEECH
park	[pak]	[park]	[pɑrk]
Harvard	[havəd]	[harvəd]	[hɑrvɚd]
sharp	[ʃap]	[ʃarp]	[ʃɑrp]
farm	[fam]	[farm]	[fɑrm]
far	[fa]	[far]	[fɑr]
army	[amɪ]	[armɪ]	[ɑrmɪ]
harm	[ham]	[harm]	[hɑrm]
harp	[hap]	[harp]	[hɑrp]
cart	[kat]	[kart]	[kɑrt]

	NEW ENGLAND	/a/ PLUS /r/	CAREER SPEECH
Arthur	[aθə]	[arθə]	[ɑrθɚ]
partridge	[patrɪdʒ]	[partrɪdʒ]	[pɑrtrɪdʒ]
marvelous	[mavələs]	[marvələs]	[mɑrvələs]
garter	[gadə]	[gardə]	[gɑrtɚ]
harmonize	[hamənaɪz]	[harmənaɪz]	[hɑrmənaɪz]
arson	[asən]	[arsən]	[ɑrsən]
pardon	[padn̩]	[pardn̩]	[pɑrdn̩]

Use of [ɒ]

Refer to the discussion on the production of [ɒ] with the accompanying representative words and sentences (Chapter 6, pp. 115–116). In some areas of New England, this sound is distorted by opening the mouth too wide and using excessive lip action.

Addition of /r/

Frequently, the New Englander adds /r/ to the end of a word ending with the letter *w* or after /ɔ/ (as in "law"), especially when a vowel follows. Also, the New Englander often changes /ɔ/ to [ɒ] or /a/. This is particularly true when a word ending with /ɔ/ is followed by another word beginning with a vowel or a diphthong. For example, in the sentence "The winter thaw is beginning," the New Englander is likely to say "The winter thawr [θɒr] is beginning" because of the following vowel /ɪ/ in "is." But the same person probably would *not* say, "Hey, Robert, you're still waiting for the spring thaw(r)!" (But sometimes he does!)

Read aloud the following selections several times using negative practice. Do not hesitate to overdo the pronunciation of words so that you can feel the addition as well as the omission of /r/.

1. He didn't draw it today.

Career:	[hɪ ˈdɪdn̩t drɔ ɪt təˈdeɪ]
New England:	[hɪ ˈdɪdn̩t drɒr ɪt təˈdeɪ]
Career:	[hɪ ˈdɪdn̩t drɔ ɪt təˈdeɪ]

2. Steve was injured by the clawing tiger.

Career:	[stiv wəz ˈɪndʒɚd baɪ ðə ˈklɔɪŋ ˈtaɪgɚ]
New England:	[stiv wəz ˈɪndʒəd baɪ ðə ˈklɒrɪŋ ˈtaɪgə]
Career:	[stiv wəz ˈɪndʒɚd baɪ ðə ˈklɔɪŋ ˈtaɪgɚ]

3. Antigone had a flaw in her character.

Career:	[ænˈtɪgəni hæd ə flɔ ɪn hɚˈkærəktɚ]
New England:	[ænˈtɪgəni hæd ə flɒr ɪn ə ˈkærəktə]
Career:	[ænˈtɪgəni hæd ə flɔ ɪn hɚˈkærəktɚ]

4. A cawing bird can be very aggravating.

Career:	[ə kɔɪŋ bɝd kæn bi vɛri ˈægrəvetɪŋ]
New England:	[ə kɒrɪŋ bɝd kæn bi vɛri ˈægrəvetɪŋ]
Career:	[ə kɔɪŋ bɝd kæn bi vɛri ˈægrəvetɪŋ]

5. If you get tired, draw up a chair.

Career:	[ɪf ju gɛt taɪrd drɔ ʌp ə tʃɛr]
New England:	[ɪf jə gɛt taɪəd drɒr ʌp ə tʃeə]
Career:	[ɪf ju gɛt taɪrd drɔ ʌp ə tʃɛr]

6. Draw a picture.

Career:	[drɔ ə ˈpɪktʃɚ]
New England:	[drɒɹ ə ˈpɪtʃə]
Career:	[drɔ ə ˈpɪktʃɚ]

Intervocalic /r/

New Englanders do not omit all of their /r/ phonemes. Often the connecting or intervocalic /r/ is used when a word ending in /r/ or /ɚ/ (as in "after") is followed by a word beginning with a vowel, especially the vowel /ɪ/ (as in "bit").

In the following sentences, note when the /r/ or /ɚ/ is omitted or retained relative to the next sound.

This is Arthur's house. [ðɪs ɪz aθəz haʊs]
Arthu<u>r is</u> Greek. [aθ<u>ɚɪ</u>z grik]
Did you hear what I said? [dɪd ju hiə ʌʌt aɪ sɛd]
I hea<u>r it.</u> [aɪ h<u>ɪɹɪ</u>t]
I got a call from Aunt Martha. [aɪ gɒt ə kɔl frəm ant maθə]
Aunt Marth<u>a is</u> coming to dinner. [ant maθ<u>ɚɪ</u>z kʌmɪŋ tʊ dɪnə]

Substitution of /ɚ/ for /ə/

Another very recognizable and imitative New England speech characteristic is the substitution of the /ɚ/ for the schwa when it is the last sound in a word. President John F. Kennedy often used this sound.

Read aloud the following word list using negative practice. Do not hesitate to exaggerate the pronunciation because this will help you to feel the production.

	CAREER	NEW ENGLAND	CAREER
Asia	[eʒə]	[eʒɚ]	[eʒə]
pneumonia	[nɪumonjə]	[nɪumonjɚ]	[nɪumonjə]
idea	[aɪdiə]	[aɪdiɚ]	[aɪdiə]
stamina	[stæmɪnə]	[stæmɪnɚ]	[stæmɪnə]
umbrella	[əmbrɛlə]	[əmbrɛlɚ]	[əmbrɛlə]
euphoria	[jufɔrɪjə]	[jufɔrɪjɚ]	[jufɔrɪjə]
regalia	[rɪgeɪljə]	[rɪgeɪljɚ]	[rɪgeɪljə]
sofa	[sofə]	[sofɚ]	[sofə]
Alabama	[æləbæmə]	[æləbæmɚ]	[æləbæmə]
Cuba	[kjubə]	[kjubɚ]	[kjubə]

Substitution of /ɜ/ for /ɝ/

This distinguishing characteristic is slowly disappearing in New England. Some residents of parts of Maine, New Hampshire, Vermont, and Cape Cod still retain it and pass it along to their children. (For exercises, refer to the discussion of /ɜ/ on p. 103.)

Substitution of /ə/ for /ɚ/

This substitution is also characteristic of London speech. Read aloud the following word list using negative practice. Exaggerate the pronunciation so that you feel the production.

	CAREER	NEW ENGLAND	CAREER
sister	[sɪstɚ]	[sɪstə]	[sɪstɚ]
brother	[brʌðɚ]	[brʌðə]	[brʌðɚ]
mother	[mʌðɚ]	[mʌðə]	[mʌðɚ]
father	[faðɚ]	[faðə]	[faðɚ]
actor	[æktɚ]	[ækðə]	[æktɚ]
keeper	[kipɚ]	[kipə]	[kipɚ]
talker	[tɔkɚ]	[tɒkə]	[tɔkɚ]
walker	[wɔkɚ]	[wɒkə]	[wɔkɚ]
minister	[mɪnɪstɚ]	[mɪnɪstə]	[mɪnɪstɚ]
mister	[mɪstɚ]	[mɪstə]	[mɪstɚ]

Substitution of /a/ for /æ/

This substitution is typical of New England speech. Record the following words using negative practice.

	CAREER	NEW ENGLAND	CAREER
half	[hæf]	[haf]	[hæf]
bath	[bæθ]	[baθ]	[bæθ]
last	[læst]	[last]	[læst]
aunt	[ænt]	[ant]	[ænt]
ant	[ænt]	[ãnt][1]	[ænt]
fast	[fæst]	[fast]	[fæst]
cast	[kæst]	[kast]	[kæst]
passed	[pæst]	[past]	[pæst]
flask	[flæsk]	[flask]	[flæsk]
calf	[kæf]	[kaf]	[kæf]

Excessive Assimilation Nasality

New England speech often exhibits excessive assimilation nasality, although this characteristic is by no means limited to this region. You will remember that the modifying mark for nasality, [˜], is placed over the affected phoneme. (Refer to the drills on excessive assimilation nasality on pp. 67–70.)

EXERCISES FOR NEW ENGLAND AND CAREER SPEECH

Read aloud the following sentences, and exaggerate the pronunciation. Feel what the articulators are doing in the production of the sounds.

1. Asia and Africa are large continents.

Career:	[ˈeʒə ænd ˈæfrɪkə ɑr lɑrdʒ ˈkantənənts]
New England:	[ˈeʒɚ æ̃nd ˈæfrɪkɚ a ladʒ ˈkɒntn̩nts]
Career:	[ˈeʒə ænd ˈæfrɪkə ɑr lɑrdʒ ˈkantənənts]

2. Martha had the idea of bringing the umbrella to the beach.

---

[1]The New Englander distinguishes between "aunt" and "ant." (She resents being called an insect!) In addition, the New Englander tends to nasalize the vowel in "ant." You will notice that in career speech, the relative and the insect are pronounced the same—and without nasality on /æ/.

Career:	[ˈmɑrθə hæd ði aɪˈdiə əv ˈbrɪŋɪŋ ði əmˈbrɛlə tə ðə bitʃ]
New England:	[ˈmaθə hæd ði aɪˈdiɚ əv ˈbrɪŋɪŋ ði əmˈbrɛlə tə ðə bitʃ]
Career:	[ˈmɑrθə hæd ði aɪˈdiə əv ˈbrɪŋɪŋ ði əmˈbrɛlə tə ðə bitʃ]

3. Harvey must have had a lot of stamina to wear all that underwater regalia.

Career:	[ˈhɑrvɪ mʌst həv hæd ə lɑt əv ˈstæmɪnə tə wer ɔl ðæt ˈʌndɚˈwɑtɚ rəˈgeljə]
New England:	[ˈhavɪ mʌst həv hæd ə lɒt əv ˈstæmɪnə tə weə ɒl ðæt ˈʌndəˈwɒdə rəˈgeljɚ]
Career:	[ˈhɑrvɪ mʌst həv hæd ə lɒt əv ˈstæmɪnə tə wer ɔl ðæt ˈʌndɚˈwɑtɚ rəˈgeljə]

4. Since Margo had pneumonia, she was resting on the sofa.

Career:	[sɪns ˈmɑrgo hæd nɪuˈmonjə ʃɪ wəz ˈrɛstɪŋ ɑn ðə ˈsofə]
New England:	[sɪns ˈmago hæd nɪuˈmonjɚ ʃɪ wəz ˈrɛstɪŋ ɒn ðə ˈsofɚ]
Career:	[sɪns ˈmɑrgo hæd nɪuˈmonjə ʃɪ wəz ˈrɛstɪŋ ɑn ðə ˈsofə]

5. Georgia and Alabama are not too far from Cuba.

Career:	[ˈdʒɔrdʒə ænd æləˈbæmə ɑr nɑt tu fɑr frəm ˈkjubə]
New England:	[ˈdʒɒdʒɚ ænd æləˈbæmɚ a nɒ tu fɑ frəm ˈkjubɚ]
Career:	[ˈdʒɔrdʒə ænd æləˈbæmə ɑr nɑt tu fɑr frəm ˈkjubə]

In the following sentences, the New England sounds appear above the appropriate letters.

    ə ɜ   eə   ɜ   ɒ ɒ   ɜ
6. Mister Earl prepared herbs for all the servants.

     ɜ   ɜ   ɜ
7. The nurse was irked by the unworthy patient.

   ɜ   a ə   a ə a   a   ɒ   ɒ ɒ   a   ə   a ə
8. To avert disaster, the Master asked the aunt not to walk on the grass near the harbor.

     ə   ɜ   ɜ   ɜ   ɜ ɒ   ə
9. Richard Burton purchased an ermine fur for his sister.

     ɜ   ɜ   ɜ   ə   ɜ
10. Shirley was certain that she would smirk at the minister's sermon.

   eː   ɜ   a   a ə
11. Where is this person called Ma Barker?

    ɜ   ə   ɒ   ɜ   ɜ
12. Research the records for Myrtle's birthday.

In the following two selections, New England sounds are transcribed above the appropriate letters. Record it as you would usually say it. Then, emphasize the New England characteristics that magnify those phonemic elements characteristic of the dialect. Focus on the sound discrimination and production.

           a   ə
13. The ghost of Hãmlet's father speaks.

       a   ə
I ãm thy father's spirit;

      ɒ   ɜ   ɜ   ɒ
Doom'd for a certain term to walk the night,

    ɒ   a   ə
Ãnd, for the day, confin'd to fast in fires,

                            ə
Till the foul crimes done in my days of nature

        a   3   3   ə
Are burnt ãnd purg'd away. But that I ãm forbid

To tell the secrets of my prison-house,

                        3
I could a tale unfold whose lightest word

Would harrow up thy soul, freeze thy young blood,

          a   a   ə   ə
Make thy two eyes, like stars, start from their spheres,

        D   D   a
Thy knotted ãnd combined locks to part,

        ə   ə   ə   D
Ãnd each particular hair to stãnd on end,

          D   D
Like quills upon the fretful porpentine:

          3
But this eternal blazon must not be

                    ə
To ears of flesh ãnd blood—List, list, O list!

            ə   iə   a   ə
If thou didst ever thy dear father love— . . .

                    3   ə
Revenge his foul ãnd most unnatural murder.

From HÃMLET

William Shakespeare

                ə   D
14. Remember me when I ãm gone away,
     D   a
Gone far away into the silent lãnd;

                  ə
When you cãn no more hold me by the hãnd,
    D   a   3   3
Nor I half turn to go, yet turning stay.

        ə   ə
Remember me when no more, day by day,

      a   ə
You tell me of our future that you plãnned;

         ə   ə
Only remember me; you understãnd

                    D
It will be late to counsel then or pray.

             ə
Yet if you should forget me for a while

     a   ə   ə   ə   D
Ãnd afterwards remember do not grieve:
    D   a
For if the darkness ãnd corruption leave

               D
A vestige of the thoughts that once I had,

Better by far you should forget ãnd smile

Thãn that you should remember ãnd be sad.

REMEMBER

Christina Rossetti

In the following selections, there is room for you to add the symbols for the New England sounds above the appropriate letters. These selections were written for New England characters. Record the selections with your habitual speech and then with a New England dialect. These exercises are recommended for students who wish to acquire a New England dialect for special reasons.

15. *Mr. Webb:* Well, ma'am, I wouldn't know what you'd call much. Satiddy nights the farmhands meet down in Ellery Greenough's stable and holler some. We've got one or two town drunks, but they're always having remorses every time an evangelist comes to town. No ma'am, I'd say likker ain't a regular thing in the home here, except in the medicine chest.

From OU TOWN

Thornton Wilder

16. *Cabot:* I cal'clate God give it to 'em—not yew! God's hard, not easy! Mebbe they's easy gold in the West but it hain't fur me. I kin hear His voice warnin' me agin t' be hard an' stay on my farm. I kin see his hand usin' Eben t' steal t' keep me from weakness. I kin feel I be in the palm o' His hand, His fingers guidin' me. It's a-goin' t' be lonesomer now than ever it war afore—an' I'm gettin' old, Lord, ripe on the bough. . . . Waal—what d'ye want? God's lonesome, hain't He? God's hard an' lonesome!

From DESIRE UNDER THE ELMS
Eugene O'Neill

17. For those of you who have difficulty with the phonetic transcription of "Yankonics," try the following taken from the Internet:

Pahty: A place to go drink and socialize—nothing to do with Mother Nature.
ah: The letter between "q" and "s".
ahnt: Sistah of your fathah or muthah.
bah: Serves beah and hahd likkah. "The train to Noo Yok has a bah cah".
bay-ah: Ferocious brown or black animal.
beah: Malt beverage.
bzah: Strange, odd.
Chahiz: The rivah.
chowdah: Clams, Milk, budah.
connah: Where streets intersect.
fah: Not neah heah.
fiah: Blaze.
Gahden: What they closed down last yeah (also "last cheea" a place to plant flowahs).
hahbah: What they dumped tea into in 1773.
Havid: Preppy college across the rivah.

heah: Done with the eahs. "Listen my children, and you shall heah of the
                midnight ride of Paul Reveah".
khakis: What you staht the cah with and keep on yawh key chain.
nawtheastah: Stohm that blows in from the wodah.

>>> NEW YORK CITY

The cawafee in Manhattan (dentalized, of course) is so strawang!

Although the inhabitants of Brooklyn, the Bronx, Queens, Staten Island, and Manhattan do not all have the same dialect, they do share certain speech characteristics. Some of the more frequently heard are discussed in this section. As in the New England dialect, the New York City dialect contains sound distortions, omissions, and additions.

If you speak with a New York City dialect, record the following word lists as presented, rerecord them with a New York City dialect, then with career speech, and finally with a New York City dialect. This routine gives you more practice at producing the corrected and erroneous sounds consciously. The same technique can be used by non–New Yorkers who want to acquire a New York City dialect for professional reasons. As you do this exercise, feel what is happening to your articulators.

Vowels

Substitution of /oə/ for /ɔ/

The sound /oə/ is not the exact substitution used for /ɔ/ (as in "law"), but it does approximate the vowels used by New Yorkers. An exact representation of the New York City sound would require a discussion far too complex for the purposes of this text.

Record the following word lists.

	CAREER	NEW YORK CITY	CAREER
awful	[ɔful]	[oəful]	[ɔful]
coffee	[kɔfɪ]	[koəfɪ]	[kɔfɪ]
lawless	[lɔləs]	[loələs]	[lɔləs]
salt	[sɔlt]	[soəlt]	[sɔlt]
water	[wɔtɚ]	[woədə]	[wɔtɚ]
small	[smɔl]	[smoəl]	[smɔl]
bought	[bɔt]	[boət]	[bɔt]
caller	[kɔlɚ]	[koələ]	[kɔlɚ]
faucet	[fɔsət]	[foəsət]	[fɔsət]
fought	[fɔt]	[foət]	[fɔt]

In the following sentences, the New York City sounds appear above the appropriate letters.

            oə   ə   oə
There are many authors in Boston.
   oə   oə   oəs
The Australian and the Austrian met because of chănce.
   oə   oə
The auspicious bankers insisted on an audit.
   oə   oə   oə   oə
My boss thought that the longer song was the bedə one.
   oə   oə   oə oə
The awful battle was fought for a lost cause.

Substitution of /ɛə/ for /eɪ/

One of the best exercises to work on this error is to divide the following words into additional words. Take the time to prolong the first word before pronouncing the second. Then, put them together in one monosyllabic word (except the last word, *regale*).

pay͡ill → pale
Fay͡ill → fail
day͡Lee → daily
say͡ill → sale
nay͡ill → nail
may͡ill man → mailman
Ray͡ill → rail
stay͡ill → stale
Kay͡ill → kale
bay͡ill → bail
Jay͡ill → jail
flay͡ill → flail
bray͡ill → brail
tray͡ill → trail
re gay͡ill → regale

Once you have recorded this substitution you will be more aware of it and will be able to use it if ever necessary.

	CAREER	NEW YORK CITY	CAREER
pale	[peɪl]	[pɛəl]	[peɪl]
fail	[feɪl]	[fɛəl]	[feɪl]
sailor	[seɪlɚ]	[sɛələ]	[seɪlɚ]
failure	[feɪljɚ]	[fɛəljə]	[feɪljɚ]
daily	[deɪlɪ]	[dɛəlɪ]	[deɪlɪ]
sale	[seɪl]	[sɛəl]	[seɪl]
nail	[neɪl]	[nɛəl]	[neɪl]
mailman	[meɪlmæn]	[mɛəlmæ̃n]	[meɪlmæn]
rail	[reɪl]	[rɛəl]	[reɪl]
stale	[steɪl]	[stɛəl]	[steɪl]

     ɛə   ɛə   oə
The mailmãn delivered the *New York Daily News* to me at the ball game.
oə   ɛə ə   ɛə
All of the plãns to rescue the sailors failed.
     ɛə   ɛə
The railroad stumps were for sale for forty dollars.
oə   ɛə   ɛə   ɛə   ɛə
Although the air was stale, the frail stream of smoke left a trail.
    ɛə   ɛə   ɛə
Gail put down her pail ãnd watched the boats sail by.

Substitution of /ɛə/ for /æ/

	CAREER	NEW YORK CITY	CAREER
apple	[æpl̩]	[ɛəpl̩]	[æpl̩]
mask	[mæsk]	[mɛəsk]	[mæsk]

	Career	New York City	Career
balance	[bæləns]	[bɛələns]	[bæləns]
gallon	[gælən]	[gɛələn]	[gælən]
pastoral	[pæstərl̩]	[pɛəstərl̩]	[pæstərl̩]
galaxy	[gæləksɪ]	[gɛələksɪ]	[gæləksɪ]
glad	[glæd]	[glɛəd]	[glæd]
hash	[hæʃ]	[hɛəʃ]	[hæʃ]
calf	[kæf]	[kɛəf]	[kæf]
half	[hæf]	[hɛəf]	[hæf]

    ɛə   ɛə   ɛə   ɛə
Carol gave Harry a back scratcher for his birthday.

        ɛə   ɛə   ɛə
The masked bãndit grabbed the calf ãnd rãn.

    ɛə   ɛə   oə   ɛə   ɛə
Harold has been called a rough taskmaster by his students.

 ɛə   oə   ɛə   ɛə   oə
Ask if he saw the tãn cat attack the dog.

               ɛə   ɛə
Crãmming for exãms is a bad habit.

Substitution of /æʊ/ for /ɑʊ/

Remember that /ɑʊ/ is an acceptable *allophone* of /aʊ/. Record the following list of words and sentences as transcribed. Focus on the New York City substitutions.

	Career	New York City	Career
owl	[ɑʊl]	[æʊl]	[ɑʊl]
south	[sɑʊθ]	[sæʊθ]	[sɑʊθ]
housekeeper	[hɑʊskipɚ]	[hæʊskipə]	[hɑʊskipɚ]
devout	[dɪvɑʊt]	[dɪvæʊt]	[dɪvɑʊt]
tower	[tɑʊɚ]	[tæʊə]	[tɑʊɚ]
outside	[ɑʊtsaɪd]	[æʊtsaɪd]	[ɑʊtsaɪd]
shout	[ʃɑʊt]	[ʃæʊt]	[ʃɑʊt]
drown	[drɑʊn]	[dræʊn]	[drɑʊn]
bow	[bɑʊ]	[bæʊ]	[bɑʊ]
Browning	[brɑʊnɪŋ]	[bræʊnɪŋ]	[brɑʊnɪŋ]

    æʊ   oə   æʊ   æʊ   æʊ
Howard thought it was about time to go around the house.

    æʊ   æʊ   æʊ
The mountainous terrain made it doubtful that we could go south.

    æʊ   æʊ   æʊ
Browning and Houseman are our favorite poets.

      æʊ   æʊ   æʊ
When she scowled and pouted, I went outside.

    æʊ   æʊ   æʊ
The brown cows were particularly foul smelling.

Substitution of /ɒɪ/ for /aɪ/

Record the following list of words and sentences as transcribed. Focus on the New York City substitutions.

	CAREER	NEW YORK CITY	CAREER
eye	[aɪ]	[ɒɪ]	[aɪ]
final	[faɪn̩]	[fɒɪn̩]	[faɪn̩]
daylight	[delaɪt]	[delɒɪt]	[delaɪt]
island	[aɪlənd]	[ɒɪlənd]	[aɪlənd]
stylish	[staɪlɪʃ]	[stɒɪlɪʃ]	[staɪlɪʃ]
diary	[daɪərɪ]	[dɒɪərɪ]	[daɪərɪ]
certify	[sɝtəfaɪ]	[sɝtəfɒɪ]	[sɝtəfaɪ]
biography	[baɪɑgrəfɪ]	[bɒɪɑgrəfɪ]	[baɪɑgrəfɪ]
guide	[gaɪd]	[gɒɪd]	[gaɪd]
rise	[raɪz]	[rɒɪz]	[raɪz]

    ɒɪ   ɒɪ   ɒɪ
The bicycle arrived just in time.

ɒɪ   ɒɪ   ɒɪ
Iris got a diamond ring from Byron.

      ɒɪ   ɒɪ   ɒɪ
At the height of the lightning storm they arrived.

    ɒɪ   ɒɪ   ɒɪ
The license certified that they could photograph the lions.

ɒɪ   ɒɪ   ɒɪ
I'll not ask the guide to drive the Jeep.

Substitution of /ɔ/ for /ɑr/

Record the following list of words and sentences as transcribed. Focus on the New York City substitutions.

	CAREER	NEW YORK CITY	CAREER
park	[pɑrk]	[pɔk]	[pɑrk]
Harvard	[hɑrvɚd]	[hɔvəd]	[hɑrvɚd]
cart	[kɑrt]	[kɔt]	[kɑrt]
pardon	[pɑrdn̩]	[pɔdn̩]	[pɑrdn̩]
hearty	[hɑrtɪ]	[hɔtɪ]	[hɑrtɪ]
char	[tʃɑr]	[tʃɔ]	[tʃɑr]
carving	[kɑrvɪŋ]	[kɔvɪŋ]	[kɑrvɪŋ]
Darth	[dɑrθ]	[dɔθ]	[dɑrθ]
barn	[bɑrn]	[bɔn]	[bɑrn]
lard	[lɑrd]	[lɔd]	[lɑrd]

   ɔ   ɔ   ɔ   ɔ
Park the car in Harvard Yard.

   ɔ   ɔ
Marvin slipped in the barn.

   ɔ   ɔ
Hark and hear the lark.

ɔ   ə   ɔ   ɔ
Arthur carved the turkey for the starving people.

          ɔ   ə   æʊ   ɔ   ə
The farmer's cow was farther up the road.

Substitution of /ɛɪ/ for /ɛr/

Record the following list of words and sentences as transcribed. Focus on the New York City substitutions.

	CAREER	NEW YORK CITY[2]	CAREER
their	[ðɛr][3]	[ðɛ̱ɪ]	[ðɛr][3]
wear	[wɛr][3]	[wɛ̱ɪ]	[wɛr][3]
hair	[hɛr][3]	[hɛ̱ɪ]	[hɛr][3]
fair	[fɛr][3]	[fɛ̱ɪ]	[fɛr][3]
where	[ʍɛr][3]	[ʍɛ̱ɪ]	[ʍɛr][3]
stair	[stɛr][3]	[stɛ̱ɪ]	[stɛr][3]
Claire	[klɛr][3]	[klɛ̱ɪ]	[klɛr][3]
airplane	[ɛrplen]	[ɛːplen]	[ɛrplen]
hairline	[hɛrlaɪn]	[hɛ̱ɪlɒɪn]	[hɛrlaɪn]
bear	[bɛr][3]	[bɛ̱ɪ]	[bɛr][3]

     ɛɪ   ɛɪ   ɛɪ
Claire was wearing a new hairdo.

       ɛɪ   ɔ   ɛɪ   ɛɪ
It is unfair to charge so much fare for the airplane.

          ɛɪ   ɛɪ
Billie Rich's hair went everywhere when she dãnced.

            ɛɪ   ɛɪ
If provoked, they would tear their fur.

       ɛɪ   ɛɪ
The bear cub went where?

Substitution of /ɛu/ for /o/ and /oʊ/

Record the following list of words and sentences as transcribed. Focus on the New York City substitutions.

	CAREER	NEW YORK CITY	CAREER
going	[goɪŋ]	[gɛ̱ʊɪŋ]	[goɪŋ]
follow	[fɑlou]	[fɑlɛ̱ʊ]	[fɑlou]
goat	[got]	[gɛ̱ʊt]	[got]
smoke	[smok]	[smɛ̱ʊk]	[smok]
rope	[rop]	[rɛ̱ʊp]	[rop]
slowly	[slouli]	[slɛ̱ʊli]	[slouli]
showed	[ʃoud]	[ʃɛ̱ʊd]	[ʃoud]
folder	[foldɚ]	[fɛ̱ʊldə]	[foldɚ]
almost	[ɔlmost]	[oəlmɛ̱ʊst]	[ɔlmost]
shallow	[ʃælou]	[ʃælɛ̱ʊ]	[ʃælou]
spoke	[spok]	[spɛ̱ʊk]	[spok]

     ɛʊ   ɛʊ   ɛʊ
Joe was the only one with yellow hair.

     ɛʊ   ɛʊ ɛʊ
Go and get both folders.

---

[2]Note that the addition of [ə] after [ɛɪ] is also possible (for example, [ɛɪ̱ə] or [ðɛɪ̱ə] for [ðɛɪ̱r]).
[3]These are the pronunciations used in dynamic speech rather than those used for isolated words.

εu   ɒɪ   εu   εu
Snow White sang "Heigh Ho" with Dopey.
    εu   oə   oə εu
Coal costs almost double.
    εu   εu   æu
In poker the joker does not count.

Consonants

Dentalization of /t/, /d/, /n/, and /l/

New York City speech is often dentalized, which means that the entire blade of the tongue rather than just the tip is in contact with the alveolar ridge in the production of /t/, /d/, /n/, and /l/. This articulation gives a heavier sound. Although other sounds may also be dentalized, these are certainly the most characteristic of New York City speech. Remember that the modifying mark [̪] is placed under the dentalized sound.

	CAREER	NEW YORK CITY	CAREER
tender	[tɛndɚ]	[tɛn̪də]	[tɛndɚ]
dandelion	[dændəlaɪən]	[dæn̪dəlɒɪən]	[dændəlaɪən]
undersized	[ʌndɚsɑɪzd]	[ʌn̪dəsɒɪzd̪]	[ʌndɚsɑɪzd]
tantalize	[tæntəlaɪz]	[tæn̪təlɒɪz]	[tæntəlaɪz]
tonsillitis	[tansɪlaɪtəs]	[tan̪sɪlɒɪtəs]	[tansɪlaɪtəs]
dentalize	[dɛntəlaɪz]	[d̪ɛn̪təlɒɪz]	[dɛntəlaɪz]
dictate	[dɪktet]	[d̪ɪktet]	[dɪktet]
lullaby	[lʌləbaɪ]	[l̪ʌləbɒɪ]	[lʌləbaɪ]
notate	[notet]	[n̪eutet̪]	[notet]
lollipop	[lalɪpap]	[l̪alɪpap]	[lalɪpap]

N̪an̪ette d̪id̪n̪'t̪ mean̪ to d̪o it̪.

What̪ is the mean̪ing of the word *d̪ilet̪tan̪te?*

Wil̪ma, pl̪ease pl̪ace the t̪in where Bil̪lie can̪ fin̪d̪ it.

The smel̪l̪ of t̪ar̪t̪s was t̪oo t̪an̪t̪alizing for N̪ancy.

    εu   εu   ɒɪ
Joey, d̪o you kn̪ow what̪ t̪ime it̪ is?

Substitution of /t/ for /θ/, /d/ for /ð/, and /ɔɪ/ for /ɝ/

Although these substitutions are often associated with Brooklyn and the Bronx, it is also typical of sections of many large cities, including Philadelphia, Boston, and Chicago. It is most colorfully represented in the speech of many Damon Runyon characters. For the following exercise, these substitutions will be labeled "Runyonesque."

	CAREER	RUNYONESQUE	CAREER
mother	[mʌðɚ]	[mʌdə]	[mʌðɚ]
other	[ʌðɚ]	[ʌdə]	[ʌðɚ]
weather	[wɛðɚ]	[wɛdə]	[wɛðɚ]
both	[boθ]	[bot̪]	[boθ]
either	[iðɚ]	[idə]	[iðɚ]
tooth	[tuθ]	[tut̪]	[tuθ]
this	[ðɪs]	[d̪ɪs]	[ðɪs]

	CAREER	RUNYONESQUE	CAREER
truth	[truθ]	[trut]	[truθ]
without	[wɪðɑut]	[wɪdæut]	[wɪðɑut]
thirty	[θɜˑtɪ]	[tɔɪdɪ]	[θɜˑtɪ]
		[tɜˑdɪ]	
murder	[mɜˑdɚ]	[mɔɪdə]	[mɜˑdɚ]
hurt	[hɜˑt]	[hɔɪt]	[hɜˑt]
curtain	[kɜˑtn̩]	[kɔɪtn̩]	[kɜˑtn̩]
surf	[sɜˑf]	[sɔɪf]	[sɜˑf]
smirk	[smɜˑk]	[smɔɪk]	[smɜˑk]
curt	[kɜˑt]	[kɔɪt]	[kɜˑt]
Murphy	[mɜˑfɪ]	[mɔɪfɪ]	[mɜˑfɪ]
curfew	[kɜˑfju]	[kɔɪfju]	[kɜˑfju]
Smurf	[smɜˑf]	[smɔɪf]	[smɜˑf]
Shirley	[ʃɜˑlɪ]	[ʃɔɪlɪ]	[ʃɜˑlɪ]

      ɔɪ   d d   d ə

Shirley played with the other kids.

                d ə   d ə   dæu   t

Andrea's father and mother went without a lot of things.

      d ə   εu d   εu ɒɪ d

Either Danny will go or they'll go by themselves.

    d   d   t   æu d   t

The dentist didn't tell the truth about the toothache

     dæu d   ə d   εu

Without this paper there's no proof.

EXERCISES FOR NEW YORK CITY AND CAREER SPEECH

The following sentences are transcribed into career speech and New York City speech. As you produce the sounds, listen and feel what is happening to the articulators.

1. Herb sat on the curb.

Career:	[hɜˑb sæt ɑn ðə kɜˑb]
New York City:	[hɔɪb sɛɐt ãn̯ də kɔɪb] (Runyonesque speech)
Career:	[hɜˑb sæt ɑn ðə kɜˑb]

2. You want a cup of coffee?

Career:	[ju wɑnt ə kʌp ə kɔfɪ]
New York City:	[jə wɑn̯ə kʌp ə koəfɪ]
Career:	[ju wɑnt ə kʌp ə kɔfɪ]

3. Tom is down the hall.

Career:	[tɑm ɪz dɑun ðə hɔl]
New York City:	[tɑm ɪz dæun də hoəl]
Career:	[tɑm ɪz dɑun ðə hɔl]

4. Finally, it is all done.

Career:	[faɪnəlɪ ɪt ɪz ɔl dʌn]
New York City:	[fɒɪnəlɪ ɪt̯ ɪz oəl̯ dʌn̯]
Career:	[faɪnəlɪ ɪt ɪz ɔl dʌn]

5. I couldn't care less.

Career: [aɪ kʊdn̩t kɛr lɛs]
New York City: [ɒɪ kʊdn̩t kɛː lɛs]
Career: [aɪ kʊdn̩t kɛr lɛs]

Each of the following speeches was written for a person with New York City speech. In exercise 6, the playwright attempted to indicate the New York City street dialect through spelling. The actual sound substitutions are transcribed above the letters. Room has been left above the remaining speeches to make your own phonetic notations. First, record the material as transcribed. Then, record it in your habitual speech (which we hope is career speech!), and compare it with your New York City version.

               oə   ɒɪ   oə   æks   oə

6. *Tommy:* Nah, dey're all wise tuh us. Duh minute we walk in, 'ey asks us wadda we want.

                ɛu   ɒɪ   ɒɪ   ɒɪ   ɒɪ

If we had some dough, while one uv us wuz buyin' sumpm, de udduh guys could swipe

                                                   ɛu

some stuff, see? I got faw cents, but 'at am' enough. Anybody got any dough heah? Hey,

yew, Angel, yuh got some?

From DEAD END
Sidney Kingsley

7. *Velma:* It's my mother's blood! I didn't know what to do. I don't . . . know why I did it! I don't even really remember that much, Frankie. When I got in the subway to come to work afterwards it was just like nuthin' happened, nuthin' at all! But do you know? I thought, I thought when my mother asked me to cover her piece of coffee cake with a whole lot of caviar, I thought . . . my mother . . . she thinks that my head is a hammer! That's what she thinks. And it isn't! It isn't! Tell me, Frankie, please tell me that my head is not a hammer!

From BIRDBATH
Leonard Melfi

8. *Gittel Mosca:* Sophie. Is Oscar there?—Well, listen, that hat-type friend of his last night, the long one, what's his number?—Look, girl, will you drag your mind up out of your girdle and go see if Oscar's got it written down?

From TWO FOR THE SEESAW
William Gibson

9. *Billie Dawn:* My father? Gas Company. He used to read meters, but in this letter he says how he can't get around so good anymore so they gave him a different job. Elevator man. Goofy old guy. He used to take a little frying pan to work every morning and a can of Sterno and cook his own lunch. He said everybody should have a hot lunch.

From BORN YESTERDAY
Garson Kanin

>>>
SOUTHERN

"Ah told ya to be home bah nahn or tin o'clock and don't argy with me!"

Because there are so many dialects and subdialects in Southern speech, it would be impractical to present all of them in a text on voice and articulation. The purpose of this chapter is only to give you a flavor of the four major American-English dialects.

In representing a Southerner's speech, it is common to indicate the lilting pitch. Compared with the other major American-English dialects, the Southern dialect contains many more variations in pitch. However, these changes cannot be represented by a phonetic alphabet. To show such acoustical phenomena, **suprasegmental features** (those aspects of speech that concern more than individual phonemes, such as duration and stress) must be used, but that is a topic that is beyond the scope of this chapter. Therefore, only the major phonemic substitutions and omissions will be presented here.

Vowels and Diphthongs

Many people, particularly Northerners, feel that the Southern drawl results from prolonging the sounds: "It takes them so-o-o-o-o lo-o-ong to say what they want to saaa-ay!" Actually, the Southerner takes no more time to produce an individual sound than anyone else does. This false impression stems from the many **triphthongs** used in Southern speech.

Addition of /jə/ to /ɪ/ and /æ/

These sounds are used primarily in monosyllabic words. Record the following list of words and sentences as transcribed. Focus on the Southern additions.

	CAREER	SOUTHERN	CAREER
flit	flɪt]	[flɪjət]	[flɪt]
been	[bɪn]	[bɪjən]	[bɪn]
wit	[wɪt]	[wɪjət]	[wɪt]
grip	[grɪp]	[grɪjəp]	[grɪp]
inch	[ɪntʃ]	[ɪjəntʃ]	[ɪntʃ]
tryst	[trɪst]	[trɪjəst]	[trɪst]
mince	[mɪns]	[mɪjəns]	[mɪns]
trim	[trɪm]	[trɪjəm]	[trɪm]
chip	[tʃɪp]	[tʃɪjəp]	[tʃɪp]
pick	[pɪk]	[pɪjək]	[pɪk]
man	[mæn]	[mæjən]	[mæn]
handle	[hændl̩]	[hæjəndl̩]	[hændl̩]
Fran	[fræn]	[fræjən]	[fræn]
can	[kæn]	[kæjən]	[kæn]
band	[bænd]	[bæjənd]	[bænd]
candy	[kændɪ]	[kæjəndɪ]	[kændɪ]
Nancy	[nænsɪ]	[næjənsɪ]	[nænsɪ]
bad	[bæd]	[bæjəd]	[bæd]
lamb	[læm]	[læjəm]	[læm]
trapped	[træpt]	[træjəpt]	[træpt]

   ɪjə   ɪjə   a
Pick up the mince pie.
æjə   æjə a   ɪjə   ɪjə
Andrea can buy the pig for Midge.
   æjə   æjə æjə ɪjə
Danny loves ham and pickles.
   æjə   æjə   ɪjə   ɪ
Fran was trapped amid the members.
    ɪjə ɪjə   æjə   æjə ɪjə ɪjə ɪjə
Chris gripped the brash young man with his fist.

Substitution of /a/ for /aɪ/

Record the following list of words and sentences as transcribed. Focus on the Southern substitutions.

	CAREER	SOUTHERN	CAREER
buy	[baɪ]	[ba]	[baɪ]
like	[laɪk]	[lak]	[laɪk]
smile	[smaɪl]	[smal]	[smaɪl]
hi	[haɪ]	[ha]	[haɪ]
try	[traɪ]	[tra]	[traɪ]
hide	[haɪd]	[had]	[haɪd]
spied	[spaɪd]	[spad]	[spaɪd]
tightly	[taɪtlɪ]	[tatlɪ]	[taɪtlɪ]
frightful	[fraɪtfʊl]	[fratfʊl]	[fraɪtfʊl]
cried	[kraɪd]	[krad]	[kraɪd]

         a   a   a   ə
I saw the brightest smile ever.

              a   a   a   ə
The Blythe building was slightly higher.

      a   a   æjə
Hide that frightful hat.

ıjə a   a   ə   ə
It's a crime to spy on your neighbors.

         ə a   a   a   ə
Mister Hyde tried to like Doctor Jekyll.

Substitution of /ɪ/ for /ɛ/ before the Nasal Consonants

Record the following list of words and sentences as transcribed. Focus on the Southern substitutions.

	CAREER	SOUTHERN	CAREER
men	[mɛn]	[mɪn]	[mɛn]
hem	[hɛm]	[hɪm]	[hɛm]
then	[ðɛn]	[ðɪn]	[ðɛn]
friend	[frɛnd]	[frɪnd]	[frɛnd]
blend	[blɛnd]	[blɪnd]	[blɛnd]
Flemish	[flɛmɪʃ]	[flɪmɪʃ]	[flɛmɪʃ]
chemist	[kɛmɪst]	[kɪmɪst]	[kɛmɪst]
lend	[lɛnd]	[lɪnd]	[lɛnd]
spend	[spɛnd]	[spɪnd]	[spɛnd]
phlegm	[flɛm]	[flɪm]	[flɛm]

                      ɪ   ɪ   ɪ
Blair and Beverly asked for benefits for ten men.

   ɪ   ɪ   ɪ
Penny's expensive pendant was stolen.

   ɪ   ɪ   ɪ
Ken's intention was to place emphasis on proper words.

I   I
French and chemistry were pleasant lessons.
I   I   I   I
Wendy marked the length of the hem with a pencil.

Substitution of /ə/ for /ɚ/

New Englanders make this same substitution. As a matter of fact, New Englanders and Southerners share several speech characteristics. (See the words and sentences on pp. 305–306)

Substitution of /ɜ/ for /ɝ /

This is another New England characteristic. (Refer to the selections on pp. 103–104.)

Substitution of /oə/ for /or/

This substitution is also characteristic of the New England dialect. Record the following list of words and sentences as transcribed.

	CAREER	SOUTHERN	CAREER
bore	[bor]	[boə]	[bor]
sore	[sor]	[soə]	[sor]
tore	[tor]	[toə]	[tor]
snore	[snor]	[snoə]	[snor]
chore	[ʧor]	[ʧoə]	[ʧor]
more	[mor]	[moə]	[mor]
roar	[ror]	[roə]	[ror]
lore	[lor]	[loə]	[lor]
galore	[gəlor]	[gəloə]	[gəlor]
adore	[ədor]	[ədoə]	[ədor]
shore	[ʃor]	[ʃoə]	[ʃor]

a   oə   a   oə
I adore watching Dinah Shore.
          oə   ə   oə
What more can be said about dinner chores?
       oə   oə ə   æjə
He tore the border of the map.
a   oə   ɪ   oə
I roared at the jokes and then was sore.
       oə   oə   oə
Morley snorted at the folklore.

Substitution of /e/ for /ɛ/ before /r/

Record the following list of words as transcribed.

	CAREER	SOUTHERN	CAREER
gregarious	[grəgɛrɪəs]	[grəgerɪəs]	[grəgɛrɪəs]
various	[vɛrɪəs]	[verɪəs]	[vɛrɪəs]
fairy	[fɛːrɪ]	[feːrɪ]	[fɛːrɪ]
variable	[vɛrɪəbl]	[verɪəbl]	[vɛrɪəbl]

dairy	[dɛːrɪ]	[deːrɪ]	[dɛːrɪ]
Mary	[mɛːrɪ]	[meːrɪ]	[mɛːrɪ]
prairie	[prɛːrɪ]	[preːrɪ]	[prɛːrɪ]

Substitution of /a/ or /ɑ/ for /æ/

This substitution is also characteristic of New England speech. (Refer to the word lists on p. 306

Substitution of /æʊ/ for /aʊ/

Refer to the words related to the New York City regionalism on page 312.

Consonants

Omission of /l/ When Followed by a Consonant

This omission is very typical of some Southern dialects. Record the following list of words as transcribed.

	CAREER	SOUTHERN	CAREER
film	[fɪlm]	[fɪm]	[fɪlm]
help	[hɛlp]	[hɛp]	[hɛlp]
whelp	[ʍɛlp]	[ʍɛp]	[ʍɛlp]
self	[sɛlf]	[sɛf]	[sɛlf]
alfalfa	[ælfælfə]	[æfæfə]	[ælfælfə]
themselves	[ðɛmsɛlvz]	[ðɛmsɛvz]	[ðɛmsɛlvz]

Substitution of /n/ for /ŋ/ in "-ing"

This substitution is common in sloppy speech.

	CAREER	SOUTHERN	CAREER
singing	[sɪŋɪŋ]	[sɪŋɪn]	[sɪŋɪŋ]
going	[goɪŋ]	[goɪn]	[goɪŋ]
laughing	[læfɪŋ]	[læjəfɪn]	[læfɪŋ]
walking	[wɔkɪŋ]	[wɔkɪn]	[wɔkɪŋ]
driving	[draɪvɪŋ]	[dravɪn]	[draɪvɪŋ]

EXERCISES FOR SOUTHERN AND CAREER SPEECH

1. The following 1775 speech by Patrick Henry was spoken in British English, of course. However, read the speech aloud with the transcribed Southern characteristics.

      ɜ   æjə a   ɔ   æjə e
They tell us, sir, that we are weak—unable to cope with so formidable an adversary.

   ɪ   ə   ɔ   jiə
But when shall we be stronger? Will it be the next week, or the next year? Will it be

   ɪ   a   a   ɪ   a
when we are totally disarmed, and when a British guard shall be stationed in every

æʊ   æjəə   ɪn   a   æjə æjə
house? Shall we gather strength by irresolution and inaction?

In the following sentences, the sounds substituted in Southern speech are transcribed above the appropriate letters.

a a   ɪjəin   ɪjə   æjə
2. I like sipping on mint juleps on the veranda.

æjə ə æjə ɪ   a   æʊ ɪjə
3. Pat never had any anxiety about it.

a   a   a ɪjə ɜ   o   ɪjə   ɪn
4. My, my, my, it certainly is warm this evening.

a   æjəɜ   æjə   æjə   ə
5. I'm as nervous as a long-tailed cat in a room full of rockers.

a   æjə   oə ɪn   æjə
6. Mighty glad to see you this morning ma'am.

aɪ   ɪjə ɪn   a   ɪjə
7. I can fix things up right quick.

a a   a   oə   æ a
8. Hi! I'm Dinah from North Carolina.

ɪ   ɪ   a   a   a   ɪ
9. Gentlemen, may I remind you, there are ladies present.

ɛː a   ɜ ɪn   ɜ ɪn æjə
10. Where are the Worthingtons of Birmingham?

ejə æjə   ə
11. Well, at his age it ought to be clear!

Place the phonetic transcriptions above the appropriate letters to reflect a Southern accent in the following exercises. Then, record them with the Southern pronunciation.

12. Women can take more time 'cause they've got more of it to take: like I told you, vita statistics don't lie and they have established the fact that the average woman outlives the average man by a good ten years. At least! That explains their total disregard of time coming and going, when a man's waiting for them. They secretly, in their subconscious, enjoy! revel! in their extra ten years on earth, and secretly enjoy the revel in the man's rapid decline.

æ jə
From THE FROSTED GLASS COFFIN

ɪ ɪ
Tennessee Williams

ɪ

13. *Richard Henry Lee:* I'll leave tonight—why, hell, right now, if y'like! I'll stop off at Stratford just long enough to refresh the missus, and then straight to the matter. Virginia, the land that gave us our glorious commander-in-chief, George Washington, will now give the continent its proposal on independence. And when Virginia proposes, the South is bound to follow, and where the South goes the Middle Colonies go! Gentlemen, a salute! To Virginia, the Mother of American Independence.

From 1776
Peter Stone

ɜ

14. *BirdiE:* Me, young? Maybe you better find Simon and tell him to do it himself. He's to look in my desk, the left drawer, and bring my music album right away. Mr. Marshall is very anxious to see it because of his father and the opera in Chicago. Mr. Marshall is a polite man with his manners and very educated and cultured, and I've told him all about how my mama and papa used to go to Europe for the music.

From THE LITTLE FOXES
Lillian Hellman

15. "That's a fact," Ratliff said. "A fellow can dodge a Snopes if he just starts lively enough. In fact, I don't believe he would have to pass more than two folks before he would have another victim intervened betwixt them. You folks ain't going to buy them things, sho enough, are you?"

From SPOTTED HORSES
William Faulkner

 æjə

16. *Amanda:* Ella Cartwright? This is Amanda Wingfield. How are you, honey? How is that kidney infection? Horrors . . . You're a Christian martyr, yes, honey, that's what you are, a Christian martyr.

                    æjə   ɪ   æjə
From THE GLASS MENAGERIE
ɪ   ɪ
Tennessee Williams

17. *Boss Finley:* Do you remember the clip I bought your mama? Last thing I give your mama before she died. . . . I knowed she was dying before I bought that clip, and I bought that clip for fifteen thousand dollars, mainly to make her think that she was going to get well. . . . When I pinned it on her on the night gown she was wearing, that poor thing started to crying.

                    ɜ
From SWEET BIRD OF YOUTH
ɪ   ɪ
Tennessee Williams

18. The author in the following speech attempts to indicate the Southern dialect through spelling. There are, however, additional sound substitutions that you should indicate.

Cherie: I dunno why I keep expectin' m'self to fall in love with someone, but I do. I'm beginnin' to seriously wonder if there is the kinda love I have in mind. I'm oney nineteen, but I been goin' with guys since I was fourteen. In fact, I almost married a cousin of mine when I was fourteen, but Pappy wouldn't have it.

From BUS STOP
William Inge

>>> GENERAL AMERICAN

Although *General American speech* is a much debated and, according to some experts, dated term, it has been deliberately chosen to indicate the speech generally used in the Midwest, West, and Northwest. General American contains fewer distinguishing speech characteristics than the speeches of any of the other regions. Although career speech is not synonymous with General American speech, there are some similarities.

Vowels and Diphthongs

Use of /ɔ/ Between /w/ and /r/

	GENERAL AMERICAN AND CAREER		GENERAL AMERICAN AND CAREER
war	[wɔr]	warp	[wɔrp]
warrant	[wɔrənt]	Warsaw	[wɔrsɔ]

	GENERAL AMERICAN AND CAREER		GENERAL AMERICAN AND CAREER
warble	[wɔrbl̩]	wart	[wɔrt]
ward	[wɔrd]	warmth	[wɔrmθ]
warn	[wɔrn]		

Often the Midwesterner substitutes the vowel /a/ (as in "ask") for the low-back /ɑ/ (as in "father"). Record the following list of words using negative practice.

	/ɑ/	/a/	/ɑ/
hot	[hɑt]	[hat]	[hɑt]
spot	[spɑt]	[spat]	[spɑt]
Tom	[tɑm]	[tam]	[tɑm]
Robert	[rɑbɚt]	[rabɚt]	[rɑbɚt]
grotto	[grɑto]	[grato]	[grɑto]
probably	[prɑbəblɪ]	[prabəblɪ]	[prɑbəblɪ]
motto	[mɑto]	[mato]	[mɑto]
locked	[lɑkt]	[lakt]	[lɑkt]
got	[gɑt]	[gat]	[gɑt]
cot	[kɑt]	[kat]	[kɑt]
doctor	[dɑktɚ]	[daktɚ]	[dɑktɚ]

Addition of /r/ after /ɔ/

This error, which is considered substandard, is not characteristic of most Midwestern speech. For professional purposes, however, it is a useful combination. Use negative practice in the following list of words.[4]

	CAREER	GENERAL AMERICAN	CAREER
wash	[wɔʃ]	[wɔrʃ]	[wɔʃ]
Washington	[wɔʃɪŋtən]	[wɔrʃɪŋtən]	[wɔʃɪŋtən]
cautious	[kɔʃəs]	[kɔrʃəs]	[kɔʃəs]
washroom	[wɔʃrum]	[wɔrʃrum]	[wɔʃrum]
caution	[kɔʃən]	[kɔrʃən]	[kɔʃən]
squaw	[skwɔ]	[skwɔr]	[skwɔ]
squalor	[skwɔlɚ]	[skwɔrlɚ]	[skwɔlɚ]
squash	[skwɔʃ]	[skwɔrʃ][5]	[skwɔʃ]

Substitution of /wɑ/ for /wɔ/

Record the following list of words transcribed into the General American dialect and acceptable New England vowel substitution. Either pronunciation is acceptable.

	GENERAL AMERICAN	NEW ENGLAND
wobble	[wɑbl̩]	[wɔbl̩]
wad	[wɑd]	[wɔd]
waddle	[wɑdl̩]	[wɔdl̩]

---

[4]The vowel /ɑ/ (as in "father") could also be used in career speech in some of these words.
[5]Before you say, "We don't say that!" put "squash" into a sentence with a word following it. It makes a difference in pronunciation.

water	[wɑɾɚ]	[wɔtɚ]
Waldorf	[wɑldɔrf]	[wɔldɔrf]
walk	[wɑk]	[wɔk]
wash	[wɑʃ]	[wɔʃ]
Wallace	[wɑləs]	[wɔləs]
wallet	[wɑlət]	[wɔlət]
wampum	[wɑmpəm]	[wɔmpəm]
watch	[wɑtʃ]	[wɔtʃ]

Substitution of /ɝ/ for /ʌr/

Compare the General American and Southern/New England pronunciations. The Southern/New England pronunciation is recommended for stage and television.

	GENERAL AMERICAN	SOUTHERN/ NEW ENGLAND
hurry	[hɝɪ]	[hʌrɪ]
worry	[wɝɪ]	[wʌrɪ]
hurricane	[hɝəken]	[hʌrəken]
curry	[kɝɪ]	[kʌrɪ]
burrow	[bɝo]	[bʌro]
scurry	[skɝɪ]	[skʌrɪ]
furrow	[fɝo]	[fʌro]
Murray	[mɝɪ]	[mʌrɪ]
flurry	[flɝɪ]	[flʌrɪ]
surrey	[sɝɪ]	[sʌrɪ]

Substitution of /ɻ/ for /r/

The semivowel /ɻ/ is produced like the /r/ but with the tongue tip excessively curled and extremely tense. The elevated tip is placed too far back. Midwesterners are often told that they use too much "r" in their speech. Sometimes the sound is referred to as the Midwestern "burr." In the following word lists, refresh your New England accent. To obtain career speech, some Northerners and Midwesterners will need to relax the tongue tip.

	NEW ENGLAND	GENERAL AMERICAN	CAREER
barn	[ban]	[bɑɻn]	[bɑrn]
far	[fa]	[fɑɻ]	[fɑr]
heart	[hat]	[hɑɻt]	[hɑrt]
farmer	[famə]	[fɑɻmɚ]	[fɑrmɚ]
park	[pak]	[pɑɻk]	[pɑrk]
alarm	[əlam]	[əlɑɻm]	[əlɑrm]
chart	[tʃat]	[tʃɑɻt]	[tʃart]
hearty	[hatɪ]	[hɑɻtɪ]	[hartɪ]
sparse	[spas]	[spɑɻs]	[spɑrs]
yard	[jad]	[jɑɻd]	[jɑrd]

Misarticulated /ɝ/

Sometimes General American speakers round their lips too much and elevate the tongue tip too high when articulating /ɝ/ (as in "her"). The symbol for too much rounding is [ɷ] and appears under the vowel sound, and an overly elevated tongue is indicated by [⊥]. Use negative practice in the following word list.

	CAREER	GENERAL AMERICAN	CAREER
heard	[hɝd]	[hɝ̠d]	[hɝd]
flirt	[flɝt]	[flɝ̠t]	[flɝt]
word	[wɝd]	[wɝ̠d]	[wɝd]
mirth	[mɝθ]	[mɝ̠θ]	[mɝθ]
spurt	[spɝt]	[spɝ̠t]	[spɝt]
worm	[wɝm]	[wɝ̠m]	[wɝm]
murder	[mɝdɚ]	[mɝ̠dɚ]	[mɝdɚ]
swerve	[swɝv]	[swɝ̠v]	[swɝv]
bird	[bɝd]	[bɝ̠d]	[bɝd]

Substitution of /ɑ̣/ for /ɑ/

In General American speech, the production of /ɑ/ is often excessively tense, indicated by /ɑ̣/. Use negative practice as you pronounce the following words.

	CAREER	GENERAL AMERICAN (SOMETIMES!)	CAREER
Bob	[bɑb],[bɒb]	[bɑ̣b]	[bɑb],[bɒb]
cot	[kɑt], [kɒt]	[kɑ̣t]	[kɑt], [kɒt]
cod	[kɑd], [kɒd]	[kɑ̣d]	[kɑd], [kɒd]
Tom	[tɑm], [tɒm]	[tɑ̣m]	[tɑm], [tɒm]
hot	[hɑt], [hɒt]	[hɑ̣t]	[hɑt], [hɒt]
pod	[pɑd], [pɒd]	[pɑ̣d]	[pɑd], [pɒd]
spot	[spɑt], [spɒt]	[spɑ̣t]	[spɑt], [spɒt]
pond	[pɑnd], [pɒnd]	[pɑ̣nd]	[pɑnd], [pɒnd]

 EXERCISES FOR DIALECTS

The familiar soliloquy from Hamlet *is transcribed here for all of the regionalisms discussed in this chapter. Record each one of them. Read the phonetic transcriptions as presented. Then, compare your habitual reading with career speech.*

To be, or not to be, that is the question:—
Whether 'tis nobler in the mind to suffer
The slings and arrows of outrageous fortune,
Or to take arms against a sea of troubles,
And by opposing end them?

1. New England

tə bi ɒ nɒt tə bi ðæt ɪz ðə ˈkwɛstʃən
To be, or not to be, that is the question:—

ˈʍɛðə   tɪz ˈnoblə ɪn ðə maɪnd tə ˈsʌfə
Whether 'tis nobler in the mind to suffer

ðə slɪŋz æn ˈæroz əv autˈreʤɪs ˈfɒʧun
The slings and arrows of outrageous fortune,

ɒ tu tek amz əˈgɛnstə si əv ˈtrʌbl̩z
Or to take arms against a sea of troubles,

æ̃nd baɪ əˈpozɪŋ ɛn ðɛm
And by opposing end them?

2. New York City

tə bi oə n̪ɑt t̪e bi ðɛət̪ ɪz ðə ˈkwɛsʧən
To be, or not to be, that is the question:—

ˈʍɛðᵊ t̪ɪzˈn̪ɛublə ɪŋ ðə mn̩d tə ˈsʌfᵊ
Whether 'tis nobler in the mind to suffer

ðə sl̩z æn̪ ˈɛərɛuz əf æut̪ˈreʤn̩ ˈfoʧun
The slings and arrows of outrageous fortune,

oə t̪u t̪ek ɔmz əˈgɛn̪t̪ ə si əf ˈt̪ʌbᵊ
Or to take arms against a sea of troubles,

æ̃n̪ bɒɪ əˈpɛuzɪŋ ɛn̪ ðem
And by opposing end them?

3. Southern

tə bi ɔ nat   tə bi ðæjɛt ɪjəz ðə ˈkwɛsʧne
To be, or not to be, that is   the question:—

ˈʍɛðᵊ   tɪjəz nɛublə ɪjən ðə mand– tə sʌfᵊ
Whether 'tis   nobler in the mind to suffer

ðə slɪŋz æjənˈæjərozəv æutˈreɪʤɪs ˈfɔʧun
The slings and arrows of outrageous fortune,

ɔ tu   tek amz əˈgɪnst ə si əv ˈtrʌbl̩z
Or to take arms against a sea of troubles,

æjənd ba əˈpozɪŋ ɪnd ðɪm
And by opposing end them?

4. General American

tə bi ɔɾ nat tə bi ðæt ɪz ðə ˈkwɛsʧən
To be, or not to be, that is the question:—

ˈʍɛðɚꞁ tɪz ˈnoblɚꞁ ɪn ðə maɪnd tə ˈsʌfɚꞁ
Whether 'tis nobler in the mind to suffer

ðə   slɪŋz ænd æɾoz əv autˈreʤəs ˈfɔɾʧun
The slings and arrows of outrageous fortune,

ɔɾ tu tek   ɑɾmz əˈgɛnst ə si əv ˈtrʌbl̩z
Or to take arms against a sea of troubles,

ænd baɪ   əˈpozɪŋ ɛnd ðɛm
And by opposing end them?

5. Career Speech

tə bi or nat tə bi ðæt ɪz ðə ˈkwɛsʧən
To be, or not to be, that is the question:—

ˈʍɛðɚ   tɪz ˈnoblɚ ɪn ðə maɪnd tə ˈsʌfɚ
Whether 'tis nobler in the mind to suffer

ðə slɪŋz ænd ˈærouz əv autˈreʤəs ˈfortʃun
The slings and arrows of outrageous fortune,

or tə tek ɑrmz əˈgɛnst ə si əv ˈtrʌbḷz
Or to take arms against a sea of troubles,

ænd baɪ əˈpozɪŋ ɛnd ðɛm
And by opposing end them?

W   To locate URLs and search terms for weblinks relevant to this chapter, please go to the companion website at www.cengage.com/rtf/crannell/voiceandarticulation5e and select the proper chapter.

Write the definitions for the following terms in the space below.

KEY TERMS   DEFINITIONS

Dialect

Sound Addition

Sound Distortion

Sound Omission

Sound Substitution

Suprasegmental Features

Triphthong

CHAPTER **13**

STAGE SPEECH AND SELECTED INTERNATIONAL ACCENTS

Y ou may wonder what a discussion of stage diction and international accents is doing in a basic text on voice and articulation. Because this text focuses on career speech, it is essential to include these discussions for actors as well as for professionals in communications (such as radio and television announcers). This chapter is also helpful for individuals for whom English is a second language and, thus, whose English pronunciation is influenced by their primary language. (Exercises for additional accents are located in the Appendixes.) **Ear training** (the process of developing hearing acuity), as well as the kinetic awareness of sound production, is valuable in learning the English language.

This chapter focuses on the influence of foreign languages on American-English pronunciation. By no means an exhaustive discussion, it is meant to introduce the subject to the student. With the growing interest in international communication, it is increasingly important for Americans, many of whom speak no foreign language, to become aware of foreign languages, customs, and cultures.

Some of the sounds represented in the IPA are present in foreign languages but not in English. For example, the German language contains the vowel /y/, which is the first vowel in the word *grüssen*. The umlaut (the two dots over the vowel) indicates a different pronunciation from the "u" without the umlaut. The vowel /y/ does not exist in English. Therefore, an American learning German has difficulty with this sound and, even with proper ear training and practice, can only approximate the correct pronunciation. Conversely, some sounds in English, such as the English /θ/ and /ð/, present problems for the German speaker learning English, because they do not exist in German.

In developing an international accent for performance, there are two major considerations. First, select the most characteristic aspects—do not attempt to present all the vocal

329

idiosyncracies. Yes, you want authenticity, but not at the expense of intelligibility. Second, be consistent in using the speech characteristics that you have chosen. Any audience is quick to pick up a lack of consistency.

To use any of the dialects discussed next accurately in performance, you must study the rhythm, pitch changes, tempo, and other acoustical phenomena in that dialect. Because it is virtually impossible to describe all these aspects in print, you should listen to recordings by professional performers so that you can learn these nonphonemic aspects.

>>> STANDARD STAGE SPEECH

You will certainly discover that there are many similarities between career speech and standard stage speech. Remember that career speech does not come from a particular area of the United States. **Standard stage speech,** also called *London Speech,* is the speech that should be used in a play requiring a British dialect. Stage speech is the speech often used in British plays or plays in translation (both classical and modern) when a particular dialect is unnecessary.

For most American plays, standard stage speech would be out of place. For example, a production of George S. Kaufman and Moss Hart's *The Man Who Came to Dinner* would not use stage speech, although certain characters might use it.

Career speech and stage speech are not synonymous. Both, however, represent the best standards of American and British English.

Vowels and Diphthongs

Substitution of /ɜʊ/ for /oʊ/

The sound /ɜʊ/ can be achieved by rounding the /o/ (as in "go") even more, tensing both lips, and keeping the tongue tip behind the lower teeth. Record the following list of words and sentences as transcribed. Focus your attention on the difference between career and stage speech.

	CAREER	STAGE	CAREER
go	[goʊ]	[gɜʊ]	[goʊ]
slow	[sloʊ]	[slɜʊ]	[sloʊ]
whole	[hoʊl]	[hɜʊl]	[hoʊl]
home	[hoʊm]	[hɜʊm]	[hoʊm]
toe	[toʊ]	[tɜʊ]	[toʊ]
spoken	[spoʊkn̩]	[spɜʊkn̩]	[spoʊkn̩]

In the following sentences, the substitution of /ɜʊ/ for /oʊ/ is notated above the appropriate letters. Use career speech, stage speech, and then career speech again.

   ɜʊ   ɜʊ   ɜʊ
I told you, Mona, I won't do it!

   ɜʊ   ɜʊ   ɜʊ
No one stole the Holmes book.

         ɜʊ ɜʊ
The wind is so cold.

   ɜʊ   ɜʊ
Noel, fold the napkin properly.

     ɜʊ ɜʊ   ɜʊ
The ghost roamed through the whole house.

Production of /ɔ/ with Tongue Elevated

Compared with career speech, the tongue is placed higher in stage speech in pronouncing /ɔ/, in a position similar to that for /o/ (as in "g<u>o</u>"). Record the following list of words.

	CAREER	STAGE	CAREER
fall	[fɔl]	[fɔ⊥l]	[fɔl]
cough	[kɔf]	[kɔ⊥f]	[kɔf]
lost	[lɔst]	[lɔ⊥st]	[lɔst]
taught	[tɔt]	[tɔ⊥t]	[tɔt]
naughty	[nɔtɪ]	[nɔ⊥tɪ]	[nɔtɪ]

In the following sentences, the variation of /ɔ/ is notated above the appropriate letters. Use stage speech between two career speech pronunciations.

    ɔ⊥   ɔ⊥   ɔ⊥
Thomas's daughter was getting increasingly naughty.

     ɔ⊥   ɔ⊥
He taught the coughing students.

  ɔ⊥   ɔ⊥   ɔ⊥
Toss the ball to Flossie.

     ɔ⊥   ɔ⊥
The mauling tiger was painted on the wall.

  ɔ⊥   ɔ⊥
Call to the sailors on the yawl.

Substitution of /ɑ/ for /æ/

In stage speech, /ɑ/ (as in "f<u>a</u>ther") is used in many words in which /æ/ (as in "c<u>a</u>t") is used in career speech. New Englanders substitute /ɑ/ for /æ/ in the same words. Read each of the words in the following list, and compare the pronunciations.

	NEW ENGLAND	STAGE	CAREER
laugh	[lɑf]	[lɑf]	[læf]
bath	[bɑθ]	[bɑθ]	[bæθ]
half	[hɑf]	[hɑf]	[hæf]
last	[lɑst]	[lɑst]	[læst]
aunt	[ɑnt]	[ɑnt]	[ænt]
fast	[fɑst]	[fɑst]	[fæst]
cast	[kɑst]	[kɑst]	[kæst]
passed	[pɑst]	[pɑst]	[pæst]
calf	[kɑf]	[kɑf]	[kæf]
flask	[flɑsk]	[flɑsk]	[flæsk]

Stage speech retains /æ/ in the following phonetic environments:

1. before /ʃ/ (for example, "cash" [kæʃ], "gash" [gæʃ], and "flash" [flæʃ])
2. before the letters *ct* (for example, "fact" [fækt] and "actor" [æktə])
3. before the nasals /m/ and /n/ except in the words *dance, chance,* and *France* (for example, "fan" [fæn] and "dandy" [dændɪ])
4. in *and* words except "demand" and "command" (pronounced [dɪmɑnd] and [kəmɑnd])

Substitution of /ɜ/ for /ɝ/

See the words and drills on pages 99–100.

Substitution of /ə/ for /ɚ/

See the words and drills on page 306.

Substitution of /ɒ/ for /ɑ/

See the words and drills on pages 115–116.

Consonants

Use of Intervocalic /ɾ/

The one-tap trilled /r/ (/ɾ/) is used to link one syllable to another or at the end of a word when the next word begins with a vowel. This is also called the **intervocalic** /ɾ/. Read aloud the following list.

	CAREER	STAGE	CAREER
very	[vɛɾɪ]	[vɛɾɪ]	[vɛɾɪ]
sorry	[sɔɾɪ]	[sɔ⊥ɾɪ]	[sɔɾɪ]
worry	[wʌɾɪ]	[wʌɾɪ]	[wʌɾɪ]
syrup	[sɪrəp]	[sɪɾəp]	[sɪrəp]
lyric	[lɪrɪk]	[lɪɾɪk]	[lɪrɪk]
choric	[korɪk]	[kɔ⊥ɾɪk]	[korɪk]
virile	[vɪrəl]	[vɪɾəl]	[vɪrəl]
irrigate	[ɪrəget]	[ɪɾəget]	[ɪrəget]
irritate	[ɪrətet]	[ɪɾətet]	[ɪrətet]
pyramid	[pɪrəmɪd]	[pɪɾəmɪd]	[pɪrəmɪd]
marry	[mærɪ]	[mæɾɪ]	[mærɪ]
merry	[mɛrɪ]	[mɛɾɪ]	[mɛrɪ]

Say the following phrases and sentences using the intervocalic /r/ (/ɾ/):

far into the forest [fɑɾ ɪntʊ ðə fɔ⊥ɾəst]

her intention [həɾ ɪntɛnʃən]

fear of the Merry Men [fɪɾ əv ðə mɛɾɪ mɛn]

Steer it straight. [stɪɾ ɪt stret]

Here it is. [hɪɾ ɪt ɪz]

Maura is a Sister of Mercy. [mɔ⊥ɾə ɪz ə sɪstəɾ əv mɜsɪ]

The Nile River is in Africa. [ðə nɑɪl rɪvəɾ ɪz ɪn ɑfrɪkə]

(((EXERCISES FOR STAGE SPEECH

The following is a list of common words that are pronounced differently in British English than in American English. Record the words as you would pronounce them in American English and then as they are transcribed in stage speech.

AMERICAN ENGLISH	STAGE	AMERICAN ENGLISH	STAGE
clique	[klik]	lever	['livə]
capsule	['kæpsjul]	herb	[ɜb]
leisure	['lɛʒə]	medicine	['mɛdsɪn]
schedule	['ʃɛdjul]	vase	[vɑz]

either	['aɪðə]	patriot	['pætrɪət]
neither	['naɪðə]	massage	[mæ'sɑʒ]
been	[bin] or [bɪn]	tomato	[tə'mɑto]
glacier	['glesjə]	patent	['petənt]
again	[ə'gen] or [ə'gɛn]	mirage	[mɪ'rɑʒ]
process	['prosɛs]	sexual	['sɛksuəl]
barrage	[bæ'rɑʒ]	patronize	['petrənaɪz]
privacy	['prɪvəsɪ]	missile	['mɪsaɪl]
nephew	['nɛvju]	Derby	['dɑbɪ]
laboratory	[lə'bɔrətrɪ]	clerk	[klɑk]
against	[ə'genst]	tissue	['tɪsju]
garage	['gærɑʒ]	figure	['fɪgə]
hostile	['hɔ⊥staɪl]	lieutenant	[lɛf'tɛnənt]
futile	['fjutaɪl]	issue	['ɪsju]

In the following selections, transcribe the stage substitutions above the appropriate letters. The intervocalic /ɾ/ has already been supplied. Record the entire selection. Work to increase speed, which will help to ease any self-consciousness.

           ɾ   ɾ

1. Once upon a midnight dreary, while I pondered, weak and weary,

                 ɾ

Over many a quaint and curious volume of forgotten lore—

From THE RAVEN
   ɾ
Edgar Allan Poe

2. *Hamlet:* Speak the speech, I pray you, as I pronounced it to you, trippingly on the

tongue: but if you mouth it, as many of your players do, I had as lief the town crier

spoke my lines. Nor do not saw the air too much with your hand thus; but use all

           ɾ   ɾ   ɾ

gently; for in the very torrent, tempest, and, as I may say, whirlwind of your passion,

     ɾ   ɾ

you must acquire and beget a temperance that may give it smoothness. O, it offends

                ɾ   ɾ   ɾ

me to the soul to hear a robustious periwig-pated fellow tear a passion to tatters, to

     ɾ

very rags, to split the ears of the groundlings, who for the most part are capable of
nothing but inexplicable dumb shows and noise.

From HAMLET
William Shakespeare

                   ɾ   ɾ

3. *Lady Bracknell:* I'm sorry if we were a little late, Algernon, but I was obliged to call

         ɾ   ɾ

on dear Lady Hadbury. I hadn't been there since her poor husband's death. I never saw

a woman so altered; she looks quite twenty years younger. And now I'll have a cup of

tea, and one of those nice cucumber sandwiches you promised me.

From THE IMPORTANCE OF BEING EARNEST
Oscar Wilde

4. One I love,

Two I love,

   ſ

Three I love I say,

   ſ

Four I love with all my heart,

Five I cast away,

Six he loves,

Seven she loves,

Eight they want to wed,

     ſ

Nine they tarry,

     ſ

Ten they marry

Is what the daisy said.

Anonymous

⟩⟩⟩
COCKNEY

Because a great deal of literature has been written for characters with a cockney accent, we have included the cockney dialect in this chapter.

Vowels and Diphthongs

Substitution of /æʊ/ for /o/ and /oʊ/

This substitution is very characteristic of cockney. Record the following list of words and sentences. Focus on the difference between career speech and cockney.

	CAREER	COCKNEY	CAREER
don't	[doʊnt]	[dæʊnt]	[doʊnt]
grown	[groʊn]	[græʊn]	[groʊun]
bloat	[bloʊt]	[blæʊt]	[bloʊt]
sold	[soʊld]	[sæʊld]	[soʊld]
stove	[stoʊv]	[stæʊv]	[stoʊv]
cold	[koʊld]	[kæʊld]	[koʊld]
row	[roʊ]	[ræʊ]	[roʊ]
soap	[soʊp]	[sæʊp]	[soʊp]
most	[moʊst]	[mæʊst]	[moʊst]
rogue	[roʊg]	[ræʊg]	[roʊg]

     æʊ   æʊ

Hold the soap in your hands.

       æʊ   æʊ   æʊ

Flossie sold the stove to the rogue.

    æU   æU
Most of the kitchen was moldy with ashes.
    æU æU æU   æU
Row, row, row your boat.
       æU   æU
Some folks like to take to the high roads.

Substitution of /ʌɪ/ for /i/

This substitution is sometimes difficult for Americans to produce. Do not confuse it with /aɪ/. Record the following list of words and sentences. Focus on the difference between /i/ and /ʌɪ/.

	CAREER	COCKNEY	CAREER
me	[mi]	[mʌɪ]	[mi]
eager	['igɚ]	['ʌɪgə]	['igɚ]
agreed	[ə'grid]	[ə'grʌɪd]	[ə'grid]
meet	[mit]	[mʌɪt]	[mit]
scene	[sin]	[sʌɪn]	[sin]
feet	[fit]	[fʌɪt]	[fit]
kneel	[nil]	[nʌɪl]	[nil]
beach	[bitʃ]	[bʌɪtʃ]	[bitʃ]
sleep	[slip]	[slʌɪp]	[slip]
please	[pliz]	[plʌɪz]	[pliz]

    ʌɪ   æU ʌɪ
Please don't sleep.

  ʌɪ   ʌɪ   ʌɪ
Eve feels defeated.

  ʌɪ   ʌɪ   ʌɪ
Lee's a conceited beast!

   ʌɪ   ʌɪ   ʌɪ æU
She didn't believe the machine broke.

  ʌɪ   ʌɪ   ʌɪ   ɔː
Jean heeded the team's warning.

Substitution of /aɪ/ for /e/ and /eɪ/

This is one of the most common characteristics of the cockney dialect. Record the following list of words and sentences. Focus on the difference between career speech and cockney. Note that in the career speech columns, both the /eɪ / and /e/ sounds are correct.

	CAREER	COCKNEY	CAREER
stay	[steɪ]	[staɪ]	[steɪ]
wait	[weɪt]	[waɪt]	[weɪt]
great	[greɪt]	[graɪt]	[greɪt]
fail	[feɪl]	[faɪl]	[feɪl]
sale	[seɪl]	[saɪl]	[seɪl]
mail	[meɪl]	[maɪl]	[meɪl]
sake	[seɪk]	[saɪk]	[seɪk]
famous	[feɪməs]	[faɪməs]	[feɪməs]
faith	[feɪθ]	[faɪf]	[feɪθ]
waist	[weɪst]	[waɪst]	[weɪst]

    aɪ   aɪ   æʊ
I'm afraid she stayed at home.
   aɪ aɪ   aɪ
James made a mistake.
   aɪ æʊ faɪf   aɪ
Ray had no faith in the tale.
   aɪ aɪ   aɪ
Kate wasted the cake.
    aɪ   aɪ æʊ   aɪ
The famous star paid no attention to Blake.

Substitution of /ɛ/ for /æ/

	CAREER	COCKNEY	CAREER
taxi	[tæksɪ]	[tɛ̱ksɪ]	[tæksɪ]
am	[æm]	[ɛ̱m]	[æm]
hand	[hænd]	[hɛ̱nd]	[hænd]
back	[bæk]	[bɛ̱k]	[bæk]
grapple	[græpl̩]	[grɛ̱pl̩]	[græpl̩]
pan	[pæn]	[pɛ̱n]	[pæn]
wrap	[ræp]	[rɛ̱p]	[ræp]
lad	[læd]	[lɛ̱d]	[læd]
hat	[hæt]	[hɛ̱t]	[hæt]
that	[ðæt]	[ðɛ̱t]	[ðæt]

 ɛ   ɛ   ɛ ɛ
Andrea, have some ham and eggs.
   ɛ   ɛ   ɛ
Becka sat in the back of the taxi.
  ɛ   ɛ   ɛ   ɛ
Hey, laddy, hand me the fancy pants.
 æʊ æʊ ʌɪ ɛ ɛ ɛ
Joe, don't be mad at dad,
 ɛ   ɛ ɒ   ɛ
Dan, put my hat on the rack.

Substitution of /a/ for /ʌ/

Record this straightforward substitution in the following list of words and sentences. Focus on the differences between career speech and cockney.

	CAREER	COCKNEY	CAREER
love	[lʌv]	[la̱v]	[lʌv]
some	[sʌm]	[sa̱m]	[sʌm]
mummy	[mʌmɪ]	[ma̱mɪ]	[mʌmɪ]
mother	[mʌðɚ]	[ma̱ðɚ]	[mʌðɚ]
fudge	[fʌʤ]	[fa̱ʤ]	[fʌʤ]
judge	[ʤʌʤ]	[ʤa̱ʤ]	[ʤʌʤ]
luck	[lʌk]	[la̱k]	[lʌk]
cut	[kʌt]	[ka̱t]	[kʌt]
runner	[rʌnɚ]	[ra̱nə]	[rʌnɚ]
duck	[dʌk]	[da̱k]	[dʌk]

    a   a   a   a
Mummy, carve the lucky duck.
    a   ə   a   a
She loves her husband, the judge.
      a   a   ə a
Drink from some other jug.
      æU   ɛ   a   a
The old man rubbed his stomach.
    ʌɪ   ɛ   a   af
Steve had done nothing wrong.

Substitution of /ɒɪ/ for /aɪ/ or /ɑɪ/

This substitution is evident in some New York City speech. Record the following list of words and sentences. Focus on the differences between career speech and cockney.

	CAREER	COCKNEY	CAREER
spy	[spaɪ]	[spɒ̱ɪ]	[spaɪ]
alive	[əˈlaɪv]	[əˈlɒ̱ɪv]	[əˈlaɪv]
crime	[kraɪm]	[krɒ̱ɪm]	[kraɪm]
abide	[əˈbaɪd]	[əˈbɒ̱ɪd]	[əˈbaɪd]
china	[ˈtʃaɪnə]	[ˈtʃɒ̱ɪnə]	[ˈtʃaɪnə]
apply	[əˈplaɪ]	[əˈplɒ̱ɪ]	[əˈplaɪ]
file	[faɪl]	[fɒ̱ɪl]	[faɪl]
light	[laɪt]	[lɒ̱ɪt]	[laɪt]
rhyme	[raɪm]	[rɒ̱ɪm]	[raɪm]
quite	[kwaɪt]	[kwɒ̱ɪt]	[kwaɪt]

    ɒɪaɪ   ɛ   aɪ
Friday is fish and chips day.
       ɛ   aɪ   ɒɪ   ɒɪ   ɛ
Look at the stripes on the guide's shirt.
       ɒɪ   aɪ   ɒɪ
There's quite a lot of daylight left.
      ɒɪ   ɒɪ   ɒɪ
In the night, silence is sublime.
     ɒɪ ɔ ə   ɒɪ   ɒɪ
My father is the wisest man alive.

Substitution of /æU/ for /ɑU/ or /aU/

Refer to the drills on page 312.

Substitution of /ə/ for /ɚ/

Refer to the drills on page 306.

Substitution of /ɜ/ for /ɝ/

Refer to the discussion on page 103 and the /ɝ/ word list and exercises on pages 99–100.

Consonants

Substitution of Glottal Stop [ʔ] for /h/ before Initial Vowels

Glottalization is an articulation that involves the use of the space between the vocal folds. Record the following list of words and sentences. Feel the stoppage of breath at the larynx.

	CAREER	COCKNEY	CAREER
half	[hæf]	[ʔaf]	[hæf]
habit	[hæbɪt]	[ʔabɪt]	[hæbɪt]
Harry	[hærɪ]	[ʔarɪ]	[hærɪ]
handsome	[hænsəm]	[ʔansəm]	[hænsəm]
hold	[hold]	[ʔæʊd]	[hold]
heaven	[hɛvn̩]	[ʔɛvm̩]	[hɛvn̩]
heard	[hɝd]	[ʔɝd]	[hɝd]
hand	[hænd]	[ʔɛnd]	[hænd]
high	[haɪ]	[ʔɒɪ]	[haɪ]
happy	[hæpɪ]	[ʔɛpɪ]	[hæpɪ]

    ʔæʊ   æʊʔ ʔ   aɹ
How about it, Harry?

        ʔ   ʔʊ   ʔʌɪ
The hospital was heated.

ʔɝʊ   ə   ʔɛ aʊ a
Whoever did that has no heart.

      æʊ   ʌɪ   əɹ a
Anyhow she's left her husband!

ʔʌɪ ʔɪ ʔɪ   ʔɪ   ɝ ʔɛ
He hit it with his hand.

Substitution of [ʔ] for Medial and Final /t/ and /u/ for Final /l/

	CAREER	COCKNEY	CAREER
bitter	[bɪtɚ]	[bɪʔə]	[bɪtɚ]
battle	[bætl̩]	[bɛʔu]	[bætl̩]
matter	[mætɚ]	[mɛʔə]	[mætɚ]
butter	[bʌtɚ]	[baʔə]	[bʌtɚ]
cattle	[kætl̩]	[kɛʔu]	[kætl̩]
bottle	[batl̩]	[bɒʔu]	[batl̩]
metal	[mɛtl̩]	[mɛʔu]	[mɛtl̩]
better	[bɛtɚ]	[bɛʔə]	[bɛtɚ]
got it	[gat ɪt]	[gaʔɪ]	[gat ɪt]
sit on	[sɪt an]	[sɪʔɒn]	[sɪt an]
put it	[pʊt ɪt]	[pʊʔɪ]	[pʊt ɪt]

Substitution of /f/ for /θ/ and /v/ for /ð/

Record the following words, and make the suggested substitution.

	CAREER	COCKNEY	CAREER
whether	[ʍɛðɚ]	[wɛvə]	[ʍɛðɚ]
leather	[lɛðɚ]	[lɛvə]	[lɛðɚ]

with us	[wɪð əs]	[wɪv̱ əs]	[wɪð əs]
birthday	[bɝˑθdeɪ]	[bɝf̱daɪ]	[bɝˑθdeɪ]
both of us	[boθ əv ʌs]	[bau̱f əv as]	[boθ əv ʌs]
smother	[smʌðɚˑ]	[smav̱ə]	[smʌðɚˑ]
something	[sʌmθɪŋ]	[samf̱ɪŋk]	[sʌmθɪŋ]
father	[fɑðɚˑ]	[fav̱ə]	[fɑðɚ]
mother	[mʌðɚˑ]	[mav̱ə]	[mʌðɚˑ]
worth it	[wɝˑθ ɪt]	[wɝf̱ʔɪ]	[wɝˑθ ɪt]

((((• EXERCISES FOR A COCKNEY ACCENT

1. Read the following poem with a cockney accent. As you read aloud the poem, remember that it must be understood by an audience. The poet has not included all of the sound substitutions. Transcribe cockney sounds above the appropriate letters.

   A muvver was barfin' [bathing] 'er biby one night,

   The youngest of ten and a tiny young mite,

   The muvver was poor and the biby was thin,

   Only a skelington covered in skin;

   The muvver turned rahned for the soap off the rack,

   She was but a moment, but when she turned back,

   The biby was gorn; and in anguish she cried,

   "Oh, where is my biby?"—The angels replied:

   "Your biby 'as fell dahn the plug-ole,

   Your biby 'as forn dahn the plug;

   The poor little thing was so skinny and thin

   'E oughter been barfed in a jug;

   Your biby is perfeckly 'appy,

   'E won't need a barf any more,

   Your biby 'as fell dahn the plug-ole,

   Not lorst, but gorn before."

   BIBY'S EPITAPH
   Anonymous

2. In the following selection, the first stanza is transcribed into phonetics. Transcribe the second stanza. (The refrain has been omitted.) As you rerecord the selection, increase your speed and work for continuity and proper inflection.

   jə maɪ tɔː ə dʒɪn ən bɪə
   You may talk o' gin and beer

   wɛn jə   kwɔˑʔəd saɪf æʊʔ ɪə
   When you're quartered safe out 'ere,

   ɛn jə   sɛnt tə pɛni fɔɪts ən ɔɪdəʃˑɒ ʔɪ
   An' you're sent to penny fights an' Aldershot it;

bəˀ wɛnˀɪ kamz tə slɔˀə
But when it comes to slaughter

jə wɪ du jɔ wɜk ɒn wɒˀə
You will do your work on water,

ɛn jəl lɪk və blɪumɪn buts əv əm vɛts gˀɒˀɪ
An' you'll lick the bloomin' boots of 'im that's got it.

næʊ ɪn ɪnʤəz sanɪ klɒɪm
Now in Injia's sunny clime,

wɛr ɒɪ just tə spɛn mɒɪ tɒɪm
Where I used to spend my time

ə sɜvɪn əv ər mɛʤɛstɪ və kwʌɪn
A-servin' of 'Er Majesty the Queen,

əv ɔl vɛm blɛkfaɪst krɪu
Of all them blackfaced crew

və fɒɪnɪst mɛn ɒɪ nɪu
The finest man I knew

wəz æʊə rɛʤɪmɛˀu bʌɪstʌɪ gʌŋgə dʌɪn
Was our regimental bhisti,[1] Gunga Din.

The uniform 'e wore

Was nothin' much before,

An' rather less than 'arf o' that be'ind,

For a twisty piece o' rag

An' a goatskin water-bag

Was all the field-equipment 'e could find.

When the sweatin' troop-train lay

In a sidin' through the day,

Were the 'eat would make your bloomin' eyebrows crawl,

We shouted "Harry By!" "Harry By"—

"O, brother!" Till our throats were bricky-dry,

Then we wopped 'im 'cause 'e couldn't serve us all.

From GUNGA DIN
Rudyard Kipling

The following selections were written for cockney characters. Transcribe the cockney sounds above the appropriate letters.

3. *Kathleen:* Sent me to the country once, all them trees. Worse 'n people. Gawd. Take them off if I could get them on again. Can't understand why they let me have laces. Took me belt as well. Who they think I'm going to strangle? Improved my figure it did—the belt. Drew it in a bit.

---

[1]*Bhisti:* water carrier.

From HOME
aɪ   ɾ
David Storey

4. In the following speech, Shaw fairly successfully approximated a cockney accent through spelling.

Bill: Aw did wot Aw said Aw'd do. Aw spit in is eye. E looks ap at the skoy and sez, "Ow that Aw shold be fahned worthy to be spit upon for the gospel's sike!" e sez; an Mog sez "Glaory Allellooher!"; an then e called me Braddher.

aɪ   ə   ɔ
From MAJOR BARBARA
George Bernard Shaw

5. *Iris:* Cheek! Watched every move I made. I don't like being watched. Never have. Still, I knew it was no good getting my knickers in a twist over that. More important was to find out where I was. I hadn't got the foggiest idea. See, geography was never my best thing.

From JOHNNY BULL
Kathleen Betsko

ʔɔ   ɒ   ə
6. *Artful Dodger:* Don't fret your eyelids on that score. I know a 'spectable old genelman as lives there, wot'll give you lodgings for nothink—that is, if any genelman he knows interduces you. And don't he know me? Oh, no! Not in the least! By no means!

From OLIVER TWIST
Charles Dickens

aɪ   ʔɪ   u
7. *Eliza Doolittle:* I tell you it's easy to clean up here. Hot and cold water on tap, just as much as you like there is. Woolly towels, there is. And a towel horse so hot, it burns your fingers. Soft brushes to scrub yourself. And a wooden bowl of soap smelling like primroses. Now I know why ladies is so clean.

aɪ
From PYGMALION
George Bernard Shaw

8. *Dogberry:* Dost thou not suspect my place? Dost thou not suspect my years? O that he were here to write me down an ass! But, masters, remember that I am an ass. Though it not be written down, yet not forget that I am an ass. No, thou villain, thou art full of piety, as shall be proved upon thee by good witness. I am a wise fellow; and which is more, an officer; and which is more, a householder; and which is more, as pretty a piece of flesh as any in Messina.

æʊ   f   k
From MUCH ADO ABOUT NOTHING
aɪ
William Shakespeare

>>>
SCOTTISH

There are several Scottish dialects; the following discussion pertains to the Edinburgh dialect.

Vowels and Diphthongs

Substitution of /ɛř/ for /ɝ/

This use of the trilled /ř/ is perhaps the most recognizable characteristic of the Scottish dialect. The /ř/ is a longer trill than the one-tap trill /ɾ/ used in stage speech. If you have difficulty in producing /ř/, say the word *three* and increase the number of taps of the tongue tip on the alveolar ridge. The closest American-English sound is /ɾ/ in the /θɾ/ combination. In recording the following list of words and sentences, magnify the difference between /ɛř/ and /ɝ/.

	CAREER	SCOTTISH	CAREER
working	[wɝˑkɪŋ]	[wɛřkɪn]	[wɝˑkɪŋ]
thirty	[θɝˑtɪ]	[θɛřtɪ]	[θɝˑtɪ]
heard	[hɝˑd]	[hɛřd]	[hɝˑd]
squirt	[skwɝˑt]	[skwɛřt]	[skwɝˑt]
journey	[ʤɝˑnɪ]	[ʤɛřnɪ]	[ʤɝˑnɪ]
curse	[kɝˑs]	[kɛřs]	[kɝˑs]
world	[wɝˑld]	[wɛřld]	[wɝˑld]
word	[wɝˑd]	[wɛřd]	[wɝˑd]
first	[fɝˑst]	[fɛřst]	[fɝˑst]
bird	[bɝˑd]	[bɛřd]	[bɝˑd]

     ɛř   ɛř   ɛř
Don't smirk during the sermon.

       ɛř   ɛř   ɛř
The nurse was irked by the perfect patient.

          ɛř   ɛř
The blackbird was sitting on the perch.

      ɛř   ɛř   ɛř
Many girls are learning to assert themselves.

       ɛř   ɛř   ɛř ɛř
The verb occurs in the first verse.

Substitution of /əř/ for /ɚ/

Record the following list of words and sentences, and distinguish between /ɚ/ and /əř/.

	CAREER	SCOTTISH	CAREER
sister	[sɪstɚ]	[sɪstəř]	[sɪstɚ]
brother	[brʌðɚ]	[břʊðəř]	[brʌðɚ]
overage	[ovɚeʤ]	[ovəřeʤ]	[ovɚeʤ]
boundary	[baʊndɚɪ]	[baʊndəřɪ]	[baʊndɚɪ]
southern	[sʌðɚn]	[sʊðəřn]	[sʌðɚn]
razor	[rezɚ]	[rezəř]	[rezɚ]
camera	[kæmɚə]	[kaməřə]	[kæmɚə]
perhaps	[pɚhæps]	[pəřhaps]	[pɚhæps]
government	[gʌvɚnmənt]	[gʊvəřnmənt]	[gʌvɚnmənt]
number	[nʌmbɚ]	[nʊmbəř]	[nʌmbɚ]

         əř   əř
Anthony, history is interesting.

       əř ʔ   əř   ř
I wonder what the average grade was.

       əř   əř
His father was an actor.

    ʊ   əř   əř   əř   əř
Mother cooked her favorite dinner.
    əř a   əř   ʊ əř   ʊ
Perhaps my sister and brother will come.

Substitution of /a/ for /æ/

This is a substitution that is also characteristic of New England speech. Record the following list of words as transcribed.

	CAREER	SCOTTISH	CAREER
mask	[mæsk]	[ma̱sk]	[mæsk]
stamp	[stæmp]	[sta̱mp]	[stæmp]
calf	[kæf]	[ka̱f]	[kæf]
glad	[glæd]	[gla̱d]	[glæd]
bombastic	[bɑmbæstɪk]	[bəmba̱stɪk]	[bɑmbæstɪk]
half	[hæf]	[ha̱f]	[hæf]
chance	[tʃæns]	[tʃa̱ns]	[tʃæns]
grass	[græs]	[gra̱s]	[græs]
alas	[əlæs]	[əla̱s]	[əlæs]

(Refer to the exercises on page 306.)

Substitution of /u/ for /ʊ/

Record the following list of words and sentences. Listen for other English words when the substitution is made.

	CAREER	SCOTTISH	CAREER
would	[wʊd]	[wu̱d]	[wʊd]
full	[fʊl]	[fu̱l]	[fʊl]
book	[bʊk]	[bu̱k]	[bʊk]
foot	[fʊt]	[fu̱t]	[fʊt]
put	[pʊt]	[pu̱t]	[pʊt]
butcher	[bʊtʃɚ]	[bu̱tʃəř]	[bʊtʃɚ]
pull	[pʊl]	[pu̱l]	[pʊl]
cookie	[kʊkɪ]	[ku̱kɪ]	[kʊkɪ]
Brooklyn	[brʊklɪn]	[břu̱klɪn]	[brʊklɪn]
stood	[stʊd]	[stu̱d]	[stʊd]

      u   u   u
The cook took the pudding.
     əř   u   ř   u
Reverend Woods spoke from the pulpit,
      u   u
The wooden keg was full.
         u   u   u əř
Frank shook the hook on the pushcart.
    əř u   u
Mr. Hood was told he could do it.

Substitution of /u/ for /aʊ/

Record the following words and sentences. This is a sound substitution typical of the Scottish speaker.

	CAREER	SCOTTISH	CAREER
house	[haʊs]	[hus]	[haʊs]
mouse	[maʊs]	[mus]	[maʊs]
mountain	[maʊntn̩]	[muntn̩]	[maʊntn̩]
sound	[saʊnd]	[sund]	[saʊnd]
bounty	[baʊntɪ]	[buntɪ]	[baʊntɪ]
found	[faʊnd]	[fund]	[faʊnd]
down	[daʊn]	[dun]	[daʊn]
hound	[haʊnd]	[hund]	[haʊnd]
cloudy	[klaʊdɪ]	[kludɪ]	[klaʊdɪ]
now	[naʊ]	[nu]	[naʊ]

　　　u　　ʔ　e　　u　　　a
Now what have you found, Hank?
　ř　u　　　u
Fran counted on the bounty.
　　　　　　　　u　　　u
Meg climbed down the mountain.
　　　　　　u　　　u
Kay made the sound of a mouse.
　　　　u　　　　u　　řu
On a cloudy day, Kip plowed the ground.

Substitution of /ʊ/ for /ʌ/

This is a common Scottish characteristic. As you record the following words and sentences, focus on the substitution as transcribed.

	CAREER	SCOTTISH	CAREER
love	[lʌv]	[lʊv]	[lʌv]
such	[sʌtʃ]	[sʊtʃ]	[sʌtʃ]
double	[dʌbl̩]	[dʊbl̩]	[dʌbl̩]
money	[mʌnɪ]	[mʊnɪ]	[mʌnɪ]
punish	[pʌnɪʃ]	[pʊnɪʃ]	[pʌnɪʃ]
judge	[ʤʌʤ]	[ʤʊʤ]	[ʤʌʤ]
flood	[flʌd]	[flʊd]	[flʌd]
young	[jʌŋ]	[jʊŋ]	[jʌŋ]
hundred	[hʌndrəd]	[hʊndřəd]	[hʌndrəd]
muttering	[mʌtɚɪŋ]	[mʊtəřɪŋ]	[mʌtɚɪŋ]

　　　ʊ　　　ʊ　　ʊ　　　　εř
The young puppy dug in the dirt.
　ʊ　　　ʊ　　ʊ　　　　ʊ
Double bubble gum bubbles double.
　　　ʊ　　　εř　　　　　ʊ
The judge determined the punishment.
　　　　ʊ　　ʊ　　　　ʊ
A skunk stood on a stump.
　ʊ　əř　ʊ　　　ʊ　　　　　ř
Mother and Uncle Ned jumped into the car.

Consonants

Glottalization

One of the distinguishing characteristics of Scottish is the use of glottalization. Refer to the drills for cockney on page 338.

Substitution of /ɪç/ for Letters *ight*

The consonant /ç/ is also a sound found in German. It is roughly made by forming the vowel /ɪ/ and immediately producing /k/. The feeling of producing the sound ought to be like the reflex action when a fish bone is caught in your throat. Although this does not produce a very pleasant sound, it is very accurate! The sound /x/ is made the same way, except that it occurs after back vowels and is made farther back in the throat than /ç/.

Record the following list of words. Notice that in all of the words the substitution takes place in the final position.

	CAREER	SCOTTISH	CAREER
light	[laɪt]	[lɪç̱t]	[laɪt]
bright	[braɪt]	[břɪç̱t]	[braɪt]
right	[raɪt]	[řɪç̱t]	[raɪt]
slight	[slaɪt]	[slɪç̱t]	[slaɪt]
night	[naɪt]	[nɪç̱t]	[naɪt]
fight	[faɪt]	[fɪç̱t]	[faɪt]
sight	[saɪt]	[sɪç̱t]	[saɪt]
fright	[fraɪt]	[fřɪç̱t]	[fraɪt]
blight	[blaɪt]	[blɪç̱t]	[blaɪt]
might	[maɪt]	[mɪç̱t]	[maɪt]

Substitution of /ř/ for /r/ in All Positions

Record the following list of words. The trill is usually easier to produce for Americans when used in the blends /př/ and /gř/.

	CAREER	SCOTTISH	CAREER
ripe	[raɪp]	[ṟ̌aɪp]	[raɪp]
around	[əraʊnd]	[əṟ̌ʊnd]	[əraʊnd]
barren	[bærən]	[baṟ̌ən]	[bærən]
brag	[bræg]	[bṟ̌ag]	[bræg]
drum	[drʌm]	[dṟ̌ʊm]	[drʌm]
correct	[kərɛkt]	[kəṟ̌ɛkt]	[kərɛkt]
comfort	[kʌmfɚt]	[kʊmfəṟ̌t]	[kʌmfɚt]
Araby	[ærəbɪ]	[aṟ̌əbɪ]	[ærəbɪ]
prim	[prɪm]	[pṟ̌ɪm]	[prɪm]
pride	[praɪd]	[pṟ̌aɪd]	[praɪd]
grim	[grɪm]	[gṟ̌ɪm]	[grɪm]

Omission of /θ/ and /ð/ in Final Position

Record the following list of words. Then, add a word so you feel the sound omission (for example, [wɪ ʌs] for "with us").

	CAREER	SCOTTISH	CAREER
with	[wɪð], [wɪθ]	[wɪ]	[wɪð], [wɪθ]
mouth	[maʊθ]	[mu]	[maʊθ]

	CAREER	SCOTTISH	CAREER
youth	[juθ]	[ju]	[juθ]
truth	[truθ]	[třu]	[truθ]
cloth	[klɔθ]	[klɔ]	[klɔθ]
breathe	[brið]	[bři]	[brið]
bathe	[beð]	[be]	[beð]

 ## EXERCISES FOR A SCOTTISH ACCENT

In the following selections, the writers attempted to approximate the dialect through spelling. Phonetically transcribe the sounds over the appropriate letters.

       ç

1. *Lachie:* I'm nae much of a mon on the surface, boot I've a great and powerful will tae wurk. I've a wee butt-in-ben in Scotland which ye know aboot. Ma' health is guid, regardless of the Colonel's spite. I've a fearful temper, boot I dinna think I'll ever make ye suffer fur it.

                ař

From THE HASTY HEART
     ř

John Patrick

    ař

2. *Sarah:* I'm not sure which I'm wantin' maist—a wee flower for the window there or a bright new bonnet. Whit wud ye do—get the bonnet or the flower? Mrs. MacLeod has a braw new bonnet but now she has it, she canna enjoy it. Every time she puts it on, she's fairly sick wie the price of it.

      ř   ř

From SPRING O' THE YEAR

     ř   əř

W. H. Robertson

3. It mak's a change in a'thing roon'

When mither's gane.

The cat has less contented croon,

The kettle has a dowie tune,

There's naething has sae blythe a soon,

Sin' mither's gane.

The bairnies gang wi' ragged claes,

Sin' mither's gane.

There's nane to mend their broken taes,

Or laugh a' their pawky ways,

The nichts are langer than the days,

When mither's gane.

   ř   e

From WHEN MITHER'S GANE
Anonymous

4. Auld Daddy Darkness creeps frae his hole,

Black as a blackamoor, blin' as a mole;

Stir the fire till it lowes, let the baimie sit,

Auld Daddy Darkness is no want it yet.

See him in the corners hidin' frae the licht,

See him at the window gloomin' at the nicht;

Turn up the gas licht, close the shutters a',

An' Auld Daddy Darkness will flee far awa'.

a   ař
AULD DADDY DARKNESS
εř
James Ferguson

u
5. *Dowey:* I've never been here before. If you know what it is to be in sic a place without a friend. I was crazy with glee, when I got my leave, at the thought of seeing London at last, but after wandering its streets for four hours, I would almost have been glad to be back in the trenches.

ř   ɪ̌ɛ
From THE OLD LADY SHOWS HER MEDALS
aɪ
James M. Barrie

GERMAN

There are a few languages whose general pronunciations are important to Americans for political and social reasons. These include German, Spanish, French, and Russian.

To many people, the German language is intimidating because of its long words, lots of capital letters, and those two dots (umlauts) that seem to be everywhere. Some of the words are long because they are compounds made up of two or more words. For example, *Schuh* means "shoe," *Hand* means "hand," and *Handschuh* means "glove"—a shoe for the hand. Keep in mind that every noun in German has a capital letter, and the umlaut over a vowel indicates a different pronunciation. The umlaut is sometimes transcribed into English as an *e* that follows the umlauted vowel; thus the word *König* can be written as *Koenig*.

The following discussion of the German dialect is in no way exhaustive. The intent is to indicate characteristic sounds and substitutions that will help a professional communicator (actor or newsperson) who must be familiar with the language. The information will also be useful for Germans who are learning English pronunciation.

German Trill

The German language uses a trill that is different from the British or Scottish trill, which is made with the tongue tip. The German trill, which is also used in French, is produced with the back of the tongue against the uvula. This intensifies the guttural sound often associated with the German language. This uvular trill is very difficult for most Americans to produce because it does not exist in English and because its articulatory adjustment cannot be observed easily.

This trill, designated /ʀ/, is made by contact between the back of the tongue and the uvula. To produce this sound, gargle so that you can feel what is happening in your throat. If you cannot manage this trill with the back of the tongue, feel free to use the Scottish trill. A little trill is better than no trill!

The following is an attempt to indicate the sound of gargling rather than the word itself. Produce the gargling sound and carry it over into the pronunciation of the word.

gaaaaaaarrn-rrr ⟶ run
gaaaaaaarntrrr ⟶ rough
gaaaaaaarrrrrrr ⟶ rich

Now shorten the "gargle" and say the following words with a uvular /ʀ/:

rhyme	arrest	proud	trip	cream	frown
ripe	very	problem	trick	crime	frame
rent	horrible	brown	trunk	craft	Frances
rob	arrive	brought	drip	grim	French
range	around	bright	dream	green	freeze

Vowels and Diphthongs

Substitution of /ɑ/ for /æ/ and /ʌ/

This is a common substitution in many foreign languages. Record the following list of words and sentences. Focus on the vowel substitution.

	CAREER	GERMAN	CAREER
cat	[kæt]	[kɑt]	[kæt]
mass	[mæs]	[mɑs]	[mæs]
flash	[flæʃ]	[flɑʃ]	[flæʃ]
ask	[æsk]	[ɑsk]	[æsk]
half	[hæf]	[hɑf]	[hæf]
laugh	[læf]	[lɑf]	[læf]
class	[klæs]	[klɑs]	[klæs]
fast	[fæst]	[fɑst]	[fæst]
smashing	[smæʃɪŋ]	[smɑʃɪŋ]	[smæʃɪŋ]
damp	[dæmp]	[dɑmp]	[dæmp]

ɑ   ɑ   ɑ
Take a chance and command the child to stay off the grass.
ɑ   ɑ
On behalf of my good friend Eberhard Hoffman, I congratulate you.
ɑ   ɑ   ɑ
Rosemarie advanced into the alabaster bathroom.
ɑ   ɑ
Jürgen took a chance and glanced at Greta.
ɑ   ɑ
The photograph of Dr. Rainer amazed the class.

	CAREER	GERMAN	CAREER
double	[dʌbl̩]	[dɑbl̩]	[dʌbl̩]
money	[mʌnɪ]	[mɑnɪ]	[mʌnɪ]
come	[kʌm]	[kɑm]	[kʌm]

judge	[ʤʌʤ]	[ʒɑʒ]	[ʤʌʤ]
young	[jʌŋ]	[jɑŋ]	[jʌŋ]
puppy	[pʌpɪ]	[pɑpɪ]	[pʌpɪ]
humbug	[hʌmbʌg]	[hɑmbɑg]	[hʌmbʌg]
ugly	[ʌglɪ]	[ɑglɪ]	[ʌglɪ]
punish	[pʌnɪʃ]	[pɑnɪʃ]	[pʌnɪʃ]
studied	[stʌdɪd]	[stɑdɪd]	[stʌdɪd]

    ɑ   ɑ   ɑ
The young puppy dug in the dirt.
    ɑ   ɑ   ɑ
Double bubble gum bubbles double.
      ɑ   ɑ
The judge made the punishment fit the crime.
        ɑ   ɑ   ɑ   ɑ   ɑ   ɑ
The hamburg was on an ugly-looking bun covered with mustard. Humbug on the hamburg!
      ɑ   ɑ   ɑ
Have you studied much about the hummingbird?

Substitution of /ɛʀ/ for /ɝ/

This is a difficult substitution for Americans to say. Record the list of words and sentences. Remember to gargle.

	CAREER	GERMAN	CAREER
earth	[ɝθ]	[ɛʀs]	[ɝθ]
nerve	[nɝv]	[nɛʀf]	[nɝv]
work	[wɝk]	[vɛʀk]	[wɝk]
stir	[stɝ]	[ʃtɛʀ]	[stɝ]
verdict	[vɝdɪkt]	[fɛʀdɪçt]	[vɝdɪkt]
mercy	[mɝsɪ]	[mɛʀsɪ]	[mɝsɪ]
Irving	[ɝvɪŋ]	[ɛʀfɪŋ]	[ɝvɪŋ]
deserving	[dɪzɝvɪŋ]	[dɪzɛʀfɪŋk]	[dɪzɝvɪŋ]
confirm	[kɔnfɝm]	[kɔnfɛʀm]	[kɔnfɝm]
avert	[əvɝt]	[əfɛʀt]	[əvɝt]
Eric	[ɛrɪk]	[ɛʀɪç]	[ɛrɪk]

    ɛʀ   ɛʀ   ɛʀ   ɛʀ
The verb occurs in the first verse.
               ɛʀ   ɛʀ   ɛʀ
Rainer was sure he would smirk during the sermon.
    ɛʀ   ɛʀ
Research the records for Hans's birthday.
        ɛʀ   ɛʀ
The blackbird was sitting on the perch.
        ɛʀ   ɛʀ   ɛʀ
Many girls are learning to assert themselves.

Additional Vowel Sounds

German has three vowel sounds that do not exist in English. Although a German learning English would not need to use them, a number of careers require some use of the German language. An obvious example is the television newscaster who might have to pronounce German words for a news story.

1. Use the vowel /œ/ when *ö* is followed by two or more consonants, including double consonants. The vowel /œ/ is made by saying the vowel /ɛ/ with rounded lips. To hear and feel the German vowel, make certain that you form and think /ɛ/ while rounding the lips. Say:

/œ/ /œ/ /œ/ /œ/ /œ/

Now produce that vowel while reading the following German words:

Löffel ['lœfəl] (n.): spoon
Löschblatt ['lœʃblɑt] (n.): blotting paper
Mönch [mœnç] (n.): monk
Mörder ['mœʀdəř] (n.): murderer
nördlich [nœrtlɪç] (adj.): northern
öffentlich ['œfəntlɪç] (adj.): public
öffnen ['œfnən] (v.): to open
schöpfen ['ʃœpfən] (v.): to ladle
tröpfeln ['trœpfəln] (v.): to trickle

The following German proper names are pronounced with /œ/:

Böcklin ['bœkliːn], the painter
Böll [bœl], the author
Goebbels [gœbəls], the politician
Goethe ['gœtə], the poet
Hölderlin ['hœldəřlin], the poet
Mössbauer ['mœsbaʊəř], the physicist
Röntgen ['ʀœntgən], the physicist

2. Use the vowel /ø/ when *ö* is followed by a single consonant in the same syllable. The sound /ø/ is made by producing the vowel /e/ (as in "m<u>a</u>de") with rounded lips. To hear and feel the German vowel, make certain that you form and think /e/ while rounding the lips. Say:

/ø/ /ø/ /ø/ /ø/ /ø/

Now produce that vowel while reading the following German words:

dröhnen ['dʀøːnən] (v.): to roar
Gelöbnis [gə'løpnis] (n.): promise
Getöse [gə'tøːzə] (n.): noise
Höhe ['høːə] (n.): height
hörig ['høːrɪç] (adj.): a slave to
Köder ['køːdəř] (n.): lure
König ['køːnɪç] (n.): king
lösen ['løːzən] (v.): to loosen
nötigen ['nøːtɪgən] (v.): to compel
öde ['øːdə] (adj.): bleak, dull
Störer ['ʃtøːʀəř] (n.): one who disturbs

The following German proper nouns are pronounced with /ø/:

Böhm [bøːm], the conductor
Döblin [dø'bliːn], the author
Mörike ['møːřikə], the poet

3. Use /y/ when *ü* is followed by a single consonant or a double <u>s</u> within the same syllable. The vowel /y/ is made by producing the vowel /i/ (as in "<u>see</u>") with rounded lips. To hear and feel the German vowel, make certain that you form and think /i/ while rounding the lips. Say:
/y/ /y/ /y/ /y/ /y/

Now produce that vowel while reading the following German words:

bücken ['byːkən] (v.): to stoop:
Büffel ['byfəl] (n.): buffalo
Büro [by'ʀo] (n.): office
Gemüt [gə'myːt] (n.): mind, feeling
glück [glyk] (n.): good luck
tüchtig ['tyçtɪç] (adj.): clever
überführen ['yːbəř'fyːʀən] (v.): to convey
würde ['vyʀdə] (n.): dignity
würgen ['vyʀgən] (v.): to strangle
wüten ['vyːtən] (v.): to rage

The following German proper nouns are pronounced with /y/:

Brüssel ['bʀysəl], the city
Dürer ['dyːʀəř], the painter
Düsseldorf ['dysəldɔʀf], the city
Grünewald ['gřyːnəvɑlt], the painter
Heissenbüttel ['hɑɪsənbytəl], the poet
Lübeck ['lyːbɛk], the city
München ['mynçən] (n.): Munich
Nürnberg ['nyʀnbɛʀk], the city

4. In German, the letter combination *ie* is pronounced /i/ (as in "s<u>ee</u>"); the letter combination *ei* is prounounced /aɪ/ (as in "<u>i</u>ce").

Consonants

Substitution of /t/ or /s/ for /θ/ and /d/ or /z/ for /ð/

Record the following list of words, using career speech and German pronunciation.

	CAREER	GERMAN	CAREER
theme	[θim]	[t̠im], [s̠im]	[θim]
youthful	['juθfʊl]	['jut̠fəl], ['jus̠fəl]	['juθfʊl]
thought	[θɔt]	[t̠ɔt], [s̠ɔt]	[θɔt]
thin	[θɪn]	[t̠ɪn], [s̠ɪn]	[θɪn]
through	[θru]	[t̠ʀu], [s̠ʀu]	[θru]
mouth	[maʊθ]	[maʊt̠], [maʊs̠]	[maʊθ]
them	[ðɛm]	[d̠ɛm], [z̠ɛm]	[ðɛm]
either	['iðɚ]	['id̠ə], ['iz̠ə]²	['iðɚ]
weather	['wɛðɚ]	['vɛd̠ə], ['vɛz̠ə]²	['wɛðɚ]
breathe	[brið]	[bʀid̠], [bʀiz̠]	[brið]
feather	['fɛðɚ]	['fɛd̠ə], ['fɛz̠ə]²	['fɛðɚ]

Substitution of /v/ for /w/ and /ʍ/

This is a simple substitution. Record the following list of words, using career speech and German pronunciation.

	CAREER	GERMAN	CAREER
walk	[wɔk]	[v̠ɔk]	[wɔk]
when	[ʍɛn]	[v̠ɛn]	[ʍɛn]

---

²Final /r/ phonemes are often omitted in German.

	CAREER	GERMAN	CAREER
unworthy	[ən'wɝ·ðɪ]	[ən'v̠ɛʀzɪ]	[ən'wɝ·ðɪ]
liquid	['lɪkwɪd]	['lɪkv̠ɪd]	['lɪkwɪd]
wife	[waɪf]	[v̠aɪf]	[waɪf]
woman	['wʊmən]	['v̠ʊmən]	['wʊmən]
why	[ʍaɪ]	[v̠aɪ]	[ʍaɪ]
highway	['haɪˌwe]	['haɪˌv̠e]	['haɪˌwe]
anyone	['ɛnɪˌwʌn]	['ɛnɪˌv̠an]	['ɛnɪˌwʌn]
require	[rɪ'kwaɪr]	[ʀɪ'kv̠aɪə]	[rɪ'kwaɪr]

Record the following German proper nouns, shown with the transcriptions of their correct pronunciations:

Wagner ['vagnəř], the composer
Weill [vaɪl], the composer
Weizsäcker ['vaɪtszɛkəř], the physicist
Weser ['veːzəř], the river
Wien [viːn], Vienna
Wiesbaden ['viːsbadn̩], the city
Wilhelm ['vɪlhɛlm]
Wolfgang ['vʊlfgaŋ]
Zweig [tsvaɪk], the author
Schwartzwald ['ʃvatsvalt]

Substitution of /f/ for /v/

	CAREER	GERMAN	CAREER
very	['vɛrɪ]	['f̠ɛʀɪ]	['vɛrɪ]
vain	[ven]	[f̠en]	[ven]
David	['devɪd]	['def̠ɪt]	['devɪd]
eve	[iv]	[if̠]	[iv]
groove	[gruv]	[gʀuf̠]	[gruv]
prevent	[prɪ'vɛnt]	[pʀɪ'f̠ɛnt]	[prɪ'vɛnt]
avoid	[ə'vɔɪd]	[ə'f̠ɔɪd]	[ə'vɔɪd]
vanity	['vænətɪ]	['f̠anətɪ]	['vænətɪ]
evil	['ivl̩]	['if̠əl]	['ivl̩]
love	[lʌv]	[laf̠]	[lʌv]

Record the following German words, shown with the transcriptions of their correct pronunciations:

Vaterland ['faːtəřlant], fatherland
Beethoven ['beːtofən], composer
verboten [fɛř'botən], forbidden
Volkswagen ['fɔlksvaːgən], people wagon

Substitution of /x/ for Letters *ch* and *g* Following a Back Vowel, and of /ç/ Otherwise

In German, substitute the phoneme /x/ for the letters *ch* and *g* when they follow a back vowel. In all other instances use the /ç/ phoneme. The production of /x/ is mentioned in the discussion of the Scottish dialect on page 345. If you have difficulty in making either /x/ or /ç/, consider them interchangeable.

The following German proper names are shown with the transcriptions of their correct pronunciations:

Bach [bɑx], the composer
Barlach ['bɑřlɑx], the sculptor
Becher ['bɛçəř], the poet
Bloch [blɔx], the philosopher
Brecht [bʀɛçt], the writer
Eichendorff ['aɪçəndɔřf], the writer

Substitution of /ts/ for /z/

	CAREER	GERMAN	CAREER
zoo	[zu]	[<u>ts</u>u]	[zu]
zipper	['zɪpɚ]	[<u>ts</u>ɪpəř]	['zɪpɚ]
zinc	[zɪŋk]	[<u>ts</u>ɪŋk]	[zɪŋk]
xylophone	['zaɪləfon]	['<u>ts</u>aɪləfon]	['zaɪləfon]
zany	['zenɪ]	['<u>ts</u>enɪ]	['zenɪ]

Substitution of /ʃ/ for /ʧ/ and /ʒ/ for /ʤ/

Record the following list of words. This substitution usually occurs in the initial position and is common in some European languages.

	CAREER	GERMAN	CAREER
church	[ʧɝʧ]	[ʃɛRʃ]	[ʧɝʧ]
Chuck	[ʧʌk]	[ʃak]	[ʧʌk]
punch	[pʌnʧ]	[panʃ]	[pʌnʧ]
char	[ʧɑr]	[ʃɑr]	[ʧɑr]
chopping	['ʧɑpɪŋ]	['<u>ʃ</u>ɑpɪŋ]	['ʧɑpɪŋ]
jail	[ʤeɪl]	[ʒeɪl]	[ʤeɪl]
jump	[ʤʌmp]	[ʒɑmp]	[ʤʌmp]
joke	[ʤok]	[ʒok]	[ʤok]
jelly	['ʤɛlɪ]	['<u>ʒ</u>ɛlɪ]	['ʤɛlɪ]
gem	[ʤɛm]	[ʒɛm]	[ʤɛm]

Substitution of /ʃt/ and /ʃp/ for /st/ and /sp/

This substitution is very characteristic of the German dialect, especially in the initial position. Read aloud the following words, using both career speech and German pronunciation.

	CAREER	GERMAN	CAREER
student	['stɹudn̩t]	['<u>ʃ</u>tudənt]	['stɹudn̩t]
street	[strit]	[<u>ʃ</u>třit]	[strit]
strict	[strɪkt]	[<u>ʃ</u>třɪçt]	[strɪkt]
stripe	[straɪp]	[<u>ʃ</u>třaɪp]	[straɪp]
stable	['stebl̩]	['<u>ʃ</u>tebl̩]	['stebl̩]
stack	[stæk]	[<u>ʃ</u>tɑk]	[stæk]
stallion	['stæljən]	['<u>ʃ</u>tɑljən]	['stæljən]
stamp	[stæmp]	[<u>ʃ</u>tɑmp]	[stæmp]
stand	[stænd]	[<u>ʃ</u>tɑnt]	[stænd]
state	[stet]	[<u>ʃ</u>tet]	[stet]

	CAREER	GERMAN	CAREER
span	[spæn]	[ʃpɑn]	[spæn]
spot	[spɑt], [spɒt]	[ʃpɔt]	[spɑt], [spɒt]
speak	[spik]	[ʃpik]	[spik]
space	[spes]	[ʃpes]	[spes]
spoon	[spun]	[ʃpun]	[spun]
spicy	['spaɪsɪ]	['ʃpaɪsɪ]	['spaɪsɪ]
spin	[spɪn]	[ʃpɪn]	[spɪn]
spine	[spaɪn]	[ʃpaɪn]	[spaɪn]

The following German proper nouns are shown with the transcriptions of their correct pronunciations:

Einstein ['aɪnʃtaɪn], the scientist
Strauss [ʃtřaʊs]
Stuttgart ['ʃtutgɑřt], the city

EXERCISES FOR A GERMAN ACCENT

Try your hand at pronouncing German in the following translations of stanzas from English poems.

1. Tiger, Tiger, lohendes Licht,
Das dutch die Nacht der Walder bricht,
Welches Auge, welche unsterbliche Hand
Hat dich furchtbar in dein Ebenmass gebannt?

fʀ
From TIGER, TIGER
v
William Blake

2. Das Jahr, wenns fruhlingt,
und der Tag wird geborn
morgens um sieben,
der Hand, taubeperlt
die Lerche beschwingt,
die Schecke am Dorn:
Gott in Seinem Himmel—
Gut stehts um die Welt!

From PIPPA PASSES
Robert Browning

In the following exercises, transcribe the German substitutions above the appropriate letters before practicing aloud.

3. *Fräulein Schneider:* "Lina," my friends used to say to me, "however can you? How can you bear to have strange people living in your rooms and spoiling your furniture, especially when you've got the money to be independent?" And I'd always give them the same answer. "My lodgers aren't lodgers," I used to say. "They're my guests."

ɛʀ i
From A BERLIN DIARY
vu
Christopher Isherwood

4. *Fräulein Schneider:* Upset? Yes, I am upset. You go off on a trip of the whole world. You can afford to do that. But me, I have had to wait for my money, because you were too hard up sometimes to pay me. And now you throw me the china and the glass as a tip. The china and the glass. . . . I will throw them from the windows after your taxi as you go away. That is what I think from your china and your glass. And from you too.

From I AM A CAMERA

John Van Druten

5. *Fräulein Schneider:* Herr Schultz! Can I believe what I see? But this is too much to accept. So rare so costly—so luxurious . . . a pineapple for me!

From CABARET

Joseph Masteroff, John Kander, Fred Ebb

6. *Agnes:* That was a bitter time. From morning till night we heard nothing but the sounds of marching feet—the troops of the victor. The city had fallen. The enemy was here. His pennants fluttered against the dark sky like streamers of blood. It was noon on a day in spring; it was May, but the sky was dark with ashes and smoke.

From WHEN THE WAR WAS OVER

Max Frisch

7. *Einstein:* Well, Chonny, where do we go from here? We got to think fast. The Police! They got pictures of that face. I got to operate on you right away. We got to find someplace—and we got to find someplace for Mr. Spinalzo, too. . . . We can't leave a dead body in the rumble seat! You shouldn't have killed him, Chonny. He's a nice fellow—he gives us a lift and what happens?

From ARSENIC AND OLD LACE

Joseph Kesselring

8. But you must go to München. You have not seen Germany if you have not been to München. All the Exhibitions, all the Art and Soul life of Germany are in München. There is the Wagner Festival in August, and Mozart and a Japanese collection of pictures—and there is the beer! You do not know what good beer is until you have been to München.

From GERMANS AT MEAT

Katherine Mansfield

SPANISH

Because there has been such an influx of Spanish speakers into the United States, it has become increasingly important for Americans to speak and understand Spanish. Like German, Spanish spelling is very consistent with its pronunciation, once you know the rules.

Vowels

Substitution of /i/ for /ɪ/

This substitution is common in a number of languages. Record the following list of words and sentences. Focus on the differences in the transcriptions.

	CAREER	SPANISH	CAREER
pins	[pɪnz]	[p<u>i</u>nz]	[pɪnz]
chip	[ʧɪp]	[ʧ<u>i</u>p]	[ʧɪp]
wind	[wɪnd]	[w<u>i</u>nd]	[wɪnd]
lift	[lɪft]	[l<u>i</u>ft]	[lɪft]
since	[sɪns]	[s<u>i</u>ns]	[sɪns]
ship	[ʃɪp]	[ʧ<u>i</u>p][3]	[ʃɪp]
pretty	[prɪtɪ]	[př<u>i</u>t<u>i</u>]	[prɪtɪ]
business	['bɪznɪs]	['b<u>i</u>zn<u>i</u>s]	['bɪznɪs]
mistletoe	['mɪsl̩ˌtoʊ]	['m<u>i</u>sl̩toʊ]	['mɪsl̩ˌtoʊ]
fifty	['fɪftɪ]	['f<u>i</u>ft<u>i</u>]	['fɪftɪ]

     i i
Keep it simple.

    i   i   i i
Michele did the dishes quickly.

       i i   i
Where is Lizzie's kitten?

i   i i   i   i
Is he still sitting on his broken hip?

    i   i   i
Kip had a fit when he got bitten.

Substitution of /u/ for /ʊ/

Record the following list of words and sentences. Focus on the differences in the transcriptions.

	CAREER	SPANISH	CAREER
pudding	['pʊdɪŋ]	['p<u>u</u>dɪŋ]	['pʊdɪŋ]
put	[pʊt]	[p<u>u</u>t]	[pʊt]
good	[gʊd]	[g<u>u</u>d]	[gʊd]
mistook	[mɪs'tʊk]	[mis't<u>u</u>k]	[mɪs'tʊk]
looked	[lʊkt]	[l<u>u</u>kt]	[lʊkt]
could	[kʊd]	[k<u>u</u>d]	[kʊd]
tourist	['tʊrɪst]	['t<u>u</u>řist]	['tʊrɪst]
book	[bʊk]	[b<u>u</u>k]	[bʊk]
cooking	['kʊkɪŋ]	['k<u>u</u>kiŋ]	['kʊkɪŋ]
stood	[stʊd]	[st<u>u</u>d]	[stʊd]

  i   u   u   u
Miss Crook looked at the wolf.

  u   u   u
Put the hook on the hood of the car.

 ř   u   i   u
Larry made a good pass with the football.

---

[3] Often /ʧ/ is substituted for /ʃ/.

u   u   u   ř
Debbie pushed the cushion at Fred.
ř   u   u   ř
Where are the hooks for the woolen rugs?

Substitution of /ɑ/ for /æ/

The vowel /æ/ does not exist in Spanish. Record the following list of words and sentences. Focus on the difference between /ɑ/ and /æ/.

	CAREER	SPANISH	CAREER
catch	[kætʃ]	[kɑtʃ]	[kætʃ]
rack	[ræk]	[řɑk]	[ræk]
bandit	['bændɪt]	['bɑndit]	['bændɪt]
mad	[mæd]	[mɑd]	[mæd]
apple	['æpl̩]	['ɑpl̩]	['æpl̩]
scrap	[skræp]	[skřɑp]	[skræp]
master	['mæstɚ]	['mɑstəř]	['mæstɚ]
laugh	[læf]	[lɑf]	[læf]
class	[klæs]	[klɑs]	[klæs]
plastic	['plæstɪk]	['plɑstik]	['plæstɪk]

ɑ   i   ɑ   ɑ   řɑ
The cat will catch the fat rat.
řɑ   ɑ   i   ɑ
Take Fran's hand in class.
ɑ   ɑ   ɑ   əř
Half the apples were passed over.
ɑ   i   u   ɑ   ɑ   i
The bandit said to put the cash in the plastic box.
ɑ   ɑ əř i   əř   ɑř   əř
The Mad Hatter is a humorous character.

Substitution of /ɑ/ for /ʌ/

The vowel /ʌ/ does not occur in Spanish. Record the following list of words and sentences. Focus on the substitutions.

	CAREER	SPANISH	CAREER
duck	[dʌk]	[dɑk]	[dʌk]
hungry	['hʌngrɪ]	['xɑngři]	['hʌngrɪ]
onion	['ʌnjən]	['ɑndʒən]	['ʌnjən]
brush	[brʌʃ]	[břɑtʃ]	[brʌʃ]
nuts	[nʌts]	[nɑts]	[nʌts]
must	[mʌst]	[mɑst]	[mʌst]
pump	[pʌmp]	[pɑmp]	[pʌmp]
gun	[gʌn]	[gɑn]	[gʌn]
lucky	['lʌkɪ]	['lɑki]	['lʌkɪ]
hunt	[hʌnt]	[xɑnt]	[hʌnt]

dʒ   ɑ   ɑ   d   əř   ɑ
You must pump the water gun.
řɑtʃ   ɑ   id   d   ɑ   o
Brush the duck with the nutty sauce.

ɑ ʤ   ɑ   ɑ   d xɑ   in ɛř
Have you studied much about the hummingbird?
ɑd řɑ   d ɑ   əř řd ɑ ʧ
Mother rushed to the dumbwaiter for the fudge.
ɑ ʧɑ ɑ   ɑ   in
I can jump and touch the ceiling.

Consonants

Substitution of /s/ for Initial /θ/

These substitutions occur in several languages. Record the following list of words. Focus on the substitutions

	CAREER	SPANISH	CAREER
thought	[θɔt]	[sɔt]	[θɔt]
think	[θɪŋk]	[siŋk]	[θɪŋk]
thanks	[θæŋks]	[sɑŋks]	[θæŋks]
thin	[θɪn]	[sin]	[θɪn]
thick	[θɪk]	[sik]	[θɪk]
thigh	[θaɪ]	[saɪ]	[θaɪ]
thread	[θrɛd]	[sřɛd]	[θrɛd]
theft	[θɛft]	[sɛft]	[θɛft]
thing	[θɪŋ]	[siŋ]	[θɪŋ]
thaw	[θɔ]	[so]	[θɔ]

Substitution of /d/ for /ð/

	CAREER	SPANISH	CAREER
these	[ðiz]	[diz]	[ðiz]
that	[ðæt]	[dɑt]	[ðæt]
though	[ðoʊ]	[doʊ]	[ðoʊ]
loathes	[loðz]	[lodz]	[loðz]
lather	['læðɚ]	['lɑdəř]	['læðɚ]
leather	['lɛðɚ]	['lɛdəř]	['lɛðɚ]
either	['iðɚ]	['idəř]	['iðɚ]
weather	['wɛðɚ]	['wɛdəř]	['wɛðɚ]
bathes	[beðz]	[bedz]	[beðz]
with	[wɪð]	[wid]	[wɪð]

Substitution of /x/ for /h/

Because there is no /h/ phoneme in Spanish, a native Spanish speaker often substitutes /x/ for /h/ when speaking English. The primary difference between /x/ and /ç/ is that /x/ is produced farther back in the throat. (Remember that the sound /x/ can be produced by the action of dislodging a fish bone from the throat!) Record the following list of words. Focus on the substitutions.

	CAREER	SPANISH	CAREER
high	[haɪ]	[xaɪ]	[haɪ]
hand	[hænd]	[xɑnd]	[hænd]
hat	[hæt]	[xɑt]	[hæt]
heaven	['hɛvən]	['xɛβən]	['hɛvən]

hold	[hold]	[x̲old]	[hold]
hit	[hɪt]	[x̲ɪt]	[hɪt]
inhale	[ɪnhel]	[ɪnx̲el]	[ɪnhel]
somehow	['sʌmhaʊ]	['samx̲aʊ]	['sʌmhaʊ]
exhale	['ɛkshel]	['ɛksx̲el]	['ɛkshel]
behave	[bɪ'hev]	[bi'x̲ev]	[bɪ'hev]

Substitution of /β/ for /b/ and /v/

The consonant /β/ is a vocalized bilabial fricative made by the escape of vibrating air between the vibrating lips. To produce the /β/ phoneme, make /v/ without allowing the upper teeth to touch the bottom lip. Instead, the two lips touch and vibrate. Record the following list of words and sentences. Focus on the substitutions.

	CAREER	SPANISH	CAREER
base	[bes]	[β̲es]	[bes]
bay	[beɪ]	[β̲eɪ]	[beɪ]
above	[ə'bʌv]	[aβ̲aβ̲]	[ə'bʌv]
habit	['hæbɪt]	['xaβ̲it]	['hæbɪt]
stable	[stebl̩]	[steβ̲l̩]	[stebl̩]
valley	['vælɪ]	['β̲ali]	['vælɪ]
vain	[veɪn]	[β̲eɪn]	[veɪn]
David	['devɪd]	['deβ̲id]	['devɪd]
stove	[stov]	[stoβ̲]	[stov]
love	[lʌv]	[laβ̲]	[lʌv]

β   ɑ   xaβ   i
Steve doesn't have any.
β i i xaβ   βi   xə βanə kuβə
Vicki, have you been to Havana, Cuba?
xaβ   d   aβ   əř
Have you met the governor, Katie?
βaβ   xaβ   β   β
Bob told me not to have a baseball game.
x   xaβ   xaβ   ɑ   β   i
Why do we have to have a fuss about it?

Substitution of /ř/ for /r/

Refer to the list of words on page 345.

EXERCISES FOR A SPANISH ACCENT

Read and tape the word pairs aloud, and replay making certain you are differentiating between the sounds being presented. If you are having difficulty discriminating between the sounds, refer to the appropriate section of the CD.

(p-b)

INITIAL		MEDIAL		FINAL	
peat	beat	dips	dibs	rip	rib
pit	bit				

pet	bet				
pat	bat	rapid	rabid	cap	cab
par	bar	cops	cobs	lop	lob
Paul	ball				
pull	bull				
plume	bloom	loops	lubes	loop	lube
purr	burr			Earp	herb
putt	but	pups	pubs	cup	cub
pace	base			ape	Abe
pie	by			tripe	tribe
poi	boy				
pout	bout				
pole	bowl	roping	robing	rope	robe

(b-v)

INITIAL		MEDIAL		FINAL	
beat	veep	Eben	even		
bicker	vicar				
berry	very	ebber	ever		
bat	vat				
boom	voom				
bale	vale	cable	caver		
buy	vie				
Boyd	void				
bough	vow				
boat	vote	lobes	loaves	robe	rove

(ʃ-ʧ)

INITIAL		MEDIAL		FINAL	
sheet	cheat	leashes	leaches	quiche	Keach
ship	chip	wishing	witching	dish	ditch
share	chair				
shad	Chad	masher	matcher	cash	catch
shop	chop	washer	watcher	wash	watch
shuck	Chuck	bushes	butches	bush	Butch
shoe	chew				
shuck	Chuck			mush	much
Shane	chain				
shore	chore	kosher	coacher		

(t-θ)

INITIAL		MEDIAL		FINAL	
tree	three	eater	ether	heat	heath
trill	thrill	mitts	myths	wit	with
tread	thread	tents	tenths	debt	death
tank	thank	batless	bathless	mat	math
				swat	swath
taught	thought	forts	fourths	brought	broth
true	through	roots	Ruth's	toot	tooth
				dirt	dirth
tug	thug				
tie	thigh	fates	faiths	fate	faith
tow	throw				

(d-ð)

INITIAL		MEDIAL		FINAL	
		breeds	breathes	seed	seethe
den	then				
Dan	than	ladder	lather		
		fodder	father		
		wordier	worthier		
		udder	other		
day	they				
die	thy	riding	writhing		
dough	though	loads	loathes		

(s-ʃ)

INITIAL		MEDIAL	
see	she	leases	leashes
sip	ship		
said	shed	messed	meshed
sack	shack	massed	mashed
sock	shock		
sort	short		
		pussy	pushy
sue	shoe		
sun	shun		
say	shay		
sigh	shy		
sour	shower		
so	show		

In the following exercises, transcribe the phonetic substitutions used in a Spanish accent as indicated above the appropriate letters. As you become more adept at making the substitutions increase your rate of speed. Work for continuity.

1. In the following speech, the playwright has attempted to indicate a Spanish accent through spelling. Add any remaining substitutions needed.

   Certamente. . . . And to him who bids the 'ighest, shall go ze little paper and he shall come wiz me while I show 'im where se oil she is 'iding. To him what does not bid ze 'ighest, he shall stay 'ere wiz Pedro until eight o'clock tonight.

     ř   d   a   a
   From THE BAD MAN

             ɛř   ř
   Porter Emerson Brown

     d   i   i
2. *The Gypsy:* I'll show you how to take a shot of tequila. It dilates the capillaries. First you sprinkle salt on the back of your hand. Then lick it off with your tongue. Now then, you toss the shot down. And then you bite into the lemon. That way, it goes down easy, but what a bang!—You're next.

   From CAMINO REAL
   Tennessee Williams

3. *Googie Gomez:* You boy really know how to cheer a girl up when she's dumps in the down. My boyfriend Hector see me do that: ay! cuidado! He hates you maricones, that Hector! . . . You know why you're not a producer? You're too nice to be a producer. But I'm gonna show them all, mister, and tonight's the night I'm gonna do it. One day you gonna see the name Googie Gomez in lights and you gonna say to yourself: "Was that her?" And you gonna answer yourself, "That was her!" But you know something, mister? I was always her, just nobody knows it. Yo soy Googie Gomez, estrellita del futuro!

     ř   d   ři
   From THE RITZ
   Terence McNally

4. *Tomas:* Perhaps, after the mass, when the women have come home, you and I could stop in the saloon and celebrate the coming of a phonograph to El Carmen. Perhaps you can even buy us a large glass of beer in celebration . . . ten cent glasses.

     ř   s ř ʧ β
   From TOOTH OR SHAVE
   Josephina Niggli

5. *Maria:*

   One thing always gives me laughter

   Pancho Villa[4] the morning after

   Ay, there go the Carranzistas

   Who comes there?

   Why the Villistas.

   Ay, Pancho Villa, ay Pancho Villa,

   Ay, he can no longer walk.

   ---

   [4]For the letters *ll*, use /j/.

Because he lacks now, because he has not

Any drug to help him talk! Ay-yay!

εř

From SOLDADERA
Josephina Niggli

>>> RUSSIAN

Russian is a particularly difficult language for Westerners because it contains few similarities to familiar languages such as French, Italian, and Spanish. Furthermore, Russian is written with a different alphabet, the Cyrillic. This is why Russian appears to have sideway and backward letters.

Because learning another alphabet in addition to the IPA would be too demanding, this unit will only discuss some characteristics of a Russian accent in English. In addition, some Russian proper nouns will be transcribed into our alphabet and the IPA.

Vowels and Diphthongs

Substitution of /i/ for /ɪ/

This is a substitution found in Spanish. Record the following list of words. Focus on the pronunciation according to the transcriptions. Additional words appear on page 90.

	CAREER	RUSSIAN	CAREER
hit	[hɪt]	[hit]	[hɪt]
mitten	[mɪtn̩]	[mitn̩]	[mɪtn̩]
film	[fɪlm]	[film]	[fɪlm]
split	[splɪt]	[split]	[splɪt]
tin	[tɪn]	[tin]	[tɪn]
simple	['sɪmpl̩]	['simpl̩]	['sɪmpl̩]
list	[lɪst]	[list]	[lɪst]
him	[hɪm]	[him]	[hɪm]

To realize the importance of distinguishing /i/ from /ɪ/, compare the following word pairs:

/i/		/ɪ/	
green	[grin]	grin	[grɪn]
scream	[skrim]	scrim	[skrɪm]
read	[rid]	rid	[rɪd]
meat	[mit]	mitt	[mɪt]
neat	[nit]	knit	[nɪt]
lead	[lid]	lid	[lɪd]
Jean	[dʒin]	gin	[dʒɪn]
seed	[sid]	Sid	[sɪd]
teen	[tin]	tin	[tɪn]
scene	[sin]	sin	[sɪn]

Substitution of /ɔ/ for /o/

This substitution is rarely found in other languages. Record the following list of words and sentences. Focus on their transcriptions.

	CAREER	RUSSIAN	CAREER
coat	[kot]	[kɔ̲t]	[kot]
fellow	['fɛlo]	['fɛljɔ̲]	['fɛlo]
blow	[blo]	[blɔ̲]	[blo]
hold	[hold]	[hɔ̲lt]	[hold]
scold	[skold]	[skɔ̲lt]	[skold]
moat	[mot]	[mɔ̲t]	[mot]
slow	[slo]	[slɔ̲]	[slo]
low	[lo]	[lɔ̲]	[lo]
rowed	[rod]	[rɔ̲t]	[rod]
alone	[ə'lon]	[ə'lɔ̲n]	[ə'lon]

Refer to the comparison of /ɔ/ and /o/ on page 111.

    ɔ   ɔ   ɔ   ɔ

The opening of *Oklahoma!* was loaded with celebrities.

    ɔ   ɔ   ɔ

Snow White sang "Heigh Ho" along with Dopey.

    ɔ   ɔ   ɔ   ɔ ɔ

The phoney old man was rowing toward the other rowboat.

    ɔ   ɔ   ɔ

Go and bring me the folders from both desks.

        ɔ   ɔ   ɔ   ɔ

The short stories by Poe are often odious, woeful, and sorrowful.

Substitution of /u/ for /ʊ/

This substitution also appears in Spanish. Record the following list of words and sentences as transcribed. Additional words and sentences appear on pages 113–114.

	CAREER	RUSSIAN	CAREER
full	[fʊl]	[fu̲l]	[fʊl]
bush	[bʊʃ]	[bu̲ʃ]	[bʊʃ]
mistook	[mɪstʊk]	[mistu̲k]	[mɪstʊk]
would	[wʊd]	[vu̲d]	[wʊd]
wool	[wʊl]	[vu̲l]	[wʊl]
book	[bʊk]	[bu̲k]	[bʊk]
hood	[hʊd]	[hu̲t]	[hʊd]
could	[kʊd]	[ku̲t]	[kʊd]
bookcase	[bʊkes]	[bu̲kes]	[bʊkes]
pudding	[pʊdɪŋ]	[pu̲dɪŋk]	[pʊdɪŋ]

   U U   U   U I I   U I

The cook took the sugar and put it in the pudding.

   U   U   U

The wolf stole the pullet and forsook the farm.

   U   U

The wooden keg was full of beer.

   U   I   U   I   U

The butcher withstood the insults as long as he could.

     U   U   U

He shook the hook from the pushcart.

Substitution of /ɑ/ for /æ/

This substitution is common in several languages. Record the following list of words and sentences as transcribed.

	CAREER	RUSSIAN	CAREER
mad	[mæd]	[mɑ̠d]	[mæd]
chap	[tʃæp]	[tʃɑ̠p]	[tʃæp]
grab	[græb]	[gř̠ɑ̠b]	[græb]
track	[træk]	[tř̠ɑ̠k]	[træk]
add	[æd]	[ɑ̠d]	[æd]
rather	[ræðɚ]	[ř̠ɑ̠dəř]	[ræðɚ]
latch	[lætʃ]	[lɑ̠tʃ]	[lætʃ]
man	[mæn]	[mɑ̠n]	[mæn]
snack	[snæk]	[snɑ̠k]	[snæk]
laughed	[læft]	[lɑ̠ft]	[læft]

    ɑ   ɑ   ɑ   ɑ

The man's manners seemed radical to the chapter.

    ɑ   ɑ   i   ɑ   ɑ   ɑ

Ask Andy if he saw the tan cat attack the dog.

    ɑ   i   ɑ   i   ɔ ɑ

Candid Camera is a popular program.

    ɑ   ɑ   i   ɑ   ɑ ɑ ɑ

The masked bandit grabbed half the calf and ran.

   ɑ   ɑ   i   i   ɑ xɑ i

Cramming for examinations is a bad habit.

Substitution of /ɛř/ for /ɝ/

This substitution is also common in other languages. Record the following list of words and sentences as transcribed. Additional words and sentences appear on page 342.

	CAREER	RUSSIAN	CAREER
deserve	[dɪˈzɝv]	[diˈzɛ̠řv]	[dɪˈzɝv]
learn	[lɝn]	[lɛ̠řn]	[lɝn]
hurt	[hɝt]	[hɛ̠řt]	[hɝt]
reverse	[rɪˈvɝs]	[riˈvɛ̠řs]	[rɪˈvɝs]
word	[wɝd]	[vɛ̠řd]	[wɝd]
worth	[wɝθ]	[vɛ̠řt]	[wɝθ]
reserve	[rɪˈzɝv]	[riˈzɛ̠řv]	[rɪˈzɝv]
girl	[gɝl]	[gɛ̠řl]	[gɝl]
dirt	[dɝrt]	[dɛ̠řt]	[dɝrt]

Consonants

Dentalization of /t/, /d/, and /n/

To produce dentalization, remember to place the blade of the tongue in contact with the back of the top teeth. To eliminate dentalization, refer to the discussion on page 315. Record the following list of words, comparing the differences between career speech and the Russian dialect.

	CAREER	RUSSIAN	CAREER
today	[təˈdeɪ]	[t̪əˈd̪eɪ]	[təˈdeɪ]
don't	[dont]	[d̪ont̪]	[dont]

numb	[nʌm]	[n̪ɑm]	[nʌm]
dough	[doʊ]	[d̪ɔ]	[doʊ]
past	[pæst]	[past̪]	[pæst]
trust	[trʌst]	[t̪řʌst̪]	[trʌst]
wed	[wɛd]	[vɛd̪]	[wɛd]
cat	[kæt]	[kɑt̪]	[kæt]
wade	[wed]	[ved̪]	[wed]
once	[wʌns]	[vɑn̪s]	[wʌns]

Substitution of /tʃ/ or /ʒ/ for /dʒ/

This substitution is very characteristic of the Russian dialect. Record the following list of words and sentences, comparing the differences between career speech and the Russian dialect.

	CAREER	RUSSIAN	CAREER
jump	[dʒʌmp]	[tʃʌmp], [ʒɑmp]	[dʒʌmp]
jaw	[dʒɔ]	[tʃɔ]	[dʒɔ]
judge	[dʒʌdʒ]	[tʃʌtʃ]	[dʒʌdʒ]
gentle	['dʒɛntl̩]	['tʃɛntl̩]	['dʒɛntl̩]
bridge	[brɪdʒ]	[břɪtʃ], [břɪʒ]	[brɪdʒ]
badge	[bædʒ]	[batʃ], [baʒ]	[bædʒ]
magic	['mædʒɪk]	['matʃik], ['maʒik]	['mædʒɪk]
joke	[dʒok]	[tʃok], [ʒok]	[dʒok]

      tʃ   ř ɔ   ř tʃ
The angels wrote down the strategy.
tʃ   tʃɑ   ř   ɑ i
Judy jumped from the chair she sat in.
tʃi   ɑtʃ   ɔ
Jim sent the badge to the police.
      ř tʃ tʃɑ   i   ɑř tʃ
The stranger jumped into marriage.
    ɑtʃ   tʃɔ   tʃ
Madge played the joke on John.

Substitution of /v/ for /w/

This substitution is also common in the German dialect. Record the following list of words. Focus on the substitutions.

	CAREER	RUSSIAN	CAREER
web	[wɛb]	[vɛb]	[wɛb]
way	[weɪ]	[veɪ]	[weɪ]
wasp	[wɔsp]	[vɔsp]	[wɔsp]
wavy	[wevɪ]	[vevi]	[wevɪ]
wall	[wɔl]	[vɔl]	[wɔl]
waste	[west]	[vest]	[west]
weather	['wɛðɚ]	['vɛdəř]	['wɛðɚ]
weak	[wik]	[vik]	[wik]
when	[ʍɛn]	[vɛn]	[ʍɛn]
white	[ʍaɪt]	[vaɪt]	[ʍaɪt]

For additional words, refer to pages 351–352.

Substitution of /d/ for /ð/

Refer to the words on page 358.

Substitution of /ř/ for /r/

Refer to the words on page 345.

Addition of /k/ to /ŋ/ in Words with More Than One Syllable

Record the following words and sentences, comparing career speech with the Russian dialect.

	CAREER	RUSSIAN	CAREER
going	['goɪŋ]	['goɪŋk]	['goɪŋ]
tying	['taɪɪŋ]	['taɪɪŋk]	['taɪɪŋ]
slaving	['slevɪŋ]	['slefɪŋk]	['slevɪŋ]
bowing	['bauɪŋ]	['bauɪŋk]	['bauɪŋ]
	['bɔɪŋ]	['bɔɪŋk]	['bɔɪŋ]
failing	['felɪŋ]	['felɪŋk]	['felɪŋ]
stating	['stetɪŋ]	['stetɪŋk]	['stetɪŋ]
jumping	['dʒʌmpɪŋ]	['tʃampɪŋk]	['dʒʌmpɪŋ]
clanking	['klæŋkɪŋ]	['klaŋkɪŋk]	['klæŋkɪŋ]
teaching	['titʃɪŋ]	['titʃɪŋk]	['titʃɪŋ]
loving	['lʌvɪŋ]	['lafɪŋk]	['lʌvɪŋ]

ɪŋk ɑ   ɪŋk ɑ   ɪŋk
Dividing and gliding and sliding.
ɑ   ɪŋk ɑ   ř   ɪŋk ɑ   ř   ɪŋk
And falling and brawling and sprawling,
ɑ   ř   ɪŋk ɑ   ř   ɪŋk ɑ   ř   ɪŋk
And driving and riving and striving
ɑ   řɪŋk ɪŋk ɑ   ɪŋk ɪŋk ɑ   řɪŋk ɪŋk
And sprinkling and twinkling and wrinkling.

Substitution of /t/ for Final /d/

Record the following transcriptions, comparing career speech with the Russian dialect.

	CAREER	RUSSIAN	CAREER
had	[hæd]	[hɑt̪]	[hæd]
jade	[dʒed]	[tʃet̪]	[dʒed]
sound	[saʊnd]	[sɑʊn̪t̪]	[saʊnd]
braided	[bredəd]	[bředət̪]	[bredəd]
said	[sɛd]	[sɛt̪]	[sɛd]
nude	[nɪud]	[n̪ɪut̪]	[nɪud]
opened	[opənd]	[ɔpən̪t̪]	[opənd]
patted	[pætəd]	[pɑt̪ət̪]	[pætəd]
bad	[bæd]	[bɑt̪]	[bæd]

Substitution of /f/ for Medial or Final /v/

This substitution also appears in the German dialect. Record the following list of words as transcribed. Additional words are given on page 352.

	CAREER	RUSSIAN	CAREER
leave	[liv]	[lif]	[liv]
lovely	[ˈlʌvlɪ]	[ˈlafli]	[ˈlʌvlɪ]
above	[əˈbʌv]	[əˈbaf]	[əˈbʌv]
forgive	[fɔrˈgɪv]	[fɔřgif]	[fɔrˈgɪv]
prove	[pruv]	[přuf]	[pruv]
serve	[sɝv]	[sɛřf]	[sɝv]
waves	[wevz]	[vefs]	[wevz]
move	[muv]	[muf]	[muv]
oven	[ˈʌvn̩]	[ˈafən]	[ˈʌvn̩]
shove	[ʃʌv]	[ʃaf]	[ʃʌv]
carve	[kɑrv]	[kɑřf]	[kɑrv]

Substitution of /x/ or /ç/ for /h/

The /h/ phoneme does not exist in Russian. Refer to the words on pages 358–359.

EXERCISES FOR A RUSSIAN ACCENT

1. Pronounce the following Russian nouns according to the phonetic transcriptions; use the primary stress indicated:

babushka [ˈbɑbuʃkə]: grandmother
Bolshoi [ˈbalʃɔɪ]: the ballet company
borscht [bɔřʃ]: a vegetable and beet soup
dacha [ˈdɑtʃə]: a country house
Gulag [ˈgulɑg]: the group of concentration camps
nyet [n̠jɛt̠] or [n̠ɪɛt̠]: no
samizdat [sɑmɪzˈdɑt̠]: an underground political paper

The following are commonly encountered proper names:

Aleksei [ɑlɪkˈseɪ]
Boris [bɑˈřis]
Chekhov [ˈtʃɛkxɒf]
Ekaterina [ɪkət̠ɪřˈin̠ə]
Galina [gɑˈlin̠ə]
Godunov [gədುˈn̠ɒf]
Gogol [ˈgɔgəl]
Grigori [gřɪˈgɔři]
Ivan [iˈfɑn̠]
Ivanova [iˈfɑn̠ɑvɑ]
Ivanovich [iˈfɑn̠əfitʃ]
Moussorgsky [ˈmuzəřski]

Nabokov [nɑˈbɒkɒf]
Prokofiev [přɑˈkɔfjɛf]
Rasputin [řasˈput̠in̠]
Rimski-Korsakov [ˈřimski ˈkɔřsikɔf]
Shostakovich [ʃəst̠əˈkɔfitʃ]
Solzhenitsyn [sɔlʒəˈnit̠sin̠]
Stanislavski [st̠ɛn̠ɪsˈlɑfski]
Stravinsky [st̠řəˈfin̠ski]
Tchaikovsky [tʃeˈkɒfski]
Tolstoi [ˈt̠ʌl̩st̠ɔi]
Vladimir [vl̩ɑˈdimɛř]

In the following exercises, transcribe the phonetic substitutions used in a Russian accent above the appropriate letters. As you become more adept at making the substitutions, increase your rate of speech. Work for continuity.

   d   ř a   a

2. *The Grand Duchess:* Ali, Kolenkhov, our time is coming. My sister Natasha is studying to be a manicurist. Uncle Sergi they have promised to make floor-walker, and next month I get transferred to the Fifth Avenue Childs'. From there it is only a step to Schraffts', and then we will see what Prince Alexis says.

ř a   i   id
From YOU CAN'T TAKE IT WITH YOU
        x   a t ʧ
Moss Hart and George Kaufman

2. *Kolenkhov:* He should have been in Russia when the Revolution came. Then he would have stood in line—a bread line. Ali, Grandpa, what they have done to Russia. Think of it! The Grand Duchess, Olga Katrina, a cousin of the Czar, she is a waitress in Childs' restaurant! I ordered baked beans from her only yesterday. It broke my heart.

ř a   I   id
From YOU CAN'T TAKE IT WITH YOU
        x   a t ʧ
Moss Hart and George Kaufman

3. *Ikonenko:* Herr Busch, your attitude, even though it is impossible to understand, does you no credit. I must warn you against the terrible danger of being incomprehensible in the future. I shall give the order tonight for Soviet troops to begin operations for the occupation of the castle at dawn tomorrow, so that it may pass back into the hands of its legitimate owners, the people!

ř a   d   af   af
From THE LOVE OF FOUR COLONELS
Peter Ustinov

4. *Romanoff:* We have a perfect right to criticize each other. It is a pastime encouraged by the party. You have been criticizing me since your arrival. Now it's my turn. My criticism will take the form of a history lesson. Don't interrupt me—I am sure you know many more dates than I do, but I know more about our revolution than you do, because I was there!

ř a   ř   a t ʧ
From ROMANOFF AND JULIET
Peter Ustinov

5. *Spy:* A confession of only eight pages? It appears as though you were still attempting to conceal something. Comrade Kotkov's recent confession ran to two hundred and fourteen typewritten pages, and was written in a clear, concise, functional style. At the end, the reader had a vivid impression of the author's inner rottenness. It was a model of how such documents should be prepared.

ř a   ř   a t ʧ
From ROMANOFF AND JULIET
Peter Ustinov

6. The former empress of Russia believes that she has finally found her long lost granddaughter Anastasia.

Malenkaia! Malenkaia! Malenkaia! I couldn't believe it at first. You've come from so far away and I waited and waited and waited. Don't cry—don't say anything—you are warm, you are alive—that is enough. I can stand no more for now. Can't you hear how that weary old heart of mine is beating? I must go—but don't be afraid—I shall come back—I need you. Let go of my dress. That is what you used to do as a child. Be sensible, Malenkaia. I'll go as I used to—speaking to you as I left the side of your little bed. We will go, tomorrow if you like, to my old palace in Finland. It is still there and still mine. There is a very old man there—our lamplighter. Each evening he goes from one room to another lighting the empty lamps—until for him the great dark rooms are ablaze with light. The other servants take no notice—they realize that he is childish. And perhaps that is true of us all—and we are lighting dead lamps to illumine a life that is gone. Goodnight, Anastasia—and please—if it should not be you—don't ever tell me.

From ANASTASIA
Marcelle Maurette, adapted by Guy Bolton

W To locate URLs and search terms for weblinks relevant to this chapter, please go to the companion website at www.cengage.com/rtf/crannell/voiceandarticulation5e and select the proper chapter.

Write the definitions for the following terms in the space below.

KEY TERMS	DEFINITIONS
Ear Training	
Glottalization	
Intervocalic /r/	
Standard Stage Speech (London Speech)	

APPENDIX A

ENGLISH PRONUNCIATION FOR ASIAN-LANGUAGE SPEAKERS

For students who are pursuing a career in the communications arts, Chapter 13 (Stage Speech and Selected International Accents) might prove helpful. That chapter includes accents that are of particular interest to actors (standard stage speech, cockney, and Scottish) and pronunciations of interest to radio and television anchors (German, Spanish, and Russian). However, any Western normative English speakers with any of these particular accents would find the discussions and exercises very useful.

Because of the influx of Asian immigrants into the United States, discussions of English pronunciations for speakers of Chinese, Japanese, Korean, and Vietnamese appear in this Appendix. Because the languages of Japan, Korea, and Vietnam are based on the Chinese language, many of its distinctive characteristics appear in the other Asian languages. Special characteristics of each language are included.

Chapters 6 through 10 are particularly useful because they focus on individual American-English sounds, pronunciations, and speech dynamics, both verbal and non-verbal. As in Chapter 13, the page numbers of appropriate drill exercises that appear elsewhere in the text are given.

>>>
Chinese

Distinctive Characteristics of the Chinese Language

The two major dialects of the Chinese language are Cantonese and Mandarin. Cantonese is the language of Hong Kong and is by far the most widely spoken dialect. Mandarin is the dialect of northern China and of its capital, Beijing. Although the dialects are similar in structure, they are different in intelligibility. Both dialects present the same problems for Chinese who are attempting to learn English: the same sound substitutions occur.

The Chinese (as well as other Asians) have special needs that are related not only to their language but also to their culture. Chapters 9 and 10 include both information about the English language and exercises that can help Chinese people to adapt more successfully to their new language. Among the cultural differences that Chinese English-speakers experience is the verbal and nonverbal overtness of Americans. First, most Asians are not used to the physical freedom Americans display in both face and body; the Chinese feel quite uncomfortable using their faces (especially the eyes). Further, most Asians are unaccustomed to (and are very self-conscious about) producing any sound that requires them to reveal their tongues or move their lips. To most Asians the tongue is a private organ. And so, in addition to learning the particular sounds of English, attention must be given to these cultural differences. For these reasons it may be helpful to work on articulatory exercises such as those that appear in Chapter 7.

Chinese dialects are composed of monosyllabic words that often end in vowels and diphthongs. Because no Chinese words end with /l/, /r/, /f/, /v/, /s/, /ʃ/ (as in "<u>ship</u>"), or /tʃ/ (as in "<u>church</u>"), the Chinese dialects have few final consonant sounds. Therefore, when learning English pronunciation, Chinese speakers must make certain that they finish their words. The tendency is to omit final consonants.

Record the following words, paying close attention to the final consonant closures:

/l/	/r/	/f/	/v/	/s/	/ʃ/	/tʃ/
coo<u>l</u>	fea<u>r</u>	bee<u>f</u>	e<u>ve</u>	mi<u>ss</u>	a<u>sh</u>	pi<u>tch</u>
pu<u>ll</u>	he<u>re</u>	hal<u>f</u>	lo<u>ve</u>	ni<u>ce</u>	di<u>sh</u>	wi<u>tch</u>
sti<u>ll</u>	caree<u>r</u>	Clif<u>f</u>	sho<u>ve</u>	ri<u>ce</u>	wi<u>sh</u>	ben<u>ch</u>
you'<u>ll</u>	nea<u>r</u>	tou<u>gh</u>	sto<u>ve</u>	hou<u>se</u>	ca<u>sh</u>	bea<u>ch</u>
mi<u>ll</u>	tea<u>r</u>	cou<u>gh</u>	mo<u>ve</u>	ki<u>ss</u>	wa<u>sh</u>	ma<u>tch</u>

Other characteristics of the Chinese language also make it difficult to learn English.

1. Chinese uses only the present tense. Changes in time are indicated by accompanying words. For example, "I will go to school tomorrow" is simplified in Chinese to "I go school tomorrow." (And this certainly simplifies the thought.) "I went to school yesterday" becomes "I go school yesterday."

   Say the following sentences:

   a. I will tell you tomorrow.

   b. He gave me the money yesterday.

   c. Last Monday I put the picture there.

   d. Next week will be very warm.

   e. It was a very interesting day.

2. In Chinese and other Asian languages, prepositions and articles are omitted. Therefore, the Chinese speaker is likely to say "I do place book table" rather than "I *did* place *the* book *on the* table."

Prepositions with definite and indefinite articles are written in English and phonetics below. Please note that the prepositions and articles are usually not stressed in English. Read the following phrases. The stressed words are underlined.

	STRESSED	UNSTRESSED
about	It's <u>about</u> time.	It's about <u>time</u> Tim came.
	[ɪts ə'baʊt taɪm]	[ɪts ə'baʊt taɪm tɪm kem]
above	The *sky* is <u>above</u>.	The <u>sky</u> is above.
	[ðə skaɪ ɪz ə'bʌv]	[ðə skaɪ ɪz ə'bʌv]
across	It's <u>across</u> the street.	It's across the <u>street</u>.
	[ɪts ə'krɔs ðə strit]	[ɪts ə'krɔs ðə strit]
after	Come <u>after</u> lunch.	Come after <u>lunch</u>.
	[kʌm 'æftɚ lʌntʃ]	[kʌm 'æftɚ lʌntʃ]
against	Put it <u>against</u> the door.	Put it against the <u>door</u>.
	[pʊt ɪt ə'gɛnst ðə dor]	[pʊt ɪt ə'gɛnst ðə dor]
among	<u>among</u> the people	among the <u>people</u>
	[ə'mʌŋ ðə 'pipl̩]	[ə'mʌŋ ðə 'pipl̩]
around	<u>around</u> the house	around the <u>house</u>
	[ə'raʊnd ðə haʊs]	[ə'raʊnd ðə haʊs]
at	<u>at</u> the moment	at the <u>moment</u>
	[æt ðə 'momənt]	[ət ðə 'momənt]
before	<u>before</u> the time is over	before the time is <u>over</u>
	[bɪ'for ðə taɪm ɪz 'ovɚ]	[bɪ'for ðə taɪm ɪz 'ovɚ]
below	<u>below</u> the line	below the <u>line</u>
	[bə'lo ðə laɪn]	[bə'lo ðə laɪn]
between	<u>between</u> us	between <u>us</u>
	[bə'twin əs]	[bə'twin ʌs]
by	close <u>by</u>	<u>close</u> by
	[klos baɪ]	[klos baɪ]
down	<u>down</u> the street	down the <u>street</u>
	[daʊn ðə strit]	[daʊn ðə strit]
during	<u>during</u> the day	during the <u>day</u>
	['dʊrɪŋ ðə de]	['dʊrɪŋ ðə de]
except	<u>except</u> you and me	except you and <u>me</u>
	[ɪk'sɛpt ju ənd mi]	[ɪk'sɛpt ju ənd mɪ]
for	<u>for</u> a minute	for a <u>minute</u>
	[fɔr ə 'mɪnɪt]	[fɔr ə 'mɪnɪt]
from	<u>from</u> you and me	from you and <u>me</u>
	[frɑm ju ən mi]	[frɑm ju ən mi]
in	<u>in</u> the house	in the <u>house</u>
	[ɪn ðə haʊs]	[ɪn ðə haʊs]
inside	<u>inside</u> the car	inside the <u>car</u>
	['ɪn 'saɪd ðə kɑr]	['ɪn 'saɪd ðə kɑr]
off	<u>off</u> the bus	off the <u>bus</u>
	[ɔf ðə bʌs]	[ɔf ðə bʌs]
out	<u>out</u> in the yard	out in the <u>yard</u>
	[aʊt ɪn ðə jɑrd]	[aʊt ɪn ðə jɑrd]
since	<u>since</u> yesterday	since <u>yesterday</u>
	[sɪns 'jɛstɚˌde]	[sɪns 'jɛstɚˌde]
through	<u>through</u> the wall	through the <u>wall</u>
	[θru ðə wɔl]	[θru ðə wɔl]
to	<u>to</u> the front	to the <u>front</u>
	[tu ðə front]	[tu ðə front]

	STRESSED	UNSTRESSED
toward	toward the south	toward the south
	[tord ðə sauθ]	[tord ðə sauθ]
underneath	underneath the bridge	underneath the bridge
	[ˌʌndɚ ˈniθ ðə brɪʤ]	[ˌʌndɚ ˈniθ ðə brɪʤ]
until	until now	until now
	[ˌʌnˈtɪl nau]	[ˌənˈtɪl nau]
up	up the stairs	up the stairs
	[ˈʌp ðə stɛrz]	[əp ðə stɛrz]
upon	once upon a time	once upon a time
	[wʌns əˈpɒn ə taɪm]	[wəns əˈpɒn ə taɪm]
with	pay with cash	pay with cash
	[pe wɪð kæʃ]	[pe wɪð kæʃ]
within	within an hour	within an hour
	[wɪˈðɪn ən aur]	[wɪˈðɪn ən aur]
without	without warning	without warning
	[wɪðˈaut ˈwɔrnɪŋ]	[wɪðaut ˈwɔrnɪŋ]

3. Unlike in English, the meaning of Chinese words changes according to changes in pitch. In Chinese, the same word can have many meanings depending upon the tone used. In time, native Chinese speakers can learn English pitch ranges.

Additional Distinctions of Chinese

ENGLISH SOUNDS NOT IN CHINESE	CHINESE SUBSTITUTIONS	EXERCISES IN TEXT
Vowels		
/ɪ/ as in "bit"	/i/ as in "see"	pp. 89–91
/æ/ as in "cat"	/ɑ/ as in "father"	pp. 94–96
/ɝ/ as in "her"	/ɑr/ as in "farm"; or /ɛr/ as in "air"	pp. 98–100
/ɚ/ as in "after"	/ə/ as in "about"	pp. 100–103
/ʌ/ as in "cut"	/ɑ/ as in "father"	pp. 103–105
/ʊ/ as in "put"	/u/ as in "true"	pp. 110–111
Consonants		
/b/ as in "but"	/v/ as in "van"	pp. 134–135
/ʧ/ as in "chop"	/ts/ as in "boats"	pp. 141–142
	or	
	/ʃ/ as in "ship" (in initial position)	
/ʤ/ as in "jump"	/dz/ as in "toads"	pp. 141–142
	or	
	/ʃ/ as in "ship" (in initial position)	
/f/ as in "fan"	/ɸ/; does not appear in English[1]	pp. 143–144
/v/ as in "van"	/β/ as in "Havana"	pp. 143–144
/θ/ as in "bath"	/t/ as in "top"	pp. 144–146
	or	
	/s/ as in "so"	
/ð/ as in "them"	/d/ as in "dog"	pp. 144–146
	or	
	/z/ as in "zoo"	

---

[1]The sound /ɸ/ is the voiceless cognate of /β/. See Spanish accent (p. 359) for comments on the production of /β/.

/ʒ/ as in "a<u>z</u>ure"	/z/ as in "<u>z</u>oo"	pp. 153–155
/l/ as in "<u>l</u>ay"[2]	/r/ as in "<u>r</u>ay"	pp. 155–158
/r/ as in "<u>r</u>ay"	/l/ as in "<u>l</u>ay"	pp. 158–161
/w/ as in "<u>w</u>ay"	sound omitted	pp. 161–163
/m/ as in "<u>m</u>ay"	/n/ as in "<u>n</u>o" (medial and final positions)	pp. 164–166

/l/ AND /r/ WORD PAIRS

<u>l</u>ake	<u>r</u>ake	<u>l</u>ack	<u>r</u>ack	<u>l</u>ead	<u>r</u>eed
<u>l</u>ong	<u>wr</u>ong	<u>l</u>ate	<u>r</u>ate	<u>l</u>ead	<u>r</u>ed
<u>l</u>eek	<u>r</u>eek	<u>l</u>ag	<u>r</u>ag	<u>l</u>ather	<u>r</u>ather
<u>l</u>ined	<u>r</u>ind	<u>l</u>ap	<u>r</u>ap	<u>l</u>eer	<u>r</u>ear
<u>l</u>ay	<u>r</u>ay	<u>l</u>amp	<u>r</u>amp	<u>l</u>egal	<u>r</u>egal
<u>l</u>ace	<u>r</u>ace	<u>l</u>aughed	<u>r</u>aft	<u>l</u>evel	<u>r</u>evel

Substitution of /n/ for /m/

Say the following words and feel the lips coming together in the formation of the nasal /m/.

someti<u>me</u>,	*not*	sun<u>t</u>ine
ho<u>me</u>,	*not*	ho<u>ne</u>
ga<u>me</u>,	*not*	gai<u>n</u>
fo<u>am</u>,	*not*	phone
autu<u>mn</u>,	*not*	autu<u>n</u>

/aʊnt/ and /aʊnd/

This is one of the most problematic English sound combinations for Chinese people. They substitute the common combination /ɑŋ/ in Chinese for /aʊnt/ and /aʊnd/. One of the reasons for this substitution is the tremendous frequency of the phoneme /ŋ/ (as in "si<u>ng</u>") in Chinese. Further, making the sound combination requires using the front of the tongue for /n/, /t/, and /d/, a tongue position that is very "unnatural" for speakers of Chinese. Before you read aloud the following exercises, complete the exercises dealing with the diphthong /aʊ/ on pages 120–123. In reading aloud the following exercises, make certain that you produce the entire diphthong /aʊ/ before using the front of the tongue. Although /n/ is a common phoneme in Chinese, the /nt/ and /nd/ combinations do not occur. Unfortunately for native speakers of Chinese, these are very common sound combinations in English.

1. Prolong the /au/ diphthong as written. Then, being careful not to touch the back of the tongue to the soft palate, place the tongue tip on the alveolar ridge behind the upper front teeth and produce /n/; then, add /t/ or /d/, which have a similar tongue placement to /n/.

   aaaaaaaaaʊʊʊʊʊʊʊ ➡ nnnnnnnnnnnnnn
   aaaaaaaaaʊʊʊʊʊʊʊ ➡ nnnnnnnnnnnnnn
   aaaaaaaaaʊʊʊʊʊʊʊ ➡ nnnnnnnnnnnnnn

---

[2]Chinese dialects have the lateral glide /l/, but the tongue does touch the alveolar ridge. Although there appears to be a simple substitution of /l/ for /r/ and /r/ for /l/, this is not always the case. In the final position, the /l/ is often produced with a tongue tip that is raised but does not touch the alveolar ridge. Therefore, there is influence of the /r/ phoneme on the /l/ and vice versa.

2. Now shorten the time from one sound to the next as indicated:

aaaaaaʊʊʊʊʊʊʊnnnnnn   aaaaaaʊʊʊʊʊʊʊnnnnnn
aaaʊʊʊnnn   aaaʊʊʊnnn   aaaʊʊʊnnn   aaaʊʊʊnnn
aʊn   aʊn aʊn   aʊn aʊn   aʊn   aʊn

3. Add the consonant at the beginning of the word as indicated:

taaaʊʊʊnnn [taʊn]-town   daaaʊʊʊnnn [daʊn]-down
gaaaʊʊʊnnn [gaʊn]-gown   nnaaaʊʊʊnnn [naʊn]-noun

4. Decrease the time given to the sounds as indicated:

aaaaʊʊʊʊnnnnt   aaaaʊʊʊʊnnnnnt   aaaaʊʊʊʊnnnnnt
aaʊʊnnt   aaʊʊnnt   aaʊʊnt
aʊnt   aʊnt   aʊnt

aaaaʊʊʊʊnnnnnd   aaaaʊʊʊʊnnnnnd   aaaaʊʊʊʊnnnnnd
aaʊʊnnd   aaʊʊnnd   aaʊʊnnd
aʊnd   aʊnd   aʊnd

5. Read aloud the following exercise as it appears:

mmmmaaaaʊʊʊʊnnnnt   [maʊnt]-mount
kkkkaaaaʊʊʊʊnnnnt   [kaʊnt]-count
ammaaaaʊʊʊʊnnnnt   [əmaʊnt]-amount
ffffaaaaʊʊʊʊnnnnntn   [faʊntn̩]-fountain
mmmmaaaaʊʊʊʊnnnnntn   [maʊntn̩]-mountain

ssssaaaaʊʊʊʊnnnnnd   [saʊnd]-sound
mmmmaaaaʊʊʊʊnnnnnd   [maʊnd] mound
rrrraaaaʊʊʊʊnnnnnd   [raʊnd]-round
araaaaʊʊʊʊnnnnnd   [əraʊnd]-around
ffffaaaaʊʊʊʊnnnnnd   [faʊnd]-found
hhhhaaaaʊʊʊʊnnnnnd   [haʊnd]-hound
wwwwaaaaʊʊʊʊnnnnnd   [waʊnd]-wound

p → aaaaʊʊʊʊnnnnnd   [paʊnd]-pound

b → aaaaʊʊʊʊnnnnnd   [baʊnd]-bound

Read aloud the following word list designed to be front vowel practice for all normative English speakers:

/i/		/ɪ/		/e/		/ɛ/		/æ/	
reed	[rid]	rid	[rɪd]	raid	[red]	red	[rɛd]	rad	[ræd]
lead	[lid]	lid	[lɪd]	laid	[led]	led	[lɛd]	lad	[læd]
feed	[fid]			fade	[fed]	fed	[fɛd]	fad	[fæd]
he'd	[hid]	hid	[hɪd]			head	[hɛd]	had	[hæd]
keyed	[kid]	kid	[kɪd]			ked	[kɛd]	cad	[kæd]
neat	[nit]	nit	[nɪt]	Nate	[net]	net	[nɛt]	gnat	[næt]
seed	[sid]	Sid	[sɪd]			said	[sɛd]	sad	[sæd]
teed	[tid]					Ted	[tɛd]	tad	[tæd]
weed	[wid]			weighed	[wed]	wed	[wɛd]		
beet	[bit]	bit	[bɪt]	bait	[bet]	bet	[bɛt]	bat	[bæt]
seat	[sit]	sit	[sɪt]	sate	[set]	set	[sɛt]	sat	[sæt]
meet	[mit]	mitt	[mɪt]	mate	[met]	met	[mɛt]	mat	[mæt]
Pete	[pit]	pit	[pɪt]	pate	[pet]	pet	[pɛt]	Pat	[pæt]
feet	[fit]	fit	[fɪt]	fate	[fet]	fait (Fr)	[fɛt]	fat	[fæt]

Mandarin (Chinese) Word Pairs

Read and tape the word pairs aloud, and replay making certain you are differentiating between the sounds being presented. If you are having difficulty discriminating between the sounds, refer to the appropriate section of the audio file.

(p-b)

INITIAL		MEDIAL		FINAL	
peat	beat	dips	dibs	rip	rib
pit	bit				
pet	bet				
pat	bat	rapid	rabid	cap	cab
par	bar	cops	cobs	Iop	Iob
Paul	ball				
pull	bull				
plume	bloom	loops	lubes	loop	lube
purr	burr			Earp	herb
putt	but	pups	pubs	cup	cub
pace	base			ape	Abe
pie	by			tripe	tribe
poi	boy				
pout	bout				
pole	bowl	roping	robing	rope	robe

(t-d)

INITIAL		MEDIAL		FINAL	
team	deem	liter	leader	beat	bead
till	dill	bitter	bidder	bit	bid
tell	dell	betting	bedding	bet	bed
tan	Dan	matter	madder	bat	bad
tot	dot	rots	rods	pot	pod
tall	Dahl	daughter	dauber		
tomb	doom	moots	moods	moot	mood
turn	Dern	hurts	herds	Bert	bird
ton	dun	butting	budding	cut	cud
tame	dame	eights	aids	late	laid
tie	dye	rights	rides	bite	bide
toil	Doyle			Voight	void
tout	doubt	pouter	powder	lout	loud
toll	dole	coating	coding	boat	bode

(l-r)

INITIAL		MEDIAL		FINAL	
leap	reap	flee	free		
limb	rim	miller	mirror	dale	dare
lead	read	belly	berry	dell	dare
lamp	ramp	clash	crash		
lock	rock	clock	crock		
law	raw	claw	craw	wall	war
look	rook	pulling	purring	pull	poor
loom	room	clue	crew	duel	doer

INITIAL		MEDIAL		FINAL	
lung	rung	clutch	crutch		
lace	race	belated	berated		
light	right	filling	firing	dial	dire
loyal	royal				
lout	rout	clown	crown	owl	hour
low	row	glow	grow	mole	more

(t-θ)

INITIAL		MEDIAL		FINAL	
tree	three	eater	ether	heat	heath
trill	thrill	mitts	myths	wit	with
tread	thread	tents	tenths	debt	death
tank	thank	batless	bathless	mat	math
				swat	swath
taught	thought	forts	fourths	brought	broth
true	through	roots	Ruth's	toot	tooth
				dirt	dirth
tug	thug				
tie	thigh	fates	faiths	fate	faith
tow	throw				

(d-ð)

INITIAL		MEDIAL		FINAL	
		breeds	breathes	seed	seethe
den	then				
Dan	than	ladder	lather		
		fooder	father		
		wordier	worthier		
		udder	other		
day	they				
die	thy	riding	writhing		
dough	though	loads	loathes		

(s-z)

INITIAL		MEDIAL		FINAL	
seal	zeal	ceasing	seizing	peace	peas
sip	zip	gristle	grizzle	fierce	fears
				pence	pens
sag	zag			ass	as
Saar	Czar				
				sauce	saws
sue	zoo	looses	loses	deuce	dues
				hearse	hers
		buses	buzzes	bus	buzz
same	zane	lacy	lazy	face	faze
		prices	prizes	ice	eyes
sounds	zounds	dousing	dowsing	Boyce	boys
sewn	zone	doses	dozes	dose	doze

JAPANESE

Distinctive Characteristics of the Japanese Language

The Japanese language is considered relatively consistent in terms of sound production and sentence structure. It is a language composed of approximately 100 syllabic sounds that are invariable and contain all of the phonetic possibilities. There are only five vowel sounds in Japanese; they are similar to the American-English /ɑ/ as in "father," /i/ as in "see," /ɛ/ as in "bed," /o/ as in "go," and /u/ as in "true." Each is shorter than its American-English counterpart. The five vowel sounds compare with a minimum of fifteen American-English vowel sounds plus the diphthongs. Because Western languages compare with American English, tending to have more vowel sounds, Europeans, for example, are more intelligible to the American ear than are many Asians.

The syllabic declensions of the /k/, /s/, and /t/ groups are:

/kɑ/	/ki/	/ku/	/ke/	/ko/
/sɑ/	/ʃi/[3]	/su/	/se/	/so/
/tɑ/	/tʃi/[3]	/tsu/[3]	/te/	/to/

Because the Japanese vowels are much shorter in duration, Japanese has a more staccato flavor. Prolong the vowels as you work with the sounds that follow. Unlike English, Japanese does not rely on degrees of stress and changes of rate for clarification of meaning. Japanese is regular in rhythm, stress, and rate but has four levels of pitch.

Because Japanese is derived from Chinese, the linguistic and pronunciation characteristics noted in that discussion are often applicable to Japanese.

ENGLISH SOUNDS NOT IN JAPANESE	JAPANESE SUBSTITUTIONS	EXERCISES IN TEXT
Vowels		
/ɪ/ as in "bit"	/i/ as in "see"	pp. 89–91
/ɛ/ as in "met"	/ɑ/ as in "father"	pp. 92–94
/æ/ as in "cat"	/ɑ/ as in "father"	pp. 94–96
/ɝ/ as in "her"	/ɑ/ as in "father"	pp. 98–100
/ɚ/ as in "after"	/ɑ/ as in "father"	pp. 100–103
/ʌ/ as in "cut"	/ɑ/ as in "father"	pp. 103–105
/ə/ as in "about"	/ɑ/ as in "father"	pp. 105–108
/ʊ/ as in "put"	/u/ as in "true"	pp. 110–111
/ɔ/ as in "law"	/o/ as in "go"	pp. 113–115
Consonants		
/f/ as in "feet"	/h/ as in "house"	pp. 143–144
/v/ as in "vine"	/β/ (see Spanish accent)	p. 359
/θ/ as in "theme"	/s/ as in "some"	pp. 144–146
/ð/ as in "them"	/z/ as in "zoo"	pp. 144–146
/ʒ/ as in "azure"	/z/ as in "zoo"	pp. 153–155

/b/ AND /v/ WORD PAIRS

berry	very	bail	veil
bat	vat	ballet	valet

---

[3]For explanations, refer to exercises.

Bali	valley	ban	van
bane	vein	bile	vile
base	vase	bend	vend
bent	vent	best	vest

/l/ as in "lay"   *See pp. 155–158 and Chinese drill, p. 5.*
/r/ as in "ray"   *See pp. 158–161 and Chinese drill, p. 5.*

Additional Distinctions of Japanese

1. Consecutive consonant sounds do not appear in Japanese. Because Japanese is composed of syllabic sounds, there is a tendency to place a vowel (either /ə/ as in "about" or /u/ as in "true") between the consecutive consonants (for example, [bəlak] for [blæk] in "black" or [sətand] for [stænd] in "stand").

scarf	[skɑrf]	tremble	[trɛmbl]
school	[skul]	break	[brek]
sleeps	[slips]	please	[pliz]
stew	[stu]	crash	[kræʃ]
truck	[trʌk]	strip	[strɪp]

2. If an English word ends in a consonant, Japanese speakers tend to add a schwa (/ə/ as in "about") or a more definite vowel like /u/ as in "true." In the following words, do not add a vowel to the final consonant.

start	[stɑrt]	church	[tʃɝtʃ]	dream	[drim]
Pat	[pæt]	paid	[ped]	worth	[wɝθ]
said	[sɛd]	failed	[feld]	circus	['sɝkəs]
jump	[dʒʌmp]	surf	[sɝf]	flirt	[flɝt]
watch	[wɑtʃ]	thin	[θɪn]	sing	[sɪŋ]

3. The only consonant sound that occurs at the end of a word following a vowel sound is "n" as in *kaban* ("box"). However, this sound is produced with the back of the tongue against the velum, which makes its articulatory adjustments similar to /ŋ/ as in "sing." In Japanese, there is the syllabic nasal /n/ that is produced with the back of the tongue. Therefore, when Japanese or Chinese speakers are learning English, they will often see the phoneme /n/ and produce it with the back of the tongue and velum as if it were a Chinese or Japanese syllabic /n/. In a word like *sand*, Japanese speakers are more likely to use the back of the tongue for the production of /n/. Like their Chinese counterparts, Japanese speakers end most of their words with vowels. The Chinese and Japanese share their difficulties with the /aʊnt/ and /aʊnd/ combinations. Refer to the discussions of these sounds on pages 5 and 6.

4. Japanese speakers often omit the phoneme /r/ when it appears after a vowel and before a consonant. Pronounce the following words, making certain that the /r/ sound is produced.

dark	[dɑrk]	mark	[mɑrk]
Marty	[mɑrtɪ]	alarm	[ə'lɑrm]
heart	[hɑrt]	charm	[tʃɑrm]
swarm	[swɑrm]	warm	[wɑrm]
barge	[bɑrdʒ]	large	[lɑrdʒ]

5. Frequently, the /u/ is substituted for the medial and the final /l/. See exercises on pages 2 and 5 to correct this.

6. The /s/ is mispronounced as /ʃ/ as in "sheep" when it appears before /i/ as in "see."

seep	[sip]	asleep	[ə'slip]
seed	[sid]	seem	[sim]

seal	[sil]	cedar	['sidɚ]
ceiling	['silɪŋ]	season	['sizən]
seek	[sik]	seen	[sin]

7. The /t/ is mispronounced as /tʃ/ as in "<u>ch</u>urch" when it appears before /i/ as in "s<u>ee</u>."

tease	[tiz]	steam	[stim]
team	[tim]	steal	[stil]
teen	[tin]	steep	[stip]
teach	[titʃ]	steeple	[stipl̩]
teeth	[tiθ]	Steve	[stiv]

8. The /t/ is mispronounced as /ts/ before /u/ as in "tr<u>ue</u>."

tonight	[tu'naɪt]	tooth	[tuθ]
tool	[tul]	toupee	[tu'pe]
tomb	[tum]	toothpick	['tuθpɪk]
tune	[tun]	tulip	['tulɪp]
tube	[tub]	tuna	['tunə]

>>>

KOREAN

Geographical, historical, ethnological, and linguistic sources all agree that the Korean language was derived from the Ural-Altaic family and, especially, the Mongolian, Turkish, and Tungusic languages:

> Ancient Korean can be classified broadly into the Puyo language in the north and the Han language in the south, which were closely akin to each other. The Puyo language was spoken by tribes which settled in the general region of Manchuria and northern Korea. . . . The prolonged political and cultural influence of the Chinese upon Korea through the dynasties left an indelible mark upon the written and spoken Korean language. A substantial portion of the Korean language comes from Chinese culture, especially its Confucian classics, . . . that have been assimilated into Korean, at least phonetically, if not in meaning.[4]

Some linguists believe that about half of the active Korean vocabulary consists of words that are definitely of Chinese origin.

There are also cultural differences within Korea. For instance, the people in the southern provinces are much more outgoing.

It is important to know that Korean words do not distinguish gender, case, or number. Gender is shown with a character that indicates sex. Number is denoted by adding a particle that indicates plurality. The basic order of words is subject, object, and predicate. Adjectives come before nouns and adverbs precede verbs.

Before studying this section, it is suggested that you complete the earlier exercises for Chinese speakers.

ENGLISH SOUNDS NOT IN KOREAN	KOREAN SUBSTITUTIONS	EXERCISES IN TEXT
Vowels		
/ɪ/ as in "b<u>i</u>t"	/i/ as in "s<u>ee</u>"	pp. 89–91
/æ/ as in "c<u>a</u>t"	/ɑ/ as in "f<u>a</u>ther"	pp. 94–96
/ɝ/ as in "h<u>er</u>"	/ɑr/ or /ɛr/	pp. 98–100

---

[4]A Hand book of Korea, (Korean Overseas Information Service Ministry of Culture and Information, 4th. ed) Lee Kwang Pyo: Minister of Culture, Seoul, 1982, p. 42

/ɚ/ as in "after"	/ə/ as in "about"	pp. 100–103
/ʌ/ as in "cut"	/ɑ/ as in "father"	pp. 103–105
/ə/ as in "about"	/ɑ/ as in "father"	pp. 105–108
/ʊ/ as in "put"	/u/ as in "true"	pp. 110–111
/ɔ/ as in "call"	/o/ as in "go"	pp. 113–115

Consonants

/f/ as in "fine"	/ɸ/ (see /β/ in Spanish accent)	p. 359
/v/ as in "vine"	/β/ (see Spanish accent)	p. 359
/θ/ as in "theme"	/t/ as in "to"	pp. 144–146
/ð/ as in "them"	/dʒ/ as in "judge"	pp. 144–146
/z/ as in "zoo"	/s/ as in "soon"	pp. 151–152
/r/ as in "run"	/l/ as in "lion"	pp. 158–161
/l/ as in "lion"	/r/ as in "run"	pp. 155–158

Korean Word Pairs

Read and tape the word pairs aloud, and replay making certain you are differentiating between the sounds being presented. If you are having difficulty discriminating between the sounds, refer to the appropriate section of the audio file.

(p-f)

INITIAL		MEDIAL		FINAL	
peat	feet	leaps	leafs	leap	leaf
pit	fit	ripped	rift	rip	riff
pear	fair	leapt	left	tip	tiff
pan	fan	napper	raffer	lap	laugh
par	far				
pall	fall				
pull	full				
pool	fool			proof	roof
pearl	furl				
pun	fun	cups	cuffs		
pace	face				
pie	fie				
poi	foy				
Powell	foul				
pole	foal			lope	loaf

(b-v)

INITIAL		MEDIAL		FINAL
beep	veep	Eben	even	
bicker	vicar			
berry	very	ebber	ever	
bat	vat			
boom	voom			
bale	vale	cable	caver	
buy	vie			

Boyd	void				
bough	vow				
boat	vote	lobes	loaves	robe	rove

(l-r)

INITIAL		MEDIAL		FINAL	
leap	reap	flee	free		
limb	rim	miller	mirror	bill	been
lead	read	belly	berry	dale	dare
lamp	ramp	clash	crash		
lock	rock	clock	crock		
law	raw	claw	craw	wall	war
look	rook	pulling	purring	pull	poor
loom	room	clue	crew	duel	doer
lung	rung	clutch	crutch		
lace	race	belated	berated		
light	right	filing	firing	dial	dire
loyal	royal				
lout	rout	clown	crown	owl	hour
low	row	glow	grow	mole	more

(t-th)

INITIAL		MEDIAL		FINAL	
tree	three	eater	ether	heat	heath
trill	thrill	mitts	myths	wit	with
tread	thread	tents	tenths	debt	death
tank	thank	batless	bathless	mat	math
				swat	swath
taught	thought	forts	fourths	brought	broth
true	through	roots	Ruth's	toot	tooth
				dirt	dirth
tug	thug				
tie	thigh			fate	faith
tow	throw				

(d-th)

INITIAL		MEDIAL		FINAL	
		breeds	breathes	seed	seethe
den	then				
Dan	than	ladder	lather		
		fodder	father		
		wordier	worthier		
		udder	other		
day	they				
die	thy	riding	writhing		
dough	though	loads	loathes		

(s-z)

INITIAL		MEDIAL		FINAL	
seal	zeal	ceasing	seizing	peace	peas
sip	zip	gristle	grizzle	fierce	fears
				pence	pens
sag	zag			ass	as
Saar	Czar				
				sause	saws
sue	zoo	looses	loses	deuce	dues
				hearse	hers
		buses	buzzes	bus	buzz
sane	Zane	lacy	lazy	face	faze
		prices	prizes	ice	eyes

Additional Distinctions of Korean

1. Although there are no final consonant sounds in Chinese, there are some in Korean: /ŋ/ as in "sing," /m/, /l/, /n/, /t/, /k/, and /p/. However, exercises for final consonants are encouraged for Koreans learning English (see p. 10).
2. Dentalization of /t/, /d/, /l/, and /n/ also occurs in Korean.
3. The Japanese language shows its influence on Korean with the addition of vowels between consecutive consonants. Pronounce and record the words in the list in (1) on page 10. Make certain that there is no vowel between two consecutive consonant sounds.
4. In Korean, the main thought is placed at the beginning of the sentence. (Americans usually place the main thought at the end of the sentence.)
5. Korean words do not have gender, number, or case. Gender is expressed by a character prefix denoting sex. Number is expressed by adding a particle denoting plurality. Both the gender prefix and number particle are omitted unless indispensable. Case is determined by particles known as postpositions.
6. The basic word order in a sentence is subject–object—predicate. Adjectives come before nouns, and adverbs come before verbs.
7. Adjectives and verbs undergo no declensional or conjugational changes. Instead, special particles are added to the stem to indicate the tense or voice.

>>> VIETNAMESE

Vietnamese, like Japanese and Korean, has its beginnings in Chinese. Therefore, many of the Chinese influences discussed previously have a direct relationship to the Vietnamese language.

ENGLISH SOUNDS NOT IN VIETNAMESE	VIETNAMESE SUBSTITUTIONS	EXERCISES IN TEXT
Vowels		
/ɪ/ as in "b<u>i</u>t"	/i/ as in "s<u>ee</u>"	pp. 89–91
/æ/ as in "c<u>a</u>t"	/ɑ/ as in "f<u>a</u>ther"	pp. 94–96
/ɝ/ as in "h<u>er</u>"	/ɑr/ or /ɛr/	pp. 98–100
/ɚ/ as in "aft<u>er</u>"	/ɑ/ as in "f<u>a</u>ther"	pp. 100–103
/ʌ/ as in "c<u>u</u>t"	/ɑ/ as in "f<u>a</u>ther"	pp. 103–105

/ə/ as in "about"	/ɑ/ as in "father"	pp. 105–108
/ʊ/ as in "put"	/u/ as in "true"	pp. 110–111
/ɔ/ as in "call"	/o/ as in "go"	pp. 113–115

Consonants

/ʧ/ as in "chain"	/ts/ as in "boats"	pp. 141–142
/θ/ as in "theme"	/t/ as in "to"	pp. 144–146
/ð/ as in "them"	/d/ as in "deep"	pp. 144–146
/z/ as in "zoo"	/s/ as in "soon"	pp. 151–152
/ʃ/ as in "ship"	/s/ as in "soon"	pp. 153–155
/ʒ/ as in "treasure"	/s/ as in "soon"	pp. 153–155
/w/ as in "wife"	sound omitted	pp. 161–163
/j/ as in "yard"	sound omitted	pp. 163–164

Additional Distinctions of Vietnamese

1. Unlike other Asian languages, Vietnamese contains the /l/ and /r/ phonemes, which may be the result of the French influence. However, the production of these phonemes is often incomplete. Remember that the tip of the tongue must touch the ridge behind the upper teeth when producing /l/ (for production and exercises, see pp. 155–158).

2. Because Vietnamese, like Chinese, is a monosyllabic language, it is important to do drills on English words that contain more than one syllable. Pronounce the words in the lists accompanying each vowel and diphthong in the text. In addition, the tense (that is, requiring a tense tongue) English vowels should be stressed.

NEWS, SPORTS, WEATHER, AND COMMERCIAL COPY

>>>

NEWS COPY

THE VERDICT IS IN . . . AFTER 5 AND A HALF DAYS IN DELIBERATION JURORS FOUND 25-YEAR-OLD _____ GUILTY.

THE NEW HAMPSHIRE MAN WAS FOUND GUILTY OF 14 OUT OF 16 CHARGES, INCLUDING GUILTY OF ARMED HOME INVASION. BACK IN FEBRUARY _____ INVADED A HOME IN SALEM AND HELD THE SMITH FAMILY HOSTAGE FOR FOUR HOURS. _____ WILL BE SENTENCED ON NOVEMBER 9TH.

MASSACHUSETTS NOW HAS ONE OF THE TOUGHEST GUN LAWS IN THE COUNTRY. IT BANS ASSAULT WEAPONS THAT WERE MADE AFTER SEPTEMBER 1994. GUN OWNERS WILL NOW FACE STIFF FINES IF THEIR GUNS ARE NOT PROPERLY LOCKED AND SAFELY STORED.

THE FLOODING IN TEXAS HAS NOW CLAIMED THE LIVES OF TWO DOZEN PEOPLE. PEOPLE STRANDED ON ROOFTOPS ARE BEING RESCUED BY HELI-COPTERS AND BOATS. PRESIDENT CLINTON HAS DECLARED 20 COUNTIES DISASTER AREAS.

A FORMER HIGH-RANKING SOVIET OFFICIAL SAYS HE WAS A U.S. SPY. FIFTY-THREE-YEAR-OLD ARKADY SHEVCHENKO SAYS HE WAS A TOP CIA

INFORMANT FOR THIRTY-TWO MONTHS BEFORE HE DEFECTED TO THE UNITED STATES IN 1978. . . . SHEVCHENKO WROTE ABOUT HIS SPYING EXPERIENCE IN THE BOOK . . . BREAKING WITH MOSCOW . . . TO BE PUBLISHED SOON. . . . THE EX-SOVIET ADVISOR SAYS HE GAVE THE U.S. INFORMATION ON SOVIET INVOLVEMENT IN AFRICA, CENTRAL AMERICA, AND CHINA. . . . SHEVCHENKO IS THE HIGHEST-RANKING SOVIET DIPLOMAT TO DEFECT SINCE WORLD WAR TWO.

HEALTH OFFICIALS HAVE DECLARED AN EMERGENCY. . . . AS THEY SCRAMBLE TO FIND OUT EXACTLY HOW THIS STARTED. WHAT THEY DO KNOW IS IT STARTED IN MEXICO. . . . WHERE AT LEAST 149 PEOPLE HAVE DIED . . . AND ANOTHER 16 HUNDRED ARE SICK. . . . RIGHT NOW . . . HEALTH OFFICIALS BELIEVE THE STRAIN MAY HAVE COME FROM SOMEONE WORKING WITH PIGS . . . IN MEXICO. SPAIN, FRANCE AND CANADA ARE ALSO REPORTING A CASE.

CHECK OUT THE SURVEILLANCE VIDEO. . . . THE SUSPECT IS SEEN DEMANDING MONEY FROM THE CLERK. POLICE SAY IT HAPPENED AROUND 1:30 SUNDAY MORNING AT THE—MOBIL ON THE RUN—GAS STATION ON ROUTE ONE-THIRTY-SIX. NO WORD—HOW MUCH MONEY WAS STOLEN. POLICE ARE LOOKING FOR A WHITE VAN . . . SEEN LEAVING THE SCENE. ANYONE WITH INFORMATION IS URGED TO CALL SWANSEA POLICE. . . .

AND NEW INFORMATION ON AN EMERGENCY LANDING AT LOGAN AIRPORT IN BOSTON. . . . FROM OVER THE WEEKEND. THE DELTA AIRLINES FLIGHT FROM NEW YORK WAS HEADED TO TEL AVIV ON FRIDAY WHEN A 22-YEAR OLD ISREALI MAN IS ACCUSED OF RUSHING THE PLANE'S COCKPIT. PASSENGERS AND CREW WERE ABLE TO SUBDUE THE MAN. . . . HE WAS GREETED BY POLICE. . . . ON THE GROUND . . . AND ARRAIGNED TODAY IN COURT.

A RADICAL ENVIRONMENTAL GROUP SETS A VAIL RESORT ON FIRE.

IN COLORADO, A VAIL RESORT HAS SUFFERED TWELVE MILLION DOLLARS IN DAMAGES.

THE EARTH LIBERATION FRONT ADMITTED STARTING THE FIRE AT THE NATION'S BUSIEST SKI RESORT.

KCR-FM COLORADO PUBLIC RADIO RECEIVED AN E-MAIL FROM THE GROUP SAYING THEY STARTED THE FIRES IN PROTEST.

VAIL ASSOCIATES ARE MOVING FORWARD WITH A CONTROVERSIAL EIGHT-HUNDRED-AND-EIGHTY-ACRE SKI EXPANSION.

THE ENVIRONMENTALISTS SAY THE LAND BEING USED IS VITAL FOR SURVIVAL OF THE NATURAL HABITAT.

NATO FORCES:

IF IT FAILS THE FIRST TIME TRY AND TRY AGAIN.

THAT WAS THE ATTITUDE OF THE SECRETARY OF STATE, WHO SENT REPRESENTATIVES TO BELGRADE TO PERSUADE THE SERBIAN PRESIDENT TO RENEW PEACE TALKS BETWEEN SERBIA AND ALBANIA.

U-S OFFICIALS HAVE CONFIRMED THE WITHDRAWAL OF SERBIAN TROOPS TO THEIR BARRACKS.

U-N SECRETARY GENERAL KOFI ANNAN HAS ISSUED AN INCLUSIVE REPORT ON SERB COMPLIANCE WITH U-N CEASEFIRE DEMANDS.

WEATHER REPORT:

RAIN RAIN GO AWAY.

THAT WAS THE CHANT BY MANY AS HEAVY RAINS POUNDED THE AREA.

HEAVY RAINS CAUSED FLOODING AND DELAYED TRAFFIC THROUGHOUT BOSTON.

TODAY THE HIGH WAS SEVENTY-THREE WITH THE LOWS EXPECTED TO BE IN THE FIFTIES.

TOMORROW EXPECT THE RAIN TO GO AWAY WITH CLOUDS SCATTERED THROUGHOUT.

THE HIGHS SHOULD REACH THE MID-SIXTIES WITH THE LOWS IN THE FORTIES.

KANSAS STORMS:

AS THE SUN ROSE THIS MORNING MORE DEATH AND MAYHEM FELL ON OKLAHOMA.

SIX INCHES OF RAIN FELL ON THE CITY OF TULSA, CAUSING FLOODING IN THE CENTRAL AND EASTERN PARTS OF THE STATE.

MEANWHILE IN KANSAS, FIVE PEOPLE ARE DEAD AFTER STORMS RIPPED THROUGH THE AREA EARLIER YESTERDAY.

AUTHORITIES ARE STILL SEARCHING FOR MISSING PEOPLE.

SPOOKY WORLD:

NO SPRINKLERS, NO TRICK OR TREAT . . .

THAT IS WHAT AUTHORITIES ARE SAYING TODAY AFTER OWNERS OF THE SPOOKY WORLD THEME PARK REFUSED TO INSTALL THEM IN THREE ATTRACTIONS.

TWO WEEKS AGO THE CITY OF WORCESTER DEMANDED SPRINKLERS BE PUT IN OR THE ATTRACTIONS WOULD BE CLOSED.

SPOOKY WORLD ALSO HAD THE OPTION OF PAYING TWO HUNDRED DOLLARS AN HOUR FOR A MANNED FIRE TRUCK ON THE SCENE.

FRIDAY SPOOKY WORLD FILED FOR BANKRUPTCY.

DESPITE THIS, SPOOKY WORLD WILL REMAIN OPEN THROUGH HALLOWEEN.

JOE BOXER/KICKER:

DO YOU EVER FIND YOURSELF LOOKING FOR CLEAN UNDERWEAR?

WELL THERE IS A SOLUTION FOR THAT PROBLEM . . . UNDERWEAR IN A CAN.

NEXT MONTH JOE BOXER CORPORATION PLANS TO UNVEIL VENDING MACHINES THAT WILL DISPENSE MEN'S UNDERWEAR.

FLEET:

FLEET HAS JUST ANNOUNCED THAT ALL NEW ENGLAND BRANCHES WILL BE CUTTING THEIR INTEREST RATES.

INTEREST RATES ON SHORT-TERM BORROWING WILL BE CUT ONE QUARTER OF A PERCENT.

THE NEW RATE WILL BE EIGHT AND ONE QUARTER PERCENT.

FLEET HAS NOT ANNOUNCED HOW SOON THESE CUTS WILL GO INTO EFFECT.

IN OTHER BUSINESS NEWS, THE DOW JONES HAS FALLEN SINCE THE INTEREST CUTS WERE ANNOUNCED YESTERDAY,

TODAY THE DOW WENT DOWN TWO HUNDRED POINTS.

MICROSOFT:

IN WASHINGTON MICROSOFT HAD ITS FIRST DAY IN COURT.

THE LARGEST SOFTWARE COMPANY IN THE WORLD WENT TO COURT TODAY IN THE JUSTICE DEPARTMENT'S ANTITRUST SUIT.

WHILE C-E-O BILL GATES DID NOT ATTEND HE DEFENDED HIS COMPANY WITH VIDEOTAPED TESTIMONY.

MICROSOFT VICE PRESIDENT WILLIAM NEUKOM SAID THAT EVERY COMPANY OUGHT TO BE ABLE TO INNOVATE.

ANALYSIS DOES NOT SEE ANY MAJOR CHANGES IN THE MARKET IF MICROSOFT WINS.

MICROSOFT VEHEMENTLY DENIES THE GOVERNMENT'S CLAIMS AND STANDS BY ITS RIGHT TO INNOVATE PRODUCTS.

SOUTH AFRICA:

THE AFRICAN NATIONAL CONGRESS (ANC) IS HEADING FOR A DECISIVE VICTORY IN SOUTH AFRICA'S GENERAL ELECTION, TAKING MORE THAN TWO-THIRDS OF THE VOTE SO FAR.

WITH MORE THAN 12 MILLION VOTES COUNTED, THE ANC HAS 67 PERCENT.

THE MAJOR OPPOSITION PARTIES ARE TRAILING WELL BEHIND—THE DEMOCRATIC ALLIANCE WITH 16 PERCENT AND THE NEWLY FORMED CONGRESS OF THE PEOPLE (COPE) HAS 7.6 PERCENT.

NEWS FROM TRINIDAD AND TOBAGO:

THE PEOPLE OF TRINIDAD AND TOBAGO ARE BEING TOLD TO BRACE THEMSELVES FOR JOB LOSSES AND LAYOFFS AND A STALLED ECONOMY.

CENTRAL BANK GOVERNOR DOCTOR EWART WILLIAMS YESTERDAY PAINTED WHAT MANY SAY IS A VERY GLOOMY PICTURE OF THE COUNTRY'S ECONOMY.

HE SAYS THERE IS NO RECESSION BUT ECONOMIC GROWTH IS NOT LIKELY THIS YEAR.

ACCORDING TO GOVERNOR WILLIAMS THINGS ARE WORSE THAN INITIALLY PROJECTED.

DOCTOR WILLIAMS MADE THE STATEMENTS WHILE PRESENTING THE BANK'S SEMI-ANNUAL MONETARY POLICY.

THE EDUCATION MINISTER IS TOLD TO STOP MAKING EXCUSES, AND MAKE SURE REPAIRED SCHOOLS OPEN ON TIME.

THE TRINIDAD AND TOBAGO UNIFIED TEACHERS ASSOCIATION PRESIDENT ROUSTON JOB SAYS THE MINISTRY CAN DO MORE TO ENSURE THE TIMELY OPENING OF ALL SCHOOLS, EVEN IF THERE ARE EXTENSIVE REPAIRS DONE.

MINISTER ESTHER LE GENDRE YESTERDAY SAID THE TWO-MONTH AUGUST VACATION IS NOT ENOUGH TO COMPLETE SOME OF THE REPAIRS.

SHE WAS NOT SURE WHAT KIND OF IMPACT THAT SITUATION WOULD HAVE ON SCHOOLS THIS YEAR.

BUT PRESIDENT JOB BELIEVES THE MINISTRY SHOULD CONSIDER OTHER OPTIONS IN AN ATTEMPT TO AVOID DELAYS.

MINISTER LE GENDRE SAID THE EDUCATION FACILITIES COMPANY IS MONITORING THE SITUATION AND WOULD DETERMINE HOW THE REPAIR SYSTEM WILL WORK THIS.

AND:

PRESIDENT BARACK OBAMA HAS TOLD THE U.S. CREDIT CARD IN-DUSTRY TO SCRAP UNFAIR INTEREST RATE HIKES AND TO BE MORE TRANS-PARENT AND ACCOUNTABLE.

HE TOLD BOSSES OF 13 CARD ISSUERS HE WANTED TO KEEP THE CREDIT CARD MARKET BUT TO "ELIMINATE SOME OF THE ABUSES."

POLITICIANS HAVE EXPRESSED ANGER THAT MANY OF THE BANKS ISSUING CREDIT CARDS WITH HIGH FEES ARE THE SAME BANKS THAT HAVE RECEIVED GOVERNMENT BAILOUT MONEY. BANKS SAY TIGHTER RULES WOULD REDUCE INCOME AT A DIFFICULT TIME FOR THEM.

>>>
SPORTS COPY

THE BALTIMORE RAVENS CAME TO LAMBEAU FIELD FOR THE FIRST TIME EVER YESTERDAY AND WERE HOPING TO MEET THE BRETT FAVRE THAT HAS THROWN THREE INTERCEPTIONS IN EACH OF THE LAST THREE WEEKS.

INSTEAD THEY MET THE THREE-TIME MVP BRETT FAVRE, WHO PRO-CEEDED TO SHRED THE RAVENS' DEFENSE, THROWING TWO TOUCHDOWN PASSES AND RUNNING FOR ONE.

AS PATS' HEAD COACH, PETE CARROLL HAS NOT LOST TO THE MIAMI DOLPHINS—A PERFECT 3 AND 0. THEY MET AGAIN SUNDAY WITH THE HOPES OF UNLEASHING DREW BLEDSOE AND THE HIGH-POWERED PATRIOTS' OFFENSE ON JIMMY JOHNSON'S SQUAD.

UNFORTUNATELY FOR THE PATS, THE DOLPHIN DEFENSE HELD NEW ENGLAND TO JUST 3 FIELD GOALS IN REGULATION.

BUT THE PATS PUT UP A SIMILAR GIFT. THIS ONE WENT TO OVERTIME KNOTTED AT NINE APIECE.

IT WAS IN OVERTIME WHERE THE DOLPHINS TACKED ON THAT FOURTH FIELD GOAL AND WON IT 12 TO 9.

IN HOCKEY, THE B'S TOOK THEIR SOLID START ON THE ROAD VERSUS THE NEW JERSEY DEVILS.

IN THE FIRST PERIOD, THE DEVILS STRUCK FIRST BLOOD, TAKING A ONE TO NOTHING LEAD.

THE BRUINS WOULD BATTLE BACK AND TIE THE GAME LATER IN THE SECOND.

THEN WITH THE SECOND PERIOD COMING TO AN END THE DEVILS WOULD PUT A CONTROVERSIAL GOAL BEHIND DALLAS AND WOULD NEVER LOOK BACK.

THE DEVILS TAKE THIS ONE BY A FINAL COUNT OF 2 TO 1.

BASKETBALL:

THE CELTICS HAD THEIR CHANCES BUT NOW MAKE IT HARD ON THEM-SELVES BY ALLOWING THE BULLS TO TIE THE SERIES.

KEVIN GARNETT CHEERING ON HIS CELTICS TEAMMATES . . . C'S WITH A SHORT BENCH SO THE STARTERS PLAYED A LOT OF MINUTES.

RAJON RONDO ANOTHER HUGE GAME . . . DRIVING IN FOR THE LAY-UP. RONDO HAS BEEN THE MVP OF THE SERIES SO FAR.

DEREK ROSE WITH THE WRAP-AROUND PASS TO TYRUS THOMAS . . . THE BULLS UP 7 . . .

THE CELTS COME BACK AND RAY ALLEN DRILLS A TRIPLE WITH EIGHT TENTHS OF A SECOND LEFT IN THE HALF . . . CELTS BY ONE AT THE BREAK.

PAUL PIERCE HAD A BIG GAME . . . DRILLING A THREE TO HELP GIVE THE CELTS A FIVE-POINT LEAD AFTER THREE.

THE FOURTH QUARTER BEGAN WITH SOME PUSHING AND SHOVING . . . BIG BABY THE SAVE BUT BRAD MILLER GETS THE BALL . . . BIG BABY THE HARD FOUL AND MILLER SHOVES HIM . . . REFS GIVE MILLER A TECHNICAL FOUL.

RONDO DELIVER AGAIN . . . A TRIPLE DOUBLE WITH 25 POINTS, 11 BOARDS AND 11 ASSISTS. HE PLAYED 55 MINUTES.

BEN GORDON STEPPED UP BIG TIME . . . BANKING HOME TWO OF HIS 22 POINTS.

CELTS DOWN 3 WITH 10 SECONDS LEFT WHEN ALLEN TIES IT WITH A TRIPLE . . . RAY WITH 28 . . . IT'S ON TO OVERTIME.

IN THE O-T . . . ALLEN NAILS THE JUMPER AND THE CELTS HAD A FIVE-POINT LEAD AND THE MOMENTUM.

BUT GORDON COMES UP HUGE . . . KNOCKING DOWN THE TREY TO TIE THE GAME AT 110-ALL . . . IT'S ON TO A SECOND O-T.

THE BULLS TAKE A FOUR-POINT. LEAD BUT EDDIE HOUSE FINDS BIG BABY FOR THE SLAM . . .

AND WHEN PIERCE NAILS A THREE FROM THE WING, THE CELTS WERE DOWN A ONE . . . PIERCE PLAYED 52 MINUTES.

ONE MORE CHANCE FOR PIERCE TO TIE BUT JOHN SALMONS THE BLOCK . . . BULLS WIN 121-118 TO TIE THE SERIES AT TWO HEADING BACK TO BOSTON TUESDAY.

MEANWHILE, THE L-A LAKERS HELD OFF A LATE FIGHTBACK BY THE UTAH JAZZ TO BOOK THEIR PLACE IN THE NBA WESTERN CONFERENCE FINALS WITH A TENSE 108-105 ROAD VICTORY.

KOBE BRYANT LED THE WAY WITH THIRTY-FOUR POINTS . . . EIGHT REBOUNDS AND SIX ASSISTS AS THE LAKERS WON THE SEMI-FINAL SERIES 4-2 ON SATURDAY.

DEXTER TO BEIJING:

THERE WAS NO INTERNET ACCESS LAST NIGHT WHEN DEXTER ST. LOUIS LET LOOSE A FIERCE BACK-HAND SMASH TO DEFEAT MARCOS MADRID OF MEXICO AND JOIN THE ELITE GROUP PF LATTU [LATIN AMERICAN TABLE TENNIS UNION] QUALIFIERS FOR THE OLYMPICS IN BEIJING, CHINA. IT WAS A GRUELLING MATCH WITH DEXTER LEADING SEVERAL TIMES AT DEUCE IN THE SECOND GAME BEFORE GOING DOWN AT 15-17. MARCOS MADRID PLAYED HIS HEART OUT AND WITH THE GAME TIED 3-3 AND MARCOS LEADING AND SERVING AT 9-7 IN THE SEVENTH, THERE WAS NO STOPPING DEXTER. HIS MENTAL STRENGTH TO FIGHT IN TIGHT SITUATIONS SUCH AS THIS WAS SUPERIOR AND MARCOS DID NOT GET ANOTHER POINT. THE GAME SAW DEXTER AT HIS BRILLIANT BEST WITH HIS TRADEMARK POWER-BLOCKS AND PERFECTLY EXECUTED SMASHES. DEXTER WON 4-3. EARLIER DEXTER DEFEATED PAVEL OXAMENDY OF CUBA 4-0 TO SET UP HIS MATCH WITH MADRID. TOP SEED IN DEXTER'S GROUP HUGO HOYAMA OF BRAZIL EXITED EARLY TO DIMEY GONGARA OF CUBA. THE OTHER MALE QUALIFER WAS THIAGO MONTERO OF BRAZIL WHO DEFEATED PABLO TABACHINIK OF ARGENTINA 4-2.

TODAY, IN THE THIRD AND LAST ROUND OF THE OLYMPIC QUALIFIER KNOCKOUT KHALEEL ASGARALI LOST TO PAUL DAVID OF GUYANA IN HIS FIRST MATCH 2-4.

CURTIS HUMPHREYS ALSO BOWED OUT TO OMAR FLORES OF GUATEMALA 0-4 IN HIS FIRST MATCH THIS MORNING.

RHEANN CHUNG BEAT ANGELA MORI OF PERU 4-2 IN THE FIRST KNOCKOUT ROUND OF 32. SHE THEN ADVANCED TO THE QUARTER-FINALS WHEN SHE WHIPPED JERICA MARERO OF PUERTO RICO 4-2. SHE LOST HER QUARTER-FINAL MATCH-UP WITH PAULA MEDINA OF COLOMBIA 1-4.

THE TEAM EVENTS START TOMORROW. AFTER THIS DEXTER BATTLES WITH THE NEXT FIVE LATTU QUALIFIERS IN A SUPER-SIX TO CROWN THE 2008 LATTU CHAMPION WHO WILL AUTOMATICALLY QUALIFY FOR THE WORLD CHAMPIONSHIPS 2008 IN CHINA.

SOCCER:

SIR ALEX FERGUSON IS CONFIDENT HIS MANCHESTER UNITED SIDE CAN SECURE A CHAMPIONS LEAGUE SEMI-FINAL SPOT AFTER A 2-0 FIRST-LEG LAST-EIGHT WIN AT ROMA.

CRISTIANO RONALDO AND WAYNE ROONEY EACH SCORED VITAL A WAY GOALS TO PUT UNITED IN POLE POSITION AHEAD OF THE SECOND LEG AT OLD TRAFFORD ON 9 APRIL.

THE SCOT SAID UNITED WOULD HAVE TO BE WARY OF THE RETURN OF ROMA CAPTAIN AND TALISMAN FRANCESCO TOTTI NEXT WEDNESDAY.

ARSENAL GOALKEEPER JENS LEHMANN IS ON THE BRINK OF SIGNING FOR GERMAN SIDE STUTTGART AFTER MEETING WITH CLUB OFFICIALS ON MONDAY MORNING.

THE THIRTY-EIGHT-YEAR-OLD DISCUSSED A MOVE BEFORE FLYING TO MALLORCA WITH THE GERMAN SQUAD TO BEGIN THEIR EURO 2008 PREPARATIONS.

IT IS BELIEVED LEHMANN WANTS TO SORT OUT HIS FUTURE BEFORE NEXT MONTH'S EUROPEAN CHAMPIONSHIPS IN AUSTRIA AND SWITZERLAND.

STUTTGART REQUIRES A NEW GOALKEEPER AFTER RAPHAEL SCHAFER, WHO WAS SIGNED FROM NURNBERG LAST SUMMER, FAILED TO LIVE UP TO EXPECTATIONS.

HOWEVER, GENERAL MANAGER HORST HELDT TOLD GERMANY'S BILD NEWSPAPER HE WILL NOT BE HELD TO RANSOM IN HIS BID TO SIGN LEHMANN.

"IF HE WANTS TO EARN AS MUCH AS HE DID AT ARSENAL, THEN WE HAVE NO CHANCE," SAID HELDT.

STUTTGART, WHO FINISHED SIXTH IN THE BUNDESLIGA, ARE THOUGHT TO BE OFFERING A ONE-YEAR CONTRACT, WITH AN OPTION FOR A SECOND YEAR.

VOLLEYBALL:

LAST NIGHT IN THE OPENING OF THE FIRST INTERNATIONAL WOMEN'S VOLLEYBALL LEAGUE . . . HOSTED BY THE T&T VOLLEYBALL FEDERATION AT THE JEAN PIERRE COMPLEX . . . GLAMORGAN AND WEST SIDE STARS BOTH WON THEIR RESPECTIVE MATCHES.

GLAMORGAN BEAT BIG SEPOS IN THREE STRAIGHT SETS . . . 25-12 . . . 25-14 . . . AND 25-10 . . . WHILE WEST SIDE STARS. . . . BEAT NATIONAL CHAMPI-ONS UTT IN FIVE SETS . . . 25-23 . . . 14-25 . . . 25-22 . . . 12-25 AND 15-12.

IN THIS EVENING'S ACTION. . . . IN A GAME THAT STARTED AT SIX. . . . GLAMORGAN IS TAKING ON CHALLENGERS . . . AND FROM EIGHT . . . BIG SEPOS FACES WEST SIDE STARS.

TENNIS:

RAFAEL NADAL CLINCHED HIS FIRST HAMBURG MASTERS TITLE WITH A HARD-FOUGHT 7-5, 6-7 (3-7), 6-3 WIN OVER THE DEFENDING CHAMPION AND TOP SEED ROGER FEDERER.

THE WORLD NUMBER TWO NEEDED TWO HOURS AND FIFTY-TWO MINUTES TO BEAT THE WORLD NUMBER ONE IN A GRUELLING AND TENSE MATCH.

HE CAME BACK FROM 5-1 DOWN TO CLINCH THE FIRST SET, WHILE FEDERER ALSO LET AN ADVANTAGE SLIP IN THE SECOND BEFORE TAKING THE SET IN THE TIE-BREAK.

NADAL BROKE TWICE IN THE THIRD AS HE CLAIMED THE 26TH TITLE OF HIS CAREER.

BOTH PLAYERS SPOKE AFTER THE MATCH.

MEANWHILE, WORLD NUMBER SIX ANDY RODDICK HAS WITHDRAWN FROM THE FORTHCOMING FRENCH OPEN WITH A SHOULDER INJURY.

THE AMERICAN, WHO HAS LOST IN THE FIRST ROUND AT ROLAND GARROS FOR THE LAST TWO YEARS, EXPECTS TO BE FIT FOR THE START OF THE GRASS-COURT SEASON AT QUEEN'S.

CRICKET:

HEAVY RAIN DENIED AUSTRALIA A WIN AGAINST A JAMAICA XI IN THEIR THREE-DAY FIXTURE AT TRELAWNY.

SET A MERE NINETY-SIX RUNS TO BEAT THEIR HOSTS, THE AUSTRALIANS WERE COASTING ALONG AT SIXTY-FIVE FOR ONE WHEN RAIN ENDED PLAY AT APPROXIMATELY 4:30 LOCAL TIME YESTERDAY.

SPINNERS SIMON KATICH AND STUART MACGILL PUT THE AUSSIES IN A WINNING POSITION AFTER SHARING SEVEN WICKETS BETWEEN THEM TO RESTRICT THE JAMAICANS' SECOND INNINGS TO 194 ALL OUT. CARLTON BAUGH TOP SCORED WITH THIRTY-SIX WHILE XAVIER MARSHALL MADE THIRTY-ONE. KATICH HAD BRILLIANT FIGURES OF FOUR FOR FIFTEEN OFF 5.2 OVERS WITH MACGILL TAKING THREE FOR FIFTY.

AUSTRALIA HAD SECURED A NINETY-NINE-RUN FIRST INNING'S ADVANTAGE ON SATURDAY WHEN THEY SCORED 396 ALL OUT IN REPLY TO JAMAICA'S FIRST INNINGS SCORE OF 297.

THE TOURISTS WILL COMMENCE THEIR TOUR OF THE CARIBBEAN ON THURSDAY WHEN THEY FACE THE WEST INDIES IN THE FIRST OF A THREE-TEST SERIES AT SABINA PARK IN JAMAICA. THEY ALSO PLAY AT 20/20 MATCH AT THE KENSINGTON OVAL IN BARBADOS ON TWENTIETH JUNE BEFORE THE START OF THE FIVE ODI SERIES AT ARNOS VALE IN ST VINCENT ON TWENTY-FOURTH JUNE.

MEANWHILE, SHIVNARINE CHANDERPAUL, RAMNARESH SARWAN, AND DWAYNE BRAVO ARE EXPECTED TO JOIN THE REST OF THE WEST INDIES SQUAD IN ANTIGUA TODAY FOR THE TEST AFTER THEIR PARTICIPATION IN THE IPL IN INDIA.

THE THREE PLAYERS HAD MISSED THE WEST INDIES ONE-WEEK TRAINING CAMP IN ANTIGUA.

WHILE CHANDERPAUL AND SARWAN LEFT INDIA ON SATURDAY, BRAVO LEFT YESTERDAY AFTER HE LED HIS MUMBAI INDIANS SIDE TO A COMPREHENSIVE TWENTY-FIVE-RUN WIN OVER THE DECCAN CHARGERS. BRAVO HAD BEST BOWLING FIGURES OF THREE FOR TWENTY-FOUR AND ALSO HIT A VALUABLE THIRTY RUNS AS MUMBAI WERE WINNING THEIR SIXTH STRAIGHT MATCH ON THE TROT TO STAY ON COURSE FOR THE KNOCKOUT STAGE.

>>>
WEATHER COPY

THE BEAUTIFUL, VERY WARM MID-SPRING WEATHER WILL CONTINUE. TONIGHT WILL BE CLEAR TO PARTLY CLOUDY, WITH TEMPS DIPPING INTO THE 50'S AND THEN LEVELLING OFF IN THE LOW TO MID 50'S. THERE MAY BE SOME FOG ON CAPE COD THIS EVENING. IT'S GOING TO WARM BACK UP AGAIN TOMORROW, WITH HIGHS AWAY FROM THE COAST WELL INTO THE 80'S. IT SHOULD BE BETWEEN 85-90 INLAND, AND IN THE UPPER 70'S TO LOW 80'S AT THE COAST.

>>>
COMMERCIAL COPY

1. BY THE TIME YOU REACH 50, YOU'VE MADE A REAL CONTRIBUTION THROUGH A LIFETIME OF PRODUCTIVITY. AND SAVE FIRST THINKS YOU DESERVE SOME PRIVILEGES. THAT'S WHY WE OFFER YOU THE SPECIAL PRIVILEGES OF ELDERLY BANKING WHEN YOU'RE ONLY 50! ELDERLY BANKING GIVES YOU A FREE INTEREST CHECKING ACCOUNT, FREE TRAVELERS' CHECKS, AND NOTARY SERVICE, ESTATE PLANNING, A BONUS RATE ON CDS . . . , AND SO MUCH MORE. SO IF YOU'RE 50 OR OVER, CALL OR VISIT SAVE FIRST TODAY. AND LET THE PRIVILEGES OF ELDERLY BANKING BENEFIT YOU.

2. EVERY TIME MY RELATIVES VISIT, THEY EAT ME OUT OF HOUSE AND HOME. THERE'S MY UNCLE LOUIE. WHENEVER WE HAVE A COOKOUT, HE HAS TWO DOUBLE CHEESEBURGERS, THREE HELPINGS OF BAKED BEANS, HALF A DOZEN HOT DOGS AND A DIET SODA. IT'S RIDICULOUS. OH, AND TALK ABOUT "LIKE FATHER LIKE SON." YOU SHOULD SEE COUSIN FREDDIE. EVERY TIME I TURN AROUND HE'S GOT HIS FACE IN THE FRIDGE. THIS GUY JUST DOESN'T SNACK BETWEEN MEALS. HE SNACKS BETWEEN THE SALAD AND THE ENTRÉE. I'M SURE GLAD I SHOP AT MA'S DELI, BECAUSE THEY HAVE LOW PRICES ON EVERYTHING IN THE STORE. MEAT, PRODUCE, BAKED BEANS, EVERYTHING. HEY, IT'S IMPORTANT FOR ME TO SAVE MONEY ON GROCERIES. ESPECIALLY WHEN MY AUNT SOPHIE'S IDEA OF A LIGHT LUNCH IS ANYTHING SHE CAN PICK UP WITH A FORK. SO, FROM THE BOTTOM OF MY POCKET BOOK, MA'S DELI, I THANK YOU.

3. MY HUSBAND IS A COUCH POTATO. IN FOURTEEN YEARS, HE'S WORN OUT THREE RECLINERS. CAN'T REMEMBER OUR ANNIVERSARY, BUT HE'S GOT THE TV SCHEDULE MEMORIZED. ONE TIME I TOOK THE BATTERIES OUT OF HIS REMOTE CONTROL. HE CALLED 911. LAST WEEK HE COMES HOME

FROM WORK, PLOPS DOWN ON HIS RECLINER, THROWS IT INTO LIFTOFF POSITION AND TELLS ME THAT HIS BOSS IS GIVING A DINNER PARTY AND WE'RE SUPPOSED TO BRING DESSERT. SO I SAID, "GREAT. WHAT ARE *YOU* GONNA MAKE?" THAT BROUGHT HIM TO HIS FEET. HE GOES, "GEE, HONEY, I THOUGHT YOU'D MAKE YOUR FAMOUS STRAWBERRY SHORTCAKE." "THINK AGAIN," I SAID. "HE'S YOUR BOSS. YOU COOK SOMETHING." HE WAS SMARTER THAN I THOUGHT. WENT TO MA'S DELI/BAKERY AND PICKED UP A CHEESECAKE. WELL, HIS BOSS'S WIFE RAVED OVER IT. SO HE SAYS, "THANK YOU. I MADE IT FROM SCRATCH."

4. A NEW SHOW IS BORN. . . . EYEWITNESS TO HISTORY. . . . CHARLES ROBERT DARWIN. . . . A MAN AND HIS ORIGIN . . . JOURNEY ON THE BEAGLE . . . THE ORIGIN OF SPECIES. . . . WHAT DARWIN ACHIEVED . . . GET INSIDE THE DELIVERY ROOM AND BE A PART OF THE BIRTH. . . . EYEWITNESS TO HISTORY. . . . CHARLES ROBERT DARWIN. . . . NARRATED BY JEROME LEWIS. . . . ON 195.5. . . . THE MOST INFLUENTIAL NAME IN RADIO

EYEWITNESS TO HISTORY IS NOW ON THIS FREQUENCY. . . . TRAVEL ALONG WITH US AS WE EXPLORE THE MASTERS OF THE UNIVERSE . . . THEIR THEORIES . . . THEIR MESSAGE AND THEIR WISDOM . . . RIDE WITH US AS WE GO DEEP INSIDE THE HEARTS AND MINDS OF THE GREAT WARRIORS OF OUR TIME . . . EYEWITNESS TO HISTORY . . . NOW PLAYING ON THE TAKE TWO SHOW ON 195.5. . . . THE MOST INFLUENTIAL NAME IN RADIO

THREE CENTURIES AGO SHE WAS STOLEN FROM GHANA AND TAKEN TO SAINT VINCENT AND THE GRENADINES. . . . TWENTY-THREE YEARS LATER SHE WAS A FREE WOMAN IN THIS COUNTRY . . . IN THE NEXT EPISODE OF EYEWITNESS TO HISTORY . . . WE FOLLOW THE PATH OF AFRICAN SLAVE MARIA . . . HER LIFE AT CAPE COAST STONE CASTLE IN GHANA. . . . HER JOURNEY THROUGH THE DOOR OF NO RETURN. . . . AND HER FINAL DAYS IN TRINIDAD AND TOBAGO . . . THE PATH OF AFRICAN SLAVE MARIA . . . ON THE NEXT EPISODE OF EYEWITNESS TO HISTORY . . . VOICES FROM THE PAST . . . ON-AIR AT 195.5 . . . THE MOST INFLUENTIAL NAME IN RADIO.

VOICE AND SPEECH EVALUATION FORMS

>>>

VOICE AND SPEECH EVALUATION FORM

Name _____   Campus address _____

Date _____   _____

Course/section _____   _____

Major/class _____   Telephone _____

Evaluator's name _____   Social Security # _____

The evaluator should check all those characteristics that are relevant to the speaker.

Voice

Quality
☐ Breathiness
☐ Denasality
☐ Excessive assimilation nasality
☐ Hypernasality
☐ Glottal shock
☐ Harshness
☐ Hoarseness
☐ Stridency
☐ Thinness
☐ Throatiness
☐ Vocal fry
☐ Vocal tension

Rate
☐ Too fast
☐ Too slow
☐ Needs variety
☐ Adequate variety

Breathing Habits
☐ Clavicular
☐ Diaphragmatic
☐ Nasal inhalation
☐ Thoracic
☐ Uncontrolled exhalation

Pitch
☐ Adequate
☐ Too high
☐ Too low
☐ Investigate optimum pitch

Loudness
☐ Too loud
☐ Too soft
☐ Adequate

Sounds

Use check marks to indicate correct sound production. For sound substitutions, supply phonetic symbols. Use a star to indicate sound distortion.

CONSONANTS

Plosives:
☐ pea   ☐ bay
☐ tea   ☐ day
☐ Kay   ☐ go
☐ choy   ☐ jay

Fricatives:
☐ fin   ☐ Vin
☐ thin   ☐ then
☐ sin   ☐ zool
☐ shoe   ☐ azure
☐ he   ☐ why

Lateral: ☐ lie

Semivowels:
☐ wise
☐ red
☐ yes

Nasals:
☐ may
☐ nay
☐ song

VOWELS

☐ see   ☐ heard   ☐ put
☐ bit   ☐ after   ☐ so
☐ made   ☐ cut   ☐ law
☐ met   ☐ about   ☐ hot
☐ cat   ☐ true   ☐ father
☐ ask

Diphthongs:
☐ house   ☐ useful
☐ try   ☐ ray
☐ boy   ☐ go
☐ stay

Speech

Check boxes that apply.

☐ Patterned inflection
☐ Lacks variety
☐ Poor articulation
☐ Staccato speech
☐ Affected speech
☐ Poor phrasing

Problems
☐ Additions
☐ Distortions
☐ Omissions
☐ Dentalization
☐ Blends

Regionalism _____

Foreign accent _____

Nonverbal

Check boxes that apply.

☐ Vocalized pause
☐ Lacks confidence
☐ Too confident

☐ Lacks desire to communicate
☐ Lacks eye contact
☐ Lacks control of nervousness

COMMENTS:

_____

_____

_____

>>>
VOICE AND SPEECH RATING SCALE I (INITIAL EVALUATION)

Name _____

Date _____

Course/section _____

Circle the number that best reflects the performance:

	High		Medium		Low
Voice					
Presence of open throat	1	2	3	4	5
Controlled exhalation	1	2	3	4	5
Used diaphragmatic breathing	1	2	3	4	5
Vocal tension	1	2	3	4	5
Pleasant quality	1	2	3	4	5
Loudness: easily heard	1	2	3	4	5
Variety of loudness	1	2	3	4	5
Use of optimum pitch	1	2	3	4	5
Speech					
Clarity of sound production	1	2	3	4	5
Appropriate rate	1	2	3	4	5
Variety of rate	1	2	3	4	5
Appropriate pitch	1	2	3	4	5
Variety of pitch	1	2	3	4	5
Distinctness of articulation	1	2	3	4	5
Variety of inflection	1	2	3	4	5
Nonverbal					
Use of:					
Vocalized hesitations	1	2	3	4	5
Facial expressions	1	2	3	4	5
Eye contact	1	2	3	4	5
Appropriate gestures	1	2	3	4	5
Appropriate stance/posture	1	2	3	4	5
Attitudes					
Interest in subject	1	2	3	4	5
Self-confidence	1	2	3	4	5
Desire to communicate	1	2	3	4	5
Control of nervousness	1	2	3	4	5

COMMENTS:

_____

_____

_____

>>>

VOICE AND SPEECH RATING SCALE II (FINAL EXAMINATION)

Name _____

Date _____

Course/section _____

Circle the number that best reflects the performance:

	High		Medium		Low
Voice					
Presence of open throat	1	2	3	4	5
Controlled exhalation	1	2	3	4	5
Used diaphragmatic breathing	1	2	3	4	5
Vocal tension	1	2	3	4	5
Pleasant quality	1	2	3	4	5
Loudness: easily heard	1	2	3	4	5
Variety of loudness	1	2	3	4	5
Use of optimum pitch	1	2	3	4	5
Speech					
Clarity of sound production	1	2	3	4	5
Appropriate rate	1	2	3	4	5
Variety of rate	1	2	3	4	5
Appropriate pitch	1	2	3	4	5
Variety of pitch	1	2	3	4	5
Distinctness of articulation	1	2	3	4	5
Variety of inflection	1	2	3	4	5
Nonverbal					
Use of:					
Vocalized hesitations	1	2	3	4	5
Facial expressions	1	2	3	4	5
Eye contact	1	2	3	4	5
Appropriate gestures	1	2	3	4	5
Appropriate stance/posture	1	2	3	4	5
Attitudes					
Interest in subject	1	2	3	4	5
Self-confidence	1	2	3	4	5
Desire to communicate	1	2	3	4	5
Control of nervousness	1	2	3	4	5

COMMENTS:

_____

_____

_____

COMPARISON OF PRESENTATIONS:

_____

_____

_____

_____

>>>
STUDENT INFORMATION SHEET

Name _____   Phone _____

Course/section _____   Class _____

E-mail address _____

Why are you taking this course? _____

List any other oral communication courses that you have taken._____

_____

Where were you born? _____   How long did you live there? _____

Where were your parents born? _____

What are your career goals? _____

_____

What are your expectations of this class? (Personal goals, grade, skill level to attain, etc.) _____

_____

_____

What is your speech and performance background? _____

_____

Relatives and friends say the following about my voice and speech: _____

_____

I am ☐ satisfied ☐ unsatisfied with my voice and speech and would like to make the following changes:

_____

_____

How sensitive are you to constructive criticism of your speech /voice? _____

_____

What language(s) do you and /or your parents speak in addition to English? _____

_____

What are your hobbies? _____

_____

What books or magazines have you read lately? _____

_____

Are you employed? _____ Where? _____ Hours per week? _____

Have you had speech or voice therapy? _____

When? _____ Diagnosis _____

How long did you attend the sessions? _____

What would you like me to know about you? _____

_____

What have you heard about this course? _____

_____

General comments or questions: _____

_____

_____

_____

GLOSSARY

Acoustic Pertaining to sound, the sense of hearing, or the science of sound.

Adam's Apple The bump on the front of the thyroid cartilage.

Aesthetic Distance The physical and psychological distance the artist has to the art object.

Affected Speech/Voice Spoken or vocal characteristics that are not yet habitual. Any deviation or change in current speech and voice habits will seem affected; once such changes have been developed, they seem "natural."

Affricate A speech sound composed of a plosive followed by a fricative.

Allophone A specific variation of a phoneme, some of which are acceptable and others are unacceptable. Several variations of the same phoneme may be called a set.

Alveolar Ridge The bony ridge behind the upper teeth.

Alveoli Tiny air sacs in the lungs that conduct the air to the bloodstream. Upon inhalation, oxygen enters the bloodstream; during exhalation, carbon dioxide is released from the bloodstream through the alveoli.

Anaptyxis A linguistic error in which a vowel, usually the schwa, is placed between two consonants, thereby adding an extra syllable (for example, [ˈlaɪtənŋ] for [ˈlaɪtnɪŋ]).

Articulation The production of sounds—namely, vowels, diphthongs, and consonants.

Articulatory Adjustment The manipulation of anatomical structures to produce sounds, such as placing the tongue tip on the alveolar ridge and vocalizing, which produces the consonant /l/.

Arytenoid One of the two pyramid-shaped cartilages of the larynx.

Aspirate A sound composed predominantly of breath.

Assimilation The influence of one speech sound on another.

Assimilation Nasality A vocal quality in which vowels appearing before, after, or between nasal sounds take on nasal characteristics.

Audience Feedback Signals given to a speaker during a speech occasion; such signals include restlessness, attentiveness, or smiles of enjoyment.

Auditory Discrimination The ability to hear differences among sounds.

Auditory Sense The sense of hearing.

Autistic Mannerisms Unconscious muscular movements usually caused by nervousness.

Bilabial Pertaining to the two lips.

Breathiness A vocal quality characterized by the release of excessive breath because the vocal folds are not brought closely enough together during phonation; also caused by lack of breath support.

Bronchioles Small branches at the end of the bronchi.

Bronchus (*bronchi,* plural; *bronchial,* adjective) One of the two tubular divisions of the trachea.

Canned Speech Speech that sounds memorized or spoken many times and is therefore devoid of vocal or mental dynamics.

Career Speech Voice and speech that are of professional quality; trained speech.

Cartilage A tough, white fibrous tissue attached to the surfaces of bones.

Clavicular Breathing Respiration in which the upper chest and shoulders are elevated and lowered; named for the clavicles (collarbones).

Cleft Palate Speech Hypernasality exhibited in the speech of individuals who have palatal problems; excessive nasality.

Cognate Pairs Two sounds having the same articulatory adjustment; one is unvoiced and the other is voiced.

Connotation The associational or suggestive value of a word (for instance, connotations for *horse* could be "stallion," "mount," and "horsey").

Consonant A speech sound produced when the flow of breath is stopped either partially or totally by the articulatory organs and is then released. The consonants give spoken language clarity.

Continuant A classification of sound in which there is a free flow of breath through the articulatory mold; except for the plosives, all sounds are continuants. A speech sound capable of being prolonged.

Conversational Speech Speech habits learned through observation, informal speech.

Countenance The face, including the eyes; in the context of speech, the use of the face to communicate messages.

Cricoid The signet-ring-shaped cartilage of the larynx.

Denasality A vocal quality characterized by insufficient nasal resonance.

Denotation The explicit meaning of a word according to the dictionary.

Dental Pertaining to the teeth.

Dentalization The erroneous use of the teeth in the production of sounds.

Dentalized Pertaining to the articulation error (dentalization), resulting when the teeth are inappropriately used in the production of a sound.

Diadochokinesis The ability to produce difficult sound combinations with rapidity and precision.

Dialect The general pronunciation practiced in a particular region by people who speak the same language.

Diaphragm A double, dome-shaped muscle of respiration that forms the floor of the thorax (chest) and the ceiling of the abdomen. The most important muscle used in abdominal breathing.

Diaphragmatic Breathing (Abdominal Breathing) Respiration in which the muscles of the abdomen, including the diaphragm, are used; the preferred form of breathing for speech. In addition, diaphragmatic breathing involves lateral movement of the lower ribs.

Diction   The choice and use of words (*dictionary*). An individual should have both written and oral diction. A secondary definition of *diction* involves the distinctness of speech.

Diphthong   A speech sound composed of two vowel sounds but perceived as one. Any two vowels coming together within the same syllable constitute a diphthong.

Direct Performance Occasion   A situation in which the speaker talks directly to an audience and expresses his or her own ideas and emotions. (open situation)

Dolce et utile   From the Italian, meaning "sweet or entertaining" and "useful, informational, or educational."

Dynamic Speech   Conversational or performance speech.

Ear Training   The process of developing hearing acuity; good ear training contributes to the ability to distinguish sounds.

Empathy   Feeling what another person feels; "feeling into."

Epiglottis   The spoon- or leaf-shaped cartilage of the larynx.

Exhalation   That part of the breathing process in which carbon dioxide is expelled from the lungs.

Explosion   The release of impounded breath in the production of a plosive.

Extemporaneous Speech   A speech that has had some time for preparation. The time may vary considerably.

Eye Contact   The degree to which a speaker looks into the eyes of audience members.

Fricative   A speech sound in which breath or sound waves pass through a narrow opening in the oral cavity, creating frictional noises.

Fundamental Tone   The sound produced by the vibration of the vocal folds as a whole unit.

Fused   Joined together.

Gesture   Upper body movement, including use of the arms and hands, used to amplify a speaker's words.

Glide   See *semivowel*.

Glottalization   Stopping the breath at the glottis (the space between the true vocal folds); an articulation that involves the use of the glottis; a characteristic of Scottish and cockney dialects.

Glottal Shock or Stop   A vocal quality in which the vocal folds are forced apart by breath that has been held back, resulting in an explosion of sound, usually on an initial vowel or diphthong.

Glottis   The space between the true vocal folds.

Habitual   Pertaining to that which is customary or usual. In describing voice and speech, it refers to your current verbal characteristics. Something made habit through repetition.

Habitual Pitch (Modal Pitch)   The pitch that you use most frequently.

Haplology   A linguistic error in which a repeated sound or syllable is omitted (for example, ['laɪbɛrɪ] for ['laɪbrɛrɪ]).

Hard Palate   The first third of the roof of the mouth, composed of bone and membrane.

Harshness   A quality of voice characteristic of gross tension accompanied by loud breathing noises and low pitches.

Hoarseness   A quality of voice caused by strain.

Homograph   One of two or more words that are spelled the same way but differ in meaning, pronunciation, or derivation.

Homonym   One of two or more words that have the same sounds and, often, the same spelling but that have differences in meaning.

Homophenous Sounds   Sounds that look alike on the lips (for example, /p/, /m/, and /b/).

Homophenous Words   Words that use homophenous consonants with the same vowel or diphthong (for example, *pan, man,* and *ban*).

Homophone   A type of homonym in which the sounds are the same but the words are spelled differently.

Homophonous Words   Words that sound exactly alike (for example, *vain, vane,* and *vein*).

Hyoid Bone   The small bone from which the larynx is suspended.

Implosion   The coming together of the articulators and the buildup of breath without the release of the impounded breath in the production of a plosive.

Impromptu Speech   A speech that has had no time for preparation.

Indirect Performance Occasion   A situation in which a speaker recreates fictional characters and presents their thoughts and feelings. (closed situation)

Inflection   A vocal technique that brings attention to thoughts and ideas through variations of pitch. These changes of stress, tempo, and pitch occur without speech interruption and support, enhance, reflect, and amplify meaning.

Inhalation   The initial part of the breathing process in which oxygen rushes into the lungs in order to equalize the atmospheric pressure.

Intercostal Muscles   Muscles located between the ribs that, when contracted, elevate the rib cage. These are important muscles in diaphragmatic breathing.

International Phonetic Alphabet (IPA)   An alphabet of visual symbols that represent sounds. The American-English portion is found on the inside cover of the text.

Intervocalic /ɾ/   The one-tap trilled /ɾ/ linking one syllable or word to another.

Introduction   The opening of a speech occasion during which the audience becomes acquainted with the speaker and the nature of the presentation.

Kinesics   The study of the role of body movements in communication.

Kinesthesis (*kinesthetic,* adjective)   The sensory perception of muscular movement.

Kinesthetic Sense   The sense related to small muscular movements.

Labio-dental   A sound made by lips and teeth.

Lambda   An unacceptable /l/ allophone made with the tongue tip resting behind the lower front teeth.

Laryngectomy   The surgical removal of the larynx.

Laryngitis   The inflammation of the larynx (voice box).

Larynx   Commonly called the voice box, it is located at the top of the trachea and houses and protects the vocal folds. It is composed of five major cartilaginous structures and muscles, including the vocal folds.

Lateralization   The improper escape of air from the sides of the mouth and over the sides of the tongue, as in a lateralized sibilant.

Lectern   A wooden or a metal stand upon which a speaker's notes are placed; it is not intended to be an object clenched by nervous speakers until their knuckles turn white. A lectern is often incorrectly called a *podium*, which is the dais upon which the feet rest or a platform upon which a speaker stands.

Lingua-alveolar   Pertaining to the tongue and alveolar ridge.

Lingua-dental   A sound made by tongue and teeth.

Lingua-palatal   Pertaining to the tongue and the palate.

Lingua-velar   Pertaining to the tongue and the velum.

Loudness   The perception of the intensity or expansiveness of sound vibrations; volume.

Lung   One of a pair of thoracic organs filling the chest cavity. The lung is the basic organ of respiration.

Mandible   The lower jaw.

Maxilla   The upper jaw.

Medulla Oblongata   The lowest (most posterior) part of the brain, located at the top of the vertebral column.

Metathesis   A *linguistic* error in which sounds are reversed in the pronunciation of a word (for example, "prespiration" for "perspiration").

Mimesis (*mimetic*, adjectival)   Imitation.

Molar   A tooth with a flattened surface.

Monosyllabic   A word composed of one syllable.

Muscle   A fibrous tissue capable of being contracted and relaxed.

Muscle Memory   The ability to reproduce a remembered muscular activity.

Nasal   Pertaining to the nose or to a speech sound in which the vibrating air resonates in the nose.

Nasal Cavity   The cavity in the head, located above the soft and hard palate, that leads to the nose. The entrance but not the size of this cavity can be adjusted.

Nasality   A vocal quality in which too much sound resonation escapes through the nose during phonation.

Nasal Resonance   An amplification and modification of the fundamental tone in the nose.

Nasal Spurs   Growths in and around the nasal cavity that interfere with the flow of breath.

Natural   Pertaining to that which is not artificial. The only truly natural characteristics are those with which you were born. In regard to voice and speech, the anatomical, physiological, and muscular systems are natural. These are, however, capable of being trained and developed. Because speech is a learned process, it is artificial. (We "speechies" do not like to admit that, so keep it a secret!)

Negative Practice   The learning technique that involves "consciously" practicing an error.

Nodule   A membranous mass; a polyp.

Nonverbal   Pertaining to everything in communication that is not spoken, such as gestures, facial expressions, and so on.

Open Throat   Optimal pharyngeal resonance; a relaxed throat that produces a relaxed sound.

Optimum Pitch   The best pitch for your voice, as determined by your physical structure. The best sound produced with the least effort.

Oral   Pertaining to the mouth.

Oral Cavity   The buccal or mouth cavity; the size of this cavity can be adjusted.

Oral Recidivism   The tendency to relapse into a previous condition or mode of oral behavior.

Oral Resonance   An amplification and modification of the fundamental tone in the mouth.

Overly Open Throat   A voice quality that sounds too relaxed and includes a yawning quality.

Pace   A form of speech emphasis in which changes in speed of verbalization are used for contrast and highlight.

Partials (Overtones, Segmentals, Harmonics)   The components of a vibrating agent that are related mathematically. These components are said to be the partials of the fundamental tone produced by that vibrating agent. The partials give the voice its particular quality and are usually higher in pitch than the fundamental tone.

Pause   A form of speech emphasis in which there is an absence of speech before or after an utterance.

Performance Studies   The study of oral performance through many kinds of literature.

Pharyngeal Resonance   An amplification and modification of the fundamental tone in the throat.

Pharynx (*pharyngeal*, adjectival)   The throat cavity located between the esophagus and the opening to the nasal cavity; the size of this cavity can be adjusted. It is also called the *throat*.

Phonation   The sound made by the vibration of the vocal folds.

Phoneme   A sound family that conveys meaning within languages; the individual sound components of a word. The smallest unit of recognizable speech sound.

Phonetics   The science of speech sounds.

Pitch   A factor of sound related to frequency, or the number of vibrations per unit of time. The perception of the highs and lows of sound.

Plosive   A speech sound in which breath under pressure reaches a peak in the articulatory adjustment and is released in a small puff of air when the articulators are relaxed.

Polysyllabic   A word composed of three or more syllables.

Projected Scene   A technique for differentiating characters that are being suggested during an indirect speech occasion. The speaker focuses at a point slightly above and slightly behind the audience so that when each character is represented the speaker faces the audience at different angles of direction.

Projection   The act of controlling loudness.

Pronunciation   The combination of vowels, consonants, and diphthongs to form words.

Prosody   "The art or science of patterning in poetry"[1]; prosody includes patterns of meter and images as well as other repetitions.

Quality   A factor of sound determined by the complexity of vibrations per unit of time. The subjective interpretation of sound determined by the complexity of the vibration; the amplification of the partials—the overtones that individualize a voice.

Rate   The amount of time that is given to a speech utterance as well as silences. How quickly or slowly speech is produced.

Rectus Abdominus   The sheath of muscle going from the sternum down to the pelvis.

---

[1]Wallace Bacon, *The Art of Interpretation*, 3d ed. (New York: Holt, Rinehart & Winston, 1979), 548.

Resonance   The process that amplifies and modifies the intensity of tone. In the production of speech sounds, this amplification occurs primarily in the cavities of the mouth, nose, and throat because of either forced or sympathetic vibration. These three cavities constitute the vocal resonators. The size, shape, and physical makeup of the cavities determine the kind of amplification. In other words, the fundamental tone produced at the vocal folds is "re-sounded" within these cavities.

Resonance Cavities   The cavities in which sound can resonate. For voice production, the mouth, nose, and throat cavities are the most important.

Respiration   The process of breathing; the exchange of oxygen and carbon dioxide.

Restressing   The changing of a vowel due to a change in stress; frequently a schwa turns into /ʌ/ instead of retaining the original vowel. For example, in its restressed form, "was" becomes [wʌz] instead of [wɑz] or [wɒz].

Rib Cage   The bony boundary of the chest, or thorax.

Schwa   A middle-central and unstressed vowel.

Semivowel (Glide)   A speech sound in which there is a gliding movement of the tongue, the lips, or both.

Septum   The dividing wall of the nose.

Sibilant   A speech sound in which breath passes through a narrow opening, creating a hissing noise.

Signature Story   A story or part of a story that makes your speech yours. It deals with personal experience, thoughts, or vignettes.

Singer's Nodes   Small growths on the vocal folds due to vocal strain; they are fairly common among singers.

Singing Voice   Prolongation of vowels at particular pitches.

Skeleton   The bony or more or less cartilaginous framework of the body.

Slide   A movement through steps; in inflection, sliding occurs through changes in voice quality and projection as well as in pitch.

Sound Addition   See *anaptyxis*.

Sound Distortion   The simulation of a specific speech sound that is usually identifiable but lacking in clarity because of excessive nasality or incorrect articulation (for example, the excessive nasalization of /æ/ in [mæn]).

Sound Omission   The omission of a sound (for example, ['mnɪstɚ] for "minister").

Sound Substitution   The use of one sound for another (for example, [wæbɪt] for "rabbit").

Speech   The result of the production, combination, and presentation of the individual components of vocal sound.

Speech Environment   The circumstances surrounding a speaking occasion, including the audience and nature of the event. The speech environment determines the style of speech to be used.

Speechreading   The technique of understanding oral communication primarily through visual cues.

Spontaneity   A manner that is natural and unstudied.

Spoonerism   The transposition of sounds in different words.

Standard Stage Speech (London Speech)   Professional speech used by vocally trained actors in plays that benefit aesthetically from the use of a standard British accent.

Step   The interval between two adjoining pitches.

Sternum   The breastbone.

Stress   The amount of intensity given to a sound, syllable, or word. In speech it is a form of speech emphasis in which attention is given to words that are important to meaning. This form of emphasis has also been called *force*. In broadcasting, this form of emphasis is called *punching*.

Strident   A quality of voice characterized by harshness and (usually) high pitch.

Suprasegmental Features   Those aspects of speech, such as duration, stress, and juncture, that concern more than individual phonemes.

Sympathetic Vibration   The vibration of one vibrating agent caused by another vibrating agent without direct contact between them; this results when two or more vibrating agents have the same pitch. This phenomenon is easily observed when one strikes a tuning fork and places it near another fork that is capable of vibrating at the same pitch; the second fork then vibrates at the same pitch, even though there is no direct contact between the two.

Tactile Sense   The sense of touch.

Tempo   The rate at which words are spoken. The tempo affects rhythm.

Thorax (Thoracic Cavity)   The chest or chest cavity.

Thyroarytenoid Muscles   The vocal folds.

Thyroid Cartilage   The largest cartilage of the larynx; it is shield-shaped.

Tight Throat   Excessive tension in the throat; the opposite of an open throat.

Tongue   The largest muscle in the mouth.

Trachea   The windpipe; a cartilaginous tube located between the throat and the bronchial tubes.

Transcribe   To write a word, phrase, or sentence phonetically.

Triphthong   Three vowels coming together within the same syllable, an unacceptable pronunciation in career speech.

Turbinates   Three spiral-shaped bones located behind the nose that warm, moisten, and filter the air during vegetative breathing.

Upper Thoracic Breathing   Respiration while elevating the sternum and often pulling in the lower ribs.

Uvula   The hanging tip of the velum.

Vegetative Breathing   Respiration in order to sustain life.

Velum (*velar*, adjectival)   The back two-thirds of the palate, composed of muscle and membrane; commonly called the *soft palate*.

Ventricular Bands   The false vocal folds that grow just above the true vocal folds.

Verbal   Pertaining to words.

Vertebral Column   The spinal column.

Vibrating Agent   A physical object that can be vibrated to produce sound. Examples are the vocal folds, a reed, and the lips.

Viscera   The soft digestive organs in the abdomen.

Visualization   A technique in which a person recalls mental images of himself or herself in a nonthreatening situation.

Visual Sense   The sense of sight.

Vocal Flexibility   The ability to make changes in voice and speech to underscore changes of meaning in connected or dynamic speech.

Vocal Folds   Folds of muscle located within the larynx that, when vibrated by subglottal air pressure, cause most of the sounds of speech.

Vocal Fry (Glottal Fry)   A quality of voice characterized by a scratchy sound, usually caused by poor breathing habits and characterized by excessive opening and closing of the glottis during phonation.

Vocal Process   The projection on an arytenoid to which the back (posterior) portion of the vocal fold is attached.

Voice   The quality and condition of the sound produced at the larynx by the passage of exhaled breath between the vocal folds, which causes them to vibrate. The vocal sound is magnified and made resonant by the resonance cavities; it is here that quality becomes a factor of sound.

Voiced Sound   A sound produced by the vibration of the vocal folds; also called a *sonant, tonic, voiced, phonating,* or *vibrating* sound.

Voiceless Sound   A sound produced with no vibration of the vocal folds; also called a *surd, atonic, unvoiced, nonphonating,* or *non-vibrating* sound.

Volume   The amount of force or energy applied to the production of the vocal sound; sound intensity shown by sound waves.

Vowel   A speech sound in which there is a free, unobstructed flow of vibrating breath through the articulatory mold. The vowels are determined by the shape of the tongue and lips. Vowels give the language beauty and carrying power.

Wrenched Stress   Intentional misplacement of primary stress on a syllable; a device sometimes used in poetry.

Index of Names and Topics

INDEX OF AUTHORS AND SELECTIONS